Contracts for Paralegals

PARALEGAL SERIES

Contracts for Paralegals

Legal Principles and Practical Applications

Second Edition

Linda A. Wendling

(formerly Spagnola)

 Wolters Kluwer

Published by Wolters Kluwer in New York.

Wolters Kluwer Legal & Regulatory U.S. serves customers worldwide with CCH, Aspen Publishers, and Kluwer Law International products. (www.WKLegaledu.com)

Cover image: ilkercelik/iStock by Getty Images

To contact Customer Service, e-mail customer.service@wolterskluwer.com, call 1-800-234-1660, fax 1-800-901-9075, or mail correspondence to:

Wolters Kluwer
Attn: Order Department
PO Box 990
Frederick, MD 21705

Printed in the United States of America.

1 2 3 4 5 6 7 8 9 0

ISBN 978-1-4548-6915-3

Library of Congress Cataloging-in-Publication Data

Names: Wendling, Linda A., author.
Title: Contracts for paralegals: legal principles and practical applications / Linda A. Wendling (formerly Spagnola).
Description: Second edition. | New York: Wolters Kluwer, [2019] | Series: Paralegal series | Includes index.
Identifiers: LCCN 2018056715 | ISBN 9781454869153
Subjects: LCSH: Contracts—United States. | Legal assistants—United States—Handbooks, manuals, etc.
Classification: LCC KF801.Z9 S68 2019 | DDC 346.7302/2—dc23
LC record available at https://lccn.loc.gov/2018056715

About Wolters Kluwer Legal & Regulatory U.S.

Wolters Kluwer Legal & Regulatory U.S. delivers expert content and solutions in the areas of law, corporate compliance, health compliance, reimbursement, and legal education. Its practical solutions help customers successfully navigate the demands of a changing environment to drive their daily activities, enhance decision quality and inspire confident outcomes.

Serving customers worldwide, its legal and regulatory portfolio includes products under the Aspen Publishers, CCH Incorporated, Kluwer Law International, ftwilliam.com and MediRegs names. They are regarded as exceptional and trusted resources for general legal and practice-specific knowledge, compliance and risk management, dynamic workflow solutions, and expert commentary.

This book is dedicated to my family, whom I love beyond measure.

To my daughters, Emmelia and Katerina—the lights of my life. I have watched them grow and blossom into beautiful, witty, and intelligent young ladies from the time of the first edition until now. They mean more to me than they will ever know. My heart bursts with pride at their accomplishments and their potential for their future.

To my parents, Susan and Larry Pflum—twin pillars of strength and support. I simply would not be who I am or where I am without them. Every day they find another way to show their love and I am forever grateful.

To my husband, John Mark Bojanski—my beloved anchor and soulmate. He is always patient, always kind, and always has an open heart. He has brought so much beauty and adventure into my life. He can simultaneously let me soar and hold me safe and close—true magic.

Linda A. Wendling
December 2018

Summary of Contents

Contents xi ▪ Preface xix ▪ Art Credits xxvii ▪ About the Author xxix

PART ONE: FORMATION (THE ELEMENTS)   1

1   Offer   3
2   Consideration   41
3   Acceptance   67
4   Conditions   93
5   Third-Party Interests   113

PART TWO: DEFECTS IN FORMATION   139

6   Statute of Frauds   141
7   Capacity and Illegality   165
8   Absence of a "Meeting of the Minds"   195
9   Rules of Construction   221

PART THREE: FAILURE OF PERFORMANCE   255

10   Breach of Contract   257
11   Excuse of Performance   283
12   Changes by Agreement of the Parties   325

PART FOUR: REMEDIES   359

13   Compensatory and Related Damages   361
14   Equity and Quasi-Contract   389

PART FIVE: ARTICLE 2 OF THE UNIFORM COMMERCIAL CODE   413

15   The Uniform Commercial Code—Article 2: Sale of Goods and Dealings with Merchants   415

APPENDIXES

A   How to Prepare the Case Brief   457
B   How to Polish the Construction Contract   467

Glossary 469 ▪ Index 481

Contents

Preface xix ▪ Art Credits xxvii ▪ About the Author xxix

PART ONE: FORMATION (THE ELEMENTS)

Chapter 1: Offer   3

Mutual Assent   4
  Bilateral and Unilateral Contracts   5
  Certainty of Terms   6
  Communication to Intended Offeree   12
Method of Creation   13
Termination of the Offer   13
Summary   19
Key Terms   19
Review Questions   20
"Write" Away! Portfolio Assignment   21
Case in Point: Advertisements and Offers   22
Case in Point: Attempt to Rescind   36

Chapter 2: Consideration   41

Legal Value   42
Exceptions   44
Sufficiency of Consideration   48
Special Agreements   51
Summary   52
Key Terms   53
Review Questions   54
"Write" Away! Portfolio Assignment   55
Case in Point: Legally Sufficient Consideration   56

Chapter 3: Acceptance   67

Mirror Image Rule   68
The Mailbox Rule   71
Partial Performance/Substantial Beginning   77
Summary   80
Key Terms   81
Review Questions   81
"Write" Away! Portfolio Assignment   83
Case in Point: Counteroffers   84
Case in Point: Acceptance   90

Chapter 4: Conditions   93

Types of Conditions   94
Method of Creation   98
Summary   103
Key Terms   103
Review Questions   104
"Write" Away! Portfolio Assignment   105
Case in Point: Conditions   106

Chapter 5: Third-Party Interests   113

Types of Third-Party Interests   114
Right to Sue   117
Assignment/Delegation of Contractual Rights and Obligations
    to Third Parties   120
Summary   125
Key Terms   126
Review Questions   126
"Write" Away! Portfolio Assignment   127
Case in Point: Assignment   128
Case in Point: Third-Party Beneficiaries   131
Vocabulary Builders   136

PART TWO: DEFECTS IN FORMATION

Chapter 6: Statute of Frauds   141

Writing Requirement   142
Types of Contracts   145
Transfer of Real Property Interests   145
Contracts That Are Not Performable Within One Year   148

*Contracts in Consideration of Marriage (Prenuptial and
    Antenuptial Agreements) 150*
Sureties and Guarantees (Answering the Debt of Another) 152
*The Sale of Goods Valued over $500.00 (§ 2- 201 Uniform
    Commercial Code) 153*
Partial Performance   154
Summary   156
Key Terms   156
Review Questions   157
"Write" Away! Portfolio Assignment   158
Case in Point: The Statute of Frauds & Partial Performance   159

Chapter 7: Capacity and Illegality   165

Capacity   166
    Minority   166
    Exception for Necessities   168
    Mentally Infirm   169
    Under the Influence   171
Illegality   173
Summary   178
Key Terms   179
Review Questions   179
"Write" Away! Portfolio Assignment   180
Case in Point: Capacity   181
Case in Point: Illegality   185

Chapter 8: Absence of a "Meeting of the Minds"   195

Mistake   196
    Unilateral Mistake   196
    Mutual Mistake   197
Duress   200
Undue Influence   203
Fraud and Misrepresentation   204
Unconscionability   208
Summary   210
Key Terms   210
Review Questions   211
"Write" Away! Portfolio Assignment   212
Case in Point: Fraud in the Inducement   213

Chapter 9: Rules of Construction   221

Four Corners Doctrine   222
Business Custom and Trade Usage   226

Parol Evidence   228
Summary   234
Key Terms   235
Review Questions   235
"Write" Away! Portfolio Assignment   237
Case in Point: Trade Custom and Usage   238
Case in Point: Rules of Construction and Parol Evidence   243
Vocabulary Builders   252

PART THREE: FAILURE OF PERFORMANCE

Chapter 10: Breach of Contract   257

Anticipatory Repudiation   258
Materiality   262
Background   267
Divisibility   269
Waiver   270
Summary   272
Key Terms   273
Review Questions   273
"Write" Away! Portfolio Assignment   275
Case in Point: Materiality of Breach   276

Chapter 11: Excuse of Performance   283

Impracticality   284
Impossibility   285
   Death or Incapacity of Party   286
   Destruction of Subject Matter   287
   Supervening Illegality   289
Frustration of Purpose   291
Performance Prevented and Voluntary Disablement   293
Insolvency   294
Summary   295
Key Terms   295
Review Questions   296
"Write" Away! Portfolio Assignment   297
Case in Point: Impossibility   298
Case in Point: Frustration of Purpose   304
Case in Point: Illegality   313

Chapter 12: Changes by Agreement of the Parties 325

Mutual Rescission   326
Release   328
Accord and Satisfaction   330
Substituted Agreement/Novation   332
Modification   335
Summary   338
Key Terms   338
Review Questions   338
"Write" Away! Portfolio Assignment   340
Case in Point: Accord and Satisfaction   341
Case in Point: Novation or Modification   350
Vocabulary Builders   356

PART FOUR: REMEDIES

Chapter 13: Compensatory and Related Damages 361

Damages Not Recoverable Under Contract Law   362
    Speculative Damages   362
    Punitive Damages   364
Calculation of Compensatory Damages   365
    Expectation Damages   365
    Restitution Damages   366
    Reliance Damages   367
Duty to Mitigate   368
Consequential and Incidental Damages   370
Nominal Damages   372
Calculation of Damages   372
Liquidated Damages   375
Limitation of Damages   377
Costs   377
Summary   379
Key Terms   380
Review Questions   380
"Write" Away! Portfolio Assignment   382
Case in Point: Calculation and Award of Damages   383

Chapter 14: Equity and Quasi-Contract 389

"Action" Damages   390
   Injunctions   390
   Specific Performance   393
"Court-Ordered" Solutions   395
   Declaratory Judgment   395
   Rescission and Restitution   396
   Reformation   397
Quasi-Contracts   398
   Promissory Estoppel   398
   Prevention of Unjust Enrichment   399
Doctrine of "Unclean Hands"   401
Summary   402
Key Terms   403
Review Questions   404
"Write" Away! Portfolio Assignment   405
Case in Point: Equitable Damages   405
Vocabulary Builders   410

PART FIVE: ARTICLE 2 OF THE UNIFORM COMMERCIAL CODE

Chapter 15: The Uniform Commercial Code—Article 2: Sale of Goods and Dealings with Merchants 415

Covered Transactions   416
Merchants   419
Formation of the Contract   419
   Missing Terms Do Not Invalidate the Offer   419
   Modifications or Counteroffers Do Not Terminate the Offer   421
   Battle of the Forms   421
   Firm Offers   423
   Silence as Acceptance   424
   Warranties   424
Performance   428
Breach   429
   Acceptance   429
   Rejection   430
   Adequate Assurances   431
Remedies   432
   Seller's Remedies   432
   Buyer's Remedies   434

Summary   436
Key Terms   437
Review Questions   438
"Write" Away! Portfolio Assignment   439
Case in Point: Scope of UCC's Application and the Predominance Test "Goods
    and Services"   440
Vocabulary Builders   454

Appendixes

Appendix A: How to Prepare the Case Brief   457
Appendix B: How to Polish the Construction Contract   467

Glossary 469   ▩   Index 481

Preface

First and foremost, the student should understand that a contract is a legally enforceable promise. Our parents and kindergarten teachers instilled in us very early that we should honor our promises. The justice system echoes this sentiment in making these agreements enforceable between the parties to a contract. In order to create certainty in society when we make agreements or promises between parties who may be strangers to each other, the justice system binds parties to their contractual obligations by enforcing penalties on those who break their side of the bargain.

Contracts are not foreign abstractions to us. They are not relegated to large boardrooms filled with executives and lawyers negotiating for millions of dollars. We are surrounded by them every day—large, complex ones and tiny, simple ones. We live in a contract essentially—the social contract that allows people to interact with each other and have consistency and dependability. Our most esteemed document, the Constitution of the United States, is, at its core, nothing more than a contract. The government of the United States agrees to grant liberties and freedoms to its citizens in exchange for their promise to abide by the laws of the nation. Remedies are granted for breaches by either party. With every election, we continue the negotiation processes for changes in terms of this social contract.

On the other end of the spectrum, our morning coffee and newspaper are sales contracts. As we plunk our $1.25 on the counter, we have completed an entire contract from offer through complete performance: the entire conceptual text of this book in the blink of an eye.

While it appears that the study of contract law is not an easy one when a newly introduced paralegal student first reads the Table of Contents, be assured that the complexity is superficial. A contract can be understood by breaking it down into manageable parts.

Just as a complex jigsaw puzzle may look daunting at first, once the pieces have been sorted out, it becomes understandable and manageable. Indeed, construction of the puzzle, just like the construction of a contract, becomes formulaic. Let's suppose you and your friend set out to put a large puzzle together. First you would put the border together, much like you first need to set the parameters of a contract. Then you would fill in the important and prominent features of the picture, the material elements of the contract. Background elements like the sky or grass can then be sorted and fit in to the picture to complete the puzzle. These basic rules of construction apply just as neatly to contract formation.

If, for some reason, one or more of the pieces are found to be defective, you simply will be unable to form the puzzle. If one of the necessary elements of a valid contract is defective, you simply will be unable to form a contract.

Naturally, if either you or your friend loses or withholds any pieces, the puzzle will not be completed. Assuming the completion of the puzzle was of importance to you, the innocent party will want some sort of consequence to befall the careless or hostile co-creator. After all, you will not get the desired benefit—the completion of the puzzle—and you depended on your "friend" to help you reach that goal. Ironically, the term used in contract law to describe the desired outcome of a contractual dispute is to "make the innocent party whole"—just as the goal of the jigsaw puzzle maker is to make the project whole.

Of all the areas of the law, it is most consistent, partly due to its formulaic logic and partly because the law of contracts is a cold-hearted creature. I can recall the disgusted tone in my contracts professor's voice as she coolly responded to a question about punitive damages: "This is *not* torts class; contract law does not succumb to emotional pleas." In other words, injured parties must show that they were legally wronged and base the request for monetary judgment on a solid mathematical formula. There, of course, will be a discussion of the role of equity (the notion of justice in enforcement despite a lack of a "true" contract).

So where does contract law come from? And, perhaps more importantly for the legal student, where can it be found? The bulk of contract law can be found within case law. The practice of law is one of the oldest professions.[1] Therefore, there is a very long history of judges making decisions regarding the enforcement of promises between people. The courts have rendered innumerable decisions regarding the basic precepts of contract law. From these opinions, contract law has been distilled. Our legal system, like many others, rests upon the principle of *stare decisis*[2]; judges follow precedent, looking to past decisions to determine the rule of application in the current situation. Reliance on precedent gives contract law (and, indeed, other areas of law) its consistency. Knowing the rationale of previous decisions allows a measure of predictability in similar situations. However, the doctrine of *stare decisis* and reliance on precedent do not guarantee a certain result in any case, as the courts can distinguish the matter at hand from the precedent and find differently. This is particularly true where the court has determined that following precedent will result in an unjust result. And why have I discussed all of this with you? Because now you, the student, will understand why it is so important to learn to read and analyze case law. It is not merely a sadistic academic rite of passage for initiation into the practice of law.

---

[1] The Code of Hammurabi contains 282 "laws" and dates back to 1780 B.C.E. It prescribes, among other things, the rules for the creation and enforcement of contracts.

[2] From the Latin, meaning "to stand by things decided."

There are two notable exceptions to this generalization that contract law comes from common law: (1) the Statute of Frauds and (2) the Uniform Commercial Code. However, note that these two pieces of legislation relate to only specific types of contracts. The Statute of Frauds is discussed in Chapter 6 and the Uniform Commercial Code (Article Two—Sale of Goods) in Chapter 15.

These are the two primary sources of law (cases and statutes) and answer the question: "where does contract law come from?" Going back to case law for a moment to discuss another place to *find* contract law: You may find, quite often actually, that judges are relying on something called the *Restatement (Second) of Contracts*. While this publication from the ALI (American Law Institute) is only secondary authority, it has, for all practical purposes, the influence of primary law. As a student, you may find the comments and illustrations extremely helpful, as they explain the why's and how's of the principles of contract law.

The last place to find a secondary interpretation of the law is legal treatises. The most authoritative scholars in this area of law are Williston, Farnsworth, and Corbin.[3] These authors seek to clarify the law by detailing the development of the law and the complex principles associated with it.

This text takes a chronological approach to understanding contracts. We will discuss each contractual consideration as it would come up in the "real world." Additionally, attention must be paid during each step to the avoidance of litigation, a common and laudable goal in contractual relationships. Therefore, the text will discuss these practical matters as they arise during the course of constructing the contract in Parts One and Two of the text. Parts Three and Four deal with analyzing the failure of the contract and the remedies available to the non-breaching party. Again, emphasis will be placed on how to construct the contract to provide for remedies while avoiding litigation. This, of course, underscores the apparent dichotomy between the elements of certainty and freedom in contract. The rules of construction and enforcement are relatively confined when the court must step in to settle the dispute, while the parties, outside of litigation, are free to contract for whatever subject matter and provide for a myriad of their own remedies.

After having read all this, the paralegal student may be asking: "Yes, but what does all this have to do with me?" As a paralegal, which one day you will be, and a competent one at that I hope, you will be required to understand all the pieces of the puzzle so that you can draft an initial agreement, make appropriate changes after negotiations, perform the initial analysis of the contract to determine the rights and liabilities of the parties in the execution of the contract, and, finally, to determine the remedies available to the non-breaching party should a problem arise. This list of tasks assigned to a paralegal is not all-inclusive, but it is indicative of the importance of the work involved.

---

[3] However, the Calamari and Perillo *Hornbook* is more digestible as it is one book, whereas the others are multivolume sets. Indeed, the Williston series consists of 18 volumes and the Corbin series consists of 14.

WHAT'S NEW?

What's new in this, the second edition? While contract law is incredibly stable in theory, modern technologies have influenced how contracts are made, stored, and enforced. I have included in almost every chapter a feature called "Crypto Contracts" that discusses the impact of blockchain technology and the rise of "smart contracts."

Additionally, technology has crept into our social lives as well. I have updated cases and examples to demonstrate how social media can influence contract origination, performance, and evidence.

Also note that each case from the first edition was reviewed for continued relevance. Where there was a more illustrative or modern case, those changes were made.

ORGANIZATION OF THE TEXT

What do each of the textbook sections have in store for the paralegal student?

Part One

"The secret of getting ahead is getting started. The secret of getting started is breaking your complex overwhelming tasks into small manageable tasks, and then starting on the first one." —Mark Twain.

The first task in analyzing a contract is to determine whether the requisite elements are present. There must be a valid offer supported by legally recognizable consideration and properly accepted with conditions and third-party interests, if any, satisfactorily set forth. Without these basic elements, there is nothing for a court to enforce. An improperly formed contract is not a contract at all; the inquiry ends without a remedy in contract law.

Part Two

Once the parameters of a valid contract have been set, the student can examine the affirmative defenses that may available to the defendant. Affirmative defenses are facts and circumstances set forth that essentially defeat the plaintiff's claim, even if all the allegations against the defendant are true. Certain defects in the formation of the purported agreement will nullify the attempt at creating a legally binding contract. This means that while all the requisite elements exist; a valid offer has been made, supported by legally recognizable consideration and that the offeree has accepted, something in the surrounding circumstances has gone wrong.

This goes to the heart of enforceability of a contract. Once a party has brought the contract before the court, the party against whom the suit was filed can assert that there were defects in the formation of the contract, although it appears that the requisite elements are present, there were circumstances affecting the formation which make it impossible to enforce performance.

Part Three

Assuming that all the elements of a valid contract exist as discussed in Part One, and that there are no defenses to formation as discussed in Part Two, the parties stand on solid ground to perform their mutual contractual obligations. If the parties perform their obligations in accordance with the contract's terms, there is no further analysis needed. The contract has been executed upon and the parties owe no further legal duties to each other. Both have received the benefits they expected and have no need to resort to the legal system to resolve any issues.

However, just as *"the course of true love never did run smooth,"*[4] neither does the course of performance of many contracts. Broadly speaking, any performance that does not perfectly conform to the contract's requirements can be considered a breach of contract and potentially give rise to a claim for legal relief. Part Three is the discussion of what happens when a party does not tender "perfect performance."

Part Four

Finally, the last step in contract analysis has been reached. Now that a breach has been established, the non-breaching party needs to recover damages from the breaching party. Damages are the legal remedies available and they may take many forms. Remedies in the law attempt to put the non-breaching party in the same position they would have been in had the breach not occurred.

The first step in this process of recovery is to file a lawsuit, as any attempt at "self-help" by agreement of the parties (as discussed in the preceding chapter) has not solved the problem. Alternatively, with the rise in alternate dispute resolution, a party may elect to arbitrate the matter to avoid the expense and time involved in litigation. The non-breaching party must resort to the courts or other tribunal in order to establish the enforceable right to recoup losses incurred by the breach.

Once the lawsuit is filed, the plaintiff (non-breaching party bringing the lawsuit) will need to establish that harm has occurred due to the breach. This is the element of causation. The breach must have been the thing that caused the plaintiff's harm. If the plaintiff was harmed due to another independent occurrence then the breaching party may not be at fault for the harm. Without any real harm done by the defendant (breaching party), the plaintiff's case must be dismissed.

Lastly, this attribution of fault must show that the court can make the breaching party either pay money or perform an act to compensate the plaintiff

---

[4] Shakespeare, *A Midsummer Night's Dream* (I, i, 134)

for the harm that the defendant caused. If there is nothing the court could do to help the plaintiff recoup the losses, then there are no legal remedies available, the law is simply not equipped to act on behalf of the plaintiff. The case, therefore, must be dismissed.

Part Five

The first four parts of the text have discussed and are governed by the common law principles of contract law. Throughout this final chapter, it will appear that the Uniform Commercial Code (UCC) carves exceptions out from the stringent rules of contract law. Why? The underlying purpose of the entire UCC is practicality. These rules have been propagated in response to the very nature of commercial transactions. The "exceptions" to the general rules of contract law better reflect what really happens in commercial transactions. The UCC tries to protect and preserve these agreements and the expectations of the parties involved.

Where there appears to be leniency, do not presume weakness. The UCC also sets certain standards of conduct. While the rules governing the formation of the transaction may be more flexible, the conduct must be of a certain quality in order to merit that leniency." Certain ground rules apply to this grant of freedom in construction and performance. Article 1 of the UCC sets these ground rules. § 1-203 requires that the parties adhere to the principles of "good faith and fair dealing." § 1-204 requires "reasonableness" in response times in acting upon the agreement. And § 1-205 requires that the parties should and can rely upon the normal course of dealing and trade practices in the industry. Thereby making some assumptions taken by one or both parties reasonable in light of what normally occurs in that type of commercial transaction. Note that all of these ground rules can change depending on the particular industry involved. It may be reasonable to delay a shipment in the shoe industry by one week, but this kind of delay in the produce industry might be completely unacceptable as the goods will be destroyed in that time.

Therefore, do not think of the UCC as putting holes in the fabric of contract law, but rather as weaving a safety net. The small transgressions against the strict principles of common law may slip through unnoticed, but the larger issues will be caught.

It is completely beyond the scope and page capacity of this text to explain every section in Article 2. The most important sections are presented so that the student can gain an understanding of the general requirements of the UCC.

An alternate way to view the formation of contracts is via a timeline. The book is set up chronologically; intuitively, we know that a contract must be formed before it can be breached. The following flowchart / decision tree may prove helpful.

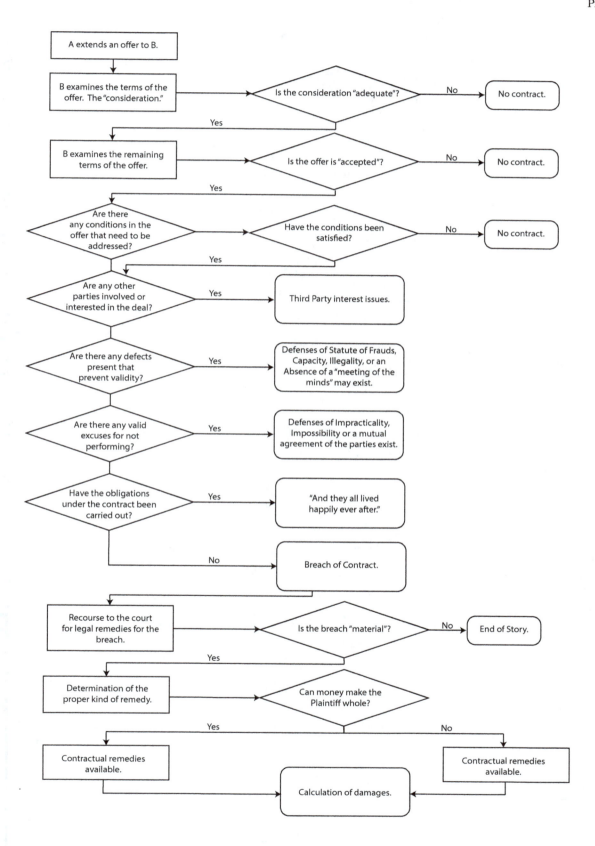

Art Credits

Archive icon, Dinosoftlabs/Adobe Stock; **Binary code**, botond1977/Adobe Stock; **Business handshake**, piyaset/iStock; **Calculator and money**, AnikaSalsera/iStock; **Common nails**, APCortizasJr/iStock; **Crumpled contract**, jeecis/iStock; **eBooks**, Bhavesh1988/Adobe Stock; **"Ethics" road sign**, JoyImage/iStock; **Fountain pen and real estate form**, RapidEye/iStock; **Keyboard with "yes" and "no" keys**, Nikolai Sorokin/Adobe Stock; **Two people talking**, icon_craft_studio/Adobe Stock; **Vision icon**, vasabii/Adobe Stock.

About the Author

Linda A. Wendling (formerly Spagnola) earned her BA in French with a minor in political science from Rutgers College and her JD from Seton Hall School of Law. She is admitted to practice in New Jersey, New York, Massachusetts, and North Carolina, where she now resides.

Upon graduation, she worked for a boutique law firm specializing in construction law. This area of law is its own peculiar creature whose practice requires attention to detail and perseverance to endure years of complex litigation. After leaving active practice in 2001, Dr. Wendling turned to academia. She joined the faculty of Union County College in Cranford, New Jersey. There, she created the Paralegal Program from the ground up and started registering students in 2003. The spring of 2006 saw her first class of graduates earning their associate degrees in Paralegal Studies.

After moving to North Carolina in 2007, Dr. Wendling (or just "W" as her students call her) could not resist the call of the classroom, except this time it was as a student. She pursued a master's degree in constitutional history at North Carolina State University. She also served as the Assistant Dean for Career Services at North Carolina Central University School of Law. The pull of hands-on teaching then led her to South University, where Dr. Wendling served not only as the Legal Studies Program Director, but also as the Chair of the Department serving campuses in ten states.

Learning never ends. Concern for the future led Dr. Wendling to Vermont Law School, where she earned an LL.M. in Environmental Law in January 2016. The culmination of her studies was an appointment to the Paris Climate Change Conference (COP21) as a U.N. delegate to assist Myanmar in preparing their position papers for international negotiation. She currently serves as the co-chair for the pro bono committee for the Environmental Law Section of the North Carolina Bar Association and an appointed member of the board of directors for the Abundance North Carolina Foundation.

Dr. Wendling is currently employed at Western Governors University as the Manager of Compliance & Accreditation for the Business and Information Technology Colleges. She works with a team of professionals monitoring regulatory affairs and ensuring academic integrity and conformity with national, state, and local standards in higher education and with a variety of programmatic accrediting bodies.

Contracts for Paralegals

Part One

Formation (The Elements)

Chapter 1: Offer

Chapter 2: Consideration

Chapter 3: Acceptance

Chapter 4: Conditions

Chapter 5: Third-Party Interests

Chapter 1

Offer

This chapter will explore the TYPE (unilateral versus bilateral), WHO (parties), WHAT (subject matter), WHEN, and the HOW (methods of creation and termination) of offers to enter into a contract. Two or more parties must both intend to enter into a binding agreement by an exchange of promises or actions. The proposal must specify who will be bound by the agreement, what will be exchanged between them, and when those obligations under the agreement must be performed. Offers may be created or terminated by a variety of methods. There may not be a need for a writing or even for words to be exchanged.

First, let's get some cumbersome vocabulary out of the way. The person who makes the offer, who initiates the potential formation of a contract, is called the **offeror**. The person to whom the offer is made is the **offeree**. As you learn about different areas of the law, you will come to notice that the

offeror
The person making the offer to another party.

offeree
The person to whom an offer is made.

3

offer
A promise made by the offeror to do (or not to do) something provided that the offeree, by accepting, promises or does something in exchange.

initiator of a transaction, the one creating the terms, is followed by the suffix "or." For example, the offeror is also referred to as the promis**or**, the person leasing space in a building is the less**or**, the person making the guarantee is the guarant**or**, and the person writing the will is the testat**or**. It then follows that the persons on the receiving ends of these transactions are, respectively, the promis**ee**, the less**ee**, the guarant**ee** (although in common usage we call this person the borrower), and the devis**ee**. The **offer** itself is the promise between these parties. According to the RESTATEMENT (SECOND) OF CONTRACTS § 24: "An offer is a promise which is in its terms conditional upon an act, forbearance or return promise being given in exchange for the promise or its performance." This legal language, of course, does the paralegal student no good as she/he reads this definition seven times trying to decipher what these people could possibly mean. What the definition really says is that two (or more) people exchange

1. Promises to do something for each other.
2. A promise to do something if the other person agrees not to do something that they might otherwise do.
3. A promise to do something if the other person simply does the act requested.

MUTUAL ASSENT

mutuality of contract
Also known as "mutuality of obligation"—is a doctrine that requires both parties to be bound to the terms of the agreement.

reasonable
Comporting with normally accepted modes of behavior in a particular instance.

These two people must intend to be legally bound upon the offeree accepting the offer with no further discussions needed. This is the principle of **mutuality of contract**—a mutual agreement to be bound by the terms of the offer. The "yes" is all it takes to form the legally binding contract. No one is surprised to be *in* a contract. (They may be surprised at the consequences but never at the mere fact they have entered into a contract.) A party must **reasonably** intend to make the offer binding at the time of the offer. The courts look at the surrounding circumstances to determine present intent to contract. The element of mutuality is absent where the offeror makes a statement that, while on its face seems to be an offer, is not intended to bind the parties to the agreement.

For example, Pete storms out of his car, slams the door, kicks the tires, and yells: "I will sell this hunk of junk to anyone who gives me a dollar!" because it has broken down yet again. Pete has not created a valid offer. Why? Because he's not seriously considering selling his car for a dollar; Pete is merely venting his frustration. Pete does not intend to be bound to someone who overhears and hands him a dollar. Additionally, Pete does not anticipate that any reasonable person who did overhear his exclamation would think that it was a valid offer.

Similarly, if words are spoken that may sound like an offer but are made in jest, there is not a valid offer. "Sure you can have my grandmother's beautiful antique brooch for a dollar." The person is obviously (objectively) being funny or sarcastic because she has no intention of parting with it for any amount of money. The standard here is reasonability. Is it objectively reasonable to think that a person would sell either of those items for a dollar? No, and no reasonable person would think that the speaker meant it. "The primary test of an offer is whether it induces a reasonable belief in the recipient that he or she can, by accepting, bind the sender. An offer is judged by its objective manifestations, not by any uncommunicated beliefs, mental reservations, or subjective interpretations or intentions of the offeror." AM. JUR. CONTRACTS § 49. A court would not force Pete to make the exchange if someone sued him because he wouldn't sign over the title to his car after the person gave him a dollar. At most the court would just make Pete give the dollar back. It is not **objectively reasonable** on either party's part that either of those statements was meant to be a legally binding offer. There can be no mutual assent if the parties know or should know it is not a valid offer to which the offeror intends to be bound. The courts have determined that an intent to enter into a contract is specific to the intention to go through with the deal. This may prove difficult where only circumstantial evidence exists. Critically, in a conspiracy to fix prices against the Sherman Act, the Court in *Bell Atl. Corp. v. Twombly*, 127 S. Ct. 1955, 167 L. Ed. 2d 929, 550 U.S. 544 (2007), determined that "[w]hile a showing of parallel 'business behavior is admissible circumstantial evidence from which the fact finder may infer agreement,' it falls short of conclusively establish[ing] agreement . . . ." *Id.* at 553 (citations omitted). This type of ambiguity—whether or not a course of conduct evidences an underlying agreement—is impermissible in contract law. If the behavior of the parties can also be explained without reference to an agreement or its terms, then the purported offer is too vague and cannot be agreed to by the parties. In the case of Bell Atlantic, the businesses that were accused of conspiring to restrain trade by inflating prices for high-speed Internet services and other billing practices could have been responding in similar fashion to the "common perceptions of the market." *Id.* at 554. Therefore, their actions could have been independent and not indicative of an agreement.

> **objectively reasonable**
> A standard of behavior that the majority of persons would agree with or how most persons in a community generally act.

Bilateral and Unilateral Contracts

As described above, there are two kinds of contracts. Numbers (1) and (2) describe a **bilateral contract**—a contract in which the parties exchange a promise for a promise.

> **bilateral contract**
> A contract in which the parties exchange a promise for a promise.

Example
Miriam offers to sell her *Contracts* book to Mark if he promises to pay her $10.00 for it. A binding legal obligation arises when Mark agrees to buy the book. Miriam is bound to sell Mark the book and Mark is bound to purchase it, even if the actual exchange of money and the book doesn't occur until the following week.

The third example, a promise to do something if the other person simply does the act requested, is a **unilateral contract**. The offeror requests that the offeree actually do something, not merely promise to do something.

> **unilateral contract**
> A contract in which the parties exchange a promise for an act.

Example

Miriam tells Mark that she will sell him her *Contracts* book if he gives her $10.00. Here Miriam wants the $10.00 handed to her before she will complete the transaction; she doesn't want Mark to merely promise to give her the money. Miriam becomes bound to Mark only after he performs on the contract by giving her the $10.00.

In the real world, common examples of unilateral contracts are offers for rewards (missing dog) and contests (best Halloween costume gets a prize). It is only when the offeree actually returns the dog or shows up in the best Halloween costume that the offeror is bound to give the reward or prize to them. They simply cannot promise to do those things and expect the reward or prize.

Further, perhaps of interest to paralegal students who will eventually be looking for employment, there is a distinction between "at-will" employment formed by a unilateral contract and employment formed by bilateral contract. At-will employment—the "day's work for a day's pay" type of job—is formed by the employee actually showing up and performing the tasks assigned. This is a unilateral contract. The employer/offeror is bound to pay the employee only when the work has been done. The employer is looking for performance, not merely the promise to do the job. In a very general way, this is why paychecks are issued for the prior week's performance. In contrast, employment that requires "good cause" for termination or other contractual provisions for a guarantee of employment term is bilateral. The court in *Flower v. T.R.A. Industries, Inc.*, 111 P.3d 1192 (Wash. Ct. App. 2005), determined that Mr. Flower's promise to accept a position with the employer, sell his house, and move to Washington, while the employer promised to terminate their relationship only for good cause, formed a bilateral contract. Why is this scenario different? The employer was looking for Mr. Flower's promises to change his position (sell his house and move), not just his performance on the job.

Fine, you say, there is an academic distinction between bilateral and unilateral contracts, but why does a paralegal have to know this? In practical application, it is important to know what kind of offer was made to determine when the parties become obligated to each other. In the first example, Miriam and Mark were obligated to each other after they exchanged their promises. Miriam cannot sell her book to someone else during the time that Mark gets his money together and actually pays Miriam. If she does, Miriam is in **breach** of the contract and Mark can pursue **legal remedies** against her. However, the same does not hold true for the second situation. Miriam is not obligated to sell Mark her book until he hands over the cash; therefore, she is free to sell her book to anyone else who comes up with the cash before Mark does and she is not in breach of contract because the contract is not formed until performance.

breach
A violation of an obligation under a contract for which a party may seek recourse to the court.

legal remedy
Relief provided by the court to a party to redress a wrong perpetrated by another party.

certainty
The ability for a term to be determined and evaluated by a party outside of the contract.

Certainty of Terms

What other common element do we see in the examples above? A contract must be **certain in its terms**. In other words, the offeree must be certain as to what he is agreeing to do. A basic rule of thumb is: the more certain the terms, the more likely it is to be a valid offer. It is very important to remember that a court will *not* correct or interpret any terms in a contract. The creation of the contract is entirely up to the parties; this is the theory of freedom of contract introduced previously. Within the limits of contract law, parties may contract for *whatever* they wish; a court cannot create the **meeting of the minds** on the terms. Therefore, if the terms are uncertain, there is no contract because there has been no valid offer.

It is generally accepted that there are four elements that must be **certain** in a contract in order for there to be a valid offer:

1. Parties
2. Price
3. Subject matter
4. Time for performance

meeting of the minds
A legal concept requiring that both parties understand and ascribe the same meaning to the terms of the contract.

Parties

Usually we know the identity of the offeror, but it takes two **parties** to create an agreement. This is not generally an issue. However, since the power to create the contract is essentially within the power of the offeree, it is important to know who is capable of accepting the offer. Generally speaking, the offeree is any person (or entity) to whom the offer is communicated and/or specified in the offer. Miriam specified that the offeree was Mark when she told him she would sell her *Contracts* book to him for $10.00. If she had posted the offer on the college's bulletin board, the offerees would have been anyone who read the offer.

The most important example of knowing the offeree's identity is a personal service contract, wherein it matters who performs the act desired by the offeror. If a theater offers $10 million for the Rolling Stones (or insert any easily recognizable and distinct band) to perform, it has to be the Rolling Stones that performs. No one else may accept that contract because the Rolling Stones is a unique set of people (albeit a rather aged and grizzly group) with unique talents. This would generally hold true for any specific performance contract.

parties
The persons involved in the making of the contract. There must be at least two; one to make the offer and the other to accept it.

SURF'S UP

As the influence of e-commerce grew, it became necessary to regulate transactions taking place entirely over the Internet. Indeed, at this writing, it appears that the vast majority of commerce takes place electronically. The legislative response was the Uniform Electronic Transactions Act of 1999. This act states that electronic records and signatures have the same weight and validity as their paper counterparts.

UETA § 2 deals with the definitions used in the act. Two significant definitions are

(2) "Automated transaction" means a transaction conducted or performed, in whole or in part, by electronic means or electronic records, in which the acts or records of one or both parties **are not reviewed by an individual in the ordinary course in forming a contract**, performing under an existing contract, or fulfilling an obligation required by the transaction.

and

(6) "Electronic agent" means a computer program or an electronic or other automated means used independently to initiate an action or respond to electronic records or performances in whole or in part, **without review or action by an individual.**

Notice how both definitions contemplate the possibility of the absence of human interaction. Who are the "parties" to the transaction that is made automatically? The anonymity of the Internet has changed some of the basics of contract law.

CRYPTO CONTRACTS

This "hands-off" approach via the Internet has become even more sophisticated with the advent of "smart contracts" that exist on the inviolable and inflexible "blockchain." Just as traditional currency has been disrupted by the advent of bitcoin, traditional contracts may also move onto this secure database platform. The contractual record would be timestamped; absolute fidelity to terms and uncompromising performance would be automatically enforced. But consider as you move through this textbook, how much of contract law depends upon context—knowing with whom you are dealing and what the customs of that relationship and/or industry are. How much automation is too much when dealing with contractual relationships? Look for more information in the Crpyto Contracts features in the upcoming chapters.

Price

price
The monetary value ascribed by the parties to the exchange involved in the contract.

Now that we know who is going to perform, the **price** must be specified in the contract. Otherwise there would be no way for the offeree to know how much he/she was expected to pay in return for the goods or services provided by the offeror. Therefore, there could be no meeting of the minds; an offeror cannot expect an offeree to accept *any* price and be legally bound by it. This is not to say that the exact monetary amount down to dollars and cents needs to be in the offer. As long as the price can be objectively determined, the offer is specific as to the price.

Example
Farmer Fred offers to sell 100 bushels of Granny Smith apples to Buyer Bob at the market price prevailing on September 1st of that year. The offer is

valid and Buyer Bob will be legally bound to pay the prevailing price on September 1st if he agrees to the contract. The market price is **objectively determinable** by both parties. The cost of the apples is precisely calculable. Buyer Bob has a pretty good idea of the price given the previous years' selling prices and has agreed to assume the risk that the price is yet to be determined to the exact penny.

Herein lies the key to certainty of price—objectivity. The price on September 1st will be an exact and certain cost; everyone who cares to look it up will find the same price. If the offer were for a "price to be determined" without any objective measure, meaning the offeror could make up any price he wanted, the offer would be an **illusory promise** to sell. It would have absolutely no meaning, just like an illusion in a magic show; it is not real and therefore is not an offer.

Subject Matter

The persons and price they will pay have been identified, but the price for *what*? The goods or services that the parties are bargaining for also must be specified in the offer. Again, the offeree must be sure of what she is getting in return for the price set by the contract. The quantity, quality, and content must be reasonably specified so that the offeree could objectively ascertain what she is to take away from the agreement. The amount of detail needed, of course, depends on the **subject matter** of the contract.

> **Example**
> Let's return to Farmer Fred and let's assume that Fred grows only one kind of apple, Granny Smiths. If Fred said to Bob: "I'll sell you 100 bushels of apples at the prevailing price on September 1st of this year," a valid offer would exist because Bob would be certain of the subject matter of the contract. Fred has offered 100 bushels of Granny Smith apples even though he didn't say that outright. It is only objectively reasonable that Fred can offer only that which he has to sell. However, if Farmer Fred grew several kinds of apples, the offer would fail for uncertainty because Bob would have no way of knowing which variety of apples he would be purchasing.

Therefore, if the subject matter could refer to more than one thing or have more than one interpretation, then the offer fails due to this ambiguity. Again, the test of whether the offer is valid is whether a reasonable person could be able to determine the subject of the contract. There are some interesting plot twists that come with this element.

If both parties are unaware of the ambiguity and there has been a meeting of the minds, the offer is still valid and the courts will uphold the contract. Ironically, it is the mutuality of the mistake that preserves the mutuality of the agreement.

> **Example**
> Farmer Fred only grows Granny Smith apples on his farm and Bob knows this. Both parties have agreed to the purchase of 100 bushels of the apples

objectively determinable
The ability of the price to be ascertained by a party outside of the contract.

illusory promise
A statement that appears to be a promise but actually enforces no obligation upon the promisor because he retains the subjective option whether or not to perform on it.

subject matter
The bargained-for exchange of goods and/or services that forms the basis for the contract.

at a certain price. Unknown to both Fred and Bob, Farmer Fred has inherited a huge apple orchard from his Uncle Frank Farmer. This farm grows a dozen different kinds of apples. While to the outside observer there may be an ambiguity in the contract, which kind of apples did Bob agree to buy? Fred has 13 different kinds of apples in his inventory; however, Fred and Bob both could only have agreed at the time to the purchase of the Granny Smith apples because they were unaware of the ambiguity in the contract. Both Bob and Fred thought they were certain in their terms.

This same scenario plays out slightly differently if only one of the parties is uncertain about the subject matter and the other is certain. If Buyer Bob is unaware of the inherited apple orchard and thinks Fred only has Granny Smiths to sell, but Fred knows he has 13 varieties to sell, then the offer was ambiguous. Fred has not identified the subject matter of the contract, and there has been no valid offer. In this case, the court may uphold the agreement based on the unknowing party's interpretation based on principles of equity that will be discussed later.

Offering alternatives does not make the offer invalid for vagueness. As long as the offeror makes the alternatives clear in the offer, the subject matter is objectively reasonably determinable. Fred may have offered Granny Smiths or red delicious apples for a certain price. Bob would have to choose between the offers. The number of choices does not make an offer ambiguous; it may be complex if many alternatives are offered, but as long as the subject matter is readily discernable, the offer is valid.

EYE ON ETHICS

Attorneys regularly face ethical decisions in advising their clients about contract formation. Most poignant is the creation of the contract establishing the attorney-client relationship. In this personal service contract, the attorney must guard against overreaching or, worse, misrepresentation or fraud.

The attorney is the offeror in this transaction and, as such, can set the terms of the offer. However, the attorney is also in a privileged and sensitive position when making this offer. The attorney has substantially more knowledge about the legal process than the potential client. This may lead the attorney to unreasonably limit the scope of representation, and the client would not be aware of this until, perhaps, it was too late. Indeed, the attorney may underestimate the degree of legal knowledge, skill, and amount of preparation that may be needed until the case is well underway. Additionally, the limitation may not negatively impact the attorney's duty to provide competent representation.

When would this underestimation in the offer rise to an ethical violation?

There are two special kinds of contracts that at first blush appear to be uncertain as to the amount of the subject matter to be purchased and therefore should fail as valid offers. They do not fail, however, because while the quantity is not specified, the quantity can be objectively determined. These two contracts are (1) **output contracts** and (2) **requirements contracts**. An output contract is certain as to the quality and content of the subject matter, but the amount is specified only as "all of the production (output) of the offeree." This would mean that Bob has agreed to buy all of the Granny Smith apples grown on Fred's farm that year. This contract focuses on how much production can occur. A requirements contract's focus is on a party's needs rather than the amount that can be produced. Essentially, the tables have turned. Fred has agreed to supply Bob with all the Granny Smith apples that Bob needs to make pies. This is unrelated to how many apples Fred can grow on his farm as long as it can meet Bob's requirements.

output contract
An agreement wherein the quantity that the offeror desires to purchase is all that the offeree can produce.

requirements contract
An agreement wherein the quantity that the offeror desires to purchase is all that the offeror needs.

SPOT THE ISSUE!

Penny Paralegal has been on her job search for months. Finally, she was offered what seemed to be her dream job. The partners forwarded her the following employment contract. Is this a valid offer? What are the missing or ambiguous elements, if any? Rewrite the contract to create a valid offer.

EMPLOYMENT CONTRACT

Agreement made this day, _____, 20___ between Penny Paralegal ("Employee") and Big Law Firm ("Employer") for employment.

Big Law Firm agrees to pay Penny Paralegal for her services. Payment shall be made every 1st and 15th of the month.

Penny Paralegal shall be provided with benefits standard in the industry.

Penny Paralegal will have 2 weeks of paid vacation and be permitted a total of 10 sick days per year.

Big Law Firm agrees to send Penny Paralegal to at least one Continuing Legal Education course per year and will pay the fees and costs associated with same.

Signed:

_____

Employee — Penny Paralegal

_____

Employer — Big Law Firm

Time for Performance

The parties (WHO) and price (HOW MUCH) they will pay for the subject matter (WHAT) have been expressed in certain terms. The last certainty must be WHEN. After a contract has been accepted, the parties do not have an indefinite period in which to fulfill their obligations under the contract. Of course, under the theory of freedom of contract, the parties may contract for any time period they choose. If a time for performance is not specified, the court will interpret this as a reasonable time. If the parties make a failed attempt at a time designation, the court cannot correct their mistake and the contract will fail for uncertainty of terms.

time of the essence
A term in a contract that indicates that no extensions for the required performance will be permitted. The performance must occur on or before the specified date.

Time of the essence clauses specify a time for performance; should the party fail to perform by the date specified, she will be in breach of contract and the "innocent" party is entitled to remedies. This is most often found in real estate contracts. After the seller accepts the buyer's offer to purchase the property, the sales contract usually sets an approximate date for the closing to occur. This date is often not the day on which the parties actually close on the property, but it does set an expectation that the closing will occur around that date. If it is imperative that the buyers or sellers close on that date—perhaps they must vacate their current home—a "time is of the essence" clause will be inserted in the contract. If the closing does not take place on (or before) that day, the party making time of the essence can avoid the contract and recover a reasonable measure of damages.

executory
The parties' performances under the contract have yet to occur.

executed
The parties' performance obligations under the contract are complete.

The timing of the performance of the requested act determines whether the contract is deemed either **executory** or **executed**. An executory contract is one in which the parties have not yet performed their obligations. The contract has not been completed. It follows then that an executed contract is one that has been completed; the parties owe no further obligations to each other because they have performed (or otherwise discharged) their obligations.

Communication to Intended Offeree

At last! It has been determined whether the contract is unilateral or bilateral and the terms (all four categories) are certain. The last element of mutuality of contract is that the offer is actually communicated to the offeree. The offeree must know of the offer in order for the offer to be valid. This seems to be an intuitive, commonsensical element that needs no explanation. However, it must be made clear that the method of communication must reasonably reach the intended audience and include all the necessary information to form a contract. This is where advertisements fail to be offers. The method of communication, whether it's the newspaper or a television ad, only conveys solicitation to patronize the business. The communication fails to include all the certain terms. The exception to this general rule is where a business identifies a particular item, specifies a certain quantity for a certain price, and identifies who may accept the offer. The prime example is a car dealership stating that they have one certain vehicle identified by the VIN selling for $10,000 and that they will sell it to the first person to come in and give them the required deposit and credit line.

Without these elements—(1) how to accept the offer (by a promise in a bilateral contract or by an act in a unilateral contract), (2) the certainty of terms (parties, price, subject matter, and time for performance), and (3) knowledge of the offer—how would the parties know what was being bargained for? There could be no "meeting of the minds" or mutual assent.

There are exceptions under the UCC for merchants—Chapter 15 deals with this in more detail.

SPOT THE ISSUE!

Mark Mason and Charles Constructor entered into a contract for Mark to lay bricks at Charles' new home building project. Things have gone awry and Mark and Charles each claim that the other is in breach of the contract and litigation might be necessary. Mark's attorney calls Charles' attorney to see if Charles would agree to go to binding arbitration instead of court. A day later, Mark calls his attorney to revoke the offer to go to arbitration. Has there been a communication to the offeree? Why or why not? Examine to whom the communications were made and in what capacity. See *CPI Builders, Inc. v. Impco Technologies, Inc.*, 94 Cal. App. 4th 1167, 114 Cal. Rptr. 2d 851 (2001).

METHOD OF CREATION

A contract (either bilateral or unilateral) may be created either expressly or impliedly. An **express contract** has been expressed in words; it can be either an oral or written memorialization of the agreement. An **implied contract** is not created by words; it is created by actions of the parties. For example, an implied contract is formed when a customer plunks down $1.25 on the counter of the convenience store for morning coffee and the newspaper. No words are spoken, but the contract exists just the same. If this were to be an express contract, the offer's wording would be something like: "I will sell you this coffee and newspaper if you pay for them." The actions of the parties indicate the existence of the contract. The exchange is understood, and the parties would not take those actions absent the unspoken agreement. The customer would be in breach of contract if she walked out without paying and the shopkeeper would be in breach if she did not provide the customer with the newspaper and coffee after the customer paid.

express contract
An agreement whose terms have been communicated in words, either in writing or orally.

implied contract
An agreement whose terms have not been communicated in words, but rather by conduct or actions of the parties.

TERMINATION OF THE OFFER

Offers do not last forever; remember, there is nothing that the law of contracts likes better than certainty. When do offers end if no expiration date is specified in the offer? There are several methods to terminate an offer:

1. Lapse of time.
2. Revocation of the offer by the offeror.
3. Rejection/counteroffer by the offeree.
4. Incapacity or death of either party.
5. Destruction or loss of the subject matter.
6. Supervening illegality.

lapse of time
An interval of time that has been long enough to affect a termination of the offer.

Of these six, only the first, the **lapse of time**, is still relatively indefinite. The uncertainty of having an offer hang out there, not knowing if it will ever be accepted, is not permitted. The courts permit an offer to remain open for a reasonable amount of time, but the "reasonability" of the time frame depends on the circumstances of the offer. The comment to RESTATEMENT (SECOND) OF CONTRACTS § 41(b) reads:

> In the absence of a contrary indication, just as acceptance may be made in any manner and by any medium which is reasonable in the circumstances (§ 30), so it may be made at any time which is reasonable in the circumstances. The circumstances to be considered have a wide range: they include the nature of the proposed contract, the purposes of the parties, the course of dealing between them, and any relevant usages of trade. In general, the question is what time would be thought satisfactory to the offeror by a reasonable man in the position of the offeree; but circumstances not known to the offeree may be relevant to show that the time actually taken by the offeree was satisfactory to the offeror.

What this language really means is that what might be reasonable in one situation may not be in another and it is dependent on the actual effect it may have on the parties and their willingness to contract given that lapse of time. For example, three days may be a very long time to accept an offer to purchase a good where the price of that good is subject to drastic price fluctuations or is perishable. However, three days to accept an offer to purchase a home is not unreasonable at all; real estate is relatively stable both in price and durability within those three days.

The next five methods of termination are easily discernable. If the offer is revoked by the offeror before the offeree has given his acceptance, the offer is withdrawn. This can take the form of revocation in the contract terms themselves — "this offer will expire in 48 hours" — or by subsequent communication to the offeree. *See, e.g., Starlite Ltd. Partnership v. Landry's Restaurants, Inc.,* 780 N.W.2d 396, 399 (Minn. App. 2010) ("When an offer specifies a deadline for acceptance and that time passes, the offeree's power to accept lapses and an offeree's late acceptance cannot create a contract."). The offeree can no longer accept and has no recourse to force the offeror to go through with the deal. The **revocation** can be either a direct statement to the offeree conveying the offeror's unwillingness to enter into a contract or indirect communication by performing acts known to the offeree that are inconsistent with the offer. Either way, there is a clear indication that the offer is no longer open. For example, Miriam tells Mark that she is not going to sell him her *Contracts* book or Miriam, in the presence of Mark, who knows Miriam only has one *Contracts* book, sells the book to Jill. Either method of communication, directly telling Mark or indirectly communicating her intent to revoke through her actions of which Mark has knowledge, is an acceptable method of revocation of the offer.

revocation
The offeror's cancellation of the right of the offeree to accept an offer.

This general rule that an offeror can revoke at any time up until acceptance has an exception in the case of unilateral contracts, where acceptance is not complete until full performance. An offeror cannot revoke the offer where the offeree has begun to perform the requested act. At that time, even though the contract has not been accepted because performance is not complete, where the offeree has made a **substantial beginning** or has changed his position in **detrimental reliance** on the offer, the power to revoke is terminated. This means that the offeree has essentially manifested his intent to be bound and to permit the offeror to revoke up until the last minute would offend our sense of fairness.

Example

Archie Architect tells Paul the Painter he will pay him $1,000 if Paul paints his house on Thursday. Archie has made a unilateral offer: He wants Paul to paint his house on Thursday, not just promise to do so. Paul buys all the supplies he needs and shows up at Archie's house on Thursday. After Paul has completed about three-fourths of the house, Archie revokes the offer. Under strict contract interpretation, Paul has not accepted the contract because he hasn't given full and perfect performance. However, the law has created the doctrine of substantial beginning to protect Paul. Archie is no longer able to revoke his offer after that point. Further discussion about fairness can be found in Chapter 14 in the discussion of equity.

In *Clodfelter v. Plaza Ltd.*, 698 P.2d 1 (N.M. 1985), homeowners entered into a unilateral real estate listing agreement. The owners would pay a commission to the Realtor if he sold the property. The court reemphasized that this kind of unilateral contract "may be revoked at will until there is partial performance by the broker." The Realtor "prepared brochures and provided advertising which resulted in inquiries and property viewings for prospective buyers. This evidence was sufficient for the trial court to find that the broker, pursuant to the agreement, had expended his time and effort to sell the property, therefore completing partial performance." *Id.* at 4.

An outright **rejection** of the offer obviously kills the offer. Additionally, a **counteroffer** terminates the original offer and creates an entirely new one in its place. The original offeror becomes the new offeree and the original offeree, who is making the counteroffer, becomes the new offeror. A **conditional acceptance** ("I accept your offer if . . .") is really a counteroffer because it changes the terms and therefore it also terminates the original offer. Sometimes, these offers and counteroffers are really part of the negotiation process and are not considered offers at that time. This can occur when a **letter of intent** (also known as a **nonbinding offer**) is sent to the offeree and if the terms are approved, will become the memorialization of the agreement. This letter contemplates a contract to be entered into at a later date. The agreement essentially only binds the parties to negotiate in good faith, not to the terms of the letter. *See, e.g., Incwebs, Inc. v. First Student, Inc.* (M.D. Fla. 2016) (The Court Order dismissed the plaintiff's complaint to find an implied-in-fact contract.). The parties had entered into a Letter of Intent and also signed a Confidentiality Agreement because First Student needed information about Incwebs's business. The confidential disclosures were made "for the purpose of permitting the parties

---

substantial beginning
An offeree has made conscientious efforts to start performing according to the terms of the contract. The performance need not be complete nor exactly as specified, but only an attempt at significant compliance.

detrimental reliance
An offeree has depended upon the assertions of the offeror and made a change for the worse in his position depending on those assertions.

rejection
A refusal to accept the terms of an offer.

counteroffer
A refusal to accept the stated terms of an offer by proposing alternate terms.

conditional acceptance
A refusal to accept the stated terms of an offer by adding restrictions or requirements to the terms of the offer by the offeree.

letter of intent/ nonbinding offer
A statement that details the preliminary negotiations and understanding of the terms of the agreement but does not create a binding obligation between parties.

to *explore the possibility* of entering into contractual arrangements upon such terms and conditions as may be acceptable to the parties." (emphasis added). *Id.* at 8. These types of letters may summarize the whole negotiation process and have all the requisite elements of the agreement, but it is still open for change; there is still the potential for counteroffers. *See, e.g., C.G. Schmidt, Inc. v. Permasteelisa N. Am.*, 825 F.3d 801 (7th Cir. 2016) (The court found that the letter of intent never became binding and no contract was formed as the parties were still negotiating the final contract price.).

IN-CLASS DISCUSSION

Apex Corporation has been in negotiations with Zenon Corporation for a few weeks regarding a licensing agreement. The following letter was sent from Apex to Zenon:

> Dear Zenon:
>
> Enclosed please find five draft copies of our proposed license agreement. As per our conversation, we believe it fully reflects our understandings. I hope it is to your satisfaction. Please return four signed copies and keep one for your records.
> Sincerely,
> Apex

Note that the details of the actual agreement are not an issue.
   Consider the following:

1. Have the parties come to an oral agreement?
2. Is there a binding contract already?
3. Is the letter an offer? Or merely a formality, memorializing the oral contract?

RESEARCH THIS

Find a case in your jurisdiction that answers the following fact scenario:
   Penny Pedestrian is hurt by Otto Auto in a motor vehicle accident. Otto offers to pay for Penny's injuries so they can settle the matter and keep it out of court. Penny says she will think about it. Two days later she calls Otto and asks if he would consider also paying for massage therapy as well.
   What effect, if any, does this have on the offer? Is the original offer still open?

---

incapacity
The inability to act or understand the actions that would create a binding legal agreement.

   The fourth method of terminating the offer is just as intuitive as the one above. If either party is not able to perform their end of the bargain due to **incapacity or death**, the offer is terminated. An essential element of a valid offer—certainty of the parties involved—is now missing. This "incapacity" may take the form of insanity and makes for an interesting analysis. A party "may have insane delusions regarding some matters and be insane on some subjects, yet capable of transacting business concerning matters wherein such subjects are not concerned, and such insanity does not make one incompetent to contract unless the subject matter of the contract is so connected with an insane delusion as to render the afflicted party incapable of understanding the nature and effect of the agreement or of acting rationally in the transaction." *See Breeden v. Stone*, 992 P.2d 1167, 1170 (Colo. 2000) (the probate court held that the stress and anxiety that compelled the decedent to commit suicide did not deprive him of testamentary capacity). *See also Hanks v. McNeil Coal Corp.*, 168 P.2d 256 (Colo. 1946) (Hanks was suffering from an insane delusion regarding a "home-brewed" horse medicine, but there was no evidence of delusions or hallucinations in connection with the transaction in question or with his other business at that time).

Similarly, the fifth way an offer is terminated is by destruction or **loss of the subject matter**. If Miriam's *Contracts* book is destroyed, lost, or stolen, she can no longer sell it to Mark.

loss of subject matter
The nonexistence of the subject matter of the contract, which renders it legally valueless and unable to be exchanged according to the terms of the contract.

SPOT THE ISSUE!

Candy Cellar offers to sell her property composed of her small retail shop and 20 acres of sugar cane fields to Gary Gamble. Gary wants to build a new casino on the site, to be called "Sweet Success." Before Gary accepts the offer, the retail shop burns to the ground. Make an argument that the offer is still valid. What factors did you consider in taking that position?

Lastly, an offer is terminated if the subject matter of the offer becomes illegal. This **supervening illegality** is different than a straightforward illegal agreement. If the offer, when made, contained provisions that were at the time perfectly legal but later became illegal due to new codes or ordinances, the offer is terminated for supervening illegality. The offeree cannot agree to the terms.

supervening illegality
An agreement whose terms at the time it was made were legal but, due to a change in the law during the time in which the contract was executory, has since become illegal.

Example
Archie the Architect offers a construction contract to Chuck the Contractor to build a five-story office building in the center of Busytown. The offer contains all the necessary elements of a valid contract and, at the time Archie makes the offer, there are no building codes or zoning restrictions in place that affect the plans. However, before Chuck accepts the offer, Busytown passes a zoning ordinance making it impermissible to construct a building over three stories tall. The once-valid offer is terminated due to supervening illegality; the acts requested cannot be performed without violating the ordinance.

An illegal agreement is not, and never was, a legally recognizable offer. A person cannot contract for a murder. Murder is per se illegal; the attempt to form an agreement on these terms is in no way valid in contract law.

irrevocable offers
Those offers that cannot be terminated by the offeror during a certain time period.

option contracts
A separate and legally enforceable agreement included in the contract stating that the offer cannot be revoked for a certain time period. An option contract is supported by separate consideration.

firm offers under the UCC
An agreement made by a merchant-offeror, and governed by the Uniform Commercial Code, that he will not revoke the offer for a certain time period. A firm offer is not supported by separate consideration.

On the opposite end of the spectrum from freely rescindable offers are **irrevocable offers**. There are two types of irrevocable offers: (1) **option contracts** and (2) **firm offers** (this will be discussed in greater detail in the last chapter on the Uniform Commercial Code). Generally and broadly speaking, these come into play only in commercial contracts. An option contract is one in which the offeror agrees to keep the offer open for a specified period of time during which she has no power to revoke the offer. An option contract must be supported by some sort of consideration for that privilege of having time in which the offer stays open for the offeree. Consideration, discussed in the next chapter, is the legal value that one party gives to the other in support of the contract. For example, if Greg offers his Cadillac for sale to Alice, but Alice needs time to get money together for the pricy car, she may offer $100 to Greg as consideration to keep the offer open for her until she can secure the financing for the car. The $100 is a separate transaction that keeps Alice's option to purchase the Cadillac open for a specified period of time. The $100 is nonrefundable as it pays for the option contract, not the car.

An option contract also may be created by detrimental reliance upon the agreement. This occurs often in construction bids. Typically, the general contractor solicits bids from subcontractors and suppliers as it prepares to bid on the whole construction project. In this context, the subcontractor's bid is an option contract—irrevocable until the general contractor has been awarded the prime contract. "Although the subcontractor does not make an explicit promise to keep its bid open, the court infers such a promise." *Arango Constr. Co. v. Success Roofing, Inc.*, 730 P.2d 720, 725 (Wash. Ct. App. 1986). A firm offer is an express promise between merchants (as defined by the Uniform Commercial Code) that an offer for the sale of goods will remain open for a specified period of time (up to three months) and the firm offer is in writing. No additional consideration is required.

Both these types of contracts stay open until the time specified has expired, or the subject matter is destroyed, thereby making it impossible to perform, or if there has been a supervening illegality. These are identical to some of the methods for terminating an offer described above. However, there are circumstances particular to option contracts and firm offers that do *not* terminate the offer where these circumstances would terminate a regular offer. Obviously, the option contract offer cannot be revoked by the offeror during the time period for which the option must remain open. Any attempt at revocation is null. Further, a counteroffer does not terminate the option contract offer. That offer remains open so that if the original offeror rejects the counteroffer, the original offeree can still accept the original offer under the option. Last, and maybe most interestingly, the death or insanity of the parties does not terminate the offer supported by the option contract. The offer remains open and will bind the "inheriting" parties. For example, Ebenezer offers to sell his horse farm to Tiny Tim and Tiny Tim gives Ebenezer $100 to keep the offer open for the next month while he secures financing. The parties have created an option contract. If Ebenezer dies within the month, the beneficiaries under his will must honor the option contract. If Tiny Tim exercises his option and accepts the offer of the horse farm, Ebenezer's beneficiaries must sell it to him despite their unwillingness to do so.

After it has been determined that a valid offer exists, with minds having met on the certain terms of parties, price, subject matter, and time for performance, termination can take many forms. The time for acceptance may lapse, it may be revoked or rejected, the parties or subject matter may no longer exist, or it may be illegal to complete performance.

Summary

When a person wishes to enter into an agreement to which he intends to be legally bound, he makes a bargain with the person(s) with whom he wants to exchange promises and actions. The initiator of the bargain is the *offeror*, the recipient of the bargain is the *offeree*, and the deal itself is the *offer*. If the offeror desires that the offeree make a mutually binding promise, it is a *bilateral* contract. On the other hand, if the offeror desires to be bound to the agreement only upon the performance (or nonperformance) of some action by the offeree, it is a *unilateral* contract. The offer may be created by *express* words (either written or oral) or *implied* by the actions of the parties. Either way, the offer must be certain in its terms. The offeree must know what he is agreeing to. The terms that must be included are

1. *Parties.*
2. *Price* (which is objectively determinable).
3. *Subject matter* (including quality and quantity; recall the certainness of quantity in output or requirements contracts).
4. *Time for performance.*

The offer does not always lead to a binding contract. The offer may terminate in a number of ways:

1. *Lapse of time.*
2. *Revocation.*
3. *Rejection/counteroffer.*
4. *Incapacity or death.*
5. *Destruction or loss of the subject matter.*
6. *Supervening illegality.*

However, there are two kinds of offers that cannot be revoked within a set time period, *option contracts* and *firm offers*.

If the offer does not terminate for any of the above reasons, and it is certain in all the requisite terms, a binding contract may be formed on the basis of this valid offer. In the next chapter, we will examine the actual bargain of the contract more closely to determine whether it forms the basis for legal consideration.

Key Terms

bilateral contract	counteroffer
breach	destruction or loss of subject matter
certainty	detrimental reliance
conditional acceptance	executed

executory

express contract

firm offers

illusory promise

implied contract

incapacity

irrevocable offers

lapse of time

legal remedy

letter of intent

meeting of the minds

mutuality of contract

objectively determinable

objectively reasonable

offer

offeree

offeror

option contracts

output contract

parties

price

reasonable

rejection

requirements contract

revocation

subject matter

substantial beginning

supervening illegality

time of the essence

unilateral contract

Review Questions

MULTIPLE CHOICE

Choose the best answer(s) and please explain *why* you choose the answer(s).

1. Identify which of the following is an offer.
   a. I may sell you my car for $5,000.
   b. I will sell you my car for $5,000.
   c. I will sell you one of my cars for $5,000.
   d. I will consider selling you my car for $5,000.

2. Identify the following as either a bilateral or unilateral contract.
   a. I promise to pay $500 for your promise to sell me your gold watch.
   b. I promise to pay $500 for your selling me your gold watch.
   c. I promise to sell you my gold watch for your promise to pay $500.
   d. I promise to sell you my gold watch for your paying me $500.
   e. I promise to pay you $500 for your refraining from smoking for five years.

3. Which of the following is a "time of the essence" clause?
   a. The closing shall take place on September 30th at the office of the buyer's attorney.
   b. The closing must take place on September 30th at the office of the buyer's attorney.
   c. The closing shall take place on September 30th at the office of the buyer's attorney. Either party may indicate that time is of the essence and give notice by September 20th.

EXPLAIN YOURSELF

All answers should be written in complete sentences. A simple "yes" or "no" is insufficient.

1. A bilateral contract is:

2. A unilateral contract is:

3. What are the essential elements of every valid offer?

4. When does the offeror of a unilateral contract lose his ability to revoke the contract?

5. Explain the difference between an output contract and a requirements contract.

6. When does a contract become executed?

7. Must an express contract be written in words?

"FAULTY PHRASES"

All of the following statements are FALSE; state why they are false and then rewrite them as a true statement. Write a brief fact pattern that illustrates your answer.

1. An offer must be written down in order to be valid.

2. An offeree can accept the original offer by "conditional acceptance."

3. Insanity always terminates an offer.

4. If the terms of the offer are legal at the time of the making of the contract, then performance on the contract must be made according to those terms.

5. An offer will always terminate within one week after the offeror makes it. The offeree will not be able to accept it after that time.

"WRITE" AWAY! PORTFOLIO ASSIGNMENT

With the explosion of new building and renovation sweeping the country, construction contracts, both good and bad, are everywhere. The "Write" Away! exercises will construct one of these contracts piece by piece, term by term, as the student is exposed to them.

In this first exercise, draft an offer from "Druid Design & Build" to Carrie Kilt, the owner of a large parcel of land on which she would like to construct her new home.

Make sure the four necessary elements are present. Do not worry about too many details; that will come later. You, the student, are in control of these details. There is no set prescription; this will be a fluid, dynamic, and changing document until the end of the book.

Case in Point   ADVERTISEMENTS AND OFFERS

88 F. Supp. 2d 116
John D.R. LEONARD, Plaintiff,
v.
PEPSICO, INC., Defendant.
No. 96 Civ. 5320(KMW).
No. 96 Civ. 9069(KMW).
United States District Court, S.D. New York.
August 5, 1999.

Page 117

OPINION & ORDER

KIMBA M. WOOD, District Judge.
Plaintiff brought this action seeking, among other things, specific performance

Page 118

of an alleged offer of a Harrier Jet, featured in a television advertisement for defendant's "Pepsi Stuff" promotion. Defendant has moved for summary judgment pursuant to Federal Rule of Civil Procedure 56. For the reasons stated below, defendant's motion is granted.

I. BACKGROUND

This case arises out of a promotional campaign conducted by defendant, the producer and distributor of the soft drinks Pepsi and Diet Pepsi. (See PepsiCo Inc.'s Rule 56.1 Statement ("Def. Stat.") ¶ 2.)[1] The promotion, entitled "Pepsi Stuff," encouraged consumers to collect "Pepsi Points" from specially marked packages of Pepsi or Diet Pepsi and redeem these points for merchandise featuring the Pepsi logo. (See id. ¶¶ 4, 8.) Before introducing the promotion nationally, defendant conducted a test of the promotion in the Pacific Northwest from October 1995 to March 1996. (See id. ¶¶ 5-6.) A Pepsi Stuff catalog was distributed to consumers in the test market, including Washington State. (See id. ¶ 7.) Plaintiff is a resident of Seattle, Washington. (See id. ¶ 3.) While living in Seattle, plaintiff saw the Pepsi Stuff commercial (see id. ¶ 22) that he contends constituted an offer of a Harrier Jet.

A. The Alleged Offer

Because whether the television commercial constituted an offer is the central question in this case, the Court will describe the commercial in detail. The commercial opens upon an idyllic, suburban morning, where the chirping of birds in sun-dappled trees welcomes a paperboy on his morning route. As the newspaper hits the stoop of a conventional two-story house, the tattoo of a military drum introduces the subtitle, "MONDAY 7:58 AM." The stirring strains of a martial air mark the appearance of a well-coiffed teenager preparing to leave for school, dressed in a shirt emblazoned with the Pepsi logo, a

---

[1]The Court's recitation of the facts of this case is drawn from the statements of uncontested facts submitted by the parties pursuant to Local Civil Rule 56.1. The majority of citations are to defendant's statement of facts because plaintiff does not contest many of defendant's factual assertions. (See Plaintiff Leonard's Response to PepsiCo's Rule 56.1 Statement ("Pl. Stat.").) Plaintiff's disagreement with certain of defendant's statements is noted in the text.

In an Order dated November 24, 1997, in a related case (96 Civ. 5320), the Court set forth an initial account of the facts of this case. Because the parties have had additional discovery since that Order and have crafted Local Civil Rule 56.1 Statements and Counter-statements, the recitation of facts herein should be considered definitive.

red-white-and-blue ball. While the teenager confidently preens, the military drumroll again sounds as the subtitle "T-SHIRT 75 PEPSI POINTS" scrolls across the screen. Bursting from his room, the teenager strides down the hallway wearing a leather jacket. The drumroll sounds again, as the subtitle "LEATHER JACKET 1450 PEPSI POINTS" appears. The teenager opens the door of his house and, unfazed by the glare of the early morning sunshine, puts on a pair of sunglasses. The drumroll then accompanies the subtitle "SHADES 175 PEPSI POINTS." A voiceover then intones, "Introducing the new Pepsi Stuff catalog," as the camera focuses on the cover of the catalog. (See Defendant's Local Rule 56.1 Stat., Exh. A (the "Catalog").)[2]

The scene then shifts to three young boys sitting in front of a high school building. The boy in the middle is intent on his Pepsi Stuff Catalog, while the boys on either side are each drinking Pepsi. The three boys gaze in awe at an object rushing overhead, as the military march builds to a crescendo. The Harrier Jet is not yet visible, but the observer senses the presence of a mighty plane as the extreme winds generated by its flight create a paper maelstrom in a classroom devoted to an otherwise dull physics lesson. Finally,

Page 119

the Harrier Jet swings into view and lands by the side of the school building, next to a bicycle rack. Several students run for cover, and the velocity of the wind strips one hapless faculty member down to his underwear. While the faculty member is being deprived of his dignity, the voiceover announces: "Now the more Pepsi you drink, the more great stuff you're gonna get."

The teenager opens the cockpit of the fighter and can be seen, helmetless, holding a Pepsi. "[L]ooking very pleased with himself," (Pl. Mem. at 3,) the teenager exclaims, "Sure beats the bus," and chortles. The military drumroll sounds a final time, as the following words appear: "HARRIER FIGHTER 7,000,000 PEPSI POINTS." A few seconds later, the following appears in more stylized script: "Drink Pepsi — Get Stuff." With that message, the music and the commercial end with a triumphant flourish.

---

[2] At this point, the following message appears at the bottom of the screen: "Offer not available in all areas. See details on specially marked packages."

Inspired by this commercial, plaintiff set out to obtain a Harrier Jet. Plaintiff explains that he is "typical of the 'Pepsi Generation' ... he is young, has an adventurous spirit, and the notion of obtaining a Harrier Jet appealed to him enormously." (Pl. Mem. at 3.) Plaintiff consulted the Pepsi Stuff Catalog. The Catalog features youths dressed in Pepsi Stuff regalia or enjoying Pepsi Stuff accessories, such as "Blue Shades" ("As if you need another reason to look forward to sunny days."), "Pepsi Tees" ("Live in 'em. Laugh in 'em. Get in 'em."), "Bag of Balls" ("Three balls. One bag. No rules."), and "Pepsi Phone Card" ("Call your mom!"). The Catalog specifies the number of Pepsi Points required to obtain promotional merchandise. (See Catalog, at rear foldout pages.) The Catalog includes an Order Form which lists, on one side, fifty-three items of Pepsi Stuff merchandise redeemable for Pepsi Points (see id. (the "Order Form")). Conspicuously absent from the Order Form is any entry or description of a Harrier Jet. (See id.) The amount of Pepsi Points required to obtain the listed merchandise ranges from 15 (for a "Jacket Tattoo" ("Sew 'em on your jacket, not your arm.")) to 3300 (for a "Fila Mountain Bike" ("Rugged. All-terrain. Exclusively for Pepsi.")). It should be noted that plaintiff objects to the implication that because an item was not shown in the Catalog, it was unavailable. (See Pl. Stat. ¶¶ 23-26, 29.)

The rear foldout pages of the Catalog contain directions for redeeming Pepsi Points for merchandise. (See Catalog, at rear foldout pages.) These directions note that merchandise may be ordered "only" with the original Order Form. (See id.) The Catalog notes that in the event that a consumer lacks enough Pepsi Points to obtain a desired item, additional Pepsi Points may be purchased for ten cents each; however, at least fifteen original Pepsi Points must accompany each order. (See id.)

Although plaintiff initially set out to collect 7,000,000 Pepsi Points by consuming Pepsi products, it soon became clear to him that he "would not be able to buy (let alone drink) enough Pepsi to collect the necessary Pepsi Points fast enough." (Affidavit of John D.R. Leonard, Mar. 30, 1999 ("Leonard Aff."), ¶ 5.) Reevaluating his strategy, plaintiff "focused for the first time on the packaging materials in the Pepsi Stuff promotion," (id.,) and realized that buying Pepsi Points would be a more promising option. (See id.)

Through acquaintances, plaintiff ultimately raised about $700,000. (*See id.* ¶ 6.)

B. Plaintiff's Efforts to Redeem the Alleged Offer

On or about March 27, 1996, plaintiff submitted an Order Form, fifteen original Pepsi Points, and a check for $700,008.50. (*See* Def. Stat. ¶ 36.) Plaintiff appears to have been represented by counsel at the time he mailed his check; the check is drawn on an account of plaintiff's first set of attorneys. (*See* Defendant's Notice of Motion, Exh. B (first).) At the bottom of the Order Form, plaintiff wrote in "1 Harrier Jet" in the "Item" column and "7,000,000" in the "Total Points" column. (*See id.*) In a letter accompanying his submission,

Page 120

plaintiff stated that the check was to purchase additional Pepsi Points "expressly for obtaining a new Harrier jet as advertised in your Pepsi Stuff commercial." (*See* Declaration of David Wynn, Mar. 18, 1999 ("Wynn Dec."), Exh. A.)

On or about May 7, 1996, defendant's fulfillment house rejected plaintiff's submission and returned the check, explaining that:

> The item that you have requested is not part of the Pepsi Stuff collection. It is not included in the catalogue or on the order form, and only catalogue merchandise can be redeemed under this program.
>
> The Harrier jet in the Pepsi commercial is fanciful and is simply included to create a humorous and entertaining ad. We apologize for any misunderstanding or confusion that you may have experienced and are enclosing some free product coupons for your use.

(Wynn Aff. Exh. B (second).) Plaintiff's previous counsel responded on or about May 14, 1996, as follows:

> Your letter of May 7, 1996 is totally unacceptable. We have reviewed the video tape of the Pepsi Stuff commercial ... and it clearly offers the new Harrier jet for 7,000,000 Pepsi Points. Our client followed your rules explicitly. . . .
>
> This is a formal demand that you honor your commitment and make immediate

arrangements to transfer the new Harrier jet to our client. If we do not receive transfer instructions within ten (10) business days of the date of this letter you will leave us no choice but to file an appropriate action against Pepsi. . . .

(Wynn Aff., Exh. C.) This letter was apparently sent onward to the advertising company responsible for the actual commercial, BBDO New York ("BBDO"). In a letter dated May 30, 1996, BBDO Vice President Raymond E. McGovern, Jr., explained to plaintiff that:

> I find it hard to believe that you are of the opinion that the Pepsi Stuff commercial ("Commercial") really offers a new Harrier Jet. The use of the Jet was clearly a joke that was meant to make the Commercial more humorous and entertaining. In my opinion, no reasonable person would agree with your analysis of the Commercial.

(Wynn Aff. Exh. A.) On or about June 17, 1996, plaintiff mailed a similar demand letter to defendant. (*See* Wynn Aff., Exh. D.)

Litigation of this case initially involved two lawsuits, the first a declaratory judgment action brought by PepsiCo in this district (the "declaratory judgment action"), and the second an action brought by Leonard in Florida state court (the "Florida action").[3] PepsiCo brought suit in this Court on July 18, 1996, seeking a declaratory judgment stating that it had no obligation to furnish plaintiff with a Harrier Jet. That case was filed under docket number 96 Civ. 5320. In response to PepsiCo's suit in New York, Leonard brought suit in Florida state court on August 6, 1996, although this case had nothing to do with Florida.[4] That suit was removed to the Southern District of Florida in September 1996. In an Order

---

[3]Because Leonard and PepsiCo were each plaintiff in one action and defendant in the other, the Court will refer to the parties as "Leonard" and "PepsiCo," rather than plaintiff and defendant, for its discussion of the procedural history of this litigation.

[4]The Florida suit alleged that the commercial had been shown in Florida. Not only was this assertion irrelevant, in that plaintiff had not actually seen the commercial in Florida, but it later proved to be false. *See Leonard v. PepsiCo*, 96-2555 Civ.-King, at 1 (S.D. Fla. Nov. 6, 1996) ("The only connection this case has to this forum is that Plaintiff's lawyer is in the Southern District of Florida.").

dated November 6, 1996, United States District Judge James Lawrence King found that, "Obviously this case has been filed in a form that has no meaningful relationship to the controversy and warrants a transfer pursuant to 28 U.S.C. § 1404(a)." *Leonard v. PepsiCo,*

Page 121

96-2555 Civ.-King, at 1 (S.D.Fla. Nov. 6, 1996). The Florida suit was transferred to this Court on December 2, 1996, and assigned the docket number 96 Civ. 9069.

Once the Florida action had been transferred, Leonard moved to dismiss the declaratory judgment action for lack of personal jurisdiction. In an Order dated November 24, 1997, the Court granted the motion to dismiss for lack of personal jurisdiction in case 96 Civ. 5320, from which PepsiCo appealed. Leonard also moved to voluntarily dismiss the Florida action. While the Court indicated that the motion was proper, it noted that PepsiCo was entitled to some compensation for the costs of litigating this case in Florida, a forum that had no meaningful relationship to the case. (*See* Transcript of Proceedings Before Hon. Kimba M. Wood, Dec. 9, 1997, at 3.) In an Order dated December 15, 1997, the Court granted Leonard's motion to voluntarily dismiss this case without prejudice, but did so on condition that Leonard pay certain attorneys' fees.

In an Order dated October 1, 1998, the Court ordered Leonard to pay $88,162 in attorneys' fees within thirty days. Leonard failed to do so, yet sought nonetheless to appeal from his voluntary dismissal and the imposition of fees. In an Order dated January 5, 1999, the Court noted that Leonard's strategy was "'clearly an end-run around the final judgment rule.'" (Order at 2 (quoting *Palmieri v. Defaria,* 88 F.3d 136 (2d Cir. 1996)).) Accordingly, the Court ordered Leonard either to pay the amount due or withdraw his voluntary dismissal, as well as his appeals therefrom, and continue litigation before this Court. (*See* Order at 3.) Rather than pay the attorneys' fees, Leonard elected to proceed with litigation, and shortly thereafter retained present counsel.

On February 22, 1999, the Second Circuit endorsed the parties' stipulations to the dismissal of any appeals taken thus far in this case. Those stipulations noted that Leonard had consented to the jurisdiction of this Court and that PepsiCo agreed not to seek enforcement of the attorneys' fees award. With these issues having been waived, PepsiCo moved for summary judgment pursuant to Federal Rule of Civil Procedure 56. The present motion thus follows three years of jurisdictional and procedural wrangling.

II. DISCUSSION

A. The Legal Framework

1. Standard for Summary Judgment

On a motion for summary judgment, a court "cannot try issues of fact; it can only determine whether there are issues to be tried." *Donahue v. Windsor Locks Bd. of Fire Comm'rs,* 834 F.2d 54, 58 (2d Cir. 1987) (citations and internal quotation marks omitted). To prevail on a motion for summary judgment, the moving party therefore must show that there are no such genuine issues of material fact to be tried, and that he or she is entitled to judgment as a matter of law. *See* Fed. R. Civ. P. 56(c); *Celotex Corp. v. Catrett,* 477 U.S. 317, 322, 106 S. Ct. 2548, 91 L. Ed. 2d 265 (1986); *Citizens Bank v. Hunt,* 927 F.2d 707, 710 (2d Cir. 1991). The party seeking summary judgment "bears the initial responsibility of informing the district court of the basis for its motion," which includes identifying the materials in the record that "it believes demonstrate the absence of a genuine issue of material fact." *Celotex Corp.,* 477 U.S. at 323, 106 S. Ct. 2548.

Once a motion for summary judgment is made and supported, the non-moving party must set forth specific facts that show that there is a genuine issue to be tried. *See Anderson v. Liberty Lobby, Inc.,* 477 U.S. 242, 251-52, 106 S. Ct. 2505, 91 L. Ed. 2d 202 (1986). Although a court considering a motion for summary judgment must view all evidence in the light most favorable to the non-moving party, and must draw all reasonable inferences in that party's favor, *see Consarc Corp. v. Marine Midland Bank, N.A.,* 996 F.2d 568, 572 (2d Cir. 1993), the nonmoving party "must do more

Page 122

than simply show that there is some metaphysical doubt as to the material facts." *Matsushita Elec.*

Indus. Co. v. Zenith Radio Corp., 475 U.S. 574, 586, 106 S. Ct. 1348, 89 L.Ed.2d 538 (1986). If, based on the submissions to the court, no rational fact-finder could find in the non-movant's favor, there is no genuine issue of material fact, and summary judgment is appropriate. *See Anderson*, 477 U.S. at 250, 106 S. Ct. 2505.

The question of whether or not a contract was formed is appropriate for resolution on summary judgment. As the Second Circuit has recently noted, "Summary judgment is proper when the 'words and actions that allegedly formed a contract [are] so clear themselves that reasonable people could not differ over their meaning.' " *Krumme v. Westpoint Stevens, Inc.*, 143 F.3d 71, 83 (2d Cir. 1998) (quoting *Bourque v. FDIC*, 42 F.3d 704, 708 (1st Cir. 1994)) (further citations omitted); *see also Wards Co. v. Stamford Ridgeway Assocs.*, 761 F.2d 117, 120 (2d Cir. 1985) (summary judgment is appropriate in contract case where interpretation urged by non-moving party is not "fairly reasonable"). Summary judgment is appropriate in such cases because there is "sometimes no genuine issue as to whether the parties' conduct implied a 'contractual understanding.' ... In such cases, 'the judge must decide the issue himself, just as he decides any factual issue in respect to which reasonable people cannot differ.' " *Bourque*, 42 F.3d at 708 (quoting *Boston Five Cents Sav. Bank v. Secretary of Dep't of Housing & Urban Dev.*, 768 F.2d 5, 8 (1st Cir. 1985)).

2. Choice of Law

The parties disagree concerning whether the Court should apply the law of the state of New York or of some other state in evaluating whether defendant's promotional campaign constituted an offer. Because this action was transferred from Florida, the choice of law rules of Florida, the transferor state, apply. *See Ferens v. John Deere Co.*, 494 U.S. 516, 523-33, 110 S. Ct. 1274, 108 L.Ed.2d 443 (1990). Under Florida law, the choice of law in a contract case is determined by the place "where the last act necessary to complete the contract is done." *Jemco, Inc. v. United Parcel Serv., Inc.*, 400 So.2d 499, 500-01 (Fla. Dist. Ct. App. 1981); *see also Shapiro v. Associated Int'l Ins. Co.*, 899 F.2d 1116, 1119 (11th Cir. 1990).

The parties disagree as to whether the contract could have been completed by plaintiff's filling out the Order Form to request a Harrier Jet, or by defendant's acceptance of the Order Form. If the commercial constituted an offer, then the last act necessary to complete the contract would be plaintiff's acceptance, in the state of Washington. If the commercial constituted a solicitation to receive offers, then the last act necessary to complete the contract would be defendant's acceptance of plaintiff's Order Form, in the state of New York. The choice of law question cannot, therefore, be resolved until after the Court determines whether the commercial was an offer or not. The Court agrees with both parties that resolution of this issue requires consideration of principles of contract law that are not limited to the law of any one state. Most of the cases cited by the parties are not from New York courts. As plaintiff suggests, the questions presented by this case implicate questions of contract law "deeply ingrained in the common law of England and the States of the Union." (Pl. Mem. at 8.)

B. Defendant's Advertisement Was Not an Offer

1. Advertisements as Offers

The general rule is that an advertisement does not constitute an offer. The *Restatement (Second) of Contracts* explains that:

> Advertisements of goods by display, sign, handbill, newspaper, radio or television are not ordinarily intended or understood as offers to sell. The same is true of catalogues, price lists and circulars, even though the terms of suggested bargains may be stated in some detail.

Page 123

> It is of course possible to make an offer by an advertisement directed to the general public (see § 29), but there must ordinarily be some language of commitment or some invitation to take action without further communication.

Restatement (Second) of Contracts § 26 cmt. b (1979). Similarly, a leading treatise notes that:

> It is quite possible to make a definite and operative offer to buy or sell goods by advertisement, in a newspaper, by a handbill, a

catalog or circular or on a placard in a store window. *It is not customary to do this, however; and the presumption is the other way. . . .* Such advertisements are understood to be mere requests to consider and examine and negotiate; and no one can reasonably regard them as otherwise unless the circumstances are exceptional and the words used are very plain and clear.

1 Arthur Linton Corbin & Joseph M. Perillo, *Corbin on Contracts* § 2.4, at 116-17 (rev. ed. 1993) (emphasis added); *see also* 1 E. Allan Farnsworth, *Farnsworth on Contracts* § 3.10, at 239 (2d ed. 1998); 1 Samuel Williston & Richard A. Lord, *A Treatise on the Law of Contracts* § 4:7, at 286-87 (4th ed.1990). New York courts adhere to this general principle. *See Lovett v. Frederick Loeser & Co.,* 124 Misc. 81, 207 N.Y.S. 753, 755 (N.Y. Mun. Ct.1924) (noting that an "advertisement is nothing but an invitation to enter into negotiations, and is not an offer which may be turned into a contract by a person who signifies his intention to purchase some of the articles mentioned in the advertisement"); *see also Geismar v. Abraham & Strauss,* 109 Misc. 2d 495, 439 N.Y.S.2d 1005, 1006 (N.Y. Dist. Ct. 1981) (reiterating *Lovett* rule); *People v. Gimbel Bros.,* 202 Misc. 229, 115 N.Y.S.2d 857, 858 (N.Y. Sp. Sess. 1952) (because an "[a]dvertisement does not constitute an offer of sale but is solely an invitation to customers to make an offer to purchase," defendant not guilty of selling property on Sunday).

An advertisement is not transformed into an enforceable offer merely by a potential offeree's expression of willingness to accept the offer through, among other means, completion of an order form. In *Mesaros v. United States,* 845 F.2d 1576 (Fed. Cir. 1988), for example, the plaintiffs sued the United States Mint for failure to deliver a number of Statue of Liberty commemorative coins that they had ordered. When demand for the coins proved unexpectedly robust, a number of individuals who had sent in their orders in a timely fashion were left empty-handed. *See id.* at 1578-80. The court began by noting the "well-established" rule that advertisements and order forms are "mere notices and solicitations for offers which create no power of acceptance in the recipient." *Id.* at 1580; *see also Foremost Pro Color, Inc. v. Eastman Kodak Co.,* 703 F.2d 534, 538-39

(9th Cir. 1983) ("The weight of authority is that purchase orders such as those at issue here are not enforceable contracts until they are accepted by the seller.");[5] *Restatement (Second) of Contracts* § 26 ("A manifestation of willingness to enter a bargain is not an offer if the person to whom it is addressed knows or has reason to know that the person making it does not intend to conclude a bargain until he has made a further manifestation of assent."). The spurned coin collectors could not maintain a breach of contract action because no contract would be formed until the advertiser accepted the order form and processed payment. *See id.* at 1581; *see also Alligood v. Procter & Gamble,* 72 Ohio App. 3d 309, 594 N.E.2d 668 (1991) (finding that no offer was made in promotional campaign for baby diapers, in which consumers were to redeem teddy bear proof-of-purchase symbols for catalog merchandise); *Chang v. First Colonial Savings Bank,* 242 Va. 388,

Page 124

410 S.E.2d 928 (1991) (newspaper advertisement for bank settled the terms of the offer once bank accepted plaintiffs' deposit, notwithstanding bank's subsequent effort to amend the terms of the offer). Under these principles, plaintiff's letter of March 27, 1996, with the Order Form and the appropriate number of Pepsi Points, constituted the offer. There would be no enforceable contract until defendant accepted the Order Form and cashed the check.

The exception to the rule that advertisements do not create any power of acceptance in potential offerees is where the advertisement is "clear, definite, and explicit, and leaves nothing open for negotiation," in that circumstance, "it constitutes an offer, acceptance of which will complete the contract." *Lefkowitz v. Great Minneapolis Surplus Store,* 251 Minn. 188, 86 N.W.2d 689, 691 (1957). In *Lefkowitz,* defendant had published a newspaper announcement stating: "Saturday 9 AM Sharp, 3 Brand New Fur Coats, Worth to $100.00, First Come First Served

---

[5] *Foremost Pro* was overruled on other grounds by *Hasbrouck v. Texaco, Inc.,* 842 F.2d 1034, 1041 (9th Cir. 1987), *aff'd,* 496 U.S. 543, 110 S. Ct. 2535, 110 L. Ed. 2d 492 (1990). *See Chroma Lighting v. GTE Products Corp.,* 111 F.3d 653, 657 (9th Cir. 1997), *cert. denied sub nom., Osram Sylvania Products, Inc. v. Von Der Ahe,* 522 U.S. 943, 118 S. Ct. 357, 139 L.Ed.2d 278 (1997).

"$1 Each." *Id.* at 690. Mr. Morris Lefkowitz arrived at the store, dollar in hand, but was informed that under defendant's "house rules," the offer was open to ladies, but not gentlemen. *See id.* The court ruled that because plaintiff had fulfilled all of the terms of the advertisement and the advertisement was specific and left nothing open for negotiation, a contract had been formed. *See id.; see also Johnson v. Capital City Ford Co.,* 85 So.2d 75, 79 (La. Ct. App. 1955) (finding that newspaper advertisement was sufficiently certain and definite to constitute an offer).

The present case is distinguishable from *Lefkowitz.* First, the commercial cannot be regarded in itself as sufficiently definite, because it specifically reserved the details of the offer to a separate writing, the Catalog.[6] The commercial itself made no mention of the steps a potential offeree would be required to take to accept the alleged offer of a Harrier Jet. The advertisement in *Lefkowitz,* in contrast, "identified the person who could accept." Corbin, *supra,* § 2.4, at 119. *See generally United States v. Braunstein,* 75 F. Supp. 137, 139 (S.D.N.Y. 1947) ("Greater precision of expression may be required, and less help from the court given, when the parties are merely at the threshold of a contract."); Farnsworth, *supra,* at 239 ("The fact that a proposal is very detailed suggests that it is an offer, while omission of many terms suggests that it is not.").[7] Second, even if the Catalog had included a Harrier Jet among the items that could be obtained by redemption of Pepsi Points, the advertisement of a Harrier Jet by both television commercial and catalog would still not constitute an offer. As the *Mesaros* court explained, the absence of any words of limitation such as "first come, first served," renders the alleged offer sufficiently indefinite that no contract could be formed. *See Mesaros,* 845 F.2d at 1581. "A customer would not usually have reason to believe that the shopkeeper intended exposure to the risk of a multitude of acceptances resulting in a number of contracts exceeding the shopkeeper's inventory." Farnsworth, *supra,* at 242. There was no such danger in *Lefkowitz,* owing to the limitation "first come, first served."

The Court finds, in sum, that the Harrier Jet commercial was merely an advertisement. The Court now turns to the line of cases upon which plaintiff rests much of his argument.

Page 125

2. Rewards as Offers

In opposing the present motion, plaintiff largely relies on a different species of unilateral offer, involving public offers of a reward for performance of a specified act. Because these cases generally involve public declarations regarding the efficacy or trustworthiness of specific products, one court has aptly characterized these authorities as "prove me wrong" cases. *See Rosenthal v. Al Packer Ford,* 36 Md. App. 349, 374 A.2d 377, 380 (1977). The most venerable of these precedents is the case of *Carlill v. Carbolic Smoke Ball Co.,* 1 Q.B. 256 (Court of Appeal, 1892), a quote from which heads plaintiff's memorandum of law: "[I]f a person chooses to make extravagant promises . . . he probably does so because it pays him to make them, and, if he has made them, the extravagance of the promises is no reason in law why he should not be bound by them." *Carbolic Smoke Ball,* 1 Q.B. at 268 (Bowen, L.J.).

Long a staple of law school curricula, *Carbolic Smoke Ball* owes its fame not merely to "the comic and slightly mysterious object involved," A.W. Brian Simpson. *Quackery and Contract Law: Carlill v. Carbolic Smoke Ball Company (1893),* in *Leading Cases in the Common Law* 259, 281 (1995), but also to its role in developing the law of unilateral offers. The case arose during the London influenza epidemic of the 1890s. Among other advertisements of the time, for Clarke's World Famous Blood Mixture, Towle's Pennyroyal and Steel Pills for Females, Sequah's Prairie Flower, and Epp's Glycerine Jube-Jubes, *see* Simpson, *supra,* at 267, appeared solicitations for the Carbolic Smoke Ball. The specific advertisement that Mrs. Carlill saw, and relied upon, read as follows:

100 £ reward will be paid by the Carbolic Smoke Ball Company to any person who contracts the

---

[6]It also communicated additional words of reservation: "Offer not available in all areas. See details on specially marked packages."
[7]The reservation of the details of the offer in this case distinguishes it from *Payne v. Lautz Bros. & Co.,* 166 N.Y.S. 844 (N.Y. City Ct. 1916). In *Payne,* a stamp and coupon broker purchased massive quantities of coupons produced by defendant, a soap company, and tried to redeem them for 4,000 round-trip tickets to a local beach. The court ruled for plaintiff, noting that the advertisements were "absolutely unrestricted. It contained no reference whatever to any of its previous advertising of any form." *Id.* at 848. In the present case, by contrast, the commercial explicitly reserved the details of the offer to the Catalog.

increasing epidemic influenza, colds, or any diseases caused by taking cold, after having used the ball three times daily for two weeks according to the printed directions supplied with each ball. 1000 £ is deposited with the Alliance Bank, Regent Street, shewing our sincerity in the matter.

During the last epidemic of influenza many thousand carbolic smoke balls were sold as preventives against this disease, and in no ascertained case was the disease contracted by those using the carbolic smoke ball.

Carbolic Smoke Ball, 1 Q.B. at 256-57. "On the faith of this advertisement," *id.* at 257, Mrs. Carlill purchased the smoke ball and used it as directed, but contracted influenza nevertheless.[8] The lower court held that she was entitled to recover the promised reward.

Affirming the lower court's decision, Lord Justice Lindley began by noting that the advertisement was an express promise to pay £ 100 in the event that a consumer of the Carbolic Smoke Ball was stricken with influenza. *See id.* at 261. The advertisement was construed as offering a reward because it sought to induce performance, unlike an invitation to negotiate, which seeks a reciprocal promise. As Lord Justice Lindley explained, "advertisements offering rewards . . . are offers to anybody who performs the conditions named in the advertisement, and anybody who does perform the condition accepts the offer." *Id.* at 262; *see also id.* at 268 (Bowen, L.J.).[9] Because Mrs. Carlill had complied with the terms of the offer, yet

Page 126

contracted influenza, she was entitled to £ 100.

---

[8]Although the Court of Appeals's opinion is silent as to exactly what a carbolic smoke ball was, the historical record reveals it to have been a compressible hollow ball, about the size of an apple or orange, with a small opening covered by some porous material such as silk or gauze. The ball was partially filled with carbolic acid in powder form. When the ball was squeezed, the powder would be forced through the opening as a small cloud of smoke. *See* Simpson, *supra,* at 262-63. At the time, carbolic acid was considered fatal if consumed in more than small amounts. *See id.* at 264.

[9]*Carbolic Smoke Ball* includes a classic formulation of this principle: "If I advertise to the world that my dog is lost, and that anybody who brings the dog to a particular place will be paid some money, are all the police or other persons whose business it is to find lost dogs to be expected to sit down and write a note saying that they have accepted my proposal?" *Carbolic Smoke Ball,* 1 Q.B. at 270 (Bowen, L.J.).

Like *Carbolic Smoke Ball,* the decisions relied upon by plaintiff involve offers of reward. In *Barnes v. Treece,* 15 Wash. App. 437, 549 P.2d 1152 (1976), for example, the vice-president of a punchboard distributor, in the course of hearings before the Washington State Gambling Commission, asserted that, "'I'll put a hundred thousand dollars to anyone to find a crooked board. If they find it, I'll pay it.'" *Id.* at 1154. Plaintiff, a former bartender, heard of the offer and located two crooked punchboards. Defendant, after reiterating that the offer was serious, providing plaintiff with a receipt for the punchboard on company stationery, and assuring plaintiff that the reward was being held in escrow, nevertheless repudiated the offer. *See id.* at 1154. The court ruled that the offer was valid and that plaintiff was entitled to his reward. *See id.* at 1155. The plaintiff in this case also cites cases involving prizes for skill (or luck) in the game of golf. *See Las Vegas Hacienda v. Gibson,* 77 Nev. 25, 359 P.2d 85 (1961) (awarding $5,000 to plaintiff, who successfully shot a hole-in-one); *see also Grove v. Charbonneau Buick-Pontiac, Inc.,* 240 N.W.2d 853 (N.D. 1976) (awarding automobile to plaintiff, who successfully shot a hole-in-one).

Other "reward" cases underscore the distinction between typical advertisements, in which the alleged offer is merely an invitation to negotiate for purchase of commercial goods, and promises of reward, in which the alleged offer is intended to induce a potential offeree to perform a specific action, often for noncommercial reasons. In *Newman v. Schiff,* 778 F.2d 460 (8th Cir. 1985), for example, the Fifth Circuit held that a tax protestor's assertion that, "If anybody calls this show . . . and cites any section of the code that says an individual is required to file a tax return, I'll pay them $100,000," would have been an enforceable offer had the plaintiff called the television show to claim the reward while the tax protestor was appearing. *See id.* at 466-67. The court noted that, like *Carbolic Smoke Ball,* the case "concerns a special type of offer: an offer for a reward." *Id.* at 465. *James v. Turilli,* 473 S.W.2d 757 (Mo. Ct. App. 1971), arose from a boast by defendant that the "notorious Missouri desperado" Jesse James had not been killed in 1882, as portrayed in song and legend, but had lived under the alias "J. Frank Dalton" at the "Jesse James Museum" operated by none other than defendant. Defendant offered $10,000 "to anyone who could prove me wrong." *See id.* at 758-59. The widow of the outlaw's son demonstrated, at trial, that the outlaw had in fact been killed in 1882. On appeal, the court held that defendant should be liable to pay the amount offered. *See id.* at 762; *see also Mears v. Nationwide Mutual Ins. Co.,* 91 F.3d 1118, 1122-23 (8th Cir. 1996) (plaintiff entitled to cost of two Mercedes as reward for coining slogan for insurance company).

In the present case, the Harrier Jet commercial did not direct that anyone who appeared at Pepsi headquarters with 7,000,000 Pepsi Points on the Fourth of July would receive a Harrier Jet. Instead, the commercial urged consumers to accumulate Pepsi Points and to refer to the Catalog to determine how they could redeem their Pepsi Points. The commercial sought a reciprocal promise, expressed through acceptance of, and compliance with, the terms of the Order Form. As noted previously, the Catalog contains no mention of the Harrier Jet. Plaintiff states that he "noted that the Harrier Jet was not among the items described in the catalog, but this did not affect [his] understanding of the offer." (Pl. Mem. at 4.) It should have.[10]

Page 127

Carbolic Smoke Ball itself draws a distinction between the offer of reward in that case, and typical advertisements, which are merely offers to negotiate. As Lord Justice Bowen explains:

> It is an offer to become liable to any one who, before it is retracted, performs the condition. . . . It is not like cases in which you offer to negotiate, or you issue advertisements that you have got a stock of books to sell, or houses to let, in which case there is no offer to be bound by any contract. Such advertisements are offers to negotiate—offers to receive offers—offers to chaffer, as, I think, some learned judge in one of the cases has said.

Carbolic Smoke Ball, 1 Q.B. at 268; *see also Lovett,* 207 N.Y.S. at 756 (distinguishing advertisements, as

invitation to offer, from offers of reward made in advertisements, such as *Carbolic Smoke Ball*). Because the alleged offer in this case was, at most, an advertisement to receive offers rather than an offer of reward, plaintiff cannot show that there was an offer made in the circumstances of this case.

C. An Objective, Reasonable Person Would Not Have Considered the Commercial an Offer

Plaintiff's understanding of the commercial as an offer must also be rejected because the Court finds that no objective person could reasonably have concluded that the commercial actually offered consumers a Harrier Jet.

1. Objective Reasonable Person Standard

In evaluating the commercial, the Court must not consider defendant's subjective intent in making the commercial, or plaintiff's subjective view of what the commercial offered, but what an objective, reasonable person would have understood the commercial to convey. *See Kay-R Elec. Corp. v. Stone & Webster Constr. Co.,* 23 F.3d 55, 57 (2d Cir. 1994) ("[W]e are not concerned with what was going through the heads of the parties at the time [of the alleged contract]. Rather, we are talking about the objective principles of contract law."); *Mesaros,* 845 F.2d at 1581 ("A basic rule of contracts holds that whether an offer has been made depends on the objective reasonableness of the alleged offeree's belief that the advertisement or solicitation was intended as an offer."); Farnsworth, *supra,* § 3.10, at 237; Williston, *supra,* § 4:7 at 296-97.

If it is clear that an offer was not serious, then no offer has been made:

> What kind of act creates a power of acceptance and is therefore an offer? It must be an expression of will or intention. It must be an act that leads the offeree reasonably to conclude that a power to create a contract is conferred. This applies to the content of the power as well as to the fact of its existence. *It is on this ground that we must exclude* invitations to deal or acts of mere preliminary negotiation, and *acts evidently done in jest* or without intent to create legal relations.

Corbin on Contracts, § 1.11 at 30 (emphasis added). An obvious joke, of course, would not give rise to a

---

[10]In his affidavit, plaintiff places great emphasis on a press release written by defendant, which characterizes the Harrier Jet as "the ultimate Pepsi Stuff award." (*See* Leonard Aff. ¶ 13.) Plaintiff simply ignores the remainder of the release, which makes no mention of the Harrier Jet even as it sets forth in detail the number of points needed to redeem other merchandise.

contract. *See, e.g., Graves v. Northern N.Y. Pub. Co.*, 260 A.D. 900, 22 N.Y.S.2d 537 (1940) (dismissing claim to offer of $1000, which appeared in the "joke column" of the newspaper, to any person who could provide a commonly available phone number). On the other hand, if there is no indication that the offer is "evidently in jest," and that an objective, reasonable person would find that the offer was serious, then there may be a valid offer. *See Barnes*, 549 P.2d at 1155 ("[I]f the jest is not apparent and a reasonable hearer would believe that an offer was being made, then the speaker risks the formation of a contract which was not intended."); *see also Lucy v. Zehmer*, 196 Va. 493, 84 S.E.2d 516, 518, 520 (1954)

Page 128

(ordering specific performance of a contract to purchase a farm despite defendant's protestation that the transaction was done in jest as "'just a bunch of two doggoned drunks bluffing'").

2. Necessity of a Jury Determination

Plaintiff also contends that summary judgment is improper because the question of whether the commercial conveyed a sincere offer can be answered only by a jury. Relying on dictum from *Gallagher v. Delaney*, 139 F.3d 338 (2d Cir. 1998), plaintiff argues that a federal judge comes from a "narrow segment of the enormously broad American socio-economic spectrum," *id.* at 342, and, thus, that the question whether the commercial constituted a serious offer must be decided by a jury composed of, *inter alia,* members of the "Pepsi Generation," who are, as plaintiff puts it, "young, open to adventure, willing to do the unconventional." (*See* Leonard Aff. ¶ 2.) Plaintiff essentially argues that a federal judge would view his claim differently than fellow members of the "Pepsi Generation."

Plaintiff's argument that his claim must be put to a jury is without merit. *Gallagher* involved a claim of sexual harassment in which the defendant allegedly invited plaintiff to sit on his lap, gave her inappropriate Valentine's Day gifts, told her that "she brought out feelings that he had not had since he was sixteen," and "invited her to help him feed the ducks in the pond, since he was 'a bachelor for the evening.'" *Gallagher*, 139 F.3d at 344. The court concluded that

a jury determination was particularly appropriate because a federal judge lacked "the current real-life experience required in interpreting subtle sexual dynamics of the workplace based on nuances, subtle perceptions, and implicit communications." *Id.* at 342. This case, in contrast, presents a question of whether there was an offer to enter into a contract, requiring the Court to determine how a reasonable, objective person would have understood defendant's commercial. Such an inquiry is commonly performed by courts on a motion for summary judgment. *See Krumme*, 143 F.3d at 83; *Bourque*, 42 F.3d at 708; *Wards Co.*, 761 F.2d at 120.

3. Whether the Commercial Was "Evidently Done In Jest"

Plaintiff's insistence that the commercial appears to be a serious offer requires the Court to explain why the commercial is funny. Explaining why a joke is funny is a daunting task; as the essayist E.B. White has remarked, "Humor can be dissected, as a frog can, but the thing dies in the process. . . ."[11] The commercial is the embodiment of what defendant appropriately characterizes as "zany humor." (Def. Mem. at 18.)

First, the commercial suggests, as commercials often do, that use of the advertised product will transform what, for most youth, can be a fairly routine and ordinary experience. The military tattoo and stirring martial music, as well as the use of subtitles in a Courier font that scroll terse messages across the screen, such as "MONDAY 7:58 AM," evoke military and espionage thrillers. The implication of the commercial is that Pepsi Stuff merchandise will inject drama and moment into hitherto unexceptional lives. The commercial in this case thus makes the exaggerated claims similar to those of many television advertisements: that by consuming the featured clothing, car, beer, or potato chips, one will become attractive, stylish, desirable, and admired by all. A reasonable viewer would understand such advertisements as mere puffery, not as statements of fact, *see, e.g., Hubbard v. General Motors Corp.*, 95 Civ. 4362(AGS), 1996 WL 274018, at *6 (S.D.N.Y. May 22, 1996) (advertisement describing automobile as "Like a Rock," was mere puffery, not a warranty of

---

[11]*Quoted in* Gerald R. Ford, *Humor and the Presidency* 23 (1987).

quality); *Lovett,* 207 N.Y.S. at 756; and refrain from interpreting the promises of the commercial as being literally true.

Second, the callow youth featured in the commercial is a highly improbable pilot, one who could barely be trusted with the

Page 129

keys to his parents' car, much less the prize aircraft of the United States Marine Corps. Rather than checking the fuel gauges on his aircraft, the teenager spends his precious preflight minutes preening. The youth's concern for his coiffure appears to extend to his flying without a helmet. Finally, the teenager's comment that flying a Harrier Jet to school "sure beats the bus" evinces an improbably insouciant attitude toward the relative difficulty and danger of piloting a fighter plane in a residential area, as opposed to taking public transportation.[12]

Third, the notion of traveling to school in a Harrier Jet is an exaggerated adolescent fantasy. In this commercial, the fantasy is underscored by how the teenager's schoolmates gape in admiration, ignoring their physics lesson. The force of the wind generated by the Harrier Jet blows off one teacher's clothes, literally defrocking an authority figure. As if to emphasize the fantastic quality of having a Harrier Jet arrive at school, the Jet lands next to a plebeian bike rack. This fantasy is, of course, extremely unrealistic. No school would provide landing space for a student's fighter jet, or condone the disruption the jet's use would cause.

Fourth, the primary mission of a Harrier Jet, according to the United States Marine Corps, is to "attack and destroy surface targets under day and night visual conditions." United States Marine Corps, Factfile: AV-8B Harrier II (last modified Dec. 5, 1995) <http://www.hqmc.usmc.mil/factfile. nsf>. Manufactured by McDonnell Douglas, the Harrier Jet played a significant role in the air offensive of Operation Desert Storm in 1991. *See id.* The jet is designed to carry a considerable armament load, including Sidewinder and Maverick missiles. *See id.* As one news report has noted, "Fully loaded, the Harrier can float like a butterfly and sting like a bee — albeit a roaring 14-ton butterfly and a bee with 9,200 pounds of bombs and missiles." Jerry Allegood, *Marines Rely on Harrier Jet, Despite Critics,* News & Observer (Raleigh), Nov. 4, 1990, at C1. In light of the Harrier Jet's well-documented function in attacking and destroying surface and air targets, armed reconnaissance and air interdiction, and offensive and defensive anti-aircraft warfare, depiction of such a jet as a way to get to school in the morning is clearly not serious even if, as plaintiff contends, the jet is capable of being acquired "in a form that eliminates [its] potential for military use." (See Leonard Aff. ¶ 20.)

Fifth, the number of Pepsi Points the commercial mentions as required to "purchase" the jet is 7,000,000. To amass that number of points, one would have to drink 7,000,000 Pepsis (or roughly 190 Pepsis a day for the next hundred years — an unlikely possibility), or one would have to purchase approximately $700,000 worth of Pepsi Points. The cost of a Harrier Jet is roughly $23 million dollars, a fact of which plaintiff was aware when he set out to gather the amount he believed necessary to accept the alleged offer. (See Affidavit of Michael E. McCabe, 96 Civ. 5320, Aug. 14, 1997, Exh. 6 (Leonard Business Plan).) Even if an objective, reasonable person were not aware of this fact, he would conclude that purchasing a fighter plane for $700,000 is a deal too good to be true.[13]

Page 130

Plaintiff argues that a reasonable, objective person would have understood the commercial to make

---

[12]In this respect, the teenager of the advertisement contrasts with the distinguished figures who testified to the effectiveness of the Carbolic Smoke Ball, including the Duchess of Sutherland; the Earls of Wharncliffe, Westmoreland, Cadogan, and Leitrim; the Countesses Dudley, Pembroke, and Aberdeen; the Marchionesses of Bath and Conyngham; Sir Henry Acland, the physician to the Prince of Wales; and Sir James Paget, sergeant surgeon to Queen Victoria. *See* Simpson, *supra,* at 265.

[13]In contrast, the advertisers of the Carbolic Smoke Ball emphasized their earnestness, stating in the advertisement that "£ 1,000 is deposited with the Alliance Bank, shewing our sincerity in the matter." *Carbolic Smoke Ball,* 1 Q.B. at 257. Similarly, in *Barnes,* the defendant's "subsequent statements, conduct, and the circumstances show an intent to lead any hearer to believe the statements were made seriously." *Barnes,* 549 P.2d at 1155. The offer in *Barnes,* moreover, was made in the serious forum of hearings before a state commission; not, as defendant states, at a "gambling convention." *Compare Barnes,* 549 P.2d at 1154, with Def. Reply Mem. at 6.

a serious offer of a Harrier Jet because there was "absolutely no distinction in the manner" (Pl. Mem. at 13,) in which the items in the commercial were presented. Plaintiff also relies upon a press release highlighting the promotional campaign, issued by defendant, in which "[n]o mention is made by [defendant] of humor, or anything of the sort." (*Id.* at 5.) These arguments suggest merely that the humor of the promotional campaign was tongue in cheek. Humor is not limited to what Justice Cardozo called "[t]he rough and boisterous joke . . . [that] evokes its own guffaws." *Murphy v. Steeplechase Amusement Co.,* 250 N.Y. 479, 483, 166 N.E. 173, 174 (1929). In light of the obvious absurdity of the commercial, the Court rejects plaintiff's argument that the commercial was not clearly in jest.

4. *Plaintiff's Demands for Additional Discovery*

In his Memorandum of Law, and in letters to the Court, plaintiff argues that additional discovery is necessary on the issues of whether and how defendant reacted to plaintiff's "acceptance" of their "offer"; how defendant and its employees understood the commercial would be viewed, based on test-marketing the commercial or on their own opinions; and how other individuals actually responded to the commercial when it was aired. (*See* Pl. Mem. at 1-2; Letter of David E. Nachman to the Hon. Kimba M. Wood, Apr. 5, 1999.)

Plaintiff argues that additional discovery is necessary as to how defendant reacted to his "acceptance," suggesting that it is significant that defendant twice changed the commercial, the first time to increase the number of Pepsi Points required to purchase a Harrier Jet to 700,000,000, and then again to amend the commercial to state the 700,000,000 amount and add "(Just Kidding)." (*See* Pl. Stat. Exh C (700 Million), and Exh. D (700 Million — Just Kidding).) Plaintiff concludes that, "Obviously, if Pepsi-Co truly believed that no one could take seriously the offer contained in the original ad that I saw, this change would have been totally unnecessary and superfluous." (Leonard Aff. ¶ 14.) The record does not suggest that the change in the amount of points is probative of the seriousness of the offer. The increase in the number of points needed to acquire a Harrier Jet may have been prompted less by the fear that reasonable people would demand Harrier Jets and more by the concern that unreasonable people

would threaten frivolous litigation. Further discovery is unnecessary on the question of when and how the commercials changed because the question before the Court is whether the commercial that plaintiff saw and relied upon was an offer, not that any other commercial constituted an offer.

Plaintiff's demands for discovery relating to how defendant itself understood the offer are also unavailing. Such discovery would serve only to cast light on defendant's subjective intent in making the alleged offer, which is irrelevant to the question of whether an objective, reasonable person would have understood the commercial to be an offer. *See Kay-R Elec. Corp.,* 23 F.3d at 57 ("[W]e are not concerned with what was going through the heads of the parties at the time [of the alleged contract]."); *Mesaros,* 845 F.2d at 1581; *Corbin on Contracts,* § 1.11 at 30. Indeed, plaintiff repeatedly argues that defendant's subjective intent is irrelevant. (*See* Pl. Mem. at 5, 8, 13.)

Finally, plaintiff's assertion that he should be afforded an opportunity to determine whether other individuals also tried to accumulate enough Pepsi Points to "purchase" a Harrier Jet is unavailing. The possibility that there were other people who interpreted the commercial as an "offer" of a Harrier Jet does not render that belief any more or less reasonable. The alleged offer must be evaluated on its own terms. Having made the evaluation,

Page 131

the Court concludes that summary judgment is appropriate on the ground that no reasonable, objective person would have understood the commercial to be an offer.[14]

D. The Alleged Contract Does Not Satisfy the Statute of Frauds

The absence of any writing setting forth the alleged contract in this case provides an entirely separate

---

[14]Even if plaintiff were allowed discovery on all of these issues, such discovery would be relevant only to the second basis for the Court's opinion, that no reasonable person would have understood the commercial to be an offer. That discovery would not change the basic principle that an advertisement is not an offer, as set forth in Section II.B of this Order and Opinion, *supra;* nor would it affect the conclusion that the alleged offer failed to comply with the Statute of Frauds, as set forth in Section II.D, *infra.*

reason for granting summary judgment. Under the New York[15] Statute of Frauds,

> a contract for the sale of goods for the price of $500 or more is not enforceable by way of action or defense unless there is some writing sufficient to indicate that a contract for sale has been made between the parties and signed by the party against whom enforcement is sought or by his authorized agent or broker.

N.Y.U.C.C. § 2-201(1); see also, e.g., AFP Imaging Corp. v. Philips Medizin Systeme, 92 Civ. 6211(LMM), 1994 WL 652510, at *4 (S.D.N.Y. Nov. 17, 1994). Without such a writing, plaintiff's claim must fail as a matter of law. See Hilord Chem. Corp. v. Ricoh Elecs., Inc., 875 F.2d 32, 36-37 (2d Cir. 1989) ("The adequacy of a writing for Statute of Frauds purposes 'must be determined from the documents themselves, as a matter of law.'") (quoting Bazak Int'l. Corp. v. Mast Indus., Inc., 73 N.Y.2d 113, 118, 538 N.Y.S.2d 503, 535 N.E.2d 633 (1989)).

There is simply no writing between the parties that evidences any transaction. Plaintiff argues that the commercial, plaintiff's completed Order Form, and perhaps other agreements signed by defendant which plaintiff has not yet seen, should suffice for Statute of Frauds purposes, either singly or taken together. (See Pl. Mem. at 18-19.) For the latter claim, plaintiff relies on Crabtree v. Elizabeth Arden Sales Corp., 305 N.Y. 48, 110 N.E.2d 551 (1953). Crabtree held that a combination of signed and unsigned writings would satisfy the Statute of Frauds, "provided that they clearly refer to the same subject matter or transaction." Id. at 55, 110 N.E.2d 551. Yet the Second Circuit emphasized in Horn & Hardart Co. v. Pillsbury Co., 888 F.2d 8 (2d Cir. 1989), that this rule "contains two strict threshold requirements." Id. at 11. First, the signed writing relied upon must by itself establish "'a contractual relationship between the parties.'" Id. (quoting Crabtree, 305 N.Y. at 56, 110 N.E.2d 551); see also O'Keeffe v. Bry, 456 F. Supp. 822, 829 (S.D.N.Y. 1978) ("To the extent that Crabtree permits

the use of a 'confluence of memoranda,' the minimum condition for such use is the existence of one [signed] document establishing the basic, underlying contractual commitment."). The second threshold requirement is that the unsigned writing must "'on its face refer to the same transaction as that set forth in the one that was signed.'" Horn & Hardart, 888 F.2d at 11 (quoting Crabtree, 305 N.Y. at 56, 110 N.E.2d 551); see also Bruce Realty Co. of Florida v. Berger, 327 F. Supp. 507, 510 (S.D.N.Y. 1971).

None of the material relied upon by plaintiff meets either threshold requirement. The commercial is not a writing; plaintiff's completed order form does not bear the signature of defendant, or an agent thereof; and to the extent that plaintiff seeks discovery of any contracts between defendant and its advertisers, such discovery would be unavailing: plaintiff

Page 132

is not a party to, or a beneficiary of, any such contracts. Because the alleged contract does not meet the requirements of the Statute of Frauds, plaintiff has no claim for breach of contract or specific performance.

E. Plaintiff's Fraud Claim

In addition to moving for summary judgment on plaintiff's claim for breach of contract, defendant has also moved for summary judgment on plaintiff's fraud claim. The elements of a cause of action for fraud are "'representation of a material existing fact, falsity, scienter, deception and injury.'" New York Univ. v. Continental Ins. Co., 87 N.Y.2d 308, 639 N.Y.S.2d 283, 662 N.E.2d 763 (1995) (quoting Channel Master Corp. v. Aluminium Ltd. Sales, Inc., 4 N.Y.2d 403, 407, 176 N.Y.S.2d 259, 262, 151 N.E.2d 833 (1958)).

To properly state a claim for fraud, "plaintiff must allege a misrepresentation or material omission by defendant, on which it relied, that induced plaintiff" to perform an act. See NYU, 639 N.Y.S.2d at 289, 662 N.E.2d 763. "General allegations that defendant entered into a contract while lacking the intent to perform it are insufficient to support the claim." See id. (citing Rocanova v. Equitable Life Assur. Soc'y, 83 N.Y.2d 603, 612 N.Y.S.2d 339, 634 N.E.2d 940 (1994)); see also Grappo v. Alitalia Linee Aeree

---

[15]Having determined that defendant's advertisement was not an offer, the last act necessary to complete the contract would be defendant's acceptance in New York of plaintiff's Order Form. Thus the Court must apply New York law on the statute of frauds issue. See supra Section II.A.2.

Italiane, S.p.A., 56 F.3d 427, 434 (2d Cir. 1995) ("A cause of action does not generally lie where the plaintiff alleges only that the defendant entered into a contract with no intention of performing it"). Instead, the plaintiff must show the misrepresentation was collateral, or served as an inducement, to a separate agreement between the parties. *See Bridgestone/Firestone v. Recovery Credit,* 98 F.3d 13, 20 (2d Cir. 1996) (allowing a fraud claim where plaintiff " 'demonstrate[s] a fraudulent misrepresentation collateral or extraneous to the contract'") (quoting *Deerfield Communications Corp. v. Chesebrough-Ponds, Inc.,* 68 N.Y.2d 954, 510 N.Y.S.2d 88, 89, 502 N.E.2d 1003 (1986)).

For example, in *Stewart v. Jackson & Nash,* 976 F.2d 86 (2d Cir. 1992), the Second Circuit ruled that plaintiff had properly stated a claim for fraud. In the course of plaintiff's negotiations for employment with defendant, a law firm, defendant represented to plaintiff not only that plaintiff would be hired (which she was), but also that the firm had secured a large environmental law client, that it was in the process of establishing an environmental law department, and that plaintiff would head the environmental law department. *See id.* at 89-90. The Second Circuit concluded that these misrepresentations gave rise to a fraud claim, because they consisted of misrepresentations of present fact, rather than future promises.

Plaintiff in this case does not allege that he was induced to enter into a contract by some collateral misrepresentation, but rather that defendant never had any intention of making good on its "offer" of a Harrier Jet. (*See* Pl. Mem. at 23.) Because this claim "alleges only that the defendant entered into a contract with no intention of performing it," *Grappo,* 56 F.3d at 434, judgment on this claim should enter for defendant.

III. CONCLUSION

In sum, there are three reasons why plaintiff's demand cannot prevail as a matter of law. First, the commercial was merely an advertisement, not a unilateral offer. Second, the tongue-in-cheek attitude of the commercial would not cause a reasonable person to conclude that a soft drink company would be giving away fighter planes as part of a promotion. Third, there is no writing between the parties sufficient to satisfy the Statute of Frauds.

For the reasons stated above, the Court grants defendant's motion for summary judgment. The Clerk of Court is instructed to close these cases. Any pending motions are moot.

Case In Point   ATTEMPT TO RESCIND*

Page 1248

561 A.2d 1248
385 Pa. Super. 587
Amos COBAUGH, Appellee,
v.
KLICK-LEWIS, INC., Appellant.
500 HSBG. 1988
Superior Court of Pennsylvania.
Argued Feb. 2, 1989.
Filed July 14, 1989.

Page 1249

[385 Pa.Super. 589] Robert M. Frankhouser, Jr., Lancaster, for appellant.
Wiley P. Parker, Lebanon, for appellee.

Before WIEAND, POPOVICH and HESTER, JJ.
WIEAND, Judge:

On May 17, 1987, Amos Cobaugh was playing in the East End Open Golf Tournament on the Fairview Golf Course in Cornwall, Lebanon County. When he arrived at the ninth tee he found a new Chevrolet Beretta, together with signs which proclaimed: "HOLE-IN-ONE Wins this 1988 Chevrolet Beretta GT Courtesy of KLICK-LEWIS Buick Chevy Pontiac $49.00 OVER FACTORY INVOICE in Palmyra." Cobaugh aced the ninth hole and attempted to claim his prize. Klick-Lewis refused to deliver the car. It had offered the car as a prize for a charity golf tournament sponsored by the Hershey-Palmyra Sertoma Club two days earlier, on May 15, 1987, and had neglected to remove the car and posted signs prior to Cobaugh's hole-in-one. After Cobaugh sued to compel delivery of the car, the parties entered a stipulation regarding the facts and then moved for summary judgment. The trial court granted Cobaugh's motion, and Klick-Lewis appealed.

Our standard of review is well established. A motion for summary judgment may properly be granted only if the moving party has shown that there is no genuine issue of material fact and that he or she is entitled to judgment as a matter of law. *French v. United Parcel Service*, 377 Pa. Super. 366, 371, 547 A.2d 411, 414 (1988); *Thorsen v.* [385 Pa. Super. 590] *Iron and Glass Bank*, 328 Pa. Super. 135, 140, 476 A.2d 928, 930 (1984). Summary judgment should not be entered unless a case is clear and free from doubt. *Weiss v. Keystone Mack Sales, Inc.*, 310 Pa. Super. 425, 430, 456 A.2d 1009, 1011 (1983); *Dunn v. Teti*, 280 Pa. Super. 399, 402, 421 A.2d 782, 783 (1980).

The facts in the instant case are not in dispute. To the extent that they have not been admitted in the pleadings, they have been stipulated by the parties. Therefore, we must decide whether under the applicable law plaintiff was entitled to judgment as a matter of law.

An offer is a manifestation of willingness to enter into a bargain, so made as to justify another person in understanding that his assent to that bargain is invited and will conclude it. *Restatement (Second) of Contracts* § 24; 8 P.L.E. Contracts § 23. Consistent with traditional principles of contract law pertaining to unilateral contracts, it has generally been held that "[t]he promoter of [a prize-winning] contest, by making public the conditions and rules of the contest, makes an offer, and if before the offer is withdrawn another person acts upon it, the promoter is bound

---

*A model case brief is supplied for this case in the Appendix. This will help the student with both formatting and content expected in the legal field.

to perform his promise." Annotation, Private Rights and Remedies Growing Out of Prize-winning Contests, 87 A.L.R.2d 649, 661. The only acceptance of the offer that is necessary is the performance of the act requested to win the prize. *Id.* See also: *Robertson v. United States*, 343 U.S. 711, 72 S. Ct. 994, 96 L. Ed. 1237 (1952) ("The acceptance by the contestants of the offer tendered by the sponsor of the contest creates an enforceable contract."); 17 C.J.S. Contracts § 46.

The Pennsylvania cases which have considered prize-winning contests support the principle that an offer to award a prize in a contest will result in an enforceable contract if the offer is properly accepted by the rendition of the requested performance prior to revocation. See: *Olschiefsky v. Times Publishing Co.*, 23 D. & C.2d 73 (Erie 1959) (overruling demurrer to action against newspaper for failure to award prize to winner of puzzle contest); *Holt v.* [385 Pa. Super. 591] *Wood, Harmon & Co.*, 41 Pitt. L. J. 443 (1894) (holding offer to award house to person submitting name selected for new housing development resulted in binding contract). See also: *Aland v. Cluett, Peabody & Co.*, 259 Pa. 364, 103 A. 60 (1918); *Palmer v. Central Board of Education of Pittsburg*, 220 Pa. 568, 70 A. 433 (1908); *Trego v. Pa. Academy of Fine Arts*, 2 Sad. 313, 3 A. 819 (1886); *Vespaziani v. Pa. Dept. of Revenue*, 40 Pa. Cmwlth 54, 396 A.2d 489 (1979).

Appellant argues that it did nothing more than propose a contingent gift and that a proposal to make a gift is without

Page 1250

consideration and unenforceable. See: *Restatement (Second) of Contracts* § 24, Comment b. We cannot accept this argument. Here, the offer specified the performance which was the price or consideration to be given. By its signs, Klick-Lewis offered to award the car as a prize to anyone who made a hole-in-one at the ninth hole. A person reading the signs would reasonably understand that he or she could accept the offer and win the car by performing the feat of shooting a hole-in-one. There was thus an offer which was accepted when appellee shot a hole-in-one. Accord: *Champagne Chrysler-Plymouth, Inc. v. Giles*, 388 So. 2d 1343 (Fla. Dist. Ct. App. 1980) (bowling contest); *Schreiner v. Weil Furniture Co.*, 68 So. 2d 149 (La. App. 1953) ("Count-the-dots" contest); *Chenard v. Marcel Motors*, 387 A.2d 596 (Me. 1978) (golf tournament); *Grove v. Charbonneau Buick-Pontiac Inc.*, 240 N.W.2d 853 (N.D. Sup. Ct. 1976) (golf tournament); *First Texas Savings Assoc. v. Jergins*, 705 S.W.2d 390 (Tx. Ct. App. 1986) (free drawing).

The contract does not fail for lack of consideration. The requirement of consideration as an essential element of a contract is nothing more than a requirement that there be a bargained for exchange. *Greene v. Oliver Realty, Inc.*, 363 Pa. Super. 534, 541, 526 A.2d 1192, 1195 (1987); *Commonwealth Dept. of Transp. v. First Nat'l Bank*, 77 Pa. Cmwlth. 551, 553, 466 A.2d 753, 754 (1983). Consideration confers a benefit upon the promisor or causes a detriment to the promisee. *Cardamone v. University of Pittsburgh*, [385 Pa. Super. 592] 253 Pa. Super. 65, 72 n. 6, 384 A.2d 1228, 1232 n. 6 (1978); *General Mills, Inc. v. Snavely*, 203 Pa. Super. 162, 167, 199 A.2d 540, 543 (1964). By making an offer to award one of its cars as a prize for shooting a hole-in-one at the ninth hole of the Fairview Golf Course, Klick-Lewis benefited from the publicity typically generated by such promotional advertising. In order to win the car, Cobaugh was required to perform an act which he was under no legal duty to perform. The car was to be given in exchange for the feat of making a hole-in-one. This was adequate consideration to support the contract. See, e.g.: *Las Vegas Hacienda, Inc. v. Gibson*, 77 Nev. 25, 359 P.2d 85 (1961) (paying fifty cents and shooting hole-in-one was consideration for prize). See also: *First Texas Savings v. Jergins*, supra (enforcing duty to award prize in free drawing where only performance by plaintiff was completing and depositing entry form).[1]

---

[1]The issue of an illegal contract, as the author of the dissent concedes, was not raised by appellant in the trial court or on appeal. Indeed, it was not pleaded as "new matter" as required by Pa. R. C. P. 1030 and was not the subject of evidence or argument at trial.

Even if, as the dissent contends, this Court may act sua sponte to refuse enforcement of an illegal contract, it should not do so unless the illegality is clear. It is not clear in this case that to offer an automobile as a prize for a hole-in-one during a charity golf tournament was to introduce illegal gambling to the tournament. Courts of other jurisdictions have found similar offers legal and enforceable. See: *Las Vegas Hacienda, Inc. v. Gibson*, supra (contest to award prize to golfer who, having paid fee, scored a hole-in-one was not gambling and, therefore, created valid and enforceable contract). See also: *State v. American Holiday Ass'n, Inc.*, 151 Ariz. 312, 727 P.2d 807 (1986) (discussing cases).

[385 Pa. Super. 593] There is no basis for believing that Cobaugh was aware that the Chevrolet automobile had been intended as a prize only for an earlier tournament. The posted signs did not reveal such an intent by Klick-Lewis, and the stipulated facts do not suggest that appellee had knowledge greater than that acquired by reading the

Page 1251

posted signs. Therefore, we also reject appellant's final argument that the contract to award the prize to appellee was voidable because of mutual mistake. Where the mistake is not mutual but unilateral and is due to the negligence of the party seeking to rescind, relief will not be granted. *Rusiski v. Pribonic*, 326 Pa. Super. 545, 552, 474 A.2d 624, 627 (1984), rev'd on other grounds, 511 Pa. 383, 515 A.2d 507; *McFadden v. American Oil Co.*, 215 Pa. Super. 44, 53-54, 257 A.2d 283, 288 (1969).

In *Champagne Chrysler-Plymouth, Inc. v. Giles*, supra, a mistake similar to that made in the instant case had been made. There, a car dealer had advertised that it would give away a new car to any bowler who rolled a perfect "300" game during a televised show. The dealer's intent was that the offer would continue only during the television show which the dealer sponsored and on which its ads were displayed. However, the dealer also distributed flyers containing its offer and posted signs advertising the offer at the bowling alley. He neglected to remove from the alley the signs offering a car to anyone bowling a "300" game, and approximately one month later, while the signs were still posted, plaintiff appeared on a different episode of the television show and bowled a

---

Finally, there was no evidence in this case that an element of chance was the dominant factor in shooting the hole-in-one. See: *Commonwealth v. Laniewski*, 173 Pa. Super. 245, 98 A.2d 215 (1953) (chance must be dominant factor). Even if this Court could legitimately consider the "facts" which the dissent introduces from a popular magazine, those statistics demonstrate that a professional golfer is generally twice as likely to shoot a hole-in-one as an amateur golfer. Under these circumstances, it cannot be said that skill is "almost an irrelevant factor." See: *Las Vegas Hacienda, Inc. v. Gibson*, supra, 77 Nev. at 29-30, 359 P.2d at 87 (where expert testified that "a skilled player will get it (the ball) in the area where luck will take over more often than an unskilled player," there was sufficient evidence to sustain a finding that the shooting of a hole-in-one was a feat of skill).

perfect game. The dealer refused to award the car. A Florida court held that if plaintiff reasonably believed that the offer was still outstanding when he rolled his perfect game, he would be entitled to receive the car. See also: Grove v. Charbonneau Buick-Pontiac Inc., supra (car dealer required to award prize to participant in 18-hole golf tournament played on nine-hole golf course where it had offered to award a car "to the first entry who shoots a hole-in-one on Hole No. 8" and plaintiff aced the hole marked No. 8 while driving from the seventeenth tee).

[385 Pa. Super. 594] It is the manifested intent of the offeror and not his subjective intent which determines the persons having the power to accept the offer. *Restatement (Second) of Contracts* § 29. In this case the offeror's manifested intent, as it appeared from signs posted at the ninth tee, was that a hole-in-one would win the car. The offer was not limited to any prior tournament. The mistake upon which appellant relies was made possible only because of its failure to (1) limit its offer to the Hershey-Palmyra Sertoma Club Charity Golf Tournament and/or (2) remove promptly the signs making the offer after the Sertoma Charity Golf Tournament had been completed. It seems clear, therefore, that the mistake in this case was unilateral and was the product of the offeror's failure to exercise due care. Such a mistake does not permit appellant to avoid its contract.

Affirmed.

POPOVICH, J., filed a dissenting opinion.

POPOVICH, Judge, dissenting:

"Golf ... is ... a game of relaxed recreation and limitless enjoyment for millions and a demanding examination of exacting standards . . ." (Robert Trent Jones, Preface of The Golf Course, Geoffrey S. Cornish and Ronald E. Whitten, The Rutledge Press, Revised Edition, 1987). In short, golf—as demonstrated by the vast majority of its practitioners who never have and never will score a round at par—is a sport requiring precise skills.

Making a hole-in-one, however, is such a fortuitous event that skill is almost an irrelevant factor. Because of that fact (an element of chance), combined with the payment of an entry fee to the East End Open

Golf Tournament (consideration) and the automobile prize (reward), my view is that the necessary elements of gambling are present thus rendering the contract sub judice unenforceable as violating [385 Pa. Super. 595] the Commonwealth's policy against gambling.[1] As

Page 1252

our Supreme Court stated eighty-five years ago in Davis v. Fleshman, 245 Pa. 224, 91 A. 489 (1914):

It is equally well settled in this jurisdiction that all mere wagering contracts are illegitimate transaction which the law declares void and which will not be enforced at the insistence of either party to the contract. It will not aid the winner to recover from the loser the amount of the stake, and it will not give assistance to the loser to recover back the amount of the bet after the transaction has been closed. It will leave the parties as it finds them. The law will not attempt to settle disputes arising between gamblers by enforcing their alleged rights arising out of an illegal transaction.

I raise this issue sua sponte since we have no jurisdiction to enforce a contract in violation of public policy. In re Estate of Pedrick, 505 Pa. 530, 534, 482 A.2d 215, 222 (1984) (public policy dictates court must raise "unclean hands" sua sponte); Rossi v. Pennsylvania State University, 340 Pa. Super. 39, 489 A.2d 828 (1985) (propriety of summary judgment raised sua sponte).

By couching this transaction in terms of a unilateral contract, the majority seems to opine that scoring a hole-in-one is an act of skill which a golfer can choose to undertake.[2] The truth is quite the opposite.

While every golfer dreams of the day when his ball flawlessly flies into the cup, few ever experience the thrill of a hole-in-one. So few in fact that "aceing" a hole is truly an act of "luck" not skill. Consider the following statistics:[3] [385 Pa. Super. 596] In 1988, approximately 21.7 million golfers played 434 million rounds of golf with only 34,469 holes-in-one being reported to the United States Golf Association. Golf Digest, using figures amassed since 1952, estimates that a golfer of average ability playing a par-3 hole of average difficulty has a mere 1 in 20,000 chance of aceing the hole.

While the chances increase for a professional golfer, the possibility of a hole-in-one, even for the world's best players, is still remote. Last year only 22 holes-in-one were recorded during the Professional Golf Association's tournament schedule.[4] With approximately 300 touring professionals playing in 47 tournaments (four rounds per tournament, four par-3's per round), the odds increased to approximately 1 in 10,000.

However, even at 10,000 to 1, the professional's chances of aceing a hole are more akin to an act of God than a demonstration of skill. Clearly, the possibility of a hole-in-one is sufficiently remote to qualify as the necessary gambling requirement of an element of chance.

Since all of the elements of gambling are present, I see no reason to enforce this so-called unilateral contract, rather I would find that an unenforceable gambling contract was created. While I recognize that there are a variety of socially acceptable forms of gambling indulged in by the public for the most charitable of purposes and the worthiest of causes, they are nonetheless illicit under Pennsylvania law. Dollar raffle tickets for the benefit of a hospital or a Little League Baseball Association are bought and sold innocuously and routinely, and, yet, raffles constitute unsanctioned gambling. Only recently, under strict control, has bingo, a popular and social form of gambling been legalized. 10 Pa. C.S.A. § 301 et seq. See also 4 Pa. C.S.A. § 325.101 et seq. (horse racing); 72 Pa. C.S.A. § 3761-1 et [385 Pa. Super. 597]

---

[1] Under Pennsylvania law, the three elements of gambling are consideration, a reward and an element of chance. *Commonwealth v. Weisman*, 331 Pa. Super. 31, 479 A.2d 1063 (1984); *In re: Gaming Devices Seized at American Legion Post No. 109*, 197 Pa. Super. 10, 176 A.2d 115 (1961). Illegal lotteries, gambling and bookmaking are strictly prohibited as delineated in 18 Pa. C.S.A. §§ 5512 (lotteries), 5513 (gaming devices, gambling) and 5514 (pool selling, bookmaking).

[2] "In order to win the car, Cobaugh was required to perform an act which he was under no legal duty to perform. The car was to be given in exchange for the feat of making a hole-in-one." Majority Op. at 1250.

[3] The statistics are courtesy of Lois Hains, Assistant Editor, and Hope Johnson, Chief of Research, *Golf Digest*, the foremost comprehensive periodical on the sport of golf.

[4] For the record, we note that female professional golfers playing in Ladies Professional Golf Association events had 20 holes-in-one in 1988.

seq. (state lottery). Millions of citizens spend billions of dollars each year on sports betting in office pools or with the local bookmaker. However,

Page 1253

only in one state, Nevada, is it legal so to do.

Thus, when such a rare case as this comes into court, it may be difficult to re-assert a public policy which everyday is violated by common experience, especially, such as here, where there probably was no thought of gambling or "breaking the law." Nevertheless, we cannot usurp the role of the legislature or turn our heads away from the fundamental substance of this transaction: it is a contract, a contract covering the context of gambling. Hence, it is unenforceable no matter how much condoned or indulged.

Chapter 2

Consideration

Chapter Objectives

The student will be able to:

- Use vocabulary regarding consideration properly.
- Discuss the requirements of valid, legal consideration.
- Identify invalid, not legally recognizable consideration.
- Differentiate between sufficiency and adequacy of consideration.
- Determine if the obligation falls within one of the four "special agreements" that do not require consideration.

This chapter will explore for WHAT PURPOSE (consideration) the parties enter into an agreement and WHETHER that is legally sufficient to support enforcement of the contract. Both parties must gain or give something in exchange for something else. This exchange is the consideration for the agreement. While contract law does not judge the value of the exchange, it does have some requirements that the consideration must satisfy in order to support a legally enforceable agreement.

There the offeror stands with his arm outstretched, an offer in his hand; all the offeree has to do is accept, right? Not so fast; let's take a closer look at what is in his hand. Remember there is no such thing as a free lunch; the offeror is going to want something in exchange. This is the substance of the agreement—the **consideration**. In legalese, *consideration* is the "bargained-for exchange" between the two parties—it is not the offeror's thoughtful concern for others. Perhaps the most important thing to remember about consideration is the *bargain*. Again, this term is given an alternate legal meaning other than its everyday

consideration
The basis of the bargained-for exchange between the parties to a contract that is of legal value.

41

usage. By bargain, the law means that the parties have exchanged things or promises of legal value, not that the subject matter of the offer is on a clearance rack. While it may be nice that people exchange promises and fully intend on keeping them, without this thing called consideration, the law will not enforce the promises.

LEGAL VALUE

Consideration is the *why* of a contract. "A consideration in its widest sense is the reason, motive, or inducement, by which a man is moved to bind himself by an agreement. It is not for nothing that he consents to impose an obligation upon himself, or to abandon or transfer a right. It is in consideration of such and such a fact that he agrees to bear new burdens or to forgo the benefits which the law already allows him." JOHN SALMOND, JURISPRUDENCE 359 (Glanville L. Williams ed., 10th ed. 1947). Why did the parties enter into an agreement? Was one of them to do something in exchange for the other person to do (or not to do) something or make a payment to the offeror? In the law, we call these obligations either a **benefit conferred** or a **detriment incurred**. The parties to the agreement must confer some desired good or service upon the other; otherwise what would be the point of entering into a contract? Simply, the benefits conferred in a simple sales contract are the act of giving money to the vendor (conferring a benefit upon him) and receiving the desired good or service (conferring a benefit upon the purchaser). It is more difficult to understand when someone would bargain for a detriment until you realize that they too receive a benefit by incurring the detriment. Perhaps it is only clear in example: Your rich Uncle Al doesn't want you to smoke (and you are over 18 so that you are legally permitted to do so). He offers you $5,000 to quit smoking and stay smoke-free for at least one year. The consideration is the benefit your uncle gets in knowing you will not be smoking and will probably kick the habit. This is valid consideration. You have incurred a detriment in that you have agreed not to do what you have a legal right to do. The **forbearance of a legal right** is a detriment incurred and is valid consideration. Additionally, the reason you agreed to incur this detriment was so that you could ultimately derive a benefit from the bargain, the $5,000. Therefore, incurring the detriment conferred a benefit on you. Motivation, the why of contract, is important in that understanding the parties' intent will reveal whether there was consideration.

Forbearing on the right to sue after a cause of action has arisen is a common example of consideration that is hard to see because it involves someone not doing something. This often occurs with loans, promissory notes, and insurance. This can take the practical form where the lender agrees to give the borrower more time in which to pay off the loan or the insured party agrees to take a settlement where the claim is in dispute. The consideration for the extension of time or the release of claim is the forbearance of the legal right

benefit conferred
The exchange that bestows value upon the other party to the contract.

detriment incurred
The exchange that burdens the party in giving the consideration to the other party to the contract.

forbearance of a legal right
Consideration that requires a party to refrain from doing something that he has the legal right to do.

to sue. Of course, this can only exist where the loan or payment has come due. In order to forbear, the two parties must have a reasonable belief that the claim is viable and that the lawsuit is ready to be commenced. *See, e.g., Crystal Colony Condo. Ass'n, Inc. v. Aspen Specialty Ins. Co.*, 6 F. Supp. 3d 1295 (S.D. Fla. 2014) (The Plaintiff accepted an insurance payment in order to expedite the claim process and release the company from any further actions that might have arisen from the same storm.). The mere fact that the lender does not commence suit (potentially forbearing from doing so) does not establish consideration; there must be a mutual agreement that the plaintiff would forbear to act on that legal right. *See, e.g., Greenwood Associates, Inc. v. Crestar Bank*, 448 S.E.2d 399 (Va. 1994). A borrower cannot assume that the delay in foreclosure is forbearance constituting consideration on an agreement to extend the loan.

CRYPTO CONTRACTS

While consideration may sound personal to the parties, technology has provided the distance and anonymity of the Internet. "Smart contracts"—those agreements that are recorded on a blockchain—provide for certain and unalterable consideration. This may be appropriate or desirable in one-time-only agreements between strangers. The code itself memorializes the obligations that each party agrees to undertake. This is the unchangeable element of consideration as the record is a permanently encrypted file. Therefore, contracts that are in aid of long-term relationships and/or are subject to changing terms or circumstances are not well suited for this simple, repetitive, inflexible, and automatic "smart contract" process.

IN-CLASS DISCUSSION

Frank loves fast food and, as a result of his habit of frequenting these establishments, has become substantially overweight. He has read the decision in *Pelman v. McDonald's*, 237 F. Supp. 2d 512 (S.D.N.Y. 2003) (a case wherein the plaintiffs alleged that the fast food chain caused obesity and subsequently death. The plaintiffs did not ultimately prevail; moreover, the court found the claim without basis to grant relief). Frank thinks this might be a good way to make some fast cash. He goes to his local "Chunky Charlie's Cheeseburger" restaurant and says that he intends to sue them for making him fat. Chunky Charlie's doesn't want any bad publicity so they agree to pay him $10,000 not to sue.

Is this valid consideration where the forbearance of the right to sue involves a dubious claim? How is this different, if at all, from claims that are likely to win?

EXCEPTIONS

Another way of describing what consideration is to tell you what it is *not*. There are five rules that indicate when the exchange is not legal consideration:

1. Gifts
2. Moral obligations
3. Illusory promises
4. Past consideration
5. Preexisting duties

mutuality of obligation
Also known as "mutuality of contract"; it is a doctrine that requires both parties to be bound to performance obligations under the agreement.

gift
Bestowing a benefit without any expectation on the part of the giver to receive something in return and the absence of any obligation on the part of the receiver to do anything in return.

moral obligation
A social goal or personal aspiration that induces a party to act without any expectation of a return performance from the recipient.

legal value
Having an objectively determinable benefit that is recognized by the court.

illusory promise
A statement that appears to be a promise but actually enforces no obligation upon the promisor because he retains the subjective option whether or not to perform on it.

The first two are the easiest to explain. (1) Gifts and (2) moral obligations are not consideration because they lack **mutuality of obligation**. If, for example, your friend wants to give you a **gift**, you have no motivation to promise her anything in return, and you will receive the gift without obligating yourself to do anything in exchange. The same holds true for **moral obligations**. If your friend feels that she *should* do something for you (maybe because you've helped her study for the Certified Paralegal Exam), you have no reason to promise anything to her. Friends do things for you simply because they want to, not because they have to—the essence of true friendship. In both these situations, gifts and morality, there is no bargain. The offeror (the person doing something for another) is performing these actions without asking for anything in return. Even if the recipient then recapitulates and does something nice for the offeror, there is still no consideration for the exchanges. No court would be able to enforce the agreement as there is no **legal value** to these exchanges.

Again, the cold heart of contracts appears; generosity and morality play no role in black letter contract law. (The sentimentalists will need to wait until the chapter on equity to feel reassured that the justice system does not fail to indeed provide justice and fairness.) Consistent with the cool logic of contracts, the third kind of exchange that is not legal consideration is an **illusory promise**. Contract law likes objectivity and definiteness. An illusory promise is neither; it may appear on its face to be a bargained-for exchange, but the promise itself, once examined, is so insubstantial that it doesn't impose an obligation on the offeror. It lacks the element of commitment. If the promisee performs, there is really no requirement that the offeror do anything. How does this come about? In practical terms, this happens when the offeror retains subjective control over the material terms of the bargain. *See, e.g., Cheek v. United Healthcare of Mid-Atlantic, Inc.*, 835 A.2d 656, 662 (Md. 2003) (Employees of United had to enter into an employment arbitration agreement; however, United "reserve[d] the right to alter, amend, modify, or revoke the [Arbitration] Policy at its sole and absolute discretion at any time with or without notice." The court found no real promise and therefore it was not sufficient consideration to uphold the agreement.).

Sheila Starlet is a rising actress and model. At this point in her career, she is seeking a personal representative and manager to catapult her to superstar status. She makes an agreement with Andrew Agent.

Determine whether there is valid consideration to support the following writing.

CONTRACT

Agreement made this day, May 8, 2005, between Sheila Starlet ("Starlet") and Andrew Agent ("Agent") for representative and managerial services to be rendered by Agent.

Starlet agrees to pay Agent for his services. Payment shall be made every quarter. All earnings of Starlet will be deemed to result from Agent's services and Agent shall receive 10% of the gross earned by Starlet. This contract will continue in force and effect for five years.

Agent will devote only as much time and attention to Starlet's affairs as he deems necessary.

Signed:

_____

Sheila Starlet

_____

Andrew Agent

Example

Greg Grocer offers to buy all of Farmer Fred's apples—a classic output contract. Greg sends the contract to Fred and it reads: "I, Greg Grocer, agree to purchase all the apples produced on Fred Farmer's Farm as long as they meet my standards for quality." There is no consideration in this offer; Greg has total subjective control over the contract. There is no way to know if Greg will ever have an obligation under the contract; what are his "standards for quality"? His promise to perform under the contract, to purchase the apples, is illusory—it has no substance whatsoever. It is merely an illusion—all smoke and mirrors, so to speak. There would be a different result if the offer was: "I, Greg Grocer, agree to purchase all the apples produced on Fred Farmer's Farm as long as they meet industry standards for grade A quality." There is an objective measure to determine if and when Greg becomes obligated to perform under the contract. There is valid consideration—each side has bargained for the exchange and has a way of objectively determining the value of the offer.

Contract law also does not like rifts in the space-time continuum. During the bargaining process, the parties cannot go back in time and rely on previous actions and promises to support the present exchange. The actions and promises occurred in the past and there they should stay. In an unusual (and real) case, *Anonymous v. Anonymous*, 740 N.Y.S.2d 341, 293 A.D.2d 406 (1st Dep't 2002), a prostitute tried to enforce an agreement for financial support from a client based on her previous provision of services. The court refused to grant relief based on the fact that the promise was based on past consideration (the fact that the subject matter was illegal also barred recovery). Weirdly similar is the case involving a man giving his wife a check for $60,000 that he said was for coming back and staying with him after their divorce. He told her that she could cash the check if something happened to him. The check was dated July 29, 1981. When decedent died in September 1999, the check was too old to cash, and a claim was asserted against the estate. The court refused to enforce a claim against the estate because the consideration for the check was past consideration—the wife had already come back and stayed with him for some time. *In re Estate of Lovekamp*, 2001 Okla. Civ. App. 71, 24 P.3d 894. The check was not given as an inducement to come back. Otherwise, it would have been valid, present consideration.

past consideration
A benefit conferred in a previous transaction between the parties before the present promise was made.

The parties cannot reuse this **past consideration** as valid consideration in the present transaction. The consideration for the bargain must relate to the current transaction. If you recall, one of the elements to a valid offer is the present intent to contract; the consideration must occur simultaneously in the present in order to form a valid offer. At the time you received the past consideration, you could not have had the present intent to contract for a possible future agreement.

Example

Last year, after a prosperous merger, ABC company gave out bonuses to all its suppliers. This year didn't go so well, but ABC company wants to order more supplies. ABC offers its bonuses from last year to pay for the current year's orders. This is not valid consideration because the bonuses were not given in consideration for the office supplies for this year. Past actions or payments do not serve as present consideration.

preexisting duty
An obligation to perform an act that existed before the current promise was made that requires the same performance presently sought.

The last exclusion from consideration is the **preexisting duty** rule. If the action upon which you are relying as consideration is something you are already legally bound to do, it is not valid consideration. You did not make any bargain. A typical example is the fact that firemen and police officers cannot offer their services to protect the public as consideration; they must already do so as terms of their employment. Additionally, Hank Handyman, with whom you have contracted to fix your leaking roof, cannot first agree to fix the roof for $5,000, then yank off your shingles and announce that he is not going to do the work for less than $7,000. You are under no obligation to pay the extra $2,000 when the contract stated that he would perform the work for $5,000.

Hank Handyman has a preexisting duty under the contract to fix the roof for $5,000. Hank has not offered you anything in return for your extra $2,000; therefore, there is no mutuality of consideration.

Of course, like any good legal principle, there are exceptions to the preexisting duty rule:

1. If *new or different consideration* is given to support the bargain. For example, if Hank agrees to upgrade the kind of roof he's going to install. He has a preexisting duty to install a roof, but the upgrade is new and/or different consideration and you will be obligated to pay for the $2,000 upgrade.

2. If the consideration supports a **voidable obligation**. For example, a 17-year-old cannot enter into an enforceable contract because he is a minor. If Hank is 17, he can still avoid this contract before turning 18, leaving you with your old roof. Interestingly, the minor can enforce the contract as against the other party, if he so chooses, but the adult cannot enforce the contract against the minor. After turning 18, Hank can use the promise to fix your roof (technically past consideration) to ratify the contract and make it enforceable. The change from voidable contract to enforceable contract by ratification upon attaining the age of 18 has a subtle effect on the past consideration, making it valid present consideration because it is like the minor (now attaining majority) enters into a slightly different agreement—one that is enforceable by both parties.

3. If the *duty is owed to a third person*, not the promisee, the consideration is valid to support the agreement between the third party and the promisor. For example, under contract, Hank has a preexisting duty to fix your roof; your neighbor, Netta Nosy, offers him $1,000 to fix your roof because she cannot stand looking at it. Hank can use his preexisting duty to fix your roof as consideration in the deal with Netta because he doesn't already owe *her* under the contract. His same action of fixing your roof supports both agreements as consideration. You and Netta each gets a different bargained-for benefit from the roof repairs.

4. **Unforeseen circumstances** make the duty substantially more difficult to fulfill; one of the parties is in for more than he bargained for. For example, Hank finds that the entire substructure of the roof is rotten and will have to be replaced. If he could not have known this from his prior inspections and could not have anticipated that this would be the case, perhaps because the existing roof was only five years old, he is not responsible for fixing the roof for the original contract price of $5,000. Due to these unforeseen circumstances and the necessity to replace the entire substructure, the cost to fix the roof will be $15,000. There is valid consideration to support this increase in cost as there is substantially more work to do.

voidable obligation
A duty imposed under a contract that may be either ratified (approved) or avoided (rejected) at the option of one or both of the parties.

unforeseen circumstances
Occurrences that could not be reasonably forecast to happen.

SPOT THE ISSUE!

Jack the construction foreman brought suit against his employer, Quick Build, Inc., alleging that Quick had breached an oral contract that Jack would receive a bonus for making efforts to complete the project on time and under budget. Jack's bonus would be one-half of the difference between the estimated and actual cost of a construction project. The final budget showed a savings of $35,000. Jack claims he is entitled to a bonus in the amount of $17,000. Is he? Why or why not?

SUFFICIENCY OF CONSIDERATION

sufficient consideration
The exchanges have recognizable legal value and are capable of supporting an enforceable contract. The actual values are irrelevant.

adequate consideration
Exchanges that are fair and reasonable as a result of equal bargaining for things of relatively equal value.

There is a distinction between **sufficient consideration** and **adequate consideration**. The first, sufficient consideration, is a factor that the courts will examine; the second, adequate consideration, the courts will not. To the layperson, they appear to be synonymous, but there is an important difference in the cool, calculating eyes of contract law. Consideration is sufficient if it can legally bind the parties to the agreement. This is what we have been discussing up to this point. The law cares little, however, if you've made a good bargain, whether the exchange of consideration was fair and relatively equal between the two parties. The monetary worth in the exchange means almost nothing to the court; *caveat emptor* and *caveat venditor* ("let the buyer beware" and "let the seller beware"). If you entered into a bad deal, that is your own fault; freedom of contract principles apply here.

Notice the wording carefully: The monetary worth means *almost* nothing. If the consideration's worth is so devalued in light of the other party's bargain, the court may suspect that there was no mutuality of consideration. There are two terms for this devalued consideration: (1) *nominal consideration* and (2) *sham consideration*. **Nominal consideration** usually reveals the intent to bestow a gift. For example, Holly Homeowner's parents want her to have the family home as they retire to Florida. They sell her the house for one dollar. This is nominal consideration because the house is worth substantially more than one dollar. Holly's consideration really has no value in light of what she is receiving and, indeed, there was no bargaining involved. This does not mean that the transfer is not legal. It is a donative transfer, not a contractual one. The legal ramification of this distinction is that Holly couldn't then sue for contractual enforcement of the transfer of the house. You cannot force someone to give you a gift. This situation is also an example of **good consideration**:

nominal consideration
The value of the things exchanged are grossly disproportionate to each other so that very little is given in exchange for something of great value.

good consideration
An exchange made based on love and affection, which have no legal value.

[G]ood consideration is that of [ ] the natural love and affection which a person has [for] his children, or any of his relatives. . . . A good consideration is not of itself sufficient to support a promise, any more than the moral obligation which arises from a man's passing his word; neither will the two together make a binding contract; thus a promise by a father to make a gift to his child will not be enforced against him. The consideration of natural love and affection is indeed good for so little in law, that it is not easy to see why it should be called a good consideration. . . .

JOSHUA WILLIAMS, PRINCIPLES OF THE LAW OF PERSONAL PROPERTY 95-96 (11th ed. 1881).

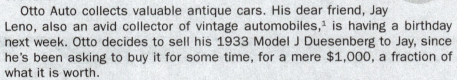

RESEARCH THIS

Find a case in your jurisdiction that answers the following fact scenario:

Otto Auto collects valuable antique cars. His dear friend, Jay Leno, also an avid collector of vintage automobiles,[1] is having a birthday next week. Otto decides to sell his 1933 Model J Duesenberg to Jay, since he's been asking to buy it for some time, for a mere $1,000, a fraction of what it is worth.

Is this a valid sales contract or is it a gift? Think about the distinction between gifts and valid contractual consideration and the courts' role in determining the sufficiency, not adequacy, of consideration.

Sham consideration is indeterminable consideration. Recall that contract law hates indefiniteness. If the contract merely recites that there is valuable consideration but does not specify what it is, the consideration is invalid, and the contract is deemed to be void for vagueness. For example, Hank agrees "to fix your roof for valuable consideration"; this is sham consideration: There is no way to know what the consideration is. Additionally, this is an illusory promise because the consideration that Hank will accept to perform the roof repairs is completely subjective.

Conditions attached to the consideration are generally regarded as valid as long as there is an objective standard to determine whether that condition has been met. Typically, the obligation to be bound under the terms of the contract is dependent on the happening (or non-happening) of an event. For example, most real estate contracts are conditioned upon the buyers' obtaining financing within a certain period of time or selling their current home. If that condition fails (the buyers do not qualify for the necessary mortgage or they cannot sell their house), then the contract is not enforceable. This is not considered a breach of the contract because the buyers tried to perform under the contract—it was not a refusal to perform. The contract specifically contemplated that the parties would be released from their obligations under the contract if this condition failed.

sham consideration
An unspecified and indeterminable recitation of consideration that cannot support an exchange.

condition
An event that may or may not happen upon which the rest of the performance of the contract rests.

---

[1]For more information on Jay's obsession, see https://www.cnn.com/2016/10/07/motorsport/jay-leno-automobile-collection-f1/index.html/. Any general search will yield similar results.

SPOT THE ISSUE!

Sam owns significant amounts of stock in Acme Co. and Carl owns the same number of shares in Generic, Inc. Sam and Carl agree to exchange their respective stock portfolios as they see this transaction as easier than selling and buying on the open market. At the time of the exchange, although they both own the same number of shares, Sam's stock is worth $1.3 million, while Carl's is worth only $10,000. Sam is reluctant to consummate the transaction because there is such a difference in the value of the consideration. Carl sues for enforcement. If you were the judge in this matter, how would you rule? Why? What factors might change your decision?

EYE ON ETHICS

An attorney is in a fiduciary relationship with the client and therefore must arrange a reasonable agreement between him/herself and the client. This may be an entirely different position than the attorney would take in drafting a contract between his/her client and a third party.

Particularly sensitive is the fee arrangement, the consideration for the rendering of these legal services. Under what circumstances are some arrangements unethical? How can a court balance the ethical considerations with its general principles of "freedom of contract" and usual unwillingness to inspect the adequacy of the parties' consideration?

Ethical rules prohibit lawyers from charging unreasonable fees and unreasonable amounts for expenses associated with the representation. "Reasonableness" of an attorney's fee is affected by several factors. An ethical board will look into the following:

(a) the amount of time and degree of skill needed for adequate representation
(b) the difficulty and uniqueness of the matter
(c) the likelihood that the matter will preclude taking on other matters in the office
(d) the fee normally charged in the relevant jurisdiction for similar matters
(e) urgency
(f) the nature of the relationship with the client
(g) the reputation and degree of experience of the attorney handling the matter

SURF'S UP

The virtual marketplace is booming. Millions of people consummate transactions each day. But the limitation on this forum is its very "virtual-ness" and the insidiousness of this forum is the arm's length and anonymous nature of the agreement.

Enjoying particular success are the Internet dating sites. They promise to supply a subscriber with the opportunity to meet and fall in love with that special someone. However, is this truly a promise that they can deliver upon? Isn't meeting your match completely subjective? There are no guarantees; what are these sites actually promising?

Go ahead; perform your own investigation. Visit the most popular sites and examine what they are offering in exchange for your subscription.

This page is just for laughs: http://gawker.com/016157/dating-in-manhattan-an-exercise-in-contract-law.

SPECIAL AGREEMENTS

We have already discussed the *exclusions* for what may be deemed valid consideration (gifts, moral obligations, illusory promises, past obligations, and pre-existing legal duties). However, there are certain circumstances where the law favors the enforcement of the promise, although not supported by consideration, where the promise *ought* to be enforced as a valid contract. So now we shall discuss the exceptions to the exceptions—where, despite the lack of valid consideration, the contract will be supported as if it did exist.

Pledges to charities are enforceable as a matter of public policy, even though they are really a gift. This is most evident during "telethons," where public television stations go on a membership drive and constantly interrupt the programming. When people call in, they are making a legally enforceable pledge to the station, despite the lack of consideration for the pledge. Charitable gifts to other kinds of institutions also can be upheld. The Massachusetts court in *King v. Trustees of Boston University*, 647 N.E.2d 1196, 1202 (Mass. 1995), recognized that "the 'meeting of minds' between a donor and a charitable institution differs from the understanding required in the context of enforceable arm's-length commercial agreements. Charities depend on donations for their existence, whereas their donors may give personal property on conditions they choose, with or without imposing conditions or demanding consideration." In this case, Coretta Scott King, the widow of the late Dr. Martin Luther King Jr. bought suit against Boston University to recover Dr. King's papers that had been donated to the university's library. The court found that a charitable gift had been made by Dr. King because the donative intent was made clear and the receiving institution had relied upon that donation. The "consideration" in cases like this is that the receiving charity relies upon that donation to continue its work for the public good.

Public policy also likes to foster the ideal that people should pay their debts. Fine moral and upstanding citizens should not shirk their monetary responsibilities. Therefore, even where a debtor has been legally discharged of his obligation to pay (say under bankruptcy or because the statute of limitations has run), the debtor can **voluntarily agree to pay back his debt**. This agreement to pay is, of course, not supported by any other consideration. The debtor has no reason to make this promise; there is no legal consequence for him if he does

pledge to charity
A legally enforceable gift to a qualifying institution.

voluntary repayment of debt
An agreement to pay back a debt that cannot be collected upon using legal means because the obligation to make payments has been discharged.

not make this payment. The debtor makes this payment because it is the right thing to do. So even though this looks like "moral consideration," which is not contractually viable as consideration, it is enforceable.

Example
Having fallen on bad times, Sheila declared bankruptcy 10 years ago. She has since gotten back on her feet. Although she is under no legal obligation to pay back her previous debts, she feels particularly guilty about the money she owed to the local furniture store that extended credit to her so she could purchase nursery furniture for her new baby. Sheila returns to the store and promises to pay in full in three monthly installments. This new obligation will be enforceable despite the lack of consideration simply because it's the right thing to do. Soon she has paid in full and has a clear conscience.

guarantee
An agreement in which a third party assures the repayment of a debt owed by another party.

Guarantees are not technically supported by consideration. A guarantee is a written agreement to pay for the debt of another person should that person fail to answer for his/her own debt. This is not the same thing as being a co-signor on a loan, the difference being that a guarantor's obligation to pay may never arise. The guarantee only becomes "enforceable" as against the guarantor after the default of the original obligor. The guarantee is made at the time the contract between the principals is made. If the guarantee comes after the loan (usually at the request of the lender because it doesn't appear that the original obligor is going to be able to pay in full), there must be some sort of additional consideration to make the guarantee as it is a separate contract.

formal contract
An agreement made that follows a certain prescribed form like negotiable instruments.

Formal contracts are the last breed of enforceable agreements without consideration. They are a strange little group consisting of negotiable instruments such as checks; they are not formal in the sense that they are written on fine paper and signed with a fancy pen. Their validity does not derive from the agreement itself; their contractual nature derives validity simply from the *form* it takes; hence, the name *formal contract*. When you write a check to pay for the groceries, you have executed a formal contract.

Summary

Consideration is the substance of the offer; it is that for which the parties have bargained. Examining the intent of the parties, why they will enter into the transaction, will usually reveal the existence or lack of valid, legally enforceable consideration. These obligations to which the parties will bind themselves are called either a *benefit conferred* or a *detriment incurred*. The forbearance of a legal right is valid consideration as it is a detriment incurred.

Consideration requires *mutuality of obligation* and must have legal value recognizable by the courts. Therefore, *gifts, moral compulsions*, and *illusory promises* are not valid consideration. Similarly, *past consideration and preexisting duties* are not valid present consideration as they do not involve current bargaining between the parties. If *new or different consideration* is added to either past consideration or the preexisting duty, it is "renewed." *Voidable obligations* can be made enforceable by the ratification of the party that can escape liability under the contract. *Duties to third parties* also may support a contract wherein the consideration has already been used between the first and second parties. Lastly, *unforeseen circumstances* can alter the conditions under which the parties came to their agreement and, if drastic enough, can provide additional consideration for the contract's modification.

While the courts do not examine the adequacy of consideration to support the contract, they do examine the sufficiency of it to determine whether the consideration is *nominal* or a *sham*. Neither of these types of consideration is considered valid as there is no bargaining involved.

The courts do acknowledge, on public policy grounds, the enforceability of certain promises that might otherwise fail for lack of consideration. They are

1. *Pledges to charities*
2. *Voluntary agreements to repay debts*
3. *Guarantees*
4. *Formal contracts*

Once the existence and validity of consideration have been determined to exist, the offeree is free to accept the offer and a binding contract will be formed.

Key Terms

adequate consideration	moral obligations
benefit conferred	mutuality of obligation
conditions	nominal consideration
consideration	past consideration
detriment incurred	pledges to charities
forbearance of a legal right	preexisting duties
formal contracts	sham consideration
gifts	sufficient consideration
good consideration	unforeseen circumstances
guarantees	voidable obligation
illusory promises	voluntary repayment of a debt
legal value	

Review Questions

MULTIPLE CHOICE

Choose the best answer(s) and please explain *why* you choose the answer(s).

1. Courts will examine the following (there can be more than one answer):
   a. The existence of consideration in the offer.
   b. The sufficiency of consideration to determine if it is really a sham.
   c. Mutuality of obligation.
   d. If the offeror has proper motives in making the offer.
   e. The adequacy of consideration.

2. Which one(s) of these best describes an illusory promise?
   a. I promise to pay you what your ring is worth.
   b. I promise to pay you what I think your ring is worth.
   c. I promise to pay you the same as you paid for your ring originally.
   d. I promise to pay you what you think your ring is worth.

3. Legal value is best described as
   a. Reasonable monetary value.
   b. Sentimental value.
   c. Objectively recognizable benefit.
   d. A loss incurred by a party.

EXPLAIN YOURSELF

All answers should be written in complete sentences. A simple "yes" or "no" is insufficient.

1. Identify the five rules that indicate when the exchange is not valid consideration.

2. Can a contract be formed when there is a lack of mutuality of obligation?

3. Describe a voidable obligation.

4. Explain the difference between nominal and sham consideration.

5. If a party is free to choose whether to perform or withdraw from the agreement or determine subjectively the meaning of any of the terms of the agreement, the court will not find consideration but a(n) _____ ____ _____.

"FAULTY PHRASES"

All of the following statements are FALSE; state why they are false and then rewrite them as a true statement. Write a brief fact pattern that illustrates your answer.

1. In every contract, there must be both a detriment incurred and a benefit conferred.

2. PBS (the public TV station) cannot sue in a court of law to recover payment for a pledge made during a telethon to raise funds because the pledge is just a gift.

3. Courts do not permit additional recovery (change in the terms of the agreement) despite the lack of new consideration due to unforeseen circumstances.

4. The reason courts enforce contracts is because performance is morally correct.

5. Forbearing from a legal right is not legal consideration because a party is not doing something and consideration must be a positive action.

"WRITE" AWAY! PORTFOLIO ASSIGNMENT

In this exercise, review your draft offer from "Druid Design & Build" to Carrie Kilt, paying close attention to the obligations of both parties. Are there any subjective elements? Does the construction have to meet objective construction industry standards or the approval of either the contractor or home owner? Does the offer specifically delineate the duties that each party has toward the other? Be mindful of Druid's preexisting duties under the offer; how are unexpected versus unforeseeable problems addressed?

Rewrite the offer to take these answers into consideration (pun intended).

Case in Point   LEGALLY SUFFICIENT CONSIDERATION

■ Case 1

407 S.W.3d 51
JUMBOSACK CORPORATION, Appellant,
v.
Bob BUYCK, Respondent.
No. ED 98134.
Missouri Court of Appeals,
Eastern District,
Division Four.
May 21, 2013.
Motion for Rehearing and/or Transfer to Supreme Court Denied June 26, 2013.
Application for Transfer Denied Aug. 13, 2013.

[407 S.W.3d 53]

Brian E. McGovern, Chesterfield, MO, for appellant.
David M. Slaby, St. Louis, MO, for respondent.
PATRICIA L. COHEN, Judge.

INTRODUCTION

JumboSack Corporation (Employer) appeals the trial court's grant of summary judgment to Bob Buyck (Employee) on its claim for breach of a non-compete agreement. Employer claims the trial court erred in granting summary judgment because: (1) the non-compete agreement was supported by valid consideration; (2) the employment agreement provided that "[a]ny changes in Employee's compensation, position or job duties subsequent to the execution of this Agreement shall in no way void or otherwise affect the remaining provisions of this Agreement"; (3) whether Employer materially breached the employment agreement is an issue of fact; (4) the parol evidence rule precluded Employee from arguing that an oral contract modified the plain and unambiguous terms of the non-compete agreement; and (5) whether Employer waived its right to enforce the non-compete agreement against Employee is an issue of fact. We reverse and remand.

FACTUAL AND PROCEDURAL BACKGROUND

Employee began working as a salesman for Employer, a supplier of large polypropylene bags used for storing and transporting "dry bulk flowable products," in August 2003. Employer agreed to pay Employee an annual salary of $70,000 plus a $500/month car allowance, sales expenses, and fuel expenses. Employer did not ask Employee to sign a non-compete agreement at the time of hire.

Approximately six months after Employee began working for Employer, Employer's president, Mike Reynoso, directed Employer's then-sales manager, Joe Wurm, to present Employee with a non-compete agreement, entitled "Employment–Confidentiality Agreement" (Agreement). The Agreement provided, in relevant part:

As a separate covenant under this Agreement, Employee covenants that he shall not, for a period of three (3) years after termination of his employment with Employer for whatever reason, directly or indirectly, on behalf of himself or any third party, make any sales contacts with, solicit or accept business from, or supervise or manage any sales activities over any customer(s) of Employer for whom Employee had sales responsibility during the period that Employee was employed by Employer, provided, however, that this restriction shall only apply to products or services which are competitive with those of Employer.

The Agreement also provided: "Any changes in Employee's compensation, position or job duties subsequent to the execution of this Agreement shall in no way void or otherwise affect the remaining provisions of this Agreement." Employee initially refused to sign the Agreement.

[407 S.W.3d 54]

However, after Wurm informed Employee that Employer would terminate his employment if he did not sign, Employee signed the Agreement on February 1, 2004. Employer did not provide Employee any additional compensation or benefit as consideration for his signing the Agreement.

Effective April 1, 2005, Employer changed Employee's compensation structure to a salary of $57,000 plus a commission rate of 1.5%. Employer later reduced Employee's rate of commission to 1.25%. Employer did not always pay Employee's commissions in a timely manner.

In January 2009, Reynoso informed Employee that Employer intended to lower Employee's salary to $50,000. On February 20, 2009, Employer announced via email a new policy pursuant to which, if a salesperson failed to obtain from a customer a signed purchase order and that customer failed to pay for its purchase, the salesperson would be responsible for one-third of the unpaid invoice. Employee resigned his employment the same day.

Employee subsequently accepted employment as a salesperson with Employer's competitor, Inter-BULK USA, LLC. On January 6, 2010, Employer filed a petition in the Circuit Court of St. Louis County seeking a temporary and permanent restraining order, injunctive relief, and damages based on Employee's alleged breach of the Agreement. Specifically, Employer alleged that Employee "is currently working as a salesperson at a competing business" and "has contacted and/or solicited business from [Employer's] customers in violation of the Employment Agreement and in so doing has utilized trade secrets and confidential information of [Employer]." The trial court granted Employer's petition for a temporary restraining order on January 15, 2010.

Employee filed a motion for summary judgment claiming he was entitled to summary judgment because: (1) the undisputed material facts established that Employer did not have trade secrets or customer contacts that were protectable under a non-compete agreement; and (2) Employer could not enforce the Agreement's non-competition clause against Employee because Employer previously breached the Agreement. The trial court granted Employee's motion for summary judgment, explaining: "[Employer] cannot enforce the non-compete agreement against [Employee] due to [Employer's] prior breach of the employment agreement and for lack of consideration." Employer appeals.

STANDARD OF REVIEW

Appellate review of summary judgment is de novo. *ITT Commercial Fin. Corp. v. Mid-Am. Marine Supply Corp.,* 854 S.W.2d 371, 376 (Mo. banc 1993). When reviewing a trial court's grant of summary judgment, this court views the record in the light most favorable to the party against whom summary judgment was entered. *Id.* This court will uphold summary judgment only if we find that there is no genuine dispute of material fact and the movant is entitled to judgment as a matter of law. *Id.*; Rule 74.04(c). An issue of material fact is genuine "only if it is real and substantial; it may not consist 'of conjecture, theory and possibilities.'" *Hanson v. Union Elec. Co.,* 963 S.W.2d 2, 4 (Mo. App. E.D. 1998) (*quoting ITT,* 854 S.W.2d at 378).

DISCUSSION

Employer presents five points on appeal. The first and third points are dispositive of the appeal. We also briefly address point two but decline to address the remaining two points.

[407 S.W.3d 55]

"The law of non-compete agreements in Missouri seeks to balance the competing concerns between an employer and employee in the workforce." *Whelan Sec. Co. v. Kennebrew,* 379 S.W.3d 835, 841 (Mo. banc 2012). As the Supreme Court recently explained, employers have a legitimate interest in "engaging a highly trained workforce without the risk of losing customers and business secrets after an employee leaves his or her employment," while employees have a legitimate interest in "having mobility between employers to provide for their families and advance their careers." *Id.* Additionally, "although the law favors the ability of parties to contract freely, contracts in restraint of trade are unlawful." *Id.*

"Missouri courts balance these concerns by enforcing non-compete agreements in certain limited circumstances." *Healthcare Servs. of the Ozarks, Inc. v. Copeland,* 198 S.W.3d 604, 610 (Mo. banc 2006). A court will enforce a non-compete only if it is reasonable, meaning "it is no more restrictive than is necessary to protect the legitimate interest of the employer." *Id.* As such, a non-compete must be narrowly tailored geographically and temporally. *Id.* Additionally, restrictive covenants are not enforceable to protect an employer from mere competition by a former employee, but only to the extent that they protect the employer's trade secrets or customer contacts. *Id.* The employer has the burden to prove that the reasonableness of the non-compete agreement. *Whelan,* 379 S.W.3d at 842.

1. Consideration

In its first point on appeal, Employer claims the trial court erred in granting Employee summary judgment because Employer provided Employee "continued employment with [Employer] (and thereby allowed him continued access to its customer relationships) for approximately five (5) years after he signed the [Agreement]." In response, Employee argues that his continued employment alone is not adequate consideration for a non-compete agreement and that Employer must also "show promotion within the company, added responsibility and increase in compensation."[1]

Like any contractual obligation, a non-compete agreement requires the support of adequate consideration. *Mayer Hoffman McCann, P.C. v. Barton,* 614 F.3d 893, 903 (8th Cir. 2010) (applying Missouri law). Consideration is "something of value that moves from one party to the other." *Sumners v. Serv. Vending Co.,* 102 S.W.3d 37, 41 (Mo. App. S.D. 2003). "A valuable consideration may consist of some right, interest, profit or benefit accruing to one party, or some forbearance, loss or responsibility given[,] suffered or undertaken by the other." *Reed, Roberts Assocs., Inc. v. Bailenson,* 537 S.W.2d 238, 240 (Mo. App. 1976) (quotation omitted). "The burden of showing legally sufficient consideration rests on the party relying on the contract." *Earl v. St. Louis Univ.,* 875 S.W.2d 234, 236 (Mo. App. E.D. 1994). Although normally the adequacy of consideration is a question of law, "if this determination necessarily turns on disputed facts, then the jury, as the arbiter of facts, must decide the issue." *Id.* at 237.

Missouri courts have recognized that continued at-will employment constitutes consideration for a non-compete agreement where the employer allows the employee "by virtue of the employment[,]

[407 S.W.3d 56]

to have *continued access* to [its] protectable assets and relationships." *Morrow v. Hallmark Cards, Inc.,* 273 S.W.3d 15, 29 (Mo. App. W.D. 2008) (emphasis in the original); *see also Nail Boutique, Inc. v. Church,* 758 S.W.2d 206, 210 (Mo. App. S.D. 1988); *Computer Sales Int'l, Inc. v. Collins,* 723 S.W.2d 450, 452 (Mo. App. E.D. 1986). In the instant case, Employee received in consideration for his covenant not to compete, access to Employer's new and existing customers, as well as continued at-will employment, salary, and commissions.[2]

---

[1] We note that Employer has not argued that Employee's continued employment alone constituted sufficient consideration.

---

[2] Employee appears to argue that his continued access to Employer's customers did not constitute consideration for his promise not to compete because Employer's customer contacts were not "protectable interests." Whether Employer had a legitimate interest in protecting its customer relationships so as to justify enforcement of the non-competition clause is a separate issue from the sufficiency of consideration. *See, e.g., Nail Boutique,* 758 S.W.2d at 209-10; *Ranch Hand Foods, Inc. v. Polar Pak Foods, Inc.,* 690 S.W.2d 437, 440, 443 (Mo. App. W.D. 1985); *USA Chem, Inc. v. Lewis,* 557 S.W.2d 15, 24 (Mo. App. 1977). However, because Employee also argued in its motion for summary judgment and as a separate ground for affirming on appeal that Employer failed to show it had protectable interests meriting protection, we address the issue here.

Employee contends that his continued employment by Employer did not constitute consideration for the non-compete agreement because his salary decreased after he signed it. In support of this argument, Employee cites *Sturgis Equip. Co., Inc. v. Falcon Indus. Sales Co.*, 930 S.W.2d 14 (Mo. App. E.D. 1996). There, the employee and the employer executed a buy-sell agreement providing that "in exchange for [the employer] agreeing to sell stock to [the employee] and buy back [the employee's] stock if he desired to sell or if his employment terminated," the employee agreed not to compete with the employer for two years following his termination. *Id.* at 16. After a demotion and a decrease in compensation, the employee terminated the employment relationship and formed a competing company. *Id.* The employer sued the employee for breach of the non-compete agreement, and the trial court entered judgment in favor of the employer. *Id.*

On appeal, the *Sturgis* court held that the non-compete agreement was unenforceable because its restrictions were "greater than fairly required for [the employer's] protection and was not supported by sufficient consideration."[3] *Id.* at 17. In regard to sufficiency of consideration, the court explained that the consideration

[407 S.W.3d 57]

of agreeing to buy back the employee's stock was insufficient to support the broad non-compete agreement. *Id.* However, the court explained that the agreement might have been enforceable if it stated that its purpose was to protect any special interest of the company, specified the additional consideration, or was part of an employment contract. *Id.* The *Sturgis* opinion, therefore, does not stand for the proposition that continued employment will only constitute consideration for a post-employment, non-compete agreement where the employee receives an increase in compensation and responsibility.

Finally, Employee argues that his continued employment was insufficient consideration to support the non-compete agreement because the non-compete agreement was not a required condition of Employee's initial employment by Employer. In other words, Employee posits that, because Employer required him to sign the Agreement subsequent to the start of the employment relationship, it is not enforceable in the absence of "extra benefits or compensation for the non-compete agreement." Missouri courts have held, however, that continued employment and the attendant access to the employer's protectable information and relationships constitutes adequate consideration for a non-compete agreement executed after the inception of employment. *See, e.g., Morrow*, 273 S.W.3d at 28-29; *Nail Boutique*, 758 S.W.2d at 210; *Computer Sales*, 723 S.W.2d at 452; *Reed, Roberts Assocs.*, 537 S.W.2d at 241. Point granted.

2. Material Breach

In point three, Employer contends that the trial court erred in basing summary judgment upon its finding that "[Employer] cannot enforce the non-compete agreement against [Employee] due to [Employer's] prior breach of the employment agreement." Specifically, Employer argues that the issue of whether Employer materially breached the Agreement and is therefore precluded from enforcing the non-competition provision is a question of fact for the fact-finder and was not appropriate for summary judgment.

"An employer that has materially breached an employment agreement before an employee has violated a covenant not to compete may not enforce the covenant." *Washington County Mem'l Hosp. v. Sidebottom,*

"An express agreement not to compete may be enforced as to employees having substantial customer contacts. It is not necessary to show that there is a secret customer list." *Osage Glass, Inc. v. Donovan*, 693 S.W.2d 71, 74 (Mo. banc 1985). In determining whether an employer's customer contacts merit the protection of a non-compete agreement, courts consider the "quality, frequency, and duration of an employee's exposure to an employer's customers." *Copeland*, 198 S.W.3d at 611; *see also Easy Returns Midwest Inc. v. Schultz*, 964 S.W.2d 450, 453 (Mo. App. E.D. 1998). Based on our review of the record, we conclude that there exist genuine issues of material fact as to the quality, frequency, and duration of Employee's customer contacts. *See, e.g., Easy Returns*, 964 S.W.2d at 454. As a result, this court cannot hold, as a matter of law, that Employer did not have a protectable interest in its customer contacts. *See id.*

[3]The Court of Appeals later explained: "The essence of the [*Sturgis*] holding is that the evidence did not support a finding of knowledge of trade secrets or of customer contact sufficient to support a restrictive covenant, and so did not justify any kind of restriction." *Alltype Fire Prot. Co. v. Mayfield*, 88 S.W.3d 120, 123-24 (Mo. App. E.D. 2002); *see also Mayer Hoffman*, 614 F.3d at 905, n. 21.

7 S.W.3d 542, 546 (Mo. App. E.D. 1999); *see also Supermarket Merch. & Supply, Inc. v. Marschuetz,* 196 S.W.3d 581, 585 (Mo. App. E.D. 2006). This is because "[a] party to a contract cannot seek to enforce its benefits where he is the first to violate its terms." *Ozark Appraisal Serv., Inc. v. Neale,* 67 S.W.3d 759, 764 (Mo. App. S.D. 2002). An employer's unilateral change to an employment agreement may constitute a material breach of the agreement if it substantially alters the manner and/or amount that the employer pays the employee. *See, e.g., Marschuetz,* 196 S.W.3d at 585; *Luketich v. Goedecke, Wood & Co., Inc.,* 835 S.W.2d 504, 507 (Mo. App. E.D. 1992); *Smith-Scharff Paper Co., Inc. v. Blum,* 813 S.W.2d 27, 29 (Mo. App. E.D. 1991); *Forms Mfg., Inc. v. Edwards,* 705 S.W.2d 67, 69 (Mo. App. E.D. 1985).

"The question of whether an employer committed a material breach is largely a factual question reserved for the trier of fact. . . ." *Marschuetz,* 196 S.W.3d at 585; *see also Adrian N. Baker & Co. v. DeMartino,* 733 S.W.2d 14, 17 (Mo. App. E.D. 1987). In *Marschuetz,* the employee had been working as a salesman for the employer for seven years when he signed a

[407 S.W.3d 58]

non-compete agreement as a condition of continued employment. *Marschuetz,* 196 S.W.3d at 583. The employer later instituted three policy changes affecting the employee's compensation,[4] and the employee resigned his employment and began working for a competitor. *Id.* at 583-84. After hearing evidence, the trial court found that the employer's unilateral changes to the employee's compensation structure did not constitute material breaches of the employment agreement and granted the employer a permanent injunction against the employee. *Id.* at 584. On appeal, the court reversed, holding that the employer materially breached the employment agreement and

was therefore barred from enforcing the terms of the non-competition clause against the employee. *Id.* at 585, 587; *cf. Ballesteros v. Johnson,* 812 S.W.2d 217, 222 (Mo. App. E.D. 1991) (affirming trial court's judgment granting injunctive relief to the employer because there was substantial evidence to support the trial court's finding that the employer did not materially breach the employment agreement).

As in *Marschuetz,* a factual question exists as to whether Employer materially breached the Agreement prior to Employee's termination.[5] In his motion for summary judgment, Employee alleged that Employer "made unilateral changes to [Employee's] employment agreement that were material in nature and [Employer] must be barred from enforcing the non-compete agreement." In support of this claim, Employee stated that Employer: "informed [Employee] that his compensation was going to be changed from $70,000 straight salary to $57,000 salary plus commission of 1 1/2%"; "never paid [Employee] the car allowance of $500 per month"; "failed to pay [Employee's] commissions on a timely basis"; later "reduced [Employee's] commission from 1.5% to 1.25%" and "reduce[d] [Employee's] compensation from an annual salary of $57,000 plus commission to an annual salary of $50,000"; and "initiate[d] a policy that would require [Employee] to pay one-third of any unpaid invoice on a custom order or possibly any order."

In response, Employer challenged the materiality of the alleged breaches and denied that it unilaterally reduced Employee's salary to $57,000, alleging that Employee had proposed the change in salary and compensation structure in an email to Employer's president. Employer also alleged in its memorandum opposing Employee's motion for summary judgment that the various changes in the amount and structure of Employee's compensation did not constitute material breaches of the Agreement because "the commission component" of Employee's salary "could cause his earnings to eclipse the $70,000 level."

---

[4]Specifically, the employer instituted a: "charge back policy" that withheld a portion of a salesperson's commissions until the customer's invoice was paid; "paid on paid invoices" policy providing for payment of a salesperson's commissions only when a customer's invoice was paid in full; and policy whereby any salesperson who left the company would only be paid commissions on customer invoices paid as of the employee's last day of employment. *Marschuetz,* 196 S.W.3d at 583-84.

[5]In *Marschuetz,* the trial court, sitting in equity and hearing the employer's action for an injunction, properly considered the question of a material breach because it was the trier of fact. *Id.* at 585. In the instant case, the trial court made this factual finding in a summary judgment proceeding. As previously stated, the existence of a genuine issue of material fact precludes the entry of summary judgment. *See Whelan,* 379 S.W.3d at 847.

[407 S.W.3d 59]

Based on our review of the pleadings, we conclude that genuine issues of fact relating to whether Employer materially breached the Agreement remain to be resolved. We therefore hold that entry of summary judgment on this ground was improper. *See, e.g., Whelan,* 379 S.W.3d at 846. Point granted.[6]

CONCLUSION

The judgment of the trial court is reversed and remanded.

LAWRENCE E. MOONEY, P.J., and KURT S. ODENWALD, J., concur.

■ Case 2

800 A.2d 271
352 N.J. Super. 476
Richard and Janet OSCAR, Plaintiff-Respondents,
v.
Chris SIMEONIDIS t/a Midtown Diner, Defendant-Appellant.
Superior Court of New Jersey, Appellate Division.
Argued Telephonically February 25, 2002.
Decided July 2, 2002.

[800 A.2d 272]

Laurence H. Olive, Montclair, argued the cause for appellant.

[800 A.2d 273]

Steven D. Plokfer, argued the cause for respondents. Before Judges PRESSLER, CIANCIA and COLEMAN. The opinion of the court was delivered by COLEMAN, J.S.C. (temporarily assigned).

The dispute in this matter arises out of a lease agreement between defendant Chris Simeonidis, the tenant, and plaintiffs Richard and Janet Oscar (hereinafter referred to as Oscar), the landlord. The trial court held a purported amendment to the lease agreement unenforceable for lack of consideration and there after determined fair market rental value as the basis for renewal of the lease under an option exercisable by the tenant. The tenant appeals. Because we disagree with the trial court's holding that the amendment was unenforceable, we reverse the order of the trial court and remand the matter for a determination of the rental pursuant to the formula contemplated by the amendment. We affirm that portion of the trial court's order that determined

---

[6]Employer argues that the trial court should not have considered whether Employer materially breached the employment agreement prior to Employee's termination because the Agreement provided that "[a]ny changes in Employee's compensation, position, or job duties subsequent to the execution of this Agreement shall in no way void or otherwise affect the remaining provisions of this Agreement." In other words, Employer maintains that its unilateral changes to the terms of Employee's employment could not, as a matter of law, constitute material breaches and therefore relieve Employee of his obligations under the non-competition clause because the Agreement provided that Employer is permitted to change Employee's "compensation, position, or job duties" without consequence. Employee counters that the trial court correctly granted him summary judgment because the Agreement "is unilateral benefiting only [Employer] and is not enforceable."

Missouri law provides that, where an agreement contains language "permitting one party to unilaterally modify the agreement such that the party could relieve itself of its promises, there is no meaningful mutuality at all, and the contract is illusory and unenforceable." *Frye v. Speedway Chevrolet Cadillac,* 321 S.W.3d 429, 442 (Mo. App. W.D. 2010), citing *Am. Laminates, Inc. v. J.S. Latta Co.,* 980 S.W.2d 12, 23 (Mo. App. W.D. 1998). "Where the apparent assurance of performance is illusory, it is not consideration for a return promise." *Restatement (Second) of Contracts* § 77 cmt. a (1981). Employer cannot take a position that renders the Agreement illusory while simultaneously seeking to enforce the Agreement's non-competition clause. Given our decision to remand, we decline to further address this matter given its limited development in the record before us.

the tenant shall be responsible for payment of real estate taxes in addition to the rental payable upon renewal.

The parties' relationship began in early 1991 when defendant Simeonidis purchased from Nick Barrise a restaurant business located in a two-story building owned by plaintiff in Montclair. As part of that purchase transaction defendant took over the lease agreement Barrise had with plaintiff. The lease agreement was for a ten-year term, beginning January 1, 1990 and ending December 31, 1999. The agreement specified "first year rent $2,500 per month to be increased annually at the rate of C.P.I. (consumer price index) with a minimum annual increase of 5%." Paragraph 32 of the lease agreement also provides: "Tenant to pay real estate taxes and any increases therein on a monthly basis, payable to the landlord, and included with the rental payment." Additionally, Paragraph 31 of the lease agreement contains a renewal option which states:

> At the termination of the within lease, the tenant is given the first option to enter into a new rental agreement with the landlord. This option will be for two consecutive five year terms with an increase based on fair market rent.

Although the lease agreement recites in Paragraph 29 that it is the full agreement of the parties that "may not be changed except in writing signed by the landlord and the tenant," from the outset the parties deviated from the terms of the agreement.[1] Simeonidis purchased the business from Barrise and assumed the lease in the second year of the term. Oscar charged Simeonidis $2500 inclusive of real estate taxes. According to Oscar, he did this to help Simeonidis develop his business. He also claims he did it as a favor to his friend Barrise. Simeonidis contends Oscar did not increase the rent or make him pay taxes as specified in the lease because the commercial rental market in Montclair was severely depressed. In any event, over the years the rent paid by Simeonidis and accepted by Oscar was below that set forth in the lease agreement. During the final two years of the lease

[800 A.2d 274]

agreement, Oscar increased the rent to $3,150 a month, inclusive of taxes. Simeonidis paid that amount without challenge.

As the ten-year term was about to expire, Oscar sent a renewal letter to Simeonidis offering to continue the lease at a new rent of $5,000, inclusive of real estate taxes. When Simeonidis did not respond to that letter, Oscar sent a time-of-the-essence letter, requesting that Simeonidis either consent to the renewal of the lease at the new rate or surrender the premises. Simeonidis still did not respond. Oscar then filed a complaint seeking possession of the premises and the matter proceeded to trial before the court in a summary action.

The proofs at trial consisted of testimony on the issue of the fair market rental value of the premises. Plaintiff presented an expert, Richard Polton, who gave a detailed market analysis, including historical trends and a comparison of similar rental properties in the area. Polton concluded that the fair market value of the premises was $22 a square foot, or a monthly rent of $5500 given the size of the premises (3000 square feet).[2] He further testified that this amount did not include real estate taxes, which were separately payable by the tenant.

Simeonidis challenged Polton's valuation of the property. He testified that he was responsible for heat, hot water and electricity and that these expenses, averaging around $2000 a month, were beyond what normally would be charged a tenant. Simeonidis further testified he was responsible for all interior repairs to the property and that he had made substantial improvements to the premises. He did not present any expert testimony on fair market value.

At the close of the proofs, it was contemplated that the parties would submit written summations; however prior to the date for such submissions, defendant Simeonidis filed a motion for leave to present

---

[1] For example, Paragraph 3 of the lease agreement provides that the tenant may not without the landlord's written consent assign the lease, sublet all or part of the rental space or permit any other person or business to use the rental space. The record does not reflect either a formal agreement or written consent from the landlord. Simeonidis' name was simply added to the lease agreement when he purchased the restaurant business from Barrise.

[2] The expert had also examined the second floor of the building, which defendant had used as an apartment, and concluded that the second floor at 1200 square feet was worth $10 a square foot. Since defendant no longer occupies or utilizes this space, it is not the subject of this appeal.

additional testimony based upon newly discovered evidence. He had learned of the existence of a document purporting to be an amendment to the lease agreement. The document had been discovered in the files of a third party, J. Roc Associates, which held a note from defendant Simeonidis in connection with his purchase of the restaurant. Pursuant to Paragraph 33 of the lease agreement, "if tenant defaults . . . Jay Roc Associates has the right to assume all rights and obligations of said lease." The trial court granted defendant's motion to reopen the proofs to permit evidence concerning the purported amendment.

When the proceedings resumed, John Meely, a partner at J. Rock, testified that he had found the document in his file relating to outstanding notes with defendant. Meely testified that his partner, Rocco Caruso, who had passed away several months prior to the trial, had handled the file and that he believed their attorney also had a copy of the document. The document is in letter format, dated March 28, 1991. It contains the signatures of Nick Barrise and Richard Oscar. It reads:

The following is an amendment to the above-mentioned lease [lease dated January 3, 1990 between Richard and Janet Oscar and Nick Barrise on the property located at 12 Church Street, Montclair, N.J. 07042]:

[800 A.2d 275]

> As of this date, the clause in paragraph 31, pertaining to an extension of this lease, which reads "Increases based upon fair market rent" will be changed to read "Increases based upon terms of the original lease."

The amendment thus directed how the rental would be determined almost nine years later in the event the tenant were to exercise the option to renew. The parties intended to revert to a simple mathematical calculation utilizing the formula specified for the rental during the original ten-year term instead of then seeking to ascertain the fair market value.

The recollections of both Barrise and Oscar were sketchy on the subject of the amendment but neither seriously disputed the authenticity of the document. Simeonidis had been unaware of the document. Barrise testified that Oscar prepared the document, brought it to him and they both signed it. Barrise believed that the amendment was related to his selling the business

to defendant Simeonidis but he was not certain who had actually requested the amendment. He responded to the following questions posed by the judge:

Q Did that [letter of March 28] change a lease provision that was then in existence? Do you understand the question?

A That's right.

Q Was—was there any benefit to the landlord, Mr. Oscar, from making that change?

A Is there any benefit to Mr. Oscar? I don't think that was the—the—the reason. The reason was to get a fairer—fairer lease for the new tenant coming in.

Q Was he simply doing it as a favor to you so you could sell the business?

A I think so, yes.

Oscar testified that he did not recall signing the document, but he did not deny that he had signed it. He just could not remember doing so. When asked whether he had received anything of value for the modification, he responded, well, "no, and that doesn't appear to be the intent of it. . . ." He did not elaborate on what was the parties' intent but did testify that Barrise often paid the rent late. Consequently, he acknowledged that it would have been in his [Oscar's] interest to have a new tenant who would be more likely to pay the rent promptly.

In a written opinion the court concluded, sua sponte, that the amendment purporting to change the rent during the period of any extension from an amount based on fair market rent to an amount based on the terms of the original lease was unenforceable because "[d]efendant presented no evidence that would constitute legal consideration." The court reasoned:

> At best, vis a vis defendant, plaintiff testified that perhaps through this change and the sale of the restaurant to defendant, that he might thereafter have a tenant who paid rent regularly. That is not legal consideration; it was what the parties had already committed themselves to do, and the enforcement of an existing obligation does not constitute legally binding consideration.

The court determined that the fair market value of the premises was $5,500 per month, accepting the opinion of plaintiff's expert witnesses with the exception of the value ascribed to an unused mezzanine. It directed the parties to ascertain the amount due and ordered that if defendant refused to pay that amount, judgment for possession would be entered; otherwise, the complaint would be dismissed.

Subsequently, defendant sought clarification as to whether the rent determined by the court was inclusive or exclusive of

[800 A.2d 276]

real estate taxes. The court reiterated that the rent was to be $5,500 per month and clarified that, pursuant to paragraph 32, the taxes were to be included with the rental payment, but are not part of the rental payment. An order dated March 28, 2001 was entered to memorialize these rulings. Defendant appeals that order both as to the rental amount and as to the payment of real estate taxes.

As a basic premise, it is true that "no contract is enforceable . . . without the flow of consideration—both sides must 'get something' out of the exchange." *Continental Bank of Pennsylvania v. Barclay Riding Academy, Inc.,* 93 N.J. 153, 170, 459 A.2d 1163, *cert. denied,* 464 U.S. 994, 104 S. Ct. 488, 78 L. Ed. 2d 684 (1983) (quoting *Friedman v. Tappan Development Corp.,* 22 N.J. 523, 533, 126 A.2d 646 (1956)). That premise applies equally to agreements to modify existing contracts as to new contracts.[3] *County of Morris v. Fauver,* 153 N.J. 80, 100, 707 A.2d 958 (1998). *See also Ross v. Orr,* 3 N.J. 277, 282, 69 A.2d 730 (1949); *Levine v. Blumenthal,* 117 N.J.L. 23, 26, 186 A. 457 (Sup. Ct. 1936), *aff'd,* 117 N.J.L. 426, 189 A. 54 (E. & A. 1937).

By the same token, "[w]hatever consideration a promisor assents to as the price of his promise is legally sufficient consideration." *Coast National Bank v. Bloom,* 113 N.J.L. 597, 602, 174 A. 576 (E. & A. 1934). "Mutual promises are sufficient consideration one for the other. They are reciprocal considerations for each other." *Id.* at 604, 174 A. 576. It has

been long accepted that the value given or received as consideration need not be monetary or substantial:

> Consideration is, in effect, the price bargained for and paid for a promise. A very slight advantage to one party, or a trifling inconvenience to the other, is a sufficient consideration to support a contract when made by a person of good capacity, who is not at the time under the influence of any fraud, imposition or mistake. Whatever consideration a promisor assents to as the price of his promise is legally sufficient consideration. *Coast National Bank v. Bloom* 113 N.J.L. 597, 174 A. 576, 95 A.L.R. 528.
>
> [*Joseph Lande & Son, Inc. v. Wellsco Realty, Inc.,* 131 N.J.L. 191, 198, 34 A.2d 418 (E. & A. 1943).]

Any consideration for a modification, however insignificant, satisfies the requirement of new and independent consideration. For example, payment of an existing rent obligation one day in advance of the due date would suffice, slight as that consideration would be. *Haynes Auto Repair Co. v. Wheels,* 115 N.J.L. 447, 448, 180 A. 836 (E. & A. 1935). "If the consideration requirement is met, there is no additional requirement of gain or benefit to the promisor, loss or detriment to the promisee, equivalence in the values exchanged, or mutuality of obligation." *Shebar v. Sanyo Business Systems Corp.,* 111 N.J. 276, 289, 544 A.2d 377 (1988) (citing *Restatement (Second) of Contracts* § 79 (1979)).

Oscar and Barrise entered into the amendment, an agreement to modify the basis for determining rent in any renewal of the lease agreement. The trial court concluded that because Barrise testified he believed Oscar had signed the

[800 A.2d 277]

amendment "as a favor" to help Barrise sell the business and because it was what the parties had already committed themselves to do, this amendment lacked consideration. Such a view is too narrow and overly exacting. Moreover, the opinion of one or both of the parties as to whether anything of value had been given or received for the modification may be informative but it is not dispositive. The determination of whether value has been given or received must ultimately be gauged by an objective examination of all of the relevant circumstances.

---

[3] In sales transactions this premise has been abrogated. Under the Uniform Commercial Code, as enacted in New Jersey, there is no requirement of new and additional consideration to support the modification of an agreement. The applicable provision, *N.J.S.A.* 12A:2-209(1) explicitly states "An agreement modifying a contract within this chapter needs no consideration to be binding."

In their original lease agreement, the parties had expressly preserved their right to modify the lease agreement so long as the terms of the modification were (1) in writing and (2) signed by the landlord and the tenant. The amendment complied with those requirements of form. *County of Morris v. Fauver, supra,* 153 N.J. at 99, 707 A.2d 958 ("Parties to an existing agreement may, by mutual assent, modify it" and "such modification can be proved by an explicit agreement to modify it or . . . by the actions and conduct of the parties, so long as the intention to modify is mutual and clear").[4]

Here, the parties adopted a formula that would permit them and any other interested person to determine the rental upon renewal of the lease by reference to objective, readily ascertainable criteria. This is itself valuable consideration sufficient to sustain the modification because the mutual agreement to abide by such a formula has the capacity to remove an element of uncertainty from the parties' future legal relationship. "It is a principle, almost universally accepted, that an act or forbearance required by a legal duty owing to the promisor that is neither doubtful nor the subject of honest and reasonable dispute is not a sufficient consideration." *Levine v. Blumenthal, supra,* 117 N.J.L. at 27, 186 A. 457 (citing *Williston on Contracts* (Rev. Ed.) §§ 103 b, 120, 130; *American Law Institute, Contracts* § 76; *Anson on Contracts (Turck Ed.)* Pp. 229, 234 et seq.). The corollary of that principle is that where a right or legal duty owing to the promisor is doubtful or the subject of honest and reasonable dispute, the clarification of such right or duty will constitute good and valuable consideration.

The amendment was executed some nine years before the option to renew was to be exercised. Although Oscar testified he signed the amendment as a favor to Barrise, neither party could have known who would actually benefit from the modification. If, as Simeonidis contended, the commercial real estate market was severely depressed at the time of the execution of the amendment or if, as was clearly possible, the market thereafter were to decline and remain in a state of decline, Oscar might have received the greater benefit of the bargain. The modification was not, as the trial court perceived, simply a free promise by Oscar to forego some benefit he was entitled to receive under the agreement. There was no fixed sum to which he was entitled. The parties, by virtue of their amendment adopting an already familiar formula, provided definition and predictability to an aspect of their future legal relationship that was otherwise ambiguous and undetermined.

[800 A.2d 278]

"Fair market rental" is not a self defining term. Obviously, we have recognized that the fair market rental value of a property can be determined even if the lease fails to articulate any guidelines or standards, but such a determination can be problematic. *See, e.g., P.J.'s Pantry v. Puschak,* 188 N.J. Super. 580, 584-85, 458 A.2d 123 (App. Div. 1983). Fair market value has been defined as the price which a willing buyer would offer and a willing seller would accept. *City of Trenton v. Lenzner,* 16 N.J. 465, 476, 109 A.2d 409 (1954), *cert. denied,* 348 U.S. 972, 75 S. Ct. 534, 99 L. Ed. 757 (1955). Thus, all of the considerations that would influence a willing buyer and willing seller in making their decisions are relevant to a determination of fair market value. *Village of South Orange v. Alden Corp.,* 71 N.J. 362, 368, 365 A.2d 469 (1976).

When an option becomes exercisable, it is not unusual that the parties are not able to agree on a fair market rental or value. As a consequence they must resort to consultants, appraisers or other experts. If a consensus still cannot be achieved, the parties find themselves subject to the substantial expense, strain and attendant delay of litigation. So viewed, the benefit of a rational and acceptable formula to define the rights and duties of the parties is tangible indeed. There is a mutual benefit, including an economic benefit, to the parties where they can bring a measure of order to their affairs by removing or reducing future uncertainty or doubt from their dealings.

Undoubtedly, one of the primary objectives for the amendment in the case now before us was either

---

[4]The Court in *County of Morris v. Fauver, supra,* 153 N.J. at 100, 707 A.2d 958 observed that the County and the Department of Corrections never clearly expressed a mutual intention to modify their contract, nor did they demonstrate knowledge and acceptance of the other party's expressed intentions. By contrast, the intention of Barrise and Oscar to modify the basis for rentals in any extension is mutual and clearly expressed. It is expressed in a writing signed by both.

to assist Barrise in the sale of his business or to assist Simeonidis in his effort to obtain financing. That does not negate the benefit to both landlord and tenant derived from the clarification of the rental value of the lease during any renewal. The added benefit to the landlord of avoiding a vacancy as a consequence of the impending failure of the business of the outgoing tenant was also a sufficient consideration to support the modification of the agreement upon mutual assent. There is no claim or suggestion that Barrise misrepresented his circumstances or contrived to deceive Oscar to induce the amendment of their agreement. They both "got something out of the exchange." In short, we find on the existing record that there was consideration for the amendment to the lease agreement and that the amendment is enforceable.

On the other hand, we reject the tenant's contention that the rental amount for the renewal term should be limited to a five percent increase over the rent actually charged at the expiration of the original lease term, rather than the amount derived by calculating the specified rental increases over the life of the lease. The concessions made by the landlord in accepting a rent different from that called for in the lease agreement constituted a waiver as to those payments for which the lower rent was accepted when due, but such prior concessions do not constitute a waiver of terms yet to be fulfilled. *See, e.g., Carteret Properties v. Variety Donuts, Inc.,* 49 N.J. 116, 129, 228 A.2d 674 (1967); *Van Allen v. Board of Commissioners of Twp. of Bass River,* 211 N. J. Super. 407, 410, 511 A.2d 1243 (App. Div. 1986). Based on the plain language of the amendment, as well as the attendant circumstances, the rental for the renewal term was to be calculated by applying the formula set forth in the original lease, namely, by adding yearly increases over the initial base rent of $2,500 at the rate of CPI or at the minimum rate of five percent per year. It remains for the parties and the court below to determine whether

[800 A.2d 279]

the C.P.I. exceeded five percent in any year during the term of the lease. If not, the renewal rate will be fixed by adding to the base rent five percent per year over the ten year term.

The argument that the trial court had no jurisdiction over the issue of real estate taxes is plainly without merit. Even though no specific prayer for relief on the tax issue was stated in plaintiff's complaint, it was clearly raised by plaintiff when he opposed defendant's request for a stay of the court's ruling. The parties were afforded an opportunity to present proof as to whether or not real estate taxes were already incorporated into the rent level to be applied to the renewal period. *Rule* 4:9-2 provides in pertinent part:

> When issues not raised by the pleadings and pretrial order are tried by consent or without the objection of the parties, they shall be treated in all respects as if they had been raised in the pleadings and pretrial order.

Defendant did not object to the trial court receiving proofs on the issue of fair market rental value of the property and the consideration of fair market value by the court appropriately encompassed the issue of whether rent would be inclusive or exclusive of real estate taxes. Plaintiff's expert testified at trial that the rental amount he determined to be fair market rent was exclusive of taxes. More fundamentally, the lease agreement contains a separate provision relating to the real estate taxes. That provision controls. We are satisfied that on this issue the court's ruling was proper and correct.

The order of the trial court is reversed in part and affirmed in part. The matter is remanded for a determination as to the effect of the C.P.I. on the calculation of the rental amount based upon the formula incorporated by the amendment to the lease agreement.

Chapter 3

Acceptance

Chapter Objectives

The student will be able to:

- Use vocabulary regarding acceptance properly.
- Discuss the "mirror image rule."
- Identify where silence may be acceptance.
- Evaluate the applicability of the "mailbox rule" and how it affects acceptance and/or rejection of an offer.
- Determine if there has been a "substantial beginning" toward partial performance of a unilateral contract, thereby binding the offeror.

This chapter will explore HOW contracts are accepted, WHEN *bilateral* contracts are accepted, and WHEN *unilateral* contracts are accepted. An offeree's acceptance must be a *mirror image* of the offer, including the means of delivering that acceptance to the offeror. Communications that deviate from the offer are not generally considered acceptances. As bilateral contracts can be accepted by making a promise, that promise—once sent, in compliance with the *mailbox rule*, to the offeror—binds the parties to their performance obligations of the agreement. However, as unilateral contracts are accepted by actual performance, the parties are not bound to their obligations until complete or *substantial* performance has been rendered.

Now that the offer has been laid bare—all the requisite terms are known and there is good and valuable consideration under the laws—the offeree may accept with merely a "yes." Indeed, he may only answer with only a "yes"; there cannot be any additional terms in the assent. If the offeree adds or modifies the terms of the offer, then it is considered a counteroffer and we need to start from Chapter 1 again.

MIRROR IMAGE RULE

mirror image rule
A requirement that the acceptance of an offer must exactly match the terms of the original offer.

This mandate that the offeree accept with only a "yes" has its basis in the **mirror image rule**. This means that the offeree's acceptance must mirror the offer exactly, without deviation or modification. This is not to say, however, that the exact words must be used in accepting, but rather that the offeror and the offeree acknowledge that they are agreeing to the same terms in the offer.

While the offeror is the *master* of the offer as he sets all the terms, the offeree is the *maker* of the contract because the contract is not formed until it is accepted. He is the "closer" of the deal. How he closes the deal also is subject to the mirror image rule in that if the offer requests a promise (a bilateral contract), the offeree must accept by making the appropriate promise. If the offeror requests a performance (a unilateral contract), the offeree must accept by performing the requested act.

For example, Cindy is struggling with her class on evidence (and what student of the law isn't?). Desiring to enter into a unilateral contract, she asks Jeff, who received an A+ in the class, to tutor her in the subject. If Cindy says she will pay Jeff $25.00 an hour for the time he helps her, she is looking for Jeff to actually perform. Jeff, by showing up in the tutoring center and teaching Cindy, makes the agreement binding at that point. If Cindy agrees to pay Jeff $250.00 a month for the semester if he promises to tutor her for 10 hours a month, she is looking for his promise of instruction. Jeff seals the deal at the moment he makes the promise. Jeff controls when the contract is formed by performing on the unilateral contract or promising to teach Cindy on the bilateral contract.

Minor variations to the offer that do not change the obligations of the parties do not inhibit the formation of the contract. They are not considered to be substantive modifications amounting to a counteroffer, but merely adaptations to circumstances in the original offer. Essentially, these "adaptations" do mirror the offer in its essential elements and therefore will be considered acceptance. However, if the proposed change in the offer alters a material term or has an impact on the performance obligations of the parties, the proposal is then considered a counteroffer. In government contracting the measurement of the proposed modification is called the "cardinal change" doctrine. It can, by analogy, be applied to any contract when a determination needs to be made whether a modification would amount to a counteroffer or not. Note that each contract and the surrounding circumstances will need to be individually analyzed. There is no hard and fast rule that signifies when a change is significant enough to be considered a counteroffer.

A cardinal change "occurs when the government effects an alteration in the work so drastic that it effectively requires the contractor to perform duties materially different from those originally bargained for." Another influential definition of the cardinal change doctrine states that: The basic standard, as the court has put it, is whether the modified job was essentially the same work as the parties bargained for when the contract was awarded. Plaintiff has no right to complain if the project it ultimately constructed was essentially the same as the one it contracted to construct. Conversely, there is a cardinal change if the ordered deviations altered the nature of the thing to be constructed. Our opinions have cautioned that the problem is a matter of degree varying from one contract to another and can be resolved only by considering the totality of the change and this requires recourse to its magnitude as well as its quality. There is no exact formula . . . . Each case must be analyzed on its own facts and in light of its own circumstances, giving just consideration to the magnitude and quality of the changes ordered and their cumulative effect upon the project as a whole. In emphasizing that there is no mechanical or arithmetical answer, we have repeated that (t)he number of changes is not, in and of itself, the test[.]

Golden Mfg. Co. v. United States, No. 12-317 C (Fed. Cl. 2012), 17-18 (internal citations omitted); *see also Gresser v. Hotzler*, 604 N.W.2d 379, 384 (Minn. App. 2000) (The offeree/prospective purchaser of real estate proposed a change in the closing date of the sales contract. The court found that the "changes directly affect[ed] [purchaser's] performance obligations under the contract, postponing his duty to perform by almost six weeks. The law of contracts is not advanced by allowing a contracting party to manipulate the finality of an obligation by rejecting an insubstantial change, but few terms are more important to sellers of real estate than the date on which they will receive the purchase money.").

In order to make the appropriate promise or perform the requested act, the offeree must have **knowledge of the offer**. This seems like a ridiculous concept to have to explain, but, of course, contract law finds a way to add a complication to what seems like common sense. Suppose the Smiths' dog, Buddy, runs away and the family posts reward notices in your neighborhood. Rudy Restaurateur notices Buddy outside his café begging for scraps and checks his tags. Rudy, a dog lover, returns Buddy to the Smiths, never having seen the reward posters. The Smiths are under no obligation to give Rudy the reward because his performance was not in response to the unilateral offer of the reward poster. Rudy had no knowledge of the offer and therefore his actions do not constitute acceptance of the offer.

knowledge of the offer
An offeree must be aware of the terms of the offer in order to accept it.

This concept is combined with the preexisting duty rule in the case of *Slattery v. Wells Fargo Armored Service Corp.*, 366 So. 2d 157 (Fla. Dist. App. 1979), wherein a polygraph operator contended he was entitled to the $25,000 reward offered by Wells Fargo for information leading to the arrest and conviction of the perpetrator of the murder of a Wells Fargo guard. The operator had no knowledge of the offer until the second day of his investigation of the perpetrator. Further, he was under a preexisting duty to interrogate the suspect and report criminal activity. Therefore, there was neither consideration nor knowledge to support the operator's claim for breach of the unilateral reward contract.

Affirmative acceptance, where the offeree did or said exactly what the offeror requested in the terms of the offer, is in direct response to a valid offer.

silence
In certain circumstances, no response may be necessary to properly accept an offer.

mutuality of assent
Both parties must objectively manifest their intention to enter into a binding contract by accepting all of the terms.

No modifications were made that would change the obligations of either party to the transaction. What if the offeree remains **silent**? We know that an offer does not stay open indefinitely; a lapse of time will terminate the offer. During the time in which the offer remains open, and the offeree remains silent, there can be no contract formed because there can be no meeting of the minds. Contract law requires **mutuality of assent**, without knowing what the offeree is thinking; will she accept or reject, or has she not yet made up her mind? This is the indefiniteness that contract law abhors and, therefore, silence is not considered acceptance. When the offeree remains silent, it is generally regarded as a rejection. The offeree has the right to speak up and accept or reject, but there is no obligation to speak if there is a rejection.

EYE ON ETHICS

Business transactions with clients are generally prohibited as a conflict of interest. There are guidelines that, if followed, will ethically permit a lawyer to enter into a business transaction with a client. As lawyers generally have the "upper hand" in dealing with the client, any business must be made on terms that are fair and reasonable, in writing, and with informed consent of the client. In practical terms this means that the client must be able to understand the terms, go have another disinterested lawyer review the agreement, and consent to all the above in writing. The attorney-client relationship must also be spelled out in detail with regard to this particular transaction.

These requirements are distinctly different from the general rules of contract law that allow parties to freely contract for whatever they wish. The ethics rules require that the disclosure to the client include

(1) the risks inherent in representation by a lawyer with a financial, business, property, or personal interest in the company, including the possible effects upon the lawyer's actions and recommendations to the client;
(2) the possible conflicts that might arise between lawyer/shareholder and client or its management and the range of possible consequences stemming from them; and
(3) any potential impact on the attorney/client privilege and confidentiality rules, particularly in communications between the client and the attorney in his role as investor rather than as counsel.

N.Y. City Bar Ass'n Ethics Op. 2000-3. Reprinted with permission from The Record of the Association of the Bar of the City of New York. © 2000 SS The Record 629.

These precautions attempt to ensure that the client can understand the offer and its ramifications prior to acceptance and that the attorney's actions are well within the ethical standards.

There are, of course, exceptions to this generalization. The Uniform Commercial Code (UCC) permits silence as acceptance between merchants where this is their normal course of dealing. For example, Fred Farmer receives an order for 25 bushels of apples from Greg Grocer. Their normal business dealings in the past leads Greg to believe that Fred will ship the apples per Greg's request even if Fred does not say anything in acceptance of the order.

The other two exceptions are relatively commonsensical. First, if the offeree has **accepted the services or goods** of the offeror without saying that she has accepted them, the law infers that the silence (nonrefusal) was indeed acceptance and the offeree will be obligated to pay for the goods or services received as the offeror supplied them with the expectation of payment.

Second, a **solicited offer** also can be accepted by silence on the part of the offeree because the offeree has such an integral role in the shaping of the offer that the offeree's acceptance is essentially redundant. In a solicited offer, the offeree has initiated the contact and invited the offeror to make him/her/it an offer. The best way to explain this is by way of example. All of the catalogs that clog your mailbox (particularly during the holiday season) are solicited offers. The offer is not made by the advertisement. The advertisements are invitations for the customers to make an offer on the terms set forth in the catalog. In reality, the customer is the offeror and the catalog company is the offeree. It is the customer who has set the quantity and type of goods that will be involved in the transaction. The catalog's advertisements fail, as all advertisements do, because they are too vague to be an offer. Therefore, the company's silence upon receipt of your order (offer) is adequate. You expect that the company will send you what you ordered without calling you upon receipt of the order and accepting.

THE MAILBOX RULE

The **mailbox rule** answers the question: "When is the acceptance effective?" This rule has a notorious reputation; however, it can be broken down into a few smaller rules. Unlike an offer, which is valid and effective when it is communicated to the offeree, an acceptance can be valid and effective (and therefore binding on the parties) *before* it is communicated to the offeror.

How can this happen? The rule states that acceptance is effective upon its **proper dispatch** to the offeror. Therefore, dropping a letter of acceptance into the mailbox (hence, the mailbox rule) is valid acceptance of a bilateral contract and, at that moment, the parties are bound as both have exchanged their promises. The real issue with this element of the mailbox rule is what constitutes "proper dispatch" of the acceptance. Courts have discussed and analyzed this element *ad nauseum* (a Latin term meaning that something has been discussed so much that everyone is sick of it to the point of nausea), and the general consensus is that a proper dispatch has the correct address and that the offeror has authorized this means of sending the acceptance. The sender must reasonably anticipate that it will reach the intended recipient. This also means that the offeror anticipates that the acceptance will be made in this manner. "It is clear

---

acceptance of services or goods
Where an offeree has taken possession of the goods or received the benefit of the conferred services, he has been deemed to have accepted the offer.

solicited offer
An invitation for members of a group to whom it is sent (potential offerors) to make an offer to the party sending the information (the potential offeree).

mailbox rule
A principle of contract law that sets the time of acceptance of an offer at the time it is posted and the time of rejection of an offer at the time it is received.

proper dispatch
An approved method of transmitting the acceptance to the offeror.

that in negotiations by mail one party must be in the dark about his contractual relations during the period for transmission of the letter. The 'mailbox rule' imposes this uncertainty on the offeror. This risk allocation is eminently reasonable when it is recognized that the offeror can shift this risk by requiring receipt of acceptance when he makes the offer. The reasonableness of this allocation is mirrored in the widespread commercial acceptability of the rule." *Worms v. Burgess*, 620 P.2d 455, 457 (Okla. App. Div. 1 1980).

The acceptance must be sent to the offeror in the way that the offer has specified, if it has specified any means. Remember, the acceptance must comply with the terms of the offer; a prescribed method of accepting the offer is a material term and will affect the validity of the acceptance. If no means of acceptance are prescribed in the offer, the courts have determined that any reasonable method of dispatching the acceptance will create the contract. *See Osprey LLC v. Kelly-Moore Paint Co., Inc.*, 984 P.2d 194, 200 (Okla. 1999) ("Use of an alternative method of notification of the exercise of a lease option does not render the notice defective if the substituted notice performed the same function or served the same purpose as the authorized method. Here, the lease provision concerned uses the permissive 'may' rather than the mandatory 'shall' and refers to personal delivery or registered or certified mail, but it does not require these methods of delivery, to the exclusion of other modes of transmission which serve the same purpose."). To that end, e-mail can be deemed as a method of delivery and receipt of notice via e-mail is presumed unless "(1) the failure of notice was due to circumstances beyond the party's or the party's representative's control and (2) the failure of notice was not due to the party's or the party's representative's fault or neglect." *Miller v. Plain Dealer Publ'g Co.*, 2015 Ohio 1016 (Ohio App. 2015) (Failure to provide an updated e-mail address in a timely manner is the fault of the receiving party as he was in a position to correct it. This was deemed failure by a party's fault or neglect. The notice e-mailed to the address on record was deemed adequate.).

Perhaps with special poetic justice, the United States Postal Service was able to avail itself of the mailbox rule in *United States v. Turley*, No. 16-7090 (10th Cir. 2017). This case involved a long-term lease with a purchase option for the property upon which the government had established a post office. Written notice of renewal of the lease was due 90 days before the new term began. Notice of the option to purchase was due a year before expiration of the lease term. There was some ongoing confusion about negotiating for another lease term and whether or not the lease had been properly renewed in 2008. The Court found the lease-renewal option was properly exercised when the notice was delivered to the proper address, even though Turley refused to retrieve it. Turley had accepted lease payments at that address prior and after this attempt at delivering the notice of renewal. Therefore, the deadline to exercise the purchase option was November 15, 2013. On November 7, 2013, the Postal Service sent a letter to that same address exercising its option to purchase the property. According to the mailbox rule, the Postal Service was bound to purchase the property once it had given notice that it was exercising its option (the *Turley* court citing *Worms, supra*).

For example, General Manufacturing Co. mailed a valid offer to purchase widgets from Gadget Co. on March 1st. On March 3rd, Gadget received the offer and agreed with the terms of the offer and mailed the signed contract back to General on March 4th. Assume also that Gadget sent the acceptance to the address specified with the proper postage. As of March 4th, a valid contract exists even though General has not yet received the contract via the mail. If General had e-mailed the offer to Gadget with the instructions that it must print the offer, sign it, and then return the hard copy to General via the mail, then Gadget would have to post its acceptance in this manner in order to validly accept the offer. If Gadget chose to e-mail its acceptance to General, it would not be a valid acceptance and no contract would be formed. General could choose to waive its "by mail" requirement, but it doesn't have to since it specified the means of acceptance in its offer.

If the acceptance is sent improperly but it is nevertheless received by the offeror, the acceptance is valid upon the receipt of the acceptance. The offeree has lost the benefit of the mailbox rule in that the offeree cannot bind the offeror at the time of transmittal, but the acceptance is still valid at a later time when the acceptance is received by the offeror. So, if General had not specified the means of sending the acceptance and Gadget mailed it to an incorrect address, a contract would only be formed if General actually received the signed agreement.

This, of course, assumes that the offer is still open. This brings us to a very interesting twist in the application of the mailbox rule. We know that an offer can be terminated by the offeror any time before acceptance, generally speaking. However, we also know that the post office, while a dependable carrier, is neither instantaneous nor perfect. So, during the time in which the acceptance is in the hands of the post office, an offeror may revoke the offer, but the offer has already been accepted, thereby making the offer irrevocable. On March 7th, three days after Gadget mailed its acceptance and thereby formed a binding contract, General, still without knowing it is in a binding contract formed on March 4th, sends an e-mail to Gadget revoking the offer. The revocation is ineffective. General may have thought that Gadget wasn't going to accept the offer and has since entered into other agreements, but none of that matters. General is bound to the terms of the original offer.

The attempted revocation is not valid as the offeror was bound to the contract without even knowing it! In an extreme circumstance where the post office loses the acceptance, the offeror is still bound to the contract even if she never receives it! But you protest: "The law of contracts likes certainty; how can this be?" This is one of the instances where the law of contracts acknowledges that life is full of uncertainty and we don't live in utopia (if we did, everyone would honor his promises and we would have no need for contract law to enforce them). The uncertainty must be shifted to one of the parties and contract law has chosen the offeror as the master of the offer to bear this burden.

Unlike acceptance, rejection of the offer is valid only *upon receipt* of the rejection by the offeree. Contract law likes to foster the creation of contracts;

therefore, it is better to assume that the contract is still open and wait until receipt of the rejection. So, if Gadget printed out the e-mail offer and mailed it with the word "rejected" (or some other unequivocal wording that indicated non-acceptance), the rejection is not valid until General receives it. This leaves the offer open during the period in which the rejection is in the mail.

A second twist in the mailbox rule arises when the offeree changes her mind. Keep the rules in mind: Acceptance is valid upon transmittal, and rejection is valid upon receipt. What happens when the offeree sends a letter of rejection, then, having a change of heart, sends an acceptance before the rejection is received? The acceptance is valid on transmittal; therefore, a contract has been formed, even though the offer was initially rejected, which as we know terminates the offer.

For clarity, let's use an example with dates. General sends an offer for an output contract to Gadget on June 1st. Gadget receives the offer, has some reservations regarding the terms, and sends a rejection letter to General on June 10th. This letter will take about two days to get to General. The next day, the 11th of June, Gadget has a change of heart; it realizes that it probably won't get a better offer, so it sends an acceptance letter to General. The contract is formed on the 11th of June, as acceptance is valid upon posting. On June 12th, General receives the rejection, but, unbeknownst to General, this rejection is not valid because the offer has been accepted by Gadget's June 11th letter.

A final twist occurs if General, relying on the acceptance, consummates a contract (made the offer and it was accepted) with another supplier of widgets on June 12th when General received what it thought was a valid rejection and was unaware of Gadget's acceptance. The courts will uphold the second contract with the other supplier of widgets because General acted in good faith.

SPOT THE ISSUE!

On May 1st, the town of Smallsville solicited bids for the construction of a new schoolhouse. The contractors all submitted their bids (offers) and Acme Construction Co. was determined to be the best bidder. On May 15th, Smallsville sent its acceptance of Acme's bid via certified mail to Acme's satellite office in Big City, even though the bid stated that notification should be sent to its office on Main Street in Smallsville. To add insult to injury, Smallsville did not have the correct postage.

On May 16th, Acme decided to withdraw its offer.

Despite these defects, Acme did in fact receive the acceptance of the bid on May 17th.

Determine whether there has been valid acceptance or an effective withdrawal of Acme's bid. [See *Town of North Branford v. AAIS*, 1995 Ct. Super. 1166 (Conn. Super. 1995).]

Like every other legal concept, there is an exception to the mailbox rule's precept that acceptance is valid upon proper dispatch. In an **option contract**, the acceptance must be received by the end of the designated time period. Recall from Chapter 1 that an option contract is an agreement that the offeror will keep the offer open for a certain period of time, after which the offer closes and can no longer be accepted. If the mailbox rule were to apply to option contracts, it would effectively lengthen the option period by at least that amount of time the postal system takes to deliver it. What if it were lost in the mail? The option would be exercised, but the offeror would never know it. This would completely frustrate the reason for entering into an option contract in the first place, to have a definite answer by a definite time.

option contract
A separate and legally enforceable agreement included in the contract stating that the offer cannot be revoked for a certain time period.

Example
On March 1st, Sam offers to sell Blackacre to Bob. As it is a valuable piece of land, Bob wants to make sure that Sam doesn't sell it to someone else while Bob gets his financing in order to see if he can afford it. Bob and Sam enter into an option contract, keeping the offer open exclusively to Bob until April 1st. Bob must send his acceptance to Sam in enough time to ensure that Sam receives it by April 1st. Sam is relying on the April 1st deadline to know that he either has sold the property to Bob or can put the land back on the market. Bob's posting of his acceptance on April 1st is not good enough. Sam must receive it by that date.

Why does the law do these things? It all rests on the concept of **reliance**. Good old contract law likes dependability: If a party in good faith (not trying to be sneaky and take advantage of the other party) takes action that is reasonable given her perception of the situation, the law will not punish that party for taking such reasonable steps. As long as the party reasonably relies on the facts known to him/her, the courts will preserve this dependence.

reliance
A party's dependence and actions based on the assertions of another party.

Of course, all of this can go out the window if the offeror simply states his own conditions in the offer that circumvent the operation of the mailbox rule. He is, after all, the master of the offer.

SURF'S UP

The section of the UETA relating to acceptance of contracts is the mailbox rule equivalent.

§ 15. Time and Place of Sending and Receipt

(a) Unless otherwise agreed between the sender and the recipient, an electronic record is sent when it:

    (1) is addressed properly or otherwise directed properly to an information processing system that the recipient has designated or uses for the purpose of receiving electronic records or information of the type sent and from which the recipient is able to retrieve the electronic record;

    (2) is in a form capable of being processed by that system; and

    (3) enters an information processing system outside the control of the sender or of a person that sent the electronic record on behalf of the sender or enters a region of the information processing system designated or used by the recipient which is under the control of the recipient.

(b) Unless otherwise agreed between a sender and the recipient, an electronic record is received when:

    (1) it enters an information processing system that the recipient has designated or uses for the purpose of receiving electronic records or information of the type sent and from which the recipient is able to retrieve the electronic record; and

    (2) it is in a form capable of being processed by that system.

(c) Subsection (b) applies even if the place the information processing system is located is different from the place the electronic record is deemed to be received under subsection (d).

(d) Unless otherwise expressly provided in the electronic record or agreed between the sender and the recipient, an electronic record is deemed to be sent from the sender's place of business and to be received at the recipient's place of business. For purposes of this subsection, the following rules apply:

    (1) If the sender or recipient has more than one place of business, the place of business of that person is the place having the closest relationship to the underlying transaction.

    (2) If the sender or the recipient does not have a place of business, the place of business is the sender's or recipient's residence, as the case may be.

(e) An electronic record is received under subsection (b) even if no individual is aware of its receipt.

(f) Receipt of an electronic acknowledgment from an information processing system described in subsection (b) establishes that a record was received but, by itself, does not establish that the content sent corresponds to the content received.

(g) If a person is aware that an electronic record purportedly sent under subsection (a), or purportedly received under subsection (b), was not actually sent or received, the legal effect of the sending or receipt is determined by other applicable law. Except to the extent permitted by the other law, the requirements of this subsection may not be varied by agreement.

CRYPTO CONTRACTS

`01100`
`10110`
`11110`

The Internet and its technical abilities once again marry with contract law's love of certainty in the newest form of electronic transaction—the "smart contract." The very purpose of blockchain technology is to determine and memorialize the parties, terms, and time of contract. Using blockchain technology, the parties have the ability to uncontrovertibly timestamp every transaction thus creating a fully automated timeline of legally significant communications. So, while physical postal stamps may no longer be relevant in the era of electronic mailboxes, the rule of acceptance upon dispatch in creating contractual obligations will remain. This technology has the capability of removing the quandary that some judges find themselves in: "When two honest and intelligent persons view the same event and come away with different versions of what occurred, the truth is hidden from a court somewhere between the two mutually exclusive stories. In such a case, a court must frequently abandon its desire for certainty and clarity and satisfy itself with deciding who is to be the winner. In doing so, it must take refuge in rules such as those that allocate the burden of proof. I have before me such a situation." *See Strickland v. Marathon Oil Co.*, 446 F. Supp. 638, 640 (E.D. La. 1978).

RESEARCH THIS

Find a case in your jurisdiction that deals with the application of the mailbox rule (which to some seems archaic) to modern electronic means of posting acceptance (fax, e-mail, etc.). Have these means been determined to be "proper dispatch"?

PARTIAL PERFORMANCE/SUBSTANTIAL BEGINNING

Of course the foregoing complexities of the mailbox rule do not apply to unilateral contracts. That is not to say that unilateral contracts do not suffer from their own quirks. Acceptance of a unilateral contract must be by performance, thereby completely obviating the need to rely on the post office for transmittal of acceptance. However, determining the exact moment of acceptance may become tricky.

Traditionally, acceptance occurred upon the completion of the requested act. This means that the offeror retains the power to revoke up until full performance. One can readily see that this may pose some hardship on the offeree who has begun to perform and, mid-performance, has the offer withdrawn. For example, Eleanor Aristocrat offered to pay Jacques the Artist to paint her portrait for display at the Contemporary Artist Gallery. Halfway through, Eleanor, always fickle, changes her mind and would rather have Juan paint her portrait. Under strict construction, Jacques did not fully perform; therefore, under the unilateral agreement, he did not yet accept and he is not entitled to payment.

Courts have modified the harsh application of this rule by adopting the theory of **substantial beginning**. Again, this goes back to "reliance." The offeree has started performing, relying on the offer and the reasonable expectation that it will stay open during the course of performance. Therefore, the courts have adopted the stance that once the offeree begins to perform, the

**partial performance/
substantial beginning**
An offeree has made
conscientious efforts
to start performing
according to the terms
of the contract. The
performance need not
be complete nor exactly
as specified, but only an
attempt at significant
compliance.

offer becomes irrevocable. This "substantial beginning" has to be more than mere preparation, however. Getting ready to start is not good enough; the offeree must start the requested act. Jacques' act of putting on his smock and preparing the canvas is not enough to accept by **partial performance**. However, once Jacques has started the actual portrait, Eleanor will be prevented from revoking the offer. *See, e.g., Weather-Gard Indus., Inc. v. Fairfield Sav. & Loan Ass'n*, 248 N.E.2d 794 (Ill. App. 1st Dist. 1969) ("Both sections [RESTATEMENT OF CONTRACTS §§ 45, 90] codify the doctrine which gives effect to the promisee's claim even though the promisor has withdrawn his offer prior to complete performance." A contractor was found not to have had to complete all of the construction work in order to enforce the unilateral contract due to his partial performance.).

SPOT THE ISSUE!

The Bakers' home was foreclosed upon by the bank for failure to make mortgage payments. The Bakers would like to repurchase their home from the bank. Unfortunately, the Butchers already put a bid on the home. The bank offered to sell the property back to the Bakers provided they convinced the Butchers to withdraw their offer, and the Bakers would have to pay the full balance of $25,000. The Bakers promised to do these two requested acts and sent a letter to the Butchers and put in applications to other banks to secure a loan for the $25,000. Two days later, the Candlestick-makers offered to purchase the home for $30,000. Can the bank accept their offer? Why or why not?
   See Knight v. Seattle First Nat'l Bank, 589 P.2d 1279 (Wash. App. 1979).

IN-CLASS DISCUSSION

Under unilateral contracts, mere preparation does not act as acceptance while a substantial beginning does. When does preparation for performance transform into a substantial beginning of the requested performance? In other words, what are the characteristics of preparation that distinguish it from performance?
   Consider this scenario:
   Hometown Hospital needs a new maternity wing and offers to pay $10 million to Buildrite Construction if it constructs the new wing within three months. Assume this is a unilateral contract and that Buildrite has all the specifications. Buildrite sent its engineer out to take some tests of the site to determine the actual scope of the project. At this point, the hospital rescinds its offer. Has Buildrite accepted, thereby terminating the hospital's right to revoke after performance? If this is only a preparation, what further steps would constitute a beginning?

Additionally, the offeror is under an obligation to accept the beginning of the act, also called a **tender of performance**. Just as it is unfair to permit the offeror to revoke the offer before the performance is completed, it is unfair for the offeror to place obstacles in front of the offeree as she stands ready, willing, and able to start the requested act.

tender of performance
The offeree's act of proffering the start of his contractual obligations. The offeree stands ready, willing, and able to perform.

Example

Greg Grocer offers to buy all of Fred Farmer's apples if and when he delivers them to Greg's store and stocks the produce aisle with them. Greg has offered to enter into a unilateral contract; his obligation to pay for the apples will arise when Fred delivers them to Greg's store and stocks them. If Greg stops the delivery truck a block from his store and refuses to let it unload at the store, Greg has prevented Fred from performing as he stood ready, willing, and able to complete the requested act. Fred has tendered performance and will be allowed to seek redress in the courts.

This tender may be seen as creating an option contract. The tender of performance, standing at the ready to fully perform, is the consideration for keeping the option contract open. It is understood that the offeror of the unilateral contract will accept the tender of performance and in good faith will keep the offer open. The offer cannot then be withdrawn until and unless the offeree manifests an intention not to fully perform on the offer. "If an offer for a unilateral contract is made, and part of the consideration requested in the offer is given or tendered by the offeree in response thereto, the offeror is bound by a contract, the duty of immediate performance of which is conditional on the full consideration being given or tendered within the time stated in the offer, or, if no time is stated therein, within a reasonable time." *See Taylor v. Multnomah County Deputy Sheriff's Ret. Bd.*, 510 P.2d 339, 343 (Or. 1973), *citing* RESTATEMENT (SECOND) OF CONTRACTS (Tent. Draft No. 1 1964) § 45.

SPOT THE ISSUE!

On February 1st, Richard and Paula enter into an agreement wherein Paula will buy Richard's orange grove for $50,000. The agreement stipulates that Richard will give Paula "good title" to the property on or before March 1st and, if Paula fails to close on the property, her $5,000 deposit will be forfeited to Richard. On February 15th, Richard sends a letter to Paula reminding her of the March 1st deadline. No further communications are made between the parties until Richard claims a breach of contract on February 28th, claiming that his February 15th letter was a tender of performance and, at that time, Paula was under an obligation to perform by rendering the full payment for the property. Is she? Why or why not? *See Pelletier v. Dwyer*, 334 A.2d 867 (Me. 1975).

Usually, the offeror knows of the performance and at that moment the offeror's obligations under the contract become due. What happens when the offeror does not know of the performance because she is at a distance? The offeree is then under an obligation to notify the offeror of the completed performance. "It is necessary for the formation of a contract that the acceptance made, outside the presence of the offeror be communicated to him. Of what value is it if the acceptance is made and the offeror knows nothing about it? The offer is a question which requires a response; and the response does not exist until it is known to him who asks for it." *Wagenvoord Broadcasting Co. v. Canal Automatic Transmission Service, Inc.*, 176 So. 2d 188, 190 (La. App. 1965).

Additionally, if the offeror has requested notification of performance, then the offeree is under a contractual obligation to so notify. If Greg is on vacation, he may need to be notified that the delivery has been made to the grocery store and then release the funds for payment to Fred.

In sum, acceptance is effective where the offeree agrees to the exact terms of the offer. The acceptance mirrors the offer. If the contract is bilateral, it is accepted upon proper dispatch of the acceptance; if the contract is a unilateral contract, it is accepted upon starting to perform.

Summary

The manifestation of the intent to be bound by a simple "yes," expressed in either words or actions, is *acceptance*. Very rarely is *silence* considered valid acceptance because it lacks the element of *mutuality of assent*. If the offeree makes the requested promise or does the requested act, the contract is formed, provided that she has *knowledge of the offer*. Both parties now have legally enforceable obligations to each other under the terms of the contract. The acceptance must be a *mirror image* of the offer; no new terms or qualifying conditions may be added, otherwise it will be considered a counteroffer, and the entire process will begin again from Chapter 1. The offeree will become the counterofferor and the original offeror will become the counterofferee.

If there is valid acceptance, when does it take effect? For the answer, we look to the *mailbox rule*. Acceptance is valid *upon posting*, and rejection is valid *upon receipt*, provided that there has been *proper dispatch* of the acceptance. The court also will look to see if there has been *reliance* on either the attempted acceptance or rejection in order to determine its effect upon the creation of the contract.

Unilateral contracts are not subject to the mailbox rule as it is very hard to drop performance into the mailbox. Once the offeree makes a *substantial beginning* of the requested performance, the offer is deemed accepted and the offeror cannot rescind the offer until the offeree has had a reasonable time to complete the performance.

Once it has been determined that a *legally enforceable contract* has come into being through a *valid offer* supported by *consideration* and *accepted by the offeree*, the remaining terms and conditions of the contract can be examined. These additional terms and conditions do not alter the fact that the contract is enforceable, they determine how and by whom the contract can be enforced.

Key Terms

acceptance	partial performance/substantial
acceptance of services or goods	beginning
knowledge of the offer	proper dispatch
mailbox rule	reliance
mirror image rule	silence
mutuality of assent	solicited offer
option contract	tender of performance

Review Questions

MULTIPLE CHOICE

Choose the best answer(s) and please explain *why* you choose the answer(s).

1. By starting to perform on a unilateral contract,
   a. The contract is accepted.
   b. The contract may be accepted.
   c. The offeror loses the ability to revoke the offer.
   d. The offeror must notify the offeree of the intention to accept the tendered performance.

2. A "solicited offer"
   a. Is a valid and binding promise to perform from the offeror.
   b. Must be acknowledged in writing by the offeror.
   c. Is an invitation to make an offer from the offeree.
   d. Can never be accepted by silence.

3. "Substantial performance" means
   a. The offeree is almost done with the requested act.
   b. The offeree has been paid for most of his work.
   c. The offeree has made efforts to perform on the work that are a clear indication of acceptance.
   d. An offeror can no longer terminate the offer.

4. Under the mailbox rule:
    a. Both rejections and acceptances are deemed valid upon the offeree's proper dispatch.
    b. Upon posting, a valid acceptance can override a previous rejection.
    c. Once the offeree sends the rejection, the offer is terminated.
    d. Upon posting, a valid acceptance can override a previous rejection as long as the acceptance arrives first.

EXPLAIN YOURSELF

All answers should be written in complete sentences. A simple "yes" or "no" is insufficient.

1. What is the mailbox rule? When is an offer accepted? When is it rejected?

2. When is silence valid acceptance in a contact *not* between merchants? (Save that for the UCC chapter!)

3. La Dolce Vita, a fabulous Italian restaurant, promised to pay Promotions International, Inc., an advertising agency, $40,000 for Promotions' planning and executing of a three-month advertising campaign for the restaurant. Promotions telephoned La Dolce Vita to say that it "accepted" the offer.
    a. Has Promotions indeed accepted the offer? How?
    b. If this is not acceptance, what would be acceptance of this contract?

4. Does the offeror of a unilateral contract ever lose his ability to revoke the contract? When?

5. Is a conditional acceptance valid acceptance of the offer? Why or why not?

6. Explain the "mirror image rule."

"FAULTY PHRASES"

All of the following statements are FALSE; state why they are false and then rewrite them as a true statement. Write a brief fact pattern that illustrates your answer.

1. Every offer for a unilateral contract is accepted by full performance.

2. As long as the offeror receives the acceptance, the contract has been validly accepted.

3. Any means of sending acceptance is valid.

4. Rewards are offers to enter into a unilateral contact and, by performing the act, the offeree is entitled to the reward.

5. A bilateral contract must always be accepted by a spoken or written promise to do the requested act in the offer.

"WRITE" AWAY! PORTFOLIO ASSIGNMENT

While Carrie agrees with most of the terms and specifications in Druid's offer, like most potential homeowners, she has some concerns about the cost and proposed timeline. In this exercise, draft a letter from Carrie to Druid Design & Build reflecting these concerns. Then identify whether this letter is an acceptance or a counteroffer. Explain your answer. Rewrite the contract to reflect all the negotiations that ensued from these communications. Be thoughtful—add more details to complete the construction contract.

DEADWOOD CANYON RANCH, LLP, Plaintiff,

v.

FIDELITY EXPLORATION AND PRODUCTION COMPANY, Defendant.
Case No. 4:10-cv-081
United States District Court for the District of North Dakota
Northwestern Division
Dated: May 10, 2012
ORDER DENYING PLAINTIFF'S MOTION
FOR PARTIAL SUMMARY JUDGMENT AND GRANTING DEFENDANT'S MOTION FOR
PARTIAL SUMMARY JUDGMENT

Before the Court are cross-motions for partial summary judgment. *See* Docket Nos. 13 and 21. The Court denies the Plaintiff's motion for partial summary judgment, and grants the Defendant's motion for partial summary judgment on the breach of contract claim.

I. BACKGROUND

The plaintiff, Deadwood Canyon Ranch, LLP ("DCR"), has three principal partners which include Stuart Pratt, Charles Steele, and the David Richards Children Trust—1977 (for which David Richards is the trustee). In 2006, DCR purchased property in Mountrail County, North Dakota. The defendant, Fidelity Exploration and Production Company ("Fidelity"), owns the mineral rights to the property.

In 2009, Fidelity contacted DCR regarding a plan to drill oil wells on the property. On September 2, 2009, Fidelity sent DCR a "Notice of Drilling Operations" which is a standard 20-day notice of its intention to drill three wells known as 44-32H, 11-33H, and 44-34H. *See* Docket Nos. 14-28, 14-29, and 14-30. The notices contained Fidelity's proposed agreements for damages associated with drilling and oil production. Fidelity offered a one-time payment ranging between

Page 2

$8,000.00 and $14,500.00 for surface damages associated with constructing access roads and the three wells sites. Fidelity also offered a one-time payment of $18,000 per well to be paid if the well

became a commercial producer of oil. *See* Docket Nos. 14-28, p. 8; 14-29, p. 8; and 14-30, p. 8.

On September 15, 2009, David Richards, on behalf of DCR, signed the receipt of the "Notice of Drilling Operations." *See* Docket Nos. 14-31, p. 4; 14-32, pp. 4-5; and 14-33, p. 1. Richards also signed the proposed agreements concerning a one-time payment for surface damages. Each of the agreements also contained an offer of a payment of $18,000 per well. Richards signed one of the three offers and accepted the payment of $18,000 if well 44-32H became a commercial producer of oil. *See* Docket No. 14-31, p. 2. However, Richards modified several other documents contained within Fidelity's proposal.

Specifically, Richards modified Exhibit B which contained conditions concerning the impact of the oil activity for all of the proposed wells. *See* Docket Nos. 14-31, p. 3; 14-32, p. 2; 14-33, p. 4. Richards also modified "Exhibit A" for wells 11-33H and 44-34H, specifically changing the offered price of $18,000 per well to $1,500,000 per well if the wells became commercial producers of oil. *See* Docket Nos. 19-1 (original for well 11-33H); 19-2 (original for well 44-34H); 19-3 (modified for well 11-33H); 19-4 (modified for well 44-34H). Richards signed the modified documents and the unmodified documents, and returned all of the documents to Fidelity. Although Richards and other partners of DCR communicated with Fidelity after Richards returned the modified documents, it is undisputed that DCR did not explicitly notify Fidelity of the significant modifications to the compensation to be paid. *See Docket No. 14-4*, pp. 33-40. As noted, Richards changed the compensation to be paid from $18,000 per well to $1.5 million dollars per well.

Page 3

On September 17, 2009, Dennis Zander, Fidelity's Regional Operations Manager, received the documents or agreements from Richards. *See Docket No. 14-34*. On the same day, Scott Kemmis, a Fidelity landman, also acknowledged receiving the signed documents from Richards. Kemmis sent an email to David Richards that stated as follow:

> David,
> I stopped by the Glendive Fidelity office this morning before leaving town for a few days (30th anniversary).
> We received the signed documents for the 3 wells that are scheduled for construction and drilling, thank you.
> I will get the payment requests processed for next week check run, where would you like the check sent? We show the Bozeman address but if elsewhere let me know.
>
> Sincerely,
> Scott A. Kemmis
> Contract Land Agent
> Fidelity E&P

See Docket No. 14-35.

On September 29, 2009, Fidelity contacted David Richards for permission to survey the property. *See Docket No. 14-38*. On September 30, 2009, and in accordance with the signed agreements, Fidelity sent DCR checks for surface damage associated with the construction of access roads and the drilling sites for the three oil wells known as 44-32H, 11-33H, and 44-34H. *See Docket No. 14-37*. On October 1, 2009, Fidelity applied for drilling permits for the wells. *See Docket Nos. 14-39; 14-40; and 14-41*. Between October 9-12, 2009, Fidelity received the permits to drill the three wells from the North Dakota Industrial Commission. *See Docket Nos. 14-39*, pp. 3-4; *14-40*, pp. 3-4; and *14-41*, pp. 3-4.

Page 4

On October 19, 2009, Scott Kemmis of Fidelity notified David Richards that Fidelity planned to begin "construction this week." *See Docket No. 14-44*, p. 4. Invoices from an excavating company, Excel Industries, Inc., show work occurred at each of the three wells from October 24, 2009, to November 11, 2009. *See Docket No. 14-42*. The work at the wells, as described in the invoice, included "[w]ell site excavation," "pit excavation," "[a]ccess road excavation," "[c]ulverts," and installation of cattleguards. *See Docket No. 14-42*.

On December 18, 2009, Scott Kemmis of Fidelity allegedly noticed for the first time that David Richards had modified Fidelity's proposal. *See Docket No. 14-47*. On December 21, 2009, Kemmis sent an email to Fidelity employees Jim Kennedy and Dennis Zander. *See Docket No. 14-46*. On December 23, 2009, counsel for Fidelity sent a letter to Richards requesting that he sign and return a copy of Fidelity's original proposal for damages of $18,000 per well if wells 11-33H and 44-34H became commercial producers of oil. *See Docket No. 14-50*. Richards did not do so.

On December 25, 2009, Fidelity began to drill the oil well known as 11-33H. *See Docket No. 14-51* (showing the "spud" date). On January 23, 2010, Fidelity began to drill the oil well known as 44-34H. *See Docket No. 14-52*. It is undisputed that both 11-33H and 44-34H became commercial-producing oil wells in 2010.

On October 19, 2010, DCR initiated a lawsuit against Fidelity in state court in Mountrail County, North Dakota. *See Docket No. 1-1*. DCR alleged in the complaint that Fidelity breached the agreements with DCR and that Fidelity owed DCR the sum of $3,000,000. On November 4, 2010, Fidelity removed the lawsuit to federal district court. *See Docket No. 1*.

On December 14, 2011, DCR moved for partial summary judgment on the breach of contract claim. *See Docket No. 13*. DCR alleges that David Richards executed a counteroffer when he

Page 5

modified Fidelity's offer for damages; that Fidelity's conduct amounted to acceptance of the counteroffer; and that Fidelity owes DCR damages in the amount of $1,500,000 per well or a total of $3,000,000 pursuant to the agreements because the oil wells 11-33H and 44-34H became commercial producers of oil. *See Docket No. 14*. On January 11, 2012, Fidelity filed a brief in opposition to the motion. *See* Docket No. 19. On February 3, 2012, DCR filed a reply brief. *See* Docket No. 26.

On January 11, 2012, Fidelity moved for partial summary judgment on the DCR's breach of contract claim. *See* Docket No. 21. Fidelity characterizes Richards's modifications as a counteroffer. Fidelity argues there are no facts which support the existence of an agreement because Fidelity timely rejected the counteroffer prior to drilling the wells. On February 3, 2012, DCR filed a responsive brief in opposition to the motion. *See* Docket No. 26. On February 28, 2012, Fidelity filed a reply brief. *See* Docket No. 28.

II. STANDARD OF REVIEW

Summary judgment is appropriate when the evidence, viewed in a light most favorable to the non-moving party, indicates no genuine issues of material fact exist and the moving party is entitled to judgment as a matter of law. *Davison v. City of Minneapolis, Minn.*, 490 F.3d 648, 654 (8th Cir. 2007); Fed. R. Civ. P. 56(a). Summary judgment is not appropriate if there are factual disputes that may affect the outcome of the case under the applicable substantive law. *Anderson v. Liberty Lobby, Inc.*, 477 U.S. 242, 248 (1986). An issue of material fact is genuine if the evidence would allow a reasonable jury to return a verdict for the non-moving party. *Id.*

Page 6

III. LEGAL DISCUSSION

The Court is sitting in diversity jurisdiction and, therefore, North Dakota substantive law applies. Under North Dakota law, a contract requires an offer, acceptance of that offer, and mutual acceptance and understanding of the offeror and offeree as to the terms of the legally enforceable obligation incurred. *Lagerquist v. Stergo*, 2008 ND 138, ¶ 15, 752 N.W.2d 168; *see also Geostar Corp v. Parkway Petroleum, Inc.*, 495 N.W.2d 61, 66 (N.D. 1993). In order to form a contract there must be a meeting of the minds between the parties with respect to all of the terms and conditions, and there must be an unqualified and absolute acceptance of an offer by either party. *See Davis v. Satrom*, 383 N.W.2d 831, 833 (N.D. 1986) (citing *Greenberg v. Stewart*, 236

N.W.2d 862 (N.D. 1975)); N.D.C.C. § 9-03-21 (requiring acceptance to be absolute). In order to form a contract, the offer and acceptance must express assent to the same thing. *Wucherpfennig v. Dooley*, 351 N.W.2d 443, 444 (N.D. 1984).

In determining whether there has been an acceptance of an offer, the order of communications is critical to an accurate analysis of the offer, counteroffer, acceptance, modification, and the like. *See B.J. Kadmas, Inc. v. Oxbow Energy, LLC*, 2007 ND 12, ¶ 14, 727 N.W.2d 270. Both parties agree that David Richards submitted a counteroffer to Fidelity when he modified Fidelity's original proposal for additional compensation in the amount of $18,000 per well. *See* N.D.C.C. § 9-03-21 ("A qualified acceptance is a new proposal."); *Cooke v. Blood Sys., Inc.*, 320 N.W.2d 124, 128 (N.D. 1982) ("An offer to be considered accepted must be accepted unconditionally. . . . A conditional acceptance of an offer is in itself a counteroffer which rejects the original offer.").

Page 7

Consent to a contract is only sufficient where the consent is (1) freely given; (2) mutual; and (3) communicated to the other contracting party. N.D.C.C. § 9-03-01. North Dakota recognizes that a party's actions may constitute consent. N.D.C.C. §§ 9-03-20 and 9-20-25 provide as follows:

> **9-03-20. Acts constituting acceptance.** Performance of the conditions of a proposal, or the acceptance of the consideration offered with a proposal, is an acceptance of the proposal.
>
> **9-03-25. Acceptance of benefit equivalent to consent.** A voluntary acceptance of the benefit of a transaction is equivalent to a consent to all the obligations arising from it so far as the facts are known or ought to be known to the person accepting.

N.D.C.C. §§ 9-03-20; 9-03-25. Unless an offer specifically prescribes the method of communicating the consent, "any reasonable and usual mode may be adopted." N.D.C.C. § 9-03-18.

DCR contends that Fidelity's conduct amounted to an acceptance of the new terms. DCR presented evidence which reveals that Fidelity constructed oil well sites, applied for drilling permits, and obtained the drilling permits concerning the wells known as 11-33H and 44-34H. As DCR's counteroffer provides, Fidelity also submitted payments to DCR for the surface damages caused by the construction of the well sites and access roads for 11-33H and 44-34H. In addition, David Richards testified that with respect to oil wells drilled on their property before this dispute, Fidelity did not sign the proposed agreements, but instead, would essentially start to construct the wells and begin drilling after Richards signed the agreements. See Docket No. 14-4, p. 35; N.D.C.C. § 9-03-18 (acceptance of a contract may be carried out by "any reasonable and usual mode").

Fidelity contends that its conduct does not amount to an acceptance of DCR's counteroffer which changed the original offer price of $18,000 per well to $1,500,000 per well if the two wells became commercial producers of oil. Fidelity argues that it was unaware of DCR's counteroffer until December 18, 2009, and promptly rejected the counteroffer on December 23, 2009. Fidelity

Page 8

contends that the rejection was effective because it had not commenced to drill the wells until after the rejection—well 11-33H was drilled on December 25, 2009, and well 44-34H was drilled on January 23, 2010.

The Court finds that Fidelity is entitled to summary judgment on DCR's breach of contract claim because no contract existed between Fidelity and DCR for the payment of additional compensation for wells 11-33H and 44-34H. The undisputed facts establish that Fidelity was unaware of DCR's $1.5 million dollar counteroffers and, therefore, never accepted the counteroffers. Absent an acceptance of DCR's counteroffers, no contract existed between Fidelity and DCR for additional compensation for wells 11-33H and 44-34H.

The uncontroverted facts establish that Fidelity never accepted DCR's counteroffers of $1,500,000 per well. Fidelity sent DCR a twenty-day "Notice of Drilling Operations" for wells 44-32H, 11-33H, and 44-34H, which contained contractual offers of $18,000 per well of additional compensation if the oil well became a commercial producer of oil. DCR accepted the additional compensation of $18,000

for well 44-32H and signed and returned that contract. However, DCR unilaterally altered Fidelity's offers for additional compensation on wells 11-33H and 44-34H. Specifically, DCR retyped the contract to look exactly the same as the original, except DCR increased the additional compensation from $18,000 per well to $1,500,000 per well. The Court finds as a matter of law that this significant and unilateral change in the amount to be paid on a contractual instrument is a material alteration which would not bind a non-consenting party.

The Court finds that DCR had no authority to make a binding offer on behalf of Fidelity to new contract terms of which Fidelity had no knowledge. DCR certainly had a right to make a counteroffer, but it could not significantly alter the original offer of $18,000 per well; increase the

Page 9

offer to $1.5 million dollars per well without Fidelity's knowledge; and then bind Fidelity to the counteroffer when it had no knowledge of the material change in terms of the compensation to be paid. DCR has failed to cite any legal authority to support its position that it had the power to make a unilateral, binding offer on behalf of Fidelity, and then accept its own significantly-increased offer, all unbeknownst to Fidelity. The Court finds as a matter of law that no contract existed between the parties because there clearly was no meeting of the minds.

In addition, Fidelity is entitled to partial summary judgment on DCR's breach of contract claim because there was no mutual consent to the payment of $1,500,000 per well as additional compensation for wells 11-33H and 44-34H. A valid contract requires the mutual consent of the parties. See N.D.C.C. § 9-01-02 (requiring mutual consent of the parties is essential to the existence of a contract). North Dakota law requires that the consent of the parties must be free, mutual, and communicated to each other. See N.D.C.C. § 9-03-01; see also Stout, 1999 ND 218, ¶ 11, 603 N.W.2d 52. Consent is not mutual unless the parties agree upon the same thing in the same manner. N.D.C.C. § 9-03-16; Thompson v. Thompson, 2008 ND 144, ¶ 11, 752 N.W.2d 624; Stout, 1999 ND 218, ¶ 11; Anderson v. Mooney, 279 N.W.2d 423, 426-27 (N.D. 1979).

In determining whether mutual consent existed, the critical issue is whether both Fidelity and DCR agreed to compensate DCR $1,500,000 per well in additional compensation for wells 11-33H and 44-34H if those wells became commercial producers of oil. In deciding whether the parties mutually consent to entering into a contract, the court must look to the actions of the parties both at the time and after the agreement was made. *Gulden v. Sloan*, 311 N.W.2d 568, 571 (N.D. 1981).

For a valid contract to exist there must be mutual consent, meaning the parties all agree upon the same thing in the same sense. N.D.C.C. § 9-03-16; *Thompson*, 391 N.W.2d 608 (N.D. 1986).

Page 10

In *Thompson*, the North Dakota Supreme Court addressed the issue of mutual consent involving a wastewater disposal well. Id. at 611. In analyzing the legal standard for determining mutual consent, the *Thompson* Court relied on *Corbin on Contracts*, which stated:

> If the court is convinced that the parties to a transaction gave different meanings to the express terms of the agreement and that neither party knew or had reason to known that fact, the holding will be that no contract was made and neither reformation nor enforcement in accordance with anybody's "meaning" will be granted.

Id. (citing *Corbin on Contracts* § 540, p. 88 (1960)). The North Dakota Supreme Court concluded the parties materially differed as to what was being conveyed in the contract. Id. Thus, the Court held there was no contract because the parties did not "agree upon the same thing in the same sense." Id. (citing N.D.C.C. § 9-03-16).

The undisputed facts clearly establish that Fidelity and DCR did not "agree upon the same thing in the same sense." *See* N.D.C.C. § 9-03-16. Fidelity reasonably believed that DCR agreed to additional compensation of $18,000 per well for wells 11-33H and 44-34H. Fidelity was not informed that DCR had changed the agreements and had made significantly-increased counteroffers in the amount of $1,500,000 per well as additional compensation. DCR claims it believed Fidelity agreed to the additional compensation of $1.5 million dollars per

well because Fidelity never rejected the counteroffer. Common sense would lead a reasonable person to conclude otherwise. In situations where the parties to a transaction gave different meanings to the terms of the agreement and neither party knew or had reason to know that fact, the court will hold that no contract was made. *See Thompson*, 391 N.W.2d at 611 (citing *Corbin on Contracts* § 540, p. 88; see *also Restatement (Second) of Contracts* § 20 (1981) (stating there is no manifestation of mutual assent to an exchange if the parties attach materially different meanings to their manifestations and neither

Page 11

party knows the meaning attached by the other). Both Fidelity and DCR assigned a significantly different meaning to the amount of additional compensation to be paid for wells 11-33H and 44-34H. The Court finds as a matter of law that no contract ever existed between the parties as to the amount of additional compensation to be paid for wells 11-33H and 44-34H if those wells became commercial producers of oil.

The Court notes that DCR is not left without a remedy. Chapter 38-11.1 of the North Dakota Century Code provides for compensation to surface owners for damage related to oil and gas production. N.D.C.C. § 38-11.1-04 states, in pertinent part:

> The mineral developer shall pay the surface owner a sum of money equal to the amount of damages sustained by the surface owner and the surface owner's tenant, if any, for loss of agricultural production and income, lost land value, lost use of and access to the surface owner's land, and lost value of improvements caused by drilling operations. The amount of damages may be determined by any formula mutually agreeable between the surface owner and the mineral developer. When determining damages, consideration must be given to the period of time during which the loss occurs and the surface owner may elect to be paid damages in annual installments over a period of time; except that the surface owner must be compensated for harm caused by exploration only by a single sum payment. The payments contemplated by this section only cover land directly

affected by drilling operations. Payments under this section are intended to compensate the surface owner for damage and disruption.

N.D.C.C. § 38-11.1-04. The determination of damages is to initially be made by the parties based upon a mutually-agreeable formula, i.e., a settlement agreement. If the parties are unable to agree on the damages to be awarded, the surface owner may sue for damages as DCR has done in this case. *Murphy v. Amoco Prod. Co.*, 729 F.2d 552, 554 (8th Cir. 1984). If the damages awarded exceed the amount offered by the mineral developer, the surface owner can recover costs and reasonable attorneys' fees. Id. (citing N.D.C.C. § 38-11.1-09). Both parties have demanded a jury trial and the trial is scheduled to commence on October 29, 2012. The surface owner's claim for

Page 12

damages under Chapter 38-11.1 remains. It will ultimately be left to a jury to determine the appropriate amount of damages associated with Fidelity's drilling activities if the parties are unable to resolve their differences. This Court has noted in the past that the damages recoverable under N.D.C.C. 38-11.1-04 are broad in scope.

III. CONCLUSION

The Court has carefully reviewed the record, the parties' briefs, and relevant case law. The Court finds that no genuine issues of material fact exist concerning the existence of a contract, and that Fidelity is entitled to judgment as a matter of law on the breach of contract claim. The Court *DENIES* DCR's partial motion for summary judgment (Docket No. 13), and *GRANTS* Fidelity's motion for partial summary judgment on the breach of contract claim (Docket No. 21). The claim for damages under Chapter 38-11.1 of the North Dakota Century Code remains.

Case in Point   ACCEPTANCE

432 P.2d 405
78 N.M. 440
A. A. MARCHIONDO, Plaintiff-Appellant,
v.
Frank SCHECK, Defendant-Appellee.
No. 8288.
Supreme Court of New Mexico.
Oct. 2, 1967.

[78 NM 441]

Page 406

Hanna & Mercer, Albuquerque, for appellant.
Marron & Houk, Dan A. McKinnon, III, Albuquerque, for appellee.

OPINION

WOOD, Judge, Court of Appeals.

The issue is whether the offeror had a right to revoke his offer to enter a unilateral contract.

Defendant, in writing, offered to sell real estate to a specified prospective buyer and agreed to pay a percentage of the sales price as a commission to the broker. The offer fixed a six-day time limit for acceptance. Defendant, in writing, revoked the offer. The revocation was received by the broker on the morning of the sixth day. Later that day, the broker obtained the offeree's acceptance.

Plaintiff, the broker, claiming breach of contract, sued defendant for the commission stated in the offer. On the above facts, the trial court dismissed the complaint.

We are not concerned with the revocation of the offer as between the offeror and the prospective purchaser. With certain exceptions (see 12 C.J.S. Brokers § 95(2), pp. 223-224), the right of a broker to the agreed compensation, or damages measured thereby, is not defeated by the refusal of the principal to complete or consummate a transaction. *Southwest Motel Brokers, Inc. v. Alamo Hotels, Inc.*, 72 N.M. 227, 382 P.2d 707 (1963).

Plaintiff's appeal concerns the revocation of his agency. As to that revocation, the issue between the offeror and his agent is not whether defendant had the power to revoke; rather, it is whether he had the right to revoke. 1 Mechem on Agency, § 568 at 405 (2d ed. 1914).

When defendant made his offer to pay a commission upon sale of the property, he offered to enter a unilateral contract; the offer was for an act to be performed, a sale. 1 *Williston on Contracts*, § 13 at 23 (3rd ed. 1957); *Hutchinson v. Dobson-Bainbridge Realty Co.*, 31 Tenn. App. 490, 217 S.W.2d 6 (1946).

Many courts hold that the principal has the right to revoke the broker's agency at any time before the broker has actually procured a purchaser. See *Hutchinson v. Dobson-Bainbridge Realty Co.*, supra, and cases therein cited. The reason given is that until there is performance, the offeror has not received that contemplated by his offer, and there is no contract. Further, the offeror may never receive the requested performance because the offeree is not obligated to perform. Until the offeror receives the requested performance, no consideration has passed from the offeree to the offeror. Thus, until the performance is received, the offeror may withdraw the offer. Williston, supra, § 60; *Hutchinson v. Dobson-Bainbridge Realty Co.*, supra.

Defendant asserts that the trial court was correct in applying this rule. However, plaintiff contends that the rule is not applicable where there has been part performance of the offer.

Hutchinson v. Dobson-Bainbridge Realty Co., supra, states:

"A greater number of courts, however, hold that part performance of the consideration [78 NM 442]

Page 407

may make such an offer irrevocable and that where the offeree or broker manifests his assent to the offer by entering upon performance and spending time and money in his efforts to perform, then the offer becomes irrevocable during the time stated and binding upon the principal according to its terms. . . ."

Defendant contends that the decisions giving effect to a part performance are distinguishable. He asserts that in these cases the offer was of an exclusive right to sell or of an exclusive agency. Because neither factor is present here, he asserts that the 'part performance' decisions are not applicable.

Many of the decisions do seem to emphasize the exclusive aspects of the offer. See *Garrett v. Richardson*, 149 Colo. 449, 369 P.2d 566 (1962); *Geyler v. Dailey*, 70 Ariz. 135, 217 P.2d 583 (1950); *S. Blumenthal & Co. v. Bridges*, 91 Ark. 212, 120 S.W. 974, 24 L.R.A., N.S., 279 (1909); Williston, supra, § 60A, note 6, and cases there cited. See also *Manzo v. Park*, 220 Ark. 216, 247 S.W.2d 12 (1952), where a listing agreement for a definite period of time was held to imply an exclusive right to sell within the time named.

Such emphasis reaches its extreme conclusion in *Tetrick v. Sloan*, 170 Cal. App. 2d 540, 339 P.2d 613 (1959), where no effect was given to the part performance because there was neither an exclusive agency, nor an exclusive right to sell.

Defendant's offer did not specifically state that it was exclusive. Under § 70-1-43, N.M.S.A. 1953, it was not an exclusive agreement. It is not the exclusiveness of the offer that deprives the offeror of the right to revoke. It is the action taken by the offeree which deprives the offeror of that right. Until there is action by the offeree—a partial performance pursuant to the offer—the offeror may revoke even if his offer is of an exclusive agency or an exclusive right to sell. *Levander v. Johnson*, 181 Wis. 68, 193 N.W. 970 (1923).

Once partial performance is begun pursuant to the offer made, a contract results. This contract has been termed a contract with conditions or an option contract. This terminology is illustrated as follows:

"If an offer for a unilateral contract is made, and part of the consideration requested in the offer

is given or tendered by the offeree in response thereto, the offeror is bound by a contract, the duty of immediate performance of which is conditional on the full consideration being given or tendered within the time stated in the offer, or, if no time is stated therein, within a reasonable time." Restatement of Contracts, § 45 (1932).

Restatement (Second) of Contracts, § 45, Tent. Draft No. 1, (approved 1964, Tent. Draft No. 2, p. vii) states:

"(1) Where an offer invites an offeree to accept by rendering a performance and does not invite a promissory acceptance, an option contract is created when the offeree begins the invited performance or tenders part of it.

"(2) The offeror's duty of performance under any option contract so created is conditional on completion or tender of the invited performance in accordance with the terms of the offer."

Restatement (Second) of Contracts, § 45, Tent. Draft No. 1, comment (g), says:

"This Section frequently applies to agency arrangements, particularly offers made to real estate brokers. . . ."

See Restatement (Second) of Agency § 446, comment (b).

The reason for finding such a contract is stated in *Hutchinson v. Dobson-Bainbridge Realty Co.*, supra, as follows:

"This rule avoids hardship to the offeree, and yet does not hold the offeror beyond the terms of his promise. It is true by such terms he was to be bound only if the requested act was done; but this implies that he will let it be done, that he will keep his offer open till the offeree who has begun can finish doing it. At least this is so where the doing of it will [78 NM 443]

Page 408

necessarily require time and expense. In such a case it is but just to hold that the offeree's part performance furnishes the 'acceptance' and the 'consideration' for a binding subsidiary promise not to revoke the offer, or turns the offer into a presently binding contract conditional upon the offeree's full performance."

We hold that part performance by the offeree of an offer of a unilateral contract results in a contract with a condition. The condition is full performance by the offeree. Here, if plaintiff-offeree partially performed prior to receipt of defendant's revocation, such a contract was formed. Thereafter, upon performance being completed by plaintiff, upon defendant's failure to recognize the contract, liability for breach of contract would arise. Thus, defendant's right to revoke his offer depends upon whether plaintiff had partially performed before he received defendant's revocation. *In re Ward's Estate*, 47 N.M. 55, 134 P.2d 539, 146 A.L.R. 826 (1943), does not conflict with this result. *Ward* is clearly distinguishable because there the prospective purchaser did not complete or tender performance in accordance with the terms of the offer.

What constitutes partial performance will vary from case to case since what can be done toward performance is limited by what is authorized to be done. Whether plaintiff partially performed is a question of fact to be determined by the trial court.

The trial court denied plaintiff's requested finding concerning his partial performance. It did so on the theory that partial performance was not material. In this the trial court erred.

Because of the failure to find on the issue of partial performance, the case must be remanded to the trial court. *State ex rel. Reynolds v. Board of County Comm'rs*, 71 N.M. 194, 376 P.2d 976 (1962). We have not considered, and express no opinion on the question of whether there is or is not substantial evidence in the record which would support a finding one way or the other on this vital issue. Compare *Geeslin v. Goodno, Inc.*, 75 N.M. 174, 402 P.2d 156 (1965).

The cause is remanded for findings on the issue of plaintiff's partial performance of the offer prior to its revocation, and for further proceedings consistent with this opinion and the findings so made.

It is so ordered.

NOBLE and MOISE, JJ., concur.

Chapter 4

Conditions

Chapter Objectives

The student will be able to:

- Use vocabulary regarding conditions properly.
- Differentiate between a covenant and a condition.
- Discuss the practical implications of conditions precedent, subsequent, and concurrent.
- Evaluate whether the condition was created expressly, impliedly in fact, or impliedly in law.
- Determine the effect of the condition on the performance required under the contract.

This chapter will explore HOW and WHEN the performance will be carried out IF at all. Conditions place requirements on the circumstances surrounding the parties' performance obligations. These requirements may have to occur before, during, or after the parties act upon their promises to each other. These conditions may be created by words, actions, unspoken intentions, or operation of law.

The offeror and offeree have shaken hands and the deal is set. The three elements of offer, consideration, and acceptance all have validity and the agreement has become a legally enforceable contract. One could think that the discussion would end here; however, nothing in the law is that simple. **Conditions** may be part of the contract. They do not necessarily affect the validity of the contract as the first three elements do; rather, conditions have to do with the timing of performance and how the other obligations under the contract are to

condition
An event that may or may not happen, but upon which the rest of the performance of the contract rests.

93

be performed. The Restatement (Second) of Contracts § 224 defines a *condition* by one of the most enigmatic sentences ever written: "an event, not certain to occur, which must occur, unless its non-occurrence is excused, before performance under a contract becomes due." Put more simply, conditions are the "strings attached" to the deal.

At the outset, it must be made clear that there is a difference between a *covenant* and a *condition*. A **covenant** is the contractual promise to perform with no strings attached. If the person does not fulfill his covenant, he is in breach. If there are other terms (aside from the performance promises) that the parties wish to incorporate, these are *conditions*. The most common condition in a contract relates to when contractual obligations become due—when do the parties actually have to do what they promised to do?

covenant
The promise upon which the contract rests.

Example

Joyce agrees to relocate with a sizable promotion to the Denver office of the Mega Company, for whom she works. Mega covenants to promote Joyce, and Joyce covenants to relocate to Denver to revitalize the business there. Joyce's relocation is conditioned upon Mega finding her a suitable house in the suburbs first. As Denver is a real estate hot-spot, Mega is unable to find a house for Joyce for months. Unless and until Mega finds a house for Joyce, the underlying covenants do not become "active." Joyce doesn't have to relocate and work in Denver and Mega doesn't have to promote her.

TYPES OF CONDITIONS

condition precedent
An event that happens beforehand and gives rise to the parties' performance obligations. If the condition is not satisfied, the parties do not have a duty to perform.

There are three types of "timing" conditions. **Conditions precedent** deal with an occurrence that must come before the party's obligation to perform. A practical example occurs in closings, wherein the buyer must obtain a mortgage commitment and the property must pass home inspection before the obligation to purchase the home (the "contracted-for" obligation) becomes due. These two events are conditions of the contract for sale. The contract is in existence and relates to the promises to sell for a specified price. However, neither party has the obligation to go through with the transaction if the conditions are not met. The seller of the home has no obligation to sell his property to someone who cannot obtain the money necessary to purchase it (the mortgage commitment condition). Similarly, the buyer has no obligation to purchase the home if the home inspection reveals that the buyer will not receive what he bargained for—an inhabitable home free from substantial defects. If either of these conditions fails, the contract is not enforceable and the parties may walk away from the transaction without penalty.

How does one determine whether a contract provision is a condition precedent or a contractual obligation? As with much of contract interpretation, it depends on the intent of the parties. A fair and reasonable reading of the language used that takes the surrounding circumstances into account should reveal the intention to create either a condition or a covenant. Where this examination still leaves a question as to the parties' intent, the more definite answer is to interpret it as a promise not a condition. "The court is mindful that '[w]here doubt exists as to whether the parties have created a promise or an express condition,' Washington precedent requires the court to 'interpret the language in question to create a promise.'" *Oliver v. Alcoa, Inc.*, Case No. C16-0741JLR (W.D. Wash. 2016), *citing Lokan & Assocs., Inc. v. Am. Beef Processing, LLC*, 311 P.3d 1285, 1289 (Wash. Ct. App. 2013) (The issue rested upon a determination whether the Plaintiff's termination was a condition precedent to receiving the enhanced severance benefit or whether Alcoa had made a promise to pay that enhanced severance when the Plaintiff signed the release of claims and agreed to work until March 31, 2016. Alcoa argued that since it refused to terminate the Plaintiff on that date, the condition was not triggered.).

EYE ON ETHICS

CONDITIONAL FEE ARRANGEMENTS

ETHICS

Notice that the typical phrasing—contingency fee—is NOT used here. A contingency fee is a kind of conditional fee. It means that the attorney will not collect a fee for the work performed on behalf of the client if the case fails to recover for the client. (Remember that the client will remain responsible for costs and court fees, though.) It is very important to remember that contingency fees are permitted in some cases, but in others, like criminal defense and domestic relations, they are not. Yes, a contingency fee arrangement is a kind of condition precedent in the retainer agreement. However, that is not the only kind of *conditional fee*. Recall that contract law allows the parties to make any kind of arrangements they would like (as long as they are legal, etc.) so other conditional arrangements can be made that delineate circumstances that will alter the contractual relationship based upon their occurrence or non-occurrence.

One such fee arrangement demonstrates the potential ethical pitfalls of such complicated conditional clauses. The court in *Rubin v. Guettler,* 73 So. 3d 809 (Fla. App. 2011) found that the particular set of conditions had a potentially unethical consequence and struck the fee arrangement despite the fact that none of the parties had foreseen it and all had agreed to it. (This is very different from the general contractual principle that parties can make as stupid a deal as they like as long as there is no fraud or illegal circumstances surrounding it.)

The terms—briefly stated:

- In the event I discharge the firm prior to resolution by judgment or settlement, or if I elect to no longer pursue the Anticipated Claims as identified herein-below, I agree to immediately thereafter pay LAW FIRM accrued hourly legal fees based upon the hourly rates [of the firm].
- I agree not to settle this matter without the prior written approval of the LAW FIRM. . . .

- I understand that time is of the essence, LAW FIRM will begin work on my behalf immediately, and I will incur fees and costs as soon as I sign this Agreement.
- I may discharge the LAW FIRM at any time.

As it turned out, the client, Guettler, dismissed all his pending cases that were the subject of this fee agreement. The attorney, of course, sought to collect his fee based upon hourly rates. The court found two ethical faults with this seemingly routine conditional contract for legal fees. First, the conditional fee arrangement that permitted a full recovery of attorney's fees at discharge resulted in a violation of Florida Rule 4-1.5(a) of the Rules Regulating the Florida Bar. The court found that a "termination-of-services clause in a contingency-fee agreement, which provides for the client to pay the discharged law firm for all services rendered up through the date of termination at the prevailing hourly rate for firm members, if the client abandons or dismisses the claim, violates rule 4-1.5 on its face." *Id.* at 813. Further, the court found that "the discharge provision had the effect of intimidating the client into not exercising her right of discharge and penalized the client for exercising this right. *Id.* at 1113. The court concluded that "[a]n attorney cannot exact a penalty for a right of discharge. To do so is contrary to our statement of policy in *Rosenberg*. . . ." *Id. See also The Fla. Bar v. Spann,* 682 So. 2d 1070, 1072-73 (Fla. 1996) (finding that a contingency-fee agreement that provided for payment based on a specified hourly rate upon termination by the client constitutes a penalty clause in violation of rule 4-1.5 because the client would be forced to pay the attorney "upon discharge even where the contingency had never been met." *Id.* at 813-814. These kinds of conditions are not enforceable in fee agreements "because a discharge clause of this type has been consistently held by the supreme court to be contrary to public policy because of the *potential* it has for chilling a client's right to change counsel." at 814. Adding what the attorney would undoubtedly term "insult to injury," the court did not allow the attorney's action for *"quantum meruit"* because it would only be proper if the condition occurred—the successful outcome and recovery for the client. This was not the case here. The client failed to recover anything, and therefore that condition precedent to attorney's fee recovery failed as well.

condition subsequent
An event that, if it happens after the parties' performance obligations, negates the duty to perform. If the condition is satisfied, the parties can "undo" their actions.

On the other end of the spectrum are **conditions subsequent**. It logically follows that these events occur after a party's performance pursuant to the contract. These conditions absolve a party from having to finish performance or totally excuse the previous performance without penalty. Now you are thinking, how and why can performance be taken back or excused once it has been accomplished? The most common examples of conditions subsequent are merchandise returns and alimony payments.

We have all changed our minds about a purchase (a completed contract of sale) at one time or another and went searching for the receipt to go back to the store. The store accepts these returns as long as the customer has the receipt and the tags are still on the merchandise and/or it is still in the packaging. These are the store's conditions subsequent to the sale that permit the excuse of the customer's performance. The customer is relieved of the obligation to pay for the merchandise. The deal becomes "undone" by the conditions subsequent to the transaction. Both parties are put back in the positions they were in before the formation of the contract. The store has the merchandise and the customer has the money.

Similarly, alimony payments made in connection with a divorce settlement (an enforceable contract) are typically subject to a condition subsequent. Alimony payments may cease, thereby terminating the performance obligation, when the party receiving the alimony remarries. Any kind of reasonable condition subsequent may apply; parties can get as specific and technical as they like. In *Mereminsky v. Mereminsky*, 188 N.Y.S.2d 771, 20 Misc. 2d 21 (2d Dep't 1959), not only did the ex-wife have to remain unmarried, but the ex-husband's obligation to pay the alimony was contingent on his remaining in the watch business and the business's profits exceeding a certain sum per year.

The third and last kind of condition is those that are **concurrent**. This simply means that the obligations to perform occur at the same time. Unless otherwise specified, the law presumes that the performances requested under the contract are concurrent conditions. Greg Grocer has an obligation to pay Fred Farmer for his apples when Fred Farmer performs on his obligation to deliver them.

concurrent condition
An event that happens at the same time as the parties' performance obligations.

SPOT THE ISSUE!

Eric Eccentric, a billionaire with delusions of grandeur, makes an agreement with a young entrepreneur, Nelly Novice, to promote Eric's new idea for a reality television show: *The Trainee*. The contract provides that Nelly will receive 10 percent of the net advertising profits as her sole means of payment for her services. Needless to say, not even the Wolf network will pick up this show and it never airs.

Nelly sues Eric, as she put a lot of effort into the development of the idea and thinks she has a case based on strict breach of contract causes of action.

Is Nelly entitled to payment under strict contract law? (Forget equity here.) Identify the condition(s), if any, in the contract and the impact on the recovery, if any.

IN-CLASS DISCUSSION

Compare and discuss the following scenarios:

1. Howard wants to remodel his kitchen and consults with Ken the kitchen designer to draw up potential plans for the renovations. Howard agrees to pay Ken $1,000 for his design services upon loan

approval from the bank that is giving Howard a home equity line of credit. The value of real estate plummets and the bank refuses to give Howard his line of credit. Is Howard under a duty to pay Ken under the design agreement?

2. Howard contacts with Renee the Realtor to sell his house. The commission of $10,000 will be due and payable upon closing of title. Renee finds a buyer for Howard's house. However, at the last minute, the buyer backs out of the deal. Is Howard under a duty to pay Renee?

3. Howard, having eventually successfully sold his home, contracts with Sheppard's Construction to build a new house. Allen the architect has designed a complex house for Howard. In the construction contract with Sheppard's, the final payment is due and owing upon the final inspection and satisfaction of Allen. After the home's completion, Allen refuses to grant his approval as he is not satisfied that the builder has constructed the home to his design vision. Other architects have visited the home and feel that it reasonably and satisfactorily complies with Allen's vision, but Allen is still not satisfied. Is Howard under the obligation to pay Sheppard's?

METHOD OF CREATION

Just as there are three types of "timing conditions," preserving the symmetry of three, there are three means of creating conditions. Conditions may be (1) *express*, (2) *implied in fact*, or (3) *implied in law*. We have seen this terminology before and thankfully it means the same thing with regard to conditions.

express conditions
Requirements stated in words, either orally or written, in the contract.

Express conditions are created when they are specifically stated in words by the parties themselves. Words such as "on the condition that . . . ," "provided that . . . ," "so long as . . . ," and similar phrases create express conditions. They are clearly intended to be a part of the contract because the parties have explicitly made them. This also means that the court cannot alter these express terms as there is no interpretation as to intent needed. Either the express conditions are fulfilled or they fail.

While the court usually interprets these express conditions strictly, conditions that are not related to the subject matter of the agreement may not be enforced so as to avoid the contract entirely. Contract law likes to preserve contracts where possible. A contract for the sale of two stores expressly conditioned the transfer upon the buyer providing the seller's attorney with evidence that certain bills had been paid and that the buyer had filed an application for a SBA loan. The court found that these express conditions of the contract bore no substantial relationship to the subject matter of the sale of the two businesses. While the express conditions were not fulfilled, they did not rise to the level of forfeiting the entire agreement. The seller's performance was put on hold until the express conditions were satisfied, but the seller could not declare the buyer in breach for the failure of these two minor conditions. *Jackson v. Richards 5 & 10 Inc.*, 433 A.2d 888 (Pa. Super. 1981).

SURF'S UP

It used to be that in order to declutter the home and make a few extra dollars, a person would set up a yard sale. Those looking to buy unusual or collector items would frequent flea markets early on Saturday mornings. These days, even this simple transaction has been incorporated into the global electronic virtual marketplace. eBay is one of many auction sites for this kind of buying and selling. However, with the addition of technology comes the addition of terms and conditions. Review the conditions attached to what seems like a "simple" transaction using an online auction site at http://pages.ebay.com/help/policies/overview.html. With one click, you agree to these terms and conditions of the user agreement.

> Before you may become a member of eBay, you must read and accept all of the terms and conditions in, and linked to, this User Agreement and the Privacy Policy. We strongly recommend that, as you read this User Agreement, you also access and read the linked information. By accepting this User Agreement, you also agree that your use of other eBay branded web sites will be governed by the User Agreement and Privacy Policy posted on those web sites.

The "agreement" is several pages long and contains links to eight other policy sites. How many people do you think actually read all of this information before using the service? This is not the only place for "do-it-yourself" commerce. Amazon has gotten into the small company market (https://services.amazon.com/content/sell-on-amazon.htm), Etsy (https://www.etsy.com/sell) provides a place to sell handcrafted items, and even Facebook has launched a "Marketplace" (https://www.facebook.com/policies/commerce). Every seller and buyer on these platforms has to submit to the terms and conditions of use.

CRYPTO CONTRACTS

Smart contracts, as they are completely automated using blockchain technology, also can be used to keep track and independently verify the fulfillment of any number of conditions before executing the contract(s). Of course, these will need to be express conditions because they need to be written into the code that makes up the contract. As good as technology may be, it cannot presume to know the minds of the parties or even what their intention may be based upon "normal" trade practices or past performance. Additionally, the smart contract cannot independently observe outside events; every element of the smart contract must be input into the blockchain in order to set the fulfillment of the conditions in motion. So, is this "self-executing" contract really as automated as the hype would have you believe? Is it really "smart" if it is (1) only really effective for relatively simple transactions and (2) dependent upon potentially erroneous/conflicting external input? There certainly are opportunities to explore its uses as this technology evolves.

implied in fact
Conditions that are not expressed in words but that must exist in order for the terms of the contract to make sense and are assumed by the parties to the contract.

Implied in fact conditions are those occurrences that must take place for the parties to perform. The parties expect these conditions without having to say them. Although it is usually good sense not to make assumptions, implied in fact conditions are assumptions that each party is aware of that will make their respective performances possible. This includes the assumptions that the parties will be alive at the time for performance (*see, e.g., Jenkins Subway, Inc. v. Jones*, 990 S.W.2d 713 (Tenn. App. 1998)) and that, if the agreement involves interest in property, the party has possession of that property. *See, e.g., CIT Group/Equipment Financing, Inc v. Integrated Financial Services, Inc.*, 910 S.W.2d 722 (Mo. App. W. Dist. 1995) (obtaining possession of an aircraft was an implied condition precedent under a loan commitment to purchase engines for that airplane). In real estate transactions, it is common to close out any existing mortgages on the property before title can transfer to the buyers. Buyers usually expect to take the property at the closing free and clear of any encumbrances such as mortgages. *See, e.g., Johnson v. Sprague*, 614 N.E.2d 585 (Ind. App. 1st Dist. 1993) (the court implied the condition that the real estate taxes would be paid off at the time of transfer in order to pass clear title to the buyer). The exception to this rule relates to quitclaim deeds, which explicitly state that there may be encumbrances on the property but the buyer is essentially taking the property "as is" with all encumbrances both known and unknown.

The evidence of the existence of these implied in fact conditions is determined by the surrounding circumstances. If you enter into a sales and delivery contract with a merchant, the express condition is that you will pay for the goods. The implied in fact condition is that you will allow the delivery person access to your home to actually deliver the goods you purchased.

It is important to note that express conditions trump implied in fact conditions. A court will not "insert terms into an agreement by implication unless the implication arises from the language employed or is indispensable to effectuate the intention of the parties." *Downtown Barre Development v. C & S Wholesale Grocers, Inc.*, 857 A.2d 263, 267 (Vt. 2004).

implied in law
Conditions that are not expressed in words but are imposed by the court to ensure fairness and justice as a result of its determination.

These first two types of conditions are compatible with the cool logical nature of contract law; however, the third type is more forgiving. Conditions **implied in law** are imposed by the court out of fairness and justice. While parties are free to contract for almost anything they'd like, the courts typically impose a condition upon their actions that they must conform to the principles of good faith and fair dealing so that they may indeed reap the benefit of the contract. This principle has been around for quite some time. The court's decision in *Frohman v. Fitch*, 164 App. Div. 231, 149 N.Y.S. 633 (1st Dep't 1914), illustrates this concept of an implied condition preserving fairness in the dealings between the parties. Very simplistically, the case involved the grant of rights from an author to a theater manager for the production of the work into a stage production. The theater manager was granted exclusive rights to produce the play in the United States and Canada. It was a great success, so the author (through his heirs) sold the rights to the new technological advancement, the moving picture. This type of means of production was not contemplated by the parties to the contract. The theater manager sued to have this type of production stopped. The court found:

> This exclusive right was to protect the plaintiff in the property which he had purchased. That the plaintiff's rights under the contract constituted property cannot be questioned. That by the aid of science it has, since the contract was executed, been made possible to produce the play in some manner not then contemplated, does not give [the defendants] the right to destroy the plaintiff's property or diminish the value of what he purchased.

Id. at 233-234.

Again, what paralegal students need to know comes from their kindergarten days. The courts and our kindergarten teachers expect people to treat others fairly and in a manner in which we would like to be treated, by implying the condition that neither party do anything to harm the other's interest in the subject matter of the agreement, nor that either party do anything to injure the other party's right to receive the fruits of the contract, "which mean that in every contract there exists an implied covenant of good faith and fair dealing." *Kirke La Shelle Co. v. Paul Armstrong Co.*, 188 N.E. 163, 167 (N.Y. 1933). In this case, fairness dictated that one party could not destroy the value of the interests transferred by taking advantage of an unforeseeable technology to do so. The facts are these: The Paul Armstrong Co., the entity representing the rights of the late playwright, was sued by the *Kirke* production company to recover its share in the profits resulting from the production of the play in the new medium of movies with sound—also known as "talkies." The original contact provided for profit-sharing of the plays. "Since 'talkies' were unknown at the time when the contract was entered into, it cannot be said that 'talkie' rights were within the contemplation of the parties." *Id.* at 165. However, Armstrong and the production company did enter into an agreement that provided that they would not "enter into any contract affecting the title to the dramatic rights exclusive of motion picture rights or the production of the play in New York City, on the road, or in stock without appellant's approval." Armstrong granted to Metro-Goldwyn-Mayer Corporation the exclusive "talkie" rights in the play and Kirke claimed its share pursuant to the profit-sharing agreement. The court found that that "since science had made it possible to produce the play in a manner not contemplated when the contract was entered into, it did not follow that the Armstrong could destroy the Kirke production company's property or diminish the value of what it had purchased." *Id.* at 167-168.

RESEARCH THIS

In many cases, contracts do not have "limiting clauses" that use the specific terms *"on condition that"* or *"provided that."* These clauses clearly indicate that the parties intend to create a condition affecting performance.

Find a case in your jurisdiction that addresses the more common scenario: How does a court interpret ambiguous language of a contract as creating a condition or a covenant?

time for performance
A condition that requires each party be given a reasonable time to complete performance.

Courts also routinely cure a missing **time for performance** term using conditions implied by law. If the contract is silent as to when a party's performance becomes due, the court will imply a reasonable time given the circumstances. The court in *Belfor U.S. Grp., Inc. v. Chicago's Best, LLC*, 13-cv-614-wmc (W.D. Wis. 2015) identified three potential issues regarding vague terms in the language of the contract: "(1) the work authorizations provide no timetable for the completion of the work; (2) the price is stated as 'TBD by estimate'; and (3) the description of the work to be completed by Belfor—'all labor, equipment and materials required to properly repair the specific real property, contents or structure.' However, none of these arguable ambiguities render the contract unenforceable. First, the lack of a completion date does not pose a problem. 'The general rule is that where there is an absence of a provision as to the time for performance, a reasonable time is implied.'" *Id.* at 17 (*citing Flores v. Raz*, 2002 WI App 27, ¶ 11, 250 Wis. 2d 306, 640 N.W.2d 159 (Wis. App. 2001), wherein the court determined that a two-year wait for approval from the landlord for the sale of a business was unreasonable.). After the lapse of a reasonable time, the waiting party may choose to terminate the agreement and avoid his own performance obligations.

SPOT THE ISSUE!

Joe's Pizzeria and Sub Shack wishes to expand its restaurant and enters into an agreement with the owner of the adjoining lot, Sam Seller, to purchase the land and begin construction. A condition precedent to the contract is Joe's ability to obtain financing from First Bank. Joe dutifully applies for the construction loan, but, as he cannot make up his mind about the new design, he isn't sure how much he needs to secure in financing. This indecision continues for three months. Needless to say, Sam becomes frustrated at Joe's fickle nature and demands that Joe make up his mind and soon! What recourse, if any, does Sam have in this situation?

Here is an example a little closer to home: Colleges essentially enter into contracts with their admitted students. The students pay for the credits in exchange for instruction. After applying for admission, the college has a reasonable time within which to notify the applicant of its decision to admit that student or not. The college is under an obligation to notify the applicant of its decision within a reasonable time if no deadline for decision has been established. What is a reasonable time in this instance? At the very least, an applicant would have to know of the decision to admit in enough time to then apply for financial aid, register for classes, and purchase textbooks.

Through an examination of the terms of the contract, the paralegal student can determine if and when performance may become due. Conditions may take many forms, and it is important that they are properly categorized so that their impact on the agreement as a whole can be determined.

Summary

Contractual conditions are those terms, other than the actual performance promises, that the parties incorporate as part of the contract. They deal with when and how the parties are to perform.

1. *Conditions precedent* deal with an occurrence that must come before the party's obligation to perform.
2. *Conditions subsequent* deal with events that occur after a party's performance pursuant to the contract and they release the parties from having to finish performance or totally excuse previous performance without penalty.
3. *Concurrent conditions* deal with obligations to perform that occur simultaneously.

Conditions may be

1. *Express.* They are specifically stated in words by the parties themselves.
2. *Implied in fact.* Those occurrences must take place in order for the parties to perform. In good faith, the parties expect these conditions without having to say them.
3. *Implied in law.* They are imposed by the court out of fairness and justice.

Key Terms

concurrent conditions
conditions
conditions precedent
conditions subsequent
covenants

express conditions
implied in fact
implied in law
time for performance

Review Questions

MULTIPLE CHOICE

Choose the best answer(s) and please explain *why* you choose the answer(s).

1. A term is considered a "condition precedent" if
   a. It takes priority over all the other terms of the contract.
   b. It describes an event that needs to occur prior to the obligation to perform.
   c. It makes the offeree perform her obligations first.
   d. It takes priority over all the other conditions in the agreement.

2. An implied in fact condition
   a. Must occur before the parties have an obligation to perform.
   b. Is a part of the contract.
   c. Is never a part of the contract.
   d. Must be agreed to by the parties.

3. A condition subsequent means that
   a. It must occur immediately following performance under the contractual terms.
   b. It can undo the performance obligations of the parties.
   c. It must never occur or else the contract is void.
   d. It will occur in the future.

EXPLAIN YOURSELF

All answers should be written in complete sentences. A simple "yes" or "no" is insufficient.

1. Describe the difference between a covenant and a condition.

2. Must conditions always be in writing to ensure that they are carried out?

3. Explain the differences between conditions precedent, conditions concurrent, and conditions subsequent.

4. When does the contract itself come into existence when there are conditions precedent?

5. Write an example of a condition that is implied in fact.

6. Write an example of a condition that is implied in law.

7. May a party prevent the occurrence of a condition to avoid his performance obligations? Why or why not?

"FAULTY PHRASES"

All of the following statements are FALSE; state why they are false and then rewrite them as a true statement. Write a brief fact pattern that illustrates your answer.

1. A condition that is "concurrent" is one that is equally important as all the other performance obligations in the contract.

2. If an event is uncertain to occur, it cannot be incorporated into the contract as a condition.

3. A failure of a condition means that the party is in breach of the contract and forfeits his performance to the non-breaching party.

4. An implied in law condition means that the judge can make the parties do whatever he sees fit; the discretion of the court is unconstrained.

5. If there are no conditions relating to a "time for performance" under the contract, the parties can take however long they choose.

"WRITE" AWAY! PORTFOLIO ASSIGNMENT

Construction contracts are never simple. Review your proposed contract between Druid and Carrie. Have you included conditions that both parties are bound to satisfy in connection with the construction? Think about the following when making your changes to the contract:

1. Financing
2. Ordering supplies
3. Getting approvals
4. Timely performance
5. Inspections
6. Change orders (modifications during the progress of the work)
7. Insurance and risk of losses

Case in Point   CONDITIONS

**HOUSTON INDEPENDENT SCHOOL DISTRICT and Michael WILLIAMS,
Successor to Robert Scott, Commissioner of Education, Appellants**
v.
Reginald SIMPSON, Appellee
NO. 03-12-00145-CV
Texas Court of Appeals, Third District, at Austin
Filed: November 1, 2013
From the District Court of Travis County, 353rd Judicial District
NO. D-1-GN-11-001924, Honorable Tim Sulak, Judge Presiding

MEMORANDUM OPINION

This administrative appeal arises from a dispute between appellee Reginald Simpson and his former employer, the Houston Independent School District (the District), in which Simpson contends that the District improperly denied his employment contract. After pursuing relief through the District's grievance process, Simpson sought administrative review of the District's decision before the Texas Commissioner of Education. See Tex. Educ. Code § 7.057(a) (providing for appeal of certain actions or decisions of any school district board of trustees). The Commissioner determined that there was no written employment contract between Simpson and the District and consequently dismissed Simpson's appeal for lack of jurisdiction. Simpson then brought suit in district court for judicial review of the Commissioner's decision. See id. § 7.057(d) (providing for appeal of decisions of Commissioner in district court). The district court reversed the Commissioner's jurisdictional ruling and remanded the cause to the Commissioner for further proceedings. On appeal,

Page 2

the District and the Commissioner assert that the trial court improperly reversed the Commissioner's decision.[1] We will affirm the district court's judgment.

BACKGROUND

Most of the background facts relevant to the issues in this appeal are undisputed. Simpson was employed by the District as a certified educator from 1999 to May 2007, when he voluntarily resigned to pursue other career opportunities.[2] In August 2007, Simpson reapplied for employment with the District. As part of the application process, the District gave Simpson the following document:

TO: HISD Employment Applicant

FROM: Beatrice G. Garza, Executive General Manager, Human Resources

RE: Memorandum of Understanding Regarding Employment on a Contingency Basis

This letter is to inform all [District] applicants that [the District] is offering you employment at this time contingent upon satisfactory results of the required local criminal background check. However, if the result of the state and national search are [sic] unacceptable, your employment may be terminated.

Your signature on this Memorandum of Understanding constitutes your agreement that you understand the conditional nature of your employment, and that your failure to fully disclose

---

[1]While the Commissioner and the District each filed a notice of appeal and brief on the same issues, we will refer to the appellants collectively as "the District."

[2]According to Simpson, at the time he resigned, he was reassured by both his principal and a representative from the District's human resources office that he would be eligible for rehire.

all criminal history records may terminate your employment with the district.

Page 3

Both Simpson and an official from the District signed the document. A week later, a human resources employee with the District gave Simpson an electronically pre-signed One-Year Employee Probationary Contract (Employee Contract), which Simpson signed and returned the same day. However, according to the District, Simpson had been issued the Employee Contract in error, and the District informed Simpson of this error the next day. The District also later told Simpson that "his criminal record precludes employment with the [District]."[3]

Simpson subsequently filed a grievance with the District's administration, alleging that his contract had been improperly denied and requesting a formal hearing. At the conclusion of the District's grievance process, including several evidentiary hearings, the District Board of Education (the Board) denied Simpson's grievance.[4] Simpson appealed the District's decision to the Commissioner pursuant to section 7.057(a)(2)(B) of the Texas Education Code.

In his petition to the Commissioner, Simpson recited the facts above and asserted that the District's "effort to invalidate [his] fully executed 2007-08 probationary teacher contract constitutes a breach of [his] contract, which causes him financial harm." Simpson's appeal was

---

[3]Prior to his employment with the District in 1999, Simpson disclosed that he had received deferred adjudication for felony theft in 1985. According to the District, under its then-existing policy, it granted Simpson a waiver that allowed him to be employed up until his resignation in 2007, despite this criminal history.

[4]The District has a three-tiered complaint system. At the final stage, the "level III grievance" decision is made by the Board. In this case, following the presentation of Simpson's grievance, and the arguments of the parties, the Board deferred to the District Superintendent to make the final decision on Simpson's grievance. On October 22, 2008, the Superintendent notified Simpson by letter that "based on the arguments presented to the board, the unique circumstances in this case, and the board's authorization to disregard the twenty-plus year old felony conviction, I have decided to grant Mr. Simpson eligibility for rehire in the [District]." However, the Superintendent also notified Simpson that his request for "back pay and all other relief" was denied.

Page 4

assigned to an administrative law judge (ALJ). After "considering the record and matters officially noticed," the ALJ issued a proposal for decision, concluding that the Commissioner lacked jurisdiction over the cause under section 7.057(a)(2)(B).

Upon considering the local record (developed through the District's grievance process) and the ALJ's proposal for decision, the Commissioner determined that (1) Simpson's employment contract was contingent on a satisfactory background check, (2) this requirement served as a condition precedent, and (3) because that condition was not met, the parties had not entered into a contract for employment for the 2007-2008 school year. Similarly, the Commissioner determined that (1) "the belief of both parties that [Simpson's] criminal history had been inspected, approved, and would not prohibit his employment was a mutual mistake," (2) "because [the District] promptly informed [Simpson] of the error and did not indicate an intention to affirm the contract, [the District] did not lose its ability to avoid the contract for mutual mistake," and (3) "due to mutual mistake, the parties did not enter into a contract for employment for the 2007-2008 school year." Concluding that the parties had not entered into a "written employment contract," the Commissioner determined that Simpson's grievance did not satisfy the jurisdictional requirements of section 7.057 of the Education Code. As a result, the Commissioner dismissed the cause for lack of jurisdiction.

Simpson filed suit in Travis County district court. After admitting the administrative record, the district court concluded that "[t]he Commissioner erred as a matter of law in holding that he did not have jurisdiction to hear [Simpson's] appeal." The district court remanded the case to the Commissioner for further action.

Page 5

STANDARD OF REVIEW

In deciding cases under his jurisdiction, the Commissioner is required to "issue a decision based on a review of the record developed at the district level under a substantial evidence standard of review." Tex. Educ. Code § 7.057(c). Similarly, on appeal, we review the judgment of the district court regarding the factual determinations of the Commissioner under a substantial-evidence standard. *Tijerina v. Alanis,* 80 S.W.3d 292, 295 (Tex. App.—Austin 2002, pet. denied).[5] Under this standard, the findings, inferences, conclusions, and decisions of the Commissioner are presumed to be supported by substantial evidence, and the burden is on the contestant to prove otherwise. *See id.* at 295 n.5. We determine whether the evidence as a whole is such that reasonable minds could have reached the same conclusion as the Commissioner in the disputed action. *See id.* On the other hand, the Commissioner's resolution of legal questions, unlike factual determinations, are not entitled to a presumption of validity and are reviewed de novo. *Weslaco Fed'n of Teachers v. Texas Educ. Agency,* 27 S.W.3d 258, 263-64 (Tex. App.—Austin 2000, no pet.).

In this case, the Commissioner determined that the dispute between the District and Simpson fell outside of his subject-matter jurisdiction. When reviewing the Commissioner's decision with respect to jurisdiction, we employ the same standard of review used when reviewing a trial court's order dismissing a cause for want of jurisdiction. *Tijerina,* 80 S.W.3d at 295. Where, as

Page 6

here, the Commissioner makes fact findings necessary to resolve the jurisdictional issue based on an evidentiary record developed through an adjudicative process, we review those fact findings under the substantial-evidence standard. *See id.* (noting that "substantial-evidence review may be appropriate when examining the Commissioner's decisions based on evidence relevant to jurisdiction"). To the extent the jurisdictional inquiry turns on an interpretation of the Education Code, we will defer to the Commissioner's interpretation of that statute, to the

---

[5]Because whether the Commissioner's order satisfies the substantial-evidence standard is a question of law, the district court's judgment is not entitled to deference on appeal. *Heritage on the San Gabriel Homeowners Ass'n v. Texas Comm'n on Envtl. Quality,* 393 S.W.3d 417, 424 (Tex. App.—Austin 2012, pet. denied); *see Texas Dep't of Pub. Safety v. Alford,* 209 S.W.3d 101, 103 (Tex. 2006) (per curiam). On appeal from the district court's judgment, the focus of the appellate review, as in the district court, is on the agency's decision. *Heritage,* 393 S.W.3d at 424.

extent it is ambiguous, if the interpretation is reasonable and does not contradict the plain language of the statute. *Tijerina,* 80 S.W.3d at 295; *see also Combs v. Health Care Servs. Corp.,* 401 S.W.3d 623, 630 (Tex. 2013) (explaining that ambiguity is "a precondition to agency deference").

ANALYSIS

Section 7.057 of the Education Code governs appeals from a local school district to the Commissioner. Subsection (a) defines the Commissioner's jurisdiction and provides:

(a)   [A] person may appeal in writing to the Commissioner if the person is aggrieved by:

(1)   the school laws of this state; or

(2)   actions or decisions of any school district board of trustees that violate:

     (A)   the school laws of this state; or

     (B)   a provision of a *written employment contract* between the school district and a school district employee, if a violation causes or would cause monetary harm to the employee.

Page 7

Tex. Educ. Code § 7.057(a) (emphasis added). Under this standard, the Commissioner examines the record developed below to determine whether the District's decision resulted from a prejudicial error of law, such as an abuse of discretion, an action taken in excess of authority, a violation of law, or fact findings that are unreasonable in light of the evidence found in the record of proceedings before the school board. *Ysleta Indep. Sch. Dist. v. Meno,* 933 S.W.2d 748, 751 n.5 (Tex. App.—Austin 1996, writ denied).

Here, in both proceedings, the Commissioner and the district court interpreted the Employee Contract and determined whether, as a threshold matter, the dispute fell within the Commission's jurisdiction under section 7.057(a)(2)(B). In determining that it did not, the Commissioner reasoned that (1) the existence of a valid "written employment contract" between the parties was a fact, the existence of which was necessary to confer jurisdiction under section 7.057(a)(2)(B), and (2) no such contract existed in this case because (a) "no contract was formed because a condition precedent was never met," and (b) alternatively, "a mutual mistake of fact by the parties shows that there was no meeting of the minds." Thus, the Commissioner necessarily interpreted the term "written employment contract" in section 7.057(a)(2)(B) to require the formation of a valid written contract. On appeal, the parties do not dispute whether the Commissioner's interpretation of section 7.057(a) is correct.[6] Assuming without deciding that the Commissioner's interpretation is correct, the resolution of this appeal turns on whether there was a "written

Page 8

employment contract" formed between Simpson and the District under section 7.057(a)(2)(B), as interpreted by the Commissioner.[7]

Under Texas law, to establish contract formation a party must prove, among other elements, an offer and acceptance and a meeting of the minds on all essential terms. *Principal Life Ins. Co. v. Revalen Dev., LLC,* 358 S.W.3d 451, 454-55 (Tex. App.—Dallas 2012, pet. denied). To create an enforceable contract, the minds of the parties must meet with respect to the subject matter of the agreement and all its essential terms. *Id.* In three issues on appeal, the District argues that the Commissioner correctly concluded that no written employment contract was formed between the parties and consequently that he had no jurisdiction. First, the District contends that the Commissioner correctly determined that obtaining satisfactory results from Simpson's background check served as an unfulfilled condition precedent to the formation of an employment contract between the District and Simpson. Second, the District contends that the record contains substantial

evidence of mutual mistake. Finally, the District argues that the record contains substantial evidence that the District's criminal-history policy restriction was not waived.

Condition Precedent

Turning to the District's first issue on appeal, we consider whether the district court erred in failing to affirm the Commissioner's ruling on the ground that Simpson's satisfactory criminal background check served as an unfulfilled condition precedent to the formation of a

Page 9

contract between the parties. A condition precedent is an event that must happen or be performed before a duty of immediate performance of a promise arises. *Hohenberg Bros. Co. v. George E. Gibbons & Co.,* 537 S.W.2d 1, 3 (Tex. 1976). There are two types of conditions precedent. *See Dillon v. Lintz,* 582 S.W.2d 394, 395 (Tex. 1979) ("A condition precedent may be either a condition to the formation of a contract or to an obligation to perform an existing agreement. Conditions may, therefore, relate either to the formation of contracts or to liability under them."); *Pearson v. Fullingim,* No. 03-03-00524-CV, 2006 Tex. App. LEXIS 1346, at *15 (Tex. App.—Austin Feb. 17, 2006, no pet.) (mem. op.). The first type is a condition precedent to the formation of a contract. *See Lintz,* 582 S.W.2d at 395. If the parties have agreed that a contract will not be effective or binding until certain conditions occur, no binding contract will arise until the conditions specified have occurred. *Parkview Gen. Hosp. v. Eppes,* 447 S.W.2d 487, 490-91 (Tex. Civ. App.—Corpus Christi 1969, writ ref'd n.r.e.). The second type of condition precedent is a condition to an obligation to perform an existing agreement. *See Lintz,* 582 S.W.2d at 395. Conditions precedent to an obligation to perform are those acts or events that must occur after the making of a contract before there is a right to immediate performance and before there is a breach of contractual duties. *Hohenberg Bros. Co.,* 537 S.W.2d at 3.

Here, it is undisputed that Simpson's background check revealed a criminal history that, under district policy at the time, was considered unacceptable. Thus, the issue is whether the parties intended for a criminal background check, conducted with

---

[6]"While the Commissioner's interpretation of his jurisdiction under section 7.057(a) is not controlling, it does merit serious consideration if it is reasonable and does not contradict the plain language of the statute." *Smith v. Nelson,* 53 S.W.3d 792, 795 (Tex. App.—Austin 2001, pet. denied) (citing *Dodd v. Meno,* 870 S.W.2d 4, 7 (Tex. 1994)).

[7]Simpson does not allege that any action or decision by the Board of Trustees violated the school laws of this state. *See* Tex. Educ. Code § 7.057(a)(2)(A). There is no dispute that, if the Commissioner has jurisdiction over Simpson's grievance, it would be pursuant to section 7.057(a)(2)(B).

satisfactory results, to act as a condition precedent to the formation of their contractual relationship. *See Parkview Gen. Hosp.,* 447 S.W.2d at 491 ("When liability on the contract depends on the performance or a happening of a

Page 10

condition precedent, the plaintiff must allege and prove that the condition has happened or has been performed or that there was a waiver of the performance of the condition precedent.").

Whether the parties intended to enter into a binding agreement is generally a question of fact. *Sadeghi v. Gang,* 270 S.W.3d 773, 776 (Tex. App.—Dallas 2008, no pet.). Likewise, whether the parties intended to create a contract only upon the satisfaction of a condition precedent is generally a question of fact. *Foreca, S.A. v. GRD Dev. Co.,* 758 S.W.2d 744, 746 (Tex. 1988). However, where the intent to form a binding agreement is clear on the face of an unambiguous writing, the issue may be determined as a matter of law. *Columbia Gas Transmission Corp. v. New Ulm Gas, Ltd.,* 940 S.W.2d 587, 589 (Tex. 1996); *John Wood Grp. USA, Inc. v. ICO,* 26 S.W.3d 12, 16 (Tex. App.—Houston [1st Dist.] 2000, pet. denied); *see Insurance Corp. of Am. v. Webster,* 906 S.W.2d 77, 80-81 (Tex. App.—Houston [1st Dist.] 1995, writ denied) ("The construction of an unambiguous writing is a question of law."). Whether a writing is ambiguous is also a question of law. *David J. Sacks, P.C. v. Haden,* 266 S.W.3d 447, 451 (Tex. 2008).

Here, the District argues that the Commissioner correctly determined that the Employee Contract and the Memorandum of Understanding created a condition precedent to the formation of an employment contract. Neither party argues that the Memorandum of Understanding or the Employee Contract is ambiguous. However, Simpson argues that the Memorandum of Understanding fails to create a condition precedent because the Memorandum of Understanding was not incorporated into the later-executed Employee Contract. We take Simpson's argument to mean that because the Memorandum of Understanding was not a part of the Employee Contract, any consideration of the Memorandum of Understanding in determining the intent of the parties is barred by the parol-evidence rule and the merger doctrine.

Page 11

Under the parol-evidence rule, extrinsic evidence is inadmissible to add to, vary, or contradict the terms of an unambiguous written contract intended by the parties to be a final expression of their agreement. *See In re H.E. Butt Grocery Co.,* 17 S.W.3d 360, 369 (Tex. App.—Houston [14th Dist.] 2000, orig. proceeding) ("The parol evidence rule precludes consideration of extrinsic evidence to contradict, vary, or add to the terms of an unambiguous written agreement absent fraud, accident, or mistake."). Similarly, in contract cases, the "merger doctrine" acts as an analogue of the parol evidence rule. *Texas A & M Univ. v. Lawson,* 127 S.W.3d 866, 872 (Tex. App.—Austin 2004, pet. denied). Under the merger doctrine, prior or contemporaneous agreements between the same parties and concerning the same subject matter are absorbed, or "merged," into another subsequent contract. *Id.* When the parties have concluded a fully integrated written agreement, parol evidence of prior or contemporaneous agreements is inadmissible if it will vary or contradict the terms of the agreement, provided that the writing is unambiguous. *David J. Sacks, P.C.,* 266 S.W.3d at 450-51; *Carr v. Christie,* 970 S.W.2d 620, 622 n. 2 (Tex. App.—Austin 1998, pet. denied).

However, parol evidence is always admissible to show the nonexistence of a contract or the conditions upon which it may become effective. *Rincones v. Windberg,* 705 S.W.2d 846, 847 (Tex. App.—Austin 1986, no writ) (citing *Baker v. Baker,* 183 S.W.2d 724, 728 (1944)). "The effect of such a condition 'is not to vary the terms of a binding instrument but merely, as a condition precedent, to postpone the effective date of the instrument until the happening of a contingency. . . .'" *Id.* Consequently, a writing evidencing an intent to create a condition precedent to contract formation is admissible for this purpose, even when it is separate and apart from the written document for which enforcement is sought. *See id.* ("It is settled that parol evidence of a condition precedent

Page 12

to a contract is admissible."). We will therefore consider the language of the Memorandum of Understanding.

Turning to the plain language of the Memorandum of Understanding, we examine whether it evidences the parties' intent to create a condition precedent to formation of a binding contract. In determining whether the District and Simpson unambiguously intended to create a condition precedent, we recognize that, because of their potential harshness, conditions precedent are disfavored. *Criswell v. European Crossroads Shopping Ctr., Ltd.,* 792 S.W.2d 945, 948 (Tex. 1990). "Although no particular words are necessary for the existence of a condition, such terms as 'if,' 'provided that,' 'on condition that,' or some other phrases that conditions performance, usually connote an intent for a condition rather than a promise." *Id.; Snyder v. Eanes Indep. Sch. Dist.,* 860 S.W.2d 692, 696 (Tex. App.—Austin 1993, writ denied).

While not singularly determinative, we note that the Memorandum of Understanding contains language that is generally indicative of intent to create a condition precedent. The Memorandum of Understanding, given to Simpson as a District "Employment Applicant" prior to his receiving a written offer of employment, states that "[the District] is offering you employment at this time *contingent* upon satisfactory results of the required local criminal background check." (Emphasis added). The document also states, "[Y]ou understand the *conditional* nature of your employment." (Emphasis added). Based on the plain language of the Memorandum of Understanding, we conclude that the document unambiguously evidences the parties' intent to create a condition precedent—that is, the District's obtaining of acceptable results from a criminal background check. This conclusion, however, does not end our inquiry. Instead, we must decide whether the condition

Page 13

precedent in the Memorandum of Understanding creates a condition precedent to formation of a contract or to obligations to perform under an existing contract. *See Dillon,* 582 S.W.2d at 395 (explaining that condition precedent may be either condition to formation of contract or to obligation to perform existing agreement).

The District contends that the Memorandum of Understanding demonstrates that the parties intended for any offer of employment by the District to be contingent

on the obtaining of a satisfactory criminal background check and thus creates a condition precedent to contract formation. However, nothing in the Memorandum of Understanding suggests that any *offer* of employment to Simpson is contingent. Instead, the Memorandum of Understanding states that "*employment* at this time" is contingent. (Emphasis added). In addition, the Memorandum of Understanding makes clear that termination of Simpson's employment could result if either (1) the criminal background check results are unacceptable or (2) Simpson fails to fully disclose all criminal history. Simpson contends, and we agree, that the Memorandum of Understanding provides that if a subsequent criminal background check proved unacceptable, one of two things would occur—(1) the District would not offer a formal employment contract, or (2) if a formal employment contract was offered and executed, as it was here, the unacceptable background check would then serve as basis for termination. In other words, under the Memorandum of Understanding, if the condition precedent of an acceptable background check is not satisfied, the District is relieved from its obligation to continue to pay and employ Simpson. Upon considering the language of the Memorandum of Understanding, viewed as a whole, we conclude that it clearly and unambiguously evidences the

Page 14

parties' intent to create a condition precedent to the District's *obligations* under the contract, rather than to its formation.

In addition, the District argues that the Employee Contract itself demonstrates that the parties intended to create a condition precedent to formation of a contract. Specifically, the District points to conditional language in the Employee Contract:

> 5. . . . This Contract is specifically subject to the policies, procedures, Standard Practice Memoranda (S.M.), rules, and regulations of the District as they exist or may be amended issued, enacted or adopted during the term of this Contract.
> 6. This Contract is conditioned on the Employee providing the necessary certification, credentials, official transcripts, original service records, medical records, and/or other records and information required by law, . . . or the District.

Assuming that this language contemplates an acceptable criminal background check as a condition precedent, we again would conclude that, at the most, the Employee Contract evidences the parties' intent to establish a condition precedent to the District's continued obligations under the contract, not to the formation of the Employee Contract itself.

Whether the District may be excused from its obligations under the Employment Contract by virtue of an unfulfilled condition precedent has no bearing on whether a valid contract between the District and Simpson was formed—the sole jurisdictional fact at issue. *See* Restatement (Second) of Contracts § 225 (1981) (explaining effects of non-occurrence of condition). We conclude, as a matter of law, that the Memorandum of Understanding and the Employee Contract do not indicate that the parties intended to create a condition precedent to the formation of an

Page 15

employment contract.[8] The District does not point to any other evidence in the administrative record as indicative of such intent; upon review of the record, we conclude that there is no such evidence. Accordingly, the Commissioner erred in dismissing Simpson's grievance for lack of jurisdiction on this basis. The District's first issue on appeal is overruled.

Mutual Mistake

In its second issue on appeal, the District argues that the trial court erred in reversing the Commissioner's jurisdictional determination because the record contains substantial evidence of mutual mistake of fact. A contract is voidable under the doctrine of mutual mistake if the parties formed the contract under a mutual misconception or mistake of a material fact. *Myra Props., Inc. v. La Salle Bank Nat'l Ass'n,* 300 S.W.3d 746, 751 (Tex. 2009). Because the issue is one of

voidability, the contract continues to have legal effect and bind the parties until the mutual mistake is judicially established by one of the parties. Restatement (Second) of Contracts § 7 (1981) (explaining voidable contracts). In contrast, when a contract is void, no one is bound, and in effect, no contract has been formed. *See id.* § 7, cmt. a (explaining void contracts); *see also id.* § 163 (when misrepresentation prevents formation of a contract), § 174 (when duress by physical compulsion prevents formation of contract).

Page 16

Even if the Commissioner correctly determined that the Employee Contract is voidable for mutual mistake, we could not conclude on this basis that the parties failed to form a contract. Whether the parties formed a contract is the only jurisdictional issue before us; therefore, we need not decide whether there is substantial evidence to support the Commissioner's conclusion that the Employee Contract was the result of mutual mistake. We conclude that, even if there is substantial evidence to support mutual mistake in this case, the Commissioner erred in dismissing for lack of jurisdiction on this basis. We overrule the District's second issue on appeal.

CONCLUSION

Because the Commissioner's finding that no valid contract was formed between Simpson and the District is not supported by substantial evidence, we conclude that the Commissioner erred in determining that he lacked jurisdiction over Simpson's grievance. We affirm the judgment of the trial court.

Scott K. Field, Justice

Before Justices Puryear, Pemberton and Field

Affirmed

---

[8]Likewise, whether any condition precedent to the District's continued obligations under the Employee Contract has been waived has no bearing on whether a valid contract between Simpson and the District was formed. *See, e.g., Sun Exploration Co. v. Benton,* 728 S.W.2d 35, 37 (Tex. 1987) (explaining that "a condition precedent may be waived" and that "the waiver of a condition precedent may be inferred from a party's conduct"). Accordingly, we need not decide the District's third issue on appeal—whether substantial evidence supports the Commissioner's determination that the criminal history requirement had not been waived.

Chapter 5

Third-Party Interests

This chapter will explore WHO, outside of the contracting parties, may have an interest in the agreement, HOW their interests are created and perfected, and WHAT effect they have on the performance obligations in the agreement. The offeror and offeree may intend at the time they make the agreement for the performance of the contractual obligations to benefit another person who is not a party to the contract. Parties may later wish to change who is responsible for the contractual obligations. If parties desire to "step out" of the agreement and substitute other persons in their place, they may either delegate their duties to perform or assign their rights.

Until now, we have been speaking of only two parties, the offeror and the offeree; those who have a direct stake in the contract and its formation. It is time to introduce another player who has a stake in the performance of the contract, although not its formation.

third-party beneficiary
A person, not a party to the contract, who stands to receive the benefit of performance of the contract.

privity
A relationship between the parties to the contract who have rights and obligations to each other through the terms of the agreement.

promisor
The party who makes a promise to perform under the contract.

promisee
The party to whom the promise of performance is made.

Let's first look at some vocabulary. A **third-party beneficiary** is a person (or entity) who stands to gain from the performance of the contract but who is not a direct party in the contract, either the offeror or offeree. In essence, the contract was made to confer some benefit onto a party who is not in **privity** to the contract. Parties are said to be in privity if they are involved in the actual making of the contract with enforceable rights. The parties in privity to the contract are the **promisor**, the person who will bestow the benefit upon the third party, and the **promisee**, the person obligating himself to the promisor. Notice in these agreements the terms *offeror* and *offeree* are replaced by *promisor* and *promisee*.

TYPES OF THIRD-PARTY INTERESTS

Classic examples of third-party contracts are wills and insurance policies. Wills are essentially contracts between the testator, the person writing the will, and the state where the testator lives. The state, the promisor, agrees to dispose of the deceased person's possessions as the testator, the promisee, has directed, and the testator benefits from the certainty of having these assets divided among her loved ones—the third-party beneficiaries. The same logic follows with respect to insurance policies as third-party contracts.

> **Example**
> Your Great Aunt Betty Bigbucks writes her will leaving the bulk of her estate to you because she is so proud of your accomplishments in your paralegal classes. After she passes, the will is submitted to the probate court, or other judicial body charged with the function of establishing the validity of a will, which is charged with establishing its validity and overseeing its proper administration. The parties to this "agreement" are your aunt and the state; the consideration is the payment of estate taxes and administrative fees for the state's assurance that the named persons in the will shall receive what your aunt gave to them. You are not a party to this "agreement," but your aunt wanted you to receive the end result of the performance of the contract. You have right and title to her possessions as a third-party beneficiary of the will.

The same scenario would play out if the agreement related to an insurance contract that your aunt took out naming you as the beneficiary.

Why are we discussing third-party interests in the first section of the text? In order to be considered valid third-party beneficiaries, the contract must have named them in the formative stage. The parties must, *at the time of contract*, intend to benefit the third party. This element is critical as it defines the third-party beneficiary contract. If a party does benefit from the contract but was not intended to benefit (it was just serendipitous that the third party happened to gain something from the transaction), he is considered an **incidental benefi-ciary** and does not have any enforceable rights under the contract.

incidental beneficiaries
Persons who may derive some benefit from the performance of a contract but who were not intended to directly benefit from the performance.

Example

Intended beneficiaries. (This example is based loosely on *Biddle v. BAA Indianapolis, LLC*, 830 N.E.2d 76 (Ind. Ct. App. 2005).) Mr. & Mrs. Quincy enjoy spending quiet time together. They recently bought a home near the city airport. In the contract for sale, the sellers included a document entitled "Noise Disclosure Statement" that put the Quincys on notice that there were noise disturbances from the operation of the airport and that the Quincys were taking the property with knowledge and acceptance of this fact. The sellers also disclosed that the airport had paid them a sum of money (10 percent of the sales price) for making that disclosure to the buyers. After the Quincys moved in, they soon discovered that the noise level was far more than they could take and decided to sue the airport for the noise disturbances, stating that it was depriving them of the value of their property. The airport claimed that it was a third-party beneficiary of the sales contract between the Quincys and the sellers, although it was not named as such. Is this possible? . . .

Yes, the court found that "one need not perform any mental gymnastics to deduce that the [Disclosure Statement] was included to protect the [Airport] from claims arising from the noise. Thus, we conclude that the **intent** of the agreement was that the [Buyers] would not seek compensation from the Airport because of the noise disturbances." *Id.* at 87 (emphasis added).

intent
Having the knowledge and desire that a specific consequence will result from an action.

Example

Incidental beneficiaries. (This example is based loosely on *Scott v. Mamari Corp.*, 530 S.E.2d 208 (Ga. App. 2000).) Ken Cabinet-Maker recently finished his installation of new custom maple cabinetry in Rob Remodeler's kitchen pursuant to their renovation contract. Rob had taken out a home equity line of credit at Local Bank for this kitchen makeover. In particular, he made an application for extension of credit in the amount of $25,000, the amount based on Ken's job estimate for the cabinets. Rob failed to pay Ken for his work, so Ken sued Local Bank for the money, stating that he was a third-party beneficiary under the contract. The court found that the loan/credit agreement "represented promises by the [homeowner] to repay the Bank and not promises by the Bank to do anything for [the contractor]." Generally, the intent to pay another third party with the loaned money does not create a beneficiary interest. There are a few cases in the nation that do give a contractor or subcontractor third-party beneficiary rights under a construction agreement in limited circumstances where justice requires, particularly where some negligence was involved.

EYE ON ETHICS

ETHICS

Conflicts of interest may occur where an attorney is providing services to two related parties, the obligor and the third-party beneficiary. This occurs often in insurance cases where the attorney represents the insurance company as the party paying the bill and the insured as the actual party represented in that particular litigation. What happens when the interests of the insurance company and the insured are not the same? To whom does the attorney owe his loyalty?

The general rule is:

A lawyer retained by a liability insurance carrier to defend a claim against the company's insured must represent the insured with undivided fidelity. For purposes of this opinion, that retention does not create an attorney-client relationship between the lawyer and the carrier. . . . [T]he insured is the client to whom the lawyer's duty of loyalty is owed.

Weitz Co., LLC v. Ohio Cas. Ins. Co., Civil Action No. 11-cv-00694-REB-BNB, page 4 (D. Colo. 2011), *citing* Colorado Formal Ethics Opinion 91 (January 16, 1993) (Opposing counsel attempted to have the insurance company attorneys disqualified under a "conflict of interest" standard arguing that they have "an attorney-client relationship not only with the insured, but also with the insurance company." Based on well-established law not only in Colorado but also across the country, this action was unsuccessful.).

However, lawyers have continued to struggle with this "third-party beneficiary" of their retainer agreement with the insurance companies where the course of the litigation/settlement does not run smoothly. *See Representing Insurance Carrier and Uncooperative Insured,* North Carolina State Bar, 99 Formal Ethics Opinion 14, approved January 21, 2000.

Opinion rules that when an insured fails to cooperate with the defense, as required by the insurance contract, the insurance defense lawyer may follow the instructions of the insurance carrier unless the insured's lack of cooperation interferes with the defense or presenting an effective defense is harmful to the interests of the insured.

Inquiry #1:

Mr. and Ms. Inlaw were passengers in an automobile being driven by their daughter-in-law, Defendant, when an accident occurred. Mr. and Ms. Inlaw were both injured and brought an action against Defendant for their damages. Insurance Company assigned Attorney D to represent Defendant in the action. Defendant is either an insured under Insurance Company's liability insurance policy or is a third-party beneficiary of the policy.

The insurance policy provides that Insurance Company has the right to defend the action and to settle the lawsuit as it deems appropriate. The policy specifically requires Defendant to cooperate with Insurance Company in the defense of the lawsuit.

Insurance Company wants Attorney D to defend the suit to avoid or minimize the damages paid to the Inlaws. Defendant does not want a defense of the lawsuit that will jeopardize the Inlaws' recovery from Insurance Company.

May Attorney D defend the lawsuit effectively, as requested by Insurance Company, against the explicit instructions of Defendant?

Opinion #1:

A lawyer who is hired by an insurance carrier to defend one of its insureds (or a third-party beneficiary) represents both the insurer and the insured (or third-party beneficiary). See RPC 91, RPC 103, and RPC 172. However, when the insured has contractually surrendered control of the defense and of the authority to settle the lawsuit to the insurance carrier, the defense lawyer is generally obliged to accept the instructions of the insurance carrier in these matters. RPC 91.

Attorney D should advise Defendant of the conditions of representation set forth in the insurance policy and should encourage Defendant to consult with independent legal counsel as to the legal consequences of her failure to cooperate with the defense of the lawsuit.

Attorney D should also inform Defendant that he cannot represent her in a coverage dispute with Insurance Company because it would be a conflict of interest. Rule 1.7(a). He must advise her to employ independent legal counsel to provide representation in a coverage dispute. RPC 91.

If Defendant insists that Attorney D limit his defense, Attorney D must determine whether Defendant's lack of cooperation will interfere with his independent professional judgment. If so, he may seek to withdraw from the representation of both parties. Rule 1.7(b).

Reprinted with the permission of the North Carolina State Bar.

RIGHT TO SUE

Another important element of the third-party contract is the fact that the third party has legally enforceable rights under the contract and, although not a party to the transaction, can sue for its enforcement. A beneficiary under a life insurance contract may sue to enforce the performance (payment) of the policy if the insurance company fails to pay a valid claim. Additionally, the original promisee retains the right to sue for enforcement for the benefit of the third party. Of course, that's not possible in the wills and life insurance contract situations where the promisee, as a condition precedent of the promisor's performance, has died!

There are essentially two categories of third-party beneficiaries: **creditors** and **donees**. The RESTATEMENT (SECOND) OF CONTRACTS has deemphasized the distinction between these two types of beneficiaries; instead, the emphasis is placed on the fact that both are *intended* beneficiaries. This underscores the importance of the intent at the time of formation of the contract. If the third party does benefit from the contract, but the parties to the contract had no intention of benefiting that party, she is an *incidental beneficiary* and has no rights under the contract.

In a *third-party creditor beneficiary contract*, the promisor agrees to pay a debt owed by the promisee. The party receiving the payment is the third-party

creditor
A party to whom a debt is owed.

donee
A party to whom a gift is given.

creditor. By way of example, your boss agrees to pay off your MasterCard® balance so that you will have enough of a credit line to buy some appropriate suits for work. Your boss is the promisor, you are the promisee (the party with the previous obligation to pay), and MasterCard® is the third-party creditor beneficiary.

The other, and more common, type of beneficiary is the *donee*. A donee receives a *gift* as a result of the transaction. The promisor confers a benefit on the donee at the request of the promisee. Again, it is easy to refer to wills: The donees are the heirs of the estate; they receive their inheritance as a gift from the testator (promisee) through the state's probate system (promisor).

SPOT THE ISSUE!

Aaron is the managing partner of a midsize law firm. In order to compete with the larger firms, he decides to upgrade all the computers and legal software. Aaron contracts with Benjamin to perform these services. Benjamin, realizing he will need help, forms an agreement with Carla wherein Benjamin will pay her as he is paid by Aaron. Both Benjamin and Carla work onsite for the next two months. After Benjamin completes one-third of the project, Aaron terminates the contract due to Benjamin's poor performance and delay. Carla has not been paid for her services, which were satisfactory, and she decides to sue Aaron based on her status as a third-party creditor beneficiary. Will she be successful? *See, e.g., Esposito v. True Color Enters. Constr. Inc.*, 45 So. 3d 554 (Fla. App. 2010).

All contracts can be canceled and/or modified according to their terms. However, there is an added complication in dealing with third-party beneficiaries. If the third-party beneficiary knows of and consents to the contract, the parties cannot cancel or modify the agreement without the beneficiary's consent. At the time the beneficiary learns of the agreement, her rights in the contract become **vested**. In a creditor situation, the beneficiary must expressly consent to the contract. Of course, a donee beneficiary is presumed to consent to the contract; everyone likes to get a gift! However, if the beneficiary does not want to receive the gift, she can refuse to accept it; this does not bear on whether the beneficiary had to originally consent to the contract at the time of its formation.

vested
Having a present right to receive the benefit of the performance when it becomes due.

SPOT THE ISSUE!

Jacob and John were the owners of Widget Works, Inc. They had been successful and wanted to retire and so sold all the stock in Widget Works, Inc., to Mark for $350,000 pursuant to the terms of a stock purchase agreement and a corresponding promissory note. Mark was to pay Jacob and John biannual payments along with 10 percent interest. Mark's payments were to be made directly to Jacob's checking account at First Bank. Mark eventually sold one-half of his stock in Widget Works to Paul and, in that agreement, Paul agreed to pay one-half of Mark's obligation to Jacob via First Bank. Who, if anyone, are the beneficiaries under these agreements? When have their rights vested, if at all? *See Olson v. Etheridge*, 686 N.E.2d 563 (Ill. 1997). *Olson* is a great case to demonstrate that while contract law is comprised of long-standing principles, they must not be blindly followed where modern practice diverges. The appellate court in *Olson* had relied on *Bay v. Williams*, 112 Ill. 91, 1 N.E. 340 (1884), as it was technically controlling precedent, but the concurring justice in his opinion "stated his belief that the Bay rule is antiquated and should be replaced by the modern approach as articulated in the RESTATEMENT (SECOND) OF CONTRACTS." *Olson*, at 566.

It has been established that a third-party beneficiary *can* sue for enforcement of the contract, but there is an issue as to *when* the right comes into being. After the beneficiary's interest is vested and performance is due from the promisor, the beneficiary can sue. *Who* can sue *whom*? Based on privity, both the promisee and promisor can sue each other. It should come as no surprise that the actual parties to any contract can sue for breach. Additionally, both the beneficiary and the promisee can sue the promisor if the promisor fails to bestow the benefit. However, the promisor cannot sue the third-party beneficiary as that party has no obligations with regard to the original obligations under the contract. The third-party beneficiary is merely the recipient of the performance with no other duty to discharge.

Example

Sylvia's parents have entered into an agreement with Curtis Construction to build a new home for her. Sylvia is directly referenced in the construction contract as the party with whom Curtis should consult regarding all design features. Sylvia's parents are merely footing the bill. After Sylvia moves in, she discovers many construction defects that affect the habitability of the home. Sylvia, as the intended third-party beneficiary of the contract, may sue Curtis for the defects. Additionally, her parents retain the right to sue Curtis for the defects as well. Alternately, if the final payment is not made, Curtis may sue Sylvia's parents because that is their duty as the promisee under the contract. However, Curtis may not sue Sylvia, the third-party beneficiary, for payment because she is under no legal duty under the contract to make payment.

The only instance where the beneficiary may sue the promisee is in the creditor situation. The creditor beneficiary may sue the promisee on the underlying debt that is the subject of the contract. As in the earlier example, MasterCard® can sue both you and your employer who promised to pay off the debt.

A donee beneficiary cannot sue the promisee; the donee beneficiary can only sue the promisor if the promisor fails to bestow the benefit. So Sylvia can sue Curtis for defects, but she cannot sue her parents for the final payment to be made to Curtis in the example above.

Along these same lines, once a lawsuit has been filed against the promisor, the promisor can **assert any defenses** that he would have if he were sued by the promisee. Here is a simple illustration using the insurance policy situation again: If the third-party beneficiary sues the insurance company for nonpayment of the benefit, the insurance company can assert that the promisee wrote bad checks and therefore the premiums were not paid. The defense really relates to the promisee's breach, but it can be asserted against the beneficiary even though the bad checks were not the fault or obligation of the beneficiary. *Any* defense available to the promisor as against the promisee may be asserted against the third-party beneficiary.

assertion of defenses
Either the original parties or a third-party beneficiary has the right to claim any legal defenses or excuses that they may have as against each other. They are not extinguished by a third party.

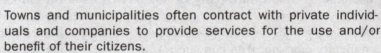

IN-CLASS DISCUSSION

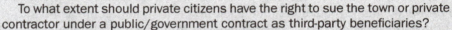

Towns and municipalities often contract with private individuals and companies to provide services for the use and/or benefit of their citizens.

To what extent should private citizens have the right to sue the town or private contractor under a public/government contract as third-party beneficiaries?

When are the citizens considered third-party beneficiaries with enforceable rights or merely incidental beneficiaries?

Contrast the results in these two cases:

McMurphy v. State, 757 A.2d 1043 (Vt. 2000).

Gorrell v. Greensboro Water-Supply Co., 32 S.E. 720 (N.C. 1899) (allowing recovery to third-party householder whose house was destroyed by fire as a result of breach of contract by the water company).

ASSIGNMENT/DELEGATION OF CONTRACTUAL RIGHTS AND OBLIGATIONS TO THIRD PARTIES

assignment
The transfer of the rights to receive the benefit of contractual performance under the contract.

delegation
The transfer of the duties/ obligations to perform under the contract.

If, at the time of making the contract, neither party contemplates that the consideration will flow to an outside party, that does not preclude such a transfer of rights and obligations. If the parties originally did not intend to benefit the third party, but rather decided to change the arrangement after the formation of the contract to include the third-party benefit, it is considered an **assignment**. If an original party who is obligated to perform is changed, it is considered a **delegation**. Either party, the offeror or offeree, may *assign their rights* to receive performance and/or *delegate their duties* to perform under the original contract to a new third party.

Since this is a new kind of relationship, there is some new vocabulary to go with it. The party who is stepping out of the transaction, so to speak, and giving his rights away is the **assignor**. The party stepping into the transaction and assuming the role vacated by the assignor is the **assignee**. The original party to the contract who remains in the contract is the **obligor**; that party is still obligated to perform.

Returning to the construction of Sylvia's new home: If Curtis owes a substantial amount of money to his sister, Claudia (she lent him money to get his construction company off the ground), Curtis, as the assignor, may assign his right to receive payment from Sylvia's parents to his sister. Sylvia's parents, the obligors, will then make payments directly to Claudia, the assignee.

The assignment scenario is most common in mortgages and other types of lines of credit. It is very common to apply for a mortgage through one company only to receive a letter a month later informing you, the mortgagor, that the mortgagee company has assigned its rights to collect your monthly payment to another company. You now write your checks to a company with whom you had no previous obligation nor with whom you had an intention to contract. Along with the assignment of the right to receive your payment goes the right to sue you if you do not pay.

In the converse situation, meaning that the duties to perform under the contract are transferred, the person delegating the duties is the **delegant** (also referred to, using the common suffix, as the **delegator**), and the person assuming the duties to be performed is the **delegate** (also referred to, using the common suffix, as the **delegatee**). The transfer of the obligations to perform is the *delegation*.

Returning to the construction of Sylvia's new home: If Curtis becomes unable to finish the work on Sylvia's home, he may contract with Zane's Zealous Construction Company to take over the job. Curtis has delegated his duties to perform and complete the construction to Zane, the delegate. Sylvia's parents remain obligors (obligated to pay under the original contract) and they now have a right to sue both Curtis and Zane if the job is not completed to the contract specifications.

The delegation scenario is commonly seen in subleases. The original tenant, the delegant, re-rents his apartment to another person, the assignee. The delegate (also known as the sublessee) steps into the shoes of the original tenant and owes the rent and any other obligations to the landlord, the obligor. Similar to beneficiaries, the delegate can sue the obligor and vice versa; the sublessee can sue the landlord if the apartment becomes uninhabitable and the landlord can sue both the original tenant as the delegant and the sublessee as the delegate. The delegation does not extinguish the delegant's liability under the contract.

Example

Chrissy, Jack, and Janet were the original tenants under the lease from the landlord, Mr. Roper. Chrissy, in an effort to find a better career opportunity, had to move. Terri, the delegate, moved in to take her place. Terri had to follow all of Mr. Roper's rules and pay Chrissy's part of the rent. Mr. Roper

assignor
The party who assigns his rights away and relinquishes his rights to collect the benefit of contractual performance.

assignee
The party to whom the right to receive contractual performance is transferred.

obligor
The original party to the contract who remains obligated to perform under the contract.

delegant/delegator
The party who transfers his obligation to perform his contractual obligations.

delegate/delegatee
The party to whom the obligation to perform the contractual obligations is transferred.

is the obligor; Terri owes him the obligations that she assumed under the delegation of the lease. If Terri fails to pay her share of the rent, Mr. Roper can sue both Terri and Chrissy for payment. Note that there was no new contract formed between Mr. Roper and Terri. If there had been a new contract formed or a novation of the existing contract, Chrissy would no longer be obligated under the original lease. (For a discussion of novation, see Chapter 12.)

The most important difference to remember between the two—assignment and delegation—is that an assignor usually is no longer liable under the contract, meaning that he is not party to a suit to enforce the assignment, whereas a delegant remains liable under the contract. This means that if Curtis assigns his right to receive payment to his sister, it is only Claudia that can sue for non-payment. Curtis has effectively stepped out of the transaction. The delegation of duties does not relieve the delegating party of his obligations should the delegate fail to perform. The original party can sue *both* for performance. Again, this means that both Zane and Curtis are responsible for the complete performance of the construction of Sylvia's house.

SPOT THE ISSUE!

Penny Paralegal has decided to continue her education through a correspondence course. She has contacted the "Perfect Paralegal Institute for Continuing Studies" because it has a great reputation and teaching staff. Penny receives the course materials and makes her first payment. She then receives a letter:

Dear Ms. Paralegal,
Kindly forward all payments to Adequate Assistants, Inc., as of July 1st. Materials will continue to be sent for your course; however, Adequate Assistants will be preparing your assignments from this date forward.

Does Penny have any recourse if she is unsatisfied with these arrangements? [*See DuPont v. Yellow Cab Co. of Birmingham, Inc.*, 565 So. 2d 190 (Ala. 1990).]

The freedom to contract also means that the parties are free to put restrictions in the contract. Ironic, isn't it? The original agreement may prohibit or invalidate any attempt at assignment or delegation. The original parties to the contract must be the ones to perform the obligations under the agreement. In the original contract, Sylvia's parents could stipulate that Curtis may not assign his rights to another party by including the typical language prohibiting assignment: "the rights under this contract are not assignable." Additional language also could be included to invalidate any attempted assignment: "all assignments under this contract are void." Therefore, if Curtis attempted to assign the rights away despite the prohibitive language in the contract, the assignment would be ineffective and unenforceable due to the invalidating language.

If the contract is *silent* as to the ability of the parties to assign their rights, it is usually assumed that assignment is *permissible if it is* **reasonable**. This means that the assignment does not substantially alter the rights and obligations of the original parties to the contract. With the modern trend of corporate takeovers, this becomes an issue in employment. When one company takes over another one, does that new company also assume all the rights of the original employer with respect to the employees?

reasonable assignment
A transfer of performance obligations may only be made where an objective third party would find that the transfer was acceptable under normal circumstances and did not alter the rights and obligations of the original parties.

RESEARCH THIS

Find a case in your jurisdiction that addresses the question of personal service contracts and the impossibility of assignment or delegation in that situation.

There is no clear "bright-line" rule either allowing or prohibiting the assignment of employment contracts; it depends on the nature of the relationship between the original employer and the employee. Generally, where the employment involves personal services (those that are unique to that employee) to be rendered to the employer with whom the employee has a "relationship of confidence," there can be no assignment without the consent of the employee. This is also true where the new employer requires substantially different performance from the employee. The more change in the terms of the employment after the transfer of management, the less likely it is for the employment contracts to be assignable.

Example

Dr. Drake, a leading-edge cardiologist, has an employment agreement with Healing Hearts Hospital that binds him to remain with the hospital for the next five years and to practice exclusively out of Healing Hearts. Recently, Healing Hearts was sold to a large health care system, Patch'em & Dispatch'em. The guiding mission of Healing Hearts was to spend all the time and money necessary to cure heart disease, a mission that was developed with the assistance of Dr. Drake. In its ruthless pursuit of profit, Patch'em & Dispatch'em emphasizes the swiftest and most cost-effective therapies. Dr. Drake's conditions of employment have substantially changed. Without a specific provision in his employment contract, Dr. Drake will not be held to the exclusivity or five-year term under the assignment. Dr. Drake can leave and/or practice elsewhere without being in violation of his previous contract. The assignment is probably neither reasonable nor valid. Conversely, Healing Hearts' employment contract with Winston the orderly is likely to be assignable because his duties include routine work such as carrying supplies and moving patients.

This is also true with respect to delegation. Returning to the apartment sublease example, generally it is assumed that Terri will be fully able to perform under the contract and Mr. Roper won't notice much of a difference; after all, rent money is rent money no matter who it comes from. Recalling the mortgage assignment example, the same holds true: Money is money; it doesn't matter to whom you write your checks; the obligation to pay your monthly mortgage payment did not change. However, personal service contracts are generally not able to be delegated as each person is unique. If part of the lease agreement provided that Chrissy had to perform at the Regal Beagle Pub in the downstairs lobby of the building that Mr. Roper owned, the delegation of the lease would be invalid. Terri, a horrible singer, could not replace Chrissy as the pub's entertainment. Similarly, if Dr. Drake tried to delegate his responsibility as head of cardiology to Winston the orderly, the hospital would lose the benefit of the original bargain. Winston is no substitute for Dr. Drake. Both these delegations (Terri for Chrissy and Winston for Dr. Drake) would substantially change the obligations owed to the original party the under the contract and therefore would be neither reasonable nor valid.

SURF'S UP

The interconnectedness of the Internet and the web of contracts creating the ability to link from site to site, support advertisements, download software, and issue licenses create innumerable third-party interests. Additionally, the ease of transmission of information and economics makes assignment and delegation essentials of the technological age. The statutory response to this information explosion was the Uniform Computer Information Transactions Act. The act "applies to the entire transaction if the computer information and informational rights, or access to them, is the primary subject matter, but otherwise applies only to the part of the transaction involving computer information, informational rights in it, and creation or modification of it." § 103. Part Five (§§ 501-506) of the act deals specifically with the transfer of interests and rights of computerized information. Bear in mind that this is a "uniform law" and has not been adopted by many states—in fact, only two as of this writing, and there are four states that have passed "anti-UCITA" laws! There is obviously significant opposition to its enactment into state contract law. What is all the hoopla about? The huge scope of what is considered "computer information" and the fact that it would be licensed rather than sold has those who are concerned about freedom of use very wary. This is comparable to the controversy surrounding net-neutrality as well, as there are significant implications for our traditional "public forums" of democratic speech, research, and culture.

CRYPTO CONTRACTS

`01100`
`10110`
`11110`

While blockchains are completely dependent on third-party verifications to operate, they are not *ipso facto* third-party contracts. However, "smart contracts" are perhaps ideally suited as the platform for third-party contracts. The veracity, stability, and security of a "smart contract" would enable the transfer of the subject to the third-party beneficiary upon the happening of the stipulated event. As noted earlier in the chapter, insurance contracts often involve third-party beneficiaries. These are the kinds of transactions that are best suited for the blockchain, and not just because the "if-then" nature of terms of insurance are easily converted to code, but also because they are immutably contained in electronic form and retrievable. In the case of life insurance, the maintenance of this digitized version would relieve the insured and the intended beneficiaries of the responsibility of retaining a paper version for years, possibly decades. A "smart life insurance policy" would gather verifiable information about the insured's death and make payments where warranted—the burden, therefore, would be lifted from the presumably grieving beneficiaries. *See* Alan Cohn, Travis West & Chelsea Parker, *Smart After All: Blockchain, Smart Contracts, Parametric Insurance, and Smart Energy Grids,* 1 Geo. L. Tech. Rev. 273 (2017) [https://perma.cc/TY7W-Q8CX].

Adding third parties to an agreement will no doubt contribute to the complexity of contractual obligations between the original parties. Adding complexity to the paralegal student's studies, these third-party interests can be created in various ways, have different effects on the performance obligations, and grant remedies to additional parties.

Summary

If the parties to a contract *intend* to have the performance, the benefit of the contract, conferred on a person not in *privity* to the contract, they have created a *third-party beneficiary contract*. The *promisor* is the person who will bestow the benefit upon the third party, and the *promisee* is the person obligating himself to the promisor.

There are essentially two categories of third-party beneficiaries: *creditors* and *donees*. At the time the beneficiary learns of the agreement, his rights in the contract become *vested*. In a creditor situation, the beneficiary must expressly consent to the contract, whereas a donee beneficiary is presumed to consent to the contract. A third-party beneficiary can sue for enforcement of the contract and the defendant can *assert any defenses* that he would have if sued by the party in privity.

After making the contract, the parties may *assign their rights* and/or *delegate their duties* under the contract to a third party. The most important difference to remember between the two—assignment and delegation—is that an assignor usually is no longer liable under the contract, meaning that he is not party to a suit to enforce the assignment, whereas a delegant remains liable under the contract. Additionally, there may be reasonable contractual limitations on assignment and/or delegation.

Key Terms

assertion of defenses	incidental beneficiary
assignee	intent
assignment	obligor
assignor	privity
creditor	promisee
delegant/delegator	promisor
delegate/delegatee	reasonable assignment
delegation	third-party beneficiary
donee	vested

Review Questions

IDENTIFICATION

Identify the parties as the obligor, promisor, promisee, third-party donee beneficiary, third-party creditor beneficiary, assignor, assignee, delegant, or delegate in the following situations. Additionally, state whether the assignment or delegation is valid and why.

1. Mr. Smith takes out a life insurance policy with State Farm Insurance Company stating that his wife and three children should receive a $500,000.00 payment upon his death.

2. Mr. Smith promises to pay Nancy Nurse $500.00 per week to take care of his elderly mother.

3. Mr. Smith contracted with Gorgeous Lawn Company for a substantial amount of landscaping to be done on his property. Mrs. Jones, his neighbor, put her house on the market and got more than she was asking because the buyer loved the beautiful views of Mr. Smith's gardens.

4. Mrs. Jones found out that Mr. Smith was unable to pay for all that landscaping and Gorgeous Lawn Company was going to pull out all the new plantings. Mrs. Jones agrees to pay for the landscaping.

5. Mr. Smith, an artist, has a contract with Connie Collector for the sale of one of his paintings. Mr. Smith tells Connie to pay Mrs. Jones directly.

6. Connie's check bounces and Mrs. Jones is distressed. To whom can she look for the money? Connie? Mr. Smith? Both?

7. It has been a very busy and prosperous season and Gorgeous Lawn is booked up; the company makes an agreement with Adequate Acreage to do the landscaping at Mr. Smith's house.

8. Adequate Acreage does not do a very good job at Mr. Smith's house. Mr. Smith wants to sue both Adequate Acreage and Gorgeous Lawn for failure of performance. Can he?

"FAULTY PHRASES"

All of the following statements are FALSE; state why they are false and then rewrite them as a true statement. Write a brief fact pattern that illustrates your answer.

1. If a contract is silent as to the ability to delegate and/or assign a contract, then all assignments and/or delegations are permissible.

2. Once a valid delegation has been made, the delegant is absolved of liability for the performance obligations of the contract.

3. All third-party beneficiaries must consent to the terms of the contract when it is made.

4. There are no differences between a third-party creditor beneficiary and a third-party donee beneficiary.

5. A third-party beneficiary may be added to the contract at any time before performance is due from either party.

"WRITE" AWAY! PORTFOLIO ASSIGNMENT

What third-party interests, if any, were created in the Druid and Carrie contract? Are the subcontractors and suppliers third-party creditor beneficiaries of the contract? Why or why not? Assume that Druid owes money to Lucky Lumber Co. In order to ensure payment, Lucky will only provide Druid with supplies for the job if it is paid directly by Carrie for the job. Draft Lucky into the contract as a third-party creditor beneficiary of the Druid and Carrie agreement.

Case in Point   ASSIGNMENT

638 A.2d 1023
432 Pa. Super. 449
FRAN AND JOHN'S DOYLESTOWN AUTO CENTER, INC., Appellant,
v.
ALLSTATE INSURANCE COMPANY.
Superior Court of Pennsylvania.
Argued January 6, 1994.
Filed March 17, 1994.

Page 1024

[432 Pa. Super. 450] George A. Gallenthin, Doylestown, for appellant.
Steven C. Shahan, Morrisville, for appellee.
Before KELLY, FORD ELLIOTT and BROSKY, JJ.
BROSKY, Judge.

This is an appeal from the Order sustaining a preliminary objection in the nature of a demurrer to appellant's second amended Complaint and dismissing the Complaint with prejudice.

On appeal, appellant queries (1) whether an insured may assign an interest which the insured has in a contract of insurance limited to a specific loss covered under the contract of insurance to a third-party beneficiary (appellant herein) without the consent of the insurer (appellee herein); and (2) whether appellant, as a third-party beneficiary to a contract of insurance between an insured and appellee, may file an action as a real party in interest and specifically for fraudulent misrepresentation. We affirm.

[432 Pa. Super. 451] Appellant initiated a cause of action against appellee grounded in fraud, for violation of the Unfair Trade Practices and Consumer Protection Law (73 P.S. §§ 201-1 et seq.) and for relief pursuant to 42 Pa. C.S.A. § 8371 for payment of interest because of appellee's alleged bad faith. This cause of action arose from appellant's repair of motor vehicles belonging to appellee's insureds. The vehicles involved had been damaged in automobile accidents. Appellee's adjustor prepared an estimate for each damaged vehicle and issued checks in the amount of the estimates. Appellant, in the process of repairing the damaged vehicles, requested supplemental sums which it claimed was necessary in order to complete the repairs. Appellee's adjustor then prepared new estimates and negotiated with appellant concerning these supplemental amounts. Apparently, appellant was dissatisfied with the negotiated supplemental amounts and filed the instant cause of action against appellee to recover sums representing the differences between the negotiated supplemental amounts to repair each of the motor vehicles and the supplemental amounts which appellant had requested from appellee.

Appellant requested each of appellee's insureds whose motor vehicles were being repaired by it to execute a document which appellant had labelled "Assignment". This document purported to assign to appellant the insureds' claim to payment for repairs from appellee under their respective contracts of insurance with appellee. The language of each "Assignment" is identical except for the name of the insured and the date of the accident and is as follows:

ASSIGNMENT

I, [name of insured] for good and valuable consideration and intending to be legally

Page 1025

bound do hereby assign and convey to Fran and John's Doylestown Auto Center, Inc. [appellant herein] *any and all* claims, rights, actions, and causes of action which I may have against Allstate Insurance Company [appellee herein] in connection with the repair of my vehicle which was damaged in an automobile accident on [date of accident]

[432 Pa. Super. 452] [signature of insured]

WITNESS:

_____

(Emphasis supplied).

The "General Provisions" page of the policy issued by appellee and in effect for each of the insureds whose motor vehicles were repaired by appellant contains a "Transfer" clause which reads in pertinent part as follows: "This policy can't be transferred to another person without *our* written consent. . . ." (Emphasis in original). Appellant acknowledges the existence of the transfer clause in each of the applicable policies but maintains that it prohibits only the transfer of the policy, itself, not a right or an interest accruing thereunder.[1] Appellant reasons that the Assignments executed by each of the insureds do not transfer the policies to appellant. Instead, appellant maintains, the assignments transfer to appellant only the insureds' contractual right to payment from appellee for repair work to their damaged vehicles. In other words, appellant attempts to argue that a distinction exists between the assignment of a contractual right to receive payment for repair of damage to a covered automobile and the transfer of the policy, itself.

Our supreme court has said that an assignment is " 'a transfer or setting over of property, or of some right or interest therein, from one person to another, and unless in some way qualified, it is properly *the transfer of one whole interest* in an estate, chattel, or other thing.' " *In re Purman's Estate*, 358 Pa. 187, 56 A.2d 86 (1948); (emphasis supplied). *Black's Law Dictionary* similarly defines "Assignment" as "[a] transfer or making over to another of *the whole* of any property. . . . The transfer by a party of all of its rights to some kind of property. . . ." At 61 (5th ed. 1979); (emphasis supplied). See also *National Mutual Aid Society v. Lupold*, 101 Pa. 111 (1882) (upholding validity of clause [432 Pa. Super. 453] prohibiting transfer of certificate of mutual benefit association without latter's consent).

Appellant does not argue that the transfer clause of the policies is ambiguous. Hence, and in that case, a court is required to give effect to the unambiguous language of the insurance policy. *Stump v. State Farm Mutual Automobile Ins. Co.*, 387 Pa. Super. 310, 564 A.2d 194 (1989). Appellant's reasoning that the Assignments in question transfer less than the insureds' entire contractual interest in or right under the policies[2] stands the transfer provision of the policies on its head. We find the language of this provision to be susceptible of no possible meaning other than to prohibit any transfer without appellee's consent. We are powerless to place upon the language of the policies in question any construction which conflicts with its plain meaning. *Timbrook v. Foremost Insurance Co.*, 324 Pa. Super. 384, 471 A.2d 891 (1984). In short, we are unpersuaded by appellant's attempt at what amounts to semantical gamesmanship.

Appellant also argues that it is nevertheless the real party in interest here because it is a third-party beneficiary to the contract of insurance between appellee and its insureds.

In *Guy v. Liederbach*, 501 Pa. 47, 459 A.2d 744 (1983), our supreme court adopted Section 302 of the Restatement (Second) of Contracts as a guide to determine whether a

Page 1026

party qualifies as a third-party beneficiary to a contract. Section 302 states:

(1) Unless otherwise agreed between promisor and promisee, a beneficiary of a promise is an intended beneficiary if recognition of a right to performance in the beneficiary is appropriate to effectuate the intention of the parties and either

[432 Pa. Super. 454]
(a) the performance of the promise will satisfy an obligation of the promisee to pay money to the beneficiary; or

_____

[1] Neither the parties nor the trial court deny that appellee has not consented to the transfer of any of the policies here involved.

[2] In fact, appellant's argument in this regard is defeated by the very terms of the Assignment set forth above. According this document, the insured assigns to appellant "*any and all* claims, rights, actions, and causes of action" which the insured may have against appellee. (Emphasis supplied). Hence, the Assignment operates as a transfer of an insured's entire contractual interest in and all contractual rights under the policy in contravention of the express terms of the policy prohibiting transfer without appellee's consent.

(b) the circumstances indicate that the promisee intends to give the beneficiary the benefit of the promised performance.

(2) An incidental beneficiary is a beneficiary who is not an intended beneficiary.

The supreme court then fashioned the following two-part test to determine whether a person qualifies as a third-party beneficiary to a contract:

(1) the recognition of the beneficiary's right must be "appropriate to effectuate the intention of the parties," and (2) the performance must "satisfy an obligation of the promisee to pay money to the beneficiary" or "the circumstances indicate that the promisee intends to give the beneficiary the benefit of the promised performance." The first part of the test sets forth a standing requirement. For any suit to be brought, the right to performance must be "appropriate to effectuate the intentions of the parties." This general condition restricts the application of the second part of the test, which defines the intended beneficiary as either a creditor beneficiary (§ 302(1)(a)) or a donee beneficiary (§ 302(1)(b)). . . . Section 302(2) defines all beneficiaries who are not intentional beneficiaries as incidental beneficiaries. The standing requirement leaves discretion with the trial court to determine whether recognition of third party beneficiary status would be "appropriate." If the two steps of the test are met, the beneficiary is an intended beneficiary "unless otherwise agreed between promisor and promisee."

Guy, supra, at 459 A.2d at 751.

We need not look any further than to the first part of the *Guy* test to determine "whether recognition of third party beneficiary status would be 'appropriate'" under the facts of this case. Id. We conclude that it would be inappropriate to confer the status of third-party beneficiary upon appellant [432 Pa. Super. 455] under the facts at bar. In *Gerace v. Holmes Protection of Philadelphia*, 357 Pa. Super. 467, 516 A.2d 354 (1986),

appeal denied, 515 Pa. 580, 527 A.2d 541 (1987), we denied third-party beneficiary status to the Essex Ring Corporation. Gerace Jewelry Store had contracted with Holmes for the installation and maintenance of a burglar alarm system at the jewelry store. Essex, through its sales representative, had left with Gerace a case of sample rings which Essex owned. The rings were stolen as a result of a robbery of the jewelry store. Essex and Gerace then instituted suit against Holmes for, inter alia, breach of contract. In denying Essex the status of third-party beneficiary, we stated that Essex had no contract with Holmes by which the latter owed the former a legal or contractual duty, nor did Essex possess any right or interest in the contract between Gerace and Holmes. The owner of Essex testified at the hearing on Holmes' Motion for summary judgment that he had no knowledge of the contract between Gerace and Holmes and had no information relating to the operation of the burglar alarm system. This court concluded that Essex was neither a creditor beneficiary under Section 302(a) of the Restatement (Second) of Contracts nor a donee beneficiary under subsection (b) thereof. Therefore, we held that conferring the status of third-party beneficiary to Essex was inappropriate under the circumstances.

In this case, we similarly conclude that it would be inappropriate to confer the status of third-party beneficiary upon appellant because the contract of insurance between appellee and its insureds does not reflect this to be the intention of the parties. Appellee owes no contractual or legal duty of performance to appellant, as the contract of insurance is for the benefit and protection of the insureds, only. See *Fizz v. Kurtz, Dowd & Nuss, Inc.*, 360 Pa. Super. 151, 519 A.2d 1037 (1987) (third party beneficiary must be owed legal duty under by contracting parties; obtaining insurance is for exclusive benefit of insured). This is evidenced by the fact that

Page 1027

the transfer provision of the instant policies prohibits transfer to any third party without the consent of appellee, which was not here obtained.

Order affirmed.

Case in Point   THIRD-PARTY BENEFICIARIES

736 P.2d 930
241 Kan. 387, 28 Wage & Hour Cas. (BNA)
412, 10 A.L.R.5th 993
Dean FASSE, Appellee,
v.
LOWER HEATING AND AIR CONDITIONING, INC., Appellant.
No. 59997.
Supreme Court of Kansas.
May 1, 1987.
Syllabus by the Court

1. Where a person makes a promise to another for the benefit of a third person,

Page 931

that third person may maintain an action to enforce the contract even though he had no knowledge of the contract when it was made and paid no part of the consideration.

2. Both K.S.A. 44-201 and the Davis-Bacon Act (40 U.S.C. § 276a et seq. [1982]) were enacted not for the benefit of contractors but to protect employees by fixing a floor under wages on public projects.

3. Courts do not require explicit statutory authorization for familiar remedies to enforce statutory obligations. When the legislature has left the matter at large for judicial determination, the court's function is to decide what remedies are appropriate in light of the statutory language and purpose and the traditional modes by which courts compel performance of legal obligations.

Stewart L. Entz, of Entz, Anderson and Chanay, of Topeka, argued the cause and Jeffrey A. Chanay, of the same firm, was with him on the brief for appellant.

Thomas H. Marshall, of Blake and Uhlig, P.A., of Kansas City, argued the cause and Michael T. Manley, of the same firm, was with him on the brief for appellee.

LOCKETT, Justice:
The plaintiff, Dean Fasse, brought this action for additional wages due him and 15 other former employees of the defendant, Lower Heating and Air Conditioning, Inc., (Lower). Fasse contends he is the intended third party beneficiary of a construction contract entered into between Lower and Washburn University. The trial court entered judgment for the plaintiff, and Lower appealed. We affirm.

Lower entered into a construction contract with Washburn University to perform the mechanical work on the Allied Health Center building on the Washburn campus. An addendum to the [241 Kan. 388] contract provided that Lower must comply with provisions of K.S.A. Chapter 44, Labor and Industries, and in particular the provisions of K.S.A. 44-201. The addendum, which included 44-201 in its entirety, concluded:

"The 'current rate of per diem wages,' for purposes of this project, shall be defined as and synonymous with the required wages and benefits for each job classification in federal and federally assisted construction projects in Shawnee County, Kansas as determined by the Secretary of Labor of the United States Government, pursuant to the Davis-Bacon Act, (42 U.S.C. 276a et seq.), current and effective upon the date of execution of the contract."

Lower began working on the project in June of 1982. During the construction, questions were raised concerning the wages being paid on the project. Representatives of Washburn met with Lower and others regarding the wages. At this meeting, Lower produced a document reflecting the wage scales paid employees on the construction project. Subsequently,

Kenneth Hackler, attorney for Washburn, wrote a letter to Lower stating that, while the labor unions and the contractors each construed the effect of Addendum No. 1 differently, the university would not interpret the contract because contract construction was a function of the court.

Lower continued to pay the wages set forth in the schedule. Plaintiff filed this action alleging that, as an intended third party beneficiary under the contract, he was to be paid wages as set by the Davis-Bacon Act (40 U.S.C. § 276a et seq. [1982]).

The trial court determined that Lower had violated the terms of the contract by failing to pay the "current rate of per diem wages" as provided in the contract addendum. After taking judicial notice of the Davis-Bacon wage scale published in the Federal Register, the trial court ordered Lower to pay the difference between the wages actually paid and the wages required under Davis-Bacon, plus prejudgment interest. Lower appeals.

Lower contends that neither the Kansas and federal wage and hour laws nor the contract intend that the workers should be third party beneficiaries. Prior to examining the applicable state and federal law and the contract, we must determine who are third party beneficiaries.

Page 932

Generally, where a person makes a promise to another for the benefit of a third person, that third person may maintain an [241 Kan. 389] action to enforce the contract even though he had no knowledge of the contract when it was made and paid no part of the consideration. *Anderson v. Rexroad*, 175 Kan. 676, 266 P.2d 320 (1954); *Burton v. Larkin*, 36 Kan. 246, 13 Pac. 398 (1887). But it is not everyone who may benefit from the performance of a contract between two other persons, or who may suffer from its nonperformance, who is permitted to enforce the contract by court action. Beneficiaries of contracts to which they are not parties have been divided into three classes: Donee beneficiaries, creditor beneficiaries, and incidental beneficiaries. Only those falling within the first two classes may enforce contracts made for their benefit. 17A C.J.S., Contracts § 519(4)b, p. 964; accord *Burton v. Larkin*, 36 Kan. 246, 13 Pac. 398. In more recent analyses of third

party beneficiary law, beneficiaries have been divided into two general classes—intended beneficiaries and incidental beneficiaries. Third party beneficiaries are discussed in 2 Williston on Contracts, § 356 (3d ed. 1959).

To be a third party beneficiary to a contract, the contract must be made for the third party's benefit as its object, and he must be the party intended to be benefited in order to be entitled to sue upon it. *Burton v. Larkin*, 36 Kan. 246, 13 Pac. 398. The third-party beneficiary can enforce the contract if he is one who the contracting parties intended should receive a direct benefit from the contract. Contracting parties are presumed to act for themselves and therefore an intent to benefit a third person must be clearly expressed in the contract. *Ronnau v. Caravan International Corporation*, 205 Kan. 154, 159, 468 P.2d 118 (1970). It is not necessary, however, that the third party be the exclusive beneficiary of all the promisor's performance. The contract may also benefit the contracting parties as well. *Martin v. Edwards*, 219 Kan. 466, 473, 548 P.2d 779 (1976); 17 Am. Jur. 2d, Contracts § 306, pp. 731-32; 17A C.J.S., Contracts § 519(4)f, p. 983.

K.S.A. 44-201 requires contractors employing workers, laborers, or mechanics on public construction projects in Kansas to pay not less than the "current rate of per diem wages" in the locality where the work is to be performed. It also requires that all contracts made by or on behalf of the State of Kansas or any governmental subdivision, which involve the employment of laborers, workers, or mechanics, contain provisions requiring the payment of per diem wages for services on the project.

[241 Kan. 390] Under K.S.A. 44-201, the "current rate of per diem wages" is the "rate of wage paid in the locality" to workers in the same trade or work of a similar nature. The statute sets a floor below which wages paid by contractors on public projects may not fall. *Andersen Construction Co. v. City of Topeka*, 228 Kan. 73, 612 P.2d 595 (1980).

The Davis-Bacon Act, originally passed in 1931, 40 U.S.C. § 276a et seq. (1982), requires the Secretary of Labor to determine the minimum wages to be paid laborers and mechanics employed by contractors on federal or federally funded construction projects. Under published regulations, the Secretary compiles wage rate information, determines the prevailing wage scales, and publishes them periodically in the Federal Register. Davis-Bacon wages must be paid by all contractors on state and local construction projects when any federal financial assistance is utilized.

The Act directs the Secretary to determine not only the hourly wage but the prevailing fringe benefit payments as well. Section 276a(b) defines "minimum wages" to include both the employee's basic hourly rate of pay and the amount paid by the contractor in fringe benefits. Fringe benefits include medical insurance, pension benefits, unemployment benefits, life insurance, disability or accident insurance, vacation and holiday pay, workers' compensation insurance, and apprenticeship and training programs or "other bona fide fringe benefits."

The Secretary of Labor has established two different types of wage determinations

Page 933

under the Act. The first type of determination is made when a federal agency awards a contract and requests the Secretary to determine the prevailing wage. The Secretary then determines wages for the work classifications involved and issues a determination for that particular project. See 29 C.F.R. § 1.5(a) (1986). The second type of determination is made by the Secretary for a particular area where large amounts of construction may be expected. These determinations are published, and once published, a contracting agency may use them without further notifying the Department of Labor. See 29 C.F.R. § 1.5(b).

For purposes of the Davis-Bacon Act wage scales, Kansas is [241 Kan. 391] divided into five wage areas. *Ritchie Paving, Inc. v. Kansas Dept. of Transportation*, 232 Kan. 346, 348, 654 P.2d 440 (1982). At trial in the present case, the plaintiff presented evidence showing that an area wage determination was prepared by the Department of Labor for the Shawnee County area. This area wage determination at the time that Washburn and Lower contracted was contained in Exhibit No. 5, which Kenneth Hackler, Washburn legal counsel, testified he had determined was the most recent wage determination for the Shawnee County area.

Both K.S.A. 44-201 and the Davis-Bacon Act were enacted not for the benefit of contractors but to protect employees by fixing a floor under wages on public projects. *Andersen Construction Co. v. City of Topeka*, 228 Kan. at 81, 612 P.2d 595. K.S.A. 44-201 clearly intends that for each day a worker labors on a contract covered by the statute, he shall be paid the current per diem rate for the type of work he is performing. *Andersen Constr. Co. v. Weltmer*, 224 Kan. 191, 577 P.2d 1197 (1978). We, however, have long recognized and approved the payment of Davis-Bacon wages in order to comply with K.S.A. 44-201. "Davis-Bacon wages are somewhat higher than 'the rate of wage paid in the locality,' computed under K.S.A. 44-201." *Andersen*, 228 Kan. at 76, 612 P.2d 595.

In order to establish that a particular individual is an intended beneficiary of the contract, a court must determine whether or not the contract provides to that individual a direct benefit by the terms of the agreement. In determining the intent of the contracting parties as to the rights of a third party beneficiary, the court must apply the general rules for construction of contracts. The contract is to be considered as a whole, not simply from the standpoint of one isolated provision. *Barnhart v. McKinney*, 235 Kan. 511, 682 P.2d 112 (1984). The intention of the parties and the meaning of the contract are to be determined from the instrument itself where the terms are plain and unambiguous. *First Nat'l Bank & Trust Co. v. Lygrisse*, 231 Kan. 595, 647 P.2d 1268 (1982). A contract is ambiguous when the words used to express the meaning and intention of the parties are insufficient in the sense the contract may be understood to reach two or more possible meanings. *Arkansas Louisiana Gas Co. v. State*, 234 Kan. 797, 675 P.2d 369 (1984). Regardless of the construction of a written instrument made by the trial court, on appeal the appellate [241 Kan. 392] court may construe the legal effect of the contract. *Hall v. Mullen*, 234 Kan. 1031, 678 P.2d 169 (1984).

Lower contends that it and Washburn did not contract to use the Davis-Bacon wage scale as a basis for wages, but only intended to comply with the "statutory floor" dictated by 44-201. Addendum No. 1 to the contract, however, specifically states that:

"The 'current rate of per diem wages,' for purposes of this project, shall be defined as and synonymous with the required wages and benefits for each job classification in federal and federally assisted construction projects in Shawnee County, Kansas as determined by the Secretary of Labor of the United States Government, pursuant to the Davis-Bacon Act, (42 U.S.C. 276a et seq.), current and effective upon the date of execution of the contract."

Where the provisions of a written contract are clear and unambiguous, there is no occasion for applying rules of construction. A contract must be enforced according

Page 934

to its terms so as to give effect to the intention of the parties, and that must be determined from the four corners of the instrument itself. *Steel v. Eagle*, 207 Kan. 146, 483 P.2d 1063 (1971).

Words will not be read into an agreement which impart an intent wholly unexpressed when the agreement was unexecuted. *Cline v. Angle*, 216 Kan. 328, 532 P.2d 1093 (1975). Here, the contract is clearly unambiguous. Even though this was not a federally funded project, the contract specifically provided that wages were to be based on the published Davis-Bacon wage scales. The district court was correct in finding that the parties to the contract intended to pay workers contract wages based on the Davis-Bacon wage scale and that the workers were third party beneficiaries under the contract.

Lower contends that 44-201 does not provide the plaintiff with a private cause of action to assert a claim for per diem wages.

Generally, the common-law procedure is regarded as the proper remedy where a right is created or a duty is required by statute and no adequate statutory remedy is provided for its enforcement or breach or where the special remedy created by statute is void. 1 Am. Jur. 2d, Actions § 75.

Courts do not require explicit statutory authorization for familiar remedies to enforce statutory obligations. When the legislature has left the matter at large for judicial determination, the [241 Kan. 393] court's function is to decide what remedies are appropriate in light of the statutory language and purpose and the traditional modes by which courts compel performance of legal obligations. If civil liability is appropriate to effectuate the purposes of a

statute, courts are not denied this traditional remedy because it is not specifically authorized. *Anderson Cattle Co. v. Kansas Turnpike Authority*, 180 Kan. 749, 308 P.2d 172 (1957). For cases from other jurisdictions see: *Montana-Dakota Co. v. Pub. Serv. Co.*, 341 U.S. 246, 71 S. Ct. 692, 95 L. Ed. 912 (1951); *State ex rel. Phillips v. Wn. Liquor Bd.*, 59 Wash. 2d 565, 369 P.2d 844 (1962); and *Branson v. Branson*, 190 Okla. 347, 123 P.2d 643 (1942).

Here, K.S.A. 44-202 and 44-205 provide fines and imprisonment for violations of 44-201 et seq. The statutes, however, provide no civil remedies for those employees damaged by an employer's failure to comply with the statute. Therefore, the employees are able to use whatever common-law remedies are available to them. A worker who claims violation of K.S.A. 44-201 may bring an action for recovery of the underpaid wages. *Ritchie Paving, Inc. v. Kansas Dept. of Transportation*, 232 Kan. at 351-52, 654 P.2d 440.

The district court was correct in finding that the workers, as third party beneficiaries, had a private cause of action to assert a claim for wages set by the contract.

Lower claims that the trial court erred in taking judicial notice of pages extracted from the Federal Register and that the Federal Register does not fall within the category of documents set forth at K.S.A. 60-409(b) for which judicial notice may properly be taken.

K.S.A. 60-409(b) provides:

"(b) Judicial notice may be taken without request by a party, of (1) private acts and resolutions of the Congress of the United States and of the legislature of this state, and duly enacted ordinances and duly published regulations of governmental subdivisions or agencies of this state, and (2) the laws of foreign countries and (3) such facts as are so generally known or of such common notoriety within the territorial jurisdiction of the court that they cannot reasonably be the subject of dispute, and (4) specific facts and propositions of generalized knowledge which are capable of immediate and accurate determination by resort to easily accessible sources of indisputable accuracy."

The Federal Administrative Procedure Act requires each federal agency to publish in the Federal Register

(1) descriptions of [241 Kan. 394] its organization and the place at which and the methods whereby the public may obtain information, make submittals or requests, or obtain decisions; (2) statements of the

Page 935

general course and method by which its functions are channeled and determined; (3) rules of procedure and descriptions of forms available or the places at which forms may be obtained; (4) substantive rules and statements of general policy; and (5) each amendment, revision, or repeal of the foregoing. 5 U.S.C. § 552 (1982). The Secretary of Labor is required by the Davis-Bacon Act to publish the Davis-Bacon wage scales in the Federal Register.

In *McAfee v. City of Garnett*, 205 Kan. 269, 469 P.2d 295 (1970), we recognized that courts could take judicial notice of Kansas administrative regulations. It is logical that since the Federal Register contains duly published regulations of federal agencies, courts should take judicial notice of federal administrative regulations, including the Davis-Bacon wage scales, as published in the Federal Register.

The trial court properly took judicial notice of the information published in the Federal Register.

Lower argues that the workers failed to prove the work classifications, tasks, or skills which would place them in comparison, for wage purposes, with other workers under the Davis-Bacon Act. Under the Davis-Bacon Act, it is the classification in which the employee works, not the employee's particular qualifications, which determines the applicable wage rates to be paid.

In *Baker v. R.D. Andersen Constr. Co.*, 7 Kan. App. 2d 568, 575, 644 P.2d 1354, rev. denied 231 Kan. 799 (1982), the court recognized that the appropriate per diem wage depends on the skill of the employee and the task being performed. Federal wage classification cases have generally held that an individual employee's classification used to determine the prevailing wages for that particular area depends on the type of work performed, not the skill or experience of the employee in performing it. In any given work classification, the ability of individual laborers will vary, as will their training and experience. For example, see Matter of Lee Roy Corley dba Corley Mechanical Contractor, [1978-81 Transfer Binder, Wages-Hours] Lab. L. Rep. (CCH) p 31,229 (March 21, 1978). The correctness of a wage classification is based not on skill or experience, but on [241 Kan. 395] the work actually performed. Matter of Hughes Aircraft Company, [1978-81 Transfer Binder, Wages-Hours] Lab. L. Rep. (CCH) p 31,316 (August 20, 1979).

At trial expert witnesses, Lower's supervisory personnel, and the workers presented evidence as to the work actually performed on the contract. Under the circumstances, there was sufficient competent evidence to support the trial court's finding that the workers on the project should be paid according to the various classifications listed in the Davis-Bacon wage scale.

The judgment of the trial court is affirmed.

VOCABULARY BUILDERS

Across

1 Agreement to pay the debt of another.
4 Termination of the offer by the offeree.
10 Offeree initiated contact to invite an offer.
13 Starting to accept a unilateral contract.
15 Being an actual party to the contract.
16 A beneficiary not intended to receive the benefit of the contract.
18 Party assuming the duties to be performed.
20 When rejection is valid.
23 Giving rights to a third party.
24 Party initiating the formation of the contract.
25 The contractual promise to perform.
26 The offeree's assent to the offer.
29 Rule that states that acceptance cannot deviate from the offer.
31 A person who stands to gain from the performance of a contract.
32 Terms of a contract that affect how the contractual terms are carried out.
40 What a court can do for the party who has been wronged.
44 What a party gives up in the bargain.
45 What a party gains from the bargain.
48 The party who can accept the contract terms.
50 Original party remaining in the contract.
54 Person making the obligation to the promisor.
55 Necessary when the offeror is at a distance from the offeree's performance.
57 The contractual promises have been fully performed.
59 Making performance of the contract substantially more difficult to fulfill.
60 Party receiving the rights.
61 Party giving away their rights under the contract.
63 Giving a duty to perform to a third party.
65 Able to be ascertained without personal intent.
67 Both parties have agreed to the terms of the contract.
68 Actual consent by both parties as to the terms of the contract.
69 Lack of a real, enforceable obligation.
70 Depending on a promise or action of another party.
71 Indefinite consideration.

Down

2 Conditions that are specifically stated in the contract.
3 The recipient of a gift.
5 Like option contracts and firm offers.
6 Party giving the benefit to the third-party beneficiary.
7 Both parties are bound by the terms of the offer.
8 Conditions that are not spoken but must occur in order to give effect to the contract.
9 A party can legally escape enforceability of the contract.
11 An agreement to purchase all the manufactured goods.
12 Conditions that must be enforced out of a sense of justice.
13 A legally enforceable gift to a charity.
14 When the intent to bestow a benefit on a third party must be made.
17 The time when the contract becomes enforceable by the third-party beneficiary.
19 The proposal for an agreement.
21 Those conditions occurring at the same time as performance.
22 Exchange of a promise for a promise.
27 Having all the material elements spelled out in the offer.
28 The party to whom a debt is owed.
30 Standard to determine when acceptance is effective.
33 The moment when courts will determine that acceptance is valid in a unilateral contract.
34 An agreement to purchase all the needs from a supplier.
35 Party giving away the duties.
36 Termination of the offer by the offeror.
37 A condition in the terms that is entirely in the control of one party.
38 The bargained-for exchange.
39 The terms have been explicitly set forth in words.
41 Usually not a method of accepting an offer.
42 When acceptance is valid.
43 The moment when the offeree stands ready to begin under a unilateral contract.
46 Those conditions occurring prior to performance obligations.
47 Valid consideration has_____.
49 Sending acceptance by the authorized method.
51 Invalid, "recycled" bargaining.
52 Something for which the party is already legally bound to do.
53 Those conditions occurring after performance.
56 Giving up a legal right.
58 The contractual promises have yet to be performed.
62 Consideration that is so devalued in light of the exchange.
64 Able to be ascertained through the actions of the parties.
66 Violation of the terms of a contract.

Part Two

Defects
in Formation

Chapter 6: Statute of Frauds

Chapter 7: Capacity and Illegality

Chapter 8: Absence of a "Meeting of the Minds"

Chapter 9: Rules of Construction

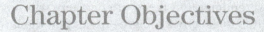

Chapter 6

Statute of Frauds

Chapter Objectives

The student will be able to:

- Use vocabulary regarding the Statute of Frauds and its application properly.
- Discuss the five types of agreements that must be in writing to comply with the statute.
- Determine whether the statute applies to a given set of facts.
- Analyze the extent of partial performance to determine whether it will take the oral agreement out from under the requirements of the statute.

This chapter will explore WHY certain types of agreements must be in writing in order to be enforced in the court, WHAT the requirements for the writing evidencing the agreement are, and HOW a party may avoid application of the Statute of Frauds by beginning performance. While oral agreements are equally as valid as written ones, there are five general categories of contracts that must be in writing in order to be enforceable in a court of law. Again, in an attempt to foster agreements and contractual performance, the writing requirement is generously interpreted in order to find an obligation. Further benevolence is demonstrated by contract law in the event that a party begins performance; despite the lack of a required writing, the performance may "substitute" for it, and the agreement may be enforceable.

While it is true that parties can generally choose whatever terms and conditions they wish under the freedom of contract theory, the nature of contract law and its desire for certainty takes the lead in certain types of contracts. Written form is more certain and concrete than verbal form. For certain types of contracts, the law requires that there be *proof in writing* of the agreement in order to be enforced through the court. This writing must be shown to be a reliable recordation of the transaction; therefore, the writing serves as proof of the agreement but also the writing itself must be proven to be reliable. There are five categories of contracts that fall under the Statute of Frauds:

1. The transfer of real property interests.
2. Contracts that are not performable within one year.
3. Contracts in consideration of marriage.
4. Sureties and guarantees (answering the debt of another).
5. Uniform Commercial Code provisions regarding the sale of goods valued over $500.00.

WRITING REQUIREMENT

An oral contract concerning these enumerated types of contracts will not be enforced in a court of law. Why? It is these types of agreements that the law of contracts, dating back to the seventeenth century, singled out as being particularly susceptible to fraud by an unscrupulous party. The Statute of Frauds is the courts' attempt to deny enforcement of dubious claims; however, as discussed later, sometimes strict enforcement of the Statute of Frauds could deny recovery for real claims and cause injustice against an innocent party. Limitations on the scope of the Statute of Frauds and lenient interpretations of it have softened potentially harsh results that would have resulted by strict adherence to the Statute of Frauds.

Be aware, however, that if an agreement would fall under the Statute of Frauds but the parties do not memorialize it in writing, it is not automatically void. The parties are free to perform on their oral contract. The Statute of Frauds merely protects parties' interests once they are involved in litigating the contractual dispute. To reiterate, people are free to make any oral promise they want and to fully perform on it. Unless the court gets involved, there is no need for the formality of a writing. In this way, the court can avoid the "he said/ she said" dilemma. Parties to a lawsuit tend to recall events and agreements in a light most favorable to them, not necessarily reflecting the facts accurately. In these five types of tempting transactions, the court takes away the reliance on fallible human memory and places it upon reliable, concrete documentation.

A note of caution: Paralegals must do their research as each state has its own statutory provisions enumerating the particular requirements for each type of contract that falls under the Statute of Frauds. It must be determined in the particular jurisdiction, first, whether the contract falls within the Statute of Frauds (whether there is a need for a writing) and second, whether the writing satisfies the requirements of the Statute of Frauds.

What type of **writing** does **satisfy the Statute of Frauds**? Must there be a long-winded formal document enumerating all the terms and conditions of the agreement? No. As long as all the requisites of certainty can be established (parties, price, subject matter, and time for performance), by a writing or multiple writings, then the Statute of Frauds is satisfied. It is possible to read several writings together to form one whole that satisfies the Statute of Frauds.

writing to satisfy the Statute of Frauds
A document or compilation of documents containing the essential terms of the agreement.

Example

Oscar does not keep his records very organized and is rather haphazard about his transactions. Recently he entered into an agreement with Peter to sell him some land Oscar owns in the Adirondacks. There is an e-mail, a brief description and crude drawing of the land on a cocktail napkin, a note on kitty cat stationery, and a receipt that all relate to the agreement. These all may be read together to form a coherent writing that satisfies the Statute of Frauds. Even if some of these "documents" are no longer truly legible or if Oscar has since lost or destroyed them, the Statute of Frauds is satisfied. The Statute of Frauds requires that the agreement be memorialized in writing, not that the writing still exist when enforcement is sought. "Where the writing has been destroyed or is presently unavailable, the parties may employ parol evidence to prove 'both its existence and contents.'" *Putt v. City of Corinth*, 579 So. 2d 534, 538 (Miss. 1991), *citing Williams v. Evans*, 547 So. 2d 54, 57 (Miss. 1989). "The 'memorandum or note' serves but to show 'a basis for believing that the offered oral evidence rests on a real transaction.'" *Id.* at 538, *citing Franklin County Cooperative v. MFC Services (A.A.L.)*, 441 So. 2d 1376, 1378 (Miss. 1983). In *Putt*, the seller of land attempted to enforce an oral contract of land. The Statute of Frauds applies in this matter, so this purported oral contract would have to be substantiated with a writing to serve as evidence of the agreement. The lower court has summarily dismissed the case due to a lack of a written agreement because a written contract could not be presented. However, the Supreme Court of Mississippi determined that the buyer's minutes of the meeting wherein the purchase was approved served as a proper "memorandum or note" that satisfied the Statute of Frauds.

SURF'S UP

Technology has altered the way in which information is transmitted and stored. No longer are we content to receive a phone call; the information is usually stored in an electronic format for ease of retrieval. "Once text is entered into a database, a 'writing' exists in fact, only to be retrieved by the party in control of such, the employer. To deny the existence of a 'writing' . . . is to ignore the very nature of electronic communications. [. . .] Thus, we [the court] may consider the effect of the UETA on this case." *Godfrey v. Fred Meyer Stores*, 124 P.3d 621, 631

(Or. App. 2005). The case revolved around a worker's compensation claim of which notice had to be given to her employer "in writing" within 90 days of the incident. The employee/claimant had telephoned her supervisor and that supervisor entered it into the company's electronic database under "employee incident report." Although the report was never printed, it was indeed considered a writing—only in electronic form.

On the other extreme, a writing may be quite extensive and clearly manifest the parties' intent to be bound to an agreement, but if it lacks the requisite specificity as to the elements of a contract, it does not satisfy the Statute of Frauds. "The question of intent to be bound is, however, distinct from the question of sufficiency under the Statute of Frauds." *Craig R. Weiner Assoc., Inc. v. Sherden*, 444 So. 2d 431, 432 (Fla. Ct. App. 1984) (The letter purporting to be a contract for the sale of real estate clearly indicated that the parties intended to be bound by the terms therein; however, the letter was not sufficiently detailed in the requisite elements to satisfy the Statute of Frauds.).

signed by the party to be charged
The writing that purports to satisfy the Statute of Frauds must be signed by the party against whom enforcement is sought.

Additionally, the writing must be **signed by the party to be charged**. This means that the writing(s) must be signed or otherwise authenticated by the person against whom enforcement is sought. Somewhere on the pieces of paper on Oscar's desk that purport to represent the agreement with Peter, Peter's signature or other indication of assent, including but not limited to Peter's initials, a memo on his letterhead, an e-mail address personal to Peter, or some other, must be present.

It must be clear from these writings that the parties did assent to the terms contained therein. There can be a plethora of writings relating to the negotiations, but they must relate to the actual, mutually agreed upon terms of the agreement. Even signed documents that relate to the purported agreement can be insufficient to satisfy the Statute of Frauds. In *Copywatch, Inc. v. American Nat'l Red Cross*, Civil Action No. 17-1219 (TJK) (D.D.C. 2018), the court determined that neither a Non-Negotiable Confidential Disclosure Agreement (NDA) nor a Memorandum of Understanding (MOU) or indeed any of the information exchanged regarding Copywatch's report about its services and cost-saving measures contained the actual agreement to terms that would bind the parties in a contractual relationship. (The NDA provided, among other things, that the parties would not disclose any "Confidential Information," defined as "certain confidential information relating to copier and printer cost recovery service." The NDA further provided that the parties would "only use the Confidential Information to the extent necessary to achieve or advance the Purpose," defined as "explor[ing] business opportunities of mutual interest." Copywatch alleged that the Red Cross used the information gained from the negotiations to the Red Cross' advantage but never formalized the contract and therefore did not pay for that information.) It is important to note that later in this text the concept of "quasi-contracts" and "unjust enrichment" will be explored as alternative means of equitable relief. As in the *Copywatch* case, there are some situations wherein a "black letter of the law" contract has not been shown to exist, but the harm suffered by the non-breaching party would be too great to allow the opposition to get away with their wrongdoing. These are non-contract remedies.

IN-CLASS DISCUSSION

After a very successful interview with Piddle and Diddle, Paula Paralegal was offered a position with the firm. The offer came via a telephone call from Mr. Piddle, wherein he told her that the employment would be for a two-year term and her starting salary would be $25,000 a year. If she performed satisfactorily for the first six months, she would receive a raise to $30,000 per year. Her second-year salary would be raised to $40,000.

A few days later, Paula received a memo from Mr. Diddle's secretary. It was a very brief note:

Employment:
Begin—January 1, 2006
$25,000 to start—6 mos. $30,000—6 months—$40,000.
2 years to make good.

Paula went to work for the first year and all went well. On June 1st, she received a payroll card indicating her raise to $30,000, initialed by the managing partner with a note next to it stating *"per agreement."*

However, Paula did not receive her next raise in January. She wants to know what her chances are if she decides to litigate the matter.

Is this agreement controlled by the Statute of Frauds? Why or why not?

Has the statute been satisfied? Why or why not?

TYPES OF CONTRACTS

A discussion of each type of contract follows, including an examination of the scope of the Statute of Frauds as it relates to that particular type of contract.

Transfer of Real Property Interests

The most obvious inclusion in this category is the actual sale of a piece of real estate. In order to purchase a house or parcel of land, the contract must be in writing. There are other "interests in real property" that qualify for inclusion under the Statute of Frauds. Mortgages, leases for a term of greater than one year, transfers of shares in real estate cooperatives, easements, liens on property as security, and the like are also included. The underlying reasoning for this is, again, contract law's love of certainty. Most of the writings relating to real property interests are recorded in a clerk's office so that the interests in the real estate are of public record. Requiring a writing under the Statute of Frauds protects that governmental interest and assures certainty and security.

Compare the following examples:

1. Charles' law school tuition is due, and he asks his girlfriend, Darlene, to lend him some cash. Darlene agrees to loan Charles money. In order to come up with that kind of cash, Darlene agrees to sell her vacation house at the Jersey shore and give Charles 20 percent of her profit on the sale of the property.
2. Darlene agrees to sell her property to Charles' law school in exchange for a tuition waiver for Charles.

The first example is not covered under the statute; the second is. Why? The underlying consideration. In the first example, the sale of the land answered *how* Darlene would come up with the money, but the sale of the land was not the underlying reason for the promise to lend money to Charles. The transfer in real estate was not the reason *why* Darlene and Charles entered into the agreement. Charles was unconcerned with where or how Darlene got the money. The second example is a transfer of an interest in real estate. It does not matter that Darlene does not receive money for it, nor does it matter that the beneficiary of the contract is not Darlene but her boyfriend Charles (recall third-party beneficiaries from Chapter 5). The transfer in real estate was the reason *why* Darlene and the law school entered into the agreement.

Where do common errors occur in determining whether the contract is an interest in land? Interestingly, a contract for the sale of the fruits of the land is not a contract for the transfer of an interest in land because, at the time the performance is due under the contract, taking the crop or other product from the land thereby separates the interest from the land. Taking something from the land is not included and neither is putting something on the land; a contract to build a house on a piece of land is not a contract tied to land and therefore is outside the Statute of Frauds.

Example

In order to supply the growing demand for fuel, Extra Oil Company enters into an output contract with Careful Growers to extract the oil that lies beneath its strawberry fields. The contract gives all right and title to all the potential oil reserves on the property. Careful Growers agrees as long as the oil company does not harm the soil or render the fields unsuitable to resume strawberry harvesting. This transfer of interest in property is not under the Statute of Frauds because the interest transferred is the moveable personal property of oil, not the land itself. Extra owns the oil, not the substance of the land. The land itself remains in the hands of Careful Growers.

However, if, for the purposes of obtaining that oil, Careful had to grant Extra an easement over its land for consideration, a recordable transaction, that agreement would have to be in writing as the grant of access over real property is a transfer of an interest in land.

Similarly, joint venture agreements to purchase land are not under the Statute of Frauds because the purpose of the contract is to form the partnership, not to deal with the land acquisition itself. However, if the partnership is formed on the premise that the partners will contribute/transfer their individual real property interests to fund the joint venture, the agreement falls within the Statute of Frauds.

Example

Richard and Jane enter into a joint venture agreement wherein they intend to purchase "fixer-uppers," renovate them, and then sell them for a much higher price than their investment, a practice known as "flipping." The joint venture agreement is not under the Statute of Frauds. The real estate transactions are how the parties intend on making money in the joint venture agreement; the transfer of real estate is not the reason why they entered into the agreement.

Richard and Jane enter into a joint venture agreement to "flip" real estate. The agreement states that both Richard and Jane will transfer their current real property interests in their individual parcels of land to fund the joint venture agreement. The agreement is based on the transfer of the individual real estate interests and, therefore, is controlled by the Statute of Frauds.

Courts also have concluded that the transfer of stock in a corporation whose sole asset is real estate is still a transfer of personal property and therefore not controlled by the Statute of Frauds. *See, e.g., Forward v. Beucler*, 702 F. Supp. 582, 585 (E.D. Va. 1988) ("The fact that the partnership's sole asset is real estate does not trigger the real property provision of the statute of frauds. Rather, [. . . those] interests are personalty whatever the nature of the partnership assets." The corpus of the transfer was the stock itself, not what the underlying asset was that gave the stock its value.). The states are not in alignment, however, where the sale of a co-op (a cooperative housing unit) is concerned. While the underlying sale is actually the transfer of shares of stock in the ownership of the cooperative building, it is in practicality the purchase of a certain unit in the building to occupy like real estate. The intent of the transfer is not actual ownership of the stock but the sale of a place to live—an interest in the physical asset, not the worth of the shares—and therefore covered under the Statute of Frauds. Therefore, in some states, like New York and New Jersey, the sale of co-op shares *is* covered under the Statute of Frauds. *See, e.g., Presten v. Sailer*, 542 A.2d 7 (N.J. Super. A.D. 1988), but in others, like Washington, acquiring the block of shares associated with a particular unit represents becoming a shareholder of the corporation that owns the apartments. *See, e.g., Firth v. Lu*, 49 P.3d 117 (Wash. 2002) (Interestingly, the Supreme Court of Washington found that shares in a co-operative corporation were not an interest in real property transferable by deed and so, reversed the decision of the appellate court which had held that the co-op shares were really a transfer of a real property interest.). What one can derive from these cases is that it is imperative for a paralegal to do the necessary research to determine which side of the Statute of Frauds their jurisdiction follows.

Contracts That Are Not Performable Within One Year

Time has the tendency to cloud recall of the particulars of an agreement. Therefore, the Statute of Frauds requires contracts to be in writing where the performance under the contract could not take place in under one year. It is very important to understand that it is the amount of time that lapses between performance and the acceptance of the contract that determines whether the contract falls under the Statute of Frauds, not how long the actual performance takes. *See* RESTATEMENT (SECOND) OF CONTRACTS § 130(1). In other words, a contract signed on January 1, 2006, agreeing to perform a day-long concert of love songs in Central Park on February 14, 2008, is under the Statute of Frauds because the performance, although it only takes one day, takes place more than one year from acceptance.

The other tricky element to this "performance within one year" requirement is that the drafter or reviewer must bear in mind not what actually does happen in the circumstance, but what *could* happen. The courts tend to limit the application of the Statute of Frauds in the "year performance" situation as much as possible. If there is a possibility, however remote or speculative, that the contract could be performed within one year, the Statute of Frauds does *not* apply.

Even if the agreement contemplates that it may be more than one year, as long as it does not prescribe that it be no less than one year, the contract is not within the Statute of Frauds. It requires a careful reading by the paralegal (or other reviewer) to determine the intent of the parties and the wording of the term limitations. *See Walker v. Tafralian*, 107 S.W.3d 665, 669 (Tex. App. 2003) (Financier Tafralian agreed to lend developer Walker purchase money for real estate purchases. The term of one of the notes was for "two years, or upon sale of any or all of the East Street property, whichever occurred first. Thus, Walker could have performed the note for improvements by repaying it within one year if he had sold the East Street property within a year.").

Example

If a contract requires a builder to construct a new house within 15 months, the contract is not within the Statute of Frauds. What?!?! How can that be? The contract clearly sets the time at 15 months, which is by mathematical definition longer than 12 months. Yes, but a lucky homeowner could have hired a very good builder who completed the house in a mere 10 months, making performance complete within one year. If the contract had not specified a time frame, and the construction had taken 15 months, it still wouldn't be under the Statute of Frauds because the possibility always existed that it *could* get done before one year passed.

The key question to be asked of these contracts is: "Would it be a breach of the contract to fully perform within one year?" Employment contracts for more than one year and covenants not to complete for more than one year after termination of employment are within the Statute of Frauds. An employee cannot fully perform on an employment contract that requires him/her to work for the employer for more than one year. It is impossible to compress time—universal laws of physics prohibit it!

Example

Paula Paralegal takes a job with Best & Brightest Law Firm. The employment contract states that Paula agrees to work for B & B for at least three years. This contract must be in writing to satisfy the Statute of Frauds. It is impossible for Paula to give B & B three years' worth of work in less than one year. If Paula were to leave her job before three years had elapsed, she would be in breach of her employment contract.

Additionally, employment contracts that contain provisions providing that the employee will not work in competition with her employer after termination for a specified period of time (at least over one year), also known as **covenants not to compete**, cannot be performed within one year. If the employee does go to work for a competitor within those years after leaving the previous employer, there is a breach, as the employee has not fully performed her obligations under the contract. Full performance can come only after the passage of the specified number of years; the Statute of Frauds applies.

covenant not to compete
An employment clause that prohibits an employee from leaving his job and going to work for a competitor for a specified period of time in a particular area.

Example

Danny the candy salesman works for Mmmmmm Candies, Inc., and his employment contract specifically states that he is not permitted to work for a competitor in this current sales territory within three years of leaving his employment with Mmmmmm Candies. This is a covenant not to compete. The company wants to protect its interests in its buyer contacts that Danny has developed. Danny leaves Mmmmmm Candies in January 2010 to work for Delish Delights, Inc., a competitor of Mmmmmm Candies. According to the covenant not to compete, Danny cannot work for this competitor in the same sales territory until January 2013. If he does, he is in breach of the contract. Therefore, it is impossible for Danny to perform on his contractual obligations not to compete with his former employer within one year.

SPOT THE ISSUE!

Paula Paralegal has been searching for a job since graduation four months ago. She interviewed with a large firm and it made her an offer for employment starting at an annual salary of $50,000. Taking this job means that Paula will have to move a considerable distance, leaving her friends and family behind. Before accepting, Paula asked for reassurances that the firm would keep her for at least two years, making it worth her while to move. During a phone call, the firm did tell her that she was highly qualified and it would love to have her in its employ for at least two years if not more! Paula, as diligent as she is, wrote the following letter:

Dear Big Firm:

Thank you for your time and interest in my professional pursuits. Although it will be hard leaving my friends and family and moving to a new city, I am looking forward to working with you. I have decided to accept your offer for $50,000 per year commencing on January 1, 2004. I understand per our conversations that my employment will be at least for a two-year period.

Signed,

Paula Paralegal

Although things went well for eight months at the new firm, Paula was terminated on August 25, 2004. Paula brought suit for wrongful termination and breach of the employment contract. Big Firm has asserted the Statute of Frauds as a defense and made a summary judgment motion based on this.

As the judge in this matter, how would you rule and why?

Contracts in Consideration of Marriage (Prenuptial and Antenuptial Agreements)

The Statute of Frauds does not apply to the mutual promise to actually marry the other person, but it does apply to all other arrangements and/or conditions attached to that agreement. This is most often recognized as either a prenuptial agreement, wherein both parties make certain decisions regarding allocation of assets and other considerations should the marriage fail, or, once the marriage has failed, an antenuptial agreement, wherein the parties make decisions regarding the dissolution. A prenuptial agreement can be likened to writing the divorce settlement before even getting married. It should be made very clear that the contract must contain conditions attached to the actual agreement to become married, not just incidental to it. The end to be attained must be the marriage and by the contract the conditions are set forth.

Example
Max Suckerfield, under the (mistaken) impression that he is as successful as Mark Zuckerberg, the CEO of Facebook, has written up a prenuptial agreement for his girlfriend, Ivana Richman. The contract states that Ivana's aging parents can live with them if she agrees to marry him and that, should the marriage dissolve, Ivana will receive 50 percent of his net worth. The consideration here is the exchange of the promise to marry for the promise to take in Ivana's parents. This agreement is controlled by the Statute of Frauds and therefore must be in writing to be enforceable. *See, e.g., Koch v. Koch*, 232 A.2d 157 (N.J. Super. App. Div. 1967).

The Statute of Frauds stays traditional and requires the actual marriage to be part of the consideration to support the purported contract. It is interesting to note that similar agreements between unmarried couples are enforceable without a writing; however, the parties are still required to demonstrate the terms of the agreement should one exist. The court in *Marra v. Nazzaro*, 2018 NY Slip Op 50004(U) (N.Y. City Ct. 2018), opined as to the difficulties one may encounter because "[t]he things done for affection and transactions made in the course of and as a natural consequence of living together in a romantic relationship do not translate well into contract law." However, in cases where an agreement appears to be sufficiently evident, the general rules of contract apply. *See, e.g., Poe v. Estate of Levy*, 411 So. 2d 253 (Fla. App. 1982) (A promise to provide support may be enforceable even though the precise amount of support is not specified, since it may be inferred that the parties intended a "reasonable" amount of support in light of their established lifestyle.). The court in *Morone v. Morone*, 429 N.Y.S. 2d 592, 595, 413 N.E.2d 1154 (N.Y. 1980) made it quite clear that contract law should be the applicable standard:

> Changing social custom has increased greatly the number of persons living together without solemnized ceremony and consequently without benefit of the rules of law that govern property and financial matters between married couples. The difficulties attendant upon establishing property and financial rights between unmarried couples under available theories of law other than contract warrant application of *Gorden*'s recognition of express contract even though the services rendered be limited to those generally characterized as "housewifely." There is, moreover, no statutory requirement that such a contract as plaintiff here alleges be in writing.

An antenuptial agreement is often used synonymously for a prenuptial agreement, although it usually only refers to what happens after divorce—like the distribution of assets and support—whereas prenuptial agreements also address the circumstances that must occur during the marriage or indeed, for the marriage to take place at all. Therefore, these contracts are enforceable only if they are in writing. These agreements are still within the language of the Statute of Frauds because they are still in consideration of marriage as that is still the reason why the parties are making the arrangements for what happens after the marriage is over. Like most contracts, it doesn't matter what the parties name their agreement, the courts will look to the form and substance and intent of the parties to make determinations.

Example

If Ivana and Max's marriage comes to an end, the parties may have agreed to the terms of the antenuptial settlement. Ivana convinced Max to agree to continue to pay for her parents' living expenses, among other things. The agreement is in contemplation of marriage—albeit the contemplation of the end of the marriage, not the beginning of it. The only reason Max and Ivana are making these arrangements is due to the marriage relationship. Therefore, the agreement must satisfy the Statute of Frauds in order to be legally enforceable.

EYE ON ETHICS

ETHICS

Many people seeking divorces are turning to alternative means to settle their dispute. Lawyers, recognizing this trend toward "alternate dispute resolution," serve as domestic relations mediators. The ethical dilemma presented is whether, following a successful mediation, the lawyer can draft the settlement agreement (which, under the Statute of Frauds, must be reduced to a writing) and necessary court pleadings to obtain a divorce for the parties.

The Utah Bar answered this issue clearly: "Never." "When a lawyer-mediator, after a successful mediation, drafts the settlement agreement, complaint and other pleadings to implement the settlement and obtain a divorce for the parties, the lawyer-mediator is engaged in the practice of law." Under this analysis, the lawyer is not merely acting as the "scrivener" to fulfill the Statute of Frauds mandate. The Bar found that the lawyer would be engaged in prohibited concurrent representation—an "ethically unacceptable practice." See Utah State Bar, Opinion Number 05-03, issued September 30, 2005.

Sureties and Guarantees (Answering the Debt of Another)

Normally, people like to hold onto their money and not pay for those things or obligations that they don't have to. Everyone likes a free lunch. However, the Statute of Frauds recognizes that there are persons who agree to pay for the debts of another party even though they don't have to. Therefore, this type of agreement must be memorialized in writing. It is a magnanimous administrator of a decedent's estate who offers to pay for the decedent's debts out of the administrator's own pocket. The obligations are tied to the remaining estate only. For example, Annie Administrator agrees to pay for Grandma Gertie's doctor's bills out of her own pocket because, perhaps, she believes that the doctor did the very best to make Gertie comfortable in her decline and the estate has no money to pay the bills. Annie's promise, as the **surety**, to pay the doctor would have to be in writing if the doctor sought collection of the bill in court.

surety
A party who assumes primary liability for the payment of another's debt.

Without delving into the intricacies of guarantees and sureties, generally speaking, where the promise to pay for the debt of another is unrelated and without gain to the promisor/guarantor, the agreement should fall within the Statute of Frauds, like the Grandma Gertie example above. Where the promise is made so that the party can obtain credit to begin with or the promisor/guarantor has something to gain from the transaction, the promise is part of the original consideration and therefore is outside the Statute of Frauds. For example, Sara's parents agree to sign a home loan agreement between Sara and National Bank as the guarantors of the loan. Should Sara be unable to make payments, the bank has a legal recourse to seek payment from Sara's parents. This guarantee, the promise to pay for the debt of another, is tied to the acquisition of the loan and is a part of the agreement itself. A guarantee is different than a co-signor. A **guarantor** is only "on the hook" for payments after the default of the primary debtor. Conversely, both co-signors of a loan are held equally responsible for the payments from the onset. There is no need to wait until one defaults. The loan would not have been made absent the guarantee from Sara's parents. Additionally, the promisors in this case, Sara's parents, also have something to gain from the transaction—Sara finally moves out!

guarantor
A party who assumes secondary liability for the payment of another's debt. The guarantor is liable to the creditor only if the original debtor does not make payment.

The Sale of Goods Valued over $500.00 (§ 2-201 Uniform Commercial Code)

While the bulk of the discussion of the Uniform Commercial Code will be in Part Five of the text, for the sake of completeness, the Statute of Frauds requirement will be discussed here.

The UCC requires that a contract for the sale of goods for a *price* over $500.00 is required to be memorialized in some written form. **Price** is stressed because there has been a change away from **value** as that is a more indefinite term. The price is the amount of money that the seller has placed on the item— the amount of money that the seller will accept to transfer the item to the buyer. The value of the item may be completely different, either higher or lower, and can be subjective.

price
The monetary cost assigned to a transaction by the parties.

value
The worth of the goods or services in the transaction as determined by an objective outside standard.

Example

Penny collects antique Italian majolica pottery; so far in her collection, she has acquired 300 different pieces. Roy owns an antique shop and carries a few pieces of this style of pottery. Roy has priced a large platter at $450. Penny considers this a bargain and agrees to purchase the platter. Penny would have paid up to $750 for this piece of majolica because she values it that highly. Other customers may consider the $450 selling price too high as they may only value the piece at $300. Under the pricing scheme of the Statute of Frauds, this transaction is not required to be in writing. If the value of the piece were the measure of determining whether the agreement to purchase was controlled by the Statute of Frauds, then it would be unclear as to whose standards of valuation would apply: the seller's? the buyer's? which buyer? Penny or the cheapskate?

Additionally, the UCC's requirements for merchants allow for some leeway in the form the writing takes. There only needs to be "some writing sufficient to indicate that a contract for the sale has been made. . . ." *See, e.g., Cohen v. Fisher*, 287 A.2d 222 (N.J. Super. 1972) (The court held that a check could constitute a writing sufficient under the Statute of Frauds and the UCC where the full contract price and the subject matter were written on the check.).

Additionally, the price may be payable in money or in exchange for property or services, thereby precluding the parties from avoiding the Statute of Frauds and UCC requirements by engaging in the barter system. "The price [for goods] can be made payable in money or otherwise. [. . .] [T]he phrase "'money or otherwise' could not be broader. Services can be the 'price' for goods. Barters are included." *See E & L Rental Equipment, Inc. v. Wade Constr., Inc.*, 752 N.E.2d 655, 659 (Ind. App. 2001) (citations omitted) (E & L provided goods, in the form of sand, limestone, and wood chips, to Wade in exchange for recycling services.).

RESEARCH THIS

In your jurisdiction, find the Statute of Frauds. What are the *particular* requirements for

1. Prenuptial agreements.
2. Conveyance of an interest in real property.
3. Guarantees and other promises to pay the debt of another.

PARTIAL PERFORMANCE

partial performance doctrine
The court's determination that a party's actions taken in reliance on the oral agreement "substitutes" for the writing and takes the transaction out of the scope of the Statute of Frauds and, thus, can be enforced.

Even if the Statute of Frauds *does apply* and the writing requirement is *not met*, the court may still give the aggrieved party who is not at fault a remedy to prevent injustice. If a party has begun to perform on an oral contract that should be in writing according to the Statute of Frauds, the party, by this **partial performance**, may have preserved her right to enforce the terms of the contract or to recoup what has been expended in her performance under the contract. It is not a bad thing to perform on your promises even if they do not conform to the Statute of Frauds. The Statute of Frauds relates solely to enforceability under traditional contract law. The court may fashion a remedy as it sees fit under the particular circumstances. It may restore the aggrieved party to the status quo by putting her in the same place she was before having performed, like making the defendant return money or the conveyance.

Example
Betty Buyer agrees to purchase Greenacre from Sam Seller. As a real estate transaction, it should be in writing according to the Statute of Frauds. However, Betty and Sam never put their agreement in writing. All seems to be going well and Betty has given Sam a check for 75 percent of the purchase price. She will give him the other 25 percent when all the inspections have finished, and she gets the keys. Sam gets another offer from Irene Interloper and, figuring that Betty doesn't have any real proof of their agreement, enters into a written contract for the sale of Greenacre to Irene. Betty learns of this deal and takes Sam to court to enforce their original agreement. Sam raises the Statute of Frauds as an affirmative defense to enforcement. The

court, however, will not let him off that easily. Using its powers in equity, the court can either force the return of the money to Betty or require Sam to convey the property to Betty despite the lack of a writing to satisfy the Statute of Frauds. The exact remedy will depend on factual details and the particulars of the situation.

Every partial performance exception to the writing requirement under the Statute of Frauds is determined on a case-by-case basis. *See Valentino v. Davis*, 270 A.D.2d 635, 637 (N.Y. App. Div. 2000). In the *Valentino* case, there was a still-to-be-finalized contract for the "boarding, breeding and care of Valentino's mares with Davis' stallions, as well as the care and ownership of any future foals, for a three-year period at the [Davis] Farm." Despite not having finalized the details of this arrangement—which would require a writing under the Statute of Frauds—Valentino sent 20 mares and their foals to the Defendant's Farm, although later he removed his mares and foals due to the poor conditions at the Davis Farm. The *Valentino* court could not find that this temporary accommodation of the mares "unequivocally" referred to the alleged three-year agreement and, therefore, partial performance was not available to save this contract from the writing requirement. *Id.* at 638. Where there is an alternative interpretation of the circumstances, then the terms of the oral contract cannot be enforced.

However, in order to avoid injustice and promote fairness, the court will allow enforcement of an oral contract that normally would be under the Statute of Frauds where the party seeking enforcement has relied on the oral agreement to her detriment. By taking positive steps toward fulfilling the oral obligation, the promisee can essentially prove the existence of the contract. The actions taken by the promisee must unquestionably relate to the oral promise. There can be no other reason that the promisee might have taken those actions. This is a "but for" test: But for the existence of the oral agreement, the promisee would not have taken those actions. The actions themselves explain the existence of the agreement and, therefore, the court can consider this a reliable means of proving the existence of the contract. This is the reason for creating the Statute of Frauds in the first place: to ensure honesty on the part of the parties to the contract.

Recall from Chapter 4 the discussion of "implied-in-fact" conditions: An entire contract may be implied in fact by the performances of the parties. However, where the parties have intended to reduce their agreement to a writing, this theory of implying the entire contract due to the surrounding actions is inapplicable. "A contract may not be implied in fact from the conduct of the parties where it appears that they intended to be bound only by a formal written agreement." *Id.* However, where the parties did not necessarily intend to reduce their agreement to a writing, performance will take the agreement outside the statute requirements: "[T]he performance, illustrated by the parties' course of dealing through the years, except[s] the agreement from the statute of frauds requirement." *See E & L Rental Equipment, supra*, at 660.

SPOT THE ISSUE!

Dr. Stanley has his own veterinary practice in New York and desires to expand his business by attracting upscale clientele. He contacts his old school buddy, Dr. Livingstone, now a famous zoologist and licensed vet. They began to discuss the terms of the partnership agreement. The original draft stated a two-year term of employment but failed to address the parties' relationship after those two years. Dr. Livingstone had some concerns and therefore did not sign this agreement. Dr. Stanley assured him that they could work these things out. Dr. Livingstone started to work with Dr. Stanley, and the two continued to work out the details. All the drafts of subsequent contracts (which were not signed) contained noncompetition clauses. Dr. Livingstone, finally fed up with Dr. Stanley, left to work for another veterinary group in the area. Is Dr. Livingstone in breach of an employment agreement? Why or why not?

Summary

Contract law's desire for certainty has placed a writing requirement on certain types of contracts to ensure against fraud. These include:

1. The *transfer of real property interests.*
2. Contracts that are *not performable within one year.*
3. Contracts *in consideration of marriage* (prenuptial and antenuptial agreements).
4. *Sureties and guarantees* (answering the debt of another).
5. *Uniform Commercial Code* provisions regarding the sale of goods *over $500.00.*

Even if the Statute of Frauds does apply and the writing requirement is not met, the court may still give the aggrieved party who is not at fault a remedy to prevent injustice if that party has *partially performed* on the agreement.

Key Terms

contracts in consideration of marriage
covenant not to compete
guarantor
"not performable within one year"
partial performance doctrine
price

signed by the party to be charged
surety
transfers of real property interests
value
writing to satisfy the Statute of Frauds

Review Questions

"SORT IT OUT"

Identify which of the following contracts fall within the Statute of Frauds and specify which provision controls.

1. Jack promises to marry Jill.

2. Jack promises to marry Jill if she promises to be a good wife.

3. Jack promises to marry Jill if she will allow his unemployed brother to live in the basement until he finds a job.

4. Sam offers to sell his farm to Joe for $400.00; he's sick of all the work it takes and just wants to get rid of it.

5. Sam offers to sell his standing trees for $400.00 to the lumber yard.

6. Sam offers to sell all his apples that year to Joe for $800.00.

7. The executrix of Mr. Smith's estate promises the funeral home that the estate will pay the burial expenses.

8. The executrix of Mr. Smith's estate promises the funeral home that she will pay the burial expenses from her own funds.

9. Rita promises Sam that if Joe cannot pay for the farm, she will pay for it.

10. Joe offers to employ Rita for life on his new farm.

11. Joe offers to employ Rita for two years with the option to renew for an additional three years after that.

"FAULTY PHRASES"

All of the following statements are FALSE; state why they are false and then rewrite them as true statements. Write a brief fact pattern that illustrates your answer.

1. The Statute of Frauds requires all contracts to be in writing in order to be valid.

2. The writing must be contained in one document in order to satisfy the proof requirement under the Statute of Frauds.

3. If a party's performance will take less than one year to complete, it is not under the Statute of Frauds.

4. Once a party begins to perform under an agreement, there is no need for a writing to satisfy the Statute of Frauds.

5. Contracts between persons who intend to get married must be in writing.

"WRITE" AWAY! PORTFOLIO ASSIGNMENT

Review the Druid and Carrie contract. Are there any elements of the transaction that need to be in writing to satisfy the Statute of Frauds? What facts could you change in the fact pattern that would change your answer? It is always good practice to memorialize any subsequent changes (there are always changes in a construction contract) to the original agreement. Draft a "Change/Extra Work Order" form for use in this transaction.

Case in Point

THE STATUTE OF FRAUDS AND PARTIAL PERFORMANCE

2017 IL App (5th) 160260-U
EMERICK FARMS, a General Partnership; FAYETTE FARMS, a General Partnership;
and Benjamin EMERICK, Individually, Plaintiffs-Appellees,
v.
James E. MARLEN and JoAnn MARLEN, Individually, and James E. MARLEN,
as Trustee of the James E. Marlen and
JoAnn Marlen Declaration of Trust Dated January 27, 2010, Defendants-Appellants.
NO. 5-16-0260
Appellate Court of Illinois Fifth District
May 2, 2017

NOTICE
Decision filed 05/02/17. The text of this decision may be changed or corrected prior to the filing of a Petition for Rehearing or the disposition of the same.
NOTICE
This order was filed under Supreme Court Rule 23 and may not be cited as precedent by any party except in the limited circumstances allowed under Rule 23(e)(1).
Appeal from the Circuit Court of Fayette County.
No. 12-L-8
Honorable MICHAEL D. MCHANEY, Judge, presiding.
JUSTICE OVERSTREET delivered the judgment of the court. Presiding Justice Moore and Justice Welch concurred in the judgment.

ORDER

¶ 1 *Held*: After a bench trial, the circuit court improperly entered money judgment in plaintiffs' favor on their breach of oral contract counts.
¶ 2 The plaintiffs, Emerick Farms and Fayette Farms, both general partnerships, along with Benjamin Emerick, filed an action in the circuit court of Fayette County, alleging damages against the defendants, James E. Marlen and JoAnn Marlen, individually, and

Page 2

James E. Marlen, as trustee of the James E. Marlen and JoAnn Marlen Declaration of Trust, dated January

27, 2010 (the Trust), for breaching oral agreements to lease lands to the plaintiffs for farming. After a bench trial, the circuit court found that the defendants breached the oral lease agreements, and the circuit court entered judgment in the plaintiffs' favor for $264,830.80, which included lost profits and costs. For the following reasons, we reverse the circuit court's judgment, and we remand the cause for further proceedings.

¶ 3 BACKGROUND

¶ 4 In the plaintiffs' second-amended complaint, filed on August 19, 2013, the plaintiffs alleged that on October 18, 2011, James verbally agreed to allow Emerick Farms to lease for farming 254 tillable acres, known as the Augsburg St. James Farm, in Fayette County, from January 1, 2012, to December 31, 2013, under the terms shown summarized in an "Amendments to Lease" dated October 14, 2010, and attached to the complaint. The "Amendments to Lease" was not signed by any of the defendants. The plaintiffs alleged that on October 18, 2011, James also verbally agreed to allow Fayette Farms to lease for farming 531 acres, known as the Butts Engele Farm, in Fayette County, from 2012 through 2013 under terms summarized in an "Illinois Cash Farm Lease," which was attached to the complaint. The "Illinois Cash Farm Lease" was also not signed by any of the defendants.
¶ 5 The plaintiffs alleged that during conversations on October 6, 2011, Benjamin, acting as tenant

and on behalf of both of the plaintiff partnerships, verbally advised James that he needed to apply fall fertilizer and perform fall tillage on the two farms, and James

Page 3

authorized and consented to the purchase and application of such fertilizer and tillage on the farms, based upon the parties' verbal agreement and mutual understanding that the plaintiffs would farm the properties in 2012 and 2013. The plaintiffs alleged that Emerick Farms and Fayette Farms thereby provided and obtained fertilizer application and fall tillage for each of the farm properties, in contemplation and in reliance on the renewal or continuance of the farm leases for the 2012 farming year.

¶ 6 The plaintiffs alleged that on December 9, 2011, James sent a letter to Benjamin disregarding the agreements previously reached. The plaintiffs alleged that this letter was received before lease renewals had been signed by both parties, but after the tillage and fertilizer were supplied on the two farms. The plaintiffs alleged that the defendants thereafter refused to perform the lease agreements and leased the property to another tenant farmer.

¶ 7 The plaintiffs alleged that their conduct in providing fertilizer and tillage constituted a significant partial performance in reliance on the oral agreements reached between the parties. Specifically, in count I, Fayette Farms and Benjamin sought judgment against James and JoAnn for $79,463.18 for tillage and fertilizer provided for the Butts Engele Farm and for lost income damages of $212,000 caused by the breach of the lease agreement. In count II, Emerick Farms sought judgment against James and the Trust for damages of $41,719.71 for fall tillage and fertilizer applied to the Augsburg St. James Farm and for loss of profits of $100,000 caused by the breach of the lease agreement.

Page 4

¶ 8 In count III, entitled "Quasi-Contract, Unjust Enrichment, Quantum Meruit," Emerick Farms alternatively alleged that in the event the court should find that the lease agreement described in count II was unenforceable, the court should nevertheless require James and the Trust to pay $41,719.71 for the reasonable value of the fall tillage and fertilizer application on the Augsburg St. James Farm. Emerick Farms alleged that James and the Trust would be unjustly enriched to retain the benefits without compensating Emerick Farms for the benefits provided under the reasonable belief that it would be farming the land in the upcoming farm year.

¶ 9 In count IV, entitled "Quasi-Contract, Unjust Enrichment, Quantum Meruit," Benjamin and Fayette Farms alternatively alleged that if the court found the oral lease agreement described in count I unenforceable, the court should nevertheless require James and JoAnn to pay $79,463.18 for the reasonable value of the fall tillage and fertilizer application on the Butts Engele Farm. Benjamin and Fayette Farms alleged that James and JoAnn would be unjustly enriched to retain the benefits without compensating Benjamin and Fayette Farms for the benefits provided under the reasonable belief that they would be farming the land in the upcoming farm year.

¶ 10 On November 7, 2013, the defendants filed an answer to counts III and IV of the plaintiffs' second-amended complaint. On the same day, the defendants filed a motion for involuntary dismissal of counts I and II of the plaintiffs' second-amended complaint. See 735 ILCS 5/2-619 (West 2012). In their motion, the defendants claimed that the plaintiffs' claims were unenforceable pursuant to the statute of frauds found in the Illinois Frauds Act. 740 ILCS 80/2 (West 2012). On December 3, 2013, the circuit court denied

Page 5

the defendants' motion to dismiss counts I and II. The court found that the plaintiffs' allegations of performing work constituted part performance to and reliance on the oral agreement, sufficient to bar the application of the statute of frauds. Thereafter, on January 23, 2014, the defendants filed their answer to counts I and II of the plaintiffs' second-amended complaint.

¶ 11 On March 14, 2016, the circuit court heard evidence on the plaintiffs' claims. The evidence revealed that in 2011, pursuant to written agreements, Benjamin and Emerick Farms leased the farm ground at issue from the defendants, but the written leases terminated by their terms on December 31, 2011. On November 3, 2011, as a result of discussions between James and Benjamin, James sent a proposed, unsigned written lease to Benjamin, but Benjamin did not return the paperwork because he was busy in the field. The proposed leases were not signed by any of the defendants. Thereafter, on December 9, 2011, James notified the plaintiffs that he would not be renewing the leases and advised the plaintiffs to disregard the forms sent on November 3, 2011.

¶ 12 At trial, the evidence also revealed that fall tillage involved turning over the weeds and farm residue on the property, mixing the material with the earth to release the nutrients into the ground and to enhance the deterioration of the material, in preparation for spring planting. The evidence suggested that the plaintiffs expended funds for tillage and fertilizer for the property in October 2011, prior to receiving notice that James would not be renewing the leases.

¶ 13 After the bench trial, the circuit court stated that it was "resolving credibility in favor of the plaintiffs and against the defendant[s]." The court further stated that "there

Page 6

was specific performance to take this out of the statute of frauds." The circuit court stated that it was "granting judgment in favor of the plaintiffs for the full amount asked for plus costs."

¶ 14 On March 21, 2016, the circuit court entered written judgment in favor of the plaintiffs and against the defendants, finding that the defendants breached the amendments to the lease for extension of the Illinois Cash Farm Lease for the Augsburg St. James Farm for the period of January 1, 2012, to December 31, 2013, and the Illinois Cash Farm Lease for the Butts Engele Farm, for the period of January 1, 2012, to December 31, 2013. The circuit court awarded judgment in the amount of $264,830. The circuit court's award included lost profits of $169,994 for the Augsburg St. James Farm in the 2012 and 2013 crop years, lost profits of $94,696 for the Butts Engele Farm in the 2012 and 2013 crop years, and costs of $140.

¶ 15 On April 15, 2016, the defendants sought leave to amend their answer to the plaintiffs' second-amended complaint to include the affirmative defense of the statute of frauds, and the circuit court granted the defendants' motion for leave to amend

their answer on May 24, 2016. On April 15, 2016, the defendants also filed a motion to reconsider the circuit court's judgment. In their motion to reconsider, the defendants noted that because the plaintiffs and the defendants did not execute written leases, the circuit court implicitly found that the parties entered into an oral lease and that partial performance removed applicability of the statute of frauds. The defendants argued, however, that the doctrine of partial performance did not apply because the plaintiffs

Page 7

sought money damages. On May 24, 2016, the circuit court denied the defendants' motion to reconsider. On June 17, 2016, the defendants filed their notice of appeal.

¶ 16 ANALYSIS

¶ 17 On appeal, the defendants argue, *inter alia*, that the circuit court erred in entering judgment for the plaintiffs on counts I and II because their actions for breach of an oral contract to lease land are barred by the statute of frauds. The defendants contend that the doctrine of partial performance, which in cases of equity may remove an oral contract from the statute of frauds, is not available because the plaintiffs alleged and offered proof of an adequate remedy at law. The plaintiffs counter that the defendants have forfeited the issue because they failed to properly raise it in the circuit court. Alternatively, the plaintiffs argue that the circuit court properly held that their partial performance removed the oral lease agreement from the statute of frauds.

¶ 18 The plaintiffs recognize that the defendants raised the statute of frauds defense in their November 7, 2013, motion to dismiss counts I and II of the plaintiffs' second-amended complaint. See *Armagan v. Pesha*, 2014 IL App. (1st) 121840, ¶ 38, n.1 (statute of frauds constitutes an affirmative matter outside of the facts alleged in a complaint and should be raised in a motion to dismiss pursuant to section 2-619(a)(7) of the Code of Civil Procedure); 735 ILCS 5/2-619(a)(7) (West 2012). The plaintiffs filed their motion to dismiss along with their answer to counts III and IV of the second-amended complaint and prior to filing their January 23, 2014, answer to counts I and II of the plaintiffs' second-amended complaint.

See *Fox v. Seiden*, 2016 IL App. (1st) 141984, ¶ 51 (affirmative defense is properly raised at or before the time to answer the complaint). In

Page 8

their motion to dismiss, the defendants alleged that the plaintiffs' claim to damages based upon breach of a verbal agreement was unenforceable under the provisions of the statute of frauds. In rejecting the defendants' statute of frauds defense, the circuit court held that the plaintiffs' "part performance pursuant to the oral agreement and in reliance upon the oral agreement" barred the application of the statute of frauds. After the bench trial, in their motion to reconsider, the defendants argued that the circuit court improperly applied the doctrine of partial performance to remove the oral lease agreement from the statute of frauds because the doctrine of partial performance cannot remove the statute of frauds bar in actions at law for monetary damages. Again, the circuit court rejected the defendants' contention. On appeal, the plaintiffs argue that the defendants waived this particular argument regarding the enforceability of the statute of frauds by failing to raise it prior to their motion to reconsider.

¶ 19 Although "[a]rguments raised for the first time in a motion for reconsideration in the circuit court are forfeited on appeal" (*Evanston Insurance Co. v. Riseborough*, 2014 IL 114271, ¶ 36), the defendants previously raised their statute of frauds defense in their motion to dismiss. To the extent that the defendants argued the bar of the statute of frauds more expansively in their motion to reconsider, this argument properly addressed the circuit court's error in its application of the law. Accordingly, the defendants did not forfeit their statute of frauds defense on appeal because they properly asserted it before the circuit court and the plaintiffs were not taken by surprise. See *Harvey v. McKinney*, 221 Ill. App. 3d 140, 142 (1991) ("The law in this State is well established that if a defendant wishes to assert an affirmative defense such as the statute of frauds at trial, he

Page 9

is required to specifically plead it so that the plaintiff is not taken by surprise."). We therefore conclude

that the defendants sufficiently raised this issue before the circuit court and did not forfeit it for purposes of appellate review.

¶ 20 The conveyance of the right to enter upon the land for the purpose of farming is a conveyance of an interest in the land itself. Contracts conveying land or an interest therein are required to be in writing pursuant to the statute of frauds, which provides as follows:

"No action shall be brought to charge any person upon any contract for the sale of lands, . . . or any interest in or concerning them, for a longer term than one year, unless such contract or some memorandum or note thereof shall be in writing[ ] and signed by the party to be charged therewith . . . ." 740 ILCS 80/2 (West 2012).

The statute of fraud's purpose is to preserve any existing interest in land from the chances of uncertainty and fraud attending the admission of parol evidence. *IMM Acceptance Corp. v. First National Bank & Trust Co. of Evanston*, 148 Ill. App. 3d 949, 956 (1986). "The statute of frauds defense is a substantive defense which defeats the cause of action." *Cain v. Cross*, 293 Ill. App. 3d 255, 258 (1997).

¶ 21 The doctrine of part performance is an equitable doctrine developed and applied in those cases where a party is seeking the equitable remedy of specific enforcement. *Phillips v. Britton*, 162 Ill. App. 3d 774, 781 (1987); see also *Anderson v. Kohler*, 397 Ill. App. 3d 773, 786 (2009) ("partial performance is an equitable doctrine, and the only contractual relief it affords is specific performance"). "The equitable remedy of specific

Page 10

performance requires a party to perform an affirmative act to fulfill a contract." *Butler v. Kent*, 275 Ill. App. 3d 217, 227 (1995).

"The basis upon which the doctrine of partial performance rests is, that when a verbal contract has been made and the promisor has knowingly permitted the promisee to do acts in part performance of the agreement, in full reliance upon it, which would not have been done without the agreement, and which are of such nature as to change the relations of the parties and prevent a restoration to their former condition or an adequate compensation for the loss to the promisee by a judgment at law for damages, then it is a fraud in the promisor to interpose the [s]tatute of [f]rauds as a bar to the completion of the contract and thus secure for himself all the benefits of the acts done in part performance, while the promisee not only loses all advantage from the bargain but is left without adequate remedy for its failure or compensation for what he has done in pursuance of it." *Flannery v. Woolverton*, 329 Ill. 424, 431 (1928).

In other words, to remove the bar of the statute of frauds, partial performance must be such that it is impossible to compensate the performing party for the value of his performance, so that any refusal to complete the engagement would constitute a fraud on the performing party. See *Prodromos v. Howard Savings Bank*, 295 Ill. App. 3d 470, 476 (1998); see also *Roti v. Roti*, 364 Ill. App. 3d 191, 197 (2006) (the partial performance must be of such a character that it is impossible or impractical to compensate the performing party for the value of his performance).

Page 11

¶ 22 Accordingly, although acts of partial performance may be sufficient to remove an oral agreement from the operation of the statute of frauds in an action at equity, acts of partial performance do not remove an action at law from the operation of the statute of frauds. *Cohn v. Checker Motors Corp.*, 233 Ill. App. 3d 839, 845 (1992); *Sjogren v. Maybrooks, Inc.*, 214 Ill. App. 3d 888, 892 (1991); Restatement (Second) of Contracts § 129 cmt. c (1981). Indeed, this court has consistently held that the doctrine of part performance is not applicable in actions at law for money damages. *John O. Schofield, Inc. v. Nikkel*, 314 Ill. App. 3d 771, 784 (2000) (party seeking application of equitable principles to defeat interposition of statute of frauds must establish that promise cannot be made whole by money damages); *Cain*, 293 Ill. App. 3d at 259 (doctrine of part performance is not applicable in actions at law for money damages); *Phillips*, 162 Ill. App. 3d at 781 (doctrine of part performance may not be invoked to sustain an ordinary action at law for damages for breach of

contract); *Gibbons v. Stillwell*, 149 Ill. App. 3d 411, 415 (1986) ("partial performance of an oral contract does not take an action of law from the operation of the [s]tatute of [f]rauds").

¶ 23 In arguing that partial performance may take an oral contract outside the statute of frauds, the plaintiffs cite *Tabora v. Gottlieb Memorial Hospital*, 279 Ill. App. 3d 108 (1996); *Melburg v. Dakin*, 337 Ill. App. 204 (1949); and *Anderson v. Collinson*, 300 Ill. App. 22 (1939). However, in *Tabora*, the appellate court concluded that the plaintiff-physician's claim that he had an oral contract for a lifetime of two-year reappointments at the defendant-hospital was properly dismissed pursuant to the statute of frauds because the plaintiff had failed to allege sufficient partial performance. *Tabora*, 279 Ill. App. 3d

Page 12

at 120. Further, *Melburg* and *Anderson* involved the defense of part performance in forcible entry and detainer suits, and as noted by the court in *Melburg*, equitable defenses may be asserted in a forcible entry and detainer proceeding. See *Melburg*, 337 Ill. App. at 211 (tenant may assert equitable defense of partial performance when plaintiff seeks possession under the forcible entry and detainer statute); *Anderson*, 300 Ill. App. at 26 (based on farmer's partial performance, court affirmed trial court order of specific performance of oral agreement to lease farm and writ of injunction restraining owner from prosecuting forcible entry and detainer suit). "A forcible entry and detainer action is a limited proceeding, focusing on the central issue of possession." *American National Bank v. Powell*, 293 Ill. App. 3d 1033, 1044 (1997). In none of these cases did the court hold that partial performance takes an oral contract outside the statute of frauds when an adequate monetary remedy is available.

¶ 24 In this case, the plaintiffs alleged that they and the defendants entered into a verbal contract to lease the two parcels of land for two years. This oral contract, never executed as a written agreement, fell within the purview of the statute of frauds. See 740 ILCS 80/2 (West 2012). The plaintiffs argued that their partial performance in performing fall tillage and fertilizing services to the lands removed their oral contract from the purview of the statute of frauds pursuant to the doctrine of partial performance.

However, in the plaintiffs' second-amended complaint, the plaintiffs pecuniarily estimated the value of their alleged partial performance, the tillage and fertilizing services, in the amounts of $41,719.71 and $79,463.18. Thus, as alleged, the plaintiffs' partial performance was of such a character that the plaintiffs could be adequately compensated for the value of their

Page 13

services. To remove the bar of the statute of frauds, partial performance must be such that it is impossible to compensate the performing party for the value of their performance. See *Roti*, 364 Ill. App. 3d at 197; *Prodromos*, 295 Ill. App. 3d at 476.

¶ 25 Moreover, pursuant to each breach of contract claim, the plaintiffs sought, and the circuit court entered judgment for, monetary damages for lost profits as a result of the defendants' failure to honor the oral agreement for which they claimed partial performance. Because the plaintiffs alleged an adequate remedy at law for damages, the doctrine of partial performance could not operate to remove the plaintiffs' breach of oral contract action to convey an interest of land from the purview of the statute of frauds. See *Gibbons*, 149 Ill. App. 3d at 415. Accordingly, the circuit court improperly invoked the doctrine of partial performance to sustain the plaintiffs' action at law for money damages for breach of an oral contract. See *John O. Schofield, Inc.*, 314 Ill. App. 3d at 784-85; *Cain*, 293 Ill. App. 3d at 259; *Phillips*, 162 Ill. App. 3d at 781. The plaintiffs' breach of oral contract actions, found in counts I and II of their complaint, were barred by the statute of frauds

and should have been dismissed on the defendants' motion.

¶ 26 After the bench trial, without delineating on which counts it was entering judgment, the circuit court implicitly entered judgment on counts I and II, finding that the defendants "breached the [a]mendments to lease for . . . the Augsburg St. James Farm . . . for the period of January 1, 2012 to December 31, 2013 . . . and . . . for the Butts/Eng[e]le Farm . . . for the period of January 1, 2012 to December 31, 2013." The circuit court awarded judgment in favor of the plaintiffs in the total amount of $264,830.80, which included lost profits and costs. The circuit court failed to address

Page 14

counts III and IV, which were actions pled in the alternative to counts I and II, and which sought recovery for the reasonable value of the tillage and fertilizer that the plaintiffs alleged unjustly benefitted the defendants' property. Accordingly, for the foregoing reasons, we reverse the circuit court's order entering judgment in the plaintiffs' favor on counts I and II, and we remand the cause for the circuit court to consider the evidence in light of the plaintiffs' allegations in counts III and IV of their second-amended complaint.

¶ 27 CONCLUSION

¶ 28 For the reasons stated, we reverse the judgment of the circuit court of Fayette County, and we remand for further proceedings consistent with this order.

¶ 29 Reversed and remanded.

Chapter 7

Capacity and Illegality

Chapter Objectives

The student will be able to:

- Use vocabulary regarding capacity and illegality properly.
- Discuss the three categories of incapacity.
- Evaluate the ramifications of each kind of incapacity on the enforceability of a contract.
- Determine if ratification or disavowal of the contract has occurred given a certain set of facts.
- Determine whether the subject matter of the contract is illegal and if so whether it is *malum in se* or *malum prohibitum*.
- Evaluate whether a court would sever an illegal clause from a contract or hold the entire contract void.

This chapter will explore WHO may create a binding legal contract and WHO may not and WHAT the agreement may pertain to and WHAT it may not. These defects in formation of the contract are **affirmative defenses** to enforcement. Essentially, the contract was never formed and therefore cannot be properly or legally performed upon. A party may avoid enforcement of an agreement if she was unable to understand the transaction at the time due to diminished capacity, either due to lack of majority or a mental infirmity, or if the subject matter of the contract is improper, either requiring a criminal or statutorily prohibited act.

affirmative defense
An "excuse" by the opposing party that does not just simply negate the allegation, but puts forth a legal reason to avoid enforcement.

CAPACITY

minors
Persons under the age of 18; once a person has reached 18, they have reached the age of majority.

mentally infirm
Persons not having the capacity to understand a transaction due to a defect in their ability to reason and, therefore, who do not have the requisite mental intent to enter into a contract.

under the influence
Persons who do not have the capacity to understand a transaction due to overconsumption of alcohol or the use of drugs, either legal or illegal, and, therefore, who do not have the requisite mental intent to enter into a contract.

Infancy doctrine
The generally accepted doctrine of contract law that permits minors to avoid contractual obligations under a public policy that minors need to be protected from potentially unfair or unscrupulous terms due to their lack of sophistication.

voidable
Having the possibility of avoidance of performance at the option of the incapacitated party.

void
A transaction that is impossible to be enforced because it is invalid.

ratification
A step taken by a formerly incapacitated person that confirms and endorses the voidable contract and thereby makes it enforceable.

There are certain circumstances under which a person cannot enter into a contract as it is deemed legally impossible. The law of contracts protects persons who are under 18 (**minors**), those who are **mentally infirm**, and those **under the influence** of drugs or alcohol. Recall that a person must have the present intent to contract. The people in these three categories are unable to make an informed decision regarding their potential contractual obligations. There may be some very savvy 17-year-olds who indeed may claim to fully understand the deal and actually be getting the better part of the bargain. But minors are not, under the law, held to have contractual capacity. A very rare example of a minor making and being held to a contract occurred in 1972 when Bill Gates sold his first computer program; he was only 17 years old. As a general policy, contract law does not want to hold impetuous teenagers to potentially overwhelming contractual promises. The same logic holds true for those with altered states of mind; the law protects those least able to protect themselves (even from themselves).

Minority

Minors (those under the age of 18) have traditionally been protected from the enforcement of contracts they have entered into under the "**infancy doctrine**." Contracts entered into by minors are **voidable**, not *per se* **void**. A voidable contract is one that *may* be invalid, but we need to wait and see. A contract that is void is invalid and *never* enforceable. A minor has the option upon attaining the age of 18 to *ratify* the contract. By ratifying the contract, the minor validates it; she acknowledges that it is valid and enforceable. It is as if the contract is newly entered into when the former minor confirms its validity. **Ratification** is not as formal of a process as it sounds. The minor, upon reaching majority, can simply continue to abide by the contract. This continued performance indicates that the former minor intends to honor the contract.

For example, if a 17-year-old signs a lease for a car (a promise to make payments) that states that the lease cannot be canceled for the first two years, she can still avoid this contract before turning 18. *See, e.g., Doenges-Long Motors, Inc. v. Gillen*, 328 P.2d 1077 (Colo. 1958) (a minor may disaffirm a contract for the purchase of a car, even where he is at fault for misrepresenting his age at the time of making the contract). After turning 18, the person can use that promise to make the lease payments (technically, past consideration) to ratify the contract and make it enforceable. Indeed, if the minor continues to make payments after reaching 18, this action ratifies the contract. There is no other reason for the former minor to make the payment unless there was the intention of carrying out a valid and enforceable contract. The change from voidable contract to enforceable contract by ratification upon attaining the age of 18 has a subtle effect on the past consideration making it valid present consideration because it is like the minor (now attaining majority) enters into a slightly different agreement—one that is enforceable by both parties.

Note that this difference, enforceability by both parties, is important. Prior to ratification, the contract is only avoidable on the part of the minor. The adult cannot claim the child's minority as a defense to enforcement. In other words, the minor can escape his obligations under the contract while the adult is bound to the contract until it is disavowed by the minor. The disavowal is the opposite of ratification. The minor can claim that the contract is invalid and not enforceable as against him. This disavowal will also permit the minor to avoid potential contract remedies against himself. Once the minor has disavowed the contract, he is permitted to return the subject of the this voidable contract and recover his consideration. "In return the minor is expected to restore **as much of the consideration** as, at the time of disaffirmance, remains in the minor's possession." *Halbman v. Lemke*, 298 N.W.2d 562, 565 (Wis. 1980) [emphasis added] However, in the *Halbman* case, the minor no longer had possession of the vehicle in its original condition; it had been subject to both disrepair and vandalism and therefore was not worth the price paid as consideration. The court was faced with a more complicated issue than merely restoring the pre-contractual status quo. The court recognized that there was no clear rule in this kind of situation as the "law regarding the rights and responsibilities of the parties relative to the consideration exchanged on a disaffirmed contract is characterized by confusion, inconsistency, and a general lack of uniformity as jurisdictions attempt to reach a fair application of the infancy doctrine in today's marketplace." *Id.* The minor cannot give up more than he has and is not responsible for making up the loss of value or depreciation of the consideration. "It seeks compensatory value for that which he cannot return. . . . [W]e believe that to require a disaffirming minor to make restitution for diminished value is, in effect, to bind the minor to a part of the obligation which by law he is privileged to avoid." *Id.* at 567. Therefore, if one party must take a loss in a voidable contract, it will not be the minor.

disavowal
A step taken by a formerly incapacitated person that denies and cancels the voidable contract and thereby makes it unenforceable.

SURF'S UP

The anonymity of the Internet also allows people to hide their true ages. Minors have potentially the same access to material as adults. How can Internet companies be sure of a contracting party's age? For certain products, it is not enough to assume that a person has to be of age to have a credit card. Eighteen-year-olds can hold a credit card in their own name yet cannot legally purchase alcohol. Further, many Internet markets cater specifically to tech-savvy teens. There are valid arguments to be made both for and against the application of the traditional "infancy doctrine." See Cheryl B. Preston, *Cyber-Infants*, 39 Pepp. L. Rev. 2 (2013), available at http://digitalcommons. pepperdine.edu/plr/vol39/iss2/1, and Juanda Lowder Daniel, *Virtually Mature: Examining the Policy of Minors' Incapacity to Contract Through the Cyberscope*, 43 Gonz. L. Rev. 239 (2008).

Tina, a 15-year-old gymnast, aspires to the U.S. Olympic Team. She has managed to obtain the coaching services of Nella Carroli—a famous Russian trainer who works at the Tumblegym. The gym required both Tina and her mother to sign a release from liability for any injuries Tina suffered at its facility. Unfortunately, Tina was hurt as she dismounted from the uneven bars. She wishes to sue Tumblegym for inadequate safety equipment, which directly affected the severity of her injuries. Can Tina sue?

See Simmons v. Parkette Nat'l Gymnastic Training Center, 670 F. Supp. 140 (E.D. Pa. 1987).

EXCEPTION FOR NECESSITIES

necessities
Goods and services that are required; basic elements of living and employment.

As with every general rule of law, there are exceptions. Let's start with the two exceptions regarding minority. The first exception to this rule of avoidability is a contract for **necessities**. If a minor enters into a contract for the acquisition of food, shelter, clothing, medical care, and the like, the minor is not permitted to disaffirm the contract. Public policy prefers that all citizens obtain the necessities of living; therefore, the law protects the suppliers of these necessities by disallowing avoidance for these things. The supplier (the adult in the contract) is protected and will receive the benefit of the contract without fear that the minor will be able to escape his/her obligations. However, it must be noted that the item contracted for be truly necessary to the minor. Where a minor has another place to live, such as at her parents' house, the rental of an apartment is not necessary and therefore is voidable by the minor. There must be an actual need for the subject matter of the contract in order to enforce it as against a minor. *See, e.g., Young v. Weaver*, 883 So. 2d 234 (Ala. Civ. App. 2003).

Example

Marvin, a 16-year-old, is a computer genius and has set up quite a lucrative "help desk" at school; other students pay him for help with their computer problems. Marvin goes on a shopping spree with his hard-earned cash, purchasing a new motorcycle and new computer hardware, and enters into a lease agreement for a little studio apartment near his school. He also sets up a line of credit at the local supermarket to deliver a steady stream of soda, chips, cookies, and frozen pizzas to his new place. Marvin may avoid all of the contracts except for the groceries. Marvin has a place to live at home and, therefore, the apartment is not a necessity. As for the motorcycle and computer supplies, they may make his life more convenient or contribute to his profitability, but they are not necessary. The groceries are, however, a consumable necessity. If the court were to let Marvin out of the contract for the food, there would be no way to compensate the store for its losses. This simply wouldn't be fair. Marvin will have to give back the other items, thereby not truly harming the motorcycle dealership or the computer store. (Unless, of course, Marvin had damaged the items and returned them with diminished value, then the dealership and store would be harmed. From the holding of *Halbman, supra*, we know that the sellers of these goods will be out of luck and could not recover restitution to make up for the loss of value.)

The second exception relates to contracts that are governed by some sort of **legislation**. It is anticipated that minors will enter into certain contracts and cannot avoid them because of their minority. These contracts include educational loan documents, military enlistments, marriage or child-support agreements, banking, and insurance contracts. Society and contract law have acknowledged that many 16- and 17-year-olds are on their own and need to enter into these kinds of agreements, and therefore also have disallowed avoidance to facilitate legally enforceable contracts between a minor and the other parties.

legislation
Regulations codified into laws by Congress.

For example, Sheila Starlet, at the tender age of 17, moves to New York City to fulfill her destiny of becoming a Broadway icon. There will be some agreements to which she will find herself bound and some to which she will not. She will need to enter into a lease for an apartment (a necessity) and open a bank account to pay her bills (statutorily enforceable). These two kinds of contracts are not voidable. However, the contract to perform in an off-Broadway play may be avoidable.

Much of the determination whether the minor can avoid the contract rests not only upon the necessity of the subject matter but also on the potential hardship that it will cause to the adult contracting party. The more likely it is that the other party will not be disadvantaged by the disavowal, the more likely a court will be to permit the avoidance.

RESEARCH THIS

In your jurisdiction, find two cases regarding a minor's capacity to contract: one that holds that a minor is liable for necessities and one that permits disavowal of the contract.

Mentally Infirm

While there is a definite demarcation between either being a minor or not (a person's eighteenth birthday), there is some grey area with respect to *mental disability*. It is not enough to show that the contracting party was under a mental disability, but also that the mental disability rendered the party *incapable of understanding the transaction*. The mental disability must relate to the capacity to contract. *See, e.g., Matter of Estate of Obermeier*, 150 A.D.2d 863 (N.Y.A.D. 3d Dep't 1989) (Despite the fact that Mrs. Obermeier was in a nursing home, was taking sedatives, and was confused at times, she was found to have had capacity at the time she signed her will as she understood the document she was signing.). The disability does not have to be permanent; if the party is incapable due to a temporary mental infirmity, the contract may be avoided or ratified upon regaining mental capacity. By the same token, if the contract was entered into at a time when the party was mentally capable of making the contract, but subsequently became mentally infirm, the contractual performance is put on hold until a time when the party regains capacity and can perform the contractual obligations.

For example, Great Aunt Nelly has become senile and she believes she is living in the 1950s. At that time, Great Aunt Nelly was quite the entrepreneur and had invested in many small businesses that have since become very prosperous. Mr. Shady decides to visit Great Aunt Nelly and try to get her to sell her interests in the businesses. Great Aunt Nelly signs the documents that Mr. Shady presents to her, but she has no idea that she is selling her business interests or what the effect of her signing the documents will have. She believes Mr. Shady is a door-to-door salesman selling encyclopedias, as was common during the 1950s. Great Aunt Nelly is not bound to the contract and it can be rescinded. She was incapable of understanding the transaction. Furthermore, courts will generally exercise their power in equity to find that persons like Mr. Shady exploited the infirm party and render the contract unenforceable for unconscionability.

The standard for mental infirmity is rather hard to meet. Advanced age coupled with senile dementia, Alzheimer's, or even clinically diagnosed depression does not get a party out of a contractual obligation merely because these conditions exist. *See Rawlings v. John Hancock Mut. Life Ins. Co.*, 78 S.W.3d 291 (Tenn. App. 2001). The party wishing to avoid the contract, or his/her representative, must show that the condition rendered that person incapable of understanding the transaction at issue. The burden of proof rests upon the party challenging capacity as capacity is presumed. This also means that a person may be mentally incapable of performing certain acts but still retain the capacity to contract.

Perhaps Aunt Gertie was eccentric as well. Her mental state may not qualify her to act in certain capacities. Indeed, most people consider her to be unable to act in a reasonable manner at all. Often she was seen wearing a chicken costume and visiting the local Children's Museum; she got a kick out of all the hands-on pieces of whimsical art. She wrote her will and left all her money to the Children's Museum. While Aunt Gertie may not have been of sound mind in general, she may very well have been of sound mind in writing her will. The will should be upheld as expressing her true and reasonable intent. Eccentricity and unreasonableness in everyday life do not automatically transfer to the capacity to contract. As long as Aunt Gertie was aware that she was indeed writing her will and that her entire estate would devolve to it, the will is a solid and valid contractual arrangement.

In the same vein, Dennis Tito, the eccentric millionaire who paid the Russians $20 million to become the first "space tourist," and Howard Hughes, the downright looney billionaire aviator, investor, and developer of Las Vegas, may seem to be entirely unreasonable and impractical to everyone around them, but as long as they were capable at the time of forming a contract, the contract will stand. Indeed, those contracts of Tito's and Hughes' have!

Even the double whammy of a mental condition that needs to be treated with mind-altering drugs may not permit a party to escape contractual responsibility if it can be shown that she had the mental capacity at the time of contract formation to understand the transaction.

SPOT THE ISSUE!

Bill is the president of Best Products and in charge of reviewing contracts and purchase orders for the company. On June 20th, Best entered into a five-year loan agreement with Big Money Company. Bill had been undergoing psychiatric treatment since January of that year and was prescribed quite a few medications with serious side effects. As a result of lithium toxicity from some of these medications, Bill suffered from "impaired cognitive function that limited his capacity to appreciate and understand the nature and quality of his actions and judgments." During this time, Best continued to make payments on the loan. Indeed, for a year after Bill recovered from the lithium toxicity, Best continued to make payments. Throwing himself back into his work, Bill reviewed the loan documents and directed Best to stop making payments.

Do Best and/or Bill have any defenses to the enforcement of the loan?

See *Wilcox Mfg. Group, Inc. v. Marketing Services of Indiana, Inc.*, 832 N.E.2d 559 (Ind. App. 2005).

Under the Influence

On the subject of mind-altering pharmaceuticals, **intoxication** by alcohol or illicit drugs or mental confusion due to **medicinal side effects** *may* render a person incapable of entering into a contract. The incapacity as a result of the intoxication must be extensive enough to deprive the person of reason and understanding. *See* 48 C.J.S. *Intoxicating Liquor* § 144. The use of alcohol or drugs that "*simply exhilarate*" the user is not a defense to contract enforcement. *See Seminara v. Grisman*, 44 A.2d 492 (N.J. Ch. 1945). True intoxication beyond the point of mere exhilaration is sometimes treated as a temporary mental incapacity. As it is a temporary incapacity, the drunkard should make every effort to disavow a purported agreement. Just as a minor, once reaching majority, must take some action to disavow the contract, the drunkard, once regaining sobriety, must take an action to disaffirm and avoid the contract.

This is perhaps the most elusive of standards with regard to capacity to enter into a contract. Many courts have little sympathy for self-induced reduction of capacity and overindulgent persons and therefore will hold them to their contractual undertakings. The one bit of consistency is that courts also will look to the other party in the transaction. If the second party had reason to know of the

intoxication
Under the influence of alcohol or drugs that may, depending on the degree of inebriation, render a party incapable of entering into a contractual relationship.

medicinal side effects
Under the influence of over-the-counter or prescription drugs having an impact on a person's mental capacity that may render a party incapable of entering into a contractual relationship.

dram-shop liability
A bar keeper or owner who negligently over-serves alcohol to a patron who is visibly intoxicated may be liable for harm that the intoxicated person causes due to his inability to control his actions.

diminished capacity of the drunkard, then the courts are less likely to uphold the contract. It is a matter of reasonableness. If a person swaggers up to the bar, downs a few shots, and then offers to sell his car for $100 to the bartender, the bartender has reason to know that the intoxicated person may not have all his wits about him. This is particularly true if the swaggering drunk owns a new Porsche. This is just a likely result flowing from **"dram-shop liability"** in tort. "The imposition of civil responsibility upon a tavern keeper for damages resulting from his negligent service of alcoholic beverages to a visibly intoxicated patron strongly serves the public interest and does not impose any undue burden, for the tavern keeper may readily protect himself by the exercise of reasonable care." *See GNOC Corp. v. Aboud*, 715 F. Supp. 644, 653 (D.N.J. 1989), *citing Soronen v. Olde Milford Inn, Inc.*, 46 N.J. 582, 594 (1966). Contract remedies are not as generous as those founded in equity, however; thorough research into your state's case law will be necessary to make this determination on a case-by-case basis. In New Jersey, the courts were faced with a rather interesting question due to the number of casinos in Atlantic City. "The crucial question in the instant case is whether the State of New Jersey imposes on a gambling casino patron a duty to protect herself from the financial injury which might occur if she gambles while her mental facilities are impaired by alcohol. Certainly the public policy of this state imposes such a duty on a negligent driver or foolhardy pedestrian through the doctrine of comparative negligence. Does the *Aboud* analogy to dram-shop liability dictate the same result for a gambler who carelessly becomes intoxicated?" *Tose v. Greate Bay Hotel and Casino Inc.*, 819 F. Supp. 1312, 1318 (D.N.J. 1993). In *Hakimoglu v. Trump Taj Mahal Associates*, 876 F. Supp. 625 (D.N.J. 1994), the court made a clear distinction between tort liability of a casino for a patron's gambling while intoxicated (which is an expected occurrence, actually) and contractual liability for encouraging a patron to take on additional debt in the form of a "marker" (a casino agrees to lend a patron credit). "When a casino comes to court to enforce a marker debt against a patron, it seeks to enforce a contractual debt. In that case, the patron is entitled to raise all the common law defenses to a contract, including that his capacity to contract was impaired by voluntary intoxication." *Id.* at 633.

Contrast the above example of the swaggering drunkard to the business-man, Donald Drunk, who is in the habit of taking "liquid lunches" and holds his liquor well. At a lunch meeting, Donald may decide to sell part of his company for less than it is worth because he is feeling particularly generous after several single-malt scotches (which were consumed prior to the lunch meeting). If his lunch mate, Bob Buyer, has no reason to know that Donald is intoxicated, Bob may enforce the contract. The courts need to decide which party to favor; in other words, who is the "innocent" party here? Bob fits that description better than Donald, who got himself into the mess by his own volition.

Compulsive intoxication may be a form of mental illness as well. This gives a person two excuses for avoidance of the contract. Of course, that party will have to prove that the incapacity directly affected the transaction; in essence, there can be no manifestation of the intent to be bound to the agreement. Therefore, drunkenness, a temporary mental infirmity, and true mental incapacity relate back to the very essence of a contract. There must be a present intent to contract. In both these situations, there is no present intent because the very nature of the transaction cannot be understood by the impaired party.

IN-CLASS DISCUSSION

Loosely based on *Lucy v. Zehmer*, 84 S.E.2d 516 (Va. 1954).

Late one Friday evening, Farmer Zuckerman was out drinking in the local tavern. He had the largest and most successful farm in the county and many other farmers had been approaching him for years to sell it to them. Miss Lucy, his neighbor, had on several occasions offered to buy the farm. This particular Friday evening, she found Farmer Zuckerman in a particularly jovial mood. She approached Zuckerman, slapped him on the back, and said: "Bet you wouldn't sell me the farm tonight for a hundred grand would you?" Zuckerman laughed and said: "Sure I would. You come up with the cash and it's yours." He then turned to his wife and whispered: "Lucy can't rub two pennies together, never mind coming up with that kind of cash! Let's just string her along." Farmer Zuckerman then flipped over his bar tab and wrote:

"We do hereby agree to sell to Miss Lucy, my neighbor, the Zuckerman farm complete with Wilbur the Pig and all other livestock, for $100,000."

Both Farmer Zuckerman and his wife signed it and they all drank a toast to the "sale" of the farm.

Miss Lucy went to the bank first thing on Saturday morning and secured financing for the farm and had her attorney examine the title to the property. On Monday morning, Miss Lucy showed up at the Zuckermans' farm with a cashier's check for $100,000. Zuckerman refused to sell the farm, stating that he "was as high as a kite" on Friday and that he only intended the writing as a joke. Miss Lucy intended a serious business transaction and understood that the transaction on Friday was made properly.

If you were the judge in this matter, how would you find and why?

What factors might change your decision?

ILLEGALITY

There are certain circumstances under which parties who are perfectly capable of understanding the transaction cannot enter into a contract as it is deemed legally impossible to contract for the performance of an illegal act. The law of contracts forbids such "evil doing" and, of course, a court of law cannot enforce that which is illegal.

An invalid contractual purpose is characterized as either *malum in se* or *malum prohibitum*. **Malum in se** is "evil in itself." It is an act that is universally recognized as immoral and repugnant, such as murder, arson, or rape. These "contracts" are absolutely unenforceable as their purpose is inherently bad and

malum in se
An act that is prohibited because it is "evil in itself."

the courts will never find any justification in them. There can never be any "innocent" party to award damages in equity.

For example, Tony Soprano cannot sue to enforce the contract for a mob "hit" on his overly ambitious cousin to keep him from taking over the "family," where the hit man failed to finish off the cousin. "Murder for hire" contracts are per se invalid and illegal.

malum prohibitum
An act that is "prohibited" by a rule of law.

Malum prohibitum is "prohibited evil," although perhaps "evil" in this case is too strong of a word. The purpose of a contract *malum prohibitum* is not morally reprehensible; it is merely prohibited as a violation of the law. Certain acts are not allowed in order to maintain a harmonious and fair society. Many of these types of prohibited acts have been characterized as being bad for society and are therefore regulated. Additionally, the court may choose how to treat these types of contracts. Sometimes, the court deems them void and unenforceable; other times, the court will try to protect an "innocent" party to the transaction or one who has relied on the contract to his/her detriment.

For example, usury, also known as "loan sharking, is prohibited because it takes unfair advantage of people in need of money. The government, through legislation, has set a legal limit on what rate of interest can be charged on a contract for a loan. If the contract is found to be usurious, requiring an exorbitant amount of interest well above the limits set by statute, then the court can either reduce the rate to the legal limit or void the contract altogether, so the debtor would pay nothing.

Gambling and liquor distribution require licenses, and, therefore, contracts to operate bars or casinos without the proper licenses are generally unenforceable. All of this harkens back to good ol' Tony Soprano. Not only is he prohibited from enforcing his "hit" contract, he will most likely be without legal remedy for loan-sharking, operating a "speak-easy" (a place that illegally sells alcohol, very popular during Prohibition), and paying his Friday night poker party debts.

Is there any time when the court will enforce these *malum prohibitum* agreements? These contracts *may* be enforced if the innocent party can show that the other party to the agreement would be unjustly enriched at the innocent party's expense. In other words, the innocent party has reasonably and detrimentally relied on the agreement, not knowing that it was violative of some law; for example, if Tony contracted with Larry, a liquor supplier, to deliver various kinds of alcohol to his speak-easy. If the illegality of the speak-easy was unbeknown to Larry, he could sue Tony for the cost of the liquor under the contract should Tony refuse to pay.

illegal scheme
A plan that uses legal steps to achieve an illegal result.

On more unclear ground are the contracts that *appear* to have a legal purpose but for which the performance is part of an **illegal scheme**. The courts must then determine whether the illegal result is closely connected to the contract in question or whether it is remotely associated with the diabolical plan and supported by independent consideration. It is not illegal to contract for the purchase of herbs; however, if the purchaser requests that these products be shipped in unmarked boxes to a country where there is a ban on importation of foreign agricultural products, the contract is part of a scheme with an illegal result. The seller cannot perform on the contract—ship the herbs—without violating the law.

CRYPTO CONTRACTS

Part of the benefit of "smart contracts" is their security and immutability. A party to a contractual transaction that will be recorded on the blockchain must be able to access that technology. This is not the realm of simple e-contracts—those that are conducted electronically over the Internet—and to which a simple click of the "I agree" button serves as the assent to the offer. (The Uniform Electronic Transactions Act (UETA) applies, and the courts have consistently applied traditional contract doctrines to those e-contracts.) The blockchain uses mathematical techniques to verify the security keys for each party and element of the transaction. Persons who are incapacitated to such a degree as not to be held responsible for their actions are less likely to have the capacity to sign in to these secure networks to make a meaningful attempt at contracting. It is also quite unlikely that an incapacitated person could have the presence of mind to hack into and manipulate the complex codes associated with these blockchains in an attempt to alter the agreement. What is conceivable is that the very nature of the blockchain's hands-off approach and anonymity may give those who wish to pursue an illegal activity a means to do so. Codes will need to be developed to detect "suspicious activity" or automatically prohibit transfers to certain persons or entities. Perhaps some time in the future this technology will be used on such a broad scale that situations in which a party claims incapacity may arise simply because everyone is using the blockchain to memorialize their agreements. Until that time, however, we are living in the reality that reserves the use of blockchain technology primarily to large investment banks to secure financial transactions and regulatory and compliance matters.

EYE ON ETHICS

An attorney and her client actually share responsibility for the progress of the case. The client directs the attorney as to the desired end result and the attorney strategizes how to best achieve that result.

Intimate knowledge of the law and the justice system affords attorneys a vantage point not easily understood by non-practitioners. Clients may wish to use this information to their benefit. Ethics rules clearly prohibit an attorney from taking advantage of their relationship to the legal system. An attorney is prohibited from assisting a client through either advice or action to commit fraudulent or criminal activities. A client must be advised of the legal consequences of any proposed actions. This does not prohibit a full explanation of all aspects of the law and its application; it does prohibit counseling as to how to avoid its proper application.

See, e.g., *The Florida Bar v. Cueto*, 834 So. 2d 152 (Fla. 2002) (The court held that disbarment was warranted where an attorney participated in an illegal kickback scheme involving settlements of injury cases with the county adjuster.).

Attorneys are afforded protection as against confidentiality claims when presented with a situation wherein a client attempts to pursue an illegal course of action. An attorney may reveal otherwise confidential information to prevent death, serious bodily harm, or criminal activity that will cause serious financial harm to another.

See, e.g., In re Marriage of Decker, 606 N.E.2d 1094 (Ill. 1992) (The court held that the privilege did not apply where attorney had information regarding client's plan to abduct her child from the legal custodial parent.).

covenants not to compete
A clause in an employment contract restricting an employee's ability to go to work for a competitor for a specified period of time in a certain geographical area.

More likely to be encountered in your own practice as a paralegal is a **covenant not to compete**. Generally speaking, public policy and fairness dictate that agreements that restrict trade, market competition, and a person's livelihood are invalid. A covenant not to compete is usually found in the employment contract. A company will attempt to control what an employee does after he/she leaves that particular company—to limit the scope of his/her subsequent employment. It prohibits the former employee from working for a competitor for a certain period of time in a certain geographical area. There are a few exceptions that allow these restrictions to be enforced, but the burden is on the company to prove that the covenant terms regarding (1) the scope of the restricted activity, (2) the period of time the former employee is limited in pursuing the same type of employment, and (3) the geographical area in which the employee is limited is *necessary* to protect a *valid* business interest. The courts generally consider these terms to be an illegal restraint of trade.

SPOT THE ISSUE!

Suzie Scientist landed a new job at Medicine Company after being let go from Famous Pharmaceuticals. She has been hired to conduct research for a new cancer drug similar to a project she participated in at Famous. Famous commences a lawsuit against Suzie asserting that she is in breach of a covenant not to compete that reads:

Employee hereby covenants and agrees that she will not seek employment with any competitor for a period of two years after she leaves the employ of Famous Pharmaceuticals. She agrees not to act as consultant to any such competitor whether for research or marketing purposes. Additionally, she agrees not to have any interest in any competing company as director, shareholder, creditor or otherwise.

As the judge in this matter, how would you rule and why?

Additionally, the court can **sever** a contract if it contains some lawful and some unlawful (*malum prohibitum*) portions. The contract's legal purposes can be enforced. This can be achieved only if the severance doesn't affect the remaining performance. The first determination must be whether the contract will make sense as separate parts. If the contract can be construed as a series of separate, identifiable "mini contracts," then the court has the option of severing the contract into these distinct pieces and getting rid of the unlawful portions. Parties can themselves provide a "severability clause" stating that, if any of the portions of the agreement are found to be illegal, then that portion only will be omitted from the contract and the remainder will be enforceable. In essence, the parties have done the work for the court in making the determination regarding severability even before it comes up.

Tying the two concepts together, the court in *John R. Ray & Sons, Inc. v. Stroman*, 923 S.W.2d 80 (Tex. App. 1996), found that the covenant not to compete was invalid and could not be severed from the stock transfer contract because it was the basis for the entire contract. The court found that the "noncompete" clause was too restrictive as it "provided that Stroman would not engage in or have an interest in any business that sold insurance policies or engaged in the insurance agency business within Harris County and all adjacent counties for a period of five years from the date of the Agreement. It also provided that Stroman would never solicit or accept, or assist or be employed by any other party in soliciting or accepting, insurance business from any of Ray & Sons' accounts." *Id*. at 83. The scope of the clause was found to be too broad. Stroman could not perform other functions in the insurance industry, not just in his former capacity. Additionally, the geographical area was too large and the time period of restraint was too long. All of these factors led the court to conclude that the covenant not to complete was invalid. These restrictions were not necessary to protect a valid business interest. Further, it could not be severed from the stock transfer because the reason Stroman was willing to enter into the covenant not to compete was the receipt of the ownership interest in Ray & Sons.

Penalty clauses that impose severe fines for breach of contract are often unenforceable; however, the purpose of the contract remains intact and enforceable. Tony's contract with Bob the Builder stipulates that if Bob does not complete the renovations on Tony's home by Labor Day weekend, Bob will have to pay Tony a million dollars in damages. There is no justification for this exorbitant amount and, therefore, this penalty clause is unenforceable. However, the remainder of the construction contract is valid, legal, and enforceable.

Cases dealing with severance always depend heavily on the particular facts surrounding the transaction. Additionally, considerations of justice and fairness to the "innocent" party in the agreement will come into play. These considerations will be explored more fully in Chapter 14, "Equity and Quasi-Contract."

In the preceding chapter, we discussed the Statute of Frauds. Contracts that deal with certain kinds of transactions must be in writing; otherwise they are

severability of contract
The ability of a court to choose to separate and discard those clauses in a contract that are unenforceable and retain those that are.

unenforceable. They are not in compliance with statutory authority and, therefore, to contract for these things without the writing is *malum prohibitum*. Of course, the only way a court will find out about these prohibited contracts will be a lawsuit brought for enforcement.

Contracts must identify with reasonable certainty the parties and subject matter of the contract. This is the first hurdle in order to make a valid claim for enforcement. The party seeking redress in the court also must overcome any defenses relating to these two contractual elements. The party may be properly identified, but that identified person also must be capable of entering into the contract. The subject matter may be properly identified; however, it must be something for which the parties can legally transact.

Summary

Contract law gives an *affirmative defense* to those parties who find themselves in a contract that they were not *capable* of making in the first place or for which the subject matter is *illegal*. In the most general sense, freedom of contract allows anyone to contract for anything; however, there are some reasonable restrictions on this laissez-faire attitude. *Laissez-faire* is from the French "to allow to do." It is a doctrine of noninterference in the affairs of others.

As far as restrictions on *who* may contract, the courts have deemed (1) *minors*, (2) the *mentally infirm*, and (3) those *under the influence* as incapable of entering into a contract. The requisite intent to contract is missing. The contract may be avoided at the option of the party deemed incapable once their capacity has been established. A minor may affirm or disavow a contract upon reaching majority; a mentally incompetent person may do the same upon reestablishing soundness of mind; and the party under the influence may take either action upon sobriety.

Minors are subject to restrictions on their ability to avoid the contract, however. If a minor contracts for *necessities* or for a certain type of *statutorily controlled transaction*, the minor is unable to avoid the contract for lack of capacity. These transactions include educational loan documents, military enlistments, marriage or child-support agreements, banking, and insurance contracts.

Courts also restrict the subject matter of the contract, *what* the parties can bargain for. Simply stated, the transaction must not involve illegal activities or illegal purposes. These prohibited activities and purposes can either be characterized as *malum in se*, an act that is morally reprehensible, or *malum prohibitum*, an act prohibited by law for the well-being of society. Courts cannot enforce *malum in se* contracts; however, under certain conditions, an innocent party may be entitled to equitable damages or partial enforcement of the *malum prohibitum* contract if the proscribed elements can be *severed* from the remainder of the contract.

Key Terms

affirmative defense
covenant not to compete
disavowal
illegal scheme
intoxication
legislation
malum in se
malum prohibitum
medicinal side effects

mentally infirm
minors
necessities
ratification
severability
under the influence
void
voidable

Review Questions

MULTIPLE CHOICE

Choose the best answer(s) and please explain *why* you choose the answer(s).

1. Courts will likely rule that a covenant not to compete is valid where
   a. The company has many competitors in the market.
   b. The company can show that the employee has special training and knowledge gained from working at the previous job.
   c. The employee can show that she cannot get a job in the state without violating the covenant.
   d. The company can show that the employee has special knowledge that if applied at another company would drive it out of business.

2. Courts will likely find that a party had capacity to contract where
   a. The person was 17½ years old.
   b. The person was completely intoxicated and it was apparent to everyone at the bar.
   c. The person was elderly and had some lapses of short-term memory.
   d. The person was heavily medicated at the time, but otherwise had no mental disability.

3. Which of the following is a valid ratification of a contract?
   a. Continuing to make payments on the lease of the apartment after the tenant turns 18.
   b. Continuing to make payments on the lease of a new car after the purchaser turns 18.
   c. Signing a contract with witnesses.
   d. Making payments toward a contract that the purchaser believes is for a life insurance contract but in reality is for a new car.

EXPLAIN YOURSELF

All answers should be written in complete sentences. A simple "yes" or "no" is insufficient.

1. Explain why courts allow certain persons to avoid the enforcement of contracts due to "incapacity."

2. Explain the difference between contracts that are *malum in se* and *malum prohibitum*. Can the courts enforce any of these contracts?

3. When are contracts "severable"?

4. What is a covenant not to compete? Are they enforceable?

5. What proof might the court look at to determine whether a person was suffering under a mental disability and therefore is able to avoid the contract?

"FAULTY PHRASES"

All of the following statements are FALSE; state why they are false and then rewrite them as true statements. Write a brief fact pattern that illustrates your answer.

1. All contracts entered into by minors are avoidable by the minor.

2. Persons must be certified by a court as mentally insane in order to avoid enforcement of a contract.

3. All contracts with intoxicated persons are voidable.

4. Minors must formally ratify their contracts by contacting the other party on their eighteenth birthday.

5. Courts will strike the entire illegal contract.

6. Covenants not to compete are unenforceable because they are *malum prohibitum* as they prohibit free commerce and employment.

7. A person is only considered under the influence if he has had too much to drink or has used illicit drugs.

"WRITE" AWAY! PORTFOLIO ASSIGNMENT

Review the Druid and Carrie contract. Are there any terms that may be subject to local building/construction regulations? Identify these terms and provide a clause to shift responsibility onto one of the parties to double check the legality of the work (*malum prohibitum*). Draft a severability clause.

Case in Point   CAPACITY

399 N.W.2d 894
FIRST STATE BANK OF SINAI, a South Dakota Banking
Corporation, Plaintiff and Appellant,
v.
Mervin HYLAND, Defendant and Appellee.
No. 15276.
Supreme Court of South Dakota.
Argued Oct. 21, 1986.
Decided Jan. 21, 1987.

Jerome B. Lammers of Lammers, Lammers, Klei-backer & Casey, Madison, for plaintiff and appellant. David R. Gienapp of Arneson, Issenhuth & Gienapp, Madison, for defendant and appellee.

Page 895

HENDERSON, Justice.

PROCEDURAL HISTORY/ISSUES

Plaintiff-appellant First State Bank of Sinai (Bank) sued defendant-appellee Mervin Hyland (Mervin) seeking to hold him responsible for payment on a promissory note which he cosigned. Upon trial to the court, the circuit court entered findings of fact, conclusions of law, and judgment holding Mervin not liable for the note's payment. Bank appeals advocating that the court erred when it ruled that

(1) Mervin was incompetent to transact business when he signed the note;
(2) Mervin's obligation to Bank was void; and
(3) Mervin did not subsequently accept/ratify the obligation.

We treat these issues seriatim. We reverse and remand.

FACTS

On March 10, 1981, Randy Hyland (Randy) and William Buck (Buck), acting for Bank, executed two promissory notes. One note was for $6,800 and the other note was for $3,000. Both notes became due on September 19, 1981.

The notes remained unpaid on their due date and Bank sent notice to Randy informing him of the delinquencies. On October 20, 1981, Randy came to the Bank and met with Buck. Buck explained to Randy that the notes were past due. Randy requested an extension. Buck agreed, but on the condition that Randy's father, Mervin, act as cosigner. One $9,800 promissory note dated October 20, 1981 (the two notes of $6,800 and $3,000 were combined) was created. Randy was given the note for the purpose of obtaining his father's signature. According to Randy, Mervin signed the note on October 20 or 21, 1981.

Mervin had transacted business with Bank since 1974. Previously, he executed approximately 60 promissory notes with Bank. Mervin was apparently a good customer and paid all of his notes on time. Buck testified that he knew Mervin drank, but that he was unaware of any alcohol-related problems.

Randy returned to the Bank about one week later. Mervin had properly signed the note. In Buck's presence, Randy signed the note, which had an April 20, 1982 due date.

On April 20, 1982, the note was unpaid. Buck notified Randy of the overdue note. On May 5, 1982, Randy appeared at the Bank. He brought a blank check signed by Mervin with which the interest on the note was to be paid. Randy filled in the check amount at the Bank for $899.18 (the amount of interest owing). Randy also requested that the note be extended.

Buck agreed, but required Mervin's signature as a prerequisite to any extension. A two-month note for $9,800 with a due date of July 2, 1982, was prepared and given to Randy.

Randy did not secure his father's signature on the two-month note, and Mervin testified that he refused to sign that note. On June 22, 1982, Randy filed for bankruptcy which later resulted in the total discharge of his obligation on the note.

On July 14, 1982, Buck sent a letter to Randy and Mervin informing them of Bank's intention to look to Mervin for the note's payment. On December 19, 1982, Bank filed suit against Mervin, requesting $9,800 principal and interest at the rate of 17% until judgment was entered. Mervin answered on January 14, 1983. His defense hinged upon the assertion that he was incapacitated through the use of liquor when he signed the note. He claimed he had no recollection of the note, did not remember seeing it, discussing it with his son, or signing it.

Randy testified that when he brought the note home to his father, the latter was drunk and in bed. Mervin then rose from his bed, walked into the kitchen, and signed the note. Later, Randy returned to the Bank with the signed note.

The record reveals that Mervin was drinking heavily from late summer through early winter of 1981. During this period, Mervin's wife and son accepted responsibility for managing the farm. Mervin's family

Page 896

testified that his bouts with liquor left him weak, unconcerned with regard to family and business matters, uncooperative, and uncommunicative. When Mervin was drinking, he spent most of his time at home, in bed.

Mervin's problems with alcohol have five times resulted in his involuntary commitment to hospitals. Two of those commitments occurred near the period of the October 1981 note. On September 10, 1981, Mervin was involuntarily committed to the Human Services Center at Yankton. He was released on September 19, 1981. On November 20, 1981, he was involuntarily committed to River Park at Pierre.

Between the periods of his commitments, September 19, 1981 until November 20, 1981, Mervin did transact some business himself. On October 3,

Mervin and Buck (Bank) executed a two-month promissory note enabling the former to borrow $5,000 for the purchase of livestock. Mervin also paid for farm goods and services with his personal check on September 29, October 1 (purchased cattle at Madison Livestock Auction), October 2, and October 5, 1981. Mervin testified that during October 1981, he had personally hauled his grain to storage elevators and made decisions concerning when grain was sold. Additionally, Mervin continued to operate his automobile, often making trips to purchase liquor.

A trial was held on October 4, 1985. Mervin was found to be entirely without understanding (as a result of alcohol consumption) when he signed the October 20, 1981 promissory note. The court pointed to Mervin's lack of personal care and nonparticipation in family life and farming business as support for finding the contractual relationship between the parties void at its inception. It was further held that Bank had failed to show Mervin's subsequent ratification of the contract. Bank appeals.

DECISION

I. and II. Mervin Incompetent to Transact Business? Promissory Note Void?

For ease of treatment, Issues I and II will be treated together. Historically, the void contract concept has been applied to nullify agreements made by mental incompetents who have contracted either entirely without understanding or after a judicial determination of incapacity had been entered. See *Dexter v. Hall*, 82 U.S. (15 Wall.) 9, 21 L. Ed. 73 (1873); SDCL Secs. 27A-2-1 and 27A-2-3; 2 S. Williston, A Treatise on the Law of Contracts, Sec. 257 (3d ed. 1959 & Supp. 1980); Restatement (Second) of Contracts Sec. 12 (1981). Incapacitated intoxicated persons have been treated similarly to mental incompetents in that their contracts will either be void or voidable depending upon the extent of their mental unfitness at the time they contracted. 2 S. Williston, supra, at Sec. 260; Restatement (Second) of Contracts Sec. 16. A void contract is without legal effect in that the law neither gives remedy for its breach nor recognizes any duty of performance by a promisor. Restatement (Second) of Contracts Sec. 7, comment a. Therefore, the term "void contract" is a misnomer because if an agreement is void, at its genesis, no contract (void or otherwise) was ever created. See J. Calamari & J. Perillo, The Law of Contracts Sec. 1-11 (2d ed. 1977).

Mervin had numerous and prolonged problems stemming from his inability to handle alcohol. However, he was not judicially declared incompetent during the note's signing. Therefore, a void contract could only exist if Mervin was "entirely without understanding" (incompetent) when he signed the note.

The phrase "entirely without understanding" has been a subject of this Court's scrutiny from at least 1902. *Mach v. Blanchard*, 15 S.D. 432, 90 N.W. 1042 (1902). It has evolved in the law to apply in those situations where the person contracting did not possess the mental dexterity required to comprehend the nature and ultimate effect of the transaction in which he was involved. See *Fischer v. Gorman*, 65 S.D. 453, 458-60, 274 N.W. 866, 870

Page 897

(1937) (citing *Jacks v. Estee*, 139 Cal. 507, 73 P. 247 (1903); *Fleming v. Consol. Motor Sales*, 74 Mont. 245, 240 P. 376 (1925); *Long v. Anderson*, 77 Okla. 95, 186 P. 944 (1920)). A party attempting to avoid his contract must carry the burden of proving that he was entirely without understanding when he contracted. *Christensen v. Larson*, 77 N.W.2d 441, 446-47 (N.D.1956); *Hauge v. Bye*, 51 N.D. 848, 855, 201 N.W. 159, 162 (1924); 17 C.J.S. Contracts Sec. 133(2) (1963). Lapse of memory, carelessness of person and property, and unreasonableness are not determinative of one's ability to presently enter into an agreement. *Hochgraber v. Balzer*, 66 S.D. 630, 634, 287 N.W. 585, 587 (1939). Neither should a contract be found void because of previous or subsequent incompetence. *Heward v. Sutton*, 75 Nev. 452, 345 P.2d 772 (1959); *Atwood v. Lester*, 20 R.I. 660, 40 A. 866 (1898); 41 Am. Jur. 2d Incompetent Persons Sec. 69 (1968). Our inquiry must always focus on the person's mental acuity and understanding of the transaction at the time contracting occurred. See *Fischer*, 65 S.D. at 459, 274 N.W. at 869-70; 41 Am. Jur. 2d, supra, at Sec. 69.

To show that he was entirely without understanding when he signed the note, Mervin points to his family's testimony that he was unconcerned with family and business, uncooperative, antisocial, and unkempt. He also notes his involuntary commitments in the Fall of 1981.

Yet, Mervin engaged in farm operations, drove his truck, executed a promissory note (on October 3, 1981, for cattle he bought, which note was paid approximately two months thereafter), and paid for personal items by check drawn on his bank circa the period that he signed the note. Obviously, Mervin had an understanding to transact business; the corollary is that he was not entirely without understanding. In addition, only Randy was present when his father signed the note, and Randy's testimony (during his deposition and at trial) was vague and inconsistent on the crucial points of Mervin's demeanor when he signed the note and the general circumstances surrounding the event. Randy did, however, testify at his December 9, 1982 bankruptcy hearing that his dad knew he was signing a note. Thirdly, Mervin was not judicially committed during the note's signing and the presumption via SDCL 27A-14-2[1] must be that his discharge from Yankton on September 19, 1981, was an indication of his improved well-being. We therefore hold that Mervin failed to carry the burden of proving his incompetence (entirely without understanding) when he signed the note and we consequently rule that his obligation to Bank was not void. In so holding, we determine that the findings of fact and conclusions of law are clearly erroneous as we are, based on the entire evidence, left with a definite and firm conviction that a mistake has been committed. *In re Estate of Hobelsberger*, 85 S.D. 282, 181 N.W.2d 455 (1970).[2]

---

[1]SDCL 27A-14-2 provides:

A patient involuntarily committed may be discharged or provisionally discharged when, in the opinion of the administrator of the community mental health center or the center, the patient's behavior is no longer that which precipitated or caused his admission. The patient may agree to continue treatment voluntarily.

[2]The trial court seemed unclear on the state of the law concerning the distinction between void and voidable contracts. In Conclusion of Law II, Mervin's obligation via the promissory note was labeled void. Subsequently, in Conclusion of Law III, the court found that "the Defendant [Mervin] did not by his later actions ratify the void contract." These statements cannot correctly coexist. If the contract was void at its inception, it may not be subsequently ratified; only voidable contracts may be ratified.

III. Was There Subsequent Acceptance/Ratification of the Note? Was There Prompt Rescission of the Note?

Contractual obligations incurred by intoxicated persons may be voidable. See 2 S. Williston, supra, at Sec. 260. Voidable contracts (contracts other than those entered into following a judicial determination

Page 898

of incapacity, or entirely without understanding) may be rescinded by the previously disabled party. SDCL 27A-2-2. However, disaffirmance must be prompt, upon the recovery of the intoxicated party's mental abilities, and upon his notice of the agreement, if he had forgotten it. *Hauge v. Bye*, 51 N.D. at 855, 201 N.W. at 162; *Spoonheim v. Spoonheim*, 14 N.D. 380, 389, 104 N.W. 845, 848 (1905); 2 S. Williston, supra, at Sec. 260; Restatement (Second) of Contracts Sec. 16, comment c. SDCL 53-11-4 is also relevant and provides that "[t]he party rescinding a contract must rescind promptly, upon discovering the facts which entitle him to rescind. . . ." See also *Kane v. Schnitzler*, 376 N.W.2d 337 (S.D.1985). This Court in *Kane* noted that a delay in rescission which causes prejudice to the other party will extinguish the first party's right to disaffirm. Id., 376 N.W.2d at 340.

A voidable contract may also be ratified by the party who had contracted while disabled. Upon ratification, the contract becomes a fully valid legal obligation. SDCL 53-3-4. Ratification can either be express or implied by conduct. *Bank of Hoven v. Rausch*, 382 N.W.2d 39, 41 (S.D.1986); 17 C.J.S. Contracts Sec. 133 (1963). In addition, failure of a party to disaffirm a contract over a period of time may, by itself, ripen into a ratification, especially if rescission will result in prejudice to the other party. See *Kane*, 376 N.W.2d 337; 2 S. Williston, supra at Sec. 260; 17 C.J.S., supra, at Sec. 133.

Mervin received both verbal notice from Randy and written notice from Bank on or about April 27, 1982, that the note was overdue. On May 5, 1982, Mervin paid the interest owing with a check which Randy delivered to Bank. This by itself could amount to ratification through conduct. If Mervin wished to avoid the contract, he should have then exercised his right of rescission. We find it impossible to believe that Mervin paid almost $900 in interest without, in his own mind, accepting responsibility for the note. His assertion that paying interest on the note relieved his obligation is equally untenable in light of his numerous past experiences with promissory notes.[3]

In addition, Mervin's failure to rescind, coupled with his apparent ratification, could have jeopardized the Bank's chances of ever receiving payment on the note. As we know, Mervin unquestionably was aware of his obligation in late April 1982. If he had disaffirmed then, Bank could have actively pursued Randy and possibly collected some part of the debt. By delaying his rescission, and by paying the note's back interest, Mervin lulled Bank into a false sense of security that may have hurt it when on June 22, 1982, Randy filed for bankruptcy and was later fully discharged of his obligation on the note.

We conclude that Mervin's obligation to Bank as not void because he did not show that he was entirely without understanding when he signed the note. Mervin's obligation on the note was voidable and his subsequent failure to disaffirm (lack of rescission) and his payment of interest (ratification) then transformed the voidable contract into one that is fully binding upon him.

We reverse and remand.

MORGAN and SABERS, JJ., and FOSHEIM, Retired Justice, concur.

WUEST, C.J., concurs in result.

MILLER, J., not having been a member of the Court at the time this action was submitted to the Court, did not participate.

---

[3]Mervin claims that he paid the interest because he owed Randy money and that this interest payment did not in any way constitute acceptance of the obligation. But Randy testified that his dad neither owed him money nor required that Randy later work off the payment. Moreover, Randy testified that the "interest was due and I didn't have the money so he [Mervin] said he'd just as well pay it." Trial Transcript at 42-43, quoting Randy's Deposition at 12.

Case in Point ILLEGALITY

109 N.J. 396
537 A.2d 1227, 77 A.L.R.4th 1, 56 USLW 2442
In the Matter of BABY M, a pseudonym for an actual person.
Supreme Court of New Jersey.
Argued Sept. 14, 1987.
Decided Feb. 3, 1988.

[Appearances omitted.]
[Pagination removed.]

The opinion of the Court was delivered by WILENTZ, C.J.

In this matter the Court is asked to determine the validity of a contract that purports to provide a new way of bringing children into a family. For a fee of $10,000, a woman agrees to be artificially inseminated with the semen of another woman's husband; she is to conceive a child, carry it to term, and after its birth surrender it to the natural father and his wife. The intent of the contract is that the child's natural mother will thereafter be forever separated from her child. The wife is to adopt the child, and she and the natural father are to be regarded as its parents for all purposes. The contract providing for this is called a "surrogacy contract," the natural mother inappropriately called the "surrogate mother."

We invalidate the surrogacy contract because it conflicts with the law and public policy of this State. While we recognize the depth of the yearning of infertile couples to have their own children, we find the payment of money to a "surrogate" mother illegal, perhaps criminal, and potentially degrading to women. Although in this case we grant custody to the natural father, the evidence having clearly proved such custody to be in the best interests of the infant, we void both the termination of the surrogate mother's parental rights and the adoption of the child by the wife/stepparent. We thus restore the "surrogate" as the mother of the child. We remand the issue of the natural mother's visitation rights to the trial court, since that issue was not reached below and the record before us is not sufficient to permit us to decide it *de novo*.

We find no offense to our present laws where a woman voluntarily and without payment agrees to act as a "surrogate" mother, provided that she is not subject to a binding agreement to surrender her child. Moreover, our holding today does not preclude the Legislature from altering the current statutory scheme, within constitutional limits, so as to permit surrogacy contracts. Under current law, however, the surrogacy agreement before us is illegal and invalid.

I. FACTS

In February 1985, William Stern and Mary Beth Whitehead entered into a surrogacy contract. It recited that Stern's wife, Elizabeth, was infertile, that they wanted a child, and that Mrs. Whitehead was willing to provide that child as the mother with Mr. Stern as the father.

The contract provided that through artificial insemination using Mr. Stern's sperm, Mrs. Whitehead would become pregnant, carry the child to term, bear it, deliver it to the Sterns, and thereafter do whatever was necessary to terminate her maternal rights so that Mrs. Stern could thereafter adopt the child. Mrs. Whitehead's husband, Richard, [Footnote omitted.] was also a party to the contract; Mrs. Stern was not. Mr. Whitehead promised to do all acts necessary to rebut the presumption of paternity under the Parentage Act. N.J.S.A. 9:17-43a(1), -44a. Although Mrs. Stern was not a party to the surrogacy agreement, the contract gave her sole custody of the child in the event of Mr. Stern's death. Mrs. Stern's status as a nonparty to the surrogate parenting agreement presumably was to avoid the application of the baby-selling statute to this arrangement. N.J.S.A. 9:3-54.

Mr. Stern, on his part, agreed to attempt the artificial insemination and to pay Mrs. Whitehead $10,000 after the child's birth, on its delivery to him. In a separate contract, Mr. Stern agreed to pay $7,500 to the Infertility Center of New York ("ICNY"). The Center's advertising campaigns solicit surrogate mothers and encourage infertile couples to consider surrogacy. ICNY arranged for the surrogacy contract by bringing the parties together, explaining the process to them, furnishing the contractual form, [Footnote omitted.] and providing legal counsel.

[. . .]

On February 6, 1985, Mr. Stern and Mr. and Mrs. Whitehead executed the surrogate parenting agreement. After several artificial inseminations over a period of months, Mrs. Whitehead became pregnant. The pregnancy was uneventful and on March 27, 1986, Baby M was born.

[. . .]

Mrs. Whitehead realized, almost from the moment of birth, that she could not part with this child. [. . .]

Nonetheless, Mrs. Whitehead was, for the moment, true to her word. Despite powerful inclinations to the contrary, she turned her child over to the Sterns on March 30 at the Whiteheads' home.

The depth of Mrs. Whitehead's despair surprised and frightened the Sterns. She told them that she could not live without her baby, that she must have her, even if only for one week, that thereafter she would surrender her child. The Sterns, concerned that Mrs. Whitehead might indeed commit suicide, not wanting under any circumstances to risk that, and in any event believing that Mrs. Whitehead would keep her word, turned the child over to her. It was not until four months later, after a series of attempts to regain possession of the child, that Melissa was returned to the Sterns, having been forcibly removed from the home where she was then living with Mr. and Mrs. Whitehead, the home in Florida owned by Mary Beth Whitehead's parents.

The struggle over Baby M began when it became apparent that Mrs. Whitehead could not return the child to Mr. Stern. Due to Mrs. Whitehead's refusal to relinquish the baby, Mr. Stern filed a complaint seeking enforcement of the surrogacy contract. [. . .]

The Sterns' complaint, in addition to seeking possession and ultimately custody of the child, sought enforcement of the surrogacy contract. Pursuant to the contract, it asked that the child be permanently placed in their custody, that Mrs. Whitehead's parental rights be terminated, and that Mrs. Stern be allowed to adopt the child, *i.e.*, that, for all purposes, Melissa become the Sterns' child.

The trial took thirty-two days over a period of more than two months. [. . .] Soon after the conclusion of the trial, the trial court announced its opinion from the bench. 217 N.J. Super. 313, 525 A.2d 1128 (1987). It held that the surrogacy contract was valid; ordered that Mrs. Whitehead's parental rights be terminated and that sole custody of the child be granted to Mr. Stern; and, after hearing brief testimony from Mrs. Stern, immediately entered an order allowing the adoption of Melissa by Mrs. Stern, all in accordance with the surrogacy contract. Pending the outcome of the appeal, we granted a continuation of visitation to Mrs. Whitehead, although slightly more limited than the visitation allowed during the trial.

Although clearly expressing its view that the surrogacy contract was valid, the trial court devoted the major portion of its opinion to the question of the baby's best interests. The inconsistency is apparent. The surrogacy contract calls for the surrender of the child to the Sterns, permanent and sole custody in the Sterns, and termination of Mrs. Whitehead's parental rights, all without qualification, all regardless of any evaluation of the best interests of the child. As a matter of fact the contract recites (even before the child was conceived) that it is in the best interests of the child to be placed with Mr. Stern. In effect, the trial court awarded custody to Mr. Stern, the natural father, based on the same kind of evidence and analysis as might be expected had no surrogacy contract existed. Its rationalization, however, was that while the surrogacy contract was valid, specific performance would not be granted unless that remedy was in the best interests of the child. The factual issues confronted and decided by the trial court were the same as if Mr. Stern and Mrs. Whitehead had had the child out of wedlock, intended or unintended, and then disagreed about custody. The trial court's awareness of the irrelevance of the contract in the court's determination of custody is suggested by its remark that beyond the question of the child's best interests, "[a]ll other concerns raised by counsel constitute commentary." 217 N.J. Super. at 323, 525 A.2d 1128.

[. . .]

The court's review and analysis of the surrogacy contract, however, is not at all in accord with ours. The trial court concluded that the various statutes governing this matter, including those concerning adoption, termination of parental rights, and payment of money in connection with adoptions, do not apply to surrogacy contracts. *Id.* at 372-73, 525 A.2d 1128. It reasoned that because the Legislature did not have surrogacy contracts in mind when it passed those laws, those laws were therefore irrelevant. *Ibid.* Thus, assuming it was writing on a clean slate, the trial court analyzed the interests involved and the power of the court to accommodate them. It then held that surrogacy contracts are valid and should be enforced, *Id.* at 388, 525 A.2d 1128, and furthermore that Mr. Stern's rights under the surrogacy contract were constitutionally protected. *Id.* at 385-88, 525 A.2d 1128.

Mrs. Whitehead appealed. This Court granted direct certification. 107 N.J. 140, 526 A.2d 203 (1987). The briefs of the parties on appeal were joined by numerous briefs filed by *amici* expressing various interests and views on surrogacy and on this case. We have found many of them helpful in resolving the issues before us.

Mrs. Whitehead contends that the surrogacy contract, for a variety of reasons, is invalid. She contends that it conflicts with public policy since it guarantees that the child will not have the nurturing of both natural parents—presumably New Jersey's goal for families. She further argues that it deprives the mother of her constitutional right to the companionship of her child, and that it conflicts with statutes concerning termination of parental rights and adoption. With the contract thus void, Mrs. Whitehead claims primary custody (with visitation rights in Mr. Stern) both on a best interests basis (stressing the "tender years" doctrine) as well as on the policy basis of discouraging surrogacy contracts. She maintains that even if custody would ordinarily go to Mr. Stern, here it should be awarded to Mrs. Whitehead to deter future surrogacy arrangements.

[. . .]

II. INVALIDITY AND UNENFORCEABILITY OF SURROGACY CONTRACT

We have concluded that this surrogacy contract is invalid. Our conclusion has two bases: direct conflict with existing statutes and conflict with the public policies of this State, as expressed in its statutory and decisional law.

One of the surrogacy contract's basic purposes, to achieve the adoption of a child through private placement, though permitted in New Jersey "is very much disfavored." *Sees v. Baber,* 74 N.J. 201, 217, 377 A.2d 628 (1977). Its use of money for this purpose—and we have no doubt whatsoever that the money is being paid to obtain an adoption and not, as the Sterns argue, for the personal services of Mary Beth Whitehead—is illegal and perhaps criminal. N.J.S.A. 9:3-54. In addition to the inducement of money, there is the coercion of contract: the natural mother's irrevocable agreement, prior to birth, even prior to conception, to surrender the child to the adoptive couple. Such an agreement is totally unenforceable in private placement adoption. *Sees,* 74 N.J. at 212-14, 377 A.2d 628. Even where the adoption is through an approved agency, the formal agreement to surrender occurs only *after* birth (as we read N.J.S.A. 9:2-16 and -17, and similar statutes), and then, by regulation, only after the birth mother has been offered counseling. N.J.A.C. 10:121A-5.4(c). Integral to these invalid provisions of the surrogacy contract is the related agreement, equally invalid, on the part of the natural mother to cooperate with, and not to contest, proceedings to terminate her parental rights, as well as her contractual concession, in aid of the adoption, that the child's best interests would be served by awarding custody to the natural father and his wife—all of this before she has even conceived, and, in some cases, before she has the slightest idea of what the natural father and adoptive mother are like.

The foregoing provisions not only directly conflict with New Jersey statutes, but also offend long-established State policies. These critical terms, which are at the heart of the contract, are invalid and unenforceable; the conclusion therefore follows, without more, that the entire contract is unenforceable.

A. Conflict with Statutory Provisions

The surrogacy contract conflicts with: (1) laws prohibiting the use of money in connection with adoptions; (2) laws requiring proof of parental unfitness or abandonment before termination of parental rights is ordered or an adoption is granted; and (3) laws that make surrender of custody and consent to adoption revocable in private placement adoptions.

(1) Our law prohibits paying or accepting money in connection with any placement of a child for adoption. N.J.S.A. 9:3-54a. Violation is a high misdemeanor. N.J.S.A. 9:3-54c. Excepted are fees of an approved agency (which must be a non-profit entity, N.J.S.A. 9:3-38a) and certain expenses in connection with childbirth. N.J.S.A. 9:3-54b. [Footnote omitted.]

Considerable care was taken in this case to structure the surrogacy arrangement so as not to violate this prohibition. The arrangement was structured as follows: the adopting parent, Mrs. Stern, was not a party to the surrogacy contract; the money paid to Mrs. Whitehead was stated to be for her services—not for the adoption; the sole purpose of the contract was stated as being that "of giving a child to William Stern, its natural and biological father"; the money was purported to be "compensation for services and expenses and in no way . . . a fee for termination of parental rights or a payment in exchange for consent to surrender a child for adoption"; the fee to the Infertility Center ($7,500) was stated to be for legal representation, advice, administrative work, and other "services." Nevertheless, it seems clear that the money was paid and accepted in connection with an adoption.

The Infertility Center's major role was first as a "finder" of the surrogate mother whose child was to be adopted, and second as the arranger of all proceedings that led to the adoption. Its role as adoption finder is demonstrated by the provision requiring Mr. Stern to pay another $7,500 if he uses Mary Beth Whitehead again as a surrogate, and by ICNY's agreement to "coordinate arrangements for the adoption of the child by the wife." The surrogacy agreement requires Mrs. Whitehead to surrender Baby M for the purposes of adoption. The agreement notes that Mr. *and Mrs.* Stern wanted to have a child, and provides that the child be "placed" with Mrs. Stern in the event Mr. Stern dies before the child is born. The payment of the $10,000 occurs only on surrender of custody of the child and "completion of the duties and obligations" of Mrs. Whitehead, including termination of her parental rights to facilitate adoption by Mrs. Stern. As for the contention that the Sterns are paying only for services and not for an adoption, we need note only that they would pay nothing in the

event the child died before the fourth month of pregnancy, and only $1,000 if the child were stillborn, even though the "services" had been fully rendered. Additionally, one of Mrs. Whitehead's estimated costs, to be assumed by Mr. Stern, was an "Adoption Fee," presumably for Mrs. Whitehead's incidental costs in connection with the adoption.

Mr. Stern knew he was paying for the adoption of a child; Mrs. Whitehead knew she was accepting money so that a child might be adopted; the Infertility Center knew that it was being paid for assisting in the adoption of a child. The actions of all three worked to frustrate the goals of the statute. It strains credulity to claim that these arrangements, touted by those in the surrogacy business as an attractive alternative to the usual route leading to an adoption, really amount to something other than a private placement adoption for money.

The prohibition of our statute is strong. Violation constitutes a high misdemeanor, N.J.S.A. 9:3-54c, a third-degree crime, N.J.S.A. 2C:43-1b, carrying a penalty of three to five years imprisonment. N.J.S.A. 2C:43-6a(3). The evils inherent in baby-bartering are loathsome for a myriad of reasons. The child is sold without regard for whether the purchasers will be suitable parents. N. Baker, *Baby Selling: The Scandal of Black Market Adoption* 7 (1978). The natural mother does not receive the benefit of counseling and guidance to assist her in making a decision that may affect her for a lifetime. In fact, the monetary incentive to sell her child may, depending on her financial circumstances, make her decision less voluntary. *Id.* at 44. Furthermore, the adoptive parents [Footnote omitted.] may not be fully informed of the natural parents' medical history.

Baby-selling potentially results in the exploitation of all parties involved. *Ibid.* Conversely, adoption statutes seek to further humanitarian goals, foremost among them the best interests of the child. H. Witmer, E. Herzog, E. Weinstein, & M. Sullivan, *Independent Adoptions: A Follow-Up Study* 32 (1967). The negative consequences of baby-buying are potentially present in the surrogacy context, especially the potential for placing and adopting a child without regard to the interest of the child or the natural mother.

(2) The termination of Mrs. Whitehead's parental rights, called for by the surrogacy contract and actually ordered by the court, 217 N.J. Super. at 399-400,

525 A.2d 1128, fails to comply with the stringent requirements of New Jersey law. Our law, recognizing the finality of any termination of parental rights, provides for such termination only where there has been a voluntary surrender of a child to an approved agency or to the Division of Youth and Family Services ("DYFS"), accompanied by a formal document acknowledging termination of parental rights, N.J.S.A. 9:2-16, -17; N.J.S.A. 9:3-41; N.J.S.A. 30:4C-23, or where there has been a showing of parental abandonment or unfitness. A termination may ordinarily take one of three forms: an action by an approved agency, an action by DYFS, or an action in connection with a private placement adoption. The three are governed by separate statutes, but the standards for termination are substantially the same, except that whereas a written surrender is effective when made to an approved agency or to DYFS, there is no provision for it in the private placement context. *See* N.J.S.A. 9:2-14; N.J.S.A. 30:4C-23.

[. . .]

As the trial court recognized, without a valid termination there can be no adoption. *In re Adoption of Children by D., supra,* 61 N.J. at 95, 293 A.2d 171. This requirement applies to all adoptions, whether they be private placements, *ibid.,* or agency adoptions, N.J.S.A. 9:3-46a, -47c.

> Our statutes, and the cases interpreting them, leave no doubt that where there has been no written surrender to an approved agency or to DYFS, termination of parental rights will not be granted in this state absent a very strong showing of abandonment or neglect. [. . .]

In this case a termination of parental rights was obtained not by proving the statutory prerequisites but by claiming the benefit of contractual provisions. From all that has been stated above, it is clear that a contractual agreement to abandon one's parental rights, or not to contest a termination action, will not be enforced in our courts. The Legislature would not have so carefully, so consistently, and so substantially restricted termination of parental rights if it had intended to allow termination to be achieved by one short sentence in a contract.

Since the termination was invalid, [Footnote omitted.] it follows, as noted above, that adoption of Melissa by Mrs. Stern could not properly be granted.

(3) The provision in the surrogacy contract stating that Mary Beth Whitehead agrees to "surrender custody . . . and terminate all parental rights" contains no clause giving her a right to rescind. It is intended to be an irrevocable consent to surrender the child for adoption—in other words, an irrevocable commitment by Mrs. Whitehead to turn Baby M over to the Sterns and thereafter to allow termination of her parental rights. The trial court required a "best interests" showing as a condition to granting specific performance of the surrogacy contract. 217 N.J. Super. at 399-400, 525 A.2d 1128. Having decided the "best interests" issue in favor of the Sterns, that court's order included, among other things, specific performance of this agreement to surrender custody and terminate all parental rights.

Mrs. Whitehead, shortly after the child's birth, had attempted to revoke her consent and surrender by refusing, after the Sterns had allowed her to have the child "just for one week," to return Baby M to them. The trial court's award of specific performance therefore reflects its view that the consent to surrender the child was irrevocable. We accept the trial court's construction of the contract; indeed it appears quite clear that this was the parties' intent. Such a provision, however, making irrevocable the natural mother's consent to surrender custody of her child in a private placement adoption, clearly conflicts with New Jersey law.

[. . .]

It is clear that the Legislature so carefully circumscribed all aspects of a consent to surrender custody—its form and substance, its manner of execution, and the agency or agencies to which it may be made—in order to provide the basis for irrevocability. It seems most unlikely that the Legislature intended that a consent not complying with these requirements would also be irrevocable, especially where, as here, that consent falls radically short of compliance. Not only do the form and substance of the consent in the surrogacy contract fail to meet statutory requirements, but the surrender of custody is made to a private party. It is not made, as the statute requires, either to an approved agency or to DYFS.

These strict prerequisites to irrevocability constitute a recognition of the most serious consequences that flow from such consents: termination of parental rights, the permanent separation of parent from child, and the ultimate adoption of the child. *See Sees v. Baber, supra,* 74 N.J. at 217, 377 A.2d 628. Because of those consequences, the Legislature severely limited the circumstances under which such consent would be irrevocable. The legislative goal is furthered by regulations requiring approved agencies, prior to accepting irrevocable consents, to provide advice and counseling to women, making it more likely that they fully understand and appreciate the consequences of their acts. N.J.A.C. 10:121A-5.4(c).

Contractual surrender of parental rights is not provided for in our statutes as now written. Indeed, in the Parentage Act, N.J.S.A. 9:17-38 to -59, there is a specific provision invalidating any agreement "between an alleged or presumed father and the mother of the child" to bar an action brought for the purpose of determining paternity "[r]egardless of [the contract's] terms." N.J.S.A. 9:17-45. Even a settlement agreement concerning parentage reached in a judicially-mandated consent conference is not valid unless the proposed settlement is approved beforehand by the court. N.J.S.A. 9:17-48c and d. There is no doubt that a contractual provision purporting to constitute an irrevocable agreement to surrender custody of a child for adoption is invalid.

[. . .]

The provision in the surrogacy contract whereby the mother irrevocably agrees to surrender custody of her child and to terminate her parental rights conflicts with the settled interpretation of New Jersey statutory law. [Footnote omitted.] There is only one irrevocable consent, and that is the one explicitly provided for by statute: a consent to surrender of custody and a placement with an approved agency or with DYFS. The provision in the surrogacy contract, agreed to before conception, requiring the natural mother to surrender custody of the child without any right of revocation is one more indication of the essential nature of this transaction: the creation of a contractual system of termination and adoption designed to circumvent our statutes.

B. Public Policy Considerations

The surrogacy contract's invalidity, resulting from its direct conflict with the above statutory provisions, is further underlined when its goals and means are measured against New Jersey's public policy. The contract's basic premise, that the natural parents can decide in advance of birth which one is to have custody of the child, bears no relationship to the settled law that the child's best interests shall determine custody. *See Fantony v. Fantony,* 21 N.J. 525, 536-37, 122 A.2d 593 (1956); *see also Sheehan v. Sheehan,* 38 N.J. Super. 120, 125, 118 A.2d 89 (App. Div. 1955) ("WHATEVER THE AGREEMENT OF THE PARENTS, The Ultimate determination of custody lies with the court in the exercise of its supervisory jurisdiction as *parens patriae*."). The fact that the trial court remedied that aspect of the contract through the "best interests" phase does not make the contractual provision any less offensive to the public policy of this State.

The surrogacy contract guarantees permanent separation of the child from one of its natural parents. Our policy, however, has long been that to the extent possible, children should remain with and be brought up by both of their natural parents. That was the first stated purpose of the previous adoption act, L. 1953, c. 264, § 1, codified at N.J.S.A. 9:3-17 (repealed): "it is necessary and desirable (a) to protect the child from unnecessary separation from his natural parents. . . ." While not so stated in the present adoption law, this purpose remains part of the public policy of this State. *See, e.g., Wilke v. Culp,* 196 N.J. Super. 487, 496, 483 A.2d 420 (App. Div. 1984), certif. den., 99 N.J. 243, 491 A.2d 728 (1985); *In re Adoption by J.J.P., supra,* 175 N.J. Super. at 426, 419 A.2d 1135. This is not simply some theoretical ideal that in practice has no meaning. The impact of failure to follow that policy is nowhere better shown than in the results of this surrogacy contract. A child, instead of starting off its life with as much peace and security as possible, finds itself immediately in a tug-of-war between contending mother and father. [Footnote omitted.]

The surrogacy contract violates the policy of this State that the rights of natural parents are equal concerning their child, the father's right no greater than the mother's. "The parent and child relationship extends equally to every child and to every parent, regardless of the marital status of the parents." N.J.S.A. 9:17-40. As the Assembly Judiciary Committee noted in its statement to the bill, this section establishes "the principle that regardless of the marital status of the parents, all children *and all parents* have equal rights with respect to each other."

Statement to Senate No. 888, Assembly Judiciary, Law, Public Safety and Defense Committee (1983) (emphasis supplied). The whole purpose and effect of the surrogacy contract was to give the father the exclusive right to the child by destroying the rights of the mother.

The policies expressed in our comprehensive laws governing consent to the surrender of a child, discussed *supra* at 1244-1246, stand in stark contrast to the surrogacy contract and what it implies. Here there is no counseling, independent or otherwise, of the natural mother, no evaluation, no warning.

The only legal advice Mary Beth Whitehead received regarding the surrogacy contract was provided in connection with the contract that she previously entered into with another couple. Mrs. Whitehead's lawyer was referred to her by the Infertility Center, with which he had an agreement to act as counsel for surrogate candidates. His services consisted of spending one hour going through the contract with the Whiteheads, section by section, and answering their questions. Mrs. Whitehead received no further legal advice prior to signing the contract with the Sterns.

[. . .]

Under the contract, the natural mother is irrevocably committed before she knows the strength of her bond with her child. She never makes a totally voluntary, informed decision, for quite clearly any decision prior to the baby's birth is, in the most important sense, uninformed, and any decision after that, compelled by a pre-existing contractual commitment, the threat of a lawsuit, and the inducement of a $10,000 payment, is less than totally voluntary. Her interests are of little concern to those who controlled this transaction.

[. . .]

Worst of all, however, is the contract's total disregard of the best interests of the child. There is not the slightest suggestion that any inquiry will be made at any time to determine the fitness of the Sterns as custodial parents, of Mrs. Stern as an adoptive parent, their superiority to Mrs. Whitehead, or the effect on the child of not living with her natural mother.

This is the sale of a child, or, at the very least, the sale of a mother's right to her child, the only mitigating factor being that one of the purchasers is the father. Almost every evil that prompted the prohibition on the payment of money in connection with adoptions exists here.

The differences between an adoption and a surrogacy contract should be noted, since it is asserted that the use of money in connection with surrogacy does not pose the risks found where money buys an adoption. Katz, "Surrogate Motherhood and the Baby-Selling Laws," 20 Colum. J.L. & Soc. Probs. 1 (1986).

First, and perhaps most important, all parties concede that it is unlikely that surrogacy will survive without money. Despite the alleged selfless motivation of surrogate mothers, if there is no payment, there will be no surrogates, or very few. That conclusion contrasts with adoption; for obvious reasons, there remains a steady supply, albeit insufficient, despite the prohibitions against payment. The adoption itself, relieving the natural mother of the financial burden of supporting an infant, is in some sense the equivalent of payment.

Second, the use of money in adoptions does not *produce* the problem—conception occurs, and usually the birth itself, before illicit funds are offered. With surrogacy, the "problem," if one views it as such, consisting of the purchase of a woman's procreative capacity, at the risk of her life, is caused by and originates with the offer of money.

Third, with the law prohibiting the use of money in connection with adoptions, the built-in financial pressure of the unwanted pregnancy and the consequent support obligation do not lead the mother to the highest paying, ill-suited, adoptive parents. She is just as well-off surrendering the child to an approved agency. In surrogacy, the highest bidders will presumably become the adoptive parents regardless of suitability, so long as payment of money is permitted.

Fourth, the mother's consent to surrender her child in adoptions is revocable, even after surrender of the child, unless it be to an approved agency, where by regulation there are protections against an ill-advised surrender. In surrogacy, consent occurs so early that no amount of advice would satisfy the potential mother's need, yet the consent is irrevocable.

[. . .]

The point is made that Mrs. Whitehead *agreed* to the surrogacy arrangement, supposedly fully understanding the consequences. Putting aside the issue of how compelling her need for money may have been, and how significant her understanding of the consequences, we suggest that her consent is irrelevant. There are, in a civilized society, some things that money cannot buy. In America, we decided long ago that merely because conduct purchased by money was "voluntary" did not mean that it was good or beyond regulation and prohibition. *West Coast Hotel Co. v. Parrish,* 300 U.S. 379, 57 S. Ct. 578, 81 L. Ed. 703 (1937). Employers can no longer buy labor at the lowest price they can bargain for, even though that labor is "voluntary," 29 U.S.C. § 206 (1982), or buy women's labor for less money than paid to men for the same job, 29 U.S.C. § 206(d), or purchase the agreement of children to perform oppressive labor, 29 U.S.C. § 212, or purchase the agreement of workers to subject themselves to unsafe or unhealthful working conditions, 29 U.S.C. §§ 651 to 678. (Occupational Safety and Health Act of 1970). There are, in short, values that society deems more important than granting to wealth whatever it can buy, be it labor, love, or life. Whether this principle recommends prohibition of surrogacy, which presumably sometimes results in great satisfaction to all of the parties, is not for us to say. We note here only that, under existing law, the fact that Mrs. Whitehead "agreed" to the arrangement is not dispositive.

The long-term effects of surrogacy contracts are not known, but feared—the impact on the child who learns her life was bought, that she is the offspring of someone who gave birth to her only to obtain money; the impact on the natural mother as the full weight of her isolation is felt along with the full reality of the sale of her body and her child; the impact on the natural father and adoptive mother once they realize the consequences of their conduct. Literature in related areas suggests these are substantial considerations, although, given the newness of surrogacy, there is little information. *See* N. Baker, *Baby Selling: The Scandal of Black Market Adoption, supra; Adoption and Foster Care, 1975: Hearings on Baby Selling Before the Subcomm. on Children and Youth of the Senate Comm. on Labor and Public Welfare,* 94th Cong. 1st Sess. (1975).

The surrogacy contract is based on principles that are directly contrary to the objectives of our laws. [Footnote omitted.] It guarantees the separation of a child from its mother; it looks to adoption regardless of suitability; it totally ignores the child; it takes the child from the mother regardless of her wishes and

her maternal fitness; and it does all of this, it accomplishes all of its goals, through the use of money.

Beyond that is the potential degradation of some women that may result from this arrangement. In many cases, of course, surrogacy may bring satisfaction, not only to the infertile couple, but to the surrogate mother herself. The fact, however, that many women may not perceive surrogacy negatively but rather see it as an opportunity does not diminish its potential for devastation to other women.

In sum, the harmful consequences of this surrogacy arrangement appear to us all too palpable. In New Jersey the surrogate mother's agreement to sell her child is void. [Footnote omitted.] Its irrevocability infects the entire contract, as does the money that purports to buy it.

III. TERMINATION

We have already noted that under our laws termination of parental rights cannot be based on contract, but may be granted only on proof of the statutory requirements. That conclusion was one of the bases for invalidating the surrogacy contract. Although excluding the contract as a basis for parental termination, we did not explicitly deal with the question of whether the statutory bases for termination existed. We do so here.

As noted before, if termination of Mrs. Whitehead's parental rights is justified, Mrs. Whitehead will have no further claim either to custody or to visitation, and adoption by Mrs. Stern may proceed pursuant to the private placement adoption statute, N.J.S.A. 9:3-48. If termination is not justified, Mrs. Whitehead remains the legal mother, and even if not entitled to custody, she would ordinarily be expected to have some rights of visitation. *Wilke v. Culp, supra,* 196 N.J. Super. at 496, 483 A.2d 420.

[. . .]

Nothing in this record justifies a finding that would allow a court to terminate Mary Beth Whitehead's parental rights under the statutory standard. It is not simply that obviously there was no "intentional abandonment or very substantial neglect of parental duties without a reasonable expectation of reversal of that conduct in the future," N.J.S.A. 9:3-48c(1), quite the contrary, but furthermore that the trial court never found Mrs. Whitehead an unfit mother and indeed affirmatively stated that Mary Beth Whitehead had been a good mother to her other children. 217 N.J. Super. at 397, 525 A.2d 1128.

Furthermore, it is equally well settled that surrender of a child and a consent to adoption through private placement do not alone warrant termination. See Sees v. Baber, supra, 74 N.J. 201, 377 A.2d 628. It must be noted, despite some language to the contrary, that the interests of the child are not the only interests involved when termination issues are raised. The parent's rights, both constitutional and statutory, have their own independent vitality. See New Jersey Div. of Youth and Family Servs. v. A.W., supra, 103 N.J. at 601, 512 A.2d 438.

Although the statutes are clear, they are not applied rigidly on all occasions. The statutory standard, strictly construed, appears harsh where the natural parents, having surrendered their child for adoption through private placement, change their minds and seek the return of their child and where the issue comes before the court with the adoptive parents having had custody for years, and having assumed it quite innocently.

These added dimensions in Sees v. Baber, supra, 74 N.J. 201, 377 A.2d 628, failed to persuade this Court to vary the termination requirements. The natural parent in that case changed her mind two days after surrendering the child, sought his return unequivocally, and so advised the adoptive parents. Since she was clearly fit, and clearly had not abandoned the child in the statutory sense, termination was denied, despite the fact that the adoptive parents had had custody of the child for about a year, and the mother had never had custody at all.

A significant variation on these facts, however, occurred in Sorentino II, supra, 74 N.J. 313, 378 A.2d 18. The surrender there was not through private placement but through an approved agency. Although the consent to surrender was held invalid due to coercion by the agency, the natural parents failed to initiate the lawsuit to reclaim the child for over a year after relinquishment. By the time this Court reached the issue of whether the natural parents' rights could be terminated, the adoptive parents had had custody for three years. These circumstances ultimately persuaded this Court to permit termination of the natural parents' rights and to allow a subsequent adoption. The unique facts of Sorentino II were found to amount to a forsaking of parental obligations. Id. at 322, 378 A.2d 18.

The present case is distinguishable from Sorentino II. Mary Beth Whitehead had custody of Baby M for four months before the child was taken away. Her initial surrender of Baby M was pursuant to a contract that we have declared illegal and unenforceable. The Sterns knew almost from the very day that they took Baby M that their rights were being challenged by the natural mother. In short, the factors that persuaded this Court to terminate the parental rights in Sorentino II are not found here.

There is simply no basis, either in the statute or in the peculiar facts of that limited class of case typified by Sorentino II, to warrant termination of Mrs. Whitehead's parental rights. We therefore conclude that the natural mother is entitled to retain her rights as a mother.

IV. CONSTITUTIONAL ISSUES

[. . .]

V. CUSTODY

Having decided that the surrogacy contract is illegal and unenforceable, we now must decide the custody question without regard to the provisions of the surrogacy contract that would give Mr. Stern sole and permanent custody. (That does not mean that the existence of the contract and the circumstances under which it was entered may not be considered to the extent deemed relevant to the child's best interests.) [. . .]

VI. VISITATION

[. . .]

CONCLUSION

This case affords some insight into a new reproductive arrangement: the artificial insemination of a surrogate mother. The unfortunate events that have unfolded illustrate that its unregulated use can bring suffering to all involved. Potential victims include the surrogate mother and her family, the natural father and his wife, and most importantly, the child. Although surrogacy has apparently provided positive results for some infertile couples, it can also, as this case demonstrates, cause suffering to participants, here essentially innocent and well-intended.

We have found that our present laws do not permit the surrogacy contract used in this case. Nowhere, however, do we find any legal prohibition against surrogacy when the surrogate mother volunteers, without any payment, to act as a surrogate and is given the right to change her mind and to assert her parental rights. Moreover, the Legislature remains free to deal with this most sensitive issue as it sees fit, subject only to constitutional constraints.

[. . .]

Chapter 8

Absence of a "Meeting of the Minds"

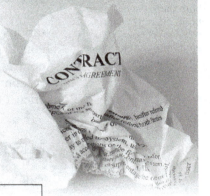

Chapter Objectives

The student will be able to:

- Use vocabulary regarding mistake, duress, undue influence, fraud, misrepresentation, and unconscionability properly.
- Determine whether there has been a "meeting of the minds."
- Discuss the difference between unilateral and mutual mistake.
- Evaluate the ramifications of each kind of formative defect on the enforceability of a contract.
- Identify the three different kinds of duress.
- Determine the intention and reasoning of the parties entering into a contract.
- Identify the differences between a finding of fraud or negligent misrepresentation.
- Evaluate whether a court might find a contract unconscionable.

This chapter will examine exactly what "agreement" means in contract law and HOW parties may avoid performance obligations based on a formative defense and WHAT those defenses are. The parties' internal perceptions of meaning of the contract need to be the same. Their minds need to meet. This is a tricky situation since this analysis relies on subjective intent rather than objectively determinable manifestations of intent. There are situations where a party's subjective intent is contrary to their outward intent to enter into the contract—in other words, if the party could have avoided entering into the contract, she would. It is a matter of free will, or lack thereof, in the formative stage of a contract.

Until now, we have been discussing the *agreement* as the *contract* between the parties. While it may appear that there is an outward manifestation of an agreement, there may not be a **"meeting of the minds."** The parties to an agreement must have the same understanding of the contractual terms and consideration for the contract. If it is discovered that there are differing interpretations of the terms or improper reasons for entering into the bargain (flawed consideration), then the courts may allow the "innocent" party to avoid the contract. There are five general types of such failures to agree on the terms or reasons for entering into the agreement: (1) mistake, (2) duress, (3) undue influence, (4) fraud and misrepresentation, and (5) unconscionability.

meeting of the minds
A theory holding that both parties must both objectively and subjectively intend to enter into the agreement on the same terms.

MISTAKE

This means of avoiding the contract is the least insidious of the five failures of a true agreement as a meeting of the minds. Where one or both parties are *innocently* mistaken as to the subject matter of the contract, there is mistake. Mistakes can be made by both parties, a mutual mistake, or made by only one party, a unilateral mistake.

Unilateral Mistake

unilateral mistake
An error made by only one party to the transaction. The contract may be avoided only if the error is detectable or obvious to the other party.

Generally, contract law turns a deaf ear on **unilateral mistakes** as it presumes that the parties have understood that which they have agreed to and, of course, contract law's love for the objective standard requires this. If the mistake will unjustly enrich one party and pose substantial hardship on the mistaken party, *equitable* principles may be applied to grant relief from performance on the contract. Unilateral mistakes can be subjective and, therefore, disfavored as a basis for granting a remedy. However, where the mistake is objectively reasonable, the courts may permit avoidance. The mistake usually involves some sort of *detectable* or *obvious* typographical or computational error. The reasoning behind this is easily understood: If there is glaring error that the other party must be aware of, they cannot then take advantage of that mistake. It is a question of honesty and fair business practice at that point.

A common example of a unilateral mistake resulting in avoidance is the computational error in a construction contract bid. Bob the Builder submits a bid to the town to construct the new schoolhouse. All the other bids submitted by other contractors were around the $2 million mark. Due to a typographical error, Bob's bid was $200,000. Apparently, Bob's secretary missed a zero as he was typing. This error is reasonably obvious to the town and it cannot take advantage of the unilateral mistake. Bob may avoid enforcement of the contract at $200,000.

On the other hand, if the computational error was not obvious, perhaps because Bob's bid came in at $1.7 million because he left out the cost of the roof, the town can enforce performance of the contract at $1.7 million. Bob's mistake was known only to him and was due to carelessness or negligence. If the bid specification required a line item bid, meaning every part of the construction had to be individually computed and set forth (like a detailed receipt), and the roof was not included on the list, the courts may determine that this was an obvious error as all buildings require a roof.

Additionally, if the mistake was due to **poor judgment**, Bob would be stuck with the consequence of his mistake. Poor judgment, generally, can only be known to the mistaken party and is not a basis for avoidance of the contract. The drafting party usually is held responsible for the content of the contract so, if there is a mistake, it is held against them. Suppose Bob underbid all his competitors because he was simply desperate for any work. He now realizes that his company will take a loss on the project and that this project conflicts with other construction projects that are already scheduled with his company. This is simply poor business judgment on Bob's part. Bob will still be held to the contract, despite the consequences to his business. Courts will not rescue a party from bad planning.

RESEARCH THIS

In your jurisdiction, find two cases regarding a unilateral mistake in terms of the contract: one that holds that the mistake entitles the parties to rescind the contract and one that holds that the mistake does not entitle the drafting party to avoid its obligations and enforces the contract.

What was the defining difference between the facts of these cases that permits avoidance of obligations in one but not in the other?

Mutual Mistake

This kind of mistake goes to the very foundation of the contract—the consideration. Both parties must have a different concept of what they are bargaining for in order to establish that there was a **mutual mistake**. These mistakes generally relate to (1) the **existence of the subject matter**, (2) the ownership or the **right to transfer** ownership, or (3) the **identity or quality of the subject matter**. There must be an actual mistake on the part of both parties that goes to the very heart of the contract, not just a disagreement as to the meaning of the terms. Where there is a disagreement on the meaning of terms, the rules of construction (discussed in the subsequent chapter) will apply.

If either party wants to avoid the contract, they may, provided that (1) the mistake relates to a **material** aspect of the contract, (2) it has a **detrimental effect** on one or both parties, and (3) it **could not have been foreseen**.

poor judgment
Contract law does not allow avoidance of performance obligations due to a mistake that was simply a bad decision on the part of one party.

mutual mistake
An error made by both parties to the transaction; therefore, neither party had the same idea of the terms of the agreement. The contract is avoidable by either party.

existence of the subject matter
The goods to be transferred must exist at the time of the making of the contract.

right to transfer
The party supplying the goods must have the legal title (ownership) or legal ability to give it to the receiving party.

identity or quality of the subject matter
The goods to be transferred must be described with sufficient clarity to allow an outside third party to recognize them.

material
A term is material if it is important to a party's decision whether or not to enter into the contact.

detrimental effect
A party's worsening of his position due to his dependence on the terms of the contract.

foreseeability
The capacity for a party to reasonably anticipate a future event.

SURF'S UP

The most relevant section of the UETA relating to the meeting of the minds issues in contracts is the disproportionate likelihood of mistake in the instantaneous electronic marketplace. We have all hit that "enter" key a little hastily.

§ 10. *Effect of Change or Error*

If a change or error in an electronic record occurs in a transmission between parties to a transaction, the following rules apply:

(1) If the parties have agreed to use a security procedure to detect changes or errors and one party has conformed to the procedure, but the other party has not, and the nonconforming party would have detected the change or error had that party also conformed, the conforming party may avoid the effect of the changed or erroneous electronic record.

(2) In an automated transaction involving an individual, the individual may avoid the effect of an electronic record that resulted from an error made by the individual in dealing with the electronic agent of another person if the electronic agent did not provide an opportunity for the prevention or correction of the error and, at the time the individual learns of the error, the individual:

    (A) promptly notifies the other person of the error and that the individual did not intend to be bound by the electronic record received by the other person;

    (B) takes reasonable steps, including steps that conform to the other person's reasonable instructions, to return to the other person or, if instructed by the other person, to destroy the consideration received, if any, as a result of the erroneous electronic record; and

    (C) has not used or received any benefit or value from the consideration, if any, received from the other person.

(3) If neither paragraph (1) nor paragraph (2) applies, the change or error has the effect provided by other law, including the law of mistake, and the parties' contract, if any.

(4) Paragraphs (2) and (3) may not be varied by agreement.

CRYPTO CONTRACTS

Throughout this text, we have been discussing the immutable nature of "smart contracts" as they exist on the blockchain. This can be either a blessing or a curse in the actual performance or enforcement of the obligations. This basic technology does not permit change is the face of a mistake, until recently. . . . A new development in the coding of blockchain contracts will permit the editing of those transactions. This is particularly important where mistakes are concerned. Without the ability to correct a mistake prior to deployment, critical mistakes can wreak havoc on the financial markets where these blockchain transactions are most often used. "A system of editing blockchain transactions has been applauded by financial participants, but others in the blockchain community have criticized editing technology as antithetical to the blockchain and symptomatic of large financial entities attempting to expropriate the blockchain for themselves in contravention of the technology's original intent." *See* Martin Arnold, *Accenture to Unveil Blockchain Editing Technique*, Fin. Times, Sept. 20, 2016.

Existence of the Subject Matter

Bob the Builder contracts with Larry Landowner for all the standing timber on Larry's property for use in his construction business. Unknown to both Bob and Larry, a recent fire has destroyed the entire lot; there is no salvageable timber. The contract is avoidable by both parties due to a mutual mistake regarding a material fact: They both thought the timber was in existence. This mistake goes to the core of the contract: Without the timber there is no reason to enter into the contract. It has a detrimental effect on Bob, as he will not get the benefit of his bargain and it could not have been reasonably foreseen that a fire would occur. This is assuming that the acreage was not in an area prone to wildfires.

Ownership of the Subject Matter

Bob and Larry may be under an incorrect assumption that Larry has both the ownership of the land and the rights to transfer ownership of the standing timber. Bob is unaware that the land that he believed was his really is part of his neighbor's parcel. At the time Larry drives his trucks to the site, the true owner, Sam, steps forward and protests at cutting down his precious forest. A surveyor is called to the site and determines that Sam's claim is valid and Bob is not the true owner of the land. Neither Bob nor Larry is responsible for the mistake and can avoid liability on the contract.

Quality of the Subject Matter

Alternatively, Bob and Larry may both be mistaken as to the quality of the timber on the land. Bob and Larry may both believe that the wood harvested will be adequate to build with. If this error cannot be attributable to either party's negligence or misrepresentation in determining the species of tree growing on the land, both may avoid the contract. They both may have relied on an incorrect agricultural report. However, a court may be reluctant to grant full relief to Bob if he was given the opportunity to inspect the trees to determine their species and grade before making the contract.

SPOT THE ISSUE!

Doug contracts with Paul for the sale of a gold mine. Doug agrees to pay Paul for mining rights out of the profits of the gold mine. Once $2 million has been paid to Paul, Paul will deed the mine over to Doug. Part of their agreement states: "not less than 250 pounds of gold shall be shipped within the first year." What assumptions are Doug and Paul making? Under what circumstances can one or both of them get out of the contract?

See *Virginia Iron, Coal & Coke Co. v. Graham*, 98 S.E. 659 (Va. 1919).

It is worth noting that where one or both parties assume a risk that the subject matter may or may not be what they think it is, there is no mistake. The uncertainty is out in the open and that uncertainty is part of the consideration; the parties are taking the risk that they will get the better end of the deal. Remember, contract law does not care if you make a good deal or use sound judgment; it is concerned only with your intention to contract for the subject matter. For example, in *Wood v. Boynton*, 25 N.W. 42 (Wis. 1885), the parties contracted for the sale of a gemstone and neither of them knew what it was. The parties were willing to risk that it may have been worth more or less than the price paid when and if it was discovered what it was. Neither party made any investigation as to its nature before the conveyance. The court would not rescind the contract when it was discovered that the plaintiff sold an uncut diamond worth 700 times the purchase price. The court determined that there was no mistake; both parties knew of the ambiguity and that was part of the consideration. As the author, I should like to point out that the inclusion of such old cases is purposeful; it underscores the stability of most principles of contract law.

DURESS

duress
Unreasonable and unscrupulous manipulation of a person to force him to agree to terms of an agreement that he would otherwise not agree to.

Leaving the innocence of mistake behind, we now venture into more sinister territory. While it may outwardly appear that the parties have come to a mutual agreement on the terms of the contract, the contract has not been freely entered into. Freedom of contract also pertains to the requirement that the parties freely entered into the agreement and there was a fair bargaining process. In the case of **duress**, there has been some sort of force or coercion by the inducing party.

Interestingly, contract law takes another departure from its objective standard in evaluating whether duress existed in the formation of the contract and therefore can result in the avoidance of the contract by the innocent/coerced party. This is a more modern development in contract law. If the innocent party to the contract subjectively felt the coercion, then duress exists, regardless of the "reasonableness" to an outside party. What may be duress to one person may not be to another, perhaps more stronger-willed, person.

There are various kinds of duress. The most obvious is **physical duress**. This harkens to a "shotgun wedding" scenario. Vito, a rather old-fashioned and protective father, finds out that Nathan has impregnated his daughter Sonia. He confronts Nathan and threatens to "do him wrong" if he doesn't "do right" by his daughter and marry her. Nathan understands that he will not like enduring the serious bodily harm that will result from his refusal, so he agrees to marry Sonia. When threatened with bodily harm, a person is more likely to agree to terms to which, in their absence, they would not normally agree. The act of holding a gun or threatened severe bodily harm to someone is considered a wrongful act and therefore can constitute physical duress.

A second kind of duress stems from a person's desire for financial security. Threats of *economic harm*, either taking away money or assets or refusing to give earned financial rewards, constitute wrongful influence over the innocent party. The fear of losing money forces the party to consent to the terms, not freedom of choice; for example, the threat to fire an employee unless that party agrees to work overtime without pay. During the hectic holiday shopping season, Bill the boss tells Lucy that she must stay after hours to complete the inventory count and she will not be paid overtime for this additional work. If she complains or refuses, she will be fired. Lucy has no choice because she has bills to pay and cannot afford to lose her job. The loss of financial stability by means of remaining employed is **economic duress** because the employee feels that she has no choice but to submit to this wrongful request. Note that the coercion must be a *wrongful threat*. It is wrong to ask an employee to work overtime without pay. A different conclusion would result if the company requested that the employee sign a covenant not to compete or else be fired. The company has a legal right to request that an employee sign a reasonable covenant; therefore, it cannot constitute a wrongful act to show duress.

In addition to threatening her physical and economic security, a person may be coerced by **mental duress**. The innocent party feels that she has no reasonable choice due to the power that the inducing party has over her. If this occurs in a close relationship, it is referred to as "undue influence," which we will discuss later in the chapter. Overt pressure to enter into the contract or else something unwanted might happen can be classified as mental duress.

For example, a **contract of adhesion** is one where one party has such control over the bargaining process that the innocent party has no choice but to agree to the deal. There has been no bargaining over the terms; the coercing party forces the terms on the weaker party and the terms are clearly slanted in favor of the controlling party.

Example

Cindy Starlet will do almost anything to break into show business. She is a great talent and any production company would be lucky to have her, but she is naïve and doesn't realize this. In an attempt to keep her from competitors and reap great profits, Magnificent Entertainment Company pressures

physical duress
The threat of bodily harm unless the aggressor's demands are met.

economic duress
The threat of harm to a party's financial resources unless demands are met.

mental duress
The threat of harm to a party's overall well-being or a threat of harm to loved ones that induces stress and action on the party of the threatened party.

contract of adhesion
An agreement wherein one party has total control over the bargaining process and therefore the other party has no power to negotiate and no choice but to enter into the contract.

her to sign its contract. Magnificent tells her that she is a marginal talent, but with their help, she could rise to the top. The terms are incredibly one-sided, giving total control of all Cindy's affairs to Magnificent in addition to a huge percentage of her earnings. Cindy feels she has no other choice but to trust Magnificent and consent to its terms.

blackmail
The extortion of payment based on a threat of exposing the victim's secrets.

Blackmail is also a form of mental duress. Imagine Suzie Socialite, who is threatened by Randy Ruthless to expose her sordid past unless she agrees to sell her treasured diamond necklace for a fraction of what it's worth. Suzie's mental anguish at the thought of having her reputation tarnished and probable banishment from her country club and social circles forces her to agree to Randy's terms. Absent this wrongful threat, Suzie would not have entered into this contract.

abuse of process
Using the threat of resorting to the legal system to extract agreement to terms against the other party's will.

Abuse of process, the threat or actual filing of a lawsuit to force a party to agree to terms against her will, constitutes mental duress. In order to be duress, the party must have as her primary intent the procurement of the consent to the contract, not the purpose for which the justice system would grant a remedy. For example, Sam Shareholder threatens to bring a suit against Clancy, the CEO of the corporation, on embezzlement charges unless Clancy agrees to sell Sam a significant amount of shares at a deep discount. Sam may very well be right in bringing a lawsuit, but his purpose for the threat is immediate personal gain, not the pursuit of justice. Sam is using the system and its processes improperly. Sam really wants to coerce Clancy into the agreement to sell the stocks, not to see the lawsuit to fruition.

In sum, lack of choice, aggressiveness to the point of wrongfulness, and unfair use of superior bargaining position all can contribute to mental duress.

CRYPTO CONTRACTS

Perhaps ironically, the defense of duress, which appears to be in-your-face and highly personal, is, in fact, one of the flaws of using the impersonal, distributed, and autonomous blockchain to serve as the contracting medium. Indeed, almost all electronic "click-wrap" and "shrinkwrap" license agreements are completely one-sided and, therefore, could be argued to be contracts of adhesion as the average user has no control over the terms. *See Comb v. Paypal, Inc.*, 218 F. Supp. 2d 1165 (N.D. Cal. 2002) (PayPal asserted that the click-through agreement incorporated both the clauses in question and any updates to them.). A contract of adhesion is a "standardized contract, which, imposed and drafted by the party of superior bargaining strength, relegates to the subscribing party only the opportunity to adhere to the contract or reject it." *Id.* at 1172, *citing Armendariz v. Foundation Health Psychcare Serv.*, 24

Cal. 4th 83, 113, 99 Cal. Rptr. 2d 745, 6 P.3d 669 (2000) (citations and internal quotation omitted). The court concluded that the agreement and questionable clauses were fundamentally unconscionable because they imposed substantial hardship upon the users.

This holding, of course, threatened to disrupt the entire method of doing business on the Internet and indeed, would dismantle the entire structure of blockchain agreements due to their nature. The electronic format of the majority of these agreements require users to simply click on a box indicating that they have read, understood, and agreed to the terms. The plaintiff in *Dejohn v. The .TV Corp. Int'l*, 245 F. Supp. 2d 913 (C.D. Ill. 2003), following the logic of the PayPal holding, argued that the website registration agreement was "an unconscionable adhesion contract because it did not result from arm's length bargaining and was an inherently unfair boilerplate agreement." *Id.* at 919. However, the *Dejohn* court determined that the use of clickwrap consent is not *de facto* unconscionable and clarified the doctrine of unconscionability and contracts of adhesion: "it is the **unfair use of**, not the mere existence of, unequal bargaining power that is determinative." *Id.* [emphasis added].

UNDUE INFLUENCE

Closely related to duress is **undue influence**. The result is almost identical: A party enters into an agreement on terms that are not necessarily what would have been chosen if not for some sort of impermissible persuasion from the other party. In duress, the dominating force is one that influences by fear of some sort. Undue influence is just the opposite: The influenced party is so charmed by the other that she is willing to enter into an agreement on terms that are unfair and/or unwarranted.

undue influence
Using a close personal or fiduciary relationship to one's advantage to gain assent to terms that the party otherwise would not have agreed to.

Undue influence occurs in close, **fiduciary relationships**. A common example is brought to light in a will contest situation. Unprincipled relatives or close friends may try to take advantage of an ailing relative to secure an unfair advantage under the will. Often these exploited relatives are elderly, physically infirm, and psychologically dependent on their exploiters. These conditions tend to make them susceptible to undue influence.

fiduciary relationship
A relationship based on close personal trust that the other party is looking out for one's best interests.

The key factor to examine in these cases is whether the person receiving the benefits under the agreement would naturally receive them or whether the benefit is at odds with normal expectations. For example, Netta Neighbor becomes more attentive as Ethel grows older and more dependent. This relationship blossoms into a very close relationship indeed. Netta has always had her eye on Ethel's land, which adjoins her own, in order to expand her garden. Netta visits Ethel quite often, going out of her way to accommodate Ethel's needs. Netta interferes with Ethel's other relationships, particularly with her children, the natural beneficiaries of Ethel's estate. To everyone's surprise, except Netta's, Ethel leaves her entire estate to Netta. Ethel's heirs have a good cause of action for undue influence.

These seemingly kind actions belie the wrongful intent to deceive and control someone who is not in a position to think reasonably or independently for herself in this powerful situation.

EYE ON ETHICS

Not only is the attorney under the ethical obligations previously discussed in contract formation, but the fiduciary relationship puts an ongoing burden on the attorney for scrupulous dealings with the client.

Examine your state's Code of Professional Conduct with regard to the drafting of wills. There is almost a presumption of undue influence where a will is written by an attorney who then takes as a beneficiary under that will.

FRAUD AND MISREPRESENTATION

The full depth of these aforementioned "evils" lies in fraud and misrepresentation—the worst of the types of deception. Some of the unscrupulous abide by the adage that you can catch more flies with honey than with vinegar; another method for convincing a party into an agreement she would not normally enter into is an outward lie. It takes a little more finesse than the "vinegary" shotgun duress method, but the contractual result is the same. "[T]he parties appear to negotiate freely; but, in fact, one party's ability to negotiate fair terms and make an informed decision is undermined by the other party's fraudulent conduct." *Digicorp, Inc. v. Ameritech Corp.*, 662 N.W.2d 652, 660 (Wis. 2003). The innocent party can avoid her obligations under the contract because there was no intent to enter into such a contract. In other words, it is voidable at the option of the innocent party. **Fraud** and **misrepresentation** are cousins; contractual fraud in the inducement has five elements, whereas its poorer cousin, misrepresentation, only has four. Simply stated, the elements of fraud are

> **fraud**
> A knowing and intentional misstatement of the truth in order to induce a desired action from another person.

> **misrepresentation**
> A reckless disregard for the truth in making a statement to another in order to induce a desired action.

1. the statement made to the other party
2. regarding a material fact
3. with the intent to deceive and
4. the lie was relied upon by the innocent party and
5. the reliance somehow harmed the innocent party.

> **intent to deceive**
> The party making the questionable statement must plan on the innocent party's reliance on the first party's untruthfulness.

The **intent to deceive** is the defining element of fraud. A person must know and intend to make a material falsehood in order to perpetrate fraud upon another party. This differs from negligent misrepresentation in that the party in error does not have this affirmative deceptive intention. A party is culpable of negligent misrepresentation where that party could or should have known of the truth regarding the material fact but did not ascertain that truth before relating the falsity to the innocent party. Thus, negligent misrepresentation is more akin to a sin of omission rather than one of commission.

Example

Linda Landbaron offers to sell her land in Florida to Delores Developer, who plans to construct a golf course on the site. Linda makes the assertion that the area consists of 150 acres, the minimum that Delores needs. In reality, the site only consists of 125 acres. For Linda to be guilty of fraud in the inducement:

1. She would have had to have known that the site consisted of only 125 acres.
2. She would have had to have known that Delores considered the size of the site to be an important fact and at least part of the reason for entering into the contract.
3. She intended to mislead Delores into believing that the site was in fact 150 acres.
4. Delores did rely on the representation of Linda.
5. Delores was harmed by virtue of the fact that she was unable to construct the golf course as she intended.

Linda is guilty of misrepresentation if she did not know whether the site actually consisted of 150 acres, but she told Delores it did in order to close the deal. Here, Linda had no intent to deceive Delores by telling her a deliberate lie; however, she was not responsible enough to ascertain the actual amount of acreage and she was in the best position to do so. Delores reasonably relied on this misrepresentation by assuming that Linda, as the landowner and a savvy businesswoman, knew the dimensions of the land. (Caveat: Some courts will question why official surveys were not produced and examined by Delores. Those courts may hold that the contract may be rescinded and order restitution, but there will be no recovery for economic losses that Delores may forecast due to the rescission.) Let's revisit mistake: If Linda had an honest, but mistaken, belief that the site did consist of 150 acres (perhaps there was a non-obvious mathematical mistake on the survey), both parties would be relieved of their respective obligations due to mutual mistake. Neither party would be "at fault."

Nondisclosure, not telling someone the whole truth, is a tricky area in fraud and misrepresentation. When a party has an obligation to disclose all information known to him/her, the intentional withholding of that information can rise to either fraud or negligent misrepresentation. This most often occurs in real estate transactions and sales of goods. In both these situations, the law imposes an **affirmative duty** to disclose the truth about the condition of the property or item. It is only where the law imposes an affirmative duty to disclose that nondisclosure is actionable. Silence often leads the other party into making certain assumptions; this conforms to the old adage "no news is good news." If the seller makes no mention of any negative aspects of that which

nondisclosure
The intentional omission of the truth.

affirmative duty
The law requires that certain parties positively act in a circumstance and not have to wait until they are asked to do that which they are required to do.

they are selling, the buyer assumes that the property or goods are in perfect condition. *Caveat emptor*: When the term "as is" is included, it relieves the seller of much of this responsibility to reveal all defects. The inclusion of "as is" puts the buyer on notice that there are or may be defects in the property or goods and that the buyer should make all reasonable efforts to find them for him/herself. The deceptively silent party is as guilty of fraud or misrepresentation as if he/she had positively asserted the assumption that the other party was correct when the seller knows that this assumption is not true.

(1)   One who fails to disclose to another a fact that he knows may justifiably induce the other to act or refrain from acting in a business transaction is subject to the same liability to the other as though he had represented the nonexistence of the matter that he has failed to disclose, if, but only if, he is under a duty to the other to exercise reasonable care to disclose the matter in question.

(2)   One party to a business transaction is under a duty to exercise reasonable care to disclose to the other before the transaction is consummated,

(a)   matters known to him that the other is entitled to know because of a fiduciary or other similar relation of trust and confidence between them; and

(b)   matters known to him that he knows to be necessary to prevent his partial or ambiguous statement of the facts from being misleading; and

(c)   subsequently acquired information that he knows will make untrue or misleading a previous representation that when made was true or believed to be so; and

(d)   the falsity of a representation not made with the expectation that it would be acted upon, if he subsequently learns that the other is about to act in reliance upon it in a transaction with him; and

(e)   facts basic to the transaction, if he knows that the other is about to enter into it under a mistake as to them, and that the other, because of the relationship between them, the customs of the trade or other objective circumstances, would reasonably expect a disclosure of those facts.

RESTATEMENT (SECOND) OF TORTS § 551.

The examples that jump to mind are those relating to the sale of real property. Homeowners have intimate knowledge of their houses and conditions that exist thereon. While not every "quirk" of a home need be reported in exacting detail, those conditions that may affect the buyer's decision whether or not to purchase the home are required to be revealed. One could hardly expect that a map of every squeaky floorboard is necessary, or, in the author's case, where the seller failed to tell me about the early spring invasion of crickets in the downstairs den. The fact that a house is not built on the most sound fill material (footings resting on large timbers subject to further rot that will eventually cause the house to collapse), or that a heavy rainstorm will flood the basement, or that a landfill is scheduled to be constructed very nearby must be revealed. Some courts have gone so far as to find an active duty to disclose whether murders had taken place in the home [*see Reed v. King*, 145 Cal. App. 3d 261, 193 Cal. Rptr. 130 (1983)] or whether the home was haunted [*see Stambovsky v. Ackley*, 169 A.D.2d 254, 572 N.Y.S.2d 672 (1991)].

Hiding the defects with new spackle and paint, that is, **active concealment**, is more heinous in that the buyer is not afforded the opportunity to question the existence of defects because they are hidden from view. Therefore, if the seller is silent, no questions will even be asked.

> [Defendant] contends that her statement to plaintiffs that the basement had one leak "effectively disclosed the existence of the flooding problem." Using the Titanic as an example, she argues that it is the quantity of water leakage, not the number of leaks, which is important. The statement that only one leak existed, however, may have left the buyers with a false sense of security. Where a plaintiff's inquiries are inhibited by a defendant's statements which create a false sense of security, the plaintiff's failure to investigate further is not fatal. Defendant argues that plaintiffs did not "seek to look behind the [basement wall] paneling which covered the disclosed defects." We find these arguments to be without merit.

> *Zimmerman v. Northfield Real Estate, Inc.*, 510 N.E.2d 409, 416, 166 (Ill. 1986) (internal citations omitted).

Clearly, proving misrepresentation or fraud is difficult as it requires proof of what was in the other party's mind at the time of contract. This can only be evidenced by the other party's actions surrounding the formation of the agreement. An examination of the facts of every case is necessary in order to evaluate whether misrepresentation or fraud exists. There are no bright-line rules in this area.

active concealment
Knowingly hiding a situation that another party has the right to know and, being hidden from them, assumes that it does not exist.

SPOT THE ISSUE!

Jacques Peacock has recently moved to America and, unfortunately, due to his limited English language skills, was only able to obtain employment earning a mere $200 a week. He must support his family of five on this meager salary but is certain that his prospects will improve once his English improves. In order to make his family feel a little more comfortable, Jacques decides to purchase some home furnishings. He goes to a store where a salesman speaks fluent French. Jacques tells his tale of woe to Slick Sylvester Salesman, who assures Jacques that he will be able to buy all the furniture he needs on installment plans. Every time Jacques wants another piece of furniture, he can buy it and the price can be paid monthly. The sales contract reads in part:

Any and all payments now and hereafter made by the Purchaser shall be credited pro rata on all outstanding contracts for purchase, bills and accounts due to the Company at the time the payments are made.

> Jacques signs these agreements, which are written in English and obscure at best to native English speakers. Months later, Jacques comes to the law office where you work and explains that all the time he has been making payments on each item of furniture under separate contracts; it never seems to result in him actually owning any of it. In other words, the effect of this provision in the contract keeps a balance due on each and every item purchased until the balance due on *all* the items has been totally paid off.
>
> Explain the theory(ies) of how you might get Jacques out of these contracts.

UNCONSCIONABILITY

unconscionable
So completely unreasonable and irrational that it shocks the conscience.

This last defect in formation is also the least certain. Courts have failed to adequately define what constitutes an **unconscionable** term, instead relying on the theory that "they'll know it when they see it." Justice Stewart, in his concurring opinion in *Jacobellis v. Ohio*, 378 U.S. 184, 197, 84 S. Ct. 1676 (1964), wrote: "I shall not today attempt further to define the kinds of material I understand to be embraced within that shorthand description; and perhaps I could never succeed in intelligibly doing so. But I know it when I see it. . . ." Since the earliest reported cases, the definition of unconscionability has been vague and has not improved; indeed, many courts continue to rely on the following definition:

> *It may be apparent from the intrinsic nature and subject of the bargain itself;* such as no man in his senses and not under delusion would make on the one hand, and as no honest and fair man would accept on the other; *which are unequitable and unconscientious bargains; and of such even the common law has taken notice; for which, if it would not look a little ludicrous. . . .*

> *Hume v. United States*, 132 U.S. 406, 10 S. Ct. 134 (1889) (emphasis added)
> (*Hume* has been cited over 400 times as of this writing).

In short, unconscionability may be found where none of the other defects in formation apply, but the court cannot permit the oppressing party to escape some liability for taking unscrupulous advantage of another. Superior knowledge and bargaining position put one party at such an advantage over the other that some protection must be afforded to the subjugated party. The court can choose a variety of remedies to either release the innocent party from her contractual obligations or to level the playing field and enforce the contract but without the offensive term so that a fair result is accomplished. *See* RESTATEMENT (SECOND) OF CONTRACTS § 208.

Example

Betty, who owns the local beauty salon, orders several hairdryers and curling irons from Scorch'em, Inc., the only supplier in the area. On the back of the order form, in very, very small print, Scorch'em disclaimed any and all warranties, which relieved the company of any and all claims relating to its products. Essentially, it couldn't be held responsible for any damages at all. After using the hairdryers and curling irons just once, they all burst into flames and caused substantial damage to both customers and the salon. In this instance, the court would most likely find that the warranty disclaimers were unconscionable. The terms were not fairly disclosed to the buyer, resulting in unfair "surprise" as to the actual terms of the agreement. *See A & M Produce Co. v. FMC Corp.*, 135 Cal. App. 3d 473 (1982). Further, being released from all responsibility is not fair to the buyer or to the public at large. It does not conform to "minimum levels of integrity" in business. *Id.* at 488, *citing Graham v. Scissor-Tail, Inc.*, 28 Cal. 3d 807, 826-827 (1981).

IN-CLASS DISCUSSION

Loosely based on *Hurwitz v. Bocian*, 670 N.E.2d 408 (Mass. App. Ct. 1996).

Stella, a very attractive account executive at Star Enterprises, was approached by the president of the company, Mr. Orion, who promised her a promotion in "the near future" and that she would share in one-half of the profits. This agreement was not reduced to a writing. Mr. Orion said he would put it in writing after his divorce was final.

She began not only working harder but started an affair with Mr. Orion. When the company began to suffer financial difficulties, Stella did not draw her salary so that payroll could be met. The assurances of Mr. Orion were enough for her.

When Mr. Orion ended the relationship (after the business began doing well again), Stella sought her share of the business and her back pay. Mr. Orion refused and said she had nothing in writing so he was off the hook and he never planned on giving her such a share in the business.

Can Stella bring an action based on any of the meeting of the minds defenses to formation? Explain your answer. What factors, if different, would change your answer?

In order for a court to uphold a contract, there must be a reasonable semblance of a meeting of the minds. Two or more parties must have engaged in some sort of meaningful dealing to decide upon the terms of the contract. The terms do not have to be fair, but they cannot be so outrageously prejudiced against one party as this leaves the court with only one conclusion: that there was not any meaningful meeting of the minds.

Summary

An "agreement" in contract law means that there has been a *meeting of the minds* with respect to all material terms of the contract. There are five general types of such failures to agree on the terms or reasons for entering into the agreement: (1) mistake, (2) duress, (3) undue influence, (4) fraud and misrepresentation, and (5) unconscionability.

Mistakes can be either mutual or unilateral. *Mutual mistakes* result in the possibility of avoidance of the contract by either party. *Unilateral mistakes,* a misunderstanding by only one party, result in the possibility of avoidance of the contract only where there is some *detectable* or *obvious* error. In both cases, the mistake must relate to some material term of the contract in order to be avoided as a failure of the meeting of the minds. Of course, both parties can assume the risk of error and the issue of avoidance is removed altogether.

Where one party has *forced* or *coerced* the other into making the contract, contract law will allow avoidance on the basis of duress. Duress can be *physical, economical,* or *mental.* Duress also can take the form of a *contract of adhesion, blackmail,* or *abuse of process.* A special form of duress that occurs in *fiduciary relationships* is *undue influence.* The person putting pressure on the other party uses the closeness of the relationship to his unfair advantage.

The cousins, *fraud* and *misrepresentation,* relate to (1) lying about (2) a material fact (3) knowing that the other party would reasonably rely on the lie and (4) in fact the reliance upon that lie harmed the innocent party. If the element of (5) the *intent to deceive* based on the lie is present, the misrepresentation rises to fraud in the inducement. *Nondisclosure* can rise to either fraud or misrepresentation if the person who does not tell the whole truth is under a legal, *affirmative duty* to disclose that information. *Active concealment* is a form of nondisclosure where the party knows of the defect and thwarts efforts of the other party to discover it.

Lastly, an *unconscionable* term is one that no reasonable person would freely agree to as it is so unfair and one-sided. It shocks the conscience of the court that anyone would actually make that type of offer or that a person could accept it.

Key Terms

abuse of process
active concealment
affirmative duty
blackmail
contract of adhesion
detrimental effect
duress

economic duress
existence of the subject matter
fiduciary relationship
foreseeability
fraud
identity/quality of the subject matter
intent to deceive

materiality
meeting of the minds
mental duress
misrepresentation
mutual mistake
nondisclosure
physical duress

poor judgment
right of transfer
unconscionability
undue influence
unilateral mistake
wrongful act

Review Questions

MULTIPLE CHOICE

Choose the best answer(s) and please explain *why* you choose the answer(s).

1. Courts will likely rule that a unilateral mistake is the basis for avoidance of the contract where
   a. One party is in a superior bargaining position.
   b. The mistake was obviously a typographical error.
   c. One party used poor judgment when entering into the contract.
   d. One party can show that the other has special knowledge that the contract will not be possible to perform if the mistake is not corrected.

2. Courts will likely rule that a mutual mistake is the basis for avoidance of the contract where
   a. One party is in a superior bargaining position.
   b. The person was completely intoxicated and it was apparent to everyone at the bar.
   c. Both parties had no idea that the subject matter of the contract was destroyed in a flood.
   d. Both parties assumed the risk that the deal might not turn out as expected.

3. Which of the following is *not* a form of duress?
   a. Farmer Fred finds out that Harry has been courting his daughter and tells Harry he really wants him to marry her. If Harry refuses, Farmer Fred will burn Harry's crops to the ground and salt the earth.
   b. Farmer Fred finds out that Harry has been courting his daughter and tells Harry he really wants him to marry her. If Harry refuses, Farmer Fred will be so disappointed that he will have to close his farm.
   c. Farmer Fred finds out that Harry has been courting his daughter and tells Harry he really wants him to marry her. Farmer Fred tells his daughter that she will be disinherited if she does not marry Harry.
   d. Farmer Fred finds out that Harry has been courting his daughter and tells Harry he really wants him to marry her. If Harry refuses, Farmer Fred will expose all of Harry's dirty family secrets to the whole town.

EXPLAIN YOURSELF

All answers should be written in complete sentences. A simple "yes" or "no" is insufficient.

1. Whenever a court wants to find in favor of one party, it can use the doctrine of unconscionability.

2. What is the difference between fraud and misrepresentation? Write a fact pattern to illustrate your answer.

3. What is the essential difference between duress and undue influence? How do they manifest themselves differently?

"FAULTY PHRASES"

All of the following statements are FALSE; state why they are false and then rewrite them as true statements. Write a brief fact pattern that illustrates your answer.

1. In order to establish undue influence, a party must show that he/she was disinherited.

2. The defining element of fraud in the inducement of a contract is to tell a lie to the other party.

3. A person selling real estate must always reveal every condition of the property known to her at the time of contract.

4. Active concealment of a defect is not the equivalent of affirmatively denying its existence.

5. The terms of the contract are evidence of a "meeting of the minds."

6. Parties can always avoid the contract based on mutual mistake.

7. Threatening to sue someone is an example of duress.

8. Requesting that an employee sign a covenant not to compete is a form of economic duress.

"WRITE" AWAY! PORTFOLIO ASSIGNMENT

What are the ramifications of mistake on the Druid and Carrie contract? Who bears the risk for mistakes? Draft a clause regarding the assumption of risk for mistake allocating the appropriate type of risk to the responsible party.

Case in Point

FRAUD IN THE INDUCEMENT

■ This case is very well known to any law student attending school since its publication. It is one of those infamous cases that so adeptly capture a principle of law.

133 N.W.2d 666
257 Iowa 613
Agnes SYESTER, Appellee,
v.
James R. BANTA, Mary L. BANTA, George B. THEISS and Forest L. THEISS,
d/b/a ARTHUR MURRAY DANCE STUDIO, Appellants.
No. 51504.
Supreme Court of Iowa.
March 9, 1965.

Page 668

[257 Iowa 615] Dickinson, Parker, Mannheimer & Raife, Des Moines, for appellants.

I. Joel Pasternak, Des Moines, for appellee.

SNELL, Justice.

This is a law action seeking damages, actual and exemplary, for allegedly false and fraudulent representations in [257 Iowa 616] the sale of dancing instruction to plaintiff. From the final judgment entered after a jury verdict for plaintiff in a substantial amount defendants have appealed.

Plaintiff is a lonely and elderly widow who fell for the blandishments and flattery of those who saw some "easy money" available.

Defendants are the owners of the Des Moines Arthur Murray Dance Studio. They have a legitimate service to sell but when their selling techniques transcend the utmost limits of reason and fairness they must expect courts and juries to frown thereon. In this case the jury has done so.

Since the beginning of recorded history men and women have persisted in selling their birthrights for a mess of pottage and courts cannot protect against the folly of bad judgment. We can, however, insist on honesty in selling. The old doctrine of caveat emptor is no longer the pole star for business.

Much of the testimony was uncontradicted. The testimony as to intentional fraud and misrepresentation as well as the motive and credibility of some witnesses was attacked but these were questions for the jury. It was for the jury to say who should be believed.

It is not for us to say who should have prevailed with the jury. It is for us to determine the sufficiency of the admissible evidence to generate a jury question and the correctness of the instructions given the jury. We will mention only as much of the testimony as is necessary for that purpose.

Page 669

Plaintiff is a widow living alone. She has no family. Her exact age does not appear but a former employee of defendants and a favorite dancing instructor of plaintiff testified "that during the period from 1957 through the fall of 1960 she was 68 years old."

After her husband's death plaintiff worked at Bishops as a "coffee girl." She first went to the Arthur Murray Studio in 1954 as a gift from a friend. On the first visit there was no attempt to sell her any lessons but she was invited to return a few days later. When she returned she was interviewed by the manager and sold a small course of dancing lessons. From that time on [257 Iowa 617] there appears to have been an astoundingly successful selling campaign.

The testimony of defendants' manager and his written summary of payments, received as Exhibit

1, are not in complete accord, but the variation is not vital. By May 2, 1955 defendants sold plaintiff 3222 hours of dancing instruction for which she paid $21,020.50. In all, according to the testimony of defendants' manager plaintiff paid $33,497.00 for 4057 hours of instruction. Because of some refunds and credits defendants' Exhibit 1 shows plaintiff's cost to be only $29,174.30. Defendants' Exhibit 1 is as follows:

"EXHIBIT 1
"SUMMARY OF "DANCE COURSES PURCHASED "BY AGNES SYESTER
HOURS IN

"DATE	SOLD BY	COURSE	AMT PAID
9-27-54	Brick	206	1709.50
10-15-54	Neidt	300	2490.00
11-4-54	Neidt	16	88.00
1-8-55	Bersch	500	3825.00
1-19-55	Bersch	1000	6800.00
5-2-55	Bersch	1200	6000.00
5-24-55	Brick	100	995.00
6-22-55	Brick	10	79.80
5-25-57	Brick-Ziegler	11	130.00
6-22-57	Brick	10	106.00
6-4-58	Carey	10	106.00
9-8-58	Carey	10	99.00
1-6-59	Erickson	4	25.00
5-27-59	Wolf	10	116.00
6-10-59	Wolf	10	112.50
6-10-59	Wolf	10	112.50
12-2-59	Carey-Kenton	25	290.00
3-2-60	Carey	625	6090.00
		$4057	$29174.30"

[257 Iowa 618] On May 2, 1955 when plaintiff bought 1200 additional hours of instruction for $6,000 she had already bought 2022 hours and had used only 261 hours.

Included in the courses offered were lifetime memberships. With the purchase of 1,000 or 1,200 hours of instruction it was the policy of defendants to give free attendance

Page 670

to weekly dances for life and two hours of instruction or practice a month to keep active on what had been learned. Included in plaintiff's purchases were three lifetime memberships. Plaintiff attended the weekly dances and incidental entertainments and admitted having fun.

Plaintiff testified that defendants' manager sold her the first lifetime membership. She testified 'He promised me all the privileges of the studio and I would be a professional dancer.' To make such a promise to a lady plaintiff's age was ridiculous. The fact that she was so gullible as to be an easy victim does not justify taking over $29,000 of her money. She may have been willing and easily sold but nevertheless a victim.

The members of defendants' staff were carefully schooled and supervised in the art of high-powered salesmanship. Mr. Carey, a witness for plaintiff, testified at length as to methods and as to his contact with plaintiff. There was evidence that Mr. Carey was a disgruntled former employee and instructor and had expressed hostility toward defendants, but his credibility was for the jury.

Defendants' studio occupies seven rooms consisting of a grand ballroom and six private studios. Each private studio is wired for sound so the manager could monitor conversations between instructor and student and without the student's knowledge correct the instructor's sales technique.

Mr. Carey had received two months training including a course on sale technique taught by the manager. Plaintiff's Exhibit H is a revised edition of defendants' "Eight Good Rules For Interviewing." It is an exhaustive set of instructions, outlines and suggested conversations covering twenty-two typewritten pages. A few pertinent parts are:

"1. How to prevent a prospect from consulting his banker, lawyer, wife or friend.
[257 Iowa 619] "2. Avoid permitting your prospect to think the matter over.
"3. Tell the prospect that has never danced before that it is an advantage and tell the prospect that has danced before that it is an advantage.
"4. To dance with the prospect and then tell the prospect that the rhythm is very good, their

animation or self confidence is good, that their natural ability is very good. That they will be an excellent ballroom dancer in much less time and that if they didn't have natural ability it would take twice as long.

"5. To summarize the prospect's ability to learn as follows: "Did you know that the three most important points on this D.A. are: Rhythm, natural ability and animation? You've been graded Excellent in all three.""

"6. In quoting the price for various courses, the instructor is supposed to say "the trouble with most people is that they dance lifelessly, but as I told you on your analysis, you have animation—vitality in your dancing. No matter what course you decide on you're going to be a really smooth dancer (men would rather be a smooth dancer—women would rather be a beautiful, graceful dancer).""

"7. To use "emotional selling" and the instructor is tutored as follows: "This is the warm-up period and is a very important part of your interview. You have proved to him by now that he can learn to dance; now you must appeal to his emotions in such a way that he will want lessons regardless of the cost.""

Theoretically, for advancing proficiency in dancing (the jury must have thought that $29,000 had something to do with it), plaintiff was awarded a Bronze Medal, then a Silver Medal and then a Gold Medal. These awards were given plaintiff all in the same year although defendants' manager testified that it takes approximately two to four years to qualify for a Bronze Medal, five to seven years for a Silver Medal and anytime after 1200 hours a student could qualify for the Gold Medal. Finally after

Page 671

considerable thought about new incentives for plaintiff to buy something more she was shown a film on Gold Star dancing. This is a difficult professional type of dancing. "The dancers on the film were brought in from Europe by Mr. Murray. The dancing is English quick step and is the type of dancing done by Ginger [257 Iowa 620] Rogers and Fred Astaire only about twice as difficult." This film had been studied 15 to 20 times to determine what parts to stress with plaintiff.

Plaintiff was easily sold a Gold Star course of 625 hours for $6,250. A few days later she came into

the ballroom, handed Mr. Carey an envelope and said "Well, it took some doing but here is the money." The money was delivered to the manager.

The Gold Star course was started although even the instructor was 'faking it' and had no idea what he was doing.

Mr. Carey testified that from 1957 through the fall of 1960 plaintiff's dancing ability did not improve. "She was 68 years old and had gone as far as she would ever go in dancing, thereon it would be merely repetitious." In his opinion "it would take 200 to 400 hours of instructions to teach her to dance in the manner she was dancing in 1960." He also testified that while he was at the studio none of his students ever failed to qualify for any of the medals. When he questioned plaintiff's ability to do the advanced type of dancing she was being sold he was remained by defendants' manager that he was an employee and that the manager made the rules.

Mr. Carey testified at length as to the attentions, inducements, promises and lies (he said they were) lavished on plaintiff. He became plaintiff's regular instructor. He was about twenty-five years old and apparently quite charming and fascinating to plaintiff. She gave him a diamond ring for his birthday in 1960.

The testimony is rather fantastic but it would unduly extend this opinion to set it forth in greater detail. It was in our opinion sufficient for the jury to find that plaintiff was the victim of a calculated course of intentional misrepresentations.

The charge for instruction varied somewhat up to $10 per hour. After some refunds, and, according to defendants' computation, plaintiff paid approximately $6.75 per hour for 3425 hours of instruction or about $23,000.

If Mr. Carey's estimate of plaintiff's ability and possibility of progress is accepted plaintiff was knowingly overcharged for 3025 hours or a total sum of $20,418.75.

Mr. Carey was discharged by defendants in the fall of 1960. [257 Iowa 621] Plaintiff quit the studio shortly thereafter. She still had 1750 hours of unused time that she had purchased. She testified that she did so because she "was unhappy because things didn't go right and I was through with dancing, and that was the only reason I quit." Defendants' manager testified that plaintiff "became unhappy over the dismissal of Mr. Carey and left the studio."

Another witness for defendants said plaintiff complained mostly about losing her instructor, Mr. Carey.

In January 1961 plaintiff employed counsel to represent her in a lawsuit against defendants. Her counsel contacted defendants. Conferences were held. Apparently a divertive campaign was planned by defendants. Mr. Carey testified:

"I next heard from Mr. Theiss in January of 1961 when he called and asked me to come down to the studio to discuss employment. I went to see him and he told me that Mrs. Syester was suing him and wanted to know if I still had any influence over her, to get her to drop the suit. I told him I felt that I still did and I would try to get her to come back in the studio and drop her legal action against him. He said he would reinstate me and pay all of my past due commissions. I accepted the position and went to Bishop's Cafeteria where Mrs. Syester was the coffee girl to see what her feelings were toward the studio. She was very cold toward me and I reported this

Page 672

to Mr. Theiss. He said not to concern myself with the studio, that my job was merely to get her to drop the lawsuit, so I went to Bishops a couple of times a day to try and talk with Mrs. Syester. Finally I succeeded and told her that I was back in the studio and that Mr. Theiss wanted her back. I told her that there would be no hard feelings on our part if she would just drop the suit and come back but she said she did not want to come back to the studio. I continued talking to her and finally got her to accept coming to a party and told her that I would be out to pick her up and escort her to the studio. This was about a week after I first contacted her, in Febuary of 1961. I told her that I was going to the party and I would save her some waltzes. I knew this was her favorite dance. And I felt that if she would pass up this waltz, she was not interested in dancing. She did not come to the studio so the next day I went down to Bishop's and told her she disappointed [257 Iowa 622] me very much. Then I started talking about all of the lessons she and I had had and

all of the months we had danced and the fun we had together. I told her how wonderful she had done. I painted word pictures and things so she could see this. I asked her if she remembered about when she got the Bronze. She kept saying that was best but all she wanted was her money back. I finally pursuaded her to come to the studio and we danced for about 45 minutes. It was at this time that she called the lawsuit off. . . . When I went to Bishop's Cafeteria to see Mrs. Syester I told her she was a good dancer and that she still had the ability to be a professional, excellent dancer. I told her that she did not need an attorney; after, all Mrs. Theiss and myself were her only friends and we wanted her back at the studio to continue with her Gold Star and reminded her of all the waltzes we would do together."

During the month of February several people contacted plaintiff at the instigation of defendants' manager, including Mr. Carey. These efforts were fruitful. Plaintiff made what defendants claim was a complete settlement. Defendants' counsel prepared a written release (defendants' Exhibit 2) and was present during one conference of the parties. Defendants' counsel did not instigate, carry on, nor make the "settlement" with plaintiff. He testified that he "did not want to get that implicated." In any event defendants' manager at plaintiff's home persuaded plaintiff to discharge her counsel by phone and agree to settle for the refund of her March 2, 1960 payment of $6,090. This was reported to defendants' counsel, who in behalf of his client, wrote settlement checks. Plaintiff's counsel received his share although there is no evidence that the settlement was ever pursuant to his advice. There is evidence that defendants were attempting to lead plaintiff away from her own counsel. Their efforts were so far beyond the limits of propriety that their own counsel hesitated to participate.

The release signed by plaintiff is a specific release of her claim based on the March 2, 1960 payment and a general release of all claims. If obtained in good faith it is a bar to all plaintiff's claims. The release was witnessed by Estella M. Smith, whose identity does not appear and by defendants' manager. [257 Iowa 623] After signing this release on March 6, 1961 plaintiff's then pending lawsuit was dismissed. Plaintiff returned to the studio and participated in the activities for several months.

A second release dated January 28, 1963 was obtained by defendants' manager. It purports to be a contractual release for $4,000. The $4,000 to be paid was to be evidenced by a note. There is no claim that anything has been paid thereon. The note provided for installment payments but instead of being signed by defendants it is signed by plaintiff. Defendants' manager testified that this was all a mistake and that the studio was to pay.

Accepting defendants' explanation that it was a mistake the most charitable thing that can be said is that plaintiff would

Page 673

sign anything requested, even a note wherein she was the payee.

The present action was filed March 12, 1963. It alleged fraud and misrepresentation in the several sales to plaintiff and in obtaining dismissal of the previous lawsuit and the releases signed by plaintiff.

Defendants denied any fraud or misrepresentations and urged the releases as a complete defense. Defendants offered evidence in support of their position. At the close of plaintiff's evidence and again at the close of all the evidence defendants moved for a directed verdict. The motions were overruled. The jury returned a verdict for plaintiff in the sum of $14,300 actual damages and $40,000 punitive damages. Defendants appealed.

I. The court told the jury to first consider the issues involved in the releases signed by plaintiff and placed on plaintiff the burden of proving by clear, satisfactory and convincing evidence that they were not binding on her. This was proper.

In five instructions, separately numbered but in sequence, the court instructed on fraud, expression of opinion as distinguished from a statement of fact, fraudulent misrepresentation, intent to mislead, consideration for releases, presumption of freedom from fraud, need for prudence in signing and failure of consideration.

On appeal defendants challenged the sufficiency of the evidence to generate a jury question but not the accuracy of the instructions.

[257 Iowa 624] Defendants argue in the absence of fraud the execution of a valid release bars a future action based on the rights relinquished. The rule is stated in Kilby v. Charles City Western Railway Company, 191 Iowa 926, 928, 183 N.W. 371 as follows:

"Where a settlement has been had between competent parties, and a release has been fairly entered into, without fraud or overreaching, it becomes binding and effectual, and will be upheld and enforced. It is undoubtedly the law that an instrument of this character can be impeached for fraud in procuring the same or where the same was executed by a party who was mentally incompetent to legally execute such an instrument. The burden of proof is on the party seeking to impeach such written instrument."

Mere failure to read an instrument before signing will not avoid its provisions. Crum v. McCollum, 211 Iowa 319, 233 N.W. 678. These propositions are not in dispute and further citation of authority is unnecessary.

Relief from the bar of a release is becoming more liberal even where there is no claim of fraud but only mistake. In Reed v. Harvey, 253 Iowa 10, 17, 110 N.W.2d 442, 446 we quoted from 71 A.L.R.2d as follows:

"There 'appears to be a definite trend in most jurisdictions towards granting relief liberally where it is made to appear that an injured party released his claim under a false impression that he was fully informed as to the nature and extent of his injuries' (page 88 of 71 A.L.R.2d)."

Reed v. Harvey was a tort action but the same rule should apply.

In Christy v. Heil, 255 Iowa 602, 606, 123 N.W.2d 408, 410, a vendor-vendee case, we said: 'The trend of recent cases is toward the doctrine that a vendor cannot shield himself from liability by asking the law to condemn the credulity of the purchaser.'

The issue involving the releases was essentially factual. That plaintiff was easily influenced appears without question. The consideration for the first release was wholly inadequate. It was only a partial return of an unconscionable overcharge. The consideration for the second release was not paid. The evidence [257 Iowa 625] was such that the jury could find that there was such a concerted effort, lacking in propriety, to obtain the releases as to constitute fraudulent

Page 674

overreaching. The jury obviously concluded that there was a predatory play on the vanity and credulity of an old lady. We find no reason for interfering with that conclusion.

II. Defendants argue that 'In an action based upon fraud, certain universally recognized elements must be alleged and shown, and the failure to establish any one or more of such elements is fatal to such action.' With this statement we agree and so did the trial court. In Instruction No. 10 the jury was told that to recover the burden was on plaintiff to establish by clear, satisfactory and convincing evidence each of the following propositions:

"1. That the defendants made one or more of the representations' claimed by plaintiff . . . .

"2. That said statements, or one or more of them, were false.

"3. That said false statements or representations were as to material matters with reference to the entering into the lesson contracts.

"4. That the defendants knew the said representations, or one or more of them, were false.

"5. That said representations were made with intent to deceive and defraud the plaintiff.

"6. That the plaintiff believed and relied upon said false representations and would not have entered into the lesson contracts, except for believing and relying upon said misrepresentations.

"7. That the plaintiff was damaged in some amount through relying on said representations.

"If you find that the plaintiff has established each and every one of the foregoing propositions, numbered 1 to 7 inclusive by evidence which is clear, satisfactory and convincing, then your

verdict will be for the plaintiff and against the defendants in such amount as you find plaintiff is justly entitled to receive.

"If you find, however, that the plaintiff has failed to establish any one or more of the foregoing propositions, numbered 1 to 7 inclusive, then your verdict will be for the defendants."

[257 Iowa 626] The instruction was adequate. Here again the problem was factual. Defendants argue that the representations proved by plaintiff were nothing more than mere expressions of opinion or 'puffing' and that the only substantial exression of opinion was in fact accomplished.

In *Christy v. Heil*, supra, we considered statements of fact as distinguished from opinion or puffing. We said "Ordinarily the question of whether the representations made are opinion or fact is for the jury to determine and depends upon the facts and circumstances in each case." (Citations) loc. cit. 608, 123 N.W.2d loc. cit. 411. "We must review the evidence in the light most favorable to the purchasers." loc. cit. 613, 123 N.W.2d loc. cit. 414.

Defendants' review of the authorities is exhaustive and scholarly but the fact remains that in the case at bar there was evidence, which if believed by the jury, would support a finding of fraud.

III. Defendants argue that there was no proof of damage. Although the court's instructions on measure of damage were closer to the "out of pocket" rule than to the "benefit of bargain" rule to which we are committed (see 37 C.J.S. Fraud § 143, page 477) defendants make no complaint. The instruction was not prejudicial to defendants. Defendants say that the rule was properly stated but suggest that the statement of the issues including the amount prayed for may have been misleading. The fact that plaintiff asked for something beyond the correct measure of damage is not reversible error if, as defendants say, the court properly instructed the jury.

Page 675

Defendants argue that there was no evidence from which the jury could find the fair and reasonable value of the instruction received other than the amount paid by plaintiff. Defendants' manager testified that plaintiff still has 899 hours of unused lessons. Mr. Carey's testimony would support a finding that plaintiff was knowingly overcharged for $3025 hours or the sum of $20,418.75. The jury's verdict for $14,300 actual damages was within the evidence. We have no means of knowing just how the jury computed the damage. It was for more than the charge for the unused time according to defendants, but less than would be due for unproductive instruction. In argument defendants [257 Iowa 627] have stressed the value of plaintiff's enjoyment. That may have entered into the jury's computation.

The verdict was not beyond the scope of the evidence or the instructions.

IV. In addition to actual damages plaintiff asked for exemplary or punitive damages. The claim was submitted to the jury and a verdict for $40,000 punitive damages was returned.

Defendants argue that the record will not support an award of punitive damages in any amount and that the issue should not have been submitted, but do not challenge the accuracy of the instructions relative thereto.

Defendants argue that in the absence of actual damages, punitive damages cannot be awarded. That proposition is well established and needs no extended discussion here for we have said in Division III, supra, that there was support for an award of actual damages. The rule is stated in 17 Iowa Law Review, 413, 414, as follows:

"It is a well settled and almost universally accepted rule in the law of damages that a finding of exemplary damages must be predicated upon a finding of actual damages. The reason for the rule lies in the theory behind exemplary damages, and this theory is ordinarily utilized by the courts in supporting their statements. As indicated by its synonyms, "exemplary" damages are a species of punishment. They are awarded to the plaintiff in the discretion of the jury as a means of retaliation against the defendant for his anti-social conduct, as a means of preventing him from acting similarly in the future, and as a means of deterring others who might be so inclined. It is argued effectively, therefore, that if no actual damages have been sustained, the defendant merits no harsh treatment, and that there is no

foundation on which exemplary damages may be based. . . ."

In the absence of malice, punitive damages cannot be awarded. The problem of what constitutes malice and the evidence necessary to support a finding has been considered in many decisions. The problem frequently arises in actions for libel but comparable confusion arises in other situations. In *Ballinger v. Democrat Company*, 207 Iowa 576, 578, 223 N.W. 375, 376, the following quotation appears: "the word 'malice' is the bugbear of the law of libel."

[257 Iowa 628] Judge Graven in *Amos v. Prom*, 115 F. Supp. 127 thoroughly analyzed the rules and supporting authorities incident to exemplary damages. We quote and adopt, but need not repeat the supporting citations for that opinion.

"[T]here is no mathematical ratio and exemplary damages may considerably exceed compensatory damages in some cases." loc. cit. 131

"Under Iowa law exemplary damages are not a matter of right but rest in the discretion of the jury." (Citations) loc. cit. 133

"Exemplary damages may be awarded where it appears that the defendant is guilty of fraud." loc. cit. 133

Page 676

"Such exemplary damages are permitted on the theory that they serve as a deterrent to wrongdoers and as punishment for wrongdoing." loc. cit. 134

Malice or wanton conduct is imputable to the principal. loc. cit. 134

"While it is not entirely clear whether the Iowa decisions regard 'malice in fact' as a descriptive term for 'legal malice' or as a synonym for 'express malice,' it is apparent that the 'malice' required to permit an award of exemplary damages is something less than actual ill-will or express malice and may be termed 'legal malice' for want of a better expression." loc. cit. 136

"It is finally said that the intentional doing of a 'wrongful act' without justification will permit an inference of the wicked state of mind. Yet it is apparent that many wrongful or illegal acts may be intentionally committed from motives wholly apart from any malice or evil intent directed toward the person who happens to suffer by the action, as where defendant is motivated by a desire for gain and has no feeling at all for those injured by him.

"Therefore, when the law reaches this last stage, as it has in Iowa, it is no longer 'malice' which is required but the 'something else' from which malice is said to be presumed. (Citations) 'It is enough (for legal malice) if it be the result of any improper or sinister motive and in disregard of the rights of others.' [*Jenkins v. Gilligan*, 131 Iowa 176] 108 N.W. at page 238 [9 L.R.A., N.S., 1087]. The rule would seem to be: exemplary damages may be awarded where defendant acts maliciously, [257 Iowa 629] but malice may be inferred where defendant's act is illegal or improper; where the nature of the illegal act is such as to negative any inference of feeling toward the person injured, and is in fact consistent with a complete indifference on the part of defendant, liability for exemplary damages is not based upon the maliciousness of the defendant but is based, rather, upon the separate substantive principle that illegal or improper acts ought to be deterred by the exaction from the defendant of sums over and above the actual damage he has caused." loc. cit. 136 and 137.

The jury award of $40,000 was large. However, the evidence of greed and avariciousness on the part of defendants is shocking to our sense of justice as it obviously was to the jury.

The allowance of exemplary damages is wholly within the discretion of the jury where there is a legal basis for the allowance of such damages. We may interfere only where passion and prejudice appear and then only by reversal.

It is not within our power to order a remittitur. *Waltham Piano Company v. Freeman*, 159 Iowa 567, 571, 141 N.W. 403; *Crum v. Walker*, 241 Iowa 1173, 1181, 44 N.W.2d 701; *Sergeant v. Watson Bros. Transportation Company*, 244 Iowa 185, 200, 52 N.W.2d 86.

We think the question of exemplary damages was properly submitted to the jury; that there was evidence to support a verdict; that there is no indication of such passion and prejudice as to require a reversal and that the case should be and hereby is

Affirmed.

GARFIELD, C.J., and HAYS, LARSON, PETERSON, THORNTON, and MOORE, JJ., concur.

THOMPSON and STUART, JJ., concur in result.

Chapter 9

Rules of Construction

Chapter Objectives

The student will be able to:

- Use vocabulary regarding the rules of construction properly.
- Discuss the "four corners" doctrine regarding the interpretation of the contract.
- Determine if the interpretation of the contract requires the application of business custom and usage of the trade.
- Differentiate among the three types of customary or trade usage actions that affect the construction of the contract.
- Explain the parol evidence rule and identify the types of evidence permitted or excluded by the parol evidence rule.
- Differentiate between a partial and complete integration.
- Evaluate whether a court would permit parol evidence in a variety of circumstances.

This chapter will examine HOW courts interpret an agreement once its validity has been challenged. Knowing these rules will allow the paralegal to understand WHY contracts are drafted in a certain way. In order to avoid pitfalls after a problem has arisen, it is important to understand how contracts are read and understood by not only the parties, but the court. Courts follow certain general rules when reviewing a contract; these are arranged hierarchically. The four corners doctrine examines the writing as a whole, then any modifications to the contract itself, then any oral explanations of the terms (parol evidence). The hierarchy is based on the idea that the most certain evidence of the agreement is considered first and the least reliable last.

certainty
The ability to rely on objective assurances to make a determination without doubt.

freedom of contract
The doctrine that permits parties to make agreements on whatever terms they wish with few exceptions.

With all the subtlety of a stampede of wild buffalo, I shall reassert the guiding principle of contract law—**certainty**. Contracts are interpreted, generally speaking, according to the same rules in order to avoid inconsistent application of the law. It is a great benefit to drafters to understand these rules of construction so they can avoid unintended results of contract enforcement.

A second doctrine, **freedom of contract**, is also part of these rules of construction in that the courts seek to enforce the contract according to the intent of the parties. The courts do not attempt to revise the contract to reflect what it thinks the best interpretation or deal could be. Rather, the court seeks to give the parties exactly what they wanted, good or bad, as long as it is not illegal. Parties are free to contract for whatever they wish, and those wishes should be crystallized by interpreting the contract consistent with their intent. A court cannot use these rules of construction as a way to hide its correction of the contract.

FOUR CORNERS DOCTRINE

four corners doctrine
A principle of contract law that directs the court to interpret a contract by the terms contained within the pages of the document.

The most certain measure of the parties' intention is the written language of the contract. When the intention of the parties is clear from the words within the "four corners of the document," there is no judicial interpretation needed—the contract speaks for itself. The court assumes that the words written within the four corners of the pages of the contract document are those that the parties chose and chose for a reason at the time of contract—the **four corners doctrine**. The court, with few exceptions, will enforce the contract by its own terms. This reflects the courts' intention of enforcing a contract as the parties intended when they created it, not after some time and difficulties have come to pass. There are problems associated with this kind of enforcement. It assumes that the contracting parties used precise language and that both parties subjectively understood the language in the same way.

> We are not unmindful of the danger of focusing only upon the words of the writing in interpreting an agreement. A court must be careful not to "retire into that lawyer's Paradise where all words have a fixed, precisely ascertained meaning; where men may express their purposes, not only with accuracy, but with fullness; and were [sic], if the writer has been careful, a lawyer, having a document referred to him, may sit in his chair inspect the text and answer all questions without raising his eyes."
>
> *In re Estate of Breyer*, 379 A.2d 1305, 1309 (Pa. 1977), *citing* 3 Corbin on Contracts § 535 n.16 (1960), *quoting* Thayer, Preliminary Treatise on Evidence 428 (1896).

However, courts have generally determined that the parties to the contract are in the best position to avoid ambiguities and use appropriate terminology, so the burden lies with them and not the court in choosing the language to memorialize the contract.

Those terms are given their **plain**, ordinary dictionary **meaning**. Courts enforce terms as they are understood objectively by the majority of parties in similar circumstances. This is consistent with the objective third-party determinative test used by the court in most interpretative situations. If the parties intended to mean something specific or special by those terms, they should specify this in the contract; otherwise, that meaning might be lost in enforcement.

plain meaning rule
Courts will use the traditional definition of terms used in a contract if those terms are not otherwise defined in the agreement.

Example

Example loosely based on *Levine v. Massey III*, 232 Conn. 272 (Conn. 1995). Testers, Inc., a lab that analyzes blood samples for local doctors, and Dr. Watson worked together to develop a new device for centrifugal blood separation in test tubes. This machine was patented in the names of Testers and Dr. Watson. Testers agreed to pay Dr. Watson one-third of the royalties received from licensing of the new machine. Testers then redeveloped a new machine that was a vast improvement on the previous machine invented with Dr. Watson and a separate patent was issued to Testers. Dr. Watson claimed that the royalty agreement covers this new machine as well. The court found that the agreement could only cover the first machine because the very language of the agreement referred to the "said invention" which was "jointly invented." The agreement only referred to one, single invention, not to all inventions emanating from the original. The court "[would] not torture words to impart ambiguity where ordinary meaning leaves no room for ambiguity." *Id*. at 279. The plain meaning of the contract rules.

SPOT THE ISSUE!

Mr. and Mrs. Hatfield own 10 acres of farmland and currently rent it to the McCoys for their use in raising long-eared Nubian goats, whose milk is high in butterfat and therefore produces very tasty cheese. The parties have entered into a "right of first refusal" agreement:

> "During the lifetime of the Hatfields, should they receive a bona fide offer for the purchase of the 10 acres currently rented by the McCoys, the McCoys may exercise their right to purchase the farmland at a cost of twice the value of the premises according to the tax assessor records at that time."

The Hatfields and McCoys intended to refer to the tax assessment as an objective third-party standard that they both understood to be customarily valued at 50 percent of the actual or market value of the land. What, if any, problems can you foresee in the enforcement of this agreement as written?

Compare the majority and dissenting opinions in *Steuart v. McChesney*, 444 A.2d 659 (Pa. 1982) (note, this case has been cited over 300 times in the relevant jurisdiction at the time of this writing.)

Additionally, the writing will be read as a whole. While lawyers may have the reputation for dissecting every last word and playing upon semantics, the rule in contracts is to look at the "big picture." Every word in the contract is given its ordinary meaning and counts toward the interpretation of the contract. In the above example, the contract was entered into for the purpose of distributing the fair share of profits from the work put into inventing the machine—not to compensate Dr. Watson in perpetuity for all other machines that are based on the original invention. One machine = one compensation. Again, the intent at the time of contract is evidenced by the terms used in the writing and given their plain meanings. Indeed, "[a]bsent the plain meaning rule, nary an agreement could be conceived, which, in the event of a party's later disappointment with his stated bargain, would not be at risk to having its true meaning obfuscated under the guise of examining extrinsic evidence of intent." *Steuart*, 441 A.2d at 663.

Of course, trying to give each provision equal weight may prove to be difficult where they are in conflict with each other. For the most part, the court will try to harmonize the terms of the entire contract. If that is not possible, there is a hierarchy of enforcement to which the court can look. Many times, contracts consist of preprinted forms. If any language is added to the form, those terms prevail. It follows that the additions truly reflect the intention of the parties as they were added after the wording of the form was found to be inadequate. On the same note, if language is added that is more specific than previous terms, the more specific terms are preferred over the more generic. Also, it is not uncommon to add handwritten notes or changes to the document right before signing to reflect last-minute negotiations or corrections. These **"last-in-time"** terms are **"first in right"**: They will be enforced over any other inconsistent clauses in the contract.

"last in time = first in right"
A principle in law that favors the most current activity or change with respect to the transaction as it is most likely the most reflective of the intent of the parties.

Example
Charles and Camilla enter into a real estate sales contract for a lovely Charleston, North Carolina, estate. The sales contract is the preprinted standard from Findit Realty. On the sales contract, there are blank lines under "fixtures included" whereon Beatrice the broker has typed in "dining room chandelier, living room tapestry drapes and washer and dryer." At closing, a computational error is found and corrected by hand; this correction prevails over the previous amount. Additionally, the washer and dryer have been taken by the previous owners. Those items have been crossed out by hand and initialed by Charles, Camilla, and the seller with a note that says: "compensation paid outside of closing by check to buyers." The controlling language is that which came last and is in handwriting. The contract is read to exclude the washer and dryer.

against the drafter
Imprecise terms and/or ambiguous wording is held against the party who wrote the document as he was the party most able to avoid the problem.

When all of the above rules do not result in a consistent interpretation of the contract, the fallback position is to construe the ambiguous terms as **against the drafter** of the document. The person who wrote the document was in the best position to avoid the confusion. This also encourages drafting parties to strive for clarity since they will not be able to take advantage of purposeful ambiguities and gain an upper hand in enforcement.

For example, as a general rule, where there is an uncertainty in an insurance coverage contract and one interpretation grants coverage and another limits or denies coverage, the court will favor the interpretation that covers the insured party. The insurance company is in control of the drafting of these complex documents and it is in the best position to avoid any questions as to interpretation. However, because insurance contracts are contracts of adhesion, when an ambiguity exists courts should interpret the contract in favor of the insured and against the insurer. Courts should examine whether more precise policy language, if chosen by the insurance company, would have "put the matter beyond reasonable question. Exclusions in insurance policies must be construed narrowly; the burden is on the insurer to bring the case within the exclusion." *Homesite Ins. Co. v. Hindman*, 992 A.2d 804, 806-807 (N.J. Super. 2010) (internal citations omitted).

Example

Harry owns a historic home in the center of town and has an insurance policy that contains a "repair or rebuild" provision. The insurance company will undertake to pay for the less expensive option of the two. Unfortunately, Harry's home is destroyed by fire, and he makes a claim. The insurance company states that it will rebuild the home using contemporary building methods, but Harry protests, stating that he wants his house built in the original manner using hand-hewn timbers and a thatched roofing system. This will be incredibly expensive. The insurance company takes the position that the "repair or rebuild" provision doesn't cover these old-fashioned methods of construction. The court may find that this language is ambiguous and will construe the term as against the drafter—the insurance company. If the insurance company intended to exclude historically accurate reconstruction, it was in the best position to so state in its own contract. Harry's home should be rebuilt to maintain its historic character.

SPOT THE ISSUE!

Wilma and Fred have been married for 25 years and have raised three lovely children, all of whom are out on their own. Now that they are alone again, they find they are no longer compatible. They agree to divorce and write the following property settlement agreement:

Fred shall pay as maintenance to Wilma the sum of $2,500.00 per month for a period of five years. Thereafter, he shall pay to Wilma the sum of $2,000.00 per month for an additional period of five years. These payments shall terminate absolutely on the death, marriage, or cohabitation of Wilma, but shall be a liability of Fred's estate in the event of his death.

When Fred reaches age 65 (10 years from the date of this Agreement), the amount of maintenance payable to Wilma, if any, shall be re-determined in light of the investment and other income of each party.

Prior to signing the agreement, the parties crossed out the word "cohabitation" and initialed this change, thus eliminating cohabitation as an event that would immediately terminate the maintenance payments.

Wilma decided to start living with her neighbor, Barney, three years after the date of the agreement. Fred brought an action to have his maintenance payments cease under the agreement.

As the judge in this matter, how would you rule and why? What evidence would you admit with regard to the change?

BUSINESS CUSTOM AND TRADE USAGE

The cliché "actions speak louder than words" has applicability in contract interpretation. Where parties may express one intention in words and another in the way they act in carrying out their required performance under the contract (or in previous transactions), their actions will influence a court's interpretation of the contract more than the actual words (or lack thereof). This rule applies to dealings between **merchants**—persons or businesses who "hold [themselves] out as having expertise peculiar to the goods in which [they] deal and [are] therefore held by the law to a higher standard of expertise than that of a non-merchant." BLACK'S LAW DICTIONARY (8th ed. 2004). The particularities that apply to merchants under the Uniform Commercial Code will be discussed at length in Chapter 15.

There are three distinct actions that will bind parties to a commercial contract: **course of performance**, **course of dealing**, and **usage of the trade**. They are listed in the order of preference as well. Courts like to look to how the parties have acted on the contract in question prior to the dispute. The actions taken under the contract reflect the understanding of the parties most accurately. Commercial agreements are composed not only of the language used by the parties but also of implied terms from the surrounding circumstances of the transaction that include the courses of performance, dealing, and usage of the trade.

For example, Owen owns a fabric shop and Sally has agreed to purchase 20 bolts of silk fabric to be shipped in four batches. The contract calls for payment by cashier's check. For the first three shipments, Fred has accepted payment by personal check; however, on this last shipment, he insists on cash. This is contrary to his prior course of performance on this contract.

Second on the totem pole is course of dealing. These are actions taken by the parties in other similar transactions but not in the one in question. Similarly, Owen has accepted personal checks from Sally for every other order she has placed with him, but this time, for no apparent reason, he insists on payment up front in cash.

merchants
Businesspersons who have a certain level of expertise dealing in commercial transactions regarding the goods they sell.

course of performance
The parties' actions taken in reliance on the particular transaction in question.

course of dealing
The parties' actions taken in similar previous transactions.

usage of the trade
Actions generally taken by similarly situated parties in similar transactions in the same business field.

If there has not been any performance on either the contract in question or similar transactions, the courts will finally look to the standards in the industry, the usage of the trade. Evidence of what other business do in similar transactions will be used to determine what the parties in the current situation intended as the term in question. The fabric wholesale industry works on 30-day invoicing with payment acceptable by personal or business check. Without language in the contract to the contrary, Sally can expect that Owen will accept the same term. Therefore, if either or both parties intend to deviate from the industry customs, it should be so specified in the contract.

SPOT THE ISSUE!

Ernie grows watermelons on Sesame Farm. Bert is a produce wholesaler. Ernie and Bert have been doing business for a long time, and this summer was no exception. Ernie called Bert to inquire as to what Bert was paying for watermelons. At the beginning of the season, Bert stated he would be paying three cents per pound to his farmers. Due to market price fluctuations, at the end of July, Bert began paying two and one-half cents per pound. Throughout the course of the watermelon season, Bert paid Ernie partial payments with the intent that, at the end of the season, Bert would settle the account according to the delivery records.

On September 1st, Bert and Ernie attempted to settle, but they could not agree whether the calculation of the amount owed was based on loaded weight at Sesame Farm or the delivered weight to the purchasers of the watermelons. Additionally, Ernie claims he was not advised that the price had dropped from three cents per pound in July and that he did not agree to the lesser price.

See *Zolman v. SEMO Produce, Inc.*, 875 S.W.2d 605 (Mo. App. S.D. 1994).

SURF'S UP

- For a thorough discussion on the Internet as "fraud's playground" and the need for "trusted sites," see A. Michael Froomkin, *The Essential Role of Trusted Third Parties in Electronic Commerce*, 75 Or. L. Rev. 49 (1996). Of course, while there have been significant developments since that time, the overall discussion in the article lays the foundation for understanding the complex issues at hand today.
- Additionally, you should think about business custom and usage in the trade issues in e-commerce: Are there any? How long will it take for them to become established? Due to the tremendous diversity of the Internet, will they ever be established?

CRYPTO CONTRACTS

01100
10110
11110

"At the end of the day, 'smart contracts' are neither smart nor contracts. They can't adapt to ambiguity and are only as good as the person coding them. . . . They carry data without knowing what that data is." The author's argument that a smart contract isn't a contract is semantic at best. Glidden argues that since a contract is an agreement, it can only live in peoples' minds, not on a hard drive. That would then suggest that any tangible evidence of an agreement is not a contract, which, of course, is the exact opposite of the definition of a traditional contract. The important idea to take away is his point that smart contracts cannot adapt to ambiguity; there is no mechanism to interpret how they will be enforced, because the enforcement of performance is completely automated. The contract will simply die in cyberspace on the blockchain, unless the matter is brought by litigation in the courts, and then, it gets treated like any other contract—its purported "smartness" rendered irrelevant. Andrew Glidden, *Should Smart Contracts Be Legally Enforceable?*, Blockchain at Berkeley Blog (Feb. 28, 2018).

PAROL EVIDENCE

parol evidence
Oral testimony offered as proof regarding the terms of a written contact.

While the courts primarily look within the four corners of the contract, finding that whatever is contained in writing constitutes the agreement between parties, there are instances where the contract cannot speak for itself due to inconsistencies, illogical interpretations, or omissions. Where the contract's voice is uncertain, another voice must tell the court what the language of the contract means. This "outside voice" is **parol evidence**. *Parol* comes from the root "parl," which means to speak. For example, the verb "to speak" in French is *parler* and in Italian is *parlate*, and a *parlor* is a room in a home where people can gather for social conversation.

explanatory
Oral testimony is permitted to clarify the terms of the contract.

Where can the court look for guidance? What can "speak" to the court as to the parties' true meaning? Often, the parties' intent may lie in their negotiation process. What did they contemplate the result of the agreement to be? When this information is imperfectly memorialized, **explanatory** evidence may be admitted to clear up the confusion. However, the courts do not let every bit of information in as a free-for-all. Otherwise, what would the point be of reducing the agreement down to a writing?

parol evidence rule
A court evidentiary doctrine that excludes certain types of outside oral testimony offered as proof of the terms of the contract.

In response to this potential for chaos, contract law has developed the **parol evidence rule**, which excludes certain kinds of extrinsic material from the determination of contractual meaning. The rule attempts to curb the parties' efforts to change the terms of the contract once it has come under scrutiny. Therefore, all **contradictory** evidence is disallowed.

contradictory
Evidence that is in conflict with the terms of the contract and inadmissible under the parol evidence rule.

The courts condition the acceptance of parol evidence on the nature of the written contract. A contract should be the final embodiment of the agreement between the parties; the courts call this an integration. All negotiations have been made part of this final writing. Further, an integration may be *partial* or *complete*. A **partial integration** contains the final agreement as to the terms that have been agreed upon by the parties but still leaves the entire contract incomplete as there are other terms to which the parties have not come to a final agreement. For example, most new home construction contracts can only be considered a partial integration as both parties, the contractor and the homeowners, know that additional decisions may need to be made, such as what tile to put in the kitchen or the final color of paint for the living room walls. The contract to construct the house is a satisfactory writing and a valid contract, but only a partial integration. By contrast, a **complete integration** contains the final and total agreement as to all terms necessary to perform on the contract.

In either case, as stated before, no evidence of prior or contemporaneous agreements can be heard that would contradict the terms of either type of integration. However, there is a difference with regard to the admissibility of **supplemental** agreements. Logically, if these additional terms are not normally included in the original contract, they must be evidenced by a supplemental agreement. A boilerplate sales contract often does not contain particular delivery options; these can be worked out as the situation warrants. Therefore, parol evidence of the delivery agreement can be admitted. *See, e.g., Gustav Thieszen Irrigation Co., Inc. v. Meinberg*, 276 N.W.2d 664 (Neb. 1979). The caveat here is to beware of the court's discretion in determining whether the original agreement is a partial or complete integration as that has an effect on these admissibility issues.

So far we have three general rules of admissibility of parol evidence:

1. Contradictory evidence is *never* permitted.
2. Explanatory evidence is *always* permitted.
3. Supplemental evidence is *sometimes* permitted depending on the nature of the integration (either partial, for which it is admissible, or complete, for which it is inadmissible).

There are different views as to when parol evidence can be admitted in circumstances other than those listed above, but as these are determined on a case-by-case basis and revolve around abstract academic theory rather than practical application, they will not be discussed here.

partial integration
A document that contains the essential terms of the contract but not all the terms that the parties may have or need to agree upon.

complete integration
A document that contains all the terms of the agreement and the parties have agreed that there are no other terms outside the contract.

supplemental
Evidence that adds to, but does not contradict, the original agreement is admissible under the parol evidence rule.

supplemental agreements
Those writings of the parties that naturally add to, but do not conflict with, the original terms of the partially integrated contract.

EYE ON ETHICS

ETHICS

The crux of the conflict-of-interest rules with regard to business transactions with clients reflects the concern for clarity and full disclosure. It is not hard to imagine a lengthy document replete with legal terms and complex structure. To avoid having the attorney take advantage of the client's position, most ethics rules prohibit attorneys from entering into business transactions with clients. There are three conditions that, if met, will remove this general prohibition:

1. The transaction must be in writing and the terms must be fair and reasonable. Further, those terms must be clearly understood by the client.
2. The client must be advised *in writing* to seek the advice of counsel who is completely independent of the transaction and unrelated to the attorney entering into the transaction.
3. The client consents *in writing* to the terms and conditions of the transaction in question, including the attorney's role as business partner, counselor, or otherwise.

Do you think that the court would be more willing to admit parol evidence in a case involving the above rule? Why or why not?

However, there are three more generally accepted reasons when such evidence would be admitted. Again, the rules above apply so that the terms of the contract will not be changed, but the parol evidence will be permitted to explain outside circumstances that affect either the formation or performance of the contract.

defects in formation
Errors or omissions made during the negotiations that function as a bar to creating a valid contract.

The first has to do with the **defects in formation** we discussed in Chapter 8. Where the party seeking to have the evidence admitted needs to prove that there was an absence of the meeting of the minds (mistake, fraud, duress, undue influence, etc.), the evidence is admissible. The state of mind is at issue. Just looking at the contract cannot reveal the mental intent of the parties. Indeed, in these circumstances, that kind of information would be intentionally concealed. Parol evidence is admissible to show the existence or lack of the necessary subjective intent to enter into the contract. For example, if Tony Soprano holds a gun to your head to sign over the deed to your house, the evidence that he indeed held a gun to your head would be admissible. This evidence is not considered an impermissible *contradiction in terms*, but rather a *contradiction in intent* and, therefore, parol evidence is admissible. The court is not determining what the terms of the contract are, but whether there was a contract formed at all.

> It is practically the universal rule that in suits to reform written instruments on the ground of fraud or mutual mistake, parol evidence is admissible to establish the fact of fraud or of a mistake and in what it consisted, and to show how the writing should be corrected in order to conform to the agreement or intention which the parties actually made or had. [. . .] Moreover, a general merger clause in a written contract, to the effect that it expresses the entire agreement and that no asserted extrinsic representations are binding, will not, of itself, bar parol evidence for the purpose of reforming the instrument on the ground of mistake.
>
> *Cain v. Saunders*, 813 So. 2d 891, 895 (Ala. Civ. App. 2001) (*cert. denied*), *citing* 66 Am. Jur. 2d Reformation of Instruments § 118 (1973) (citations omitted).

The parol evidence rule is designed to prevent parties from committing fraud upon the court by altering the terms of an agreement by false oral testimony. If the parol evidence rule were to apply to defects in formation, such as fraud, and keep out testimony relating to the making of the contract, the parol evidence rule would actually assist in perpetuating that which it was designed to prevent—fraud.

The second relates to the **consideration** of the contract. During the course of performance on the contract, consideration, the subject matter of the agreement, may fail. It may turn out that either party (or both) did not receive what they bargained for. This matter cannot be addressed by contractual terms either. The contract recites what the consideration should be but cannot speak to future events, such as the failure of consideration. For example, Farmer Fred and Greg Grocer contract for 100 bushels of Grade A granny smith apples at $10.00 per bushel to be delivered within one week after the fall harvest. This appears to be an integrated contract and evidence contrary to these terms will not be admissible. However, if Fred did not deliver the apples or delivered substandard apples, or if Greg did not pay the contractually stated price, any of this information would be permissible parol evidence as it relates to the performance of the parties under the contract. It does not contradict the terms of the contract; the evidence would show how the terms were not met.

Third, as we have discussed, explanatory evidence is permissible where the terms may be ambiguous. However, the parol evidence rule also permits explanatory evidence where it may appear to the court that there is no ambiguity, but one or both of the parties have a different understanding of the term. Parol evidence can be used to explain **technical terms, specifications, or trade/business customs**. These may be specific to the industry and therefore unknown to the court. Where the court may attach a certain meaning to the contract term using its everyday meaning, the parties may have mutually intended another meaning particular to their specialty. As courts want to enforce contracts as they were intended, parol evidence of these specialized or technical terms may be admitted.

An interesting intersection of parol evidence and the Statute of Frauds was discussed in *In re Marriage of Shaban*, 88 Cal. App. 4th 398, 105 Cal. Rptr. 2d 863 (2001). The couple were married in Egypt and, following their Islamic tradition, executed a marriage contract "in Accordance with his Almighty God's Holy Book and the Rules of his Prophet to whom all God's prayers and blessings be, by legal offer and acceptance from the two contracting parties." *Id*. at 403. The husband attempted to prove that this single-page document covered property distribution at the time of any divorce. If this was an agreement in contemplation of marriage, it would have to be in compliance with the Statute of Frauds. The court found that the terms were too vague and distant from the "transaction" to satisfy the Statute of Frauds. To show that this was the parties' intent and verify the terms of the contract to satisfy the Statute of Frauds, the husband offered expert parol evidence regarding the traditions of the Islamic religion. The court did not allow the entire content of the purported premarital agreement to be supplied by parol evidence. Quite evident is the fact that the whole reason for the Statute of Frauds would be "frustrated if any substantive

consideration
The basis of the bargained for exchange between the parties to a contract that is of legal value.

technical terms, specifications, or trade/business custom
Parol evidence is permitted to explain the meaning of special language in the contract as the parties understood it if the plain ordinary meaning of the language was not intended or was ambiguous.

portion of the agreement could be established by parol evidence" *Id.* at 405. Further:

> This appeal presents a situation that not only reaches the outer limits of the ability of a prospective married couple to incorporate by reference terms into a prenuptial agreement, but so far exceeds those limits as to fall off the edge. It is one thing for a couple to agree to basic terms, and choose the system of law that they want to govern the construction or interpretation of their premarital agreement. It is quite another to say, without any agreement as to basic terms, that a marriage will simply be governed by a given system of law and then hope that parol evidence will supply those basic terms.

> *Id.* at 400.

CRYPTO CONTRACTS

Contract law will undergo a shift in its thinking with the advent of "smart contracts"— these agreements that live as code on the blockchain. These are just a few questions that will need to be answered. (No one expects the reader of this text to have answers, but they are food for thought.)

As this new technology and its usage grows, how will the long-standing principles of contract law adapt? What will be the rules of interpretation once the coded language is "translated" for the court's use into an actual readable transcript? Is that translation actually parol evidence since it is not the embodiment of the "writing"? If smart contracts are used for the very reason that they are immutable, should there be any interpretation of their terms at all? How do collateral agreements affect a smart contract?

See Mark Hines, *Lex Disturbia: The Impact of Smart Contracts on the Law*, Gowling WLG Blog (March 16, 2016).

RESEARCH THIS

In your jurisdiction, find two cases regarding parol evidence: one that allowed extrinsic evidence to be admitted due to an ambiguity regarding a certain term and another that held that extrinsic evidence was not permissible to explain a contractual term. What were the factual differences that resulted in these contradictory outcomes?

merger clause
Language of a contract that indicates that the parties intend to exclude all outside evidence relating to the terms of the contract because it has been agreed that all relevant terms have been incorporated in the document.

To avoid the issues relating to parol evidence, the parties may choose to include an integration or *merger clause* that says that the parties agree that the written document is *all* there is and it incorporates every part of the parties' agreement. Everything that they have negotiated for has been *merged* into the contract. The parties by their own terms have excluded parol evidence.

What about conditions precedent that would not naturally become a part of the contract? An agreement may only become binding upon the happening of an event; once that event or condition has occurred, then the contractual obligations become due. Even if the parties, then, intended that the contract was an integrated agreement complete with a merger clause, the agreement is only partially integrated with respect to that oral condition precedent. In other words, the contract is only partially integrated until the condition precedent is met. After the condition has been satisfied, the contract becomes totally integrated and the merger clause has meaning. *See Cosgrove v. Mademoiselle Fashions*, 292 N.W.2d 780, 785 (Neb. 1980), *citing* RESTATEMENT (SECOND) OF CONTRACTS § 243, cmt. b (Tent. Draft No. 6, 1971).

Having said all of this, please note that the parol evidence rule applies only to **prior or contemporaneous agreements** between the parties. The negotiation process and refinement to a final, complete integration is what the parol evidence rule holds dear. Subsequent agreements are completely outside of the scope of the rule. Evidence of **subsequent agreements** that modify, contradict, or supplement the original contract is admissible without regard to this rule. They will undergo the same level of scrutiny as the original contract; all the contractual requirements discussed up until this chapter will need to be met.

prior or contemporaneous agreements
These negotiations and resulting potential terms are governed by the principles of the parol evidence rule.

subsequent agreements
Negotiations and potential terms that are discussed after the agreement has been memorialized are not covered by the parol evidence rule.

IN-CLASS DISCUSSION

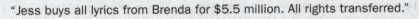

Jessica Sampson agreed to purchase song lyrics from Brenda Spars. The agreement was hastily written down on a cocktail napkin:

"Jess buys all lyrics from Brenda for $5.5 million. All rights transferred."

This may be informal, but it can be a binding legal agreement. Using the rules of construction and parol evidence, make an argument on behalf of Jessica that it is binding and enforceable and an alternate argument on behalf of Brenda that it is not enforceable as against her.

Which woman would probably prevail in court? Why?

All of the above rules of construction and parol evidence are generally accepted; however, the paralegal student must be aware that every court maintains its own prerogative to interpret each set of facts differently. These appear to be bright-line rules, but their application is not always clear. Additionally, principles of equity may come into play to sway the court's decision. Principles of equity are discussed in Chapter 14. A court's sense of fairness may influence how that decision is made, even when it appears that the court is relying on rules of construction in interpreting the contract. These rules of construction may actually be better named "general guidelines" as individual factual analysis is still vital. Where some courts may find an ambiguity and therefore apply the rules of construction, another may not find that an ambiguity exists at all and judicial intervention is not necessary at all.

Summary

Contract law's love for definiteness and desire to enforce agreements according to their makers' intent requires the parties and the court to play by certain rules of construction. When a contractual dispute arises, the court can look to these rules for guidance to assure that their determinations are consistent and that parties have a measure of certainty with regard to the outcome of the cases.

First, courts look within the *four corners* of the document itself for the meaning of the controverted term(s). There is no judicial intervention needed; the contract speaks for itself. There are rules with regard to how to read the language in the agreement. The contract should be read as a consistent whole; provisions that contradict each other will be prioritized as "*last in time, first in right*," and any irresolvable issues will be construed as *against the drafter* of the document.

Second, *merchants* may rely on business customs and trade usage as an aid to interpretation. What the parties do during the *course of performance* on the contract, or have done in their past *course of dealing*, or what is the industry's usual *usage of the trade* serves as the backdrop for the construction of the agreement.

Lastly, the rather difficult-to-apply *parol evidence rule* excludes certain outside material from bearing on the interpretation of the contract. In short, the rule

1. Excludes all *contradictory* evidence.
2. Permits all *explanatory* evidence where there is an ambiguity as to the terms in the contract.
3. Sometimes permits *supplemental* evidence depending on the nature of integration. Supplemental evidence is permitted where there is a *partial integration* and excluded where there is a *complete integration*.
4. Permits evidence of the *formative defect*—the failure of the meeting of the minds.
5. Permits evidence of failure of *consideration*.
6. Permits explanatory evidence relating to an unambiguous yet particular *technical term, specification, or trade/business custom*.

The list is much more inclusive of evidence than exclusive, which is why its application and necessity have been called into question by legal experts.

Recall also that the parol evidence rule applies solely to evidence dating either *prior to or concurrent* with the contract in question. It has no bearing on the admissibility of *subsequent agreements*.

Key Terms

against the drafter
certainty
complete integration
consideration
contradictory
course of dealing
course of performance
defects in formation
explanatory
four corners doctrine
freedom of contract
last in time = first in right

merchants
merger clause
parol evidence
parol evidence rule
partial integration
plain meaning rule
prior or contemporaneous agreements
subsequent agreements
supplemental
technical terms, specifications, or
   trade/business custom
usage of the trade

Review Questions

MULTIPLE CHOICE

Choose the best answer(s) and please explain *why* you choose the answer(s).

1. The parol evidence rule
    a. Eliminates the need for a writing to prove the terms of a contract.
    b. Admits oral testimony to prove the terms of a contract.
    c. Admits oral testimony in certain circumstances to clarify the agreement of the parties.
    d. All of the above.

2. The four corners doctrine
    a. Requires a writing in order to enforce a contract.
    b. Interprets a contract according to the ordinary meaning of the language used in the contract.
    c. Disallows handwritten changes to the contract.
    d. Is the same as the Statute of Frauds.

3. Merger clauses
    a. Must be written in every commercial contract.
    b. Can never be supplemented by outside oral testimony.
    c. Are invalid as against public policy.
    d. Indicate that the parties have included all the agreed-upon terms in the contract.

EXPLAIN YOURSELF

All answers should be written in complete sentences. A simple "yes" or "no" is insufficient. Use the following fact scenario to answer the subsequent questions.

On May 1st, Greg Grocer and Fred Farmer contract for the sale of apples; the delivery date is omitted from the writing. On May 15th, Fred agrees to have them shipped via a special carrier on July 1st.

1. Greg seeks to have this delivery date enforced. Can the evidence of the May 15th agreement be admitted?

2. Identify the kind of integration in the example above.

3. Assume that the May 15th agreement never existed and the means of delivery and date are never set forth. Is there a contract? On what terms?

4. Assume that the agreement as to means of delivery and date are made at the same time (May 1st) as the contract, but they are omitted from the writing. What is the result?

5. During the next set of negotiations, Greg adds the following language to the contract: "Contract is limited to the terms set forth herein." Assume the same scenario as above. What is the result?

6. There is a dispute as to the meaning of the term *delivery*.

7. During negotiations, Greg told Fred that if he didn't make this contract, he'd be sure that something awful would happen to his orchard. Can this evidence be admitted?

"FAULTY PHRASES"

All of the following statements are FALSE; state why they are false and then rewrite them as true statements. Write a brief fact pattern that illustrates your answer.

1. The "four corners" doctrine excludes interpretations of terms of the contract that are not part of the contract itself.

2. Courts will try to find the best provisions in the contract and enforce them over the other provisions.

3. Courts will not enforce handwritten provisions to a contract.

4. If there are inconsistent provisions in a contract, the court will construe them as against the person who brought the lawsuit.

5. Parties to a commercial contract must incorporate traditional business "usage of trade" practices in their written agreement.

"WRITE" AWAY! PORTFOLIO ASSIGNMENT

Review the Druid and Carrie contract. Are there any terms that need to be defined in order to accurately reflect the understanding between the parties? Clarify any "business customs" of Druid's that may appear in the terms of the contract (i.e., "delivery time," "standards of workmanship," etc.). Are there any changes that need to be made? Will they be in the form of a supplement or handwritten changes on the document? Do you believe a merger clause is appropriate? Should you make reference to other documents? If your answers are yes, draft the necessary documentation.

Case in Point — TRADE CUSTOM AND USAGE

■ Even the most common words can and will be misunderstood!

190 F. Supp. 116
FRIGALIMENT IMPORTING CO., LTD., Plaintiff,
v.
B.N.S. INTERNATIONAL SALES CORP., Defendant.
United States District Court S. D. New York.
December 27, 1960.

[190 F. Supp. 117]

Riggs, Ferris & Geer, New York City (John P. Hale, New York City, of counsel), for plaintiff.
Sereni, Herzfeld & Rubin, New York City (Herbert Rubin, Walter Herzfeld, New York City, of counsel), for defendant.
FRIENDLY, Circuit Judge.

The issue is, what is chicken? Plaintiff says "chicken" means a young chicken, suitable for broiling and frying. Defendant says "chicken" means any bird of that genus that meets contract specifications on weight and quality, including what it calls "stewing chicken" and plaintiff pejoratively terms "fowl." Dictionaries give both meanings, as well as some others not relevant here. To support its, plaintiff sends a number of volleys over the net; defendant essays to return them and adds a few serves of its own. Assuming that both parties were acting in good faith, the case nicely illustrates Holmes' remark "that the making of a contract depends not on the agreement of two minds in one intention, but on the agreement of two sets of external signs—not on the parties' having *meant* the same thing but on their having *said* the same thing." The Path of the Law, in Collected Legal Papers, p. 178. I have concluded that plaintiff has not sustained its burden of persuasion that the contract used "chicken" in the narrower sense.

The action is for breach of the warranty that goods sold shall correspond to the description, New York Personal Property Law, McKinney's Consol. Laws, c. 41, § 95. Two contracts are in suit. In the first, dated May 2, 1957, defendant, a New York sales corporation, confirmed the sale to plaintiff, a Swiss corporation, of

> "US Fresh Frozen Chicken, Grade A, Government Inspected, Eviscerated
> 2½-3 lbs. and 1½-2 lbs. each
> all chicken individually wrapped in cryovac, packed in secured fiber cartons or wooden boxes, suitable for export
>
> 75,000 lbs. 2½-3 lbs.........@$33.00
> 25,000 lbs. 1½-2 lbs.........@$36.50
> per 100 lbs. FAS New York
> scheduled May 10, 1957 pursuant to instructions from Penson & Co., New York."[1]

The second contract, also dated May 2, 1957, was identical save that only 50,000 lbs. of the heavier "chicken" were called for, the price of the smaller birds was $37 per 100 lbs., and shipment was scheduled for May 30. The initial shipment under the first contract was short but the balance was shipped on May 17. When the initial shipment arrived in Switzerland, plaintiff found, on May 28, that the 2½-3 lbs. birds were not young chicken suitable for broiling and frying but stewing chicken or "fowl"; indeed, many of the cartons and bags plainly so indicated. Protests ensued. Nevertheless, shipment under the second contract was made on May 29, the 2½-3 lbs. birds again being stewing chicken. Defendant stopped the transportation of these at Rotterdam.

---

[1] The Court notes the contract provision whereby any disputes are to be settled by arbitration by the New York Produce Exchange; it treats the parties' failure to avail themselves of this remedy as an agreement eliminating that clause of the contract.

This action followed. Plaintiff says that, notwithstanding that its acceptance was in Switzerland, New York law controls

[190 F. Supp. 118]

under the principle of *Rubin v. Irving Trust Co.*, 1953, 305 N.Y. 288, 305, 113 N.E.2d 424, 431; defendant does not dispute this, and relies on New York decisions. I shall follow the apparent agreement of the parties as to the applicable law.

Since the word "chicken" standing alone is ambiguous, I turn first to see whether the contract itself offers any aid to its interpretation. Plaintiff says the 1½-2 lbs. birds necessarily had to be young chicken since the older birds do not come in that size, hence the 2½-3 lbs. birds must likewise be young. This is unpersuasive—a contract for "apples" of two different sizes could be filled with different kinds of apples even though only one species came in both sizes. Defendant notes that the contract called not simply for chicken but for "US Fresh Frozen Chicken, Grade A, Government Inspected." It says the contract thereby incorporated by reference the Department of Agriculture's regulations, which favor its interpretation; I shall return to this after reviewing plaintiff's other contentions.

The first hinges on an exchange of cablegrams which preceded execution of the formal contracts. The negotiations leading up to the contracts were conducted in New York between defendant's secretary, Ernest R. Bauer, and a Mr. Stovicek, who was in New York for the Czechoslovak government at the World Trade Fair. A few days after meeting Bauer at the fair, Stovicek telephoned and inquired whether defendant would be interested in exporting poultry to Switzerland. Bauer then met with Stovicek, who showed him a cable from plaintiff dated April 26, 1957, announcing that they "are buyer" of 25,000 lbs. of chicken 2½-3 lbs. weight, Cryovac packed, grade A Government inspected, at a price up to 33¢ per pound, for shipment on May 10, to be confirmed by the following morning, and were interested in further offerings. After testing the market for price, Bauer accepted, and Stovicek sent a confirmation that evening. Plaintiff stresses that, although these and subsequent cables between plaintiff and defendant, which laid the basis for the additional quantities under the first and for all of the second contract, were predominantly in German, they used the English word "chicken"; it claims this was done because it understood "chicken" meant young chicken whereas the German word, "Huhn," included both "Brathuhn" (broilers) and "Suppenhuhn" (stewing chicken), and that defendant, whose officers were thoroughly conversant with German, should have realized this. Whatever force this argument might otherwise have is largely drained away by Bauer's testimony that he asked Stovicek what kind of chickens were wanted, received the answer "any kind of chickens," and then, in German, asked whether the cable meant "Huhn" and received an affirmative response. Plaintiff attacks this as contrary to what Bauer testified on his deposition in March, 1959, and also on the ground that Stovicek had no authority to interpret the meaning of the cable. The first contention would be persuasive if sustained by the record, since Bauer was free at the trial from the threat of contradiction by Stovicek as he was not at the time of the deposition; however, review of the deposition does not convince me of the claimed inconsistency. As to the second contention, it may well be that Stovicek lacked authority to commit plaintiff for prices or delivery dates other than those specified in the cable; but plaintiff cannot at the same time rely on its cable to Stovicek as its dictionary to the meaning of the contract and repudiate the interpretation given the dictionary by the man in whose hands it was put. See Restatement of the Law of Agency, 2d, § 145; 2 Mecham, Agency § 1781 (2d ed. 1914); *Park v. Moorman Mfg. Co.*, 1952, 121 Utah 339, 241 P.2d 914, 919, 40 A.L.R.2d 273; *Henderson v. Jimmerson*, Tex. Civ. App. 1950, 234 S.W. 2d 710, 717-718. Plaintiff's reliance on the fact that the contract forms contain the words "through the intermediary of:", with the blank not filled, as negating agency, is wholly unpersuasive;

[190 F. Supp. 119]

the purpose of this clause was to permit filling in the name of an intermediary to whom a commission would be payable, not to blot out what had been the fact.

Plaintiff's next contention is that there was a definite trade usage that "chicken" meant "young chicken." Defendant showed that it was only beginning in the poultry trade in 1957, thereby bringing itself within the principle that "when one of the parties is not a member of the trade or other circle, his acceptance of the standard must be made to appear" by proving either that he had actual knowledge of the usage or that the usage is "so generally known in the community that his actual individual knowledge of it may be inferred." 9 Wigmore, Evidence (3d ed. 1940) § 2464. Here there was no proof of actual knowledge of the alleged usage; indeed, it is quite plain that defendant's belief was to the contrary. In order to meet the alternative requirement, the law of New York demands a showing that "the usage is of so long continuance, so well established, so notorious, so universal and so reasonable in itself, as that the presumption is violent that the parties contracted with reference to it, and made it a part of their agreement." *Walls v. Bailey*, 1872, 49 N.Y. 464, 472-473.

Plaintiff endeavored to establish such a usage by the testimony of three witnesses and certain other evidence. Strasser, resident buyer in New York for a large chain of Swiss cooperatives, testified that "on chicken I would definitely understand a broiler." However, the force of this testimony was considerably weakened by the fact that in his own transactions the witness, a careful businessman, protected himself by using "broiler" when that was what he wanted and "fowl" when he wished older birds. Indeed, there are some indications, dating back to a remark of Lord Mansfield, *Edie v. East India Co.*, 2 Burr. 1216, 1222 (1761), that no credit should be given "witnesses to usage, who could not adduce instances in verification." 7 Wigmore, Evidence (3d ed. 1940), § 1954; see *McDonald v. Acker, Merrall & Condit Co.*, 2d Dept.1920, 192 App. Div. 123, 126, 182 N.Y.S. 607. While Wigmore thinks this goes too far, a witness' consistent failure to rely on the alleged usage deprives his opinion testimony of much of its effect. Niesielowski, an officer of one of the companies that had furnished the stewing chicken to defendant, testified that "chicken" meant "the male species of the poultry industry. That could be a broiler, a fryer or a roaster," but not a stewing chicken; however, he also testified that upon receiving defendant's inquiry for "chickens," he asked whether the desire was for "fowl or frying chickens" and, in fact, supplied fowl, although taking the precaution of asking defendant, a day or two after plaintiff's acceptance of the contracts in suit, to change its confirmation of its order from "chickens," as defendant had originally prepared it, to "stewing chickens." Dates, an employee of Urner-Barry Company, which publishes a daily market report on the poultry trade, gave it as his view that the trade meaning of "chicken" was "broilers and fryers." In addition to this opinion testimony, plaintiff relied on the fact that the Urner-Barry service, the Journal of Commerce, and Weinberg Bros. & Co. of Chicago, a large supplier of poultry, published quotations in a manner which, in one way or another, distinguish between "chicken," comprising broilers, fryers and certain other categories, and "fowl," which, Bauer acknowledged, included stewing chickens. This material would be impressive if there were nothing to the contrary. However, there was, as will now be seen.

Defendant's witness Weininger, who operates a chicken eviscerating plant in New Jersey, testified "Chicken is everything except a goose, a duck, and a turkey. Everything is a chicken, but then you have to say, you have to specify which category you want or that you are talking about." Its witness Fox said that in the trade "chicken" would encompass all the various classifications. Sadina, who conducts a food inspection

[190 F. Supp. 120]

service, testified that he would consider any bird coming within the classes of "chicken" in the Department of Agriculture's regulations to be a chicken. The specifications approved by the General Services Administration include fowl as well as broilers and fryers under the classification "chickens." Statistics of the Institute of American Poultry Industries use the phrases "Young chickens" and "Mature chickens," under the general heading "Total chickens." and the Department of Agriculture's daily and weekly price reports avoid use of the word "chicken" without specification.

Defendant advances several other points which it claims affirmatively support its construction. Primary among these is the regulation of the Department of Agriculture, 7 C.F.R. § 70.300-70.370, entitled, "Grading and Inspection of Poultry and Edible Products Thereof." and in particular § 70.301 which recited:

"Chickens. The following are the various classes of chickens:

(a) Broiler or fryer . . .
(b) Roaster . . .
(c) Capon . . .
(d) Stag . . .
(e) Hen or stewing chicken or fowl . . .
(f) Cock or old rooster . . .

Defendant argues, as previously noted, that the contract incorporated these regulations by reference. Plaintiff answers that the contract provision related simply to grade and Government inspection and did not incorporate the Government definition of "chicken," and also that the definition in the Regulations is ignored in the trade. However, the latter contention was contradicted by Weininger and Sadina; and there is force in defendant's argument that the contract made the regulations a dictionary, particularly since the reference to Government grading was already in plaintiff's initial cable to Stovicek.

Defendant makes a further argument based on the impossibility of its obtaining broilers and fryers at the 33¢ price offered by plaintiff for the 2½-3 lbs. birds. There is no substantial dispute that, in late April, 1957, the price for 2½-3 lbs. broilers was between 35 and 37¢ per pound, and that when defendant entered into the contracts, it was well aware of this and intended to fill them by supplying fowl in these weights. It claims that plaintiff must likewise have known the market since plaintiff had reserved shipping space on April 23, three days before plaintiff's cable to Stovicek, or, at least, that Stovicek was chargeable with such knowledge. It is scarcely an answer to say, as plaintiff does in its brief, that the 33¢ price offered by the 2½-3 lbs. "chickens" was closer to the prevailing 35¢ price for broilers than to the 30¢ at which defendant procured fowl. Plaintiff must have expected defendant to make some profit—certainly it could not have expected defendant deliberately to incur a loss.

Finally, defendant relies on conduct by the plaintiff after the first shipment had been received. On May 28 plaintiff sent two cables complaining that the larger birds in the first shipment constituted "fowl." Defendant answered with a cable refusing to recognize plaintiff's objection and announcing "We have today ready for shipment 50,000 lbs. chicken 2½-3

lbs. 25,000 lbs. broilers 1½-2 lbs.," these being the goods procured for shipment under the second contract, and asked immediate answer "whether we are to ship this merchandise to you and whether you will accept the merchandise." After several other cable exchanges, plaintiff replied on May 29 "Confirm again that merchandise is to be shipped since resold by us if not enough pursuant to contract chickens are shipped the missing quantity is to be shipped within ten days stop we resold to our customers pursuant to your contract chickens grade A you have to deliver us said merchandise we again state that we shall make you fully responsible for all resulting costs."[2] Defendant argues.

[190 F. Supp. 121]

that if plaintiff was sincere in thinking it was entitled to young chickens, plaintiff would not have allowed the shipment under the second contract to go forward, since the distinction between broilers and chickens drawn in defendant's cablegram must have made it clear that the larger birds would not be broilers. However, plaintiff answers that the cables show plaintiff was insisting on delivery of young chickens and that defendant shipped old ones at its peril. Defendant's point would be highly relevant on another disputed issue—whether if liability were established, the measure of damages should be the difference in market value of broilers and stewing chicken in New York or the larger difference in Europe, but I cannot give it weight on the issue of interpretation. Defendant points out also that plaintiff proceeded to deliver some of the larger birds in Europe, describing them as "poulets"; defendant argues that it was only when plaintiff's customers complained about this that plaintiff developed the idea that "chicken" meant "young chicken." There is little force in this in view of plaintiff's immediate and consistent protests.

When all the evidence is reviewed, it is clear that defendant believed it could comply with the contracts by delivering stewing chicken in the 2½-3 lbs. size. Defendant's subjective intent would not be significant if this did not coincide with an objective meaning of

---

[2] These cables were in German; "chicken," "broilers" and, on some occasions, "fowl," were in English.

"chicken." Here it did coincide with one of the dictionary meanings, with the definition in the Department of Agriculture Regulations to which the contract made at least oblique reference, with at least some usage in the trade, with the realities of the market, and with what plaintiff's spokesman had said. Plaintiff asserts it to be equally plain that plaintiff's own subjective intent was to obtain broilers and fryers; the only evidence against this is the material as to market prices and this may not have been sufficiently brought home. In any event it is unnecessary to determine that issue. For plaintiff has the burden of showing that "chicken" was used in the narrower rather than in the broader sense, and this it has not sustained.

This opinion constitutes the Court's findings of fact and conclusions of law. Judgment shall be entered dismissing the complaint with costs.

Case in Point

RULES OF CONSTRUCTION AND PAROL EVIDENCE

448 A.2d 48
301 Pa. Super. 557
CBS INC., d/b/a/ WCAU-TV
v.
CAPITAL CITIES COMMUNICATIONS, INC., d/b/a WPVI-TV, Appellant.
PHILADELPHIA NEW YEAR SHOOTERS AND MUMMERS ASSOCIATION, INC.
v.
CAPITAL CITIES COMMUNICATIONS, INC. d/b/a WPVI-TV and
Lawrence J. POLLOCK and Charles R. BRADLEY.
Appeal of CAPITAL CITIES COMMUNICATIONS, INC. d/b/a WPVI-TV,
Appellant.
Superior Court of Pennsylvania.
Argued Oct. 20, 1981.
Filed July 9, 1982.

Page 50

[301 Pa. Super. 562] Elihu A. Greenhouse, Philadelphia, for appellants.
Gregory M. Harvey, Philadelphia, for CBS, appellee at No. 91.
Janet M. Sonnenfeld, Philadelphia, for Philadelphia New Year at No. 92.
Before BECK, MONTEMURO and WATKINS, JJ.
BECK, Judge:

These appeals are from Declaratory Judgments entered in two actions consolidated for trial below. Appellees WCAU-TV and Philadelphia New Year Shooters and Mummers Association, Inc. (the latter appellee hereinafter referred to as Association) brought suit seeking to have a clause contained in an agreement, entered into between appellant WPVI-TV and appellee Association on October 5, 1977, declared void and unenforceable. We hold that the

Page 51

challenged "option" portion of the agreement, if enforceable at any time, had expired prior to any attempt to exercise it, and affirm judgment for appellees. Appellant WPVI-TV filed a counterclaim in the

WCAU suit claiming tortious [301 Pa. Super. 563] interference with a contractual relation. Appellee Association sought in its action a further declaration that the agreement of October 5, 1977 was voidable in its entirety for fraud, and sought an accounting. Appellant WPVI-TV filed no counterclaim in this action, but prayed in its answer for a declaration interpreting the contract in accordance with its claims.

FACTUAL BACKGROUND

In Philadelphia, tradition hails the mummers who parade annually through the city on New Year's day. For as long as any living Philadelphian can remember, the Mummers' Parade of elaborately costumed string bands, portraying serious, comic, theatrical and historical themes, with prizes awarded to those judged best in each of the traditional "divisions," has been a major New Year's day event. The parade is televised and transmitted live. It has become an anticipated and lustrous part of the City's holiday celebration.

Appellee Association is an unincorporated association of string bands whose membership is comprised of some of the string bands (24 of them) which compete in the Mummers' Parade and two string bands which do not. Some time prior to 1974, pursuant to a series of written agreements, appellant

WPVI-TV began to make payment to appellee Association in return for which it received the "exclusive right to telecast the performances" of the members of the Association during the Mummers' Parade. For many years, the Mummers' Parade was telecast by and on WPVI-TV (Channel 6) and not by any other television station.

[301 Pa. Super. 564] In September of 1977, the Vice-President and General Manager of WPVI-TV, Lawrence J. Pollock, the Program Director of WPVI-TV, Charles R. Bradley, the President of the Association, Frederick Calandra, and members of the "Television Committee" of the Association met at a restaurant. The prior written agreement between WPVI-TV and the Association, dated November 5, 1974 "expired January one, 1977" and the meeting was held in order to discuss the terms of a new agreement.

At trial, Mr. Bradley testified that he stated to Mr. Calandra that the station would like to have a "first refusal option" in the agreement and explained to him "what a first refusal option was." No other witness gave testimony with regard to the negotiation of the 1977 agreement. The written agreement was prepared by counsel for appellant WPVI-TV and was executed under date October 5, 1977.

The agreement contained a preamble describing the subject matter, and then set forth the following terms:

1. Association hereby grants STATION the exclusive right to telecast the performances of its members in the said PARADE, and to record and telecast preview programs and other programs in which the performances by its members may be shown.

Page 52

2. Subject to the provisions of paragraph 3 hereof, the STATION agrees to pay ASSOCIATION the following consideration for the said rights for the following years:
   A. $13,000.00 for the PARADE scheduled for January 1, 1978;
   B. $14,000.00 for the PARADE scheduled for January 1, 1979;
   C. $15,000.00 for the PARADE scheduled for January 1, 1980;

[301 Pa. Super. 565] and STATION agrees to supply to ASSOCIATION $10,000.00 worth of television advertising for the Mummers' Annual Show of Shows held at the City's Civic Center.

3. It is agreed that if a PARADE is not held in any year during the term of and any extensions of the term of this agreement, no consideration shall be paid for each year or years when such PARADE is not sponsored and officially recognized by the City of Philadelphia, or in any year in which the PARADE is not held.

4. Failure to telecast the PARADE in any year or years for reasons as set forth in Paragraph 3 hereof shall not effect the rights of the parties for other years during the term of this agreement or any extension hereof.

5. STATION is hereby granted the first option and privilege to renew this agreement beyond the termination date as set forth herein upon the same terms and conditions of any bona fide offer received by ASSOCIATION beyond the termination date as set forth herein.

   ASSOCIATION agrees to give STATION notice of all details of any other bona fide offer received by ASSOCIATION, and STATION is hereby granted two months after receipt of such notice in which to exercise such first refusal option by written notice of election to do so. Upon exercise of such first refusal option, the terms and conditions of this agreement shall be extended in conformity therewith.

The agreement contained no terms other than the foregoing. Despite several references to "the term of this agreement" and "the termination date as set forth herein," no term of the agreement or designated termination date is anywhere set forth in the agreement.

By letter dated February 20, 1980, appellee WCAU-TV offered terms for similar "exclusive" rights for a three-year period, including an offer of escalating payments in the annual amounts of $30,000., $35,000., and $40,000. By letter dated April 29, 1980, appellant WPVI-TV offered a five-[301 Pa. Super. 566] year agreement in terms including escalating payments in the annual amounts of $40,000., $45,000., $50,000., $55,000., and $60,000. The letter stated, inter alia, "In addition, Channel 6 will want to maintain the option and similar renewal agreement for a period beyond the proposed five years covered by this agreement, as exists in the current contract." By letter to appellee Association dated May 30, 1980, appellee WCAU-TV, by its Vice-President and General Manager, Jay R. Feldman, stated that it had been advised "that a perpetual first refusal option for exclusive broadcast rights to Mummer events, such as might be claimed on the basis of your expired contract with WPVI-TV, would constitute an unreasonable restraint of trade and therefore would not be legally enforceable." The letter again offered a three-year contract increasing the escalating annual payments to $70,000., $80,000., and $100,000. Joseph A. Purul, Chairman of the TV Committee of appellee Association, wrote to appellant WPVI-TV, by letter dated and hand-delivered June 3, 1980, "to advise that WCAU-TV" had made an offer, and describing the terms of the offer. The letter concluded: "Inasmuch as the Mummers' Association body will make a determination on Thursday, June 19, 1980, which Channel will televise the Parade, it behooves you to submit your new proposal on or before that

Page 53

date if you so desire. If you do not intend to pursue the matter any further kindly advise."

On June 16, 1980, Mr. Pollock, in behalf of appellant WPVI-TV, met with the TV Committee of the Association and read aloud letter dated June 16, 1980 addressed to the Association, "attn: Joseph A. Purul, Jr., Esquire." The letter thanked him for the June 3 letter "in which you gave us notice of the other offer, as provided in our 1977 agreement," and stated "WPVI-TV elects to exercise its first refusal option." The letter then stated, inter alia, "We offer [301 Pa. Super. 567] a three-year rights package of $75,000 the first year, $87,500 the second year, and $100,000 the third year" and offered to "match or exceed" all the terms of the WCAU-TV proposal.

Following the June 16 meeting, the Association received three additional offers:

June 18—WCAU-TV—increasing their payments to equal those set forth by appellant
June 19—KYW-TV—offering $100,000. each year for three years
June 19—WCAU-TV—increasing their payments to $100,000. per year for three years.

None of these offers was communicated to appellant WPVI-TV by appellee Association. Each of the two additional offers by appellee WCAU-TV contained language identical to the earlier offer stating its view that the "first refusal option . . . would not be legally enforceable."

On June 19, 1980, representatives of the 24 Association members who appear in the Mummers' Parade met and voted 23 to 1 to accept the June 19 offer by WCAU-TV. Accordingly, Mr. Calandra initialed WCAU's June 19 letter of intent and returned it to them. On June 23, 1980, WCAU-TV delivered to WPVI-TV its letter of the same date notifying appellant of the intent of WCAU-TV to enter into a contract with appellee Association on the terms of the June 19 letter of intent, a copy of which was enclosed. Following conversations between respective counsel for the parties, on June 30, 1980 appellees brought the separate suits against appellant which resulted in the judgment from which this appeal is taken.

The court below held that:

A. Paragraph 5 of the agreement in suit [quoted above at page (5)] could only legally be construed to require [301 Pa. Super. 568] appellee Association to give appellant notice of bona fide offers which it has determined to accept.

B. Paragraph 5 could be so construed based upon testimony by appellant's expert witness that this was the understanding in the television industry of the term "bona fide offer."

C. As so construed, the agreement was legally binding and enforceable, and it was unnecessary to consider, or rule with regard to, the expiration of the "first refusal option."

D. The purported exercise of the "first refusal option" by appellant as set forth in its letter of June 16, 1980 was ineffectual in that it did not relate to an offer which appellee Association was determined to accept.

E. Appellant was duly notified of the bona fide offer which appellee Association was determined to accept by the letter from appellee WCAU-TV dated June 23, 1980 and the filing of complaints June 30, 1980.

F. Appellant WPVI-TV failed to exercise its first refusal option during the two

Page 54

months following notice from WCAU-TV and the filing of complaints, and appellee Association is therefore free to contract with others.

Exceptions filed by appellant were denied, and judgment was entered for appellees and against appellant.

ASSERTIONS ON APPEAL

Appellant asserts that it was error to hold that it had not validly exercised its "first refusal option" by the letter dated June 16, 1980. In the alternative, appellant asserts that it was error to hold that either notice from a stranger to the contract or notice by the filing of complaint constitutes compliance with the notice requirement of the contract.

[301 Pa. Super. 569] PRINCIPLES APPLICABLE TO REVIEW OF CONTRACT PROVISION

As well stated in *Bobali Corporation v. Tamapa Company*, 235 Pa. Super. 1, 340 A.2d 485 (1975) alloc. ref. construction of contract options and rights of first refusal must be in accordance with the principles of contract construction and:

In construing the terms of a contract we are guided by well-defined and fundamental canons of construction. Our Supreme Court has adopted the following principles:

"The cardinal rule in the interpretation of contracts is to ascertain the intention of the parties and to give effect to that intention if it can be done consistently with legal principles." (Citations omitted.) "Contracts must receive a reasonable interpretation, according to the intention of the parties at the time of executing them, if that intention can be ascertained from their language. (citing cases.)" *Percy A. Brown & Co. v. Raub*, 357 Pa. 271, 287 [54 A.2d 35] (1947). *Id.*, 340 A.2d at 488.

We must first look to the writing itself, for if the terms of the agreement are clear and precise, performance must be required in accordance with the intent as expressed in the agreement without resort to rules of construction or extrinsic evidence.

The question before us is whether the clause containing the right of first refusal is ambiguous so as to require interpretation. It is established that the intent of the parties to a written contract is the writing itself and when the words are clear and unambiguous the intent is to be found only in the express (sic) language of the agreement. *Felte v. White*, 451 Pa. 137, 302 A.2d 347 (1973) (other citations omitted). Thus, it is said that the agreement that is clear and unambiguous speaks for itself and is not subject to interpretation by reference to any circumstances other than those recited in the written agreement. (citations omitted). *Steuart v. McChesney & Joyce*, 284 Pa. Super. 29, 424 A.2d 1375, 1377 (1981).

[301 Pa. Super. 570] Where, however, the terms of the agreement are ambiguous and the intent of the parties cannot be ascertained by reference to the writing, the agreement will be construed strictly against the party who prepared the agreement, particularly in the event such party is in a superior bargaining position to the other contracting party. In addition, extrinsic evidence may be introduced to show the common understanding and intent of the parties at the time the contract was entered into.

However, no extrinsic evidence may be introduced in an attempt actually to alter, amend, add to, or detract from the terms of the contract as written. Such evidence is barred by the Parol Evidence

Page 55

Rule. Similarly, the court may not construe a contract in such a manner as to write a new contract for the parties, but is confined to reasonable construction of the language as actually contained in the writing. It is well-established

that "The parties have the right to make their own contract, and it is not the function of this court to rewrite it, or to give it a construction in conflict with the accepted and plain meaning of the language used." *Hagarty v. Wm. Akers, Jr., Co., Inc.*, 342 Pa. 236, 239 [20 A.2d 317] (1941); *R. F. Felte, Inc. v. White*, 451 Pa. 137 [302 A.2d 347] (1973).

Bobali Corporation v. Tamapa Company, supra, 340 A.2d at 488.

[301 Pa. Super. 571] THE AGREEMENT IN SUIT

In the instant case, it cannot be said that the terms of Paragraph 5 of the agreement are so clear and unambiguous as to obviate the necessity for construction. Although the first segment of Paragraph 5 speaks of a "first option and privilege to renew," it is unquestioned and undisputed that it was never in the contemplation of any party to the agreement that Paragraph 5 conferred a privilege to renew the terms of that agreement. Similarly, the language of the second segment stating "the terms and conditions of this agreement shall be extended" cannot be taken to mean that either the Association or WPVI-TV was bound to extend the terms of the 1977 agreement. An ambiguity further arises as to what the notice duty of the Association is which is described as being to give WPVI-TV notice "of all details of any other bona fide offer." Reference to "any other . . . offer" could be read to mean that the provision only came into play once WPVI-TV had made an offer. Does "bona fide offer" mean every genuine offer, every offer which is not a sham offer, which is received by Association, or only such offers as interest the Association? Would the notice by WPVI-TV of an intention to meet or exceed the terms of any such offer of which it had notice terminate all further negotiations, or would a new offer followed by new notice create new rights and obligations? Finally, and we believe most importantly, during what period of time was the Association under a duty to give such notice and during what period of time did WPVI-TV have the right to exercise a right of first refusal?

Applying settled principles of contract construction to the language of this agreement will yield a reasonable interpretation capable of performance with regard to each of the ambiguities except for the lack of termination date. Thus, construing the language strictly against appellant whose attorney prepared the agreement, it may reasonably be interpreted as setting forth a right of first refusal which prevents the Association from accepting any offer by a third party without first offering the opportunity to appellant [301 Pa. Super. 572] WPVI-TV to meet the terms of the third party's offer and giving WPVI-TV two months in which to decide whether to accept the offer to contract on those terms or waive its right of first refusal.

In Gateway Trading Company, Inc. v. Children's Hospital of Pittsburgh, 438 Pa. 329, 265 A.2d 115 (1970) in construing what purported to be an option to purchase land contained in a lease, but which option contained language similar to the agreement herein, the Pennsylvania Supreme Court held that the language created a right of first refusal, "described by Professor Corbin" as creating the following result:

> If a third party should make an offer, the owner was privileged not to accept it, and also not to make any offer to the promisee. But the owner was bound by duty not to accept the offer of the third party without first giving an option to the promisee.

The court therefore held that:

> The clear import of the instant rider provision was that the lessor was obliged to give Gateway written notice of the terms of any bona fide offer which it deemed

Page 56

> acceptable and to allow Gateway to purchase the property on those terms before any sale to a third party was effected. . . .

While the cases on a right of first refusal are not many, a review of such cases together with standard provisions of contract law, establishes the following:

A right of first refusal constitutes a promise to offer the res of the right to the promisee for such consideration as the promisor determines to accept on the basis of an offer from a third party before accepting the offer of the third party. A right of first refusal does not require the promisor to offer the res at all. The right of first refusal merely requires that before the promisor accepts an offer of a third party, he must offer the res to the promisee of the right for the consideration he is willing to accept from the third party. *Ross v. Shawmut Development Corp.*, 460 Pa. 328, 333 A.2d 751 (1975); *Warden v. Taylor*, 460 Pa. 577, 333 A.2d 922 (1975); *DeVries v. Westgren*, 446 Pa. 205, 287 A.2d [301 Pa. Super. 573] 437 (1972); *Gateway Trading Co., Inc. v. Children's Hospital, supra, Sun Oil Co. v. Bellone*, 292 Pa. Super. 341, 437 A.2d 415 (1981); *Steuart v. McChesney, supra, Bobali Corporation v. Tamapa Company, supra.*

Construing the instant right of first refusal in accordance with the principles thus adopted in this Commonwealth, the provisions of Paragraph 5 carry the clear import that the Association was obliged, during the life of the right of first refusal, to offer the televising rights to WPVI-TV on the terms of any bona fide offer from a third party which it had determined to accept. WPVI-TV then had two months in which to accept that offer, thus exercising its right of first refusal, or to reject that offer, thus waiving its right of first refusal.

On this basis, we agree with the lower court that the letter of June 3, 1980 from the Association to WPVI-TV, notifying it of negotiations with WCAU-TV and inviting it to make a "new proposal" can not be interpreted as inviting appellant to exercise its right of first refusal. The letter established that there was no pending offer which it was determined to accept, but on the contrary indicated that it wished all offers to be placed before it for full study and a determination on June 19. Similarly, appellant's letter of June 16 can only fairly be read as a bid and did not constitute an acceptance of any offer made by the Association. The fact that appellant also made an attempt to bind [301 Pa. Super. 574] appellee Association by using self-serving language does not alter the overall import of the letter as an attempt to outbid WCAU-TV and finalize negotiations. As stated in the opinion by Judge Stanley Greenberg in the lower court, "Their argument that the increased payment offered was an act of generosity not required under the circumstances and for which they should not be penalized, is not only a little far fetched, but is certainly not consistent with their previous dealings with the Mummers. . . ." There was therefore no offer made by appellee Association to appellant WPVI-TV to exercise its right of first refusal, and no acceptance by WPVI-TV in the exchange of letters June 3 to June 16.

We cannot agree with the court below, however, that notice in accordance with the agreement was served upon appellant. The only offer which appellee Association determined to accept was the WCAU-

Page 57

TV offer of June 19 which it voted to accept. Appellant received no notice from appellee Association that it had received that offer. Appellant received no notice

from anyone that appellee was offering appellant the televising rights on those terms or any terms. On the contrary, appellant received notice, first by the June 23 letter from WCAU-TV and then by service of complaints, that appellee Association had accepted the WCAU-TV offer and that both appellees repudiated the right of first refusal as being unenforceable. Under these circumstances, appellant could not be expected to respond as though it had received normal notice of an offer, requiring [301 Pa. Super. 575] acceptance or rejection. Therefore, if Paragraph 5 of the agreement of October 5, 1977 was valid and enforceable and had not earlier terminated, appellant has not received the notice required by the agreement.

However, this court is of the opinion that the issue of the validity of a perpetual right of first refusal is not immaterial as held by the court below, but rather is at the center of this controversy.

TERMINATION DATE OF THE AGREEMENT

The issue of the termination date of the agreement was not argued or briefed by the parties as a result of the lower court's ruling on other issues. However, this court will consider the issue since it must consider all grounds for possible affirmance appearing from the opinion and record before it. Appellees did argue in the court below, and in fact grounded their complaints on the claim, that the lack of a termination date for the right of first refusal rendered it invalid.

Appellant WPVI-TV claimed at trial, and offered testimony and exhibits tending to support, that it drafted Paragraph 5 in accordance with other agreements in the industry containing such rights of first refusal. However, each similar agreement presented by appellant as evidence contained a fixed term of the agreement and contained reasonably clear language establishing that the right of first refusal was to be exercised within the term of the agreement. Moreover, each was negotiated with a corporate [301 Pa. Super. 576] distributor in the television industry, thus resulting in a common industry understanding of the language used. In the case of the agreement in suit, appellant WPVI-TV, who drafted the agreement, neglected to insert any designation whatsoever of the term of the agreement. With regard to the primary performance of the agreement, this creates no problem, for the central portion of the agreement relates to specific payments to be made for specific performances to be held on the three specific dates, January 1, 1978, January 1, 1979 and January 1, 1980. Some vagueness does arise with regard to the dates for "other programs" mentioned in Paragraph 1 of the agreement, resulting in a lack of clarity as to whether any portion of the agreement is expected to survive

Page 58

beyond January 1, 1980. We are here faced with language so vague, as it relates to dates in which performance of duties under the contract is required, that any attempt to construe the contract may be seen as actually rewriting the contract for the parties.

To the extent any construction is possible, the contract must be construed most strongly against the claims of appellant in light of the combination of the factors of appellant's greater sophistication in the television industry and the fact that appellant drafted the agreement and must therefore accept the burden of the uncertainty created by its omission of the "Term of the Agreement" paragraph normal to the industry.

While Paragraph 5 does use language relating to a right "to renew this agreement beyond the termination date," this must be read to mean "to enter into a new agreement for the period beyond the termination date" when it is construed with the rest of the agreement and in light of its purpose. Similarly, the language indicating that such new agreement shall be based upon an offer "received by Association beyond the termination date" cannot possibly be read to mean that appellant has the right to meet all offers in the future, but clearly must be read to mean that the appellant [301 Pa. Super. 577] had the right to meet such an offer received by the Association during the term of the agreement, for performance beyond the termination date. In short, while the parties had the right and ability to draft and enter into an agreement which could have required the performance by some party of an obligation during some specifically limited period of time after the termination date of the agreement, they did not do so. At the very most, by reference to the period of time granted appellant WPVI-TV for response to notice, the agreement may be read to extend its right for the specific two-month period after the termination date.

There remains the question of whether we can ascertain a termination date and make a determination of the specific period of time during which performance was required of the parties.

Since the latest date mentioned in the agreement is January 1, 1980, we are forced to conclude that that date is intended as the termination date of the agreement. This construction is supported by the testimony of the Vice President and General Manager of appellant WPVI-TV that the prior agreement dated November 5, 1974 had expired on January 1, 1977. Although representatives of appellant did refer to the prior contract as a "three year contract" both the above testimony and the conduct of the parties in entering into a new agreement prior to November 5, 1977 demonstrate that it was viewed as a tri-annual agreement, the three annual parades covered in the agreement setting the actual contract dates.

From all of the foregoing, we must conclude either that any obligation under the agreement imposed upon appellee Association to give notice of a bona fide offer which it was determined to accept expired at midnight on January 1, 1980, or the agreement is so vague as to termination date as to require that we hold that it was null and void for want [301 Pa. Super. 578] of a term central to the agreement. In either event, we hold that no right of first refusal existed in appellant WPVI-TV on June 19, 1980 when appellee Association received the bona fide offer which it was determined to accept. Appellee Association was therefore free at all relevant times to contract with whomever it pleased.

CONCLUSION

The Declaratory Judgment should have stated:

1. Paragraph 5 of the agreement entered into between Capital Cities Communications, Inc. (WPVI-TV) and Philadelphia New Year Shooters and Mummers Association, Inc. (Association) dated October 5, 1977 is construed to require that, during the term of the agreement, Association was required

Page 59

to give notice to WPVI-TV of any bona fide offer from a third party which Association had determined to accept, and before accepting any offer from a third party was required to offer to contract with WPVI-TV on the same terms as those offered by the third party. Upon receipt of such an offer from Association, WPVI-TV was given two months within which to accept such offer.

2. Paragraph 5 of the said agreement is either so vague with regard to the termination date that it is void for want of a term central to the agreement, or must be construed to have terminated no later than March 1980.

3. Appellant WPVI-TV had no existing right of first refusal at any time relevant to this litigation, such right having terminated no later than March 1980.

The Declaratory Judgment appealed from is modified as above set forth and, as so modified, is affirmed. Judgment for both appellees in these consolidated appeals is affirmed.

[Footnotes omitted.]

VOCABULARY BUILDERS

Across

1 A contractual purpose that is against public policy.
4 ____ terms are always admissible.
5 How other parties act in similar situations.
6 Pertaining to both parties.
8 Action that cures defect in the statute.
9 Promise to pay that must be in writing.
10 Terms that are preferred over preprinted form.
13 The kind of evidence that is sometimes admissible.
18 A person lacking capacity due to a lack of understanding from a physical disability.
21 A person under the age of 18.
22 Threatening to expose personal information against a person's best interests.
24 Only some of the terms have been finalized.
25 The kind of duress that threatens financial harm.
27 Taking advantage of a close relationship.
29 Timeframe in which to avoid the statute.
35 A contract to which minors are bound.
36 Ability of court to give party a remedy at law.
39 A contract that is completely unable to be enforced.
41 The kind of duress that threatens a person's happiness or well-being.
46 Court returns the party to precontract position.
47 UCC requires in writing if the value is over $500.
49 Intentionally lying to induce a person to enter into a contract.
52 Failing to say anything about the condition of real or personal property.
53 Hiding a fact from another in order to avoid having to say anything about its condition.
54 Where the courts look first to determine the meaning of the contract.
55 ____ of consideration is always admissible.
56 Either a mutual or unilateral misunderstanding.
57 The kind of evidence that is always permitted.
58 Threatening to sue where no cause of action exists.
59 Acknowledgment of the contract after gaining capacity.

Down

1 The mistake must relate to a _____ term.
2 Only one party harbors a misunderstanding as to the terms of the contract.
3 Court's power to enforce parts of an otherwise illegal contract.
6 Persons having expertise in the trade.
7 All the terms of the agreement have been finalized.
11 Defects in _____ are always admissible.
12 A unilateral mistake must be _____ in order to avoid the contract.
14 Outside material that may help interpret the meaning of a contract.
15 Able to be disaffirmed.
16 What contract law loves best.
17 The kind of duress that threatens bodily harm.
19 Sale of _____ _____ must comply with the statute.
20 Ambiguous terms are construed _____.
23 A contractual promise that restrains trade.
26 One party has so much control over the bargaining process.
28 Parties have agreed to all material terms of the contract and both parties are satisfied with the terms.
30 Avoids parol evidence issues entirely.
31 Statute of Frauds requires that certain contracts be in _____.
32 The terms of the contract are so unfair as to shock the conscience of the court.
33 How the parties have acted in other similar agreements.
34 An agreement in consideration of marriage.
37 How the parties have acted in the agreement.
38 The kind of evidence that is never admissible.
40 Lacking capacity due to alcohol or drugs.
42 Failing to ascertain the truth of your assertion regarding a term or fact of the contract.
43 Person not at fault.
44 First in right.
45 Excessive pressure to enter into a contract.
48 Avoidance of the contract after gaining capacity.
50 A contractual purpose that is inherently evil.
51 Terms that are preferred over all others on the contract.

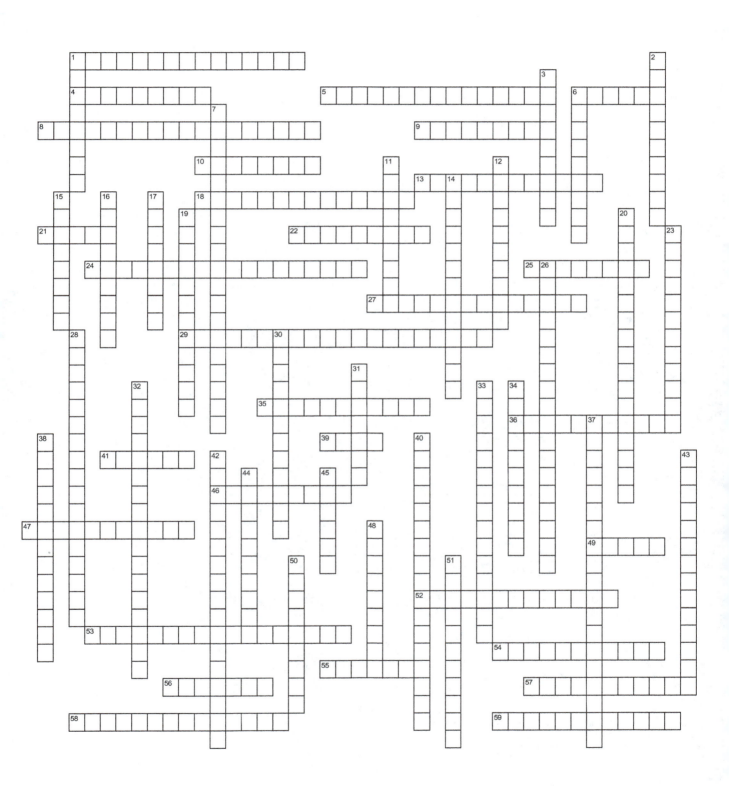

Part Three

Failure of Performance

Chapter 10: Breach of Contract

Chapter 11: Excuse of Performance

Chapter 12: Changes by Agreement of the Parties

Chapter 10

Breach of Contract

Chapter Objectives

The student will be able to:

- Use vocabulary regarding breach of contract properly.
- Discuss the theory of "anticipatory repudiation" giving the party a right to sue prior to the breach.
- Determine if the breach is material and total or nonmaterial and/or partial.
- Explain the recourses available to the non-breaching party.
- Identify the factors a court will consider in determining materiality.
- Recognize the divisibility of a contract to determine the extent of the breach and extent of recourse available to the non-breaching party.
- Determine whether there has been a knowing and intentional waiver after a breach has occurred.

This chapter will examine HOW courts determine IF and WHEN a material breach of a contract has occurred and HOW that breach affects the viability of the entire contract. After one or both parties have tendered performance on the contract, one or both of them may find that they received less than they originally bargained for. The question then arises, "what should be done about it?" This chapter discusses the option of resorting to the courts. Before going to the court, however, it is helpful to understand how the court will analyze the situation. Once it has been established that there indeed does exist a valid contract and no defenses to performance exist, the parties are expected to fulfill their promises by performance. Contract law examines the given performance in light of the expectations of the parties. Where there is a significant deviation from the expectation of the "innocent" party, the party at fault is in **breach**.

ANTICIPATORY REPUDIATION

Contract law metes out swift justice where breach of contract issues arise; however, that is not to say that the legal system moves swiftly! Indeed, in certain circumstances where certain elements are met, it affords a remedy to an aggrieved party even before the time of performance has arrived. That is the element of **anticipation**. The aggrieved party anticipates that the performance is not forthcoming. By permitting the aggrieved party to sue before performance is actually due, the potential damages can be mitigated. Instead of waiting for the future breach and thereby accruing additional damages, contract law would rather permit immediate relief that lessens the damage caused by the repudiating party. As between merchants in the course of business, one party may request **adequate assurances** that performance will be forthcoming if that party has reasonable doubts about the potentially breaching party's ability to perform. (This topic will be discussed further in Chapter 15 on the Uniform Commercial Code.)

What are these "certain circumstances" that allow a party to seek relief for **anticipatory repudiation**? If a party has **positively and unequivocally** stated that she will not or cannot perform on the contract, that party has repudiated the contract. There can be no room for second-guessing the intention of the repudiating party. If there is an uncertainty as to that party's intention or capability to fulfill her obligations under the contract, the party has *not* repudiated. Contract law favors not only definiteness, but also the preservation of agreements.

Additionally, a party's actions, not words, may repudiate a contract. If a party **transfers interest** in the subject matter or an essential element of the transaction making subsequent performance or transfer impossible, the party has repudiated the contract. For example, in *LeTarte v. West Side Development, LLC*, 855 A.2d 505 (N.H. 2004), a housing developer and a landscaper entered into an agreement whereby the landscaper would receive a particular lot in partial compensation for his work. Midway through the project, the developer sold that parcel of land to a third party. The court determined that the conveyance amounted to total anticipatory breach of contract because the developer's obligations to the landscaper were impossible to perform and a clear indication of his intent not to perform. Further demonstration of how much contract law loves consistency over time; the *LeTarte* case is one of hundreds that rely on an old and reliable contract principle espoused over 100 years ago in *Roehm v. Horst*, 178 U.S. 1, 20 S. Ct. 780, 44 L. Ed. 953 (1900). "It is not disputed that if one party to a contract has destroyed the subject-matter, or disabled himself so as to make performance impossible, his conduct is equivalent to a breach of the contract, although the time for performance has not arrived; and also that if

---

breach
A party's performance that deviates from the required performance obligations under the contract.

anticipation
An expectation of things to come that has reasonable basis for the conclusion.

adequate assurances
Under the UCC, merchants may request of each other further promises that performance will be tendered.

anticipatory repudiation
Words or acts from a party to the contract that clearly and unquestionably state the intent not to honor his contractual obligations before the time for performance has arrived.

positively and unequivocally
In order to treat a party's statement as an anticipatory repudiation, the statements or actions from the potential repudiator must clearly and unquestionably communicate that intent not to perform.

transfer of interest
In a purchase agreement, a preliminary requirement is that the seller has legal title to the subject matter and authority to transfer it to the seller. If the seller transfers his interest to a third party, this preliminary requirement can no longer be met.

a contract provides for a series of acts, and actual default is made in the performance of one of them, accompanied by a refusal to perform the rest, the other party need not perform, but may treat the refusal as a breach of the entire contract, and recover accordingly." *Id.* at 8. Indeed, this principle stated in *Roehm* referred to many previous cases dating back to the mid-1800s.

Further, any **affirmative acts** taken by a party that would make performance of her obligations under the contract impossible constitute anticipatory repudiation. The action taken by the repudiating party does not necessarily have to directly relate to the subject matter of the contract; the action may affect another material aspect of the agreement. This can easily be seen in a corporate dissolution. "There can be little doubt that [the corporation] intended the assignment and dissolution to be a complete and final termination of its business enterprise rather than a mere change in its form or structure. The liquidation of the corporate assets and distribution of those assets to the shareholders, under the facts of this case, was an express repudiation of the [contract]. The corporation was voluntarily placing itself in a position in which it could not perform its obligations and was therefore in breach of the [contract]. A party is guilty of a breach of contract when either he places himself in such a position that it is beyond his power to perform his part of the contract or if he fails to perform all the obligations which he agreed to undertake." *Rauch v. Circle Theatre*, 374 N.E.2d 546, 552 (Ind. App. 1st Dist. 1969) (internal citations omitted).

Let's take each of these three anticipatory repudiation scenarios in turn.

> **affirmative acts**
> Knowing and conscious efforts by a party to the contract that are inconsistent with the terms of the agreement and that make contractual obligations impossible to perform.

1. *Unequivocal statement of anticipatory repudiation.* On May 1st, Rachel and Ross contract with Will and Grace to purchase their chic, custom-made living room furniture. The sale is to take place in Will's apartment on July 1st. On June 1st, the couples get into a huge fight over some trivialities. Rachael and Ross tell Will and Grace that the deal is off. They refuse to purchase the furniture at any price and say that they will no longer have any dealings with the other couple. Unequivocally and positively, Rachel and Ross cancel the contract. Although the time for performance is not due, Will and Grace do not have to wait another two months to sue for breach of contract. They anticipate the repudiation of the contract. They are immediately entitled to institute a lawsuit.

2. *Transfer of interest in the subject matter.* Same basic facts as above, but, instead of fighting with Rachel and Ross, Will and Grace sell their furniture to Monica and Chandler on June 1st. This transfer of ownership makes the sale to Rachel and Ross impossible. In this scenario, it is Will and Grace who anticipatorily repudiate, and Rachel and Ross have the right to sue.

3. *Affirmative acts to repudiate the contract.* Again, Rachel and Ross desire Will and Grace's unique furniture. On May 5th, in a raucous Cinco de Mayo celebration, Will and Grace deliberately set fire to their furniture. They have thereby willfully rendered their contractual duty to sell the furniture impossible. Rachel and Ross have an immediate right to commence a lawsuit.

immediate right to commence a lawsuit
The aggrieved party does not have to wait until the time when performance would be due under the contract term where there has been an anticipatory repudiation.

cancel the contract
The aggrieved party has the right to terminate the contractual relationship with no repercussions.

ignore the repudiation
If the repudiating party has not permanently made his performance impossible, the aggrieved party can wait to see if the repudiator changes his mind and does perform.

Just as there are three types of actions that constitute anticipatory repudiation, there are three actions that the aggrieved party can take in response to the repudiation. Perhaps contract law likes symmetry as much as consistency. First, as already mentioned, the aggrieved party has an **immediate right to commence a lawsuit**, despite the fact that performance is not yet due. In all three of the scenarios described above, the non-breaching parties have the right to file a complaint for anticipatory breach of contract. The non-breaching parties have *certain* knowledge that the other parties *will not* perform.

Second, the aggrieved party can simply **cancel the contract** and walk away. If Rachel and Ross find furniture they like better than Will and Grace's, they can simply shrug their shoulders and forget the whole deal. If the non-breaching party feels there is no point in pursuing performance or the remedies for nonperformance, they can just pretend the contract never existed in the first place.

Last is the "wait and see" option. The aggrieved party may choose to **ignore the repudiation** and urge the potentially breaching party to reconsider and perform. If the repudiating party does not perform in the contractually allotted time, the aggrieved party may then sue for breach of contract based on the nonperformance, not the anticipatory repudiation. Perhaps Will and Grace are willing to see whether or not Rachel and Ross will change their minds, make up with them, and buy the furniture. Will and Grace may wait until July 1st, the time when the original performance was due; if Rachel and Ross still refuse to perform, then Will and Grace can sue for breach of contract. This is not a suit based on anticipatory repudiation; it is an actual material breach at the time for performance, not before it.

The aggrieved party's best response depends on the nature of the consideration or subject matter. Immediately commencing a lawsuit is the best option where the loss of the subject matter is easily quantifiable in monetary value. This can either be the cost of the subject matter itself or the money the aggrieved party will lose due to the failure of performance. Generally, in a simple sales contract, as above, the value of the goods is the measure of damages caused by the anticipatory repudiation. The damages in the above examples are either the value of Will and Grace's furniture or the cost to buy replacement furniture. In other situations, the damages also may be lost profits or lost opportunities and out-of-pocket expenditures of the aggrieved party in carrying out her contractual obligations prior to the repudiation. For example, if Rachel and Ross had hired a moving company to pick up the furniture and put a nonrefundable deposit down, they might be entitled to that lost deposit money from Will and Grace. A full discussion of calculation of damages follows in Chapter 13.

Simply walking away is the best option where there are no damages to claim in a lawsuit. Recall, contract law will not award remedies for a mere wrongdoing on the part of one party; there must be some lost money to be recovered. "It is an elemental rule of law that, while a plaintiff will not be denied a recovery merely because of uncertainty as to the amount or valuation, in dollars, of the injury suffered, he is limited, ultimately, only to such relief as the evidence will support. The fundamental rule of damages . . . is that the party injured by the breach of contract is limited in recovery to the loss actually suffered by the breach." *See Rauch v. Circle Theatre*, 374 N.E.2d at 553.

Where the subject matter is unique or the aggrieved party will not be able to be fully compensated monetarily or the aggrieved party will not be able to find another "substitute contract" in time, the aggrieved party may choose the "wait and see" option and try to convince the repudiator to perform.

There are two things to keep in mind when determining whether a party is attempting repudiation. First, "a **mere request for a change** in the terms or a request for cancellation of the contract is not in itself enough to constitute a repudiation." *Harrell v. Sea Colony, Inc.*, 370 A.2d 119 (Md. 1977), *citing* 6 CORBIN ON CONTRACTS § 73. If Rachel and Ross asked if the selling price or time for delivery could be changed, that is not a repudiation of the contract. They have merely indicated that other terms might be more convenient for them. If Will and Grace say no, Rachel and Ross are still bound and still intend to be bound by the original agreement.

Second, until the aggrieved party notifies the repudiating party or takes some action in reliance on this repudiation, the repudiator can change her mind and **retract the repudiation**. Contract law encourages parties to fulfill their contractual obligations and therefore does not consider an anticipatory repudiation to be "final" until the aggrieved party "accepts" the repudiation by notice to the repudiator or changes her position due to the repudiation. Until Will and Grace resell, set fire to, or otherwise dispose of the furniture, Ross and Rachel can change their minds and retract their repudiation and continue with the contract obligations. *See Truman L. Flatt & Sons Co., Inc. v. Schupf*, 649 N.E.2d 990 (Ill. App. 1995) (Purchaser sent a letter to the seller that *may* have been an attempt at repudiation, but it was ambiguous as to the purchaser's intent to go through with the deal unless the price were reduced. The seller sent a letter back indicating that he was not interested in selling at the reduced price. The purchaser then sent another letter, five days later, indicating his willingness to go through with the purchase as provided in the contract. The court determined that the first letter from the seller was not a repudiation; the letter from the seller was not a notice to the purchaser that the seller intended to treat the contract as rescinded by anticipatory repudiation; and, even if the first letter from the purchaser repudiated the contract, the second letter effectively retracted it.).

mere request for a change
A party's interest in renegotiating the terms of the contract does not amount to anticipatory repudiation.

retract the repudiation
Until the aggrieved party notifies the repudiator or takes some action in reliance on the repudiation, the repudiator has the right to "take it back" and perform on the contract.

IN-CLASS DISCUSSION

Julie has decided to open up her own boutique to sell her fine jewelry and other handcrafted items supplied by other artists. On September 1st, she goes to the local bank for a small business loan to finance her dream. First National Bank enters into loan commitments with Julie that require her to fulfill some conditions precedent to the final loan disbursement. Julie has until December 31st of that year to get the necessary documents and business plan together. The deadline comes and goes but the bank says nothing to her. Julie continues to work on the business plan. The bank manager tells Julie: "I am not pleased with your delay; this is unacceptable." He does not tell her when the new deadline is for submitting her documentation. Julie is not certain she can ever get these documents in order. In fact, Julie is not certain that her plan is economically viable. Even if she got the loan, how would she ever be able to pay it back? Given what the bank manager told her, Julie just gives up.

Which party is in breach? Did the bank or Julie anticipatorily repudiate the contract?

Is there a remedy for the non-breaching party? If so, what is it?

Does it make sense that "[t]he holder of the duty based upon condition precedent cannot profit from an anticipatory repudiation of a contract that he would have breached himself"?

See *Craigside, LLC v. GDC View, LLC*, 74 So. 3d 1087, 1090 (Fla. App. 2011).

MATERIALITY

material
An element or term that is significant or important and relates to the basis for the agreement.

While any deviation in the expected performance under contract is a breach, because perfection along with certainty is also preferred, contract law grants a remedy only for those deviations that are **material** (important or significant). In other words, a material breach is an inexcusable failure by the breaching party to do what was required of him under the terms of the contract. In reality, it makes the whole purpose of the contract null as the aggrieved party will not get what she bargained for. The freedom of contract principles (that parties are free to contract for whatever terms they wish) does not translate to freedom of performance of contract. The parties must give and receive *almost* exactly what they bargained for.

SURF'S UP

The most relevant issue in Part Three relating to electronic contracts is software licensing. We've all been online surfing, found a great piece of software or music, and then hit the "download now" button. The Internet is a great tool for obtaining information, but it also allows parties to breach these—largely unread—license agreements.

The biggest difficulty in curtailing this freewheeling disregard for these types of contractual terms is that the Internet affords anonymity. It is only through very careful tracking that a breaching party can be "brought to justice." It may not seem as though one teenager downloading a few songs is a material breach, but the accumulation of all these "little breaches" adds up to a big infraction.

Perhaps the most famous breaches of contract via the Internet were the *Napster* cases. There are still many court battles regarding this issue of copyright infringement; *A&M Records, Inc. v. Napster, Inc.*, 239 F.3d 1004 (9th Cir. 2001), is only a small representation of that type. The nature of the breach did not merely involve nonpayment of license fees but also the transfer of single-user software via file sharing or hard-copying and unauthorized use of the licensed material.

For information regarding the change in Napster's terms of use due to this litigation, please visit Napster's terms page at: www.napster.com/terms.html (last updated June 2017 as of this writing).

It is this fuzzy concept of "almost" getting what the parties bargained for that causes problems of determining what constitutes materiality in a breach. RESTATEMENT (SECOND) OF CONTRACTS § 241 best explains the factors in determining whether a failure of performance is material. They are

(a) the extent to which the injured party will be **deprived of the benefit which he reasonably expected**;

(b) the extent to which the injured party can be **adequately compensated** for the part of that benefit of which he will be deprived;

(c) the extent to which the party failing to perform or to offer to perform will suffer **forfeiture**;

(d) the likelihood that the party failing to perform or to offer to perform **will cure** his failure, taking account of all the circumstances including any reasonable assurances;

(e) the extent to which the behavior of the party failing to perform or to offer to perform comports with **standards of good faith and fair dealing**.

Fortunately, contract law does act consistently and these factors are looked at **objectively**, rather than by the subjective response of the aggrieved party, who is likely to interpret the consequences of the breach more severely. The doctrine of **substantial compliance** covers instances where the performance was not perfect; however, when examined objectively, using the above factors, it appears that the party endeavored to perform to the best of his or her ability and the performance was very close to compliance with the contract specifications. The court will most likely then hold that there was no breach because the party substantially complied with the terms of the contract. Perhaps one of the oldest lawsuits over materiality of the nonconformity of performance and substantial compliance involved Leonardo da Vinci. The Confraternity of the Immaculate Conception commissioned Leonardo to paint an altarpiece of the Virgin Mary in 1483. There were very detailed specifications written into the contract including coloring, style, and various details regarding symbolism to be included. It has been speculated for a long time that they sued him when he took longer than the contract called for and that he failed to meet the full approval of the Confraternity. The proceedings lasted for 10 years; eventually Leonardo created another painting. The original from the mid 1480s hangs

deprived of expected benefit
A party can reasonably expect to receive that for which he bargained; if he does not receive it, the breach is considered material.

adequate compensation
A party denied the benefit of his bargain may be paid or otherwise put in a position equivalent to where he would have been had performance been in compliance with the contractual terms.

forfeiture
An unreasonable loss.

ability to cure
A breaching party may be able to fix the defective performance.

standards of good faith and fair dealing
A party's performance will be judged in light of the normal or acceptable behavior displayed generally by others in a similar position.

objective
Impartial and disinterested in the outcome of the dispute.

substantial compliance
A legal doctrine that permits close approximations of perfect performance to satisfy the contractual terms.

in the Louvre in Paris; the second, which dates at about 1508, in the National Gallery in London.

As always, contract law also will heed the **intent of the parties'** terms in the contract itself. If the parties have specified the conditions that will be mutually considered a material breach of contract, the contractual provision prevails even if the court would have determined that the breach was not material.

After a material breach has occurred, the non-breaching party is **excused from performance**. It is only the non-breaching party that can sue on the breach regardless whether the breaching party suffers damages from the non-breaching party's nonperformance. A material breach is considered a **total breach**, even though not every term of the contract may have been breached. Totality refers to the impact it has on the entire contract. A total or material breach renders the rest of the contract inert.

If the breach is not material, then the non-breaching party is not excused from performance. A nonmaterial breach is also considered a **partial breach**; it does not affect the remainder of the contract terms and conditions. The remainder of the contractual obligations can still be carried out with little effect on the end result. That party must carry through with his or her contractual obligations as if no breach had occurred. However, the non-breaching party has recourse to sue for the damages incurred due to the nonmaterial breach.

intent of the parties
Almost always the controlling factor in determining the terms and performance of an agreement.

excused from performance
The non-breaching party is released from her obligations to perform due to the other party's breach.

total breach
A failure of performance that has a substantial effect on the expectations of the parties.

partial breach
A failure of performance that has little, if any, effect on the expectations of the parties.

CRYPTO CONTRACTS

By now, you, the reader, should be familiar with the principles underlying "smart contracts" and the basics of how the blockchain works in this context. However, what we have been dealing with in this chapter on breach has a lot to do with interpretation and flexibility in performance; these two concepts are foreign to the language of the blockchain. So here, the technology lets us down. As the computer code is really a set of "if-then" commands, there is also a binary result in enforcement and performance. Either the contract is fulfilled or there is a breach. There is no room for standards of good faith and fair dealing or substantial compliance as these are subject to a case-by-case review. So, are smart contracts always a smart idea when complex agreements are entered into? Are they always suited to the parties and their personal or business tolerance for flexibility and performance being "good enough"? *See generally* Jeremy Sklaroff, *Smart Contracts and the Cost of Inflexibility*, 166 U. Pa. L. Rev. 263 (2017).

SPOT THE ISSUE!

Ned and Nina Newlywed enter into a construction contract with Bob the Builder for the construction of a new center-hall colonial-style home on a five-acre lot for $500,000. The work will be completed by June 15th. As with every building contract, some difficulties arise. First, the lot was resurveyed and found not to be five acres; the lot actually measured 4.75 acres. Second, Bob was not able to obtain the building permit but broke ground anyway so that he would not get behind schedule. Third, keeping in character with the surrounding houses, Bob decides to build a craftsman-style bungalow, but the house still has the same square footage. Fourth, Bob obtains, at great expense, the Canadian cedar shakes for the exterior of the house as per the Newlyweds' specifications.

On July 1st, Bob reveals the house to the Newlyweds, who have been away for the entire time on their honeymoon in Paris. The Newlyweds are, needless to say, "surprised" at the appearance of their new home. What if the Newlyweds had called on May 30th from Paris to say that they were never going to return?

As the judge in this matter, how would you analyze the materiality of these "difficulties"?

A traditional example illustrating the difference between material and non-material breach is a construction contract. On January 2nd, after recovering from the New Year's Eve party, Bob the Builder agrees to remodel Ned and Nina Newlywed's kitchen by April 1st for $50,000. The basic terms are that the kitchen will be entirely reconfigured, giving them a different layout and more space, with maple cabinetry and modern, commercial-style appliances. Referring back to the RESTATEMENT's factors:

1. Simply refacing the existing cabinets is a material breach as the Newlyweds are *deprived of the benefit that they reasonably expected.* Additionally, project delays of one month may not be material—inconvenient, yes, but not material. However, delays of four months are material— after all, that doubles the time frame that the Newlyweds are without a kitchen. Whether or not an expectation is *reasonable* is an objective standard used by the courts on a case-by-case basis.

2. Building a center workstation topped with high-grade butcher-block that measures 9.5 square feet instead of 10 is not a material breach as the Newlyweds *can be adequately compensated for the part of that benefit of which they will be deprived.* If the workstation is valued at $200 per square foot, then the deprivation of one-half of a square foot is $100, which Bob will have to pay as damage. Again, the adequacy of the compensation is measured objectively. If Nina is an obsessive-compulsive perfectionist and is fixated on the fact that she has one-half square foot less of counter space and she personally feels that no amount of money can make up for this loss, the court will disregard her personal eccentricity and look at what the standard would be for *adequate* compensation. It is not judged by the individual's standard.

3. Bob fails to install maple cabinetry, instead putting in birch (which is very similar in appearance and other characteristics). This failure will not be treated as a material breach as Bob would suffer *forfeiture* if this

alternate installation were not accepted. Since Bob has already installed and paid his supplier for these cabinets, he needs to collect the purchase price from the Newlyweds in order to complete the transaction. The Newlyweds are retaining the benefit of the installation and should not be allowed to do so without paying for it. To permit this would make Bob suffer forfeiture. He has forfeited his expected benefit—the money for the cabinets and their installation.

4. Bob incorrectly installs dark mahogany cabinets (very different in appearance and other characteristics). However, despite this potentially material breach, Bob assures the Newlyweds that he will order and install the maple cabinets. This breach is not material because there is a likelihood *that the party failing to perform or failing to offer to perform will cure his failure.* The idea of *cure* is "making good" on the promise. The desire to satisfy the customer (non-breaching party) elicits another promise in furtherance of the originally promised performance. Bob's promise to fix his mistake "cures" his nonconforming performance (installing dark mahogany cabinets). This further promise to cure must be objectively likely to occur. Vague assurances or empty promises without real intention of following through with them are not cures.

5. Bob installs King appliances instead of Emperor because Emperor has discontinued manufacturing residential appliances. King and Emperor appliances look very similar and have the same performance ratings and warranties. This breach is not a material failure if Bob's substitution *comports with standards of good faith and fair dealing.* This is measured by what other contractors would have done in the same situation. If this is a standard practice, then Bob's substitution was reasonable and nonmaterial.

RESEARCH THIS

In your jurisdiction, find a case regarding materiality involving a contractor's nonconforming performance on a construction/building contract. How did the court determine whether the performance and potential breach of the contractor was material or not? What factual differences do you think would have resulted in the opposite outcome?

EYE ON ETHICS

Attorneys essentially are running a business; therefore, they need to enter into many different kinds of contracts. Already we have had our eye on attorney-client relationships, but what about attorney-attorney relationships and how they affect legal services rendered to the client? Attorneys, when in breach of contract, also may be in breach of the Rules of Professional Responsibility.

Read and discuss this potential "double-whammy" in an excerpt from *Davies v. Grauer*, 684 N.E.2d 924 (Ill. App. 1st Dist. 1997):

> Plaintiff, attorney William T. Davies (Davies), filed suit against defendant, attorney Paul W. Grauer (Grauer), seeking one-half of the attorney fees Grauer received in connection with two oral joint venture agreements between Davies and Grauer. Grauer moved for summary judgment pursuant to section 2-1005 of the Code of Civil Procedure (735 ILCS 5/2-1005 (West 1992)), on the ground that the oral joint venture agreements were unenforceable. Grauer argued that the two oral joint venture agreements violated Rule 2-107 of the Illinois Code of Professional Responsibility, entitled "Division of Fees Among Lawyers." The trial court granted Grauer's motion for summary judgment, from which Davies appeals.
>
> We reverse and remand.

BACKGROUND

Davies is an attorney licensed to practice in the State of Illinois. As a sole practitioner, Davies' general practice includes divorce, real estate and criminal cases, with 20% of his practice devoted to personal injury matters. In 1985, Davies and Grauer entered into two oral joint venture agreements to represent Norman Rosser and John Metz in their respective personal injury suits.

An instructive case is *Phillips v. Joyce*, 169 Ill. App. 3d 520, 120 Ill. Dec. 22, 523 N.E.2d 933 (1988). In *Phillips*, the court, in upholding a fee-splitting agreement, made an extensive analysis of the development of Disciplinary Rule 2-107 of the Illinois Code of Professional Responsibility, entitled "Division of Fees Among Lawyers." 107 Ill. 2d R. 2-107. In deciding the case, the *Phillips* court wrote:

> "To determine which agreements violate the canons of ethics, then, we must consider the underlying policy considerations and the harm to be avoided by the particular disciplinary rule.
>
> Disciplinary Rule 2-107 aims to preserve the fiduciary relationship between a client and his attorney through disclosure of fee-sharing arrangements, thereby leading to greater accountability. In addition, the rule contains a proportionality concept, which can be viewed as protecting the client from unearned or excessive fees. Requiring a relationship between the fee claimed and services or responsibility assumed also ensures that the attorney will have the incentive to use his best efforts to resolve the case.
>
> It is readily apparent that DR 2-107 mandates disclosure to the client whenever his attorney enters into an agreement with another attorney to share fees and responsibility for the legal matters entrusted to the first attorney. Hence, the client's right to be represented by the attorney of his choosing is preserved. No attorney whom the client has not retained will be entitled to payment from the client via a secret deal with the client's

attorney. Instead, the client must consent in writing to the shared fee and shared responsibility.

* * *

We believe, however, that a standard of substantial compliance is preferable because it comports with practical realities. In fact, such a standard is consonant with the Illinois Supreme Court's opinion in *Kravis v. Smith Marine, Inc.* and other cases that have considered the scope of the disclosure requirement. One court, faced with a similar question involving the disclosure of a fee-sharing agreement to a client, found that the client presumably knew of the arrangement, if not the details, stating, 'This method of dealing admittedly may not strictly comport with the guidelines of section DR 2-107 of the Code of Professional Responsibility, but it certainly does not fall far from this section's ethical parameters.' *Carter v. Katz, Shandell, Katz and Erasmous* (1983), 465 N.Y.S.2d 991, 997, 120 Misc. 2d 1009, 1015 (construing ABA version of the disciplinary rule)." *Phillips*, 169 Ill. App. 3d at 529-31, 120 Ill. Dec. 22, 523 N.E.2d 933. [Emphasis omitted.]

In the instant case, we believe that the admitted facts establish that the disclosures made to Rosser and Metz constitute substantial compliance with Rule 2-107. Such a standard of substantial compliance is consonant with *Phillips*, 169 Ill. App. 3d 520, 120 Ill. Dec. 22, 523 N.E.2d 933, and also with the Illinois Supreme Court's opinion in *Kravis v. Smith Marine, Inc.*, 60 Ill. 2d 141, 324 N.E.2d 417 (1975).

In the instant case, oral disclosures were made to both Rosser and Metz regarding the fee-sharing arrangement between Davies and Grauer. Further, both Rosser and Metz retained Davies as their attorney, not Grauer, in the first instance. In Metz's sworn affidavit, he stated that he knew Davies and Grauer were to split the attorney fees equally and that, when he signed the contingent fee agreement, he thought Davies was included because he assumed the word "associates" in "Paul Grauer & Associates" included Davies. Rosser, in his sworn affidavit, also admitted to knowing that Davies and Grauer would split the fees. We believe both Rosser and Metz had sufficient information regarding the fee-sharing agreement between Davies and Grauer to be fully protected under Disciplinary Rule 2-107 and that the aims of Disciplinary Rule 2-107 have been fulfilled.

In our view, Illinois public policy cannot reward Grauer's alleged misconduct in this case. Both Rosser and Metz affirmed that they had retained Davies and that they knew that Davies and Grauer would split the attorney fees. Grauer admitted for the purpose of his summary judgment motion that he entered into both oral joint venture agreements and that he was to draft the attorney-client agreement disclosing joint representation. However, Grauer admitted that he failed to draft the agreement. Grauer further admitted that he did not include Davies in the attorney-client agreements that Rosser and Metz signed, which he was required to do under the oral fee-sharing agreement. Accordingly, in the instant case, Grauer cannot invoke Disciplinary Rule 2-107 as a shield against living up to an allegedly substantively unobjectionable contractual arrangement with Davies.

DIVISIBILITY

In an attempt to salvage what it can from a potential breach, contract law has fashioned the idea of **divisibility**, also known as **severability**. A contract often covers a series of transactions between the parties. If these transactions can be separated from each other, the contract is considered to be divisible. In this way, the breach is only partial and contained to that part of the contract; the rest of the contract can go on as if nothing happened.

Typically this occurs in lease agreements; an annual rental for an apartment can be broken into 12 individual contracts. Nonpayment of one month's rent is a material breach of that month's obligation to pay, but it does not destroy the entire lease.

Other kinds of contracts are found to be divisible—severed into their component parts. The court looks at the intention of the parties with respect to the divisibility of the contract. The fact that the subject matter can be divided up is not the issue. Usually, a party agrees to take on an obligation to the other party after one party has performed on that divisible part. It is like the theory in physics that says every action has an equal and opposite reaction. In the lease example, after each month's rent payment, the landlord agrees to furnish the tenant with adequate shelter and amenities. Further, both the tenant and landlord (usually) do not intend for a late or nonpayment of rent in one month to result in immediate eviction (termination of the contract for material breach).

This *intention of the parties* is controlling. Generally speaking, courts disfavor dividing contracts; the presumption is that the parties created one cohesive contract. Even where a contract is easily divisible, the parties may have intended a complete and single transaction. For example, installment payments during the construction of a home do not make it divisible. The contract calls for an entire house, not parts, and the progress payments are not based on the value of work done during that period, but rather reflect a periodic payment schedule and nothing more. For example, in *Four Parks Conservation Trust v. Bianco*, 892 A.2d 258, 260 (Vt. 2006), the lease agreement provided that the tenant would maintain the easement "*at all times*" across the landlord's property to access the leased portion. While this was a separate obligation from paying rent, it was inexorably linked to the lease. Once the lease was terminated, the former tenant had no further obligation to maintain the easement for "*all time.*" Despite the separateness of the performance obligations, the parties did not intend for the easement obligation to survive the lease agreement.

In complex divorce settlements, there are many issues that must be addressed. These contracts can be held to be severable where *separate assent* is needed for each element of the settlement agreement. The parties come to an agreement regarding alimony, child support, division of real and personal

divisibility/severability
A contract may be able to be compartmentalized into separate parts and be seen as a series of independent transactions between the parties.

property, insurance, retirement assets, and many others. If one of these elements is held to be invalid, the remaining elements are left intact. The offensive clause is struck, and the remainder of the agreement continues in full force and effect.

SPOT THE ISSUE!

The local children's hospital entered into an agreement with Dr. Berry, a well-known pediatrician. The contract provided that Dr. Berry would reimburse the hospital for the money advanced to him for relocation and other costs. Dr. Berry would pay an amount equal to whatever income exceeded his set salary and expenses each month. This amount would vary depending on the billing activity for each month. Dr. Berry failed to make a payment in June and July despite having income that exceeded the specified amount. Is Dr. Berry in total breach of the contract?

See *Carswell v. Oconee Regional Medical Center, Inc.*, 605 S.E.2d 879 (Ga. App. 2004).

WAIVER

waiver
A party may knowingly and intentionally forgive the other party's breach and continue her performance obligations under the contract.

Despite all the problems and heartaches that may plague the course of performance on a contract, including a potentially fatal material breach, a party may choose to carry on as if the contract were in full force and effect. This **waiver** of the breach may take the form of words or actions on the part of the non-breaching party. The effect that this waiver has is to excuse the performance of the breaching party—as if the "innocent" party says, "that's OK; I'll finish my part of the bargain anyway." Of course, this means that the waiving party must *know* of the breach in order to *intentionally* waive it. A breaching party cannot benefit from his concealment of the breach in order to induce the non-breaching party to continue with her part of the performance. Compare the two following scenarios:

Julie designs fine jewelry and enters into a contract with Main Street Store to sell her jewelry exclusively. Julie will supply the store with inventory and the store will only sell her jewelry and give her 50 percent of the profits from those sales. The store, in breach of this agreement, also begins to sell Carla's costume jewelry. Julie discovers this breach one day as she visits the store; however, Julie's pieces are selling well and even some of the customers buying Carla's jewelry are also buying Julie's. Julie says nothing about it during her visit, nor during any of her other visits. By knowing about this nonconforming performance and voluntarily acquiescing to the breach, Julie has waived her rights with respect to enforcing the exclusivity of the contract at a later date.

Same agreement as above, however, the store hastily stashes all of Carla's jewelry away when Julie comes to visit the store. Julie has no way of knowing about the nonconforming sales of Carla's jewelry, so, by saying nothing about it at her visit, there can be no waiver. The store is in breach and continues to be in breach. The breaching party cannot hide the evidence and then claim that Julie waived her rights with respect to the store's sales of Carla's jewelry. It must be a **knowing and intentional** acquiescence in order to operate as a waiver.

knowing and intentional
A party must be aware of and plan on the outcome of his words or actions in order to be held accountable for the result.

After all this has been said, it may appear that the waiving party is playing "Mr. Nice Guy" and has nothing to show for his performance on a "breached" contract. However, the waiving party does not waive the right to pursue a contractual remedy after performance. The aggrieved party still has the right to recover damages that flowed from the breach of the contract. The waiver only applies to the obligation for the aggrieved party to continue performance despite the breach by the other party. "In general, by accepting benefits under a contract with knowledge of a breach, the non-breaching party waives the breach; but mere efforts on the part of an innocent party to persuade the promisor, who repudiates his agreement, to reject that repudiation and proceed honorably in the performance of his agreement do not involve a waiver of the innocent party's right to avail himself of the breach after the efforts finally prove unsuccessful." *94th Aero Squadron of Memphis, Inc. v. Memphis-Shelby County Airport Authority*, 169 S.W.3d 627, 636 (Tenn. Ct. App. 2004).

Julie may be able to recover some losses incurred due to the breach of exclusivity if she could prove them with reasonable certainty.

Assume that Julie's waiver of the exclusivity agreement worked out well for her. With all of her profits from her jewelry sales, Julie decides to purchase a house. She contracts with Paul to purchase his vacation house on Sanibel Island off the west coast of Florida. After the home inspection report revealed that some work needed to be done on the roof, Julie decided to complete the work herself (with the help of a local handyman). Julie noticed some other work that she could get done prior to the closing date to make it easier to move in. She decided to add French doors to the patio and a new bay window, refinish the hardwood floors, and update the bathroom fixtures. Paul was not notified of these renovations to the home and had no way of knowing of them as he had ceased using the vacation home. At closing, Julie attempted to rescind the contract, stating that the house needed too many repairs and upgrades. This attempt at rescission of the contract would be ineffectual as Julie has taken actions that indicate her assent to the contract and further act as a waiver of any "defects" as she was treating the home as her own. In making these improvements, Julie essentially waived their defective nature. She did not ask Paul to fix them; she, of her own accord, with full knowledge of the situation, voluntarily and intentionally addressed them.

Waiver is akin to "speaking now or forever holding your peace." If a person lets the opportunity to bring up problems pass by, then she has waived her right to do so at a later time.

SPOT THE ISSUE!

The O'Haras contracted with Butler Builders for the construction of their new home. Midway through the construction, it was discovered that the house was built over an easement. This has serious implications for the O'Haras as they will not have clear marketable title. However, the O'Haras closed on the house believing that they would be in default of their construction loan and subject to foreclosure if they did not go through with the contract.

Did the O'Haras waive the defect(s) in Butler Builders' performance?
See Young v. Oak Leaf Builders, Inc., 626 S.E.2d 240 (Ga. App. 2006).

There are many considerations to be taken into account when determining whether a redressable breach has occurred. Breach is not merely a broken promise or imperfect performance. There must be some tangible and significant consequence of the breach and no excuse for the failure of the contractual requirements.

Summary

Nonconforming performance of contractual obligations is a *breach*. These breaches can be either *material* and total or minor and *partial*.

If a party positively and unequivocally states that she will not continue and tender the expected performance *before* the time when performance is due, this is *anticipatory repudiation*. The repudiation can be a written or verbal communication, a transfer of contractual rights that make performance impossible, or an action that indicates this intent to repudiate. The aggrieved party has an immediate right to sue based on this anticipatory repudiation, or may choose to cancel the contract, or may choose to continue with the contract and urge the repudiating party to reconsider and perform.

After the time for performance is due, a party may evaluate the tendered performance and, if it is not what she bargained for, the breach may be considered material. To determine the extent of the breach, there are five objective factors to consider:

1. *Deprivation of the benefit expected.*
2. *Adequacy of compensation.*
3. *Forfeiture.*
4. *Ability* or likelihood *of cure.*
5. *Good faith and fair dealing.*

If a breach is not material, the performing party may be found to be in *substantial compliance* and not in breach, or the breach may be partial and does not affect the remainder of the contract. The non-breaching party's remedies for the partial breach lie in compensation for the damages caused by the breach.

A breach may be segregated from the remainder of the contract in order to salvage the agreement. This is the theory of *divisibility* of contract. It is as if the segment that has been breached is quarantined from the rest so as not to spread the infection. The *intention of the parties* controls whether the contract can be divided.

Another method of saving contracts is to simply ignore the breach. In this circumstance, the non-breaching party has *waived* the effect of the breach insofar as the obligation to perform is concerned. It does not waive the ability to recover damages from that breach.

Key Terms

ability to cure
adequate assurances
adequate compensation
affirmative acts
anticipation
anticipatory repudiation
breach
cancel the contract
certainty
deprivation of the reasonably
    expected benefit
divisibility
excused from performance
forfeiture
ignore the repudiation

immediate right to commence a lawsuit
intent of parties
knowing and intentional
material
mere request for change
objective
partial breach
positive and unequivocal
retract the repudiation
severability
standards of good faith and fair dealing
substantial compliance
total breach
transfer of interest
waiver

Review Questions

MULTIPLE CHOICE

Choose the best answer(s) and please explain *why* you choose the answer(s).

1. Anticipatory repudiation is best described as
   a. Declaring the other party in default before performance is due.
   b. A doctrine that allows a party to commence a lawsuit before performance is due.
   c. A positive and unequivocal declaration of the intent to commence a lawsuit before performance is due.
   d. All of the above.

2. Once a party has repudiated the contract:
   a. The non-breaching party must notify the repudiator of acceptance of the breach.
   b. He cannot retract it.
   c. The non-breaching party may choose to ignore it.
   d. He must take an action inconsistent with his performance obligations.

3. A material breach
   a. Can never be cured.
   b. Deprives the non-breaching party of the benefit he expected.
   c. Must comport with the standard of good faith and fair dealing.
   d. Excuses the breaching party from the rest of his performance obligations.

EXPLAIN YOURSELF

All answers should be written in complete sentences. A simple "yes" or "no" is insufficient.

Use the following fact scenario to answer the subsequent questions.

On May 1st, Greg Grocer and Fred Farmer contract for the sale of apples, to be delivered on May 25th. Fred knows that Greg needs these apples for the May 30th apple festival and that Greg is a major sponsor of this event.

1. On May 15th, Fred informs Greg that he may not be able to deliver the apples on the 25th.
   a. Is this a breach?
   b. Is it material? Or minor?
   c. Is it an anticipatory repudiation? Why or why not?
   d. What actions can Greg take?

2. Assume that Fred sells most of his crop to Peter PieMaker on May 15th.
   a. Is this a breach?
   b. Is it material? Or minor?
   c. Is it an anticipatory repudiation? Why or why not?
   d. What actions can Greg take?

3. On May 15th, Fred asks Greg if he can move the delivery date to May 29th.
   a. Is this a breach?
   b. Is it material? Or minor?
   c. Is it an anticipatory repudiation? Why or why not?
   d. What actions can Greg take?

4. On May 20th, Fred unequivocally repudiates the contract, giving rise to Greg's claim for breach. Discuss the materiality of the breach in light of the five factors given by the RESTATEMENT.

"FAULTY PHRASES"

All of the following statements are FALSE; state why they are false and then rewrite them as true statements. Write a brief fact pattern that illustrates your answer.

1. A partial breach can never be considered material.

2. Notice of anticipatory repudiation must be in writing.

3. Materiality of the breach is determined by the subjective intent of the parties at the time they entered into the contract.

4. Once a party has repudiated a contract, the non-breaching party must commence a lawsuit or else they have waived the breach.

5. Waiver of a breach of contract cancels the performance obligations of the breaching party.

6. A contract must specifically state that it is divisible in order for a court to enforce its separate parts.

7. A party who is in substantial compliance with his performance obligations is also considered to have committed a partial breach.

8. The breaching party always has time to cure the defects in performance.

"WRITE" AWAY! PORTFOLIO ASSIGNMENT

Review the Druid and Carrie contract. Create a list of what you would consider material breaches of the contract and what would be considered as minor and potentially waivable. Construction is completed in phases of work (i.e., foundation, framing, roofing, dry-walling, finish carpentry, etc.). Draft an "Acceptance of Work" form on behalf of Druid that it would have Carrie sign in acknowledgment of substantial compliance for each phase of work.

Case in Point   MATERIALITY OF BREACH

966 P.2d 777
126 N.M. 69, 1998 -NMCA- 155
Michael FAMIGLIETTA and Frances FAMIGLIETTA, Husband and
Wife, Plaintiffs-Appellees/Cross-Appellants,
v.
IVIE-MILLER ENTERPRISES, INC., Defendant-Appellant/Cross-Appellee.
No. 17922.
Court of Appeals of New Mexico.
Aug. 19, 1998.
Certiorari Denied, No. 25, 361,
Oct. 13, 1998.

Page 779

Roger Moore, Law Office of Roger Moore, Albuquerque, for Appellees/Cross-Appellants.
Michael L. Danoff, Albuquerque, for Appellant/Cross-Appellee.

OPINION

FLORES, JUDGE.

¶ 1 This case involves the sale of a tortilla chip distributorship business. Michael and Frances Famiglietta (Sellers) entered into an agreement to sell the distributorship to Ivie-Miller Enterprises, Inc. (Buyer). Sellers filed a complaint against Buyer alleging that Buyer breached the contract by failing to pay installment payments due under the contract and promissory note that was executed at the time the business was purchased. Buyer answered and counterclaimed, arguing that Sellers were not entitled to recover under the contract because Michael Famiglietta (Famiglietta) breached the contract first. In addition, Buyer argued that Sellers were also liable for additional damages under alternate theories of breach of contract, negligent misrepresentation, fraudulent inducement, and prima facie tort. The trial court ruled that although Famiglietta breached the contract, the breach was not material. Therefore, the trial court ruled that Buyer was liable for the remaining balance due under the contract and promissory note. Buyer appeals the trial court's ruling. Sellers also cross-appeal, arguing

that the trial court should have awarded them attorney fees. For the reasons that follow, we affirm in part, reverse in part, and remand.

FACTUAL BACKGROUND

¶ 2 On January 29, 1993, the parties entered into a contract for the sale of a Mi Ranchito Mexican Food Products distributorship for $50,000 plus interest. Buyer agreed to pay Sellers an initial payment of $10,000 and the remaining $40,000 plus interest by three subsequent installment payments. The contract also provided that the agreement was contingent upon Famiglietta's obligation to remain with the distributorship for a period of five years in the capacity of sales. About eighteen months after the parties entered into the contract, Famiglietta left the distributorship.

¶ 3 Buyer's president, Bob Meek, testified that during his initial discussions concerning the purchase of the distributorship he told Famiglietta that he would only consider purchasing the business if Famiglietta remained with the business because Famiglietta had been in the business for many years, was good at the job, and knew the market. Mr. Meek also testified that it was important for Famiglietta to remain with the distributorship because he knew the store personnel, was an aggressive salesman, and was able to maintain display space in the stores.

¶ 4 Famiglietta testified that he was aware of his obligation to stay with the distributorship for five years. He also acknowledged that he did not fulfill his five-year obligation even though Buyer wanted him to remain with the business because of his experience and contacts in the business. Famiglietta also recognized that at the time the parties entered into the contract his agreement

Page 780

to remain with the distributorship for five years was a material part of the contract.

¶ 5 Famiglietta testified that he was contemplating opening his own bagel shop. He also testified that his relationship with Mr. Meek was good and he could just orally inform Buyer that he was leaving. Famiglietta first told Buyer that he was leaving the distributorship in June of 1994. Famiglietta testified that Mr. Meek said he understood, but was concerned about other employees taking over Famiglietta's routes.

¶ 6 Mr. Meek testified at trial that he did not agree to release Famiglietta from his five-year obligation and he informed Famiglietta that Famiglietta would be breaking the contract if he left. Mr. Meek further testified that from the time Famiglietta informed him of his desire to leave until he finally left on June 24, 1994, that Mr. Meek informed Famiglietta at least three times that Famiglietta would be breaking the contract by leaving the business. On the day that Famiglietta left, Mr. Meek testified that he told Famiglietta he would probably be hearing from Buyer's attorney. Famiglietta claimed, however, that Mr. Meek voiced no objections to Famiglietta's departure during their conversations in June of 1994. Famiglietta contended that if Buyer had objected he would have remained with the distributorship.

¶ 7 Less than six months later in December of 1994, Buyer's attorney sent a letter to Famiglietta informing him that his departure from the business was a breach of the contract and that the contract should be rescinded. Buyer's letter also offered to return the business to Famiglietta within 60 days. Famiglietta acknowledged receiving the letter but elected not to return to the business. Famiglietta also maintained that the December letter was the first time he was informed of Buyer's objections to Famiglietta's departure from the business.

¶ 8 Mr. Meek testified at trial that Famiglietta's absence from the distributorship caused a substantial decrease in business. In particular, Mr. Meek maintained that in Famiglietta's absence the distributorship's volume of business decreased and the distributorship suffered $10,000 in lost profits. Mr. Meek also claimed that the value of the distributorship dropped in value from $50,000 to $29,000. However, Mr. Meek also acknowledged that the distributorship realized a profit during the time that it was owned by Buyer. Mr. Meek also conceded on cross-examination that much of the loss of sales after Buyer purchased the distributorship was the result of individual corporate retailers' decisions to reduce or terminate the Mi Ranchito product line and that those decisions were not related to Famiglietta's departure from the distributorship. There was also evidence showing that declining sales were already occurring during the time that Famiglietta was working for the distributorship.

¶ 9 Because Buyer refused to pay any of the remaining installment payments due under the contract and promissory note, Sellers ultimately filed suit against Buyer to recover the remaining amounts due. Buyer answered, asserting several affirmative defenses and counterclaims. While the case was pending in the district court, Buyer attempted to sell the Ivie-Miller corporate assets, including the Mi Ranchito distributorship, to a third party. Although Sellers sought injunctive relief from the district court to stop the sale, ultimately Buyer was allowed to sell all of its corporate assets. At the hearing to resolve Sellers' request for injunctive relief, Mr. Meek indicated that the distributorship was valued at $29,000. However, at the time of trial, Mr. Meek testified that no value was attached to the distributorship when it was sold with the rest of the corporate assets. In any event, the trial court stated at trial that it would not consider the effect of the sale of the business in reaching its decision because Famiglietta did not present any evidence on the point.

¶ 10 After trial, the trial court ruled that although Famiglietta breached the contract by leaving the business before his five-year obligation expired, the breach was not material. The trial court's findings also focused on the fact that Buyer did not suffer any direct damage as a result of Famiglietta's breach. Therefore, the trial court ruled that Buyer was liable for the remaining amounts due under the contract and promissory note.

Page 781

The trial court also ruled that the parties were responsible for their own attorney fees.

DISCUSSION

I. BUYER'S RIGHT TO RESCIND THE CONTRACT

¶ 11 Buyer maintains that it should not be held liable for the outstanding balance due under the contract and promissory note because Famiglietta failed to fulfill his five-year obligation to work for the distributorship. In essence, Buyer argues that because of Famiglietta's conduct it should be entitled to rescind the contract. Buyer advances two theories in support of its claim for rescission.

A. Nonoccurrence of a Condition in the Contract

¶ 12 Buyer begins by arguing that the trial court unnecessarily focused on whether Famiglietta's breach of the contract was material. Instead, Buyer suggests that Famiglietta's five-year obligation under the contract was a condition precedent to Buyer's continued performance of its obligations under the contract. See *Western Commerce Bank v. Gillespie*, 108 N.M. 535, 538, 775 P.2d 737, 740 (1989) (right to repudiate contract if condition precedent not met). Because Buyer characterizes Famiglietta's five-year obligation as a condition precedent, Buyer contends that the materiality of the five-year obligation was irrelevant. See generally E. Allan Farnsworth, II Farnsworth on Contracts § 8.2, at 345 (1990) (parties are not restricted by any test of materiality with regard to conditions in contract) [hereinafter Farnsworth on Contracts].

¶ 13 We first note our hesitation to accept Buyer's characterization of Famiglietta's five-year obligation under the contract as a condition precedent. See *Western Commerce Bank*, 108 N.M. at 537, 775 P.2d at 739 (condition precedent generally is an event that must occur subsequent to formation of contract which must occur before there is right to immediate performance). Many commentators and courts have noted the difficulty in classifying a condition in a contract as precedent or subsequent. See, e.g., *K.L. Conwell Corp. v. City of Albuquerque*, 111 N.M. 125, 129-30, 802 P.2d 634, 638-39 (1990); Farnsworth on Contracts, supra, § 8.2, at 347-51; Restatement (Second) of Contracts § 224 cmt. e and § 230 cmt. a [hereinafter Restatement]. In any event, we need not address the substance of Buyer's arguments on this point because Buyer failed to adequately preserve the issue below. Following the bench trial in this matter, Buyer's requested findings and conclusions framed the question for the trial court as one of material breach. Only after the trial court issued its findings and conclusions to the effect that Famiglietta's breach was not material did Buyer raise the notion that Famiglietta's five-year obligation was a condition of the contract unaffected by considerations of materiality. Indeed, Buyer did not even begin using condition-precedent terminology until the matter was briefed in this Court. Under these circumstances, we will not review Buyer's argument on appeal that the materiality of Famiglietta's breach was irrelevant. See *Cox v. Cox*, 108 N.M. 598, 602-603, 775 P.2d 1315, 1319-20 (Ct. App. 1989) (where party's requested findings asked court to award alimony, party cannot challenge award of alimony on appeal but is limited to challenging amount of alimony); *Platero v. Jones*, 83 N.M. 261, 262, 490 P.2d 1234, 1235 (Ct. App. 1971) (party cannot complain about findings he requested); see also *American Bank of Commerce v. United States Fidelity and Guar. Co.*, 85 N.M. 478, 478, 513 P.2d 1260, 1260 (1973) (party cannot change theory on appeal where alternate theories were not raised in trial court until submitted in requested findings three months after trial).

B. Uncured Material Breach

¶ 14 Buyer also argues that if Famiglietta's five-year obligation simply was a promise in the contract, the uncured breach of that promise relieved Buyer of any further obligations under the contract. We agree that if Famiglietta committed a material breach of the contract which remained uncured, Buyer was not required to perform its remaining obligations under the contract. See generally Farnsworth on Contracts, supra, § 8.18; see also *Horton v. Horton*, 487 S.E.2d 200, 204 (Va.1997) (material breach excuses nonbreaching party from performing his contractual obligations); *Ervin Constr. Co. v. Van*

Page 782

Orden, 125 Idaho 695, 874 P.2d 506, 511 (Idaho 1993) (rescission available when party commits material breach which destroys purpose of contract).

¶ 15 Here, the district court found that Famiglietta's breach did not cause Buyer any direct monetary damage. However, the existence or extent of monetary damage caused by a breach of contract is not necessarily dispositive of the question of materiality. See *Horton*, 487 S.E.2d at 204 (proof of specific amount of monetary damages not required when "breach was so central to the parties' agreement that it defeated an essential purpose of the contract"); *J.P. Stravens Planning Assocs., Inc. v. City of Wallace*, 129 Idaho 542, 928 P.2d 46, 49 (Idaho Ct. App. 1996) (where nonbreaching party seeks to be relieved of his obligations under the contract he must prove that breach was material but need not prove damages or amount of damages); *cf. Eldin v. Farmers Alliance Mut. Ins. Co.*, 119 N.M. 370, 379, 890 P.2d 823, 832 (Ct. App. 1994) (Hartz, J., dissenting in part and concurring in part) (materiality depends on potential for breach to cause prejudice but does not require proof prejudice actually occurred).

¶ 16 Although we believe the district court incorrectly analyzed the question of materiality, we recognize that New Mexico case law provides very little guidance on the subject. For example, the few New Mexico cases which discuss the materiality of a breach have focused on the facts of the particular case and have not provided general guidance on how materiality should be determined. See, e.g., *Montgomery v. Cook*, 76 N.M. 199, 204-05, 413 P.2d 477, 481 (1966); *Winrock Inn Co. v. Prudential Ins. Co.*, 1996-NMCA-113 p 28, 122 N.M. 562, 928 P.2d 947. Understandably, the fact-specific nature of our case law is driven by the reality that the materiality of a breach is a specific question of fact. See *Lukoski v. Sandia Indian Management Co.*, 106 N.M. 664, 665, 748 P.2d 507, 508 (1988). But the district court's decision was flawed because it focused solely on the lack of direct damage flowing from the breach without considering other factors that are relevant to the question of materiality.

¶ 17 The challenge presented by this case is to determine what constitutes a material breach of contract. Some courts have described a material breach as the "failure to do something that is so fundamental to the contract that the failure to perform that obligation defeats an essential purpose of the contract." *Horton*, 487 S.E.2d at 204. Put another way, a material breach "is one which touches the fundamental purpose of the contract and defeats the object of the parties in entering into the contract." *Ervin Constr. Co.*, 874 P.2d at 510. Other courts have noted that a material breach occurs when there is a breach of " 'an essential and inducing feature of the contract[ ].' " *Lease-It, Inc. v. Massachusetts Port Auth.*, 33 Mass. App. Ct. 391, 600 N.E.2d 599, 602 (Mass. App. Ct. 1992) (quoting *Bucholz v. Green Bros. Co.*, 272 Mass. 49, 172 N.E. 101, 102 (Mass. 1930)).

¶ 18 The Restatement also provides a useful framework for analyzing whether a breach of contract is material. In particular, the Restatement sets forth five factors that courts should consider when deciding the materiality of a breach of contract. See Restatement, supra, § 241. One factor to examine is the extent to which the injured party will be deprived of the benefit he or she reasonably expected to receive from the contract. Another factor considers the extent to which the breaching party will suffer forfeiture if the breach is deemed material. Courts should also explore whether the injured party can be adequately compensated in damages for the breach. A fourth factor focuses on the likelihood that the breaching party will cure his or her failure to perform under the contract. And the fifth factor evaluates whether the breaching party's conduct comported with the standards of good faith and fair dealing.

1. Buyer Was Deprived of a Significant Benefit It Reasonably Expected to Receive Under the Contract

¶ 19 Buyer argues that the contract unambiguously demonstrates that Famiglietta's promise to work for the distributorship for five years was a key reason why Buyer decided to buy the distributorship. Sellers

Page 783

do not dispute the unambiguous nature of the contract. See *Nearburg v. Yates Petroleum Corp.*, 1997-NMCA-069, pp 7 & 8, 123 N.M. 526, 943 P.2d 560 (where parties do not argue that agreement is ambiguous appellate court may interpret agreement de novo as a question of law). Indeed, the contract language agreed to by the parties plainly states that the purchase of the distributorship was contingent upon Famiglietta's fulfillment of the five-year term. Under those circumstances, there is little doubt that Buyer was deprived of a significant benefit that it reasonably expected to receive under the contract. The fact that Buyer may not have suffered any direct monetary damage as a result of Famiglietta's breach does not alter our conclusion. *Cf.* Restatement, supra, § 241 cmt. b (all relevant circumstances must be considered as there is no simple rule based on ratio of contract price to monetary loss).

2. Sellers' Forfeiture Under the Contract Can Be Minimized

¶ 20 As we discussed above, if a breach is found to be material, the nonbreaching party is entitled to rescind the contract and is relieved of its obligations under the contract. However, as a practical matter, if the nonbreaching party is relieved of all of its obligations under the contract, the breaching party may suffer the forfeiture of benefits it should otherwise receive under the contract in exchange for obligations he has already fulfilled. The Restatement recognizes this dilemma by encouraging courts to look at the extent to which the breaching party will suffer forfeiture if the breach is deemed material. See id. § 241 cmt. d. In this case, however, Famiglietta's forfeiture is minimized by the fact that Buyer has already paid about half of the amount contemplated under the contract. Moreover, Buyer attempted to return the distributorship to Sellers but they refused. Under those circumstances, we do not believe that Sellers' forfeiture is so extensive that the breach should not be considered material.

¶ 21 We recognize that Sellers challenge Buyer's right to retain and then sell the distributorship without having to pay the remaining installments contemplated by the contract or account for the profits and proceeds Buyer received from the operation and sale

of the business. See Restatement, supra, § 374 (party in breach is entitled to restitution for benefits he has conferred by way of part performance in excess of loss caused by breach). However, Sellers were unwilling to take back the business, and we agree that Buyer could properly sell the business in an effort to mitigate its damages. See *Elephant Butte Resort Marina, Inc. v. Wooldridge*, 102 N.M. 286, 292, 694 P.2d 1351, 1357 (1985) (nonbreaching party has duty to use reasonable diligence to mitigate damages). We also realize that Buyer contends it is entitled to recover the payments it has already made under the contract as part of its right to rescind the contract. However, Buyer's requested findings and conclusions did not seek this relief below. Therefore, this argument will not be considered on appeal. See *Woolwine v. Furr's, Inc.*, 106 N.M. 492, 496, 745 P.2d 717, 721 (Ct. App. 1987) (argument must be raised below to be considered on appeal).

3. Damages Will Not Compensate Buyer for Famiglietta's Breach

¶ 22 The district court's own findings demonstrate that it would be difficult if not impossible to compensate Buyer with damages for Famiglietta's breach. Buyer could not demonstrate actual monetary damages that were caused by Famiglietta's early departure from the distributorship. However, the contract itself demonstrates that Buyer was not solely concerned with the extent to which Famiglietta could maintain or increase the profitability of the distributorship. For example, Buyer agreed in the contract that even if business declined to the point that the distributorship would be forced to lay off personnel, Famiglietta would be the last one to remain with the business. This supports Buyer's claim that it relied on Famiglietta to work with the distributorship because of his experience and contacts with local markets irrespective of whether Famiglietta was able to increase or maintain the distributorship's profitability. In short, the trust and reliance that Buyer placed in Famiglietta's agreement to work with the business

Page 784

for five years is difficult if not impossible to value and compensate with monetary damages. *Cf.* Restatement, supra, § 241 cmt. c (difficulty of proving loss of benefit occasioned by breach affects adequacy of compensation).

4/5. Famiglietta Refused to Cure His Intentional Breach

¶ 23 The last two factors to consider under the Restatement approach also demonstrate the materiality of Famiglietta's breach. The record leaves no doubt that although Famiglietta acknowledged that he did not fulfill his five-year obligation under the contract, he had no intention of curing that breach. The record also reveals that Famiglietta ignored Buyer's warnings not to leave the business and refused Buyer's request to return to the business. And despite Sellers' unwillingness to take the business back, Sellers nevertheless attempted to prevent Buyer from selling the distributorship. Faced with Famiglietta's willful breach of the contract and his steadfast unwillingness to cure that breach, in combination with the other factors discussed above, we are compelled to hold that the breach was material.

¶ 24 We recognize that Famiglietta claimed he was not aware of Buyer's objections to his departure in June of 1994. However, the trial court apparently rejected this claim by rejecting Sellers' requested findings to the effect that Buyer waived or modified the five-year obligation by failing to object. See *Landskroner v. McClure*, 107 N.M. 773, 775, 765 P.2d 189, 191 (1988) (trial court's failure to make finding regarded as finding against party seeking to establish that fact). Moreover, Famiglietta's failure to return to the business after receiving the December letter also established Famiglietta's intentional, uncured breach of the contract. In short, the record in this case leads to one conclusion: Famiglietta's breach was material. As such, the district court erred by ruling that Buyer nevertheless was obligated to pay Famiglietta the remaining amounts due under the contract.

II. ADDITIONAL DAMAGES FOR FAMIGLIETTA'S BREACH OF CONTRACT

¶ 25 Buyer also maintains that he was entitled to additional damages that flowed from Famiglietta's breach of the contract in the form of lost profits. See *Camino Real Mobile Home Park Partnership v. Wolfe*, 119 N.M. 436, 443, 891 P.2d 1190, 1197 (1995) (party who breaches contract is "responsible for all damages flowing naturally from the breach"); *Shaeffer v. Kelton*, 95 N.M. 182, 187, 619 P.2d 1226, 1231 (1980) (damage awards should fully compensate injured party). However, as we noted above, Buyer's claim of lost profits resulting from Famiglietta's departure was contradicted by other evidence in the record. In light of these conflicts in the evidence, we affirm the district court's refusal to award Buyer damages for Famiglietta's breach. See *Zemke v. Zemke*, 116 N.M. 114, 118, 860 P.2d 756, 760 (Ct. App. 1993) (when there is conflicting evidence, appellate court views evidence in light most favorable to support the judgment).

III. BUYER'S ALTERNATIVE THEORIES OF RECOVERY

¶ 26 Buyer suggests that it still should be allowed to recover damages from Famiglietta under Buyer's alternative theories of recovery for fraudulent inducement or negligent misrepresentation. However, Buyer failed to summarize in its brief any of the evidence that may have been relevant to its tort claims. Therefore, we decline to address these arguments on appeal. See *Martinez v. Southwest Landfills, Inc.*, 115 N.M. 181, 186, 848 P.2d 1108, 1113 (Ct. App. 1993) (appellate court will not consider sufficiency of the evidence issues where appellant fails to "include the substance of all the evidence bearing upon a proposition" in the brief in chief). Moreover, Famiglietta testified that at the time he entered into the contract with Buyer he was not planning to leave the business. Under our standard of review for these factual issues, this testimony alone would support the trial court's rejection of Buyer's claims for negligent misrepresentation and fraudulent inducement. See *Zemke*, 116 N.M. at 118, 860 P.2d at 760.

IV. ATTORNEY FEES

¶ 27 Buyer argues that because Famiglietta materially breached the contract,

Page 785

Buyer is entitled to attorney fees under the contract. We agree. The contract explicitly called for attorney fees upon default by either party. We also award attorney fees on appeal. See *Dennison v. Marlowe*, 108 N.M. 524, 526-27, 775 P.2d 726, 728-29 (1989) (contractual provision which authorizes award of attorney fees includes fees on appeal). Therefore, we remand this matter to the district court for a reconsideration of Buyer's claim for attorney fees, which should include an award of attorney fees for this appeal. We also necessarily reject the claim that Sellers raise for attorney fees in their cross-appeal.

CONCLUSION

¶ 28 We reverse the trial court's judgment holding Buyer liable for the remaining installment payments due under the contract. We affirm the trial court's judgment rejecting Buyer's claim for additional damages. We remand to the trial court for a determination of an appropriate attorney fee award for Buyer. Sellers' cross-appeal is affirmed.

¶ 29 IT IS SO ORDERED.

PICKARD and ARMIJO, JJ., concur.

Chapter 11

Excuse of Performance

Chapter Objectives

The student will be able to:

- Use vocabulary regarding excuse of performance properly.
- Discuss the theory behind excusing performance rather than declaring it a breach.
- Identify the objective standards used to determine whether an excuse for performance exists.
- Differentiate between impossibility of performance and impracticality of performance.
- Determine if the contract's purpose has become frustrated.
- Explain the difference between performance prevented and voluntary disablement.
- Evaluate whether a party's performance is excused due to insolvency.

This chapter will examine WHEN performance on a contract is "excused"—a party's nonperformance is not considered a breach—and WHAT those excuses for nonperformance are. While contract law prefers performance, either perfect or in substantial compliance, as the culmination of the agreement, there are times when events beyond either one or both parties' control occur and thereby relieve a party of her obligations to perform. These occurrences are not considered a breach, but rather this failure of performance is excused without fault. While there may not be an allocation of fault as in breach, there may be some damages for these failures for which a party is responsible. Akin to the adage that you "cannot get blood from a stone," you cannot get performance from a party where

1. The required performance is *impractical*.
2. The required performance is *impossible*.
3. The contract's *purpose is frustrated*.
4. Performance is *prevented* or there has been *voluntary disablement*.
5. A party has become *insolvent*.

All of these excuses reflect contract law's awareness of reality. Just as it is not reasonable to think that parties can act perfectly in their performance obligations, it is unreasonable to think that the circumstances surrounding them will remain constant or predictable.

IMPRACTICALITY

impracticality
An excuse for performance based upon uselessness or excessive cost of the act required under the contract.

excessive and unreasonable cost
A court will only consider excusing performance based on impracticality if the additional expense is extreme and disproportionate to the bargain.

Without contract law's sternly *objective* nature, this excuse for failure of performance would be a very gray area indeed. **Impracticality** as an excuse means that the obligations could only be fulfilled at **excessive and unreasonable cost**. This excessiveness and unreasonableness must be beyond what either party could have anticipated and therefore could not have considered as part of their bargain. The objectiveness is applied to the inability of the party to furnish the required performance. If no party in the same position could reasonably tender that performance, then the party is excused for impracticality. If, on the other hand, it is only that party for her own individual reasons who cannot perform, the excuse of impracticality does not apply. It is merely subjectively impractical in that instance.

Additionally, the court will consider whether either party assumed a risk with regard to the circumstance. Many commercial contracts either specifically address certain future events or conditions or these contracts are governed by the general practices in the trade. The circumstances creating the impracticality must not have been under the control of the party claiming this excuse. The courts have been strict in applying the excuse of impracticality, finding that even an OPEC oil embargo does not necessarily create impracticality. *See Eastern Air Lines, Inc. v. Gulf Oil Corp.*, 415 F. Supp. 429, 438 (S.D. Fla. 1975) (The doctrine of impracticality is not available when the circumstance creating the difficulty "is sufficiently foreshadowed at the time of contracting to be included among the business risks which are fairly to be regarded as part of the dickered terms, either consciously or as a matter of reasonable, commercial interpretation from the circumstances.").

Let's refer to Boston's Big Dig[1] as an example. The Massachusetts Turnpike Authority (MTA) contracted with Bechtel/Parsons Brinckerhoff (BPB) to construct a huge underground highway system to alleviate traffic congestion

---

[1]For more information on this fascinating project visit www.mass.gov/the-big-dig.

through the city. One of the most challenging feats of engineering was construction of highway tunnels under the existing highway and underneath the subway train tracks that would have to stay in use during the entire project! BPB's solution was to actually freeze the dirt so it wouldn't cave in as they pushed the tunnel sections through it. If it turned out that BPB could not construct this tunnel as planned due to inordinate, unforeseeable difficulties and astronomical increases in cost, then performance may have been excused due to impracticality.

The impracticality can arise either at the time the contract was made or at the time the performance is due. If the impracticality of performance was present at the time of making the contract, the party claiming it as an excuse for failing to perform must show that the circumstances making it impractical were unknown and unknowable at the time of contract. In the Big Dig example, if the proposed excavation would destroy an ancient Totant[2] Indian tribal ground and extensive modifications and relocations would have to be made to preserve the sanctity of the area pursuant to the laws of Massachusetts, the performance would be rendered impractical. This impracticality existed at the time of the making of the contract. Indeed, it existed for a long time prior to that! However, it is not something that the parties could have known at the time of contract; therefore, it is a viable excuse.

On the other hand, if the impracticality arises at the time when performance comes due, the party wishing to be excused must show that the circumstances have changed significantly and unforeseeably and these changes were beyond that party's control. These circumstances rendering the performance impractical must go to the essence of the contract. If, due to a natural disaster occurring after the making of the contract, the Big Dig simply could not be completed without an astronomical increase in cost, then performance has been rendered impractical. The parties could not have foreseen this natural disaster and it arose at the time performance became due.

One note with regard to changed circumstances: Most of us are aware that market conditions and financial status can be unstable. Therefore, a change in a party's finances or the market price for goods and services under a contract is not unforeseeable and therefore these financial strains are not generally considered a valid excuse. It may be costly and upsetting to perform, but it does not rise to contract law's requirement of **objective impracticality**.

objective impracticality
A party's performance is excused only when the circumstances surrounding the contract become so burdensome that any reasonable person in the same situation would excuse performance.

IMPOSSIBILITY

There are three instances where the capacity to perform rises beyond impracticality to **impossibility**:

1. *Death or incapacity of a party* (or other person needed to complete the performance).

impossibility
An excuse for performance based upon an absolute inability to perform the act required under the contract.

---

[2]A tribe associated with the area in and around modern Boston.

2. *Destruction of the subject matter* (or of a specific thing necessary for performance).
3. *Supervening illegality.*

Death or Incapacity of Party

death or incapacity of a party
An excuse for performance on a contract due to the inability of the party to fulfill his obligation.

The first excuse—**death or incapacity of a party**—may seem to be self-evident. However, the language of the contract or the type of contract may dictate otherwise. While most people do not like to consider their mortality while drawing up a contract, clauses indicating that the agreement will survive even though the parties do not are valid. The contract may provide for contingent performers to fulfill the original, but now deceased, party's obligations. Similarly, if it is determined that the contract is not "personal" in nature, meaning that only that party is capable or desirable to perform, then the contract can be carried out by the deceased's estate or personal representatives. The typical example in this scenario is a contract for the sale of real estate. It does not matter to the buyer that the seller is no longer alive. The estate is perfectly capable of transferring the real estate interest and, depending upon the terms of the contract, the estate indeed may be forced to transfer the real estate.

Recall our discussion of capacity; it relates to the capacity to perform as well. A person who has become mentally infirm is not required to perform unless and until the mental infirmity passes and the party regains capacity. Many cases revolve around insurance contracts in this regard. If a policy holder becomes physically or mentally disabled, he may not have the capacity to give the required notice of a disability claim under the policy. Failure to give such notice may result in forfeiture of the claim. Of course, the insurance company would like to avoid payment of the claim due to this technical difficulty; however,

[w]ere we to adopt the reasoning of [the insurance company] that an insured-beneficiary must show not only that it was not reasonably possible for him to give notice but that no one else could have acted for him, there would seldom be a case where the failure to give notice would be excused. An insured could probably see to the giving of notice of disability by calling a meeting of his acquaintances soon after taking out his policy and saying to them: "I have taken out a policy in the New York Life Insurance Company. If I become insane, some one of you must see that notice of such disability is furnished the company." Such conduct, however, would not be reasonable. When insanity overtakes an insured he is then in no state of mind to procure others to furnish the company with notice. In this respect mental incapacity differs from physical inability. If an insured were to appoint an agent to act for him in matters pertaining to his insurance, or in other respects, such agency would be terminated by his insanity. 2 C.J.S., Agency, page 1179, § 88. Upon what theory can the rights of this insured be forfeited or prejudiced by the failure to act of some third party who is under no legal or contractual right or obligation to act for him?

Levitt v. New York Life Ins. Co., 297 N.W. 888, 891-892 (Iowa 1941).

SPOT THE ISSUE!

Wilbur, an octogenarian, entered into a contract with the Out-to-Pasture Nursing Home. The contract provided that upon payment of $100,000 (the bulk of Wilbur's estate), Out-to-Pasture would take care of Wilbur for the rest of his life, providing shelter and all necessities. Wilbur paid the sum and Out-to-Pasture made the arrangements for his residence. However, two days before actually moving in, Wilbur passed away. The estate approaches your firm in an attempt to recover the money Wilbur paid, relying on the theory of impossibility due to Wilbur's death.

The senior attorney has asked you to review the contract and render your opinion as to the estate's claim of impossibility and recovery of the money. Are there any other possible defenses or excuses for performance available to the estate? *See Gold v. Salem Lutheran Home Ass'n of Bay Cities*, 347 P.2d 687 (Cal. 1959).

EYE ON ETHICS

Where an attorney has become incapacitated, the rules of professional responsibility require an attorney to withdraw from the representation—essentially, to terminate the contract. This is a mandatory withdrawal requirement where the physical or mental condition of the attorney has or will have a significant negative impact on the representation of the client. However, note that the Bar does not leave one of its own to fend for themselves in the face of such personal calamity. Every state has a "Lawyers Assistance Program" (LAP) in place where lawyers who are affected—either themselves or a colleague—can go for help. In 2017, the ABA Working Group to Advance Well-Being in the Legal Profession—Commission on Lawyer Assistance Programs presented its final report on these matters. The ABA adopted these findings and has redoubled its efforts along with the states' programs to address the ever-growing problem of incapacity due to physical and mental impairments caused by the stress of the legal profession. Find your state's LAP and learn about its work and available resources.

Destruction of Subject Matter

The second excuse under impossibility—**destruction of subject matter**—also seems obvious. One cannot perform the obligations of the contract if the very subject matter has been lost or destroyed. What this excuse assumes, however, is that the loss of the subject matter was not due to a foreseeable event that could have been avoided and/or the risk of loss could have been allocated in the contract. Even more important for the excuse element is that the loss was not due to the voluntary action of one of the parties. If a party has caused the

destruction of subject matter
Excuse of performance based upon the unforeseeable and unavoidable loss of the subject matter.

loss that makes performance impossible, then she cannot rely on impossibility as a defense. That would be a case of voluntary disablement, which will be discussed below.

After the collapse of two five-million-gallon water tanks, the court in *City of Littleton v. Employers Fire Ins. Co.*, 453 P.2d 810 (Colo. 1969), found that the structures were impossible to build and, therefore, relieved the contractor of the obligation to build them. In this case, the subject matter was not destroyed before performance. Rather, should performance be completed, the subject matter would still not come into existence because it would be destroyed. This "destruction" was due to an engineering fault that could not have been discovered prior to the contract. What is significant is the fact that the contractor did not and could not know of the impossibility of construction at the time of contract. The engineering defects were only discovered after construction was attempted. If the contractor knew or had reason to know at the time of making the contract that it would be impossible to construct the tanks as specified, then impossibility would be no defense to a breach of contract claim. Essentially, the contractor would have waived this defense. A person may contract to do what is considered or generally accepted as impossible in an attempt to prove that presumption wrong. However, by doing so, he has knowingly given up that as an excuse for nonperformance.

The distinction between a foreseeable event and a supervening (and excusable) cause of loss is a matter of fact for determination at trial. Two illustrative examples follow, one permitting impossibility and the other not.

Example

Rosie's Flower Shop contracts with Green Grower to purchase all her floral requirements for the upcoming season. Rosie will need a large quantity of roses for her signature arrangement and so advised Green Grower. Despite this, Grower changed his method of fertilization (without mentioning this to Rosie) and found it impossible to supply Rosie with all the roses she needed. *See, e.g., Alamance County Bd. of Educ. v. Bobby Murray Chevrolet, Inc.*, 465 S.E.2d 306 (N.C. App. 1996), *citing Canadian Industrial Alcohol Co. v Dunbar Molasses Co.*, 179 N.E. 383 (N.Y. 1932). This is not an excusable impossibility because Grower could have foreseen that the change in growing methods might cause a reduction in the flower crop.

Example

Same scenario as above, but Grower did not change his method of growing or fertilization from the previous seasons. A catastrophic infestation of a new strain of Japanese beetles invades all local rose growers. Green Grower and the other local flower nurseries could not have foreseen or prevented this infestation. Rosie will find it impossible to obtain the necessary amount of roses from Green Grower or anyone else. Green Grower is excused from his performance for impossibility.

This type of occurrence is also known as **force majeure**—*"an event or effect that can be neither anticipated nor controlled."* BLACK'S LAW DICTIONARY (8th ed. 2004). Many times these natural catastrophes are referred to as "acts of God." Unfortunately, due to the increasing effects of climate change, these catastrophic events are becoming more frequent and more severe. Although scientists can predict these increasing risks, parties are not charged with anticipating when, where, and how these events may, if at all, affect their transactions. While contract law has no preventative or mitigation measures, it can provide a legal remedy should such harm occur. Using the principle of freedom of contract, parties can insert a force majeure clause, which then allocates the risk of loss for any such occurrence. *See Ergon-West Va., Inc. v. Dynegy Mktg. & Trade*, 706 F.3d 419 (5th. Cir. 2013) (Hurricanes Katrina and Rita caused extensive damage to the gas industry's infrastructure and, therefore, suppliers invoked the force majeure clauses to protect themselves against the claims of the refineries and clearinghouses for the product.). Taking our example from before, Rosie, having been in the floral business for so many years, and knowing the risks of dealing with Mother Nature, inserts a typical force majeure clause into her contracts, which states:

> No party shall be liable for any failure to perform its obligations in connection with any action required by the Agreement, if such failure results from any act of God, riot, war, civil unrest, flood, earthquake, or other cause beyond such party's reasonable control.

force majeure
An event that is neither foreseeable nor preventable by either party that has a devastating effect on the performance obligations of the parties.

Supervening Illegality

A **supervening illegality** renders performance of a contract impossible because illegal contracts are unenforceable. In this circumstance, the subject matter of the contract was not illegal at the time of the making of the agreement, but in the time between acceptance and performance, the law itself changed. The change in the law made what was previously acceptable under the contract illegal. *Cinquegrano v. T. A. Clarke Motors*, 30 A.2d 859 (R.I. 1943) (During World War II, a governmental order banned all sales of new cars until a rationing scheme could be figured out. "When, as here, a supervening lawful order of domestic government makes performance under an existing contract illegal and the enforcement of such order for an unreasonable time admittedly interferes substantially with the expressed intention of the parties and renders impossible the performance of the terms of the original contract, a party who is not at fault is justified in demanding return of the purchase price he has paid thereunder.").

A much more recent situation has given rise to plenty of legal questions surrounding supplier contracts—that of supplying products and services in the cannabis industry. In those states where cannabis production and sales are legal, those businesses will also need a variety of supplies and professional services and some of those may come from attorneys. Are those contracts illegal because, technically, the production and sale of cannabis is still illegal

supervening illegality
A change in the law governing the subject matter of the contract that renders a previously legal and enforceable contract void and therefore excusable.

under the federal Controlled Substances Act? Further, if the attorney and/or firm is based in a state that still criminalizes cannabis, does that not only render the contract null, but also expose the attorney and/or firm to criminal liability as accessories? There is also the matter of the two federal money laundering statutes, 18 U.S.C.A. §§ 1956 and 1957, that make it illegal to conduct financial transactions (i.e., provide legal advice for the business and receive legal fees) with persons / companies that routinely deal in illegal activities. This gets really tricky for financial institutions. Most banks, even in states where cannabis is legal, will not open accounts for the producers. *See* Aaron Gregg, *How a Maryland Bank Is Quietly Solving the Marijuana Industry's Cash Problem*, Wash. Post (January 2, 2018).

For example, the Newlyweds contract with Bob to build them a new home on their one-acre lot. The home will cover 30 percent of the lot, which, at the time of entering into the agreement, was permissible under the local zoning ordinances. However, prior to the commencement of construction, the local zoning board passed a new ordinance that set the maximum lot coverage at 20 percent. The home cannot be constructed per the contract due to a supervening illegality.

CRYPTO CONTRACTS

01100
10110
11110

Given the nature of smart contracts and their immutability, how could a party ensure that the contract's subject matter would remain viable or legal? On the blockchain, matters are literally binary; there is no room for renegotiation or preservation of the agreement once a condition has failed. How would parties insert an enforceable force majeure clause? How could the code interpret impossibility or impracticability? A new condition such as intervening illegality could not be inserted into this unchangeable format, thereby permitting the potentially criminal transaction to remain in force.

SPOT THE ISSUE!

Roadies Corp. subcontracted with Ramps, Inc., for Ramps to construct entry and exit ramps for a highway project with the state. Unknown to Ramps, the state Highway Department placed a water main across the area and, unfortunately, during Ramps' work, it burst. Ramps was shut down. Further complications in the repair of the water main prevented Ramps from continuing work. It appears that Roadies knew about the state's plans but thought that the state would wait until the highway work was done. Who is at fault? Is Ramps able to avoid performance obligations? Why or why not?

EYE ON ETHICS

ETHICS

Attorneys have obligations for continuing legal education, most of which are mandated by the state in which they are licensed to practice. Failure to comply with the continuing legal education requirements may result in ethical sanctions. Part of this obligation means that they must keep up with the law to be aware of any supervening illegality that may affect their clients. An attorney has a duty to ensure that she has the pertinent current knowledge and skill required in her area of practice. Law is a constantly changing creature and clients are entitled to expect that their attorneys are responding appropriately to these changes. See Bruce E. Reinhart, *Dazed & Confused: Legal and Ethical Pitfalls in Marijuana Law*, ABA Crim. Just. Mag. (Winter 2017).

FRUSTRATION OF PURPOSE

Where both parties are able to perform on their contractual obligations, but due to changed circumstances it becomes useless for them to do so, a contract's purpose has been *frustrated*. There are some rather stringent requirements for applying the doctrine of **frustration of purpose**. The reason why the agreement was made in the first place must no longer exist; therefore, the value of the contract has become a nullity. The agreement simply just doesn't make sense anymore. It is not that the parties cannot perform; it is that there is absolutely no reason for them to perform. The changed circumstance cannot be one that was foreseeable or for which the risk of its occurrence was allocated to one party or the other.

frustration of purpose
Changes in the circumstances surrounding the contract may render the performance of the terms useless in relation to the reasons for entering into the contract.

For example, Sam Skywriter contracts with Harry's Hot Dogs to provide him with skywriting advertisement over the beach on the day of a big concert. Both Sam and Harry know that the advertising contract must be performed on that day; thousands of people will potentially see the ad and significantly boost Harry's sales. The day before the concert, the beach is closed due to water and sand contamination. Harry's purpose in contracting with Sam has been frustrated. No one will be at the beach that day to see the skywriting. Even though both Harry and Sam *could* perform their contractual obligations, there is *no reason* to go forward.

The purpose for entering into the contract must be known to the parties as well. If the party not seeking to avoid the contract has no reason to know why the other is entering into the contract, the excuse of frustration of purpose will not be available. Springing a surprise on the "innocent" party is not acceptable in the predicable world of contract law. The court in *Mel Frank Tool & Supply, Inc. v. Di-Chem Co.*, 580 N.W.2d 802 (Iowa 1998), determined that the lease of a storage and distribution building by a chemical company could not be terminated due to frustration of purpose when the city passed a new ordinance banning the storage of hazardous chemicals in that area. The change in circumstances only affected some of the company's chemicals that were stored there—not all. At the time the contract was formed, neither party made inquiries as to the suitability of the building for the storage of hazardous materials. The landlord had no knowledge that the tenant would be storing such materials.

Regarding the foreseeability or anticipation of the "frustrating" event, case law has clearly established a high bar for recognizing frustration of purpose. Where there has been *any* contemplation of even just a partial failure of the underlying purpose for the contract, there will be no excuse of obligations under the contract for frustration of purpose. In *Liggett Restaurant Group, Inc. v. City of Pontiac*, 676 N.W.2d 633 (Mich. App. 2004), a food purveyor entered into a contract with the city and the Silverdome (home of the Detroit Lions football team) to provide concession stand services during home games. The contract contemplated that there would be times when the Lions would not play the minimum of eight home games a season and therefore payments for the rental of the stadium space would be proportionally reduced. As it turned out, the Lions terminated their contract with the stadium and played *no* games there. The failure turned out to be complete but was not totally out of the realm of possibility under the terms of the agreement and, therefore, the court held that, while the purpose for the contract was known to both parties, it was not substantially frustrated by the cancellation of the Lions' games.

RESEARCH THIS

In your jurisdiction, find a case where the court excused a party from performance for either impracticality or frustration of purpose. Be sure to understand the reasoning. What factual differences do you think would have resulted in the opposite outcome—where the court would not have permitted the party to escape performance obligations?

SURF'S UP

"Click-wrap"/"shrink-wrap" and end-user license agreements for computer software are interesting creatures as they provide all the specific terms of the offer *after* acceptance. So, in reality, the consumer pays for the goods first and then, by clicking OK (or some variation of that) or unwrapping the cellophane-sealed software, assents to the conditions of sale or license after payment. How can there ever be a claim based on frustration of purpose in these arm's-length transactions? While the court in *Harris v. Blockbuster, Inc.*, 622 F. Supp. 2d 396 (N.D. Tex. 2009), based its decision on the existence of an illusory contract, it could also be argued that Harris' purpose in discretely ordering movies from Blockbuster online was frustrated by the company's practice of disseminating its customers' rental choices on their Facebook accounts through Facebook's "Beacon" program.

PERFORMANCE PREVENTED AND VOLUNTARY DISABLEMENT

In both these scenarios, one party inhibits the other from receiving the benefit of the bargain. A party may do something that either makes the other party's performance impossible or makes their own performance impossible.

A party may **prevent performance** either by an affirmative blockage of the other party's attempt to perform or by preventing a condition precedent to performance. Let's use the Newlyweds and Bob the Builder as an example again. The Newlyweds have a change of heart and do not want to clear their lot of all its trees. They have decided to become modern-day hippies and live with and in nature. As Bob pulls up in the bulldozer, they throw themselves in front of the old trees and refuse to move. Bob has been affirmatively prevented from starting construction. A second scenario: After signing the contract and paying the down payment, the Newlyweds never obtain the building permits (the lot owner's responsibility), so Bob cannot start work. His performance is prevented by the Newlyweds' failure to obtain the permits—a condition precedent to starting construction. *See, e.g., Stone Excavating, Inc. v. Newmark Homes, Inc.*, 2004 Ohio 4119 (Ohio App. 2004) (A paving contractor was unable to complete the asphalt sealing due to the developer's delay in construction; the developer could not then claim that the paving contractor did not complete the work on time.).

performance prevented
If a party takes steps to preclude the other party's performance, then the performance is excused due to that interference.

If the party prevents his own performance, it is **voluntary disablement**. The party puts himself in a position where he will be unable to perform according to the contract terms. It is not an occurrence outside of the control of that party. It is the aggrieved party that may choose to treat it as an anticipatory breach. It relieves (excuses) the aggrieved party from his obligation to perform. Intuitively, we know that one cannot transfer interest in land if one does not own it. Therefore, if Sam Seller agrees with Betty Buyer for the sale of 12 Main Street, Sam is contractually bound to transfer title to Betty. If Sam convinces Eva Interloper to purchase the property (for twice what Betty agreed to!), Sam has voluntarily disabled himself from being able to perform on the contract with Betty. It is Sam's own act that renders it impossible for him to transfer title to Betty. *See, e.g., LeTarte v. West Side Development, LLC*, 855 A.2d 505 (N.H. 2004) (A landscaping contractor entered into an agreement with a real estate developer wherein the developer would transfer ownership of one of the lots in the development in exchange for the landscaper's services. The developer then conveyed the specific lot to a third party. The developer voluntary disabled himself from the ability to convey that lot to the landscaper under the agreement.).

voluntary disablement
If a party takes steps to preclude his own performance, then the performance due from the other party is excused due to that refusal/inability to perform.

Additionally, **voluntary destruction** of the subject matter also constitutes voluntary disablement and the party will be held in breach of contract for his fault. The "innocent" party will be excused from performance obligations. In spite of an agreement for the sale of her valuable Ming vase, Marsha, in a fit of anger, grabs it and throws it to the floor, smashing it to a thousand pieces. The rare Ming vase cannot be easily replaced and, therefore,

voluntary destruction
If a party destroys the subject matter of the contract, thereby rendering performance impossible, the other party is excused from his performance obligations due to that termination.

the buyer can reasonably presume that Marsha, the seller, will be unable to complete the transaction. Of course, this is actionable as a breach of contract if the buyer has suffered any damages as a result of the loss of the benefit of the bargain.

IN-CLASS DISCUSSION

Very loosely based on *LaGarenne v. Ingber*, 273 A.D.2d 735, 710 N.Y.S.2d 425 (App. Div. 3d Dep't 2000).

Suppose the following situation is happening in the law office where you are employed as a paralegal:

Two of the lawyers, Oscar and Felix, enter into an agreement to purchase a large plot of land. They intend to subdivide the lot and Oscar agrees to front all the money; Felix will pay him back with his portion of the profits from the subsequent subdivided lot sales. Indeed, Felix already owed Oscar a substantial amount of money and he promised to use the profits to pay off that debt as well. The partners entered into a contract for sale of one of the parcels to ShopHere Mall. However, before that sale could be consummated, the partners received a notice that the state was taking part of the property to widen the road. This action of governmental taking of private property for public use is perfectly legitimate. Felix is looking to get out of the original agreement and the mall is looking to get out of the sales contract. Oscar comes to talk to you about the situation.

What excuses might the parties try to use and what is the likelihood of their success?

INSOLVENCY

insolvency
A party's inability to pay his debts, which may result in a declaration of bankruptcy and put all contractual obligations on hold or terminate them.

If a party declares bankruptcy (**insolvency**), everything that the defunct party has or is involved in is put on hold. The declaration of bankruptcy stops all transactions in their tracks in order to maintain the status quo until the resolution of the bankruptcy. Unlike the previously discussed "excuses" for nonperformance, bankruptcy is not automatically considered an anticipatory breach entitling the aggrieved party to avoid her own performance and to pursue appropriate remedies.

forfeiture
A loss caused by a party's inability to perform.

How can the aggrieved party know whether his performance obligations are excused or merely suspended? It must be determined whether the bankruptcy amounts to **forfeiture**—that party's unequivocal inability to perform. Courts do not favor a declaration of forfeiture and this determination must be made on a case-by-case basis; unfortunately, there is no clear-cut rule in this situation. Given the nature of the airline industry, one can imagine the number of contracts that have been called into question due to a declaration of bankruptcy. Each passenger has a contract in the form of a ticket; each employee, each supplier, the airports, and so forth, all have contracts with the airline that are affected by the airline's insolvency. Whether the passengers are able to cancel their bookings, whether the pilots and other employees can cease working, whether the fuel suppliers can cancel delivery—all of these may be an excuse of their performance due to the insolvency, but this is a matter for a court's determination.

On a final note, in many of the cases that come under the auspices of this chapter, relief may be based on other theories of recovery such as mistake. Additionally, you may notice that there may be several theories of recovery. In that event, the aggrieved party may choose the ground on which she will rely.

Summary

An aggrieved party may be released from the obligation to perform according to the terms of the contract if

1. The required performance is *impractical*. If, from an objective standpoint, the performance would require unforeseeable, *excessive and unreasonable cost* or a burden on a party, the performance may be excused.
2. The required performance is *impossible*. If a party has *died* or become otherwise *incapable* of performance, if the *subject matter has been destroyed*, or if the required *performance*, since the making of the contract, *has become illegal*, the performance may be excused.
3. The contract's purpose is *frustrated*. If the very reason for entering into the contract no longer exists, the performance may be excused.
4. *Performance is prevented* or there has been *voluntary disablement*. If a party either does something that makes the other party's performance impossible or that makes his own performance impossible, the "innocent" party's performance may be excused.
5. A party has become *insolvent*. If a party declares bankruptcy, the other party's performance may be excused.

Key Terms

death or incapacity of a party
destruction of subject matter
excessive and unreasonable cost
force majeure
forfeiture
frustration of purpose
impossibility

impracticality
insolvency
objective impracticality
performance prevented
supervening illegality
voluntary destruction
voluntary disablement

Review Questions

EXPLAIN YOURSELF

All answers should be written in complete sentences. A simple "yes" or "no" is insufficient.

Use the following fact scenario to answer the subsequent questions.

On May 1st, Greg Grocer and Fred Farmer contract for the sale of apples to be delivered on May 25th. Fred knows that Greg needs these apples for the May 30th apple festival and that Greg is a major sponsor of this event.

1. Fred's apple pickers go on strike and Fred cannot get anyone else to cross the picket line for less than triple the normal hourly rate. Can Fred get out of the contract? Why?

2. Sadly, Fred had to call Greg and report that something awful happened to his orchard and all the apples are ruined. Can Fred get out of the contract? Why?

3. Greg calls Fred and tells him that the apple festival has been canceled. Is there any impact on the contract? Why or why not?

4. Greg finds out that Fred has been sponsoring the local Democratic candidate. Greg, a staunch Republican, decides on a scheme to curtail the contributions and sets fire to the orchard. Aside from the arson charges, is there any impact on the contract? Why or why not?

5. Greg's business has been failing since the local Super-Duper Store has moved into town. On May 15th, he has no other choice but to declare bankruptcy.

WRITE

1. Create a fact scenario where you believe a court would find that performance on an agreement may be aggravating, but it does not rise to the level of impracticality. What additional factors would make a court determine that your situation was impractical?

2. Create a fact scenario where you believe a court would find the impracticality of the situation rose to such a level that it was deemed impossible.

"FAULTY PHRASES"

All of the following statements are FALSE; state why they are false and then rewrite them as true statements. Write a brief fact pattern that illustrates your answer.

1. There is no difference between impossibility and impracticability.

2. Courts will consider a party's viewpoint as to the impracticality of performance.

3. Courts will always enforce a contract no matter what the extra cost to the parties.

4. Death of a party always releases the parties from obligations under the doctrine of impossibility.

5. All natural occurrences fall under the theory of "force majeure."

6. Parties can simply walk away from a contract if they become frustrated.

7. Both prevention of performance and voluntary disablement are valid methods of terminating a contractual relationship.

8. Financial stress of a party enables him to avoid performance of a contract due to insolvency.

"WRITE" AWAY! PORTFOLIO ASSIGNMENT

Review the Druid and Carrie contract. Create a list of what you would consider valid excuses for impracticality, impossibility, and frustration of purpose. Construction very rarely goes as originally planned. Unexpected events need to be addressed. Draft a "Change Order" form on behalf of Druid that it would have Carrie sign in such an event that might otherwise excuse performance by Druid due to an unforeseen circumstance.

Case in Point   IMPOSSIBILITY

192 Misc. 2d 743
746 N.Y.S.2d 790
Alexandra BUSH, Plaintiff,
v.
ProTRAVEL INTERNATIONAL, INC., et al., Defendants.
August 9, 2002.

Mound, Cotton, Wollan & Greengrass, New York City (Craig Stephen Brown of counsel), for defendants. Chelli & Bush, Staten Island (Marvin Ben-Aron of counsel), for plaintiff.

[192 Misc. 2d 744]

OPINION OF THE COURT

ERIC N. VITALIANO, J.

Dreams of a honeymoon safari in East Africa dashed offer fresh evidence of how the terror attack on the World Trade Center of September 11, 2001 has shredded the lives of ordinary New Yorkers and has engendered still continuing reverberations in decisional law. What might have ordinarily warranted summary disposition in favor of the safari company and its travel agent, pinning on the traveler the economic burden of trip cancellation, cannot, in the wake of September 11th, be sustained here on their motion for summary judgment.

Defendant Taicoa Corporation, doing business as Micato Safaris (Micato), acknowledges that plaintiff Alexandra Bush contacted Micato about booking a safari. By its admission, Micato referred the plaintiff to defendant ProTravel International, Inc. (ProTravel), a retail travel agent, to arrange for a reservation on one of the various safaris offered by Micato. It is undisputed that, on or about May 8, 2001, the plaintiff booked an African safari travel package for herself and her fiancé through ProTravel with Micato. At that time, it is also undisputed, the plaintiff gave ProTravel an initial 20% deposit in the amount of $1,516. Micato admits that it received the plaintiff's deposit from ProTravel on May 15, 2001. The safari Alexandra Bush selected for husband to be

and herself was scheduled to begin on November 14, 2001.

Sixty-four days before the safari's start, September 11, 2001, the world, as we knew it, came to an end. As a result of the attack on the World Trade Center, other terrorism alerts and airline scares, the plaintiff and her fiancé decided almost immediately to cancel their trip. Further, the plaintiff claims, she endeavored to notify ProTravel of her decision, but, as a result of the interruption of telephone service between Staten Island, where she had fled to safety, and Manhattan, where ProTravel maintained an office in midtown, she was physically unable to communicate her cancellation order until September 27, 2001. ProTravel agrees that the plaintiff did contact it that day and avers it passed along her request to Micato orally and in writing. Micato acknowledged receiving a fax from ProTravel to that effect on October 4, 2001. Thereafter, when the defendants refused to return her deposit, Alexandra Bush sued in this action to get it back.

The defendants, by their Manhattan and Massachusetts counsel, now move for summary judgment dismissing this action. The court notes that it has granted a separate motion permitting counsel from the Massachusetts firm of Rubin, Hay

[192 Misc. 2d 745]

& Gould, P.C. to appear pro hac vice to argue this motion for summary judgment. In support of the motion, counsel have appeared for oral argument and submitted four affidavits and two memoranda of law. The court notes that the second affidavit of Patricia Buffolano, dated June 7, 2002, and received by the court on June 10, 2002, is clearly a late submission. Counsel appeared on the June 6, 2002 submission date and did not request an adjournment in order to submit further papers. Nevertheless, the court has considered this affidavit in deciding the motion.

The defendants' motion hangs on a registration form. A copy of a completed form executed by Alexandra Bush was annexed to the moving affidavits of Joseph Traversa and Patricia Buffolano. Mr. Traversa, the employee of ProTravel who made the plaintiff's travel arrangements, states that the plaintiff completed and signed the form when she booked the safari on May 8, 2001. The form contained the following provision: "I confirm that I have read and agree to the Terms and Conditions as outlined in our brochure." Also annexed to the moving affidavits was an excerpt the defendants contend was in the "brochure" referenced in the registration form, and which the plaintiff claims she never received, setting forth Micato's cancellation policy for the safari booked by Ms. Bush. The policy imposes a $50 per person penalty for a cancellation occurring more than 60 days prior to departure. For a cancellation occurring between 30 and 60 days prior to departure, the traveler was subject to a penalty equal to 20% of the total retail tour rate. There is no disagreement that the deposit given by the plaintiff was in an amount equal to 20% of the tour rate.

With a departure date of November 14, 2001, for Alexandra Bush the days of moment under the cancellation policy were September 14, 2001 and October 15, 2001. A cancellation order given by her on or before September 14, 2001, the 61st day prior to departure, would have subjected her to, at worst, a $50 per person, i.e., a $100 penalty. Any cancellation after that date but on or before October 15, 2001 would subject her to the greater 20% penalty under the cancellation policy. Using either the September 27, 2001 date Mr. Traversa admits ProTravel received Ms. Bush's notice of cancellation or the October 4, 2001 date Micato's general manager, Patricia Buffolano, claims in her affidavit that Micato received written confirmation of the cancellation from ProTravel, the plaintiff's trip cancellation came within the 30- to 60-day prior to departure window that would trigger a 20% penalty for cancellation. On the strength

[192 Misc. 2d 746]

of those facts, neither defendant returned the deposit to Alexandra Bush and both now seek summary judgment dismissing her claim.

Without conceding that the cancellation policy the defendants advance as their sword and buckler is either valid or binding on her, Ms. Bush states in her affidavit submitted in opposition to the motion that, beginning on September 12, 2001 and continuing for days thereafter, she attempted to contact the travel agency and that due to difficulties with telephone lines, access to Manhattan and closures of its office, she was unable to speak to someone from ProTravel until September 27, 2001. All of the phone calls made by the plaintiff to ProTravel were placed from Staten Island. While ProTravel's reply affidavit protests that it was open for business from September 12th and onward and supplies phone records to show its phones were able to make and receive calls, no evidence is offered to dispute the plaintiff's claim that it was virtually impossible for many days after the terrorist attack to place a call from Staten Island if such call was transmitted via the telephone trunk lines in downtown Manhattan.

In any event, the defendants ultimately argue that all of the horror, heartbreak and hurdles for communications and commerce visited on Alexandra Bush and all New Yorkers in the aftermath of September 11th doesn't matter, for the thrust of their motion is that a contract is a contract, and that since the cancellation call was received, at best, 13 days late, the plaintiff is not entitled, as a matter of law, to her refund. In an equitable bolster to its position, the defendants also assert that Micato imposes the cancellation penalties to cover costs which it incurs in planning and preparing for a customer's safari. However, upon oral argument, defendants were unable to set forth what, if any, expenses had been incurred towards plaintiff's trip, nor when such expenses were incurred. Thereafter, the defendants submitted, in an untimely manner, the further affidavit of Patricia Buffolano, dated June 7, 2002, restating the contention that, prior to receiving notice that Ms. Bush wished to cancel her trip, Micato was required to pay certain expenses. The affidavit, nonetheless, is silent as to when these expenses, and more specifically, whether any such expenses were incurred on or before September 14, 2001, whether any were incurred between September 14 and September 27, 2001 or whether any were incurred during the one-week delay between the time ProTravel received notification of the cancellation, September 27, 2001, and when Micato claims it received notification from ProTravel, October 4, 2001.

[192 Misc. 2d 747]

When the residue has been poured away, the issue distilled here is whether the attack on the World Trade Center and the civil upset of its aftermath in the days that immediately followed excuses Alexandra Bush's admittedly late notice of cancellation. More to the point, given that effective cancellation on or before September 14, 2001 would have absolved the plaintiff of the 20% cancellation penalty, does Ms. Bush's sworn statement that she attempted to phone her cancellation notice to ProTravel beginning on September 12, 2001 but did not get through until September 27, 2001 raise a triable issue of fact, which, if resolved in her favor, entitles her to relief from the cancellation penalty provision of the contract?

It is in this context that the motion for summary judgment brought on by the defendants must be considered and it is in this context that they, as the moving parties, must demonstrate that there is no genuine issue of material fact and that they are entitled to judgment as a matter of law pursuant to CPLR 3212. Since summary judgment deprives the litigant of her day in court and is considered to be a drastic remedy, it should not be granted where there is any doubt as to the existence of a material and triable issue of fact. (See *Krupp v Aetna Life & Cas. Co.,* 103 AD2d 252 [2d Dept 1984]; see *also Rotuba Extruders v Ceppos,* 46 NY2d 223 [1978]; *Van Noy v Corinth Cent. School Dist.,* 111 AD2d 592 [3d Dept 1985].)

A movant for summary judgment has the burden to set forth evidentiary facts sufficient to entitle that party to judgment as a matter of law, tendering sufficient evidence to eliminate any material issues of fact. Failure to make such a showing requires denial of the motion. (*Winegrad v New York Univ. Med. Ctr.,* 64 NY2d 851 [1985].) "[O]nce a moving party has made a prima facie showing of its entitlement to summary judgment, the burden shifts to the opposing party to produce evidentiary proof in admissible

form sufficient to establish the existence of material issues of fact which require a trial of the action." (*Garnham & Han Real Estate Brokers v Oppenheimer,* 148 AD2d 493, 494 [2d Dept 1989]; see *Friedman v Pesach,* 160 AD2d 460 [1st Dept], *appeal dismissed* 76 NY2d 935 [1990].)

Though it is true that the black letter of the law establishes the rule that "once a party to a contract has made a promise, that party must perform or respond in damages for its failure, even when unforeseen circumstances make performance burdensome" (*Kel Kim Corp. v Central Mkts.,* 70 NY2d 900, 902 [1987]), the rule is not an absolute. Where the "means of performance" have been nullified, making "performance

[192 Misc. 2d 748]

objectively impossible," a party's performance under a contract will be excused. (*Id.* at 902; see *Conversion Equities v Sherwood House Owners Corp.,* 151 AD2d 635, 636 [2d Dept 1989].)

Counsel for the defendants at oral argument claimed to understand the difficulties encountered by literally every New Yorker in the wake of the disaster at the World Trade Center, but argue that those difficulties do not constitute a valid excuse for the failure of the plaintiff to cancel the safari before September 15, 2001. The delay until September 27, 2001, they contend, is inexcusable. Putting aside the sheer insensitivity of their argument, the argument fails to come to grips with Alexandra Bush's sworn claim that the disaster in lower Manhattan, which was unforeseen, unforeseeable and, certainly, beyond her control, had effectively destroyed her ability and means to communicate a timely cancellation under the contract for safari travel she had booked through and with the defendants. To the point, Alexandra Bush claims she could not physically take the steps necessary to cancel on time. Micato and ProTravel, to the contrary, claim she was simply a traveler too skittish to travel after September 11th, who wanted to stick the travel professionals she had retained with the bill for her faint heart. Should the defendants establish that to be the case to the satisfaction of the jury or at a bench trial, they will be entitled to judgment. (See *Evanoski v All Around Travel,* 178 Misc 2d 693 [App Term, 2d Dept 1998].) They certainly have not established that as a matter of law now.

Furthermore, the plaintiff's claim of excuse because of the frustration of the means of performance is supported, underscored and punctuated by the official actions taken by civil authorities on September 11, 2001 and in the days that followed. On the day of the attack, a state of emergency had been declared by the Mayor of the City of New York, directing the New York City Commissioners of Police, Fire and Health and the Director of Emergency Management to "take whatever steps are necessary to preserve the public safety and to render all required and available assistance to protect the security, well-being and health of the residents of the City." (NY City Legis Ann, at 355.)[1] Simultaneously, the Governor of the State of New York declared a state disaster emergency, directing state officials to "take all appropriate actions to . . . provide

[192 Misc. 2d 749]

. . . assistance as necessary to protect the public health and safety." (Executive Order [Pataki] No. 113 [9 NYCRR 5.113] [2001].)[2]

[192 Misc. 2d 750]

Particularly on the days at the focal point of the argument here, September 12, 13 and 14, 2001, New York City was in the state of virtual lockdown with travel either forbidden altogether or severely

---

[1] The full text of Mayor Rudolph W. Giuliani's proclamation of a state of emergency is as follows:

"PROCLAMATION OF A STATE OF EMERGENCY
"Date: September 11, 2001

"§ 1. Pursuant to the powers vested in me by Executive Law § 24, I hereby declare a State of Emergency.
"§ 2. This State of Emergency has been declared because of terrorist attacks on the World Trade Center causing a great many deaths, injuries and extensive damage to buildings and infrastructure in Lower Manhattan. These conditions imperil the public safety.
"§ 3. During the State of Emergency, the following orders shall be in effect:
  "a. All pedestrian and vehicular traffic, except essential emergency vehicles and personnel, shall be prohibited in the following areas: Manhattan-South of 14th Street.
  "b. The occupancy and use of buildings in the following areas is prohibited: Manhattan-Below 14th Street, except for emergency or essential personnel who have been authorized by the Police Commissioner, Fire Commissioner or the Director of Emergency Management.
  "c. . . .
"§ 4. I hereby direct the Police, Fire and Health Commissioners and the Director of Emergency Management to take whatever steps are necessary to preserve the public safety and to render all required and available assistance to protect the security, well-being and health of the residents of the City.
"§ 5. Any person who knowingly violates any provision of this Order is guilty of a class B misdemeanor.
"§ 6. This Order shall take effect immediately. It shall remain in effect for 5 days unless it is terminated at an earlier date.
"/s/_____ "Rudolph W. Giuliani "Mayor"

The proclamation by the Mayor was extended seasonally thereafter with no change in any of the declarations relevant to this action.

[2] The full text of Governor George E. Pataki's Executive Order No. 113 declaring a state disaster emergency is as follows:

"No. 113
"EXECUTIVE ORDER
"Declaring a Disaster Emergency in the State of New York
"WHEREAS, unspeakable atrocities have occurred today in New York City, our nation's capital and Pennsylvania that have taken the lives and injured unknown numbers of innocent people and have caused calamitous and pervasive damage to property; and
"WHEREAS, these events appear to be deliberate and coordinated acts of terrorism committed by despicable and cowardly persons or groups unknown;
"NOW, THEREFORE, I GEORGE E. PATAKI, Governor of the State of New York, do hereby find that a disaster has occurred for which the affected local governments are unable to respond adequately. Therefore, pursuant to the authority vested in me by the Constitution and the Laws of the State of New York, including Section 28 of Article 2-B of the Executive Law, I hereby declare a State Disaster Emergency effective September 11, 2001 within the territorial boundaries of the State of New York;
"FURTHER, pursuant to Section 29 of Article 2-B of the Executive Law, I direct the implementation of the State Disaster Preparedness Plan and authorize, effective September 11, 2001 and continuing, the State Emergency Management Office, the Department of Transportation, the New York State Thruway Authority, the State Police, the Division of Military and Naval Affairs, the Department of Environmental Conversation, the Department of Health, the Office of Mental Health, the State Department of Correctional Services, the Public Service Commission, the Office of Fire Prevention and Control, the Department of Labor, the Office of Parks, Recreation and Historic Preservation and all other State agencies and authorities over which I exercise Executive authority to take all appropriate actions to assist in every way all persons killed or injured and their families, and protect state property and to assist those affected local governments and individuals in responding to and recovering from this disaster, and to provide such other assistance as necessary to protect the public health and safety; and
"FURTHER, I have designated Edward F. Jacoby, Jr., Director of the State Emergency Management Office (SEMO) as the State Coordinating Officer for this disaster."

restricted. Precedent is plentiful that contract performance is excused when unforeseeable government action makes such performance objectively impossible. (*See Matter of A&S Transp. Co. v County of Nassau,* 154 AD2d 456, 459 [2d Dept 1989]; *Metpath, Inc. v Birmingham Fire Ins. Co.,* 86 AD2d 407, 411-412 [1st Dept 1982].) Further, in the painful recognition of the obvious and extraordinary dimensions of the disaster that prevented the transaction of even the most time sensitive business during the days and weeks that followed the September 11th atrocities, the Governor even issued an Executive Order extending the statute of limitations for all civil actions in every court of our state for a period well beyond the times Alexandra Bush claims to have communicated her cancellation and Micato acknowledges it received it. (Executive

[192 Misc. 2d 751]

Order [Pataki] No. 113.7 [9 NYCRR 5.113.7] [2001].)[3] In such light, to even hint that Alexandra Bush has failed to raise

[192 Misc. 2d 752]

a triable issue of fact by her argument that the doctrine of impossibility excuses her late cancellation of the safari she booked through ProTravel with Micato borders on the frivolous.

It is not hyperbole to suggest that on September 11, 2001, and the days that immediately followed, the City of New York was on a wartime footing, dealing with wartime conditions. The continental United States had seen nothing like it since the Civil War and, inflicted by a foreign foe, not since the War of 1812. Accordingly, it is entirely appropriate for this court to consider and follow wartime precedents which developed the law of temporary impossibility. Stated succinctly, where a supervening act creates a temporary impossibility, particularly of brief duration, the impossibility may be viewed as merely excusing performance until it subsequently becomes possible to perform rather than excusing performance

---

[3] The full text of the Governor's Executive Order of September 12, 2001 superceding statutes of limitations through New York State is as follows:

"No. 113.7
"EXECUTIVE ORDER
"Temporary Suspension and Modification of Statutory Provisions Establishing Time Limitations on Actions and Time in which to Take an Appeal
"WHEREAS, on September 11, 2001, I issued Executive Order Number 113 declaring a disaster emergency in the State of New York;
"NOW, THEREFORE, I, GEORGE E. PATAKI, Governor of the State of New York, by virtue of the authority vested in me by the Constitution and Laws of the State of New York, do hereby continue Executive Order No. 113, dated September 11, 2001, except that such Executive Order is amended to read as follows:
"FURTHER, pursuant to the authority vested in me by Section 29-a of Article 2-b of the Executive Law to temporarily suspend specific provisions of any statute, local law, ordinance, orders, rules or regulations, or parts thereof, of any agency during a State disaster emergency, if compliance with such provisions would prevent, hinder or delay action necessary to cope with the disaster, I hereby temporarily suspend, from the date the disaster emergency was declared, pursuant to Executive Order Number 113, issued on September 11, 2001 until further notice, the following laws:
"Section 201 of the Civil Practice Law and Rules, so far as it bars actions whose limitation period concludes during the period commencing from the date that the disaster emergency was declared pursuant to Executive Order Number 113, issued on September 11, 2001, until further notice, and so

far as it limits a courts authority to extend such time, whether or not the time to commence such an action is specified in Article 2 of the Civil Practice Law and Rules;
"Section 5513 of the Civil Practice Law and Rules, so far as it relates to a limitation period that concludes during the period commencing from the date that the disaster emergency was declared pursuant to Executive Order Number 113, issued on September 11, 2001;
"Sections 30.10 and 30.30 of the Criminal Procedure Law, so far as it bars criminal prosecutions whose limitation period concludes during the period commencing from the date that the disaster emergency was declared pursuant to Executive Order Number 113, issued on September 11, 2001, until further notice;
"Sections 460.10, 460.30, 460.50 and Article 460 of the Criminal Procedure Law, so far as it relates to a limitation of time to appeal in which a limitation period concludes during the period commencing from the date that the disaster emergency was declared pursuant to Executive Order Number 113, issued on September 11, 2001, until further notice;
"In addition, I hereby temporarily suspend and modify, for the period from the date of this Executive Order until further notice, any other statute, local law, ordinance, order, rule or regulation or part thereof, establishing limitations of time for the filing or service of any legal action, notice or other process or proceeding that the courts lack authority to extend through the exercise of discretion, where any limitation of time concludes during the period commencing from the date that the disaster emergency was declared pursuant to Executive Order Number 113, issued on September 11, 2001, until further notice."

By his amended order of October 4, 2001, the Governor extended the suspension of the statutes of limitations through October 12, 2001, giving yet additional factual support to the disaster conditions still obtaining in New York City at that time.

altogether. (See generally Annotation, *Modern Status of the Rules Regarding Impossibility of Performance in Action for Breach of Contract,* 84 ALR2d 12, § 14 [a] [1962].)

The law of temporary and/or partial impossibility flows from the theory that when a promisor has obligated himself to perform certain acts, which, when taken together are impossible, the promisor should not be excused from being "called upon to perform in so far as he is able to do so." (*Miller v Vanderlip,* 285 NY 116, 124 [1941].) The First Department's opinion in the World War I era case of *Erdreich v Zimmermann* (190 App Div 443 [1st Dept 1920]) is extremely instructive. In *Erdreich,* the plaintiff purchased German war bonds, which, at the time of purchase on December 14, 1916, was entirely lawful since the United States had not yet entered the conflict. Because of the war, however, the bonds could not

[192 Misc. 2d 753]

be delivered due to a naval blockade. In April 1917, after a state of war had been declared between the United States and Germany, the plaintiff demanded his money back for the defendant seller's failure to deliver the bonds. Almost two years later, with the bonds essentially worthless, the plaintiff sued for rescission and return of his purchase payment. Appellate Term held that the delivery of the bonds, though legally contracted for, would have been unlawful under wartime rules and, therefore, the contract should have been rescinded for impossibility. The Appellate Division reversed, holding that "at most, performance of [the] contract was suspended during the existence of hostilities" (at 452), and the performance, which had been temporarily excused for impossibility during hostilities, was now required. The plaintiff was entitled, therefore, to his worthless bonds, but not the return of his purchase payment. This holding is in harmony with even earlier precedents acknowledging the fog of war and its upset of civil society:

"Where performance can be had, without contravening the laws of war, the existence of the contract is not imperiled, and even if performance is impossible the contract may still, when partly executed, be preserved by ingrafting necessary qualifications upon it, or suspending its impossible provisions [i.e., physical

impossibility to cancel timely] . . . . If the contract . . . can be saved while the war lasts, it should be." (*Mutual Benefit Life Ins. Co. v Hillyard,* 37 NJL 444, 468-469.)

So too here, if Alexandra Bush can establish objective impossibility of performance at trial, she is entitled to, at minimum, a reasonable suspension of her contractual obligation to timely cancel, if not outright excuse of her untimely cancellation.[4]

Clearly, the plaintiff has raised, in any event, sufficient material issues of fact concerning both her inability to cancel by September 15, 2001 the safari she had booked and the reasonableness of her cancellation on September 27, 2001, all as a result of the terrorist attack on the World Trade Center, the

[192 Misc. 2d 754]

damage the attack caused to communications and transportation in the City of New York and the actions of government in declaring and enforcing a state of emergency in the city and beyond. Moreover, the failure of the defendants to establish that they sustained any loss whatsoever on account of the plaintiff's failure to act in the 13-day intervening period between September 14 and September 27, 2001 further supports the reasonableness of the plaintiff's late cancellation as well as the court's determination that triable issues of fact are present.

In the instant matter, the court finds that the plaintiff has raised sufficient material issues of fact concerning her inability to cancel the contract by September 15, 2001, which would, if established, provide a defense to the argument of the defendants, so as to warrant denial of this motion. Accordingly, for the reasons stated in the opinion of the court, the motion of defendants ProTravel and Micato for summary judgment dismissing this action is denied in its entirety.

---

[4] Without resolving whether actions or omissions by one or both of the defendants in reliance upon the plaintiff's silence in the period September 12 through September 27, 2001 can, to any extent, work an equitable estoppel of the plaintiff's claim of impossibility, it is significant to note that the defendants have offered no proof either in the timely or untimely affidavits submitted by them on this motion that the position of either defendant changed in any detrimental way during the period the plaintiff claims she was objectively unable to communicate her cancellation order.

Case in Point   FRUSTRATION OF PURPOSE

909 P.2d 408
184 Ariz. 341
7200 SCOTTSDALE ROAD GENERAL PARTNERS dba Scottsdale Plaza Resort, Plaintiff-Appellant,
v.
KUHN FARM MACHINERY, INC., a Foreign Corporation, Defendant-Appellee.
No. 1 CA-CV 93-0052.
Court of Appeals of Arizona,
Division 1, Department D.
May 2, 1995.
Reconsideration Denied June 23, 1995.
Review Denied Jan. 17, 1996.*

Page 409

[184 Ariz. 342] O'Connor, Cavanagh, Anderson, Westover, Killingsworth and Beshears, P.A. by Steven M. Rudner, Frank W. Moskowitz, Christopher Robbins, Phoenix, for plaintiff-appellant.
Fennemore Craig by Roger T. Hargrove, Ann-Martha Andrews, Phoenix, for defendant-appellee.

Page 410

[184 Ariz. 343]

OPINION

TOCI, Judge.

Kuhn Farm Machinery, Inc. ("Kuhn") contracted with 7200 Scottsdale Road General Partners dba Scottsdale Plaza Resort (the "resort"), to use the resort's facilities for a convention at which Kuhn's European personnel were to present new products to Kuhn's dealers and employees. In this appeal from the granting of a summary judgment for Kuhn, we consider the following issue: did the risk to air travel to Scottsdale, Arizona, posed by the Gulf War and Saddam Hussein's threats of worldwide terrorism, substantially frustrate the purpose of the contract?

Reversing the trial court's grant of summary judgment for Kuhn, we hold as follows. First, the resort did not contract with the understanding that Kuhn's European personnel were crucial to the success of Kuhn's convention. Thus, even if the attendance of the Europeans at the Scottsdale convention was thwarted by the threat to international air travel, their nonattendance did not excuse Kuhn's performance under the contract. Neither did the risk to domestic air travel posed by the Gulf War entitle Kuhn to relief. Although that risk may have rendered the convention uneconomical for Kuhn, the threat to domestic air travel did not rise to the level of "substantial frustration." Finally, Kuhn's cancellation based on the perceived risk of terrorism was not an objectively reasonable response to an extraordinary and specific threat. Consequently, Kuhn is not entitled to relief on the theory of "apprehension of impossibility."

I. FACTS AND PROCEDURAL HISTORY

A. Background

On February 9, 1990, the resort and Kuhn signed a letter agreement providing that Kuhn would hold its North American dealers' convention at the resort. The agreement required the resort to reserve, at group rates, a block of 190 guest rooms and banquet

---

* Corcoran, J., of the Supreme Court, did not participate in the determination of this matter.

and meeting rooms for the period from March 26, 1991, to March 30, 1991. Kuhn, in turn, guaranteed rental of a minimum number of guest rooms and food and beverage revenue of at least $8,000 from the use of the meeting and banquet rooms.

The agreement contained remedies protecting the resort if Kuhn canceled the meeting. Kuhn was required to pay liquidated damages for any decrease after January 25, 1991, of ten percent or more in the reserved room block. Additionally, the resort agreed to accept individual room cancellations up to seventy-two hours prior to arrival without penalty so long as total attrition did not exceed five percent. The agreement also provided that, because the loss of food and beverage revenues and of room rentals resulting from cancellation were incapable of estimation, cancellation would result in assessment of liquidated damages.

Because Kuhn refused to hold its dealers' meeting at the resort at the time specified in the agreement, the resort sued for breach of contract, seeking the liquidated damages provided for in the agreement. The resort then moved for partial summary judgment to obtain a ruling in its favor on the issue of liability. Kuhn filed a cross motion for summary judgment, alleging that its performance was discharged or suspended pursuant to the doctrines of impracticability of performance and frustration of purpose.

B. Additional Facts Established by Kuhn's Motion

In support of its motion for summary judgment, Kuhn offered the following facts. Kuhn S.A., the parent of Kuhn, is headquartered in France, where it manufactures farm machinery. Both companies engage in international

Page 411

[184 Ariz. 344] sales of farm machinery manufactured by Kuhn S.A. They sell their products through direct sales by their employees and through independent dealerships.

Kuhn and Kuhn S.A. planned to use the North American dealers' convention to introduce new products to Kuhn's sales people and dealers, stimulate enthusiasm for the new products, and provide its sales people and dealers with information to effectively market and sell the products. To accomplish these goals, Kuhn invited its top 200 independent dealers from the United States and Canada ("North Americans"), as well as some of its overseas suppliers, to attend the meeting. Approximately twenty-five Kuhn and Kuhn S.A. employees and suppliers from the United States, Europe, and Australia were to host the convention and present the new products.

Kuhn considered the overseas personnel ("Europeans") crucial to the presentation and success of the dealers' meeting. Of all of Kuhn's personnel, they were the most familiar with the design, manufacture, and production of the new products. Kuhn intended the Europeans to play the primary role in presenting the products and leading the discussions at the convention.

On August 2, 1990, Iraq invaded Kuwait. A few days later, the United States began sending troops to the Middle East. On January 16, 1991, the United States and allied forces, in Operation Desert Storm, engaged in war with Iraq. As a result, Saddam Hussein and other high-ranking Iraqi officials threatened terrorist acts against the countries that sought to prevent Iraq's takeover of Kuwait. Hussein stated, "hundreds of thousands of volunteers . . . [would become] missile[s] to be thrown against the enemy . . . ." and "the theater of operations would [include] every freedom fighter who can reach out to harm the aggressors in the whole world. . . ."

Because many newspapers reported a likelihood of terrorism, Kuhn became concerned about the safety of those planning to attend the convention. Kuhn was particularly concerned about international travel, but Kuhn also perceived a risk of terrorism within the United States.

Kuhn discovered that, apparently because of the war, convention attendance would not meet expectations. Many of Kuhn's employees who were to attend the meeting were concerned about the safety of air travel. Timothy Harman, general sales manager of Kuhn, personally spoke with several dealers who voiced their apprehension about traveling during the war. Because tentative registration was lower than Kuhn had anticipated when it signed the agreement, in late January—two months prior to the date of the planned convention—Kuhn reduced the reserved room block by more than twenty-five percent.

Interest in the proposed convention continued to wane. From February 4 to February 14, 1991, several of Kuhn's top dealerships who had won all-expense-paid trips to the convention canceled their plans to attend. By mid-February, eleven of the top fifty dealerships with expense-paid trips had either canceled their plans to send people to the convention or failed to sign up.

Kuhn S.A. wrote to the resort on February 14, 1991, requesting cooperation in rescheduling the meeting for a later date. Among other things, the letter stated that Kuhn was concerned with the safety of its people, that the dealers were reluctant to travel, and that attendance had decreased to a level making it uneconomical to hold the convention.

Without waiting for the resort's response, Kuhn decided to postpone the scheduled meeting. On February 18, 1991, Kuhn notified all potential convention participants that the dealers' meeting had been postponed. Although Kuhn and the resort did attempt to reschedule the meeting for the following year, the rescheduling negotiations broke down. The convention was never held at the resort.

C. The Resort's Response to Kuhn's Motion

The resort did not dispute Kuhn's description of the planned convention; rather, the resort contested the extent of the threat to air travel. Specifically, the resort noted that the articles cited by Kuhn indicated either

Page 412

[184 Ariz. 345] that there was little risk or that the risk was primarily to overseas locations.

The resort also contested the inferences to be drawn from the facts presented by each party. The resort asserted that the facts did not establish that the threat of terrorism frustrated the ability of Kuhn associates to fly to Scottsdale. Although conceding that several dealers canceled because of fear of terrorism, the resort emphasized that nearly all of the approximately 150 dealers registered for the meeting signed up after the Operation Desert Storm attack on Iraq. In the resort's view, Kuhn's January 29, 1991, request for a reduction in the room block to 140 rooms impliedly reconfirmed the convention after the commencement of the war. The resort argued

that these facts, taken with all others that had been presented, demonstrated as a matter of law that the defenses of impracticability of performance and frustration of purpose were inapplicable.

The trial court granted summary judgment to Kuhn, ruling that Kuhn proved both of its defenses. Before formal judgment was entered, the resort filed a motion for reconsideration, asking the trial court to consider certain new evidence it had obtained through discovery. The trial court denied the motion. The resort appeals from the summary judgment ruling, from the denial of its motion for reconsideration, and from the denial of a request it made to strike certain evidence that Kuhn had presented.

II. IMPRACTICABILITY DISTINGUISHED FROM FRUSTRATION OF PURPOSE

The trial court held that the contract was discharged under the doctrines of impracticability of performance and frustration of purpose. These are similar but distinct doctrines. See Restatement (Second) of Contracts ("Restatement") § 265 cmt. a (1981) (discussing the differences between impracticability of performance and frustration of purpose). Impracticability of performance is, according to the Restatement, utilized when certain events occurring after a contract is made constitute an impediment to performance by either party. See Restatement § 261. Traditionally, the doctrine has been applied to three categories of supervening events: death or incapacity of a person necessary for performance, destruction of a specific thing necessary for performance, and prohibition or prevention by law. *Id.* cmt. a.

On the other hand, frustration of purpose deals with "the problem that arises when a change in circumstances makes one party's performance virtually worthless to the other. . . ." Restatement § 265 cmt. a. "Performance remains possible but the expected value of performance to the party seeking to be excused has been destroyed by a fortuitous event, which supervenes to cause an actual but not literal failure of consideration." *Lloyd v. Murphy*, 25 Cal. 2d 48, 153 P.2d 47, 50 (1944). While the impact on the party adversely affected is the same regardless of which doctrine is applied, frustration of purpose, unlike the doctrine of impracticability, involves no true failure of performance by either party.

Notwithstanding, some cases speak of a contract as "frustrated" when performance has become impossible or impracticable. See, e.g., *Matheny v. Gila County*, 147 Ariz. 359, 360, 710 P.2d 469, 470 (App. 1985) (doctrine of commercial frustration is not necessarily limited to strict impossibility). This usage is inaccurate. "[F]rustration is not a form of impossibility even under the modern definition of that term, which includes not only cases of physical impossibility but also cases of extreme impracticability of performance." *Lloyd*, 153 P.2d at 50; see also Arthur Anderson, Frustration of Contract—A Rejected Doctrine, 3 DePaul L. Rev. 1, 3-4 (1953) ("[T]he concepts of frustration of purpose and impossibility or impracticability of performance are mutually in opposition.").

Turning to the contract between Kuhn and the resort, Kuhn clearly has no claim for impossibility or impracticability. The contract required the resort to reserve and provide guest rooms, meeting rooms, and food and services. In return, Kuhn was required to pay the monies specified in the

Page 413

[184 Ariz. 346] contract. Kuhn does not allege that it was impossible or impracticable to perform its contractual duty to make payment for the reserved facilities. Rather, it contends that the value of the resort's counter-performance—the furnishing of convention facilities—was rendered worthless because of the Gulf War's effect on convention attendance. This is a claim of frustration of purpose.

III. FRUSTRATION OF PURPOSE

A. *Krell v. Henry*

The doctrine of frustration of purpose traces its roots to *Krell v. Henry*, [1903] 2 K.B. 740. There, the owner of a London apartment advertised it for rent to observe the King's coronation parade. Responding to the advertisement, the renter paid a deposit and agreed to rent the apartment for two days. When the coronation parade was postponed, the renter refused to pay the balance of the rent. The court held that the contract to rent the apartment was premised on an implied condition—the occurrence of the King's coronation parade. *Id.* at 754. Accordingly, when the

parade was canceled, the renter's duty to perform was discharged by the frustration of his purpose in entering the contract. *Id.*

Several aspects of *Krell* are worth noting. First, the owner of the apartment was prepared to render the entire performance promised by him; the postponement of the coronation procession did not diminish the value of the contract to the owner. Second, the renter could have performed by simply paying the rental fee for the apartment. In other words, there was no impediment to the renter's performance of the contract. The renter's sole grievance was that his intended benefit from the contract had not been realized. See Anderson, supra, at 2.

The complaint that a contracting party did not realize the benefit he intended to realize from the contract has been described as "frustration-in-fact." *Id.* Frustration-in-fact results when, because of events subsequent to formation of a contract, the desirability of the performance for which a party contracted diminishes. *Id.* at 3. The issue then becomes: should legal consequences flow from a contracting party's failure to realize the expected benefit from a contract?

B. Frustration of Purpose and the Equitable Doctrine of *Lloyd*

Significantly, the very courts that created the doctrine of frustration of purpose have questioned its soundness. *Lloyd*, 153 P.2d at 49. In this country, some commentators have asserted that the doctrine rests on a tenuous rationale for shifting the burdens of unexpected events from the promisor to the promisee. See Edwin W. Patterson, Constructive Conditions in Contracts, 42 Colum. L. Rev. 903, 950-954 (1942); T. Ward Chapman, Comment, Contracts-Frustration of Purpose, 59 Mich. L. Rev. 98, 110-117 (1960).

Despite this criticism, many authorities, including the courts of Arizona, extend limited relief for frustration-in-fact through an extraordinary legal remedy closely resembling relief in equity. See 18 Samuel Williston, A Treatise on the Law of Contracts § 1954, at 129 (Walter H.E. Jaeger ed., 3d ed. 1978) (frustration doctrine may be viewed as equitable defense asserted in an action at law); *Cf. Opera Co. of Boston v. Wolf Trap Found. for the Performing Arts*, 817 F.2d 1094, 1099 (4th Cir.1987) (same assertion regarding impossibility doctrine). As Justice Traynor pointed out in his frequently cited opinion in *Lloyd*:

> The question in cases involving frustration is whether the equities of the case, considered in the light of sound public policy, require placing the risk of a disruption or complete destruction of the contract equilibrium on defendant or plaintiff under the circumstances of a given case, and the answer depends on whether an unanticipated circumstance, the risk of which should not be fairly thrown on the promisor, has made performance vitally different from what was reasonably to be expected.

Page 414

[184 Ariz. 347] 153 P.2d at 50 (citations omitted). Virtually all Arizona cases applying the doctrine have approved of this approach. See *Mohave County v. Mohave-Kingman Estates, Inc.*, 120 Ariz. 417, 422-23, 586 P.2d 978, 983-84 (1978); *Mobile Home Estates, Inc. v. Levitt Mobile Home Sys., Inc.*, 118 Ariz. 219, 222, 575 P.2d 1245, 1248 (1978); *Matheny*, 147 Ariz. at 360, 710 P.2d at 470; *Garner*, 18 Ariz. App. at 182-83, 501 P.2d at 23-24.

C. The Restatement Approach to Frustration of Purpose

Although the modern doctrine of frustration of purpose appears in Restatement § 265 and the comments, see *Washington State Hop Producers, Inc. v. Goschie Farms*, 112 Wash. 2d 694, 773 P.2d 70, 73 (1989) (quoting Restatement § 265 cmt. a as the appropriate test), past Arizona cases applying the doctrine of frustration of purpose have relied on *Lloyd* rather than on the Restatement. See *Mohave County*, 120 Ariz. at 422-23, 586 P.2d at 983-84; *Mobile Home Estates*, 118 Ariz. at 222, 575 P.2d at 1248; *Matheny*, 147 Ariz. at 360, 710 P.2d at 470; *Garner*, 18 Ariz. App. at 182-83, 501 P.2d at 23-24. Applying *Lloyd*'s rationale that the "purpose of a contract is to place the risks of performance upon the promisor," 153 P.2d at 50, Arizona courts have stated that " '[t]he doctrine of frustration has been severely limited to cases of extreme hardship so as not to diminish the power of parties to contract. . . .' " *Matheny*,

147 Ariz. at 360, 710 P.2d at 470 (quoting *Garner*, 18 Ariz. App. at 183, 501 P.2d at 24).

Nevertheless, neither *Lloyd* nor the Arizona cases that have relied upon it are inconsistent with Restatement section 265. The reporter's note to Restatement section 265 cites *Lloyd* as authority for illustration 6 of that section. Furthermore, in line with the Arizona cases of *Matheny* and *Garner*, the requirements for the doctrine of frustration of purpose stated in comment a provide adequate protection for the power to contract. Consequently, we follow Restatement section 265, particularly comment a, in this case. See *City of Phoenix v. Bellamy*, 153 Ariz. 363, 366, 736 P.2d 1175, 1178 (App.1987) (in the absence of law to the contrary, Arizona generally follows the Restatement).

D. Standard of Review

The trial court granted Kuhn's cross-motion for summary judgment on the theory that the purpose of Kuhn's contract with the resort was frustrated. In reviewing an order granting summary judgment, we must determine whether there is a genuine issue of disputed material fact. *In re Estate of Johnson*, 168 Ariz. 108, 109, 811 P.2d 360, 361 (App. 1991). Where the facts are not in dispute, we analyze the record to determine if the trial court correctly applied the law to the undisputed facts. *Heartfield v. Transit Management of Tucson, Inc.*, 171 Ariz. 181, 182, 829 P.2d 1227, 1228 (App. 1991). We are not bound by the trial court's conclusions of law. *Gary Outdoor Advertising Co. v. Sun Lodge, Inc.*, 133 Ariz. 240, 242, 650 P.2d 1222, 1224 (1982).

Here, the underlying facts are undisputed. Both sides conceded below that there were no additional factual matters to be developed beyond those presented in the motions for summary judgement; each party asserted that the court should rule on the questions of frustration of purpose as a matter of law. We, too, "fail to find any disputed factual inferences which arise from the undisputed facts in this case. Rather, it is the legal conclusions to be drawn from these facts that are in actual dispute." *Scottsdale Jaycees v. Superior Court*, 17 Ariz. App. 571, 574, 499 P.2d 185, 188 (1972).

Whether a party to a contract is entitled to relief under the doctrine of frustration of purpose is generally treated as a question of law. Restatement ch. 11

introductory note, at 310. As noted above, frustration of purpose is essentially an equitable doctrine, and the power to grant relief under that doctrine is reserved to the court. Arizona courts have frequently followed this general rule. See *Mohave County,* 120 Ariz. at 422-23, 586 P.2d at 983-84; *Matheny,* 147 Ariz. at 360, 710 P.2d at 470; *Korman v. Kieckhefer,* 114 Ariz. 127, 129-30, 559 P.2d 683, 685-86 (App. 1976); *Garner,* 18 Ariz. App. at 183, 501 P.2d at 24. Thus, the issues to be considered here—principal purpose and substantial frustration—are questions of law for the court.

Page 415

[184 Ariz. 348]

IV. RESOLUTION OF THIS CASE

A. Requirements for Relief

Restatement section 265 comment a lists four requirements that must exist before relief may be granted for frustration of purpose. First, "the purpose that is frustrated must have been a principal purpose of that party" and must have been so to the understanding of both parties. Restatement § 265 cmt. a. Second, "the frustration must be substantial . . . ; [it] must be so severe that it is not to be regarded as within the risks assumed . . . under the contract." *Id.* Third, "the non-occurrence of the frustrating event must have been a basic assumption. . . ." *Id.*; see Restatement § 261, cmt. b. Finally, relief will not be granted if it may be inferred from either the language of the contract or the circumstances that the risk of the frustrating occurrence, or the loss caused thereby, should properly be placed on the party seeking relief. Restatement § 265 cmt. b; see Restatement § 261 cmt. c.

Kuhn contends that the Gulf War with its attendant threats of terrorism was an "event the non-occurrence of which was a basic assumption" of the contract. The resort, on the other hand argues that these events were merely normal incidents of life in the modern world. We conclude, however, that under Restatement section 265 comment a, the parties "basic assumption" is only relevant if the other requirements listed in comment a are satisfied. Here, because we find no substantial frustration of

a principal purpose entitling Kuhn to relief, we need not decide if the nonoccurrence of the Gulf war and Saddam Hussein's threats of terrorism was a basic assumption of the parties.

B. Principal Purpose

1. A Forum for European Personnel

Kuhn contends that its principal purpose in scheduling the convention was to provide a forum for its European personnel to introduce new and innovative products to its North American dealers. The resort acknowledged that the primary threat of terrorist activity was to the United States' international interests rather than domestic targets. Even if we take this as an implied concession by the resort that it was too dangerous for Kuhn's European personnel to fly to Scottsdale, Kuhn is not entitled to relief for frustration of purpose on this ground.

For Kuhn to obtain relief based on the frustration of its plans for its European employees to introduce new products, those plans must have been understood by the resort as Kuhn's "principal purpose" in entering the contract. As the court noted in *Krell,* to establish that "the object of the contract was frustrated," it must be shown that the frustrated purpose was "the subject of the contract . . . *and was so to the knowledge of both parties.*" [1903] 2 K.B. at 754 (emphasis added). It is not enough that the promisor "had in mind some specific object without which he would not have made the contract." Restatement § 265 cmt. a. "The object must be so completely the basis of the contract that, *as both parties understand,* without it the transaction would make little sense." *Id.* (emphasis added). In *Krell,* for example, the "coronation procession and the relative position of the rooms [was] the basis of the contract as much for the lessor as the hirer." [1903] 2 K.B. at 751.

Here, Kuhn never established that both parties had a common understanding that Kuhn's principal purpose in entering the contract was a convention at which the European personnel would be present. First, the contract itself makes no mention of any particular purpose for the convention. Second, neither the deposition and affidavit of Timothy Harman—Kuhn's general sales manager responsible for scheduling the convention—nor the deposition of William

Kilburg—the resort's vice president—raised any factual inference that the resort knew of Kuhn's plans concerning the European personnel. Harman's affidavit only related Kuhn's understanding of the purpose of the convention. The only other reference in the record to the purpose of the convention is Harman's deposition testimony that his role was to find a venue for a North American dealers' meeting.

In sum, although Kuhn thought that attendance of the Europeans was crucial to the success of the convention, the record is devoid

Page 416

[184 Ariz. 349] of any evidence that the resort contracted with that understanding. Neither does the record establish any reasonable inference that, when the parties contracted, the resort knew or had reason to know that its counter-performance—the furnishing of resort facilities—would make little sense without the presence of the Europeans. We conclude, therefore, that Kuhn's principal purpose—the attendance of the European personnel—was not so completely the basis of the contract, as understood by the resort, that without such attendance the transaction was meaningless. Accordingly, Kuhn is not entitled to relief on that theory.

2. Attendance of Most Invited Personnel

Nevertheless, Kuhn argues that the parties contracted with the idea that "all or most" of Kuhn's employees and dealers would come to Scottsdale for the meeting. We agree that this was a principal purpose of Kuhn's contract with the resort. Nevertheless, nothing in this record establishes that the resort contracted with the understanding that all or most of Kuhn's dealers and employees would attend the convention. Kuhn's degree of success was not of primary concern to the resort. To the contrary, the resort clearly contemplated that the convention might not meet Kuhn's expectations. Not only does the contract include a provision for attrition in attendance and outright cancellation, it assigns the risk of such events to Kuhn. Thus, as with the attendance of the European employees, the attendance of all or most of Kuhn's dealers and employees was not so completely the basis of the contract, as understood by the resort, that

without such attendance the transaction would make little sense.

Kuhn did establish, however, that the resort contracted with knowledge that a principal purpose of Kuhn was a convention at which some of Kuhn's employees and dealers would attend. If that purpose was substantially frustrated by the Gulf War, Kuhn is entitled to relief. Consequently, we next consider whether the Gulf War and Saddam Hussein's threats of terrorism substantially frustrated a convention for some of Kuhn's employees and dealers.

C. Substantial Frustration

Kuhn argues that its purpose was effectively frustrated because air travel was unexpectedly rendered unreasonably dangerous. The resort, on the other hand, while essentially conceding that Kuhn's decision to cancel was made in good faith, contends that the general threat of terrorism was not sufficient to justify Kuhn's cancellation of the convention. We agree with the resort.

Preliminarily, as discussed above, Kuhn cannot rely on the absence of the Europeans as a basis for canceling the contract. Kuhn never established that both parties had a common understanding that Kuhn's principal purpose in entering the contract was a convention at which the European personnel would be present. Thus, in resolving this issue, we do not consider the threat posed to the European employees traveling internationally by air.

On the other hand, the threat to domestic air travel is a relevant consideration. Most of those invited to the convention resided in the United States and in Canada. Furthermore, the resort did not controvert Kuhn's assertion in its statement of facts that "the parties assumed that Kuhn personnel could and would travel to Scottsdale." Consequently, if the Gulf War effectively precluded domestic air travel, Kuhn could not have hosted a convention attended by even some of its dealers and employees. Under such circumstances, the resort's furnishing of its facilities would have been rendered valueless to Kuhn. We could then say that Kuhn's purpose in entering the contract was substantially frustrated. We conclude, however, that the contrary is true.

We begin our analysis on this point with the proposition that substantial frustration means frustration "so severe that it is not fairly to be regarded as within the risks . . . assumed under the contract." Restatement § 265 cmt. a. Furthermore, "it is not enough that the transaction has become less profitable for the affected party or even that he will sustain a loss." Id. The value of the counter-performance to be rendered by the promisee must be "totally or nearly totally destroyed" by the occurrence of the event. *Lloyd*, 153 P.2d at 50.

Page 417

[184 Ariz. 350] Here, the conduct of Kuhn and its dealers clearly demonstrates that the value of the resort's counter-performance—the furnishing of its facilities for Kuhn's convention—was not totally or nearly totally destroyed by terrorist threats. In late January, after the United States attacked Iraq and when the threat of terrorism was at its highest level, Kuhn implicitly confirmed the convention date by reducing the reserved room block from 190 to 140. Furthermore, although several dealers canceled in early February, the uncontroverted record demonstrates that over one hundred dealers registered for the convention after the commencement of Operation Desert Storm on January 16, 1991. Thus, the frustration was not so severe that it cannot fairly be regarded as one of the risks assumed by Kuhn under the contract.

Kuhn argues, however, that even if the jointly understood purpose in holding the convention was not substantially frustrated by the actual risk of terrorism, it was entitled to cancel the convention because of its perception of a serious risk to air travel. For this proposition, Kuhn relies primarily on the wartime shipping cases. See *North German Lloyd (Kronprinzessin Cecilie) v. Guaranty Trust*, 244 U.S. 12, 37 S. Ct. 490, 61 L. Ed. 960 (1917); *The Styria v. Morgan*, 186 U.S. 1, 22 S. Ct. 731, 46 L. Ed. 1027 (1902); *The Wildwood v. Amtorg Trading Corp.*, 133 F.2d 765 (9th Cir. 1943).

These cases, however, are not frustration of purpose cases. The wartime shipping cases are the source of the rules governing impossibility or impracticability of performance in the original Restatement of Contracts ("First Restatement") section 465 (1932). See Restatement § 261 reporter's note, at 323 (citing Kronprinzessin Cecilie as basis of doctrine). This doctrine, referred to by the First Restatement as "apprehension of impossibility," was

followed by the Supreme Court of Alaska in *Northern Corp. v. Chugach Electric Ass'n*, 518 P.2d 76, 81 n. 10, vacated on other grounds, 523 P.2d 1243 (Alaska 1974), cited by Kuhn, and was subsequently incorporated into comment d of Restatement section 261. See Restatement § 261 reporter's note, at 322-23.

The wartime shipping cases essentially held that a ship captain is entitled to take reasonable precautions, including abandoning the voyage, in the face of a reasonable apprehension of danger. Read together, they establish that the promisor's decision not to perform must be an objectively reasonable response to an extraordinary, specific, and identifiable threat. See *Kronprinzessin Cecilie*, 244 U.S. at 20-24, 37 S. Ct. at 490-492 (German passenger ship justified in turning back from voyage to England on the day the German Emperor declared war (World War I)); *The Styria*, 186 U.S. at 9, 22 S. Ct. at 734 (during Spanish-American war, "reasonable prudence" justified cancellation of voyage within sight of Spanish coast with a cargo of sulfur where captain knew men-of-war were ordered to interdict sulfur); *The Wildwood*, 133 F.2d at 768 ("reasonable apprehension" of "actual and substantial" danger of running a World War II naval blockade justified cancellation of ship's voyage in light of the seizure of a ship carrying identical cargo to the same destination). The degree of danger is judged in light of the facts available at the time, First Restatement section 465 comment b, but "[m]ere good faith . . . will not excuse" cancellation of performance. The Styria, 186 U.S. at 10, 22 S. Ct. at 734.

Assuming solely for the purposes of argument that the above authorities cited by Kuhn are applicable to frustration of purpose, they do not help Kuhn. Even though Kuhn canceled the convention in good faith, under the cited authorities Kuhn's cancellation did not excuse its performance of the contract with the resort. Press reports in circulation at the time Kuhn canceled the convention indicated that the risk to domestic air travel was slight. Moreover, the United States government announced that it was taking measures to insure the safety of domestic air travel and that travelers should not be put off by the threat of terrorist activity.

Furthermore, the record establishes that by the time Kuhn canceled the convention, the risk of terrorism, if any, was diminishing. First, the danger, publicized since October

Page 418

[184 Ariz. 351] 1990, had failed to materialize. Second, Kuhn itself recognized that even its French employees could possibly travel as early as April. Finally, even after the commencement of Operation Desert Storm, more than 100 of Kuhn's dealers expressed their willingness to travel to Scottsdale.

We conclude that Kuhn's cancellation of the convention because of the perceived threat of terrorism was not an objectively reasonable response to an extraordinary and specific threat. The slight risk to domestic air travel by vague threats of terrorism does not equate with the actual and substantial danger of running a naval blockade in time of war. Consequently, Kuhn gains nothing by recasting its frustration of purpose argument as one of "apprehension of impossibility."

Finally, we consider whether Kuhn is entitled to relief on the ground that fear of terrorist activities resulted in less than expected attendance, which in turn made the convention uneconomical. Although economic return may be characterized as the "principal purpose" of virtually all commercial contracts, mere economic impracticality is no defense to performance of a contract. See Restatement § 265 cmt. a. ("it is not enough that transaction has become less profitable for affected party or even that he will sustain a loss"); see also *B.F. Goodrich Co. v. Vinyltech Corp.*, 711 F. Supp. 1513, 1519 (D.Ariz.1989) (applying Arizona law); See *Louisiana Power & Light Co. v. Allegheny Ludlum Indus.*, 517 F. Supp. 1319,

1324 (E.D. La. 1981). Thus, although the Gulf War's effect on the expected level of attendance may have rendered the convention uneconomical, Kuhn was not on this ground relieved of its contractual obligation.

V. PROCEDURAL DISPOSITION

The only issues raised by Kuhn in its response to the resort's motion for summary judgment on liability were its claims for relief under the doctrines of impracticability of performance and frustration of purpose. Because we conclude that Kuhn is not entitled to relief under these doctrines, partial summary judgment must be granted to the resort. See *Anderson v. Country Life Ins. Co.*, 180 Ariz. 625, 628, 886 P.2d 1381, 1384 (App. 1994). Consequently, we need not consider the resort's claim that the trial court erred in denying both the resort's motion to strike certain evidence and its motion for reconsideration in light of new evidence.

VI. CONCLUSION

We conclude that Kuhn is not entitled to relief from the contract under either the doctrine of impracticability of performance or the doctrine of frustration of purpose. Accordingly, we reverse the judgment in favor of Kuhn, order that partial summary judgment on the issue of liability be entered in favor of the resort, and remand for further proceedings consistent with this decision.

Finally, we grant the resort attorneys' fees on appeal subject to compliance with Rule 21(c), Arizona Rules of Civil Appellate Procedure.

FIDEL, P.J., and GERBER, J., concur.

[Endnotes omitted.]

Case in Point   ILLEGALITY

■ Pay special attention to section 5. "Contraband"/Public Policy

163 F. Supp. 3d 821
THE GREEN EARTH WELLNESS CENTER, LLC, Plaintiff,
v.
ATAIN SPECIALTY INSURANCE COMPANY, Defendant.
Civil Action No. 13-cv-03452-MSK-NYW
United States District Court, D. Colorado.
Signed February 17, 2016

[163 F. Supp. 3d 823]

Daniel Patrick Barton, Barton Law Firm, Hunter Milam Klein, Robert Dale Green, Robert D. Green & Associates, PC, Houston, TX, for Plaintiff.

Lauren Petrash Shannon, Melissa A. Ogburn, Pryor Johnson Carney Karr Nixon, P.C., Greenwood Village, CO, for Defendant.

OPINION AND ORDER GRANTING AND DENYING, IN PART, PENDING MOTIONS FOR SUMMARY JUDGMENT

MARCIA S. KRIEGER, Chief United States District Judge

THIS MATTER comes before the Court pursuant to the Defendant's ("Atain") Motion for Summary Judgment (# 72), the Plaintiff's ("Green Earth") response (# 81), and Atain's reply (# 88); Atain's "Motion to Determine Question of Law Regarding Legal Interpretation of Police Provision" (# 74), Green Earth's response (# 83), and Atain's reply (# 86); Atain's "Motion to Determine Question of Law Regarding Application of Federal Law and Public Policy" (# 75), Green Earth's response (# 80), and Atain's reply (# 87); and Green Earth's Motion for Partial Summary Judgment (# 77), Atain's response (# 84), and Green Earth's reply (# 89).

FACTS

The Court offers a brief factual recitation here, and elaborates as appropriate in its analysis.

Green Earth operates a retail medical marijuana business and an adjacent growing facility in Colorado Springs, Colorado. In April 2012, Green Earth sought commercial insurance for its business from Atain. Atain issued Green Earth a Commercial Property and General Liability Insurance Policy (hereinafter "the Policy") that became effective June 29, 2012.

A few days earlier, on June 23, 2012, a wildfire started in Waldo Canyon outside of Colorado Springs. Over the course of several days, the fire advanced towards the city. The fire did not directly affect Green Earth's business, but Green Earth contends that smoke and ash from the fire overwhelmed its ventilation system, eventually intruding into the growing operation and causing damage to Green Earth's marijuana plants.

In November 2012, Green Earth made a claim under the Policy for the smoke and ash damage. Atain hired several agents, including an adjuster and an investigator, to assess the claim. The investigation extended over several months. Finally, in July 2013, Atain formally denied the claim, finding that: (i) although Green Earth claimed that the smoke and ash damage occurred beginning on July 1, 2012, smoke and ash from the fire would have been

[163 F. Supp. 3d 824]

drawn into the business premises by June 23 or 24, 2012, prior to the effective date of the Policy; (ii) Green Earth's misrepresentations about the date of the loss constituted material misrepresentations under the Policy voiding any coverage; (iii) Green Earth did not mitigate its losses because its personnel did not take any measures to protect Green Earth's plants from incoming ash and soot between June 23 and July 1; and (iv) Green Earth failed to give Atain timely notice of its loss, waiting until November 25, 2012 to make a claim.

Separately, on June 7, 2013, thieves entered Green Earth's grow facility through a vent on the roof and stole some of Green Earth's marijuana plants. At some unspecified point in time, Green Earth made another claim on the Policy for damage to the roof and ventilation system. Atain investigated the claim. On September 13, 2013, Atain denied the claim, finding that the damage to the roof and ventilation system amounted to approximately $2,400, less than the Policy's $2,500 deductible.

On December 20, 2013, Green Earth commenced this action, asserting three claims: (i) breach of contract by failure to pay the claims Green Earth made under the Policy; (ii) what appears to be a statutory claim for bad faith breach of insurance contract under C.R.S. § 10-3-1104(h)(VII); and (iii) a claim for unreasonable delay in payment under C.R.S. § 10-3-1115.

Having now concluded discovery, both parties have filed a variety of dispositive motions. Atain filed a Motion for Summary Judgment **(# 72)**, arguing: (i) as to Green Earth's bad faith claim, Green Earth cannot show that Atain acted unreasonably in investigating either the fire claim or the theft claim; (ii) if Atain acted unreasonably in handling either claim, Green Earth cannot show that it did so knowingly or recklessly; (iii) as to the delayed payment claim, Green Earth cannot show that its delay or denial in authorizing payment of the claim(s) was unreasonable, for essentially the same reasons as set forth regarding the bad faith claim; and (iv) as to the breach of contract claim, Green Earth's claim for benefits relating to damage to potted marijuana plants is barred by the "growing crops" exclusion in the Policy and the damage to the roof and ventilation system is barred by the "theft" exclusion in the Policy.

Atain filed two separate "Motion[s] for Determination of Question[s] of Law." The first **(# 74)** is fairly abbreviated, apparently requesting that the Court construe the Policy's term "commencing" consonantly with the construction given that term in *Cher-D, Inc. v. Great American Alliance Ins. Co.*, 2009 WL 943530

(E.D. Pa. Apr. 7, 2009). The other **(# 75)** is considerably more elaborate, requesting that the Court resolve two questions: (i) "Whether, in light of [Colorado's Medical Marijuana Act], federal law, and federal public Policy, it is legal for Atain to pay for damages to marijuana plants and products, and if so, whether the Court can order Atain to pay for these damages"; and (ii) "Whether, in light of [those same authorities], the Policy's Contraband Exclusion removes Green Earth's marijuana plants and marijuana material from the Policy's coverage" (and arguing that the answer to the first is "no" and the answer to the second is "yes").

Green Earth filed its own Motion for Partial Summary Judgment **(# 77)**, arguing that: (i) as a matter of law, it is entitled to coverage for the loss of or damage to marijuana plants because they constitute "Stock" under the terms of the Policy; and (ii) Green Earth is entitled to summary judgment on Atain's affirmative defense of "Policy limitations," because neither the "growing crops" or "contraband" exclusions prevent coverage of the damaged plants.

[163 F. Supp. 3d 825]

ANALYSIS

A. Standard of Review

Rule 56 of the Federal Rules of Civil Procedure facilitates the entry of a judgment only if no trial is necessary. *See White v. York Intern. Corp.*, 45 F.3d 357, 360 (10th Cir. 1995). Summary adjudication is authorized when there is no genuine dispute as to any material fact and a party is entitled to judgment as a matter of law. Fed. R. Civ. P. 56(a). Substantive law governs what facts are material and what issues must be determined. It also specifies the elements that must be proved for a given claim or defense, sets the standard of proof and identifies the party with the burden of proof. *See Anderson v. Liberty Lobby, Inc.*, 477 U.S. 242, 248, 106 S. Ct. 2505, 91 L. Ed. 2d 202 (1986); *Kaiser-Francis Oil Co. v. Producer's Gas Co.*, 870 F.2d 563, 565 (10th Cir. 1989). A factual dispute is "genuine" and summary judgment is precluded if the evidence presented in support of and opposition to the motion is so contradictory that, if presented at trial, a judgment could enter for either party. *See Anderson*, 477 U.S. at 248, 106

S. Ct. 2505. When considering a summary judgment motion, a court views all evidence in the light most favorable to the non-moving party, thereby favoring the right to a trial. See *Garrett v. Hewlett-Packard Co.*, 305 F.3d 1210, 1213 (10th Cir. 2002).

If the movant has the burden of proof on a claim or defense, the movant must establish every element of its claim or defense by sufficient, competent evidence. See Fed. R. Civ. P. 56(c)(1)(A). Once the moving party has met its burden, to avoid summary judgment the responding party must present sufficient, competent, contradictory evidence to establish a genuine factual dispute. See *Bacchus Indus., Inc. v. Arvin Indus., Inc.*, 939 F.2d 887, 891 (10th Cir. 1991); *Perry v. Woodward*, 199 F.3d 1126, 1131 (10th Cir. 1999). If there is a genuine dispute as to a material fact, a trial is required. If there is no genuine dispute as to any material fact, no trial is required. The court then applies the law to the undisputed facts and enters judgment.

If the moving party does not have the burden of proof at trial, it must point to an absence of sufficient evidence to establish the claim or defense that the non-movant is obligated to prove. If the respondent comes forward with sufficient competent evidence to establish a *prima facie* claim or defense, a trial is required. If the respondent fails to produce sufficient competent evidence to establish its claim or defense, then the movant is entitled to judgment as a matter of law. See *Celotex Corp. v. Catrett*, 477 U.S. 317, 322-23, 106 S. Ct. 2548, 91 L. Ed. 2d 265 (1986).

This case involves cross-motions for summary judgment. "Because the determination of whether there is a genuine dispute as to a material factual issue turns upon who has the burden of proof, the standard of proof and whether adequate evidence has been submitted to support a *prima facie* case or to establish a genuine dispute as to material fact, cross motions must be evaluated independently." *In re Ribozyme Pharmaceuticals, Inc., Securities Litig.*, 209 F. Supp. 2d 1106, 1112 (D. Colo. 2002); see also *Atlantic Richfield Co. v. Farm Credit Bank of Wichita*, 226 F.3d 1138, 1148 (10th Cir. 2000); *Buell Cabinet Co. v. Sudduth*, 608 F.2d 431, 433 (10th Cir. 1979) ("Cross-motions for summary judgment are to be treated separately; the denial of one does not require the grant of another.").

Rather than address the motions *seriatim*, the Court finds it more appropriate to sort the issues raised by the parties based on the two insurance claims Green Earth made on Atain, and then to address the various issues raised by the parties' motions that are pertinent to each claim.

[163 F. Supp. 3d 826]

B. The Waldo Canyon Fire Claim

To understand the context in which this dispute arises, the Court detours briefly into an examination of Green Earth's growing operation. The parties entered into a joint stipulation of facts **(# 71)**, designed to facilitate the Court's consideration of the summary judgment motions. The stipulation provides that Green Earth's claim relating to the Waldo Canyon fire seeks coverage for losses relating to several different classifications of plants: "mother plants," "flower plants," "veg plants," "clones," and "finished product," all of which were allegedly damaged by smoke and ash. The parties' stipulation does not elaborate on the particular function that each of these classifications serve in the production process; it states only that all of these are "potted plants" which are "grown indoors under artificial lighting in pots."

Green Earth's motion attaches an affidavit from its expert, Vincent Hanson. Mr. Hanson's affidavit recites "certain universal steps that all [marijuana] growers utilize" to produce product, and attests that Green Earth follows those same steps. Greatly summarizing Mr. Hanson's description, "mother plants" are plants of each individual strain of marijuana that Green Earth offers. Mother plants are not cultivated to produce useable marijuana on their own; rather, they are maintained by the grower solely for the purpose of producing a constant and reliable supply of genetically-identical "clones." A clone is a portion of the mother plant that is cut off and planted in a growing medium until it produces its own root, becoming a viable marijuana plant in its own right. The clones then grow to maturity. Mature clones are kept by the grower in one of two states: a "vegetative" (or "veg") state, in which the plant is kept under near constant lighting to prevent it from flowering; and a "flowering" state, in which the plant is subject to intermittent light and darkness in order to induce it to produce flowers and buds. At the appropriate time, the grower harvests the flowering clone, cutting off flowers and buds (and sometimes other portions of the plants), drying that material, and selling it.

For purposes of this case, Green Earth's claim under the Policy relating to the Waldo Canyon fire can be broken into two parts: a claim for more than $200,000 in damage to Green Earth's grow operation, namely its growing mother plants and clones, and a claim for approximately $40,000 in damage to buds and flowers that had already been harvested and were being prepared for sale.

Green Earth's summary judgment motion seeks judgment in its favor on its breach of contract claim, arguing that both losses were covered under the Policy's grant of coverage over Green Earth's "Stock." Atain seeks summary judgment on Green Earth's breach of contract claim relating to the Waldo Canyon fire claim, arguing: (i) that the Policy provision covering "Stock" does not apply to the growing plants; (ii) that any grant of coverage that may exist regarding the growing plants is subject to an exclusion from coverage of "growing crops"; (iii) a somewhat unclear argument to the effect that Green Earth's losses commenced prior to the coverage period; (iv) that any coverage of growing or finished marijuana is subject to an exclusion of coverage as "Contraband"; and

[163 F. Supp. 3d 827]

(v) that a contention that any grant of coverage is, essentially, void as against public Policy. The Court takes these arguments in turn.

1. Policy Interpretation Generally

The parties have not addressed what jurisdiction's law governs the Policy, but both rely on Colorado law. The "Service of Suit Endorsement" in the Policy itself seems to suggest that disputes between the parties will be governed by the law of the state in which the suit is brought—here, Colorado. In Colorado, interpretation of a contract's terms presents a question of law to be resolved by the Court. *Compass Ins. Co. v. City of Littleton*, 984 P.2d 606, 613 (Colo. 1999).

When construing the terms of a contract, the Court's ultimate objective is to give effect to the parties' mutual intentions. *East Ridge of Fort Collins, LLC v. Larimer & Weld Irrig. Co.*, 109 P.3d 969, 973 (Colo.2005). Absent some showing that the parties intended otherwise, the Court indulges in the assumption that the plain and ordinary meanings of the words used in the contract reflect the parties' agreement. *Id.*; *Level 3 Communications, LLC v. Liebert Corp.*, 535 F.3d 1146, 1154 (10th Cir. 2008). Where the plain language is, of itself, insufficient to compel an unambiguous interpretation, the Court turns to a variety of additional rules help shape its analysis, including various canons of construction—*e.g.* that the Court should examine a given phrase in the context of the agreement as a whole, not in isolation; that specific provisions addressing an issue trump more general ones; that the Court should avoid constructions that render a provision superfluous or nonsensical; and the Court must not add to or subtract from the agreement's terms. *Id.*; *Cyprus Ama x Minerals Co. v. Lexington Ins. Co.*, 74 P.3d 294, 299 (Colo. 2003). Extrinsic evidence may be relevant in demonstrating whether particular language is or is not ambiguous. *Id.* If the Court still cannot ascertain the appropriate interpretation after all this, it defaults to the rule that ambiguities must be resolved against the drafter of the language, here, Atain. *State Farm Mut. Auto Ins. Co. v. Nissen*, 851 P.2d 165, 166 (Colo. 1993).

2. "Stock"

The Policy provides that it covers, among other things, Green Earth's "Business Personal Property located in or on the [covered] building[s]," including "Stock," which the Policy defines as "merchandise held in storage or for sale, raw materials and in-process or finished goods, including supplies used in their packing or shipping." The parties agree that the finished product—the harvested flowers and buds—allegedly damaged by the smoke and ash qualify as "Stock" (although Atain disputes that such product is covered for other reasons discussed below). The first question thus presented is whether the damaged mother plants and clones (whether in veg or flowering states) are covered as "Stock."

The Policy defines "Stock" to include "raw materials and in-process or finished goods." A "raw material" is "the basic material from which a product is manufactured or made; unprocessed material." *Oxford English Dictionary*, 3d Ed. The Court has some difficulty with the notion that growing plants could be considered "raw materials." In common vernacular, producers of agricultural products do not typically refer to their growing plants as "raw materials," and Green Earth certainly has not pointed to notable examples of such a use of the language. Green Earth points only to a single example of the phrase "raw materials" being used to refer to growing agricultural products: the *Merriam-Webster Dictionary* (10th Ed.) uses the example "wheat . . . is raw material for the flour mill." Atain points out, somewhat

[163 F. Supp. 3d 828]

persuasively, that this sentence is probably referring to wheat that has been harvested and transported to the mill for processing, not a crop of wheat that remains growing in the field.

Neither party's argument does much to advance the analysis beyond this point. Neither party, for example, points to any discussions or correspondence between the parties about the scope of any insurance policy that would ultimately issue, nor do the parties point to other extrinsic evidence that would demonstrate that they shared some mutual understanding as to what might be covered by the term "Stock."

Although the use of the term "raw material" to describe a growing agricultural product appears somewhat idiosyncratic, the Court is not prepared to say, particularly at the summary judgment stage, that it would require a construction of the Policy that excludes growing plants as a matter of law. A cursory internet search reveals occasional instances where authors have used the phrase "raw materials" in a context that could refer to growing plants. Although these examples are infrequent and the term "raw materials" is used somewhat obliquely, the Court is satisfied that there is at least a colorable argument to be made that the term "raw materials" can sometimes include an agricultural producer's growing plants. This would permit a conclusion that the term "Stock" as used in the Atain Policy could cover Green Earth's growing plants.

3. *"Growing Crops"*

This does not end the inquiry, however. Assuming that the Policy extends coverage to the mother plants and clones as "Stock," it nevertheless excludes coverage if the plants are "growing crops." Such exclusion is found in Paragraph A(1) of the Building and Personal Property Coverage Form, which states that "Covered Property means the type of property [covered by Paragraph] A.1"—which includes the provision extending coverage to "stock"—"and limited in [Paragraph] A.2, Property Not Covered." Paragraph A.2 operates to exclude any coverage for "Land (including land on which the property is located), water, growing crops or lawns." The question becomes whether Green Earth's plants constitute "growing crops."

The *Oxford English Dictionary* defines "crop," in this context, as "the yield or produce of some particular cereal or other plant in a single season or in a particular locality," "the whole of the plants which engage the agricultural industry of a particular district or season," (*i.e.* "this year's orange crop") or "the produce of the land, either while growing or when gathered; harvest" (*e.g.* "the farmer's corn crops were decimated by the hail"). *See also Merriam-Webster Dictionary* 10th Ed. ("a

[163 F. Supp. 3d 829]

Plant . . . that can be grown and harvested extensively for profit or subsistence").

Green Earth argues that "crops," by definition, must grow in outdoor soil, and that plants raised indoors in containers—such as its mother plants and clones—do not fit that definition. For the most part, the dictionary definitions of "crop" do not support this assertion—they make no particular distinction between plants grown indoors or outdoors. Although one of the *Oxford English Dictionary*'s definitions does use the term "produce of the land," the Court understands that reference to be referring to plants generally, in the sense that plants rise out of soil (*i.e.* "the land"), whether that soil is on the ground or in a pot. In other words, the Court understands reference to "produce of the land" makes clear that a "crop of sheep" or other animals would be an incorrect usage, as the animals do not grow out from soil.

The Court sees nothing in the plain meaning of the word "crop" that would seem to differentiate between "crops" growing naturally in the solid earth and "crops" of plants growing in pots or otherwise in artificial conditions such as an indoor greenhouse. Indeed, a search of Westlaw reveals many instances in which courts have casually used the term "crops" to refer to plants growing in controlled indoor environments. *See e.g. Coastal & Native Plant Specialties, Inc. v. Engineered Textile Products, Inc.*, 139 F. Supp. 2d 1326, 1340 (N.D.Fl.2001) ("These grants were in part used to construct and modify greenhouses and to hydroponically grown crops, such as onions"); *Avila v. Lin*, 2014 WL 6432279 (Ca. App. Nov. 17, 2014) ("Jiang destroyed two greenhouses before he realized there were growing crops within them."); *see also Stuart v. Haughton High School*, 614 So. 2d 804, 805 (La. App. 1993) ("Mr. Stuart began growing tomatoes hydroponically in the controlled environment [of a hothouse] which allowed year-round tomato production . . . a hole in the plastic sheeting could cause the loss of the entire tomato crop as the result of a sudden change in temperature"); *In re Sunnyland Farms, Inc.*, 517 B.R. 263, 265 (N.M. Bankr. 2014) ("The only crop ever produced in the [hydroponic greenhouse complex] was a crop of tomatoes produced in 2005."). This is considerable evidence that the common use of the term "crops" does not distinguish between plants growing indoors and plants growing outdoors.

Interpreting "growing crops" as excluding coverage for Green Earth's mother and clone plants is also consistent with the parties' pre-Policy actions. In April 2012, Atain issued a quote for insurance to Green Earth; among the terms of that quotation is a provision that reads "Coverage does not extent to growing or standing plants." The record suggests that Green Earth apparently accepted this offer, as the parties then entered into a "binder"—a temporary contract of insurance pending issuance of the formal Policy. The binder also contained a provision reading that "Coverage does not extent to growing or standing plants." Although the quote and binder are extrinsic to (and ultimately superseded by) the Policy itself, Colorado law permits the Court to consider extrinsic evidence for the purpose of ascertaining whether an ambiguity exists in the Policy language. *Level 3*, 535 F.3d at 1155. Here, these documents suggest that the parties have consistently understood that the ultimate Policy would not cover Green Earth's marijuana plants, and thus, construing "growing crops" to be ambiguous would inexplicably deviate from the parties' prior course of dealing.

Green Earth offers several arguments as to why the term "growing crops" should be found to be ambiguous, and further, why the Court should find that it does not extend to the plants themselves.

[163 F. Supp. 3d 830]

Only the first of these arguments directly engages the "growing crops" language in the Policy. Green Earth argues that the "growing crops" exclusion should be construed according to the doctrine of *noscitur a sociis* ("it is known by its associates"). This doctrine suggests that the Court should "avoid ascribing to one word a meaning so broad that it is inconsistent with its accompanying words." *Yates v. U.S.*, __ U.S. __, 135 S. Ct. 1074, 1084, 191 L. Ed. 2d 64 (2015). Green Earth argues that the phrase "growing crops" should be given a construction that shares a common character with the other terms—"land," "water," and "lawns"—used in that exclusion. It argues that all three of these terms seem to be describing real property: the solid earth, bodies of water found on it, and outdoor areas of grass attached to the earth. From this, Green Earth urges that the phrase "growing crops" should be limited to those crops that grow in and attached to the surface of the earth, not to crops that are grown in pots.

The Court is not persuaded that the other terms used in the Policy warrant the assumption that the term "growing crops" describes only plants growing outdoors, but more importantly, the Court rejects the argument because the doctrine of *noscitur a sociis* may not be used to create an ambiguity where one otherwise does not exist. *Dillabaugh v. Ellerton*, 259 P.3d 550, 554 (Colo. App. 2011). Finding that there is no inherent ambiguity in the phrase "growing crops," the Court declines to resort to *noscitur a sociis* to force a different conclusion.

Second, Green Earth argues that marijuana plants cannot be considered "crops," based on various definitions found in federal and state statutes. For example, it points to regulations implementing the Federal Crop Insurance Act, 40 C.F.R. § 180.1, and notes that those regulations do not enumerate marijuana among its "crop groups." It points to a March 25, 2015 notice from the Colorado Department of Agriculture, articulating that agency's "Policy regarding the criteria for pesticide use that would not be a violation of the label when used for the production of marijuana" in Colorado. The notice recites that the Department attempted to determine "which pesticides, if any, might be used legally on marijuana," because "pesticide labels will specify the particular crops . . . to which they can be applied." The Department consulted the various crop groups in that same federal regulation and, not surprisingly, concluded that "[n]owhere . . . is marijuana listed under any crop grouping." Green Earth also cites to the regulations of the Colorado Department of Revenue, pointing out that in various locations, these regulations dictate that growing plants "shall be considered plant inventory" or "shall be accounted for as inventory." From these, Green Earth argues that, legally, growing marijuana cannot be described as "crops." The Court rejects this argument entirely. The fact that various regulatory agencies might refer to marijuana plants as "inventory" for one purpose or decide that they do not fit within existing definitions of "crop groups" for another purpose is irrelevant for the purpose of determining the parties' intentions as to how the particular language in this Policy should be construed. Neither the Policy nor the communications between the parties even remotely suggest that these references were pertinent to or considered by the parties at the time the policy terms were negotiated.

Green Earth's final, and most elaborate, argument is that it intended and expected that the Policy would cover the plants, and thus, the Policy should be construed to extend such coverage. This argument springs from a perfectly reasonable premise—Green Earth sought to insure its plants through the purchase of business insurance. From that, Green Earth points

[163 F. Supp. 3d 831]

out that Colorado law adheres to the "reasonable expectations" doctrine: that courts will honor the reasonable expectations of an insured where circumstances attributable to an insurer have deceived a objectively reasonable insured into believing that it is entitled to coverage for a certain loss. *Bailey v. Lincoln General Ins. Co.*, 255 P.3d 1039, 1053 (Colo. 2011). But the reasonable expectations doctrine is not applicable here. The doctrine requires an insured to show "that its expectations of coverage are based on specific facts which make these

expectations reasonable"; "bare allegations of Policyholders that they expected certain coverage" is not, of itself, sufficient. *Id.* at 1054. Green Earth offers nothing but a bare statement of its expectation that the Policy would cover its growing plants—the affidavit of Chris Fallis, one of its owners, states that "It was my understanding and my intention that the Policy of insurance provide coverage for the potted marijuana plants" and "It was absolutely not my intention to seek insurance coverage that excludes the very plants that are my business." Mr. Fallis' affidavit is notable for its carefully chosen language, as he does not assert that he expressed his intention to Atain, much less suggest that Atain understood and agreed to meet the expectation. To the contrary, the extrinsic evidence in the record indicates that Atain repeatedly, plainly, and conspicuously advised Green Earth that growing plants would not be covered, and there is no evidence that Green Earth ever objected.

Finally, Green Earth offers an appeal to common sense: that there would be little point to it obtaining insurance if the insurance did not going to cover its plants. This might be true if the Policy provided no benefit to Green Earth. But the Policy is far from worthless to Green Earth even if it did not cover growing plants. The Policy still insured Green Earth against general liabilities that could arise from operation of a commercial storefront and insured Green Earth against damage to non-plant business property, such as lighting systems, irrigation systems, ventilation systems, timers, computers and business machines, and so on. In this sense, the scope of the intended coverage is somewhat reflected in the questions and answers on Attain's "Medical Marijuana Dispensary Supplemental Application." This supplemental application is a one-page form primarily focuses on operation of Green Earth's dispensary business: *e.g.* "Do you utilize security doors?," "Does the applicant have a weapon on premises?," "Do you utilize private security guards?," etc. Only one question on the application even inquires about growing plants—"Do you grow Marijuana or other cannabis plants on the premises?"—and it does not ask for elaboration in the event of a "yes" answer. If, as Green Earth argues, it would be common sense for an insurance Policy written for a marijuana business to cover growing plants, one would also assume that the insurer's marijuana-specific application form would make detailed inquiries about the number, types, and values of the plants it was going to insure. The fact that Atain never sought details about Green Earth's grow operation further refutes any contention that Green Earth's expectations that the Policy would cover its growing plants was a reasonable one.

Accordingly, the Court finds that the Policy's exclusion of coverage for "growing

[163 F. Supp. 3d 832]

crops" unambiguously encompasses any body of plants tended for their agricultural yield, at least until they are harvested. This term clearly encompasses Green Earth's mother plants and clones.

This means that the only plants that are covered by the Policy are those that are "Stock", but not "growing crops." Thus, the Court finds that mother plants or clones are growing crops, and therefore are not covered by the Policy.

4. "Commencing"

Green Earth's claim from the Waldo Canyon fire also includes a claim for coverage of approximately $40,000 worth of "finished product"—that is, harvested buds, flowers, and other plant material. Atain essentially concedes that this material falls within the grant of coverage for "Stock" and is not excluded by the "growing crops" exclusion.

However, Atain argues that Green Earth's loss "commenced" as early as June 26, 2012 prior to the Policy taking effect on June 29. It points to a Policy provision that provides that the Policy "cover[s] loss or damage *commencing* during the Policy period." Atain argues that the Court should construe the term "commencing," as meaning "beginning." Green Earth does not dispute this meaning, but argues that there is a disputed question of fact as to when its losses from the Waldo Canyon fire began.

Given that both Atain and Green Earth agree that the term "commencing," as used in the Policy, means "beginning," the Court declines to construe the term. The Court agrees that the parties' dispute is one of fact—when did Green Earth's losses actually begin to occur? Both parties have identified evidentiary support for their own answers to this question, and thus, a trial is required.

5. "Contraband"/Public Policy

Finally, Atain argues that application of another exclusionary provision in the Policy excludes coverage for lost harvested buds and flowers. It invokes the exclusion of coverage for "Contraband, or property in the course of illegal transportation or trade" and argues that public policy requires that coverage be denied, even if the Policy would otherwise provide it.

The Policy does not define the term "Contraband," so the Court turns to the common and ordinary meaning of that term: "goods or merchandise whose importation, exportation, or possession is forbidden." *Meriam-Webster Collegiate Dictionary* (10th Ed.). The Court accepts Atain's observation that the possession of marijuana for distribution purposes continues to constitute a federal crime under 21 U.S.C. § 841(a)(1) and (b)(1)(D). But, as the parties are well-aware, the nominal federal prohibition against possession of marijuana conceals a far more nuanced (and perhaps even erratic) expression of federal Policy. The Court will not attempt to explain nor summarize, the conflicting signals that the federal government has given regarding marijuana regulation and enforcement since 2009. It is sufficient to

[163 F. Supp. 3d 833]

recognize that as early as 2009, and again mere weeks before Atain formally denied Green Earth's claim from the Waldo Canyon fire, federal authorities had made public statements that reflected an ambivalence towards enforcement of the Controlled Substances Act in circumstances where a person or entity's possession and distribution of marijuana was consistent with well-regulated state law. Other than pointing to federal criminal statutes, Attain offers no evidence that the application of existing federal public policy statements would be expected to result in criminal enforcement against Green Earth for possession or distribution of medical marijuana, nor does Atain assert that Green Earth's operations were somehow in violation of Colorado law. In short, the Policy's "Contraband" exclusion is rendered ambiguous by the difference between the federal government's *de jure* and *de facto* public policies regarding state-regulated medical marijuana.

With that ambiguity in mind, the Court turns to the parties' mutual intention regarding coverage of

Green Earth's saleable marijuana inventory. Just as the extrinsic evidence strongly suggested that the parties intended to exclude coverage for growing plants, the same evidence strongly suggests that the parties mutually intended to include coverage for harvested plants constituting Green Earth's inventory. Atain's repeated pre-Policy statements that it was refusing to cover "growing plants" suggests, by negative implication, that it was willing to extend coverage to harvested plants and other inventory. Moreover, unlike its apparent disinterest regarding the scope and value of the grow operation, Atain's Medical Marijuana Dispensary Supplemental Application asks several questions about the amount and value of inventory that Green Earth keeps on its premises—e.g. "How much inventory is displayed to customers?" (with instructions to deny insurance if more than 25% is displayed); "How much [by value] of inventory do you keep on premises during non-business hours?"; "After business hours, is all inventory stored in a locked safe . . . ?" These questions indicate that some form of coverage of Green Earth's inventory was something contemplated by both parties.

More fundamentally, it is undisputed that, before entering into the contract of insurance, Atain knew that Green Earth was operating a medical marijuana business. It is also undisputed that Atain knew—or very well should have known—that federal law nominally prohibited such a business. Notwithstanding that knowledge, Atain nevertheless elected to issue a policy to Green Earth, and that policy unambiguously extended coverage for Green Earth's inventory of saleable marijuana. Nothing in the record ever indicates that Atain sought to disclaim coverage for Green Earth's inventory, much less that Atain ever informed Green Earth of its position that such inventory was not insurable. In such circumstances, the Court finds that the record suggests that the parties shared a mutual intention that the Policy would insure Green Earths' marijuana

[163 F. Supp. 3d 834]

inventory and that the "Contraband" exclusion would not apply to it.

Under these circumstances, the Court finds that the "Contraband" exclusion is ambiguous such that

Atain is not entitled to summary judgment on Green Earth's claim for breach of contract arising from Atain's refusal to pay for harvested plants damaged by the Waldo Canyon fire.

This leaves Atain's "public Policy" requests. Atain "asks for some direction and assurances from this Court" as to how it should proceed. It "asks the Court to rule on" a specific question: "Whether, in light of [federal and state law], it is legal for Atain to pay for damage to marijuana plants and products, and if so, whether the Court can order Atain to pay for these damages."

These requests present problems. First, the Court does not and cannot give "assurances" to a party about the legality of engaging in particular conduct, nor does the Court intend to offer any particular opinion as to "whether . . . it is legal for Atain to pay for damages to marijuana plants and products." The Court assumes that Atain obtained legal opinions and assurances on these points from its own counsel before ever embarking on the business of insuring medical marijuana operations. Nor does the Court provide "direction" to parties as to how they should proceed. The Court's function here is purely adjudicatory—applying Colorado law. Green Earth alleges that Atain made contractual promises, then breached them. With regard to such claim, the Court merely interprets and applies the terms of the Policy, and where there is a material factual dispute, directs that matter be set for trial. Any judgment issued by this Court will be recompense to Green Earth based on Atain's failure to honor its contractual promises, not an instruction to Atain to "pay for damages to marijuana plants and products."

The unarticulated sub-text to this argument appears to be a request that the Court declare the Policy unenforceable as against public policy. Atain submits several cases in which courts have tried to reconcile federal and state law with regard to marijuana. Most of these cases are off-point, as they do not involve contractual claims in which both parties had a mutual

[163 F. Supp. 3d 835]

intent to treat marijuana products as insurable commodities, only to have one party unilaterally seek to abandon that position later. Only *Tracy v. USAA Cas. Ins. Co.*, 2012 WL 928186 (D. Hi. Mar. 16, 2012), involves the question of whether an insurer is liable for breach for failing to pay an insurance claim for loss or damage to marijuana plants. There, the court found that an insured whose possession of marijuana plants was in conformance with state regulations had an insurable interest in those plants. The court ultimately concluded that the federal Controlled Substances Act nevertheless prevailed over state law, such that enforcing the terms of the insurance Policy "would be contrary to federal law and public Policy," and granted summary judgment to the insurer on the insured's breach of contract claim. *Id.*

For the reasons discussed above, and particularly in light of several additional years evidencing a continued erosion of any clear and consistent federal public policy in this area, this Court declines to follow *Tracy*. Accordingly, the Court declines Atain's indirect invitation to declare the Policy void on public policy grounds. Atain, having entered into the Policy of its own will, knowingly and intelligently, is obligated to comply with its terms or pay damages for having breached it.

Thus, the Court finds that Green Earth's breach of contract claim with regard to the approximately $40,000 claim made by Green Earth for damage to harvested marijuana buds and flowers damaged in the Waldo Canyon fire must be tried. Bcause Green Earth's claim that Atain breached the contract remains colorable, the Court denies Atain's motion for summary judgment on Green Earth's statutory claims for bad faith breach and unreasonable delay in payment relating to that portion of the Waldo Canyon claim. Those claims shall proceed to trial as well.

C. Theft Claim

This claim arises from an incident on June 7, 2013, in which thieves entered Green Earth's grow facility through a roof vent and stole various plants. Green Earth made a claim on Atain for benefits under the Policy because of that incident. Green Earth did not seek coverage for the stolen marijuana plants, but did assert that the thieves caused damage to the roof and ventilation system, and that those losses occasioned certain consequential losses in the form of damage to drywall and other interior contents of the building from water that came through the hole the thieves created in the building's roof. Atain seeks summary judgment on Green Earth's claims arising out of this incident.

Atain first points to language in the Policy that excludes coverage for "loss or damage caused by or resulting from theft." However, it concedes that this exclusion is in turn subject to certain limitations, most notably, that coverage does exist for "Building damage caused by the breaking in or exiting of burglars." Atain argues that Green Earth cannot show that the building damage caused by the thieves was caused in the course of the thieves "breaking in or exiting" the building. It also makes an abbreviated argument that Green Earth cannot show that the amount of covered damage arising from the theft exceeds the Policy deductible of $2,500.

In response, Green Earth tenders the affidavit of Justin Flowers that unambiguously states that Green Earth (and not its landlord) was the owner of the ventilation system, and that he observed security camera footage showing the thieves entering the building through a hole they created in that system. Green Earth also tenders the report of David Poynter, a contractor, who opines that the damage to the roof and duct work is approximately $8,000.

[163 F. Supp. 3d 836]

Atain does not meaningfully dispute these assertions in its reply, nor does it point to any contrary evidence as to causation. At most, it refers to remarks that its own adjuster valued the claim differently than did Mr. Poynter. Thus, there is a triable dispute as to whether the damage caused by this incident is covered by the Policy and whether the amount of that loss exceeds the Policy's deductible. Atain's motion seeking summary judgment on Green Earth's breach of contract claim as it relates to the theft claim is denied.

However, the Court finds it appropriate to grant summary judgment to Atain on Green Earth's bad faith breach of contract claim and unreasonable delay in payment claim as it relates to the theft claim. Both of these claims require a showing that the insurer acted "unreasonably" in denying the claim or refusing to pay benefits. To prove that an insurer acted unreasonably, an insured must come forward with evidence (typically from an expert) that the insurer's conduct violated industry standards, and the determination of reasonableness is an objective one. *Estate of Morris v. COPI C Ins. Co.*, 192 P.3d 519, 524 (Colo. App. 2008). Here, Atain's original basis for denying the theft claim was that its adjuster valued the claim at approximately $2,400, below the Policy's $2,500 deductible. Green Earth certainly disagrees with Atain's adjuster's valuation, but Green Earth has not come forward with evidence to show that Atain's valuation was objectively unreasonable—it does not, for example, tender an expert who opines that no reasonable contractor or adjuster could believe that the identified damages could be fully repaired for as little as $2,400, or demonstrate that Atain's adjuster conspicuously overlooked substantial components of the claim that would have been covered.

Green Earth relies on Senior Judge Matsch's order denying summary judgment in *Jewkes v. USAA Cas. Ins. Co.*, D.C. Colo. Case No. 13-cv-01673-RPM (Jun. 26, 2014). There, Judge Matsch denied an insurer's motion for summary judgment on an insured's bad faith claim, explaining that "[t]o grant this motion this Court must find that an insurance company's reliance on expert reports is itself a sufficient showing of a reasonable basis for denial of benefits." *Id.* Judge Matsch went on to find that an adjuster's subjective evaluation of a claim is insufficient to establish reasonableness under the objective standard, and that "the veracity of the opinions expressed in . . . expert reports, the quality of the investigations done and the competence of the investigators are relevant issues [that] should be [decided] by a jury." *Id.*

This Court disagrees. Under Colorado law, the party asserting the bad faith claim has the burden of proof, and thus the burden of demonstrating the un reasonableness of the insurer's actions lies with the insured. *See Pham v. State Farm Mut. Automobile Ins. Co.*, 70 P.3d 567, 572 (Colo. App. 2003). Judge Matsch improperly placed the burden on the insurer to demonstrate that its position was reasonable as a matter of law, when the proper allocation of proof requires the insured to demonstrate that the insurer's position is unreasonable. It is not sufficient for an insured to simply tender a different valuation of a claim; indeed, were the Court to hold that a mere

disagreement between parties as to the valuation of a claim created a triable bad faith claim, essentially every insurance dispute would proceed to trial on such a claim, as disputes between the insurer and insured over the proper valuation of the loss are routine.

Because Green Earth has not come forward with evidence to demonstrate that Atain's valuation of the losses covered under the theft claim was unreasonable,

[163 F. Supp. 3d 837]

Atain is entitled to summary judgment on Green Earth's bad faith claims relating to the theft claim.

CONCLUSION

For the forgoing reasons, Atain's Motion for Summary Judgment **(# 72)** and "Motion to Determine Question of Law Regarding Application of Federal Law and Public Policy" **(# 75)**, and Green Earth's Motion for Partial Summary Judgment **(# 77)** are each **GRANTED IN PART** and **DENIED IN PART** as follows: Atain is entitled to summary judgment on Green Earth's claims as they relate to damage to growing marijuana plants and Green Earth's claims for bad faith breach of contract or unreasonable delay in payment as they relate to Green Earth's insurance claim arising out of the June 2013 theft.

Green Earth's breach of contract, bad faith, and delayed payment claims will proceed to trial with regard to Green Earth's claim for benefits arising out of damage to harvested marijuana buds and flowers allegedly caused by the Waldo Canyon fire, and Green Earth's claim for breach of contract only will proceed to trial with regard to Green Earth's claim for insurance benefits arising out of the June 2013 theft. Atain's "Motion to Determine Question of Law Regarding Legal Interpretation of Policy Provision" **(# 74)** is **DENIED**.

Although the Court would normally direct the parties to begin preparation of a Proposed Pretrial Order and schedule a Pretrial Conference at this point in the litigation, given the narrowing of the claims as set forth above, the Court instead finds it appropriate to set the matter for an Interim Case Management Conference pursuant to Fed. R. Civ. P. 16(c)(2). At that conference, the parties shall be prepared to enter into all appropriate factual stipulations so as to alleviate the need for evidentiary presentation of undisputed facts, to resolve any claims or portions of claims for which no further dispute exists, and to otherwise narrow and sharpen the case further before investing further time and resources into pretrial preparation. The Court will conduct this Interim Case Management Conference at **10:00 a.m.** on **May 10, 2016**.

Chapter 12

Changes by Agreement of the Parties

Chapter Objectives

The student will be able to:

- Use vocabulary regarding changes in contact terms or performance properly.
- Identify when consideration is necessary for the change(s).
- Determine a party's right to sue and when it is waived by the subsequent agreement.
- Differentiate among the five types of agreements that can alter the terms of performance.

This chapter will examine HOW parties can terminate the contractual relationship by making changes to the existing agreement and WHAT terms must be included in order to effectuate the valid and enforceable termination. Full satisfactory performance and breach are two ways that a contract comes to an end. There is another alternative: The parties themselves may change the contract, which then escapes either result. The "new" or alternate contract changes the requirements for performance. This alternative still requires that certain elements be present in order to enforce the "new" end result.

Renegotiation of the contract, in an attempt to salvage what they can of the agreement, can take many forms, all of which avoid recourse to the court system. The incentive to reach a "new" agreement lies in the costly and time-consuming nature of litigation and/or the parties' need to maintain their relationship. These methods of reformation include

1. Mutual rescission
2. Release
3. Accord and satisfaction
4. Substituted agreement/novation
5. Modification

MUTUAL RESCISSION

If both parties agree to surrender their respective rights under the contract without holding the other "at fault," and responsible in any way, then they have mutually rescinded the contract. It should be stressed that the agreement to terminate the contract must be mutual; both parties, through words or actions, must assent to the abandonment of the performance obligations. If rescission is inferred from the actions and circumstances surrounding the contract, then those actions must be inconsistent with the continuing existence of the contract. It is as if they throw their hands up in despair and say: Never mind, let's just call this whole deal off. *See Puma v. Gordon*, 402 N.E.2d 110, 115 (Mass. App. Ct., 1980) It became clear that the parties "considered the deal between them dead. The fact that the judge could not pinpoint the actual date of abandonment does not detract from the conclusion that the parties gradually drew apart, manifesting an intent to be no longer bound by the agreement. An agreement to rescind a contract need not be made in any formal, express terms. Rather, mutual assent to a rescission may be inferred from the attendant circumstances and conduct of the parties."

mutual rescission
An agreement by mutual assent of both parties to terminate the contractual relationship and return to the pre-contract status quo.

Contract law applies the term **mutual rescission** to the cancellation of a contract where neither party has performed, or if there has been some performance, it is minimal. Calling off the contract in its early stages poses less of a risk for loss for unjust enrichment of a party. The parties recognize that the deal is no longer worth pursuing and there is nothing to be gained or lost by the agreement to end the contract by this means. If any consideration has been exchanged, it is returned and the parties return to the position they were in prior to the agreement as if nothing had happened. If the party seeking the rescission cannot put the other party in the same position she was in prior to the contract, then rescission is not appropriate. "As a general rule, a party is not allowed to rescind where he is not in a position to put the other *in statu quo* by restoring the consideration passed." *Opsahl v. Pinehurst Inc.*, 344 S.E.2d 68, 74 (N.C. App. 1986) (internal citations omitted).

EYE ON ETHICS

When must an attorney seek rescission of the contract? As previously noted, an attorney may withdraw (be excused) from the contract of representation if she becomes incapacitated. On a further note, if an attorney does not seek mutual rescission in a case where she has become incapacitated, ethical sanctions should follow. *See In re Horwitz*, 154 A.2d 878, 879 (Conn. Super. Ct. 1959) (internal citations omitted).

> An attorney at law is an officer of court, exercising a privilege or franchise to the enjoyment of which he has been admitted, not as a matter of right, but upon proof of fitness, through evidence of his possession of satisfactory legal attainments and fair private character. For the manner in which this privilege or franchise is exercised he is continually accountable to the court, and it may at any time be declared forfeited for such misconduct, whether professional or nonprofessional, as shows him to be an unfit or unsafe person to enjoy the privilege conferred upon him and to manage the business of others in the capacity of an attorney. The power to declare this forfeiture is a summary one inherent in the courts, and exists, not to mete out punishment to an offender, but that the administration of justice may be safeguarded that the courts and the public [are] protected from the misconduct or unfitness of those who are licensed to perform the important functions of the legal profession.

A mutual rescission also acts as a **covenant not to sue** for breach as it acknowledges that there has been consent by both parties to forgo any legal remedies. This should also sound like consideration. The reason this mutual rescission "sticks" is due to the support of new, valid, legal consideration. The freedom of contract principles that make it possible for parties to create almost any contractual relationship by mutual consent also permit parties to freely terminate their contractual relationship by mutual consent. Similar to other contractual intent principles, the mutual rescission must be "clear, positive, unequivocal, and decisive, and it must manifest the parties' actual intent to abandon contract rights." *Dunn Indus. Group, Inc. v. City of Sugar Creek*, 112 S.W.3d 421, 429 (Mo. 2003).

A typical covenant not to sue is provided in Figure 12.1.

How are these covenants used? For example, the Newlyweds and Bob the Builder enter into an agreement for the construction of their new home in suburban Chicago. After signing the contract but prior to breaking ground, the Newlyweds change their mind about the house; they are simply not ready to be homeowners yet. Bob, a nice guy, doesn't want to force the young couple into emotional and financial turmoil so, instead of suing for enforcement, he agrees to rescind the contract and executes a covenant not to sue for their benefit. No harm—no foul; both parties walk away from the deal owing each other nothing. *But see Overton v. Kingsbrooke*

covenant not to sue
An agreement by the parties to relinquish their right to commence a lawsuit based on the original and currently existing cause of action under the contract.

FIGURE 12.1 ▶
TYPICAL COVENANT
NOT TO SUE

This COVENANT NOT TO SUE dated: _____ between FIRST PARTY COVENANTOR ("Smith") and SECOND PARTY COVENANTEE ("Jones").

In consideration of $_____ paid to Smith by Jones, the receipt of which is acknowledged, Smith covenants as follows:

(1) Smith as the Covenantor will never institute any action or suit at law or in equity against Jones as the Covenantee, nor institute, prosecute or in any way aid in the institution or prosecution of any claim, demand, action, or cause of action for damages, costs, loss of services, expenses, or compensation for or on account of any damage, loss or injury either to person or property, or both, whether developed or undeveloped, resulting or to result, known or unknown, past, present or future, arising out of [INSERT THE CONTRACTUAL CAUSE OF ACTION].

(2) It is understood by Smith that the payment made in consideration of this covenant is not to be construed as an admission of liability on the part of Jones.

(3) Smith reserves all rights of action, claims and demands against any and all persons other than Jones who may have been involved in the underlying cause of action for which this covenant was procured. This instrument is a covenant not to sue the individual Jones and not a release as to all claims against other parties involved in the cause of action.

(4) This covenant shall inure to the benefit of Jones and his heirs, assigns and legal representatives and shall bind Smith and his heirs, assigns and legal representatives.

(5) Merger clause: This instrument reflects the entire covenant between Smith and Jones. No statements that are not contained in this covenant not to sue shall be valid or binding.

Development, Inc., 788 N.E.2d 1212 (Ill. App. 2003) (Homeowners had to sue for court-ordered rescission of the contract for the construction of the home where the contractor was unwilling to rescind; contractor would be forced to return all deposit monies and pay damages in order to return the homeowners to the status quo.). If the parties cannot come to a mutual agreement with regard to rescission, a party can sue for the court to order a rescission of the contract, thereby permitting the party seeking rescission to disavow the contract and return to the pre-contract status quo.

RELEASE

release
A discharge from the parties' performance obligations that acknowledges the dispute but forgoes contractual remedies.

Where there is a disagreement as to the contractual obligations of the parties and at least one party does have the right to sue the other under the contract, that party may nevertheless voluntarily relinquish the right and **release** the other party of the obligations of the agreement. The main difference between a release and mutual rescission is the existence of a dispute. In a mutual rescission, the parties have agreed that there are no elements in contention and that both parties can walk away. Where a release is involved, there is a dispute as to the obligations of one or both parties. The release and accompanying covenant not to sue acknowledge that there are unresolved questions of obligation and liability but do not impose a contractual remedy. A release gives up a current legal remedy that has accrued; therefore, it is retrospective in action. A covenant not to sue is a continuing legal obligation that looks prospectively. Usually, for a party to enter into a release, some additional consideration changes hands. The releasing party usually receives monetary compensation for granting a release to the potentially liable party.

There are a few rules regarding releases. The first is logical: The release, to be enforceable, must be in writing. This is not a Statute of Frauds issue but rather one of proof of intent. The second falls under the rules of construction. A release is construed in favor of the releasing party as the law assumes that parties do not give up their legal rights lightly. This also applies with regard to the terms of the release. The words should be specific with regard to the rights that are relinquished and refer to the clear intent of the parties to give up those rights. Merely entitling a document a "release" does not make it one; there must be a clear indication that a party intended to release the potentially breaching party from liability. *See generally Shay v. Aldrich*, 790 N.W.2d 629 (Mich. 2010)

A typical release is provided in Figure 12.2.

◀ **FIGURE 12.2**

TYPICAL RELEASE

This RELEASE dated: _____ between FIRST PARTY RELEASOR ("Smith") and SECOND PARTY RELEASEE ("Jones").

(1) I, Smith, residing at _____, in consideration of the payment to me at this time of the sum of $ _____ dollars, the receipt of which I hereby acknowledge, do hereby release and forever discharge Jones and his agents, successors and assigns, heirs, personal representatives, and all other persons, firms and corporations, of and from any and all actions, causes of action, claims, demands, damages, costs, loss of service, expenses and compensation, which I now have, or may hereafter have, on account of, or arising out of any matter or thing which has happened, developed, or occurred, before the signing of this release, and particularly: [INSERT THE CONTRACTUAL CAUSE OF ACTION].

(2) I accept the above-mentioned sum in full settlement and satisfaction of all claims or demands whatsoever, for harm known, and unknown.

(3) I further understand and agree that this settlement is the compromise of a disputed claim, and that the payment made is not to be construed as an admission of liability on the part of the party or parties hereby released by whom liability is expressly denied.

(4) Merger clause: This instrument reflects the entire release agreement between Smith and Jones. No statements that are not contained in this release shall be valid or binding.

For example, after Bob believes he has completed the work on the Newly-weds' home, the Newlyweds find some defects that they would like corrected to conform to the building contract specifications. Bob does not want to complete this work, but he also doesn't want to get sued by the Newlyweds for potentially nonconforming work. The Newlyweds also would rather avoid litigation and just get the work done. The Newlyweds propose a release wherein they agree to forgo their right to sue for strict contract specification compliance if Bob will agree to pay them $1,000. The consideration supporting this release is the exchange of the Newlyweds' right to sue for $1,000.

Releases are one of the most common agreements. People sign them regularly. When a patient is admitted into the hospital, the patient must sign a release for just about every procedure; insurance companies prepare releases with regard to personal injury claims; and recreation facilities require patrons to release them from liability for certain actions of patrons or accidents.

RESEARCH THIS

In your jurisdiction, find two cases involving releases, one in which the court found that the release was valid and enforceable and the other in which the release was not. What were the facts that made the difference in the court's reasoning? What factual differences do you think would have resulted in the opposite outcomes for the two cases?

ACCORD AND SATISFACTION

We know that consideration traditionally gets used only once; if parties desire to come to another agreement, even if it is directly related to the first, there must be some other additional or different consideration—just as in the concept of release discussed above. It is difficult to find the different or additional consideration in **accord and satisfaction** because the exchange looks very similar to the original agreement.

accord and satisfaction
An agreement to accept the imperfectly proffered performance as a fulfillment of the contractual obligations.

This resolution occurs where two parties are in dispute as to what their mutual obligations are under the contract. One or both parties state that they have not received what they bargained for, but they cannot come to any agreement as to the deficiency. Instead of resolving the dispute in court, the parties "agree to disagree." Essentially, they agree to modify their original agreement to fit the situation at hand. The parties come to an *accord* (amicable arrangement) that the different nonconforming performance will *satisfy* the originally required performance. Put into plain English: "Good enough, let's not keep arguing about it."

An accord and satisfaction must comply with all the requirements for any contractual agreement, which means that the parties must intend to enter into this kind of settlement of their dispute. "In order to support a plea of accord and satisfaction, it must clearly appear from the evidence that there was in fact and in reality a meeting of the minds in accord and satisfaction. The conclusion of accord and satisfaction should not be supported by mythical or theoretical reasoning. An accord and satisfaction is the result of an agreement between the parties, and, like all other agreements, must be consummated by a meeting of the minds of the parties." *Fast Motor Co. v. Morgan*, 52 P.2d 25, ¶ 18 (Okla. 1935). This does not always equate to a written document in this instance, like a mutual rescission but unlike a release. The conduct of the parties may indicate assent to the implied terms of the accord and satisfaction.

SPOT THE ISSUE!

Twinkle Toes, Inc., has contracted with Happy Taps Co. for the distribution of Happy Taps Tap Shoes for a five-year period; shipment and payment installments would be made every two months.

In January, Happy Taps delivered 1,000 pairs of shoes to Twinkle Toes' warehouse for distribution to various retail stores. In March, Twinkle Toes began to receive complaints about the shoes. Happy Taps attempted to repair the defective shoes, which sounded more like a thud than a crisp rap. For several months, Happy Tap and Twinkle Toes attempted to repair and sell the reconditioned shoes. On June 1st, Twinkle Toes sent a letter to Happy Taps:

> "Enclosed please find a check in the amount of $5,000.00, which represents full and final payment for all shoes reconditioned and sold by us. With this correspondence, we are considering all open issues and further business closed with Happy Taps."

The check had "Final payment" written on the memo line and was endorsed and deposited to Happy Taps' account.

See *MKL Pre-Press Electronics, Inc. v. La Crosse Litho Supply, LLC*, 840 N.E.2d 687 (Ill. App. 2005).

So where is the consideration? Each party has exchanged mutually agreed-upon promises that rest on the previous contract. Remember that past consideration is no consideration and a preexisting legal duty (the party is under a legal duty to tender performance) cannot be used as consideration for a new agreement. The accord and satisfaction, however, does not suffer from a failure of consideration based on past consideration because both parties have submitted new consideration into the bargain—they have **forgone their legal right to sue**.

For example, Fred Furnisher contracts with Carl the Carpenter to fabricate Ming dynasty–style furniture with very rare and expensive pheasant tail wood for the cost of $100,000. Carl believes he has constructed the furniture to Fred's specifications, but Fred claims that Carl has substituted ironwood, a slightly softer and lighter (and cheaper) wood than pheasant tail but very similar in appearance. Carl insists that he has used pheasant tail. Instead of litigating the

forgoing a legal right to sue
Valid consideration as it has recognized legal value to support a contractual obligation.

matter, Carl and Fred agree to settle the matter by accord and satisfaction. They restructure the agreement to fit the actual occurrence—Carl will construct furniture out of the species of premium Chinese hardwood used in Ming furniture with a feather-like iridescent grain for the cost of $85,000. Both parties can agree that this is what happened, and they both agree that this performance satisfies the obligations under the original agreement. Additionally, they have both contributed additional consideration, the forbearance of suit.

By now, you should be noticing that this forbearance from suit is always going to be the new, additional consideration for all of these types of agreements in this chapter.

SUBSTITUTED AGREEMENT/NOVATION

substituted agreement
A replacement of a previous agreement with a new contract with additional but not inconsistent obligations.

merger
Combining previous obligations into a new agreement.

A **substituted agreement** is a very simple concept as it occurs at almost every flea market and garage sale. The old arrangement is consumed by the new one; it doesn't go away but **merges** with the subsequent contract. The subject matter is similar enough that the new contract is a *substitute* for the old one. Implicitly then, the subsequent contract alters the obligations but does not directly contradict them; otherwise, it would be an entirely new contract and the old contract would have to be terminated by some means already discussed.

> ### Example
> In an attempt to furnish her new home, Netta Newlywed goes to a large local flea market. She finds a coffee table she likes and agrees to pay $50 for it. Before making it to the cash register, she spots two end tables priced at $25 each. Netta makes a deal with Frank, the flea market purveyor, to take all three tables for $80 (thereby saving her $20). The bargain to take all three for $80 substitutes for her original deal of $50 for the coffee table. Her obligation to pay $50 for the coffee table is subsumed by the three tables for $80 deal. Netta has still perfectly performed by tendering money for the furniture and Frank has perfectly performed by delivering furniture.

A substituted agreement is not an accord and satisfaction because it does not allow for imperfect or defective performance to replace full and perfect performance on the contract as accord and satisfaction does. A substituted agreement keeps the original perfect performance obligations intact while subsuming them into another agreement. Therefore, the original intent and agreement is still enforceable as part of the substituted agreement. The new substituted agreement is consistent with the terms of the performance obligations of the parties in the original contract. This is not the case in the other types of agreements. A mutual rescission is exactly the opposite, by letting the parties off the hook for their performance obligations. Releases also contemplate a dispute as to the performance obligations of the parties and allow the parties to avoid liability for their imperfect performance. Substituted agreements still require perfect performance.

The term **novation** refers to making a new agreement that terminates the previous obligations, with the parties accepting the new promises of performance in lieu of the original performance. A novation is the only way to "switch out" the parties to the contract. Instead of substituting the subject matter, novation is a substitution of parties. The contract is "made new" by transferring the duties of the old party to the new one. The duties of the old party are mutually and voluntarily discharged and assumed by the new party.

There are a few rules or conditions that must exist in order for there to be a valid novation. First, there must be a legally binding **present obligation** that has not been breached by either party. Second, all parties to the arrangement must **consent** to the substitution of the new party. Last, the new obligations must rest solely on the new party, **extinguishing liability** of the old party. This is where there may be some complications. There must be a clear intent to extinguish the previous liability of the parties.

novation
An agreement that replaces previous contractual obligations with new obligations and/or different parties.

present obligation
The performances under the contract must not have been carried out but must still be executory in order to be available for a novation.

consent
All parties to a novation must knowingly assent to the substitution of either the obligations or parties to the agreement.

extinguishment of liability
Once a novation has occurred, the party exiting the agreement is no longer obligated under the contract.

CRYPTO CONTRACTS

Recall the immutability and stability of smart contracts. As a simple "if-then" set of instructions, there is no room for accord and satisfaction, substitutions, or novations. It lives in its binary state of full performance or breach. What added value then does a smart contract bring to transactions? Reputational context. By openly recording these failed contracts, there is a shared record of the parties' ability to fulfill contracts to exacting specifications. As Tony Sabat points out in his article "Could Blockchain Be the Missing Link for the AEC/Built World Industry?," AECNEXT Blog (April 20, 2018)

Well, as is common in the construction industry, What if the work promised does not match the conditions of the smart contract? By our previous logic, the contract would not execute and the subcontractor would not be paid. This discrepancy or lack of quality—the subcontractor's failure to meet the terms of the contract—can also be recorded on the Ethereum blockchain. If a subcontractor consistently underdelivers, the results could be tied to the blockchain and average out over time to develop a reputational ledger for future parties to base their operational decisions upon.

In a large industry like construction, there are multiple parties who can promise any kind of work, but it can be difficult to trust their standard of quality. This is why there are several software companies developing prequalification standards for bidding purposes. This kind of prequalification can be a dicey process, but when integrated with the Ethereum blockchain, the process becomes binary: does the subcontractor meet the qualification standards or not?

Renegotiations are not always novations. The trend to take advantage of the lowest interest rates by renegotiating a loan may not be a true novation. It must be the intent of the parties to completely cancel all terms in the prior agreement and substitute an entirely new contract in its place. *See Sullivan Builders & Design, Inc. v. Home Lumber of New Haven, Inc.*, 834 N.E.2d 129 (Ind. App. 2005). Sullivan Builders and its owner, Joseph Sullivan, entered into a loan agreement with their suppliers, Home Lumber. The terms of the original loan required a personal guarantee from Joseph. Sullivan Builders claimed that the parties entered into a novation regarding new credit terms and that Joseph's personal guarantee was no longer in effect. Home Lumber argued that there was no novation because the parties had not intended to extinguish Joseph's personal guarantee. There was no discussion as to the other terms regarding the personal guarantee; therefore, there could be no intent to enter into a novation.

Novation differs from a delegation, as discussed in Chapter 5. Recall that a delegation does *not* extinguish the original party's liability under the contract. A delegation does not make the contract new, like a novation. A delegation redirects primary responsibility for performance of a duty while maintaining secondary liability on the "old" party.

For example, let's revisit Chrissy, Jack, and Janet and their landlord, Mr. Roper. If Terri was meant to substitute for Chrissy and thereby release Chrissy from all obligations to Mr. Roper for payment of rent, a novation of the lease agreement would be appropriate, not a sublease. Now, if Terri fails to pay her share of the rent, Mr. Roper can only sue Terri, as Chrissy has been released by the novation.

What do substituted agreements look like? How can the parties be sure that they have effectively substituted the new agreement for the old one? A clause such as "This Agreement shall be in lieu of and shall supersede any other agreements existing as of the date hereof between PARTY ONE and PARTY TWO relating to the [REFERENCE TO THE AGREEMENT]" clearly manifests the intent of the parties to create a substitute. However, substituted agreements do not need to be in writing. The above language suggests a manner in writing to ensure a clear manifestation of intent to substitute; oral substitutions and/or conduct in accordance with the substituted agreement also supports the change.

How do novations differ? They are more specific as to the transfer of obligations onto the new party and extinguishment of liability of the "exiting" party.

The parties agree and stipulate that:

(1) PARTY ONE [original party] and PARTY TWO [original party] entered into a contract, referred to as the original contract, on DATE. A copy of the original contract is attached and incorporated by reference.

(2) It is agreed between the PARTY ONE and PARTY TWO that THIRD PARTY shall perform all obligations of PARTY TWO under the original contract, shall be entitled to all rights of PARTY TWO under the original contract, and that PARTY TWO shall not be liable in any way to the PARTY ONE for the performance or non-performance of the original contractual obligations by the THIRD PARTY.

(3) PARTY ONE relinquishes any claim that such party held or may have held under the terms of the original contract as against PARTY TWO.

(4) This agreement supersedes and extinguishes the original contract.

As the substituted agreement or novation takes the place of the original one, the only remedies available are those granted under the new agreement. The substituted agreement or novation extinguishes the rights and liabilities under the first contract. Therefore, if Netta discovers defects in the coffee table, she will not be able to recoup her $50 for it. The price of the table was reduced in the new deal. She will have to rely on the substituted agreement's remedy and therefore will be able to recover only $40 for the defective coffee table. This reflects the 20 percent discount she "negotiated" by taking all three tables. "[W]here the parties have clearly expressed or manifested their intention that a subsequent agreement supersede or substitute for an old agreement, the subsequent agreement extinguishes the old one. The question is simply whether the parties intended for the new contract to substitute for the old one, and that intention, if otherwise clear, need not be articulated explicitly in the new agreement." *Baldwin v. EMI Feist Catalog, Inc.*, 805 F.3d 18, 27 (2d Cir. 2015) (internal citations omitted).

SPOT THE ISSUE!

Eric Inventor entered into an agreement with Dave Distributor for the sale of Eric's patented device. Dave agreed to pay royalties to Eric in the amount of $10 for every sale. Dave would advance Eric $10,000 to be applied toward the first thousand sold. The payment would be made in five installments of $2,000 as Dave didn't have all the cash on hand at the time of signing.

After the first installment, Eric unexpectedly expired. Eric's estate requested the second installment from Dave. Dave claimed that the contract was no longer valid. He also stated that the device did not work as promised and that he would like to cancel the contract. He will return all the unsold devices and the estate can keep the $2,000. The estate refused, pressing for enforcement of the contract. Dave then offered to pay an additional $1,000 and return the goods.

Determine what actions would constitute a mutual rescission and/or a novation or an accord and satisfaction.

See *Lorentowicz v. Bowers*, 102 A. 630 (N.J. 1917).

MODIFICATION

Again, we can refer to freedom of contract principles when discussing **modification**. Parties, once they have freely entered into a contract, are not locked into those terms. Contracts are not written in stone. (Although we have seen

modification
A change or addition in contractual terms that does not extinguish the underlying agreement.

that they can be digitally impenetrable on the blockchain.) Freedom to contract includes the freedom to modify the parties' rights and obligations. A modification is much like adding a "mini-contract" to an existing one because all three requirements of a valid contract (offer, acceptance, and consideration) must be present. Requiring consideration to be present ensures that there is a valid bargain made regarding the change. Why are the parties changing the terms? Without consideration, the proposed modification is a new offer to enter into a new and different contract and terminate the previous contract. There is an exception for transactions between merchants, which will be discussed in further detail in the chapter on the UCC. Briefly, in order to facilitate commerce and ensure speedy transactions, merchants, in the course of business, may modify existing contracts without consideration for the change.

The parties must agree to alter, add, or delete any terms, but the essence of the contract, its purpose, remains unchanged. "Generally, whether the contracting parties have executed a new agreement or instead modified their original agreement is a question of fact. . . . Modification of a contract normally occurs when the parties agree to alter a contractual provision or to include additional obligations, while leaving intact the overall nature and obligations of the original agreement." *Hildreth Consulting Engineers, P.C. v. Larry E. Knight, Inc.*, 801 A.2d 967, 974 (D.C. 2002). Mutuality of contract is present in modification as well, as a party cannot unilaterally change terms.

Example

The Newlyweds have changed their minds regarding the design of the kitchen. Instead of butcher-block countertops, the Newlyweds would like granite. They approach Bob about modifying the contract to reflect this change. Bob agrees that the change is acceptable, but he will have to charge them an additional $1,000 for the upgrade. The Newlyweds and Bob have mutually agreed upon a contractual modification supported by consideration (the extra $1,000).

A first alternative scenario: If Bob decides on his own, without the input of the Newlyweds, that granite would look better in the kitchen and changes the contract, he has breached the contract. This is not a valid contract as there has been no offer, acceptance, and consideration to support the modification.

A second alternative scenario: Bob and the Newlyweds mutually agree to change the butcher-block for granite, but there is no cost associated with it. Essentially, the parties have terminated the old contract calling for butcher-block and replaced it with a new contract that requires the granite countertop. There has been no consideration for the change to granite; therefore, this is not a modification.

SURF'S UP

The infamous "click here" to accept the terms of an online agreement poses interesting problems after entry into the contract where changes are needed. Neither party has a personal or direct relationship as they have dealt at a vast electronic distance. The court in *Bellsouth Communications System, LLC v. West*, 902 So. 2d 653 (Ala. 2004), had to deal with the issue of subsequent attempts at modifications to "click-wrapped" dial-up service agreements. The terms of the agreement were modified by a posting to the service's website. The court held that the unilateral modification to the service agreement could only apply to the customer if the customer actually used the service to which the modification applied. It did not matter that the modification was in effect at the time of the lawsuit; the crux of the matter was the acceptance of the modification by use of the service, as this was an attempt at unilateral modification. Internet transactions seem to be an exception to the mutual assent rule that applies to the methods of changing an agreement.

IN-CLASS DISCUSSION

Contract law demands adherence to its strict rules; however, carrying out the requirements of every contract is not always possible. Many contracts call for written documentation signed by both parties for changes to the contractually required performances. Should oral modifications be permissible? Under what circumstances? Can the modification to the contract to permit oral modifications be in writing or can that be oral? What does this do to certainty?

   See *Richard F. Kline, Inc. v. Shook Excavating & Hauling, Inc.*, 885 A.2d 381, 390 (Md. App. 2005) ("Parties to a contract may waive the requirements of the contract by subsequent oral agreement or conduct, notwithstanding any provision in the contract that modifications must be in writing. If a provision in the contract requires modifications to be in writing, it must be shown, either by express agreement or by implication, that the parties understood that provision was to be waived.").

There are many ways for the parties to change their existing agreement in order to avoid litigation over a contractual provision. It is important for paralegals to understand these different methods in order to properly draft the required documents of change. All the methods of change must clearly state the intent of the parties and delineate the new rights and responsibilities of the parties.

Summary

Changes to a contract can take several forms. They include

1. Mutual rescission, wherein the parties decide that the contract is no longer worth pursuing. Both parties surrender their rights and no fault is assigned to nonperformance.
2. Release, wherein the party having a right to sue for nonperformance voluntarily relinquishes that right. This is often accompanied by a covenant not to sue based on the defective or nonexistent performance. These documents must be in writing, are construed in favor of the releasing party, and must reference the terms of the release with specificity.
3. Accord and satisfaction, wherein the parties agree that the tendered performance is "good enough" and change the original contract to reflect the actual occurrence.
4. Substituted agreement, wherein the parties merge the old agreement into a new one.
5. Novation, wherein one party steps completely out of the transaction and a new party is substituted for the departing party. The agreement is made new by the replacement.
6. Modification, wherein the parties mutually assent to change the terms of the contract and this modification is supported by consideration.

Key Terms

accord and satisfaction
consent
covenant not to sue
extinguishment of liability
forgoing a legal right to sue
merger

modification
mutual rescission
novation
present obligation
release
substituted agreement

Review Questions

VIVE LA DIFFÉRENCE!

In your own words, explain the difference between

1. A mutual rescission and a release with a covenant not to sue.

2. A novation and an "accord and satisfaction."

3. An "accord and satisfaction" and a modification.

4. A novation and a delegation.

5. A modification and a new offer or counteroffer.

MULTIPLE CHOICE

Choose the best answer(s) and please explain *why* you choose the answer(s).

1. Releases are best described as
   a. An agreement for additional damages in a lawsuit.
   b. A relinquishment of a right to sue based on a contractual dispute.
   c. An agreement to change the terms of the previous contract.
   d. A termination of the previous contract.

2. Mutual rescissions
   a. Must be court-ordered.
   b. Are entered into after performance has been imperfectly rendered.
   c. Allow parties to walk away from the agreement without allocation of fault.
   d. All of the above.

3. A covenant not to sue
   a. Allows parties to form a binding agreement to forgo legal remedies without resort to the courts.
   b. Is only available to parties that have fully performed their obligations under the contract.
   c. Must be supported by monetary consideration.
   d. Substitutes for a release.

4. A novation can best be described as
   a. A consensual agreement to enter into a new contract.
   b. An agreement that takes the place of a previous contract by substituting new obligations or parties.
   c. A substitution for consideration.
   d. A knowing relinquishment of a legal right to enforce a previous agreement.

"FAULTY PHRASES"

All of the following statements are FALSE; state why they are false and then rewrite them as true statements. Write a brief fact pattern that illustrates your answer.

1. Renegotiations are considered novations of a previous contract.

2. Covenants not to sue mean that the party agrees not to bring any lawsuits based on the contract.

3. Accord and satisfaction substitutes for the original contract and makes the parties accept new and additional performance obligations.

4. Simply forgoing a legal right to sue is not enough consideration to support a new agreement; money also must change hands.

5. A novation is the same as a delegation.

6. If a party wishes to get out of a contract, he can walk away by declaring a rescission.

"WRITE" AWAY! PORTFOLIO ASSIGNMENT

Review the Druid and Carrie contract. Assume that Carrie would like to make some substantial changes (which are up to your imagination). Draft a modification agreement reflecting these changes without terminating the original contract. Additionally, assume that one of the subcontractors, doing a private job for Carrie, was injured on the site. As this occurrence was outside of the scope of his regular employment, he is not covered by his workers' compensation. Draft a Release of Personal Injury Claim for Carrie.

Case in Point   ACCORD AND SATISFACTION

177 P.3d 13
217 Or. App. 551
Lawrence A. LAUDERDALE, George B. PARTRIDGE, Robert H. CARTER, Tom JOHNSON,
Melba E. STEPHENS, Sheri Marie LEWIS, and Ralph HENDRICKSON, Plaintiffs-Respondents,
Cross-Appellants,
v.
EUGENE WATER AND ELECTRIC BOARD and CITY OF EUGENE, Defendants-Appellants,
Cross-Respondents.
160320319.
A128046.
Court of Appeals of Oregon.
Argued and Submitted July 3, 2007.
Decided January 30, 2008.

Page 14

William F. Gary, Eugene, argued the cause for appellants-cross-respondents. With him on the opening brief were Susan D. Marmaduke, Caroline R. Guest, Portland, C. Robert Steringer, and Harrang Long Gary Rudnick P.C. With them on the reply brief was Sharon A. Rudnik.

Joel S. DeVore, Eugene, argued the cause for respondents-cross-appellants. On the opening brief were Martha L. Walters and Walters Chanti & Zennaché, P.C. On the reply brief were Joel S. DeVore and Luvaas Cobb.

Before LANDAU, Presiding Judge, and SCHUMAN and SERCOMBE, Judges.

SCHUMAN, J.

[217 Or. App. 553] In 1990, 2003, and 2004, the Eugene Water and Electric Board (EWEB) increased the amount that it required its retired employees to contribute to the cost of their company-sponsored retiree health care benefits and that current employees would have to contribute for those benefits when they retired. Shortly after the last increase,

Page 15

plaintiffs—five retired employees, the widow of a retired employee, and a then-current employee anticipating retirement—brought this action, alleging that the increase in cost amounted to a breach of contract and seeking specific performance of the original, pre-1990, agreement. The trial court agreed with plaintiffs that EWEB breached its contract and ordered EWEB to provide two of the plaintiffs with retirement health care benefits at the cost established in 1972 (that is, before any increase) and to provide the other plaintiffs with benefits at the cost established in 1990. EWEB appeals from the trial court's judgment on the ground that it never made an enforceable promise not to raise the cost of retiree health care benefits and that, in fact, it expressly reserved the right to do so. Plaintiffs cross-appeal, contending that the trial court should have ordered reestablishment of the 1972 costs for all of them, not just two. We affirm on appeal and cross-appeal.

The following facts are based on the trial court's express and implicit findings, which, we conclude, are supported by the evidence. In 1956, EWEB began providing employees who had worked for the company for ten years or more with the same benefits after retirement that active employees received. Those benefits were offered at no cost for the retired employee and a nominal cost for dependents. In 1972, EWEB froze the cost of dependent coverage at $7.80 per month for dependents under age 65 and $3.00 per month [217 Or. App. 554] for dependents age 65 or over, maintaining free coverage for retired employees themselves. (For convenience, we refer henceforth to benefits at that cost as "1972 retiree health care benefits.") Beginning in 1975, EWEB abandoned the ten-year requirement and promised its employees that they would continue to receive the same coverage upon retirement that active employees received, at 1972 prices, regardless of years of service. EWEB used this promise to recruit and retain employees.

No significant changes occurred for 14 years. Then, in 1989, EWEB announced that it was planning to revise the retiree benefit plan and informed employees and retirees that it had the right to modify or terminate retiree health care benefits, notwithstanding the earlier assurances to the contrary. The announcement was not well received by employees or retirees. In response to that negative reaction, EWEB formed a benefit project team consisting of active employees and retirees to address the dispute and seek a solution. Although the retirees and employees expressed "strong preference for no changes in their current contribution rates," they were informed that "a 'no change' option would not be acceptable" to EWER.

The new plan, drafted in consultation with the benefit project team, created three tiers of retirees. All three tiers' members continued to receive the same coverage as active employees; the new plan changed only the cost of that coverage. Tier I consisted of retirees who had turned 65 before January 1, 1990. Those retirees would continue to receive 1972 retiree health care benefits. Tier II consisted of retirees under age 65 on January 1, 1990, and employees who would retire between January 1, 1990 and December 31, 1993. In retirement, Tier II members would continue to receive health care benefits at no cost to themselves, but they would pay $29 per month, instead of $7.80 or $3.00, to cover their dependents. Tier III consisted of employees retiring after January 1, 1994. When they retired, they would pay between 100 percent and 25 percent of their health care premium based on the number of years they had worked for EWEB, until they reached 65, at which time they would be terminated from EWEB's benefit plan entirely. No EWEB [217 Or. App. 555] employee legally challenged

Page 16

the 1990 modifications before this action was filed in 2004.

Plaintiff Lauderdale and plaintiff Stephens's husband retired from EWEB and turned 65 before 1990. Therefore, they were in Tier I and were not affected by the 1990 modification. Plaintiff Partridge retired before 1990, but did not turn 65 until after January 1, 1990, so he was in Tier IL Plaintiff Carter was also in Tier II because he retired in 1993. He made the decision to retire at that time in reliance on written documents issued by EWEB informing employees that they would be able to lock in the health care benefits given to Tier II retirees if they retired before 1994. Plaintiffs Johnson and Lewis retired after 1994, and plaintiff Hendrickson was still employed by EWEB at the time of trial, so all three were in Tier III. The following table may clarify the various tiers and plaintiffs' positions in them:

Tier	Criteria for Membership	Plaintiff Members	Benefits under 1900 Plan
I	Retired at age 65 or older before 1/1/1990	Lauderdale (retired 1983) Stephens (husband retired 1988)	Coverage equal to active employees; cost at 1972 level
II	Retired younger than 65 before 1/1/1990 OR retired between 1/1/1990 and 12/31/1993	Carter (retired 1993) Partridge (retired 1982; not yet 65 on 1/1/1990)	Coverage equal to active employees; free for retiree; $29 per month for dependents
III	Retired after 1/1/1994	Lewis (retired 2000) Johnson (retired 2003) Hendrickson (not yet retired)	Until age 65: coverage equal to active employees, cost linked to years of service; after 65, no coverage

For approximately 18 years, EWEB implemented the 1990 plan and continued to provide employees with the retirement health care benefits that the plan established. During that period, Tier II and III plaintiffs paid the increased costs without protest (Tier I plaintiffs' costs did not increase under the 1990 plan). In 2003, however, and once again in 2004, EWEB made changes to the retiree health care [217 Or. App. 556] plan that either significantly increased the cost to retirees (including Tier I) or, also contrary to alleged earlier promises, did not provide the same coverage that active employees received. In response to these changes, plaintiffs initiated this action seeking a declaration that EWEB had breached its contract with plaintiffs; a judgment requiring EWEB specifically to perform its contract obligations; an injunction requiring EWEB to provide retiree health care benefits equal to the benefits received by its active employees at the cost promised to plaintiffs prior to 1990; and damages based on the charges EWEB imposed on plaintiffs for their health care benefits in excess of the amount that plaintiffs should have been required to pay under EWEB's original promise.

EWEB, in response, argued that it never promised plaintiffs that they would receive 1972 retiree health care benefits identical in coverage to active employees'; that, to the extent that such promises were made, they were not made by anybody with authority to do so; and that the statute of frauds rendered them unenforceable in any event. Further, EWEB contended, they were also unenforceable because they were negated by EWEB's written reservation of rights to modify or revoke retiree benefits. Therefore, according to. EWEB, the increases in 1990 and thereafter did not breach any contract. Further, even if the 1990 modification breached a contract, nonetheless, as to plaintiffs who had continued working after the 1990 modification or, if retired, had accepted the modification by paying the new premiums, any claims that those plaintiffs had to benefits promised before that time were extinguished because the 1990 modification constituted an accord and satisfaction.

Page 17

[217 Or. App. 557] EWEB filed a motion for judgment of dismissal pursuant to ORCP 54 B(2) at the close of plaintiffs' evidence and a motion for directed verdict pursuant to ORCP 60 at the close of all evidence. The trial court denied both motions. Instead, the court ruled that, before 1990, EWER repeatedly promised to provide plaintiffs with lifetime 1972 retiree health care benefits that were equal in coverage to active employees that the statute of frauds did not render the promises unenforceable; that the promises were made by EWEB employees with authority to do so and approved by the EWEB board; that plaintiffs accepted the promised benefit package and acquired a vested right to it when they began or continued working for EWEB; and that, in the time between the inauguration of the benefit plan and 1990, EWEB did not make any

"direct, affirmative, or meaningful representation" to employees or retirees that it could change retiree health care coverage costs.

The court also concluded that, after EWEB announced its intention to change the cost of retiree health care benefits and (in 1990) did so, all of the plaintiffs who continued to pay the newly established costs (that is, Tier II and III plaintiffs) signaled acceptance of the new plan. As to those employees, however, the subsequent increases that EWEB implemented *after* 1990 breached the 1990 contract, because, the court found, that contract promised that the 1990 changes were a "one time" modification. The court also concluded that Tier I plaintiffs, whose payments for retiree health care benefits remained fixed at the 1972 level even after the 1990 modifications, could not be said to have participated in an accord and satisfaction. As to those plaintiffs, the 1990 modification was a breach of contract dating from the 1975 promise to freeze costs. Thus, in summary, the court ruled that Tier I retirees had a meritorious claim to health care benefits at 1972 costs, and Tier II and III retirees and [217 Or. App. 558] employees had a meritorious claim to health care benefits at the costs established by the 1990 agreement.

On appeal, the parties appear to agree on two important premises. First, they agree that, under Oregon statutory and case law, an employer cannot unilaterally modify an employee's or retiree's vested rights in benefits. They disagree about when (or whether) the retiree health care benefits in this case became vested. Second, they agree that, some a time before 1989, EWEB promised orally and in writing that, upon retirement, plaintiffs and their dependents would receive 1972 retiree health care benefits that were identical in coverage to the benefits received by active employees. Although EWEB contested this fact at trial, the court expressly found it. That finding is supported by uncontradicted evidence in the record, and EWER does not renew its argument against it on appeal. Rather, EWEB argues that, for various reasons, the promises were unenforceable or superseded by its reservation of the right to modify or eliminate the benefit plan.

EWEB's principal argument on appeal, in other words, is that the oral and written promises to plaintiffs did not confer permanent vested rights to any retirement health care benefits. That is so, they maintain, for several reasons. First, the promises were either oral or, where written, not subscribed; therefore, evidence of the agreements was inadmissible and the agreements are unenforceable under the statute of frauds. Second, no agreements or promises were made or ratified by any person with actual or apparent authority to do, so. Third, any promises regarding unchangeable retiree health care benefits that were made contradicted

Page 18

EWEB's express reservation of rights; those reservations amounted to a fully integrated term of the agreement between plaintiffs and EWEB and therefore could not be varied or nullified by extrinsic evidence of a different agreement. Fourth, although the trial court correctly ruled that the 1990 contract replaced any earlier agreement under the theory of [217 Or. App. 559] accord and satisfaction, the court erred in ruling that the 1990 contract's "one time only" promise was admissible and enforceable so as to nullify subsequent modifications.

Plaintiffs, for their part, generally echo the trial court's findings and conclusions.

We begin with EWEB's argument that the statute of frauds renders its promises unenforceable. Under Oregon's statutory version of that common-law rule, "[a]n agreement that by its terms is not to be performed within a year from the making" is "void unless it, or some note or memorandum thereof, expressing the consideration, is in writing and subscribed by the party to be charged, or by the lawfully authorized agent of the party; evidence, therefore, of the agreement shall not be received other than the writing, or secondary evidence of its contents[.]" ORS 41.580(1), (1)(a). We agree with the trial court and EWEB that the 1972 retiree health care benefit agreement could not be performed within one year; under EWEB's retirement policies, plaintiffs were not eligible for any retirement benefits until after one year of employment. That policy relieved EWEB from performing during the first year. However, we have held that ORS 41.580(1) does not apply when *either* party has fully performed within one year. *Kneeland v. Shroyer*, 214 Or. 67, 82-88, 328 P.2d 753 (1958). And we have also held that, for purposes of the statute of frauds, when an employer offers pension benefits, the person to whom the benefits are offered completely performs his or her part of the agreement when he or she accepts the employer's job offer. *Kantor v. Boise Cascade Corp.*, 75 Or. App. 698, 704-05, 708 P.2d 356 (1985), *rev. den.*, 300 Or. 506, 713 P.2d 1058 (1986). Thus, EWEB's argument based on the statute of frauds fails because, for purposes of that rule, plaintiffs fully performed the agreement by accepting employment.

EWEB's argument based on lack of authority fails as well. Preliminarily, the argument appears to depend on the premise that no EWEB manager was authorized to contradict EWEB's reservation of the right to unilaterally change the cost of its benefit plan. Because we conclude below that [217 Or. App. 560] EWEB never effectively reserved that right, its argument fails to the extent that it is interwoven with the reservation of rights contention. To the extent that defendants make an independent argument that the EWEB board never authorized the pre-1990 policy, that argument fails as well. Plaintiffs' Exhibits 1 and 2, fact sheets entitled "Retirement Benefits" and distributed to plaintiffs, describe retiree health care benefits as being free to retirees and $7.80 or $3.00 per month for dependents. The trial court found as fact that the EWEB board approved those documents, and that finding is supported by the testimony of witnesses.

We therefore conclude that, before 1990, EWEB promised its employees that they would receive lifetime free or low-cost retirement health care benefits, and that the promise survives attacks based on the statute of frauds and on the theory that the promises came from EWEB employees without authority to make them.

EWEB, however, argues that, even if those findings and conclusions are correct, plaintiffs nonetheless cannot prevail, because Oregon law permits an employer to prospectively modify or eliminate benefits, that is, to modify or eliminate benefits the rights to which have not vested. Plaintiffs, however, assert that their entitlement to 1972 retiree health care benefits vested when, having been offered those benefits, they began working for EWEB, particularly in light of

[Page 19]

the fact that EWEB induced them to accept employment by promising them those benefits.

Plaintiffs are correct. By 1966 at the latest, the Supreme Court had rejected the "gratuity" theory of retirement benefits (that is, that employers can modify or eliminate benefits at will) and held that, when a person begins or continues employment having been promised a retirement benefit, or even if only having been "advised that he would receive" such a benefit, that benefit vests and cannot be modified or revoked. *Harryman v. Roseburg Fire Dist.*, 244 Or. 631, 634, 420 P.2d 51 (1966) (accumulated allowance for unused sick leave); *accord Oregon State Police Officers' Assn. v. State of Oregon*, 323 Or. 356, 377-78, 918 P.2d 765 (1996) [217 Or. App. 561] ("Once the employee performs services in reliance on the employer's promise to afford a particular benefit on retirement, the employer is contractually bound to honor that obligation."). The court in some cases regards the employee's act of beginning work as consideration for the employer's promise of benefits, *e.g., McHorse v. Portland General Elec.*, 268 Or. 323, 331, 521 P.2d 315 (1974); in other cases, the court regards the employee's commencement of work as an adequate tender of part performance in response to an employer's offer, *e.g., Taylor v. Mult. Dep. Sher. Ret. Bd.*, 265 Or. 445, 452-53, 510 P.2d 339 (1973). Under these cases, then, plaintiffs' right to 1972 retiree health care benefits vested when they began working for EWEB; EWEB's modifications were of existing, vested rights and were not, therefore, prospective. *Accord Adams v. Schrunk*, 6 Or. App. 580, 583-85, 488 P.2d 831 (1971) (pension; rejecting "gratuity" theory in favor of "vested right" theory); *Horton v. Prepared Media Laboratory, Inc.*, 165 Or. App. 357, 363, 997 P.2d 864, *rev. den.*, 331 Or. 283, 18 P.3d 1101 (2000) (severance pay); *Furrer v. Southwestern Oregon Community College*, 196 Or. App. 374, 379-81, 103 P.3d 118 (2004) (early retirement benefits).

Brett v. City of Eugene, 130 Or. App. 53, 880 P.2d 937 (1994), *rev. den.*, 320 Or. 507, 888 P.2d 568 (1905), does not help EWEB. That case involved accumulated leave time. When the plaintiffs began working for the city, it had a policy allowing employees to accumulate unused leave time and, on retirement, collect compensation for that time in a lump sum. The sum would be added to their last paycheck, thereby increasing the "final three-year average salary upon which their retirement benefits would be calculated, thereby increasing their potential monthly . . . retirement benefits[.]" During the period of the plaintiffs' employment, the city modified the policy by imposing a cap on the amount of leave time that could be accumulated: However, [217 Or. App. 562] "[t]he caps operate only prospectively. Employees with compensatory time balances in excess of the 80-hour cap will not lose those hours . . . . However, no new hours can be added to the balance. Employee's at or above the compensatory time cap must take all future overtime in pay or in time off during the pay period in which it is accumulated." *Id.* When the defendant announced the modification, the plaintiffs brought an action alleging breach of contract. They argued that "the *right to accrue unlimited leave* is analogous to a pension benefit and may not be modified." *Id.* at 58, 880 P.2d 937 (emphasis in original). This court concluded that, even if the right to accrue unlimited leave was a term of the employment contract, the defendant nonetheless could "modify [it] prospectively in the absence of an agreement to the contrary." *Id.* We held:

> "It is conceded that defendant could not take away any already accumulated leave or the right to receive payment for it in the last paycheck. Those benefits are protected,

Page 20

> vested property interests that may not be unilaterally modified or terminated. *Hughes v. State of Oregon*, 314 Or. 1, 838 P.2d 1018 (1992). However, the focus of this litigation is on *unaccumulated* leave. Plaintiffs contend that the right to continue to accrue leave in the future is a vested pension benefit. It is not. Unlike a pension benefit, the right to accrue leave in the future is not deferred compensation. *See Hughes v. State of Oregon, supra.* It is not even compensation. It is simply an option given employees with respect to the use of a part of their compensation. The court did not err in granting judgment to defendant."

Id. at 58-59, 880 P.2d 937 (emphasis in original).

Brett and the present case are distinguishable for several independently significant reasons. First, the focus in *Brett* was on "unaccumulated leave," that is, on benefits that served as compensation for unused leave time that had not been earned at the time of modification. Here, the focus is on benefits that came into existence *in toto* at the time plaintiffs began working for defendant. *Taylor,* 265 Or. 445, 510 P.2d 339. Put another way: A plaintiff in *Brett* would accumulate more benefits the longer he or she worked before retirement, and the modification would affect only those benefits that had not yet been earned. Here, a plaintiff who worked for EWEB for one [217 Or. App. 563] year before retirement would be entitled to the same benefit—1972 retiree health care benefits—as a plaintiff who worked for 20 years before retirement; the modifications affect benefits that are already "earned." Second, the parties here, unlike those in *Brett, did* have an agreement that employer would not modify or eliminate the disputed benefits. That agreement triggered the vesting of plaintiffs' rights. *Taylor,* 265 Or. at 450, 510 P.2d 339. And third, the right of plaintiffs to 1972 retiree health care benefits is *not* a mere "option given to employees with respect to the use of a part of their compensation"; it is, in fact, a form of "deferred compensation." Just as health care benefits are part of an active employee's compensation package, retiree health care benefits are part of a retired employee's compensation.

EWEB also claims that its position gains support from *Fish v. Trans-Box Systems, Inc.,* 140 Or. App. 255, 914 P.2d 1107 (1996). In that case, the plaintiff accepted employment from the defendant under a contract providing that, after 90 days on the job, he would be entitled to health care benefits and sick pay. After that period had elapsed, the plaintiff was injured and sought the benefits, only to learn that, in the interim, the defendant had modified the terms of employment so as to eliminate the benefits. The plaintiff continued to work for the defendant nonetheless, despite learning of the modified terms. *Id.* at 257-58, 914 P.2d 1107. In denying the plaintiff's breach of contract claim, we held that, absent a contrary agreement, an employer may "modify the employment contract so long as the modification applies only prospectively. An employee impliedly accepts such modifications by continuing employment after the modification." *Id.* at 259, 914 P.2d 1107 (quoting *Albrant v. Sterling Furniture Co.,* 85 Or. App. 272, 275, 736 P.2d 201, *rev. den.,* 304 Or. 55, 742 P.2d 1186 (1987)). EWEB argues that, as did the

plaintiff in *Fish,* plaintiffs here impliedly accepted the modification.

We disagree. *Fish* is not on point. Its holding follows from the premise that the employment contract contained no [217 Or. App. 564] agreement that the employer would *not* modify the relevant contract term. In the present case, as we have decided, there is such an agreement. That agreement is the basis for our conclusion that plaintiffs' rights vested at the start of their employment and that the modification was therefore *not* prospective. Further, *Fish,* like *Brett,* deals with benefits that an employee receives on a day-to-day basis during employment, not after retirement; retirement benefits, as we have discussed, generally vest at the commencement of employment. That difference

Page 21

is crucial. An employer's ability to change an at-will employee's current compensation cannot meaningfully be compared to an employer's ability to change vested post-employment benefits.

EWEB, then, did not have the authority under Oregon law unilaterally to modify plaintiffs' benefits, because plaintiffs' rights to those benefits vested when EWEB offered them as an inducement and plaintiffs accepted them by partial performance; the modification was of a vested right and it was not prospective. That conclusion does not end our inquiry, however, because EWEB contends that it reserved the right unilaterally to modify or eliminate the retirement benefits and that this reservation superseded or qualified its promise to provide them.

We rejected a similar claim in *Horton.* In that case, the plaintiff began working for the defendant in 1979. In 1993, the defendant adopted a policy under which the plaintiff was promised that, if she were laid off after three further years of employment, she would receive either three months' notice or three months of severance pay. 165 Or. App. at 359, 997 P.2d 864. The written policy contained the following proviso: "[The defendant] reserves the right to alter, reduce, or eliminate any pay practice, policy, or benefit without notice **except for those provisions required** by law." *Id.* (boldface in original). The plaintiff continued working for the defendant for three years and was then laid off with one day's notice. We held that "defendant employer offered a benefit to its employees in exchange for their continued work. It was, in effect, a contractual term of the employees' continued employment. [217 Or. App. 565] Plaintiff in fact continued her employment, thereby precluding defendant from revoking any benefits that had been accrued to the point of revocation. . . . Defendant certainly retained the right to revoke its severance policy, but as in *Harryman, Taylor,* and *McHorse,* that revocation cannot substantially impair plaintiff's entitlement to benefits to which she already had become entitled."

Id. at 363, 997 P.2d 864. Under *Horton,* then, even if EWEB reserved its right to modify or eliminate its retiree health care benefits, that revocation could not be applied against any employee—including plaintiffs—who had acquired a vested right to them.

We therefore affirm the trial court insofar as it ruled that EWEB offered retiree health care benefits to plaintiffs at the 1972 level; that, by commencing or continuing work for EWEB, plaintiffs accepted EWEB's offer, formed a contract, and acquired a vested right to the benefits; and that EWEB's unilateral increase in retiree costs in 1990 was a breach of that contract. Those conclusions resolve the dispute between EWEB and Tier I plaintiffs. The dispute involving Tier II and III plaintiffs, however, requires additional attention. That is because the court ruled that those plaintiffs, unlike Tier I plaintiffs, accepted the 1990 retiree health care plan as an accord and satisfaction by continuing to work for EWER (or, in the case of plaintiff Carter, by continuing to pay the increased cost) after 1990. Plaintiffs, in their cross-appeal, argue that there was no accord and satisfaction. For the following reasons, we reject that argument.

"An accord and satisfaction is a type of executed, substituted contract, which extinguishes a previous obligation. It is an affirmative defense to the original obligation with the burden of proving all its elements resting upon the one seeking to invoke its effect." *Lenchitsky v. H. J. Sandberg Co.,* 217 Or. 483, 490, 343 P.2d 523 (1959) (citations omitted). That burden requires the party to establish

"that what is given or agreed to be performed shall be offered as a satisfaction and extinction of the original [217 Or. App. 566] demand; *that the debtor shall intend it as a satisfaction of such obligation, and that such intention shall be made known to the creditor in some unmistakable manner.* It is equally essential that the creditor shall have accepted it with the intention that it should operate as a satisfaction. Both the giving and the acceptance in satisfaction are essential elements, and if they [are]

Page 22

lacking there can be no accord and satisfaction."

Id. (quoting 1 CJ 529, Accord and Satisfaction § 16 (emphasis in original)). In the context of an employment dispute, "a substitute agreement may be used to resolve good faith disputes between an employer and employee over the amount of commission, overtime, salary, or other compensation." *Erickson v. American Golf Corp.,* 194 Or. App. 672, 681, 96 P.3d 843 (2004). Whether an accord and satisfaction exists depends on the intent of the parties as "determined from all the circumstances attending the transaction." *Lenchitsky,* 217 Or. at 490, 343 P.2d 523 (quoting 1 CJ 529, Accord and Satisfaction § 16). That intent is a question of fact, and our scope of review is narrow: we cannot set aside the trial court's finding if it is supported by the evidence, including reasonable inferences drawn from it, viewed in the light most favorable to the party that prevailed on the issue at trial. *Williams v. Leatham,* 55 Or. App. 204, 207, 637 P.2d 1296 (1981) (quoting *Schlatter v. Willson,* 270 Or. 685, 688, 528 P.2d 1349 (1974), and *White v. Bello,* 276 Or. 931, 933, 556 P.2d 1362 (1976)). When the record is unclear, whether an accord and satisfaction has been formed should be resolved by the factfinder. *Lenchitsky,* 217 Or. at 493, 343 P.2d 523.

Thus, because EWEB prevailed on this issue at trial, the precise question on cross-appeal is this: Does the evidence, including circumstantial evidence and reasonable inferences, viewed in the light most favorable to EWEB, support the findings that (1) EWEB and plaintiffs had a good faith dispute over whether EWEB could modify the cost of retiree health care benefits; (2) the circumstances demonstrate that EWEB unmistakably communicated to plaintiffs that the resolution of that dispute—that is, the three-tier 1990 contract—was offered as a substitute for the existing, 1972 retiree health care benefit; and (3) plaintiffs accepted the offer? [217 Or. App. 567]

The trial court ruled that EWEB and its employees negotiated the 1990 contract in good faith; that the new contract effected a compromise, giving employees (including plaintiffs) part, but not all, of what they sought; that EWEB's intention to replace the 1972 retiree health care benefits with the new contract was unmistakably communicated; and that Tier II and III plaintiffs' acceptance of the new contract was established by the fact that they continued to work for EWEB or continued to pay the increased retiree costs and did not legally challenge the new contract for 13 years. In their cross-appeal, plaintiffs contend that, because EWES never acknowledged that plaintiffs' entitlement to 1972 retiree health care had vested and told employees that "no change" was not an option, a good faith dispute never existed. They also argue that there is no evidence in the record that EWEB unmistakably communicated to plaintiffs that the new contract extinguished the old one, and that, therefore, plaintiffs never accepted that proposition.

Although the question is close, we reject plaintiffs' arguments and affirm the trial court on cross-appeal.

The parties had a good faith dispute over the cost to retirees of their health care benefits. Plaintiffs' argument to the contrary relies on *Lenchitsky*. In that case, the plaintiff claimed that the defendant, his former employer, owed him money for unpaid compensation. 217 Or. at 485, 343 P.2d 523. The defendant offered to pay less than the plaintiff claimed, informing him that the amount offered "was all that [he] was going to get." *Id.* at 491, 343 P.2d 523 (internal quotation marks omitted). The Supreme Court held that, in those circumstances, a jury could find that the employer's offer "was merely an arbitrary declaration of intent on the part of the company to refuse to pay more on plaintiffs claim than it had previously determined to pay." *Id.* According to plaintiffs, that holding established that no good faith dispute can exist when one party had no intent to negotiate—and that is what happened here, because EWEB told its employees that the "no change" position was flatly unacceptable.

We disagree with plaintiffs for several reasons. First, *Lenchitsky* simply does not address the question

whether the parties had a good faith dispute; the issue in the [217 Or. App. 568] case was whether the defendant's proffer of less than the amount claimed by the plaintiff was

Page 23

unmistakably intended to substitute for that amount. Second, plaintiffs' argument does not account for the procedural posture of *Lenchitsky*. The defendant there assigned error to the trial court's denial of its motion for a directed verdict on the accord and satisfaction defense; the Supreme Court merely held that, because of the defendant's rigid posture, a jury "might well find" that there was no accord and satisfaction. *Id.* at 491, 343 P.2d 523. That holding does not compel the conclusion sought by plaintiffs: that an employer's rigidity or stubbornness *as a matter of law* establishes that there was no accord and satisfaction. It is merely one fact that can be considered by the factfinder. Here, EWEB negotiated with its employees from the position that it could increase the cost of retiree health care at will. The employees held the position that no increase was permitted. A compromise ensued. From those facts, a factfinder could reasonably conclude that the parties had a good faith dispute over retiree health care costs, even if EWEB's position was inflexible.

Plaintiffs are on somewhat firmer ground in arguing that EWEB never made "unmistakeably clear" its intention to substitute the 1990 costs for the 1972 costs. No document so states and no witness so testified. Indeed, EWEB's general manager testified that he never told any EWEB employees that, by accepting the new plan, they were relinquishing their claim under the old one. However, we must consider circumstantial as well as direct evidence, we must view that evidence and reasonable inferences that may be drawn from it in the light most favorable to EWEB, and, "[w]here the negotiations surrounding an alleged accord and satisfaction are doubtful and permit of conflicting deductions," we must defer to the factfinder's deduction. *Id.* at 493, 343 P.2d 523. Under that "narrow" scope of review, *Williams,* 55 Or.App. at 207, 637 P.2d 1296, the trial court's ruling must stand. As noted above, EWEB and its employees had a dispute over retiree health care costs; they negotiated, and a new plan emerged from the negotiations. Plaintiffs then continued to work for EWEB or to pay the newly established costs and, for 13 years—until EWEB proposed another revision—they did not re-new their claim to 1972 costs. From those undisputed facts alone, a factfinder could reasonably [217 Or. App. 569] infer that EWEB unmistakably indicated to plaintiffs, and plaintiffs understood, that the 1990 plan substituted for, and extinguished their claim under, the existing plan. Indeed, a contrary inference—that plaintiffs believed EWEB's 1990 plan to be only a partial accommodation to their claim to permanent 1972 costs, with complete capitulation still possible in the future—is implausible. We therefore conclude that the trial court's finding of an accord and satisfaction is not error.

We also conclude, however, that the substituted contract that EWEB offered and that plaintiffs accepted did not include authorization for EWEB to make any further modifications. The trial court found that EWEB's communication regarding the 1990 changes announced a "one time change." More specifically, the court found:

> "EWEB told plaintiffs in writing and verbally that the changes set forth on [communication to employees and retirees] were one time changes and the amounts they would be charged for retiree health coverage for themselves and their dependents were fixed for life at the time of their retirement . . . .
>
> "EWEB did not provide employees with other written communications describing these changes."

Those findings are supported by undisputed evidence. After EWEB notified employees that it was contemplating changes in retiree health care costs, but before the 1990 plan was finally adopted, EWEB distributed material explaining,

> "The new $29 amount is intended to be a <u>one time only change</u> and would remain fixed for as long as the dependent(s) remain on the plan—including after the age of 65. . . .
>
> " . . .
>
> "As you can see, there is only one change proposed in retiree health insurance contribution. That change, which would be effective January 1, 1990, is a <u>one-time increase</u> to cover dependents of retirees under 65."

Page 24

(Underscoring in original.) EWEB's board ultimately did not accept the "one time only" concept; instead, it passed a resolution stating that, with respect to Tier II and III employees [217 Or. App. 570] "The Board reserves the right to amend or terminate these policies." Thereafter, the board sent employees information about the new plan; those summaries promised a "fixed" contribution for retiree's dependent coverage, and they did not mention the board resolution purporting to reserve the right to amend or terminate.

Thus, when plaintiffs continued working for EWEB and paying the increased contributions to retiree health care benefit costs between 1990 and 2003, they plausibly did so with the understanding that the increases would not themselves be increased in the future; they were "one time" increases. The trial court could reasonably conclude, in other words, that the accord and satisfaction did not include any reservation of EWEB's right to implement further increases and that the 2003 and 2004 increases therefore breached the 1990 contract.

To summarize: In the years before 1990, EWEB offered plaintiffs retiree health care benefits at no cost to themselves, $7.80 per month for their dependents under 65, and $3.00 per month for dependents over 65. By commencing or continuing work for EWEB while that offer was in effect, plaintiffs accepted it, formed a contract with EWEB, and acquired a vested right to the benefits. Even if EWEB could reserve the right to modify vested rights, it never effectively did so. Thus, EWEB's unilateral increase in retiree cost in 1990 was a breach of its employment contract with plaintiffs. However, by continuing to work for EWEB or paying the increased cost without legal challenge, Tier II and Tier III plaintiffs accepted the 1990 contract as an accord and satisfaction substituting a new contract for the earlier one. That new contract, however, provided only that EWEB could implement a one-time increase; it did not authorize the increases in 2003 and 2004.

Affirmed on appeal and cross-appeal.

[Endnotes omitted.]

Case in Point NOVATION OR MODIFICATION

528 F. Supp. 440
Gerald J. LINDENBERG, David M. GREEN and Ouida S. GREEN, on behalf of themselves and all other persons similarly situated, Plaintiffs,
v.
FIRST FEDERAL SAVINGS AND LOAN ASSOCIATION and FULTON FEDERAL SAVINGS AND LOAN ASSOCIATION, on behalf of themselves and all other federal savings and loan associations similarly situated, Defendants.
Civ. A. No. C80-983A.
United States District Court, N. D. Georgia, Atlanta Division.
DECEMBER 8, 1981.

Joseph Lefkoff, Jerry L. Sims, Lefkoff, Pike, Fox & Sims, P.C., Atlanta, Ga., for plaintiffs.
[528 F. Supp. 441]
Trammell E. Vickery, James A. Gilbert, Hansell, Post, Brandon & Dorsey, Henry M. Hatcher, Jr., Thomas Hal Clarke, Paul H. Anderson, Mitchell, Clarke, Pate, Anderson & Wimberly, Atlanta, Ga., for defendants.

ORDER

ROBERT T. HALL, District Judge.

High interest rates and an uncertain economy over the past several years have lead to well publicized strains on the housing market. This is one of a growing number of cases around the country challenging the home mortgage lending practices of federally chartered banks and thrift institutions during this unsettled period.

Plaintiffs in this action are home purchasers, defendants are mortgagees of the purchased properties. On February 2, 1981, the court granted the defendants' motions for summary judgment on the causes of action based on the Georgia Assumption Statute, Ga. Code Ann. § 67-3002, contained in Counts II, III and V of the plaintiffs' amended complaint. 90 F.R.D. 255 (N.D. Ga. 1981). On May 26, 1981, the court denied the plaintiffs' motion for reconsideration of the summary judgment order. *Id.*

The case is presently before the court on cross-motions for partial summary judgment on the plaintiffs' allegations of usury, contained in Count IV of the amended complaint. Although the background of

the case has been given in the court's prior orders it bears a summary repetition.

I. FACTS

On March 30, 1977, defendant First Federal Savings and Loan Association ("First Federal") made a residential purchase loan to Mr. and Mrs. Perry Childers. The loan was evidenced by a note, providing for interest at the rate of 8.75% per annum, and was secured by a deed to secure debt to the residence. At the time, the maximum lawful interest rate on home loans was 9% under Georgia law.

Shortly thereafter, the Childers sold the property to Charleen Ernst who assumed the loan. On December 31, 1979, Ernst sold the property to the plaintiff, Gerald Lindenberg. Pursuant to the sale, First Federal, Ernst and Lindenberg entered into a Loan Modification and Assumption Agreement ("the Lindenberg Loan Modification") whereby First Federal released Ernst from future liability on the loan, and Lindenberg agreed to assume the loan at an increased interest rate of 10.75%.

In a similar series of transactions, on March 9, 1979, defendant Fulton Federal Savings & Loan Association ("Fulton Federal") made a residential purchase loan to Mr. and Mrs. Horace Smith. The loan was evidenced by a promissory note providing for interest at the rate of 9.75% per annum, and was secured by a deed to secure debt on the residence. At the time, the maximum lawful interest rate on home loans was 10% under Georgia law.

On May 8, 1980, the Smiths sold the property to plaintiffs David M. and Ouida S. Green. Pursuant to the sale, Fulton Federal the Smiths and the Greens entered into a Loan Modification and Assumption Agreement ("the Green Loan Modification") whereby Fulton Federal released the Smiths from future liability on the loan, and the Greens agreed to assume the loan at an increased interest rate of 12%.

In both the Lindenberg and Green loan modifications no new note or security deed was signed.

II. POSITIONS OF THE PARTIES

The plaintiffs contend that the usury limitations applicable to the loan modifications in this case are the limits which were in effect at the time the loans were originally made, rather than the limits in effect at the time of the modifications. Accordingly, they claim that the loan modifications are usurious.

Plaintiffs begin with the proposition, not contested by the defendants, that the applicable

[528 F. Supp. 442]

usury limitation in effect in the place, and at the time, a loan is made, remains the applicable limitation throughout the life of the loan, without regard to whether usury limits are subsequently changed. Ga. Code Ann. § 57-106; *Lankford v. Holton,* 187 Ga. 94, 200 S.E. 243 (1938). *See also Layton v. Liberty Loans of Waycross,* 152 Ga. App. 504, 263 S.E.2d 167 (1979). However the parties disagree sharply as to what the origination dates of the loans to the plaintiffs were.

The plaintiffs argue that because they merely assumed liability for loans previously made to other parties that the controlling origination date of the loan to them is the same as the origination date of the loan to their grantors. The heart of each plaintiff's position is that despite any modification in the terms of their loan, there was only one loan and hence, only one origination date.

The defendants concur that the debts for which the plaintiffs agreed to become liable came into existence only once — when the plaintiffs' grantors first purchased their properties. However, the defendants maintain that the origination date of the *loans to the plaintiffs* could only be at the time of the modification agreements. Defendants also contend that any state usury issue presented by this case is preempted by Pub. L.No.96-161, § 105, 93 Stat. 1233 (1979).

In support of their claims that there were single loans, each with one origination date, the plaintiffs refer to the text of the loan documents and modification agreements as well as the procedures used in effecting modifications. The plaintiffs place greatest emphasis on covenant 24 of the deeds to secure debt. This covenant provides that: "Assumption Not A Novation. Lenders acceptance of assumption of the obligations of this Deed and the Note and the release of Borrower pursuant to paragraph 17 hereof shall not constitute a novation." Fulton Federal's loan modification agreement also provides that the assumption is not a novation.

Further, both modification agreements provide that plaintiffs assume and agree to abide by all provisions of the original obligations, that the modifications only relate to interest, and that the lenders will transfer the indebtedness from the name of the seller to that of the buyer. Finally, the plaintiffs point to the fact that no new money was advanced, that no new notes were signed and that no new deeds to secure debt were executed.

The plaintiffs' most compelling argument concerns the meaning of covenant 24. According to the plaintiffs, the fact that the loan assumptions were not novations has a simple effect: As a matter of law, since the loan assumptions were not new loans, the old loans continued in effect until the expiration of their 30-year term. The plaintiffs contend that covenant 24 was inserted by the defendants for the purpose of their protecting their security interest. The plaintiffs maintain that in the absence of covenant 24, the loan modifications could be found to be novations, and that the defendants' security interest would be jeopardized. They conclude that the defendants cannot accept the benefits of the covenant for the purpose of protecting their security, but ignore the covenant or construe it away as boilerplate, when the plaintiffs assert its provisions for their benefit.

It is elementary that on a motion for summary judgment the moving party bears the burden of showing both the absence of a genuine issue as to any material fact and

[528 F. Supp. 443]

that judgment is warranted as a matter of law. Also, the evidence on the motion must be construed in favor of the party opposing the motion, and the opposing party must receive the benefit of all favorable inferences that can be drawn from the evidence.

The court has carefully considered the plaintiffs' arguments. However, even taking all facts in a light most favorable to the plaintiffs, and drawing all inferences that can reasonably be drawn in their favor, the court concludes as a matter of law, that the defendants have not charged a usurious rate of interest. Accordingly, for the reasons set forth below, the plaintiffs motion for summary judgment is DENIED and the defendants' motion for summary judgment is GRANTED.

III. DISCUSSION

A. Novation

The plaintiffs pose a dilemma for the defendants and the court. They argue that if the modifications in the instant case are new contracts, for valid consideration, and establish a new origination date for usury, then there must have been novations which destroyed the defendants' security interests in the mortgage property. Conversely, if there were no novations, the relevant origination dates were the same as those of plaintiffs' grantors.

The dilemma plaintiffs assert is false. There are middle cases between the two extremes of a novation, extinguishing the old contract and its security in its entirety, and an assumption of liability, that merely adds a new party as principal debtor with no changes in the origination date or other terms. Compare cases on novations or assumptions, *e.g.*, *Knight v. First Federal Savings & Loan,* 151 Ga. App. 447, 260 S.E.2d 511 (1979) (novation occurred) and *Chewning v. Huebner,* 142 Ga. App. 112, 235 S.E.2d 573 (1977) (novation occurred) and *Cowart v. Smith,* 78 Ga. App. 1941, 50 S.E.2d 863 (1948) (mere assumption not novation) with cases on modifications, *e.g.*, *Williams v. Rowe Banking Co.,* 205 Ga. 770, 55 S.E.2d 123 (1949) (new contract but no novation) and *Contractors Management Corp. v. McDowell-Kelley, Inc.,* 136 Ga. App. 1164, 220 S.E.2d 473 (1975) (modification). *See also* Ga. Code Ann. 20-119.

There are a host of doctrines which justify and explain how, once a contract is made between certain parties, either the contract, or the parties which it binds may be changed. These doctrines, including novation and assumption, as well as modification,

substituted agreement, accord and satisfaction, recision, and assignment, all have distinct core meanings recognized by the great contract treatises. *See* A. Corbin, Contracts (1951); Restatement (Second) of Contracts (1981), Restatement of Security (1941); S. Williston, Contracts (1957); *See also* 58 Am. Jur. 2d, Novation § 2 (1971). The treatises concede that in practice, the cases evidence more confusion than clarity in deciding what label to apply to certain transactions, and what consequences flow from the application of particular labels. *See, e.g.,* 6 A. Corbin, Contracts § 1293 (1951).

Nonetheless, from the plethora of doctrines governing changes in the parties or terms of preexisting contracts, it is self-evident that although every novation involves a new contract, not every new contract involves novation.

"Novation" is a term of art. It signifies a very particular type of accord or modification. "A novation is a complete contract within itself and has four essential requisites: (1) a previous valid obligation, (2) the agreement of all of the parties to the new contract, (3) the extinguishment of the old contract, (4) the validity of the new one." *Sutton v. General Electric Credit Corporation,* 154 Ga. App. 522, 268 S.E.2d 789 (1980). There must be a mutual intent to create a novation. *Mayer v. Turner,* 142 Ga. App. 63, 234 S.E.2d 853 (1977). The loan documents in the instant case make clear no novation was intended.

The very language of the four-part test for a novation indicates the possibility excluded by plaintiffs, of a transaction which creates a new contract without completely extinguishing the old contract or any debt

[528 F. Supp. 444]

it may have created. The terms of the loan instruments, including covenant 24, which plaintiffs advance in support of their position, simply demonstrate that the substitutions which took place here were structured to protect the defendants' security interests. Although not a novation, the transactions involved here clearly resulted in new contracts, binding on defendants as well as plaintiffs, the validity of which is to be judged at the time of their making. *See Story v. Kimbrough,* 33 Ga. 21 (1861).

The issue of novation may be relevant to the extent that had a novation occurred, the plaintiffs concede that the usury rate would be determined by the loan modification dates. The fact no novation occurred also may be significant to a mortgagee interested in protecting its security interest. But it does not follow that the absence of a novation is determinative of the origination dates of the loans to the plaintiffs.

B. Origination Dates

Although certain facts of this case are unique, the general issue presented — determining applicable usury rates after a change in the usury law — is not unprecedented. In 1755 the Governor Counsel and Assembly of the province of Georgia passed an act setting the usury limit at 10 percent, twice the statutory rate in Great Britain. Between 1755 and 1879 maximum usury rates were lowered four times and raised two times. The rates then remained unchanged until 1969 when the legislature established a separate usury rate for real estate loans and set that rate at nine percent. This rate was raised to ten percent in 1977 and made variable in 1979. *See generally Union Savings Bank v. Dottenheim,* 107 Ga. 606, 34 S.E. 217 (1898), 18 Ency. Ga. Law, Interest § 2 (1981).

The court has researched cases from the period of each increase in maximum usury limits. Noteworthy are the cases concerning the period from 1873 to 1875 when the legislature removed all limits on written agreements pertaining to interest charges.

The cases consistently hold that contracts entered into under one usury statute remain enforceable on their original terms even if the statute changes. By contrast, any contract entered into after changing the law is to be governed by the new law, even if the new contract concerns a preexisting debt. *See, e.g., Taylor v. Thomas,* 61 Ga. 472 (1878).

Indeed, even if an original loan contract was void for usury, a new promise to pay the loan after an increase in the usury limits was binding under the new limits. *Houser v. Planters Bank of Fort Valley,* 57 Ga. 95 (1876). In the instant case, the plaintiffs' promise to pay the remaining

[528 F. Supp. 445]

portion of their grantors' debt must be judged at the time of their promise.

Plaintiffs object that the cases cited concern renewals of notes already passed their maturity and are from a period when there was no maximum interest charge on written contracts. These are differences without a difference. First, in holding new, post-usury change contracts valid as of the time they were made,

the cases focus on the presence of new consideration. *See, e.g., Neil v. Bunn,* 58 Ga. 583 (1877). Post-maturity extension of time for repayment is the most likely consideration for a new contract in a two-party loan transaction. *But see Citizens & Southern National Bank v. Scheider,* 139 Ga. App. 475, 228 S.E.2d 611 (1976) (extension not consideration for post-maturity renewal). However, forebearance is not the only valid consideration for a new contract on a preexisting debt. Where three parties are involved, release of the original borrower and acceptance of a purchaser-grantee is valid consideration for a new contract at new interest rates, even before expiration of the original loan term.

Second, despite the broad language of the cases, the legislature had not ended all regulation of interest rates during the relevant period. It had merely provided for unlimited interest rates in written contracts. The rate otherwise was 7 percent. 1873 Georgia Laws 52. Whether the "legislative will" sanctions interest rate limits of 10 per cent or infinity is immaterial, so long as the challenged rate is below the sanctioned maximum. Finally, as indicated below, the loan modifications in this case were covered by the Federal preemption of state usury limits, Pub. L. 96-161.

C. Claim of Usury Personal

So long as the original borrowers are liable for a debt, they have a vested right in having interest rates remain at the rate expressed in the original promissory note for the debt. By the same token, the lender has a vested right to hold the original borrowers liable for repayment of the debt; assumption of the debt by another cannot release the borrowers from liability without the express consent of the lender. *Federal Deposit Insurance Co. v. Thompson,* 54 Ga. App. 611, 188 S.E. 737 (1936).

A plea of usury is personal. Ga. Code Ann. 67-103. Because the usury laws protect the debtor, not the debt, the parties' various rights concerning the debt belongs to them only so long as they remain within a lender-borrower relationship. The parties are free to bargain away their rights and once the borrower is released from liability, whether by novation, a loan modification or any other means, subsequent agreements for repayments of the debt are governed by the laws as of the date they are made, and not the date of the creation of the debt.

Conversely, before the sales by the original borrower-grantors, the plaintiff-grantees were total strangers to the loan agreements. Their protection under the usury law can only begin when liability for the debt is transferred to them. If the grantors were not released from liability, the grantees' rights might be derivative. But this was not the case here.

Under the plaintiffs' reasoning a modified interest rate above a preexisting maximum legal rate could *never* be achieved accept by a novation that would create a new debt and a new security interest for the lender. The transfer of liabilities and renegotiation of the terms for their repayment in light of new market conditions, a practice widespread throughout the market-place, would be severely circumscribed. This is not the law in Georgia.

IV. APPLICABLE USURY RATE

Having concluded that the loan modifications in the instant case were new contracts to be governed by the laws in effect at the time those contracts were made, the only remaining issue is what the effective usury limits were on the loan modification dates.

The applicable limits under state law were established by Ga. Code Ann. § 57-101.1, as amended. 1979 Georgia Laws 357. However, Congress preempted the state statutes by passage of Public Law 96-161.

[528 F. Supp. 446]

In passing this law Congress expressed an unmistakable intent to preempt state usury laws. *See Alessi v. Raybestos-Manhatten, Inc.*, 451 U.S. 504, 519-522, 101 S. Ct. 1895, 1904-1905, 68 L. Ed. 2d 402 (1981); *Jones v. Rath Packing Co.*, 430 U.S. 519, 525-26, 97 S. Ct. 1305, 1309-1310, 51 L. Ed. 2d 604 (1977). Public Law 96-161 provides that state usury laws do not apply to certain residential mortgage loans made between December 28, 1979, and March 31, 1980. Unless a state specifically overrides these provisions, Public Law 96-221, § 501, 94 Stat. 132, extends this preemption from April 1, 1980 on.

The parties do not dispute that Pub. L. 96-161 and Pub. L. 96-221 were valid exercises of Congressional power to preempt state legislation. Further, the loan modifications occurred after the effective date of the federal preemption.

By its own terms, Pub. L. 96-161 only applies to loans made after its effective dates. Pub. L. 96-161 § 105(a)(1)(B). *See also* 45 F.R. 1853 (Jan. 9, 1980); 45 F.R. 6166 (Jan. 25, 1980). In an argument

parallel to their state usury claims, the plaintiffs maintain that the preemption did not apply to them, because the loans for which they are liable were originally made before the effective dates of the preemption statutes. This position is without merit.

For purposes of the preemption statutes, the Home Loan Bank Board has interpreted a loan assumption, accompanied by release of the grantor and an increase in the interest rate, as constituting a new loan regulated by the statutes. Federal Home Loan Bank Board Interpretation No. 590-2 (Assumptions) 45 F.R. 6166 (Jan. 25, 1980). Although not required to give effect to an interpretative regulation, "when faced with a problem of statutory construction, this court shows great deference to the interpretation given the statute by the officers or agency charged with its administration." *Udall v. Tallman*, 380 U.S. 1, 16, 85 S. Ct. 792, 801, 13 L. Ed. 2d 616 (1965); *Roy Bryant Cattle Co. v. United States*, 463 F.2d 418, 420 (5th Cir. 1972). *Cf. General Electric Co. v. Gilbert*, 429 U.S. 125, 141-145, 97 S. Ct. 401, 410-412, 50 L. Ed. 2d 343 (1976) ("Varying degrees of deference are accorded to administrative interpretations . . .") The court's own analysis, set out above in section III, confirms the correctness of the Bank Board's position.

V. PUBLIC POLICY

In its report on permanent federal preemption of state usury laws, the Senate Banking, Housing, and Urban Affairs Committee stated the purpose of preemption as being "to ease the severity of the mortgage credit crunches of recent years . . . ." The committee believed that preemption would "enhance the stability and viability of our nation's financial system and is needed to facilitate a national housing policy and the functioning of a national secondary market in mortgage lending." S. Rep. No. 96-368, 96 Cong., 2nd Sess. 18, reprinted in 1980 U.S. Code Cong. & Ad. News 834, 852.

The public policy of Georgia is manifestly in harmony with the policy considerations which motivated the Congress in its preemption of state usury laws. A review of the legislative history of Pub. L. 96-161 and Pub. L. 96-221, relevant portions of 12 C.F.R., and other cases challenging mortgage lending practices around the country reveals the following facts:

Mortgage lenders typically carry large portfolios ("pools") of mortgages, comprised of the outstanding mortgages issued over many years of lending. So long as interest rates vary predictably or only over a narrow range lenders can adjust their lending rates so there is a positive spread between market interest rates and the weighted averages of the mortgages in their pool. However, in periods of rapidly escalating or volatile interest rates lenders with pools consisting of long term, fixed rate mortgages

[528 F. Supp. 447]

may face large negative spreads. This is so because lenders have primarily only three ways to adjust market-pool spreads: (1) to issue new loans at market rates (2) to call in old loans and (3) to offer short term or adjustable rate mortgages (ARM) instead of long term, fixed rate mortgages. Obviously these methods will be used in combinations as well as singly. For example, a combination of methods 1 and 2 is at issue in the instant case.

These three methods of adjustment are subject to regulation primarily through laws relating to usury or due on sale clauses. In particular, if usury laws prohibit issuing new loans at market rates none of these methods can be usefully employed. Moreover, lenders restricted to mortgage lending below market rates cannot participate successfully in secondary mortgage market auctions which facilitate new loans.

Even where usury laws permit lending at market rates, in periods of rapid interest rate escalation, adjusting the average pool rate is difficult because only a small proportion of loans are made at the new, higher rates. Obviously, if lenders' spreads remain negative over the long term lenders cannot continue in the business of making residential purchase loans.

Since 1969 Georgia has consistently taken steps to adjust usury laws and other regulatory policies to promote a stable and active residential mortgage lending industry. When a special category of usury restrictions for real estate loans was first established the legislature took cognizance of the fact that if usury limits are below market rates for money the funds necessary for economic activity will not be made available. 1969 Ga. Laws 33, 34.

This recognition has remained constant and has evidenced itself in a variety of contexts. See Ga. Code Ann. 57-101.1(c)(5) (VHA, FHA loans exempt from usury laws); 57-118 (for profit corporations exempt); 57-119 (loans greater than $100,000 exempt); 1977 Ga. Laws 1221 (raising real estate usury rate); 1979 Ga. Laws 357 (floating real estate usury rate). Further, the Georgia courts have been receptive to instances of federal preemption of state usury laws made in order to insure the availability of funds. See *Kennedy v. Brand Banking Co.*, 245 Ga. 496, 266 S.E.2d 154 (1980) (effectiveness of federal preemption of usury laws for federally insured state banks' business or agricultural loans of $25,000 or more); *Christian v. Atlanta Army Depot Federal Credit Union*, 140 Ga. App. 277, 231 S.E.2d 7 (1976) (federal savings and loan exempt from state usury laws).

Nor does the Georgia Assumption Statute, Ga. Code Ann. 67-3002, conflict with Georgia's long standing policy in this area. The scheme under section 67-3002 attempts to restrict loan modifications made in connection with due-on-sale clauses and thereby blocks a traditional method of adjusting mortgage pool rates. However, it does not necessarily limit a lender's ability to adjust market-pool spreads because it was: totally prospective in operation; coupled with a floating usury rate; and accompanied by changes in the traditional long term, fixed rate lending practices.

Because the loans to plaintiffs' grantors are below prevailing rates they represent a potential loss to the defendants and an attractive opportunity for profit to the plaintiffs. Plaintiffs claim that one aspect of Georgia's public policy towards mortgage lending practices is to facilitate residential home purchases. They state that in accord with this policy, the immediate effect of allowing plaintiffs to expropriate the benefits of their grantors' loan terms would be to facilitate home purchases for the plaintiff class. The plaintiffs neglect to point out, however, that the cumulative effect of such expropriations over all classes of home buyers, and over several years, would be either to destabilize the lending market or to subsidize "loan assuming" purchasers at the expense of "non-assuming" purchasers. This is not the public policy of Georgia.

For all the above stated reasons plaintiffs' motion for summary judgment is DENIED, the defendants' motion for summary judgment is GRANTED. The defendants' motions for a hearing is DENIED.

[Endnotes omitted.]

VOCABULARY BUILDERS

Across

2 The aggrieved party is entitled to a remedy even prior to the time for performance.
4 The nonbreaching party is ___ from performance.
6 May also repudiate where there are no words spoken.
9 A party's performance may not be perfect, but it is still in _____ compliance.
12 To carry on as if there were no breach.
15 The aggrieved party can _____ the repudiation and hope that the potentially breaching party reconsiders.
17 A party is completely unable to perform.
22 A party can change his/her mind and _____.
23 A novation substitutes _____.
24 A material breach is a ____ breach.
26 A party must ____ and positively state that performance is not forthcoming.
27 The agreement to accept the nonconforming performance.
29 The aggrieved party can immediately ____ for breach even though the time for performance has not yet arrived.
30 If a party forgoes the _____, it is valid consideration.
31 An excuse that the contract would have very little value at too great an expense.
35 The ability to separate the contract into parts.
38 An agreement that the releasing party will not commence litigation.
40 The parties surrender their rights under the contract.
41 A way to repudiate a contract.
42 The obligation under a novation must be a _____ one.
43 Is not a repudiation.
44 Bankruptcy.
45 The nonbreaching party voluntarily relinquishes his/her right to enforce the contract.

Down

1 The aggrieved party can ____ the contract and walk away.
3 The deciding factor as to the interpretation of terms in the contract.
5 A broken promise.
7 To make the contract new.
8 The subject matter is no longer legally valid.
10 The requirement for a valid accord and satisfaction.
11 The nonconforming performance stated in the accord.
13 The new agreement _____ for the old one where it is merged into it.
14 The reason for entering into the contract no longer exists.
16 Voluntary _____ occurs where a party makes his/her own performance impossible.
18 An event beyond the control of either party—sometimes referred to as an "act of God."
19 A contract that cannot be performed.
20 A party can be excused if his/her performance is _____.
21 A nonmaterial breach.
25 The subject matter no longer exists.
28 The parties can enter into a _____ and change the terms of the existing contract.
32 The liability of the old party is _____ under a novation.
33 A substituted agreement substitutes the _____ of the contract.
34 How the court evaluates the factors regarding materiality.
36 Parties must _____ to these kinds of changes to previous contracts.
37 The old agreement _____ into the new one in a substituted agreement.
39 Important or significant.

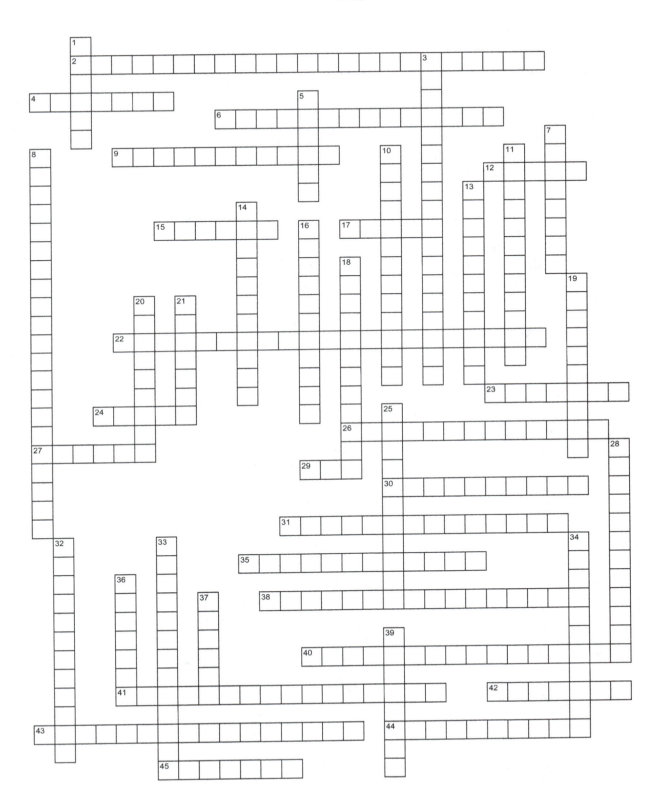

Part Four

Remedies

Chapter 13: Compensatory and Related Damages

Chapter 14: Equity and Quasi-Contract

Chapter 13

Compensatory and Related Damages

This chapter will examine WHAT kinds of monetary damages parties to a lawsuit can expect and HOW to calculate the appropriate damages. Essentially, he has broken his promise and will somehow be required to compensate the non-breaching party for the transgression. As noted in the Preface, our kindergarten teachers taught us this lesson early in our lives—if you misbehave, you will be punished.

Assume that the non-breaching party has come to the decision to file the lawsuit. What types of damages can the party recover? The law categorizes the kinds of damages available to plaintiffs based on their source. Damages can be (1) *compensatory*, (2) *consequential*, (3) *incidental*, (4) *nominal*, (5) *liquid*, and/or (6) *limited*. Each of these will be discussed in turn. Further, there are several methods for calculating these damages, all of which attempt to make the non-breaching party "whole" again.

DAMAGES NOT RECOVERABLE UNDER CONTRACT LAW

There are two kinds of damages that, while categorized, are *never* recoverable *under contract law*: (1) *speculative* and (2) *punitive*. These damages may be recovered in a primarily contractual dispute; however, the theories under which they are recovered are either tortious or statutorily imposed. If a party commits a breach of contract coupled with an intentional malicious act or a legislatively prohibited act, these damages are available and therefore are appropriate for discussion in relation to the breach.

Speculative Damages

speculative damages
Harm incurred by the non-breaching party that is not susceptible to valuation or determination with any reasonable certainty.

Speculative damages are the antithesis of contract law's love for certainty. If the amount of harm cannot be reasonably determined by objective means, then they cannot be recovered. Guessing or speculation is not permitted. The calculation does not have to be an exact mathematical certainty, but the damages must not rest on uncertain factors. This concept of uncertainty is prevalent in ascertaining future damages; after all, no one can predict the future, but objectively reasonable predictions can be made based on acceptable standards of measurement. Accounting, statistical, and economical analyses can render a probable calculation that is supported by demonstrable evidence. Certainty plays a much more significant role in determining that there was a causal link between the alleged wrongful act and the fact of damage rather than an absolute certainty as to the amount of damages. The act must have first been proven to have caused damage and then a party can estimate the amount of damages that could be awarded.

lost profits
A calculable amount of money that the non-breaching party would have made after the execution of performance under the agreement but that has not been realized due to the breach.

A common example of potentially speculative damages is **lost profits**. If Farmer Fred breaches his contract for delivery of Granny Smith apples to Greg Grocer for the apple festival, does Greg have a claim for damages of lost profits? It depends. If this were Greg's first time participating in the event, the amount of money he would have made may be completely speculative. There is nothing on which to base his claim.

Alternatively, if this were Greg's tenth year of participation, he normally makes a profit equaling about 60 percent of his selling price, and he usually sells 90 percent of the apples he brings to sell, Fred's breach would result in damages of those lost profits. Mathematically, it might look like this: number of apples brought to market = 10,000; selling price = $1.00/apple; total sales = 9,000 apples

@ $1.00 each = $9,000; 60 percent of $9,000 = $5,400 profit. This, of course, is just a projection based on past sales. In actuality, it could be more or less, but this is a reasonable expectation of lost profits.

But see El Fredo Pizza, Inc. v. Roto-Flex Oven Co., 261 N.W.2d 358 (Neb. 1978). A new pizza shop (Center Street Pizza) claimed lost profits due to a breach of contract for a new oven. It claimed lost profits based on (1) an increase in operating costs to make up for the defective oven and (2) a decrease in sales. What made this case unusual and contradictory to the above example is the nature of the business itself. This type of business doesn't take a long time to "get off the ground." The court characterized it as an "instant maturity business." *Id.* at 361. Therefore, the track record of success or failure would be relatively short and records would exist as to the profits or losses sustained. Further, the owners of Center Street Pizza owned other restaurants under the name of El Fredo Pizza, and the profitability of those restaurants would be an indicator of the profitability of Center Street.

From these records, the court determined that it cost Center Street Pizza $8,000 more in labor as it dealt with the defective oven and hired additional employees due to the inefficiency and defective nature of the oven. However, in determining the amount of damages attributable to lost retail sales, the court couldn't find dependable evidence to rely on that showed that the defective oven itself caused the lost revenue.

> Although there was some evidence that customers were dissatisfied with the pizza baked in the Roto-Flex oven, such evidence was scanty at best. In the absence of more persuasive evidence, such as that other El Fredo Pizza restaurants in fact did not have significant increases in sales after a certain period of operation, we find that it would be speculative for a jury to conclude that Center Street Pizza would have sold as much pizza when the Roto-Flex oven was in operation as it did subsequently. Although sales did increase after the Roto-Flex oven was replaced, the increase was not so dramatic as to itself imply the defective oven caused lost revenue, and there are simply too many other factors such as location, increased public awareness of a restaurant, etc., to permit a jury to conclude with reasonable certainty that the oven caused reduced sales. Therefore we believe damages cannot be recovered for lost profits allegedly caused by decreased revenue because they were not proven with reasonable certainty.

Id. at 366.

RESEARCH THIS

In your jurisdiction, find two cases regarding calculation of damages based on lost profits: one that was able to calculate the damages with a reasonable level of certainty and another that held that lost profits could not be recovered as they were too speculative. What were the factual differences that resulted in these contradictory outcomes?

Speculative damages are therefore indeterminable because there is nothing to base their calculation on. If the amount to be awarded cannot be determined, then it cannot be imposed upon a party, no matter the extent of fault. The law, no matter what area—contracts or otherwise—cannot be used to enforce arbitrary and capricious determinations.

SPOT THE ISSUE!

Diggers, Ltd., entered into an agreement with Ores "R" Us, Inc., to provide uranium mining services for three years. Ores would then sell the uranium to processors, and the profits would be shared between Ores and Diggers. Ores terminated the contract after one year after discovering the difficulties in processing the uranium. Diggers filed a complaint for the breach and sought lost profits. At trial, Diggers' expert testified that the profits could have amounted to $500,000; Ores' expert testified that the profits would have amounted to $10,000. As a judge in this matter, how would you rule and why? What factors do you consider important in making your determination? *See Ranchers Exploration and Dev. Corp. v. Miles*, 696 P.2d 475 (N.M. 1985).

Punitive Damages

punitive damages
An amount of money awarded to a non-breaching party that is not based on the actual losses incurred by that party, but as a punishment to the breaching party for the commission of an intentional wrong.

deterrent effect
The authority to assess excessive fines on a breaching party often can dissuade a party from committing an act that would subject him to these punitive damages.

statutory authority
The legislature of a jurisdiction may codify certain actions as subject to punitive damages if they occur in conjunction with a contractual breach.

Punitive damages punish the defendant's wrongdoing. They are not necessarily tied to actual losses or expenses incurred by the party who was harmed. The reason the law (not contract law) permits this type of damage is for its **deterrent effect**. Exposure to punitive damages may prevent a party from committing the act as he knows it will not be worth the extra cost. Contract law does not subscribe to this theory. Contract law remains heartless and neutral; it does not judge the degree of wrongness and mete out more severe penalties because there is a sympathetic plaintiff.

Of course, that doesn't mean that, in a contract dispute, punitive damages are prohibited from being levied on the defendant. If there is separate **statutory authority** to award punitive damages in an underlying contractual dispute, then, by the power of the statute, the court can grant a punitive damage award. For example, Bob the Builder's actions that give rise to a breach of contract action also may violate a state's Consumer Fraud Act, which may permit punitive damages to be levied against the wrongdoer. A "bait and switch" scheme designed to harm consumers generally falls under most state consumer fraud statutes. It is unlawful to plan to advertise an item at a specified price and not to sell that item for that price or intentionally substitute another more expensive alternative. So, if Bob's breach by installing expensive kitchen cabinets caused $10,000 in actual damages, a court could award treble damages (as permitted by these types of statutes in many states) as punitive damages if the court also determined that this was a part of a "scheme." Therefore, Bob would owe the Newlyweds $30,000 as a result of the breach.

Note that the various states' consumer fraud statutes are rather extensive and detailed as far as the individual requirements for a cause of action. The paralegal student should research and outline the relevant statute for his jurisdiction. Generally speaking, just because there has been error that was the defendant's fault does not mean that he acted willfully, wantonly, or in reckless disregard for the rights of the plaintiff. There must be something intentionally devious and misleading about the defendant's conduct that will give rise to a consumer fraud claim; otherwise, the plaintiff is only entitled to actual contract damages. *See Wahba v. Don Corlett Motors, Inc.*, 573 S.W.2d 357 (Ky. Ct. App. 1978) (The court determined that the car dealership was not liable under the relevant consumer fraud statute because the salesman did not act oppressively or with malice. The sales slip incorrectly stated the sales price and the manager refused to sell the car at that price. Mr. Wahba was entitled to contract damages in the amount of $875, the difference between what he contracted to pay for the car and what he paid for a substitute car. "The fraud supposedly practiced on Mr. Wahba exists only in his mind." *Id.* at 360.).

Similarly, if there is a **tortious** act that accompanied the breach of contract, the court may award punitive damages based on the intentional or negligent commission of the tort. In this case, the plaintiff would have to show the malicious intent or negligent misconduct that gives rise to the tort. For example, fraud is an intentional tort that may permit a court to award punitive damages over and above the contractual damages. Further, courts award punitive damages "only for conduct that is outrageous, either because the defendant's motive was evil or the acts showed a reckless disregard of others' rights." *Kleczek v. Jorgensen*, 767 N.E.2d 913, 922 (Ill. App. 2002).

> **tortious**
> A private civil wrong committed by one person as against another that the law considers to be punishable.

It is important to note that courts do not grant punitive damages when the plaintiff has no actual damages. The plaintiff must show that he has suffered harm before the court will award compensation beyond contractual remedies. In other words, nasty intent alone is not justification for imposing a monetary punishment. It must be on top of actual harm incurred; if there is zero dollars' worth of damages, there is zero dollars' worth of punitive damages: Three times zero is still zero.

CALCULATION OF COMPENSATORY DAMAGES

Compensatory damages compensate for the loss/harm incurred by the non-breaching party and attempt to put him in as good a position as he would have been had the contract not been breached. There are several kinds of compensatory damages: (1) *expectation damages*, (2) *restitution damages*, and (3) *reliance damages*.

> **compensatory damages**
> A payment to make up for a wrong committed and return the non-breaching party to a position where the effect of the breach has been neutralized.

Expectation Damages

Essentially, the non-breaching party expects to receive the subject matter of the contract and should be awarded damages in accordance with this expectation. Recall how much contract law likes parties to keep their promises; hence, the

expectation damages
A monetary amount that makes up for the losses incurred as a result of the breach that puts the non-breaching party in as good a position as he would have been had the contract been fully performed.

award of **expectation damages** naturally flows. Parties are expected to keep their promises and contract law will grant damages in an amount that fulfills these expectations. Therefore, the non-breaching party can receive a monetary amount that will make up for the loss or will allow him to purchase a substitute for the breached contract's subject matter. There may be some issues, such as the value of the transaction to an objective third party and at what point in time these damages are calculated, but the essence remains that the money to be awarded can be reasonably and objectively calculated and will achieve the desired result—to "make the party whole again." *Vaught v. A.O. Hardee & Sons, Inc.*, 623 S.E.2d 373, 375 (S.C. 2005).

Example

Walk This Way, Inc. (WTW), is a vacation planning company that specializes in selling walking tours of exotic locations. Fiji For Me, Inc. (FFM), is a walking tour operator based on Turtle Island among the 333 islands of Fiji. WTW and FFM entered into an agreement where FFM would design, arrange, and lead walking tours of Fiji and WTW would sell and promote all its tours of the Fiji Islands through FFM for a period of two years. The exclusivity ran both ways: WTW would exclusively sell FFM tours to its customers desiring to go to Fiji, and FFM would only work through WTW. In breach of the exclusive two-year contract, WTW began using Forage In Fiji, Inc., to arrange tours. FFM sued WTW because it was now without booked tours for the prime tourist season. At trial, the court determined that FFM expected WTW to take certain actions on its behalf and the failure of WTW to do what it was contractually bound to do resulted in real and calculable damages to FFM. FFM was entitled to damage based on its expectations as if the contract were fully performed by WTW. These expectation damages are the lost potential profits because FFM could not pursue other markets for its tours due to the exclusivity of the WTW agreement and harm to its reputation due to the canceled tours resulting directly from WTW's breach. *See Tour Costa Rica v. Country Walkers, Inc.*, 758 A.2d 795 (Vt. 2000).

Parties have expectations based on their agreements; when these fall through, parties are left not only disappointed but monetarily harmed. Expectation damages put the party in the position he would have been in had the contract been fully performed.

Restitution Damages

restitution damages
A monetary amount that requires the breaching party to return any benefits received under the contract to the non-breaching party to ensure that the breaching party does not profit from the breach.

Restitution damages focus on the breaching party's pocketbook rather than that of the non-breaching party as in expectation damages. Restitution damages essentially make the breaching party give back the benefit he may have received from the now-broken promise. If the non-breaching party has given something of value to the breaching party in compliance with the contract, the breaching party must give back that value that he gained but did not deserve. The breaching party cannot profit from his wrongdoing. For example, a store cannot take your deposit for purchase of the new, state-of-the-art television and then refuse to sell it to you without, at the very least, being on the hook for restitutionary damages in the amount of your deposit. Otherwise, parties would have an incentive to breach their promises—they could profit by keeping the deposits!

This "disgorgement" of benefit from the breaching party is exemplified in *EarthInfo, Inc. v. Hydrosphere Resource Consultants, Inc.*, 900 P.2d 113 (Colo. 1995). The parties entered into an agreement wherein Hydrosphere would collect government hydrological and meteorological information and make that information available via CD-ROMs developed by EarthInfo. Hydrosphere would receive royalty payments based on the products created from the information. A dispute arose when Hydrosphere claimed that sales of a new derivative product were subject to royalty payments, which, of course, EarthInfo challenged. All royalty payments were ceased by EarthInfo until the dispute could be resolved. Hydrosphere filed a lawsuit to rescind the contract based on the failure to make royalty payments. The court ordered EarthInfo, as a result of its breach, to pay restitutionary damages to Hydrosphere in the amount of all the profits it realized after the breach.

Restitution essentially tries to put the party back in the position he was in prior to the contract. It is as if it never happened or time has been turned back. In the above example, Hydrosphere was put back into its pre-contract position by giving up all the "ill-gotten gains" of the breach. This is different than expectation damages, which put the party in the position he would have been in had the contract been fully performed. Restitution looks backward—to put the parties back where they started; expectation looks forward—to put the parties where they should have ended.

Reliance Damages

Reliance damages focus on the non-breaching party's actions relative to the bargain. Reliance damages and expectation damages are mutually exclusive remedies. Either one or the other is determined to be the proper measure of damages because recovery under both theories would result in the receipt of "double" damages.

If the non-breaching party has changed her position in relying on the promise, then the losses that flow also can be the responsibility of the breaching party. There are some preparatory steps that parties may take to put themselves into a position where they can perform. The only reason the parties take these steps is due to their reliance on the contract. The parties have no other reason for taking these actions except to fulfill their part of the bargain. These actions are not the required performance, but they are necessary to comply with the terms of the agreement. For example, in preparation for a real estate closing, the buyer must pay for title searches and inspections. If the seller breaches, the buyer is out the cost of those services as they were undertaken based solely on the buyer's reliance on fulfillment of the contract of sale.

reliance damages
A monetary amount that "reimburses" the non-breaching party for expenses incurred while preparing to perform her obligations under the agreement but lost due to the breach.

These damages, while based on preparatory steps, may be substantial in amount. A breaching party will be responsible for amounts expended by the non-breaching party that were foreseeable and dependent on the unfulfilled representations of the contract. This also applies in situations that require forbearance from taking actions that would otherwise be contradictory to the terms of the promise relied upon. For example, in *Harmon v. State*, 62 A.3d 1198 (Del. 2013), a racing official (Harmon) had been suspended by the Delaware Harness Racing Commission because he was arrested for allegedly changing a judging sheet. The official was suspended pending the outcome of a criminal case. The official was acquitted and inquired whether he would be reinstated and the Commission agreed to do so. Almost a year after his acquittal, the Commission reneged on its promise to reinstate him, so Harmon brought an action to recover damages. "Reliance damages are intended to assure that those who are reasonably induced to take injurious action in reliance upon the non-contractual promises receive recompense for that harm. During the time that he was waiting to be reinstated, however, Harmon could not accept another job, and suffered lost income as a result. That lost income constitutes reliance damages." *Id.* at 1202 (internal citations omitted). *See also M.H. Promotion Group, Inc. v. Cincinnati Milacron, Inc.*, 1998 WL 52239 (Mass. Super. 1988) (After a lease for commercial space was signed, the "potential tenant" bought new, substantially larger and, therefore, substantially more expensive equipment in order to fully utilize the space. Before the equipment was shipped, the landlord canceled the lease agreement. The court determined that the "potential tenant" was entitled to reliance damages because he was reasonably relying on the representations of the lease when he purchased the equipment. It is important to note that, in this case, the plaintiff/tenant was not entitled to expectation damages for the breach of contract because the multiyear lease agreement was oral and, therefore, did not comply with the Statute of Frauds; the court then turned to the "next best remedy"—the reliance damages.).

The court accomplishes these goals of fulfilling the plaintiff's expectations, preventing a benefit to the breaching party, and compensating for reliance by either restoring the status quo to pre-contract conditions or making the non-breaching party whole as if the contract had been performed. One perspective on damages looks backward by restoring the status quo (restitution and reliance) and the other looks forward as if there were an absence of the breach (expectation).

DUTY TO MITIGATE

duty
A legal obligation that is required to be performed.

mitigate
To lessen in intensity or amount.

The non-breaching party has a **duty** to try to lessen the amount of harm he suffers due to the breach, thereby **mitigating** damages. The aggrieved party must make a *reasonable* effort to mitigate the damages caused by the breach. Extraordinary and potentially very expensive mitigation efforts do not necessarily have to be undertaken. The reasonableness of the aggrieved party's efforts will be determined by the court.

Example

Mr. Knight and Mr. Daye are two attorneys who have formed a partnership and rented an office building. Daye, coming from a rather wealthy family, has fronted the money for the two-year lease on the building ($500,000) and, according to the contract, Knight will pay him back through proceeds from the partnership. Knight has had second thoughts about tying his fortunes to Daye's and decided to cut his losses and breach the agreement. Daye has brought an action for the enforcement of the rental component of the agreement. Knight feels that Daye is not entitled to the full amount of rental damages ($250,000) because Daye has failed to mitigate his damages by not re-leasing the building or finding another partner. However, Daye has interviewed three attorneys over the six-month period since the "break-up" with Knight. The court will look to the reasonableness of Daye's efforts in finding a new partner or new tenant to share the cost of the building. At this juncture, Knight will be responsible for the rent until Daye does find a suitable replacement for Knight. Complicating matters is the situation where modifications or remodeling needs to take place before a new tenant can be found for the space. Are those expenses to be included in the costs associated with mitigation? It depends upon the market and reasonableness in making those changes. Are they truly necessary to re-let the space or are they just more desirable to maximize the new rental? *See Hidden Chutes, LLC v. Dick Blick Holdings, Inc.*, 2017 IL App (1st) 161070-U (Ill. App. 2017).

Another point to consider is the breaching party's burden of proof regarding the non-breaching party's duty to mitigate. The breaching party must establish the failure to mitigate as an affirmative defense. This means it is the breaching party that must show that the actions (or inactions) taken by the non-breaching party were unreasonable and that another person in that position would have done something different and more effective.

This also means that the breaching party must be able to show the correlation between the earnings after the breach and the breach itself. Even a showing that the non-breaching party was able to earn money after the breach is not necessarily applicable to reducing the damages as an effort at mitigation. For example, in the case of *Berkel & Company Contractors, Inc. v. Palm & Associates, Inc.*, 814 N.E.2d 649 (Ind. Ct. App. 2004), the contract called for surveying services to be provided by Palm. Berkel breached the contract, and Palm sued for damages. Berkel claimed, as an affirmative defense, that Palm's earnings on other surveying jobs taken after the breach mitigated the total amount of damages Palm could receive. The court denied these earnings as mitigating the Berkel contract damages.

> [W]here one person holds a contract to perform services for another and the other party wrongfully discharges the employee, then, while said employee may have a cause of action for damages resulting from the wrongful

discharge, he may not sit idly by, but must make a reasonable effort to secure other work and any income from such work may be offset against the damages sought.

We, however, recognized an exception to the above rule where the wrongfully discharged employee is not required to devote his entire time to work under the contract. We noted that the plaintiff, who was not contractually required to refrain from other work and did not agree to devote his entire time to work under the contract, would have earned the additional money even if the defendant had not terminated the contract. Thus, we held that the plaintiff's earnings from his employment after the defendant had terminated the contract did not need to be deducted as a means of mitigating his damages.

Id. at 660-61, *citing Albert Johann & Sons Co. v. Echols*, 238 N.E.2d 685, 689 (Ind. App. 1968).

While a party cannot simply sit back and let the harm get worse in order to collect more from the breaching party, in doing so, it may turn out that the non-breaching party ends up in a better deal. A school administrator was wrongfully discharged and, during the relevant contract period, obtained employment as a helicopter pilot, earning at least, if not more than, his contract salary. The court held that the administrator properly mitigated his damages but was not entitled to any damages since he was able to earn at least the amount he would have had the contract not been breached. "Note should be made of the fact that the duty to mitigate damages embodies notions of fairness and socially responsible behavior. A party whose contract has been breached is not entitled to be placed in a better position because of the breach than he would have been in had the contract been performed." *Board of Education of Alamogordo Public School District No. 1 v. Jennings*, 701 P.2d 361, 364 (N.M.1985) (citations omitted). Therefore, it can actually be a benefit to the non-breaching party to have the other party breach. Of course, this means that the breaching party is also off the hook for damages because the non-breaching party has no damages.

In the above example, if Daye had found another partner who was willing to pay even more than the necessary rental value of the building and refurnish the office because he was so sure that the partnership would flourish, then Daye would have actually benefited from Knight's breach. Knight would not have to pay any damages because Daye didn't suffer any.

CONSEQUENTIAL AND INCIDENTAL DAMAGES

consequential damages
Damages resulting from the breach that are natural and foreseeable results of the breaching party's actions.

incidental damages
Damages resulting from the breach that are related to the breach but not necessarily directly foreseeable by the breaching party.

Consequential and **incidental damages** are specific damages that go beyond compensatory damages and are incurred by the non-breaching party *after* the breach. The timing of the actions giving rise to the damages is what distinguishes consequential and incidental damages from reliance damages.

The distinction between consequential and incidental is largely a matter of academics and semantics. *Consequential damages* are those sustained by the non-breaching party that naturally and foreseeably flow from the breach; they are a direct consequence of the breach. *Incidental damages* are similar; the distinction lies in the "naturalness and foreseeability" of the actions that the non-breaching party had to take as a result of the breach and the losses and expenses incurred in doing so.

An example will make the distinction more clear (hopefully!).

Example

DoTell, a microchip manufacturer, agrees to supply Well Computers with high-speed, high-capacity silicon chips for the manufacture of their personal computers. DoTell refuses to deliver the chips, thereby materially breaching the contract. Well Computers has to stop production of its personal computers. The costs associated with the "production downtime" are consequential damages; without the microchips, the computers cannot be made and sold. Incidentally, Well Computers will have to rent additional warehouse space to store all the unfinished computers. This cost is associated with the breach, although it is not necessarily a natural and foreseeable consequence of the breach.

Contracts, by their terms, may specifically include or exclude liability for consequential and incidental damages. This is acceptable under "freedom of contract" principles to the extent that the terms of inclusion or exclusion remain reasonable. Where the terms of limitation of these remedies do not hold up under scrutiny, however, the court may award consequential and incidental damages in spite of the provision if the remedies provided for in the contract fail of their essential purpose. *See Devore v. Bostrom*, 632 P.2d 832, 835 (Utah 1981) (The plaintiff claimed damages relating to the purchase of a defective car; the court awarded insurance and license costs, interest on the purchase price, and lost wages as consequential and incidental damages, making no real distinction between the allocations of the award between the two kinds of damages associated with the breach.).

SPOT THE ISSUE!

Dr. Smith entered into an agreement with Dr. Jones, who was looking to expand his current practice and increase profits, for the purchase of Dr. Smith's chiropractic center. Dr. Smith breached the contract by refusing to hand over his current client files and equipment as part of the deal. Dr. Jones then entered into an agreement with Med Offices, Inc., to purchase empty medical office space and subsequently purchased all new equipment and incurred substantial advertising expenses to attract new clients in this location. What are the damages that Dr. Jones may be entitled to? Has Dr. Jones properly mitigated his damages? What factors should you consider in making this determination?

NOMINAL DAMAGES

nominal damages
A small amount of money given to the non-breaching party as a token award to acknowledge the fact of the breach.

Where there are really no damages to speak of, the court may still award a small sum to compensate the non-breaching party on the sole basis of being wronged. These small awards are granted where a breach has occurred but there are no other means of compensating the plaintiff. These **nominal damages** are often awarded where the plaintiff has indeed proved the fact of a breach but the evidence does not show, with as reasonable amount of certainty, the actual amount of harm suffered or indeed, if the type of damages sought are impermissible under statute. "Generally, in instances where a litigant establishes a cause of action but has not established an entitlement to compensatory damages, nominal damages may be awarded." *Mo-Jack Distrib., LLC v. Tamarak Snacks, LLC*, 476 S.W.3d 900, 907 (Ky. App. 2015). In the *Mo-Jack* case, the only damages that the plaintiff could show were attorney's fees and the costs associated with pursuing the case for fraud. Under Kentucky law, attorney's fees are not allowable as compensatory damages. "Kentucky has long adhered to the American Rule. Generally, in the absence of a statute or contract expressly providing therefor, attorney fees are not allowable as costs, nor recoverable as an item of damages." *Id.* at 906 (internal citations omitted).

CALCULATION OF DAMAGES

No matter what theory of recovery a party is relying on, the court must calculate the measure of damages to be awarded. There is a relatively simple formula for determining the amount of money that will make the plaintiff whole. Start with the value of the promise in the contract [**V**], add any foreseeable out-of-pocket expenses [**E**] and foreseeable losses due to the breach [**L**], subtract mitigation [**M**] and the value of what the non-breaching party did receive [**R**]; this will equal the potential compensatory damages [**D**]. Can this be made simpler? Yes. Let's use the letters assigned to each factor.

Value + Expenses + Losses – Mitigation – Received value = Damages
Even simpler?

V + E + L – M – R = D
Value + Expenses + Losses – Mitigation – Received value = Damages

$$V + E + L - M - R = D$$

Example

Bob the Builder agrees to construct a new home valued at $500,000 for the Newlyweds. After accepting their $50,000 deposit, he completes the foundation and framing but then walks off the job, thereby materially breaching the contract. The Newlyweds had to hire a roofer at a cost of $5,000 to get the house enclosed immediately. The Newlyweds then hired another contractor to finish what Bob started. Bob's work is valued at $25,000 and the new contractor is going to charge them $495,000 to finish the job.

$500,000 [V] + $5,000 [E] + $50,000 [L] − $495,000 [M] − $25,000 [R] = − $35,000 [D]. Therefore, the Newlyweds are entitled to $35,000 in compensatory damages from Bob.

In the example above, if the Newlyweds found a contractor to do the work per the contract specifications for $400,000, they actually would spend less in total for the house than they planned: $500,000 [V] + $5,000 [E] + $50,000 [L] − $400,000 [M] − $25,000 [R] = +$130,000 [D]. The Newlyweds are ahead of the game by $130,000; they actually saved money from Bob's breach. The court will send them on their merry way as there are no damages to award.

IN-CLASS DISCUSSION

Loosely based on *Forbes v. Rapp*, 611 S.E.2d 592 (Va. 2005).

Frank is a "flipper"; he buys run-down homes at auction and then fixes them up and resells them at a higher price. Harry has decided to put some of his investment properties up at auction. Frank bids on and wins one of Harry's properties, a house in need of repair. Frank agreed to pay $100,000 for the property, gave Harry a 10 percent deposit, and signed the contract for sale. Shortly thereafter, Frank changed his mind and attempted to cancel the contract. Harry then contacted Sally, who came in as the second-highest bidder at the auction. She agreed to purchase the property for $75,000 (significantly less than her bid at auction, but she knew Harry was desperate to unload the property). Frank argues that he should not be responsible for the total damages of $25,000 because Harry failed to mitigate damages.

Has Harry failed to mitigate damages? What could he have done to avoid them? Are there any other damages that could apply in this situation? What factors should you consider in calculating damages? What additional facts could you add that would impact the amount and kind of damages?

When dealing with a *sale of goods* as governed by the Uniform Commercial Code (and discussed in detail in Chapter 15), damages can be calculated in three different ways depending on the availability and method of mitigation. It comes down to how to **value** the goods in question.

1. **Market price**. If the goods remain unsold or are damaged or destroyed, the value of the contract is the *market value* of goods of the same or similar kind. Mitigation in this situation is not available. The market value is the price a willing buyer is ready to pay and a willing seller is ready to accept for goods of that kind. For example, Greg Grocer refuses to take delivery of the Granny Smith apples. Fred Farmer was unable to sell them on the open market before they rotted. The market value of the apples on the day that they were to be delivered can be the measure of damages.

value
The objective worth placed on the subject matter.

market price
The objective worth placed on the subject matter in the open marketplace for similar products.

cover
The non-breaching party's attempt to mitigate damages may require that he purchase alternate goods on the open market to replace those never delivered by the breaching party. The non-breaching party can recover the difference in price between the market price and the contract price.

substituted goods
The products purchased on the open market that replace those not delivered by the breaching party.

resale value
The non-breaching party's attempt to mitigate damages may require that he sell the unaccepted goods on the open market. The non-breaching party can recover the difference in price between the market price and the contract price.

2. **Cover**. The buyer, as the non-breaching party, can replace the goods by purchasing them from another supplier; this is required under the rules of mitigation. The damages are measured by subtracting the price of the **substituted goods** from the original contract price. For example, Fred refuses to deliver the apples to Greg. Greg then purchases his apple supply from Ollie's Orchard. Under the contract with Fred, Greg had to pay $10 per bushel, but Ollie charges $12 per bushel. For 100 bushels, Greg has covered his loss of supply but is entitled to damages in the amount of $200.

3. **Resale value**. The seller, as the non-breaching party, can try to sell the goods in the open market to try to recoup some of the money he would have made on the original sale. Again, this is required by the duty to mitigate. For example, Fred enticed Betty Baker to buy the apples from him for $8 per bushel. Fred has made $200 less than he would have had he sold them to Greg under the original contract.

SPOT THE ISSUE!

Gill Bates, a computer software mogul, entered into an agreement with Disc Solutions, a CD manufacturing/distribution firm. Bates will supply the original encoding and Disc Solutions will burn millions of copies onto CDs and distribute them to computer stores nationwide. In consideration, Bates will receive 25 percent of the selling price of each disc; the remainder of the profit will go to Disc.

The first batch of 10 million CDs are burned and distributed throughout the nation at various retail prices depending on the market. Bates' company has spent over $5 million in marketing and advertising. It is at this point that the CDs are discovered to be defective. Bates' company is receiving many complaints from retailers and individual customers. Indeed, the national nightly news did a cover story on this fiasco. It appears that the mighty Bates is falling and not putting out a quality product. CDs are being returned by the hundreds of thousands both to Disc and directly to Bates' company.

Behind the scenes, it is discovered that a disgruntled employee of Bates, who now is a high-level employee of Disc, purposefully and maliciously tampered with the encoding on the Bates discs.

Identify the various kinds of damages that Bates might be entitled to and determine what evidence would be needed to recover under these various theories of recovery.

SURF'S UP

Damages and electronic contracts are strange bedfellows. As previously discussed, breaches of electronic contracts are hard to detect, and it's even harder to prove and/or collect damages for the breach. Additionally, the eagerness to "click" acceptance almost always also includes not only a limitation of damages clause, but also a specific disclaimer relating to non-liability for any kind of damages whatsoever based on any theory of recovery. Therefore, the aggrieved party will most likely receive only the payments made for the products or services supplied via the Internet contract. These limitations in amount and kind of damages are essential to the basis of the bargain, and acceptance of the products or services is acceptance of these terms, as well.

The anonymity and surreptitious nature of the Internet and the talent of hackers also leave vulnerable companies doing business on the Internet. Damages may be far-reaching and difficult to calculate. In response to some of these issues, Congress has passed a civil Computer Fraud and Abuse Act, 18 U.S.C.A. § 1030 et seq., providing guidelines as to what constitutes a cause of action and the damages thereunder. *Creative Computing v. GetLoaded.com, LLC*, 386 F.3d 930 (9th Cir. 2004), involved "pirated" information about GetLoaded's website that matched truckers with available loads so they could obtain more work. Essentially, GetLoaded "copycatted" and stole operating information. The court included the Computer Fraud and Abuse Act's definition of loss as "any reasonable cost to any victim, including the cost of responding to an offense, conducting a damage assessment, and restoring the data . . . and any revenue lost, cost incurred, or other consequential damages incurred because of disruption of service." *Id.* at 934, *citing* 18 U.S.C.A. § 1030(e)(11). Creative Computing was awarded nearly three-quarters of a million dollars in damages.

LIQUIDATED DAMAGES

There is another kind of damages that has not been discussed because it does not require any calculation. Parties may agree that the damages in the event of a breach may be too difficult to calculate or the parties may wish to avoid calculation of damages at all. Without a clause in the contract setting an amount to be levied on the breaching party, these damages might be considered speculative. However, a **liquidated damages** clause is not speculative in that it merely avoids a complicated calculation; it does not set some arbitrary number for damages that may not exist at all.

A liquidated damages clause provides a disincentive to breach the contract. This disincentive must not be oppressive or unconscionable; the amount must not be disproportionate to the subject matter of the contract. Upon inspection, if the amount of damage really looks like punitive damages or speculative damages, the court may refuse to enforce it. The court generally looks at the mutual agreement of the parties to the liquidated damages clause at the time of the making of the contract, whether the intention of the parties was efficiency and reliability in the event of a breach in light of the difficulty of determining actual damages and lastly its overall reasonableness. *See Ronald A. Chisholm Ltd. v. Am. Cold Storage, Inc.*, No. 3:09-CV-00808-CRS (W.D. Ky.

liquidated damages
An amount of money agreed upon in the original contract as a reasonable estimation of the damages to be recovered by the non-breaching party.

2016). "Determining whether a clause is a liquidated damages provision is a matter of law. Liquidated damages are defined as a definite sum or amount, which has been determined by agreement of the parties or by litigation. Damages for breach by either party may be liquidated in the agreement but only at an amount that is reasonable in the light of the anticipated or actual loss caused by the breach and the difficulties of proof of loss." *Id.* at 5, *citing* RESTATEMENT (SECOND) OF CONTRACTS § 356(1) (1981). If upheld as valid, a liquidated damages clause is the easiest for a court to enforce as the non-breaching party does not have to prove his actual damages; the clause substitutes for actual damages. "While liquidated damages clauses are viewed 'as a useful commercial tool to avoid litigation to determine actual damages,' such clauses should only be enforced 'where the actual damages sustained from a breach of contract would be very difficult to ascertain.'" *Id.* (citations omitted).

For example, as a part of the franchise contract, McDougal's includes a clause setting liquid damages at $250,000 for terminating the contract prior to the end of the contract term of five years. Frank, the franchisee, terminates after only two years of owning the franchise and contests the liquidated damages clause. The court will examine whether a $250,000 award to McDougal is reasonable given the potential loss of the market share in Frank's territory, damage to the franchise's reputation, and other relevant factors to determine whether that amount is reasonable. The exact amount of damages will not and may not be able to be exactly calculated, but the liquidated damages must bear some relationship to the damages suffered.

CRYPTO CONTRACTS

As we have already discussed at length, a smart contract just follows the coded instructions in a series of "if-then" statements. Therefore, the parties will need to determine from the outset what the damages will be in case of breach of any of the parties to the contract. Not only must the smart contract try to include all of the circumstances that will nullify the obligations for the non-breaching party(ies), but also assign consequences, and in the case of this self-executing contract, those predetermined damages. The only "self-executing" remedy in contract law is a liquidated damages clause. Therefore, it could be said that smart contracts are only effective to enforce liquidated damages; otherwise, in the case of a dispute, the parties will still need to resort to the courts or another tribunal for arbitrating or mediating the case. All the other kinds of remedies require the submission of proof to a third-party neutral to assess the circumstances and calculate damages. This begs the question as to when smart contracts should be used at all where there is the possibility of breach (and quite frankly, there is almost always that possibility) as all the clauses, including liquidated damages, can be challenged in court.

LIMITATION OF DAMAGES

Parties also may opt to put a "ceiling" on the damages that can be awarded. A **limitation of damages** clause sets the amount that the actual damages will not exceed. It is not the same as liquidated damages because the non-breaching party still has to prove his actual damages. The non-breaching party will be awarded either his actual damages or the limited amount, whichever is lower. These clauses are very often found in security/fire protection systems agreements. The companies limit how much they will pay in damages should the system fail to detect theft or destruction by whatever means are covered under the policy. *Chicago Steel Rule and Die Fabricators Co. v. ADT Sec. Systems, Inc.*, 763 N.E.2d 839 (Ill. App. 2002). This limitation does not apply to third parties who may be harmed by the covered incident because they were not in privity to the original limiting contract. In other words, the fire alarm company may limit the amount of money it will pay to the covered homeowner, but that limit does not apply to the neighbor's home that goes up in flames due to the spread of the unattended fire in the covered party's home.

limitation of damages
An amount of money agreed upon in the original contract as the maximum recovery the non-breaching party will be entitled to in the event of a breach.

Example

Having moved into their lovely new home, the Newlyweds decide to enter into a home alarm system agreement with Lockdown Security Systems. The contract provides that in the event of a break-in for which the alarm system fails, it will pay damages for the loss up to $10,000. Unfortunately, the Newlyweds were burgled, and the alarm system failed. The burglars stole the Newlyweds' new stereo system valued at $7,500. Under the limitation of damages clause, the Newlyweds are entitled to the $7,500 to replace their stereo system. On the other hand, if the crafty burglars managed to get away with $25,000 in expensive jewelry and an extensive coin collection, Lockdown's liability for damages would not exceed $10,000 as per the contract.

COSTS

While it may seem that **attorney's fees and costs** associated with bringing a lawsuit in order to collect damages for a breach of contract should be normal and foreseeable consequential damages, they are *not* generally awarded. Recall the discussion of the *Mo-Jack* case, above, wherein the court refused to consider attorney's fees as consequential damages. The **American rule** states that the parties are responsible for payment of their own litigation expenses. This is in contrast to the traditional rule in England (which is, of course, where America gets its common law tradition). In 1853, "Congress undertook to standardize the costs allowable in federal litigation. In support of the proposed legislation, it was asserted that there was great diversity in practice among the courts and that losing litigants were being unfairly saddled with exorbitant fees for the victor's attorneys. The result was a far-reaching Act specifying in detail the

American rule of attorney's fees and costs
Expenses incurred by the parties to maintain or defend an action for the breach of contract are generally not recoverable as damages.

nature and amount of the taxable items of cost in the federal courts. One of its purposes was to limit allowances for attorneys' fees that were to be charged to the losing parties." *Alyeska Pipeline Service Co. v. Wilderness Society*, 421 U.S. 240, 251-252, 95 S. Ct. 1612, 1619 (1975). This case has been clearly distinguished from situations where there is an explicit statutory basis for awarding attorney's fees. There are statutes and court rules that do permit recovery for these litigation expenses, but, absent an express grant, they are not awarded as part of the damages for a breach of contract. Further, "[u]nder its inherent powers, a court may assess attorney's fees when a party has acted in bad faith, vexatiously, wantonly, or for oppressive reasons." *Id.* at 421 U.S., at 258-259, 95 S. Ct., at 1622-1623.

There is an exception to this rule. If, as a consequence of the breach, the non-breaching party is subject to a lawsuit involing a third party, the fees and costs associated with this related litigation can be recovered as against the breaching party. For example, if Well Computers was unable to fulfill contracts with its distributors due to the breach of DoTell, DoTell might be responsible for paying the attorney's fees and litigation costs associated with the lawsuit commenced by the distributors against Well Computers. It would not be responsible for Well Computer's litigation costs associated with the Well Computers versus DoTell litigation, however.

EYE ON ETHICS

Not only are ethical violations professionally costly, a legal malpractice claim will dig deep into the pockets of the attorney. Courts have a plethora of ways to grant a recovery to an injured client and are amenable to granting these damages.

If an attorney fails to properly prosecute a valid claim or collect on an obtained judgment, the client should be entitled to the value of that lost claim. This is also true where, due to the attorney's negligence, the client obtains a judgment less than the value of the claim. The attorney may be held responsible for the difference between the actual award and the value of the claim.

Where the malpractice of the attorney rises to willfulness or malicious intent, a court may impose treble damages for that intentional tort. Recall that in order to recover treble damages, the plaintiff must show that she suffered actual damages.

How does a client go about proving actual damages? The easy answer lies in a sales transaction. The loss of value to the property or its market value is the proper measure for recovery. More difficult are valuation issues that require future predictions of the market or business venture. It is in these cases that an expert is needed and, fortunately, the court also will award the costs associated with retaining those experts.

Contested cases prove even more troublesome. The court must make a determination of the merits of the plaintiff's case to determine not only the value of the claim but also the settlement value. This leads the court into a speculation as to the likelihood of settlement as well.

There are many other costs associated with suit that can be recovered by the aggrieved client. Any litigation expenses can be recovered; this includes not only the expenses incurred in the original underlying suit but also for the malpractice suit! Contrary to the general application of the American rule, clients are entitled to recover attorney's fees and costs associated with bringing the malpractice claim.

All of these elements add up to one conclusion: An attorney must exercise due care in order to preserve not only his professional standing, but his wallet as well!

Find cases in your jurisdiction that granted punitive damages to the plaintiff in a legal malpractice action. Remember to look in your jurisdiction's ethics opinions, as well. What is the element common to all the cases?

Again, returning to the "freedom of contract" principle, the parties may choose to include the award of attorney's fees to the losing party should a contract dispute arise under the agreement. All of the varied kinds of awards described in this chapter are contractual damages. Parties are free to specify any of these kinds as included or excluded should a breach action arise under the agreement. Whether or not the court will enforce these damages is, under a purely contractual analysis, an objectively reasonable determination. The following chapter will address those situations where fairness and justice are not realized by these principles.

Summary

A plaintiff can recover different kinds of damages, all stemming from the same breach of contract. Damages can be

1. *Compensatory.* Damages that put the plaintiff in as good a position as he would have been in had the breach not occurred. These damages can be based on the plaintiff's expectations, restitutionary principles, and/or reliance.
2. *Consequential.* Damages that arise from naturally and foreseeably occurring events after the breach.
3. *Incidental.* Damages that arise from unforeseeable but related events after the breach.
4. *Nominal.* A small sum of money awarded in the event of a breach where no actual damages have been sustained.
5. *Liquidated.* A certain sum of money to be awarded without the necessity of proving actual damages.
6. *Limited.* A "ceiling" that determines the maximum amount of award for damages.

A plaintiff will never recover

1. *Speculative damages*. Damages that cannot be determined or calculated.
2. *Punitive damages*, absent statutory authority or the defendant's commission of an intentional tort.

Rarely, a plaintiff can recover *attorney's fees and costs*.

With the exception of liquidated damages, a plaintiff must establish the amount of damages he actually lost due to the breach. The general formula is $V + E + L - M - R = D$. This takes the non-breaching party's *duty to mitigate* damages into account, as well. In the sale of goods, the value of the contract can be determined in three ways:

1. *Market price*, where no mitigation is available.
2. *Cover*, where the buyer is able to mitigate damages by obtaining the goods from another supplier.
3. *Resale*, where the seller is able to mitigate damages by selling the goods to another purchaser.

Key Terms

American rule of attorney's fees and costs	market price
compensatory damages	nominal damages
consequential damages	punitive damages
cover	reliance damages
deterrent effect	resale value
duty to mitigate	restitution damages
expectation damages	speculative damages
incidental damages	statutory authority
limitation of damages	substituted goods
liquidated damages	tortious
lost profits	$V + E + L - M - R = D$
	value

Review Questions

GO FIGURE

Calculate the damages in the following situations.

1. Paul contracts to paint all the rooms in Howard's house for $1,000. Paul breaches and Howard has to hire another contractor at $1,500. Further, Howard took time off from work on the day Paul was going to start painting so that Howard could let him into his home.

2. Same facts as above but Paul painted two rooms of the 10-room house and then breached.

3. Howard's new contractor is using a much higher grade of paint that costs 25 percent more than the paint called for in the contract with Paul.

4. Paul paints two rooms of the house and then Howard changes his mind and repudiates the contract. Paul, deciding he has nothing better to do, finishes painting the rooms anyway.

5. Paul refuses to finish the painting and has left the house a disaster. Howard cannot move back into his house and is forced to live in a leased apartment for two weeks while the mess gets cleaned up.

VIVE LA DIFFÉRENCE!

In your own words, explain the difference between

1. Restitution damages and reliance damages.

2. Compensatory, consequential, and incidental damages.

3. Liquidated damages and punitive damages.

"FAULTY PHRASES"

All of the following statements are FALSE; state why they are false and then rewrite them as true statements. Write a brief fact pattern that illustrates your answer.

1. Liquidated damages must accurately reflect the actual damages suffered by the aggrieved party.

2. In an action for breach of contract, the court will never award punitive damages.

3. A party may receive a recovery based on "lost profits" where the aggrieved party entered the agreement with the intention of making a profit on the transaction.

4. Expectation damages seek to put the aggrieved party in the same position he was in before the contract was entered into.

5. A party must make every effort to mitigate damages.

6. Damages for the sale of goods are always the contract price.

7. Attorney's fees are included in consequential damages, but it is foreseeable that the aggrieved party will have to hire an attorney to file suit.

"WRITE" AWAY! PORTFOLIO ASSIGNMENT

The inevitable has happened. Druid has materially breached the contract. Assume the following:

- Druid has failed to properly install the roofing tiles and leaks have erupted.
- Carrie has paid in full.
- Carrie has had to move into a rental apartment for two months while corrective work is completed.
- The correction contractor is charging $25,000 for the new roof.

Calculate Carrie's measure of damages. Draft a demand letter from Carrie to Druid for the damages.

Case in Point   CALCULATION AND AWARD OF DAMAGES

806 S.W.2d 194
Harrison McCLAIN, Plaintiff/Appellee,
v.
KIMBROUGH CONSTRUCTION COMPANY, INC., Defendant/Appellant
Appeal No. 01-A-01-9002-CH-00069
Court of Appeals of Tennessee, Middle Section, at Nashville
Filed December 19, 1990.

Attorney for Plaintiff/Appellee: James D. Kay, Jr., Donald Capparella, MANIER, HEROD, HOLLABAUCH & SMITH, Nashville, Tennessee.

Attorney for Defendant/Appellant: Steven A. Riley, Margaret C. Berry, BASS, BERRY & SIMS, Nashville, Tennessee.

William C. Koch, Jr., Judge. Samuel L. Lewis, Judge, Ben H. Cantrell, Judge, concur.

KOCH, J.

[806 S.W.2d 196]

OPINION

This appeal involves a dispute between a general contractor and a brick mason concerning work on a condominium project in Nashville. After the general contractor unilaterally terminated the subcontract before the work was complete, the brick mason filed an action in the Chancery Court for Davidson County to recover its lost profits. The contractor counterclaimed for the cost to correct portions of the brick mason's work and for overpayments. The trial court awarded the brick mason $6,798 and dismissed the contractor's counterclaim. The contractor has appealed. While we concur with the trial court's finding that the subcontractor was damaged by the general contractor's unilateral termination of the contract, we do not concur with the manner in which the trial court calculated the damages. Accordingly, we vacate the damage award and remand the case for further proceedings.

I

The Kimbrough Construction Company ("Kimbrough") was the general contractor on a condominium project in Nashville called the Woodlawn Court Condominiums. On November 6, 1987, it entered into a subcontract with Harrison McClain Masonry Company ("McClain") to do the brick work for the project. McClain agreed "to complete the work in a timely fashion and in a good and workmanlike manner," and in return, Kimbrough agreed to pay McClain $25,450.[1]

McClain began work in mid-November, 1987. Its employees laid over 20,000 bricks during the ensuing three weeks but were forced to stop work because Kimbrough had not completed the grading around the buildings. Mr. McClain and Kimbrough's project superintendent discussed the situation on December 3, 1987 and agreed that McClain's crew could begin work on another job and that Kimbrough would call them back when the brick work could be completed.

Several problems concerning the brick work arose while McClain's crew was on the job. Kimbrough's superintendent was dissatisfied with the color of the brick.[2] [806 S.W.2d 197] He also questioned several

---

[1] The parties estimated that 78,000 bricks would be required to complete the job. The amount of the contract was based on McClain charging $275 per 1,000 bricks laid and $1,000 for each "four brick chimney chase."

[2] The brick was an owner-supplied item; therefore, McClain was not responsible for the color of the brick. That matter was between Kimbrough and the brick supplier.

other portions of McClain's work, particularly a chimney chase, a "soldier course" on the top of a wall,[3] and some brick work around a garage door. While Mr. McClain agreed to replace the brick in these areas, he did not follow the superintendent's instructions to do the remedial work so that the bricks could be reused. The superintendent and Mr. McClain's brother also became involved in a heated argument concerning the chimney chase.

Kimbrough's superintendent never called McClain's crew back. Instead, he decided that McClain's work had been unacceptable and that he would retain another brick mason to complete the job. Without notice to Mr. McClain, the superintendent entered into a contract with another brick mason to complete the job and to repair or replace portions of McClain's work.[4]

Mr. McClain did not discover that Kimbrough had retained another brick mason until early February, 1988 when he observed other brick-layers working on the project. Three months later, he filed a breach of contract action against Kimbrough seeking lost profits and the retainage on the work his crew had performed. Kimbrough counterclaimed for the expenses it incurred in replacing portions of McClain's work and for overpayments.

The trial court concluded that Kimbrough breached its contract with McClain by interfering with McClain's work and by failing to give McClain an opportunity to correct its defective work or to complete the job before hiring another brick mason. The trial court also found that Kimbrough's unilateral action prevented it from recovering the additional expenses it incurred in completing the job and correcting the defective work.

II

The parties' agreement was embodied in a one-page document prepared by Kimbrough. The "subcontract agreement" identified the contracting parties, described the scope of the work, and set forth the amount of the contract and the terms of payment. It also contained the usual provisions regarding written change orders and retainage.

The subcontract did not, however, contain many of the provisions normally found in construction contracts. It did not, for example, contain a "flow down" clause tying the subcontractor's performance to the contractor to the contractor's obligations to the owner. In addition, it lacked a construction schedule, an inspection and acceptance process, and a dispute resolution procedure.

Of primary importance to this case, the subcontract did not contain a "take over" clause permitting Kimbrough to terminate the subcontract and to take over the work. Typically, a "take over" clause permits a contractor to assume control of and to carry out a defaulting subcontractor's work after giving the subcontractor reasonable notice and an opportunity to correct its defective performance.[5] In the absence of a "take over" clause, Kimbrough must find some other support for its claimed right to terminate the subcontract before its completion without first giving McClain notice and an opportunity to cure. Kimbrough has pointed to no other support, and, under the facts of this case, we can find none.

A contracting party may terminate the contract when the other party (1) is wholly unable to complete the contract, *City of Bristol v. Bostwick,* 146 Tenn. 205, 211, 240 S.W. 774, 776 (1922); (2) manifests an intent to abandon the contract, *Brady v.* [806 S.W.2d 198] *Oliver,* 125 Tenn. 595, 614, 147 S.W. 1135, 1139 (1911); (3) manifests an intent to no longer be bound by the contract, *Church of Christ Home for Aged, Inc. v. Nashville Trust Co.,* 184 Tenn. 629, 642, 202 S.W.2d 178, 183 (1947); or (4) commits fraud on the party seeking to terminate the contract. *W. F. Holt Co. v. A & E Elec. Co.,* 665 S.W.2d 722, 730 (Tenn. Ct. App. 1983).

The record contains no proof that McClain committed fraud or that he was unable to complete or intended to abandon the contract. On the contrary, McClain stopped work because Kimbrough could not provide a site suitable for finishing the job. McClain left the job with Kimbrough's assent in order

---

[3] A "soldier course" is a row of bricks laid vertically rather than horizontally.

[4] The unit prices in Kimbrough's contract with the second brick mason were less than those in the contract with McClain. Kimbrough also agreed to pay the second brick mason $4,020 to correct the portions of McClain's work that Kimbrough thought were defective.

---

[5] Examples of typical "take over" clauses can be found in Articles 3.4.1 and 7.2.1 of the "Standard Form of Agreement Between Contractor and Subcontractor," AIA Document A401 (1987 ed.).

to avoid idling its crew and was prepared to return as soon as Kimbrough gave notice that the conditions at the job site would permit him to complete the work.

III

Contracting parties should endeavor to define their respective rights and obligations precisely. See *V.L. Nicholson Co. v. Transcon Inv., Fin. Ltd.*, 595 S.W.2d 474, 482 (Tenn. 1980); *Forrest, Inc. v. Guaranty Mortgage Co.*, 534 S.W.2d 853, 857 (Tenn. Ct. App. 1975). As a practical matter, however, contracting parties are not always precise and frequently leave material provisions out of their contracts. In these situations, the courts impose obligations on contracting parties that are reasonably necessary for the orderly performance of the contract.

For example, we have required contracting parties to deal with each other fairly and in good faith, even though these duties were not explicitly embodied in their contract. *Williams v. Maremount Corp.*, 776 S.W.2d 78, 81 (Tenn. Ct. App. 1988); *TSC Indus., Inc. v. Tomlin*, 743 S.W.2d 169, 173 (Tenn. Ct. App. 1987); *Covington v. Robinson*, 723 S.W.2d 643, 645 (Tenn. Ct. App. 1986). We have also held the extent of contractual obligations should be tempered by a "reasonableness" standard. *Moore v. Moore*, 603 S.W.2d 736, 739 (Tenn. Ct. App. 1980).

In the construction context, we have imposed upon contractors the obligation to give their subcontractors a reasonable opportunity to perform. *Foster & Creighton Co. v. Wilson Contracting Co.*, 579 S.W.2d 422, 425-26 (Tenn. Ct. App. 1978). Other courts have also recognized that contractors have an implied obligation to provide their subcontractors with suitable working conditions. See 1 S. Stein, *Construction Law* para. 5.02[3][e] (1990).

Despite the importance of notice, contracting parties frequently fail to include express notice provisions in their agreements. See 6 S. Williston, *A Treatise on the Law of Contracts* § 887B (3d ed. 1962). Notice ought to be given when information material to the performance of a contract is within the peculiar knowledge of only one of the contracting parties. In the absence of an express notice provision, the courts will frequently imply an obligation to give notice as a matter of common equity and fairness. 3A A. Corbin, CORBIN ON CONTRACTS § 725 (1964).

Requiring notice is a sound rule designed to allow the defaulting party to repair the defective work, to reduce the damages, to avoid additional defective performance, and to promote the informal settlement of disputes. *Pollard v. Saxe & Yolkes Dev. Co.*, 12 Cal. 3d 374, 525 P.2d 88, 92, 115 Cal. Rptr. 648, 652 (1974); *Sturdy Concrete Corp. v. Nab Constr. Corp.*, 65 A.D.2d 262, 411 N.Y.S.2d 637, 644 (1978). Thus, even when the parties have not included a "take over" clause in their contract, courts have imposed upon contractors the duty to give subcontractors notice and an opportunity to cure before terminating the contract for faulty performance. *United States ex rel. Cortolano & Barone, Inc. v. Morano Constr. Corp.*, 724 F. Supp. 88, 98 (S.D.N.Y. 1989); see also *Cyclo Floor Machine Corp. v. National Housewares, Inc.*, 296 F. Supp. 665, 682 (D. Utah 1968) (imposing a notice requirement in a nonconstruction context).

Under the facts of this case, we find that Kimbrough had a duty to give McClain notice and a reasonable opportunity to correct its defective work before terminating the contract. Kimbrough's failure to give [806 S.W.2d 199] McClain notice constitutes a material breach unless Kimbrough was excused from performing its obligations under the subcontract.

Only McClain's uncured material failure to perform its own contractual obligations would have excused Kimbrough from performing its remaining obligations. See RESTATEMENT (SECOND) OF CONTRACTS § 237 (1979).[6] The circumstances significant in determining whether a party's failure to perform is material include:

(a) the extent to which the injured party will be deprived of the benefit which he reasonably expected;

(b) the extent to which the injured party can be adequately compensated for the part of that benefit of which he will be deprived;

(c) the extent to which the party failing to perform or to offer to perform will suffer forfeiture;

---

[6] With one exception not applicable in this case, "it is a condition of each party's remaining duties to render performances to be exchanged under an exchange of promises that there be no uncured material failure by the other party to render any such performance due at an earlier time." RESTATEMENT (SECOND) OF CONTRACTS § 237 (1979).

(d) the likelihood that the party failing to perform or to offer to perform will cure his failure, taking account of all the circumstances including any reasonable assurances;

(e) the extent to which the behavior of the party failing to perform or to offer to perform comports with standards of good faith and fair dealing.

RESTATEMENT (SECOND) OF CONTRACTS § 241 (1979).

Applying the Restatement's standards to this case, we find that the deficiencies in McClain's performance were not material and, therefore, that Kimbrough was not entitled to terminate the contract in the manner it did. McClain acted in good faith throughout its dealings with Kimbrough. If there were defects in McClain's work, they could have been corrected. In fact, McClain had already corrected several portions of its work when Kimbrough expressed dissatisfaction with them. There is no indication that McClain would not have agreed to correct any other portions of its work had it been asked to do so.

Accordingly, we find that the subcontract obligated both parties to deal with each other fairly and in good faith and to give each other notice before they unilaterally terminated the contract. Kimbrough did not give notice and had no basis for failing to do so. Therefore, Kimbrough breached the contract when it hired another brick mason to replace McClain without giving McClain notice and a reasonable opportunity to perform in the manner required by the contract.

IV

Kimbrough also asserts that McClain is not entitled to damages, even if Kimbrough breached the contract, because McClain breached the contract first. The facts do not support Kimbrough's claim.

A party who has materially breached a contract is not entitled to damages stemming from the other party's later material breach of the same contract. *John P. Saad & Sons, Inc. v. Nashville Thermal Transfer Corp.*, 715 S.W.2d 41, 47 (Tenn. 1986); *Cummins v. McCoy*, 22 Tenn. App. 681, 691, 125 S.W.2d 509, 515 (1938). Thus, in cases where both parties have not fully performed, it is necessary for the courts to determine which party is chargeable with the first uncured material breach. *See* RESTATEMENT (SECOND) OF CONTRACTS § 237 comment b (1979).

Kimbrough did not provide Mcclain's crew a suitable place to work or a reasonable opportunity to perform, and it did not give McClain notice before unilaterally terminating the subcontract and hiring another brick mason to finish the job. These breaches preceded McClain's failure to complete the work in a workmanlike manner and were of sufficient magnitude to justify McClain's failure to continue and complete its performance of the contract. Thus, McClain's failure to fully perform its contractual obligations should not prevent it from seeking damages from Kimbrough.

[806 S.W.2d 200]

V

The remaining issues involve the amount of damages the trial court awarded to McClain. Kimbrough challenges the damage award, asserting that McClain failed to prove its damages with reasonable certainty and that the trial court failed to reduce its award to McClain by the costs Kimbrough incurred in correcting the defective portions of McClain's work. We find little merit in Kimbrough's arguments. However, we have determined that the damage calculation is sufficiently flawed to require a remand for correction.

A

The subcontract obligated Kimbrough to pay McClain $275 for every 1,000 bricks laid and $1,000 for each of the four chimney chases called for in the plans. Based upon their understanding that the job would require approximately 78,000 bricks, the parties agreed that McClain would receive $25,450 for the work required by the contract.[7]

At the outset, McClain anticipated that the job would require five bricklayers and three laborers and would take twenty days to complete. Bricklayers earned $10 per hour, and laborers $6 per hour. Based on its total personnel costs for twenty days and the costs of gasoline and oil attributable to the job, McClain estimated that its total costs to complete the work would be $12,802. After subtracting

---

[7] Apparently the parties did not contemplate that minor variations in the number of bricks used would alter the amount of the subcontract.

its costs from the amount of the contract, McClain testified that its net profit would have been $12,648.

The subcontract contemplated that McClain would submit weekly draw requests based on the work performed. During the three weeks its crew was on the job, McClain's crew laid approximately 25% of the brick[8] and submitted draw requests for $6,500 (approximately 25% of the contract amount). Kimbrough paid McClain $5,850 after deducting $650, the 10% retainage authorized in the contract.

The trial court found that McClain's net profit on the job would have been $12,648. Instead of awarding McClain the full amount of its anticipated profit, the trial court deducted the progress payments McClain received and awarded McClain the difference.

B

A subcontractor may sue a contractor for damages when the contractor improperly terminates the contract after the subcontractor has partially performed. The proper measure of damages in this situation is the net profits the subcontractor would have made had it been permitted to complete the contract. *Fidelity & Deposit Co. v. Accel, Inc.*, 354 So. 2d 424, 426 (Fla. Dist. Ct. App. 1978); *Bruning Seeding Co. v. McArdle Grading Co.*, 232 Neb. 181, 439 N.W.2d 789, 791-92 (1982); *see also Inland Equip. Co. v. Tennessee Foundry & Mach. Co.*, 192 Tenn. 548, 556, 241 S.W.2d 564, 567 (1951) (recognizing lost profits as the proper measure of damages).

When lost profits are the proper measure of damages, they need only be proved with reasonable certainty, not with mathematical precision. *Swartz v. Sanders*, 56 Tenn. App. 281, 291-92, 406 S.W.2d 70, 74-75 (1966); *Black v. Love & Amos Coal Co.*, 30 Tenn. App. 377, 384-85, 206 S.W.2d 432, 435 (1948). Professor McCormick has pointed out that courts have devised three formulae with which to calculate the subcontractor's net profits:

> In this situation, three formulas have been furnished by the cases for measurement of the builder's claim: (1) The contract price (or so much as remains unpaid) less the amount that it would cost the builder to complete the

job. This is the simplest and, where the builder can prove with reasonable certainty the cost of completing, the best. (2) The profit on the entire contract (total contract price less total builder's cost of construction, both expended and to be expended) plus [806 S.W.2d 201] the cost of the work actually performed. (3) For the work done, such proportion of the contract price as the cost of the work done bears to the total cost of doing the job, plus, for the work remaining, the profit that would have been made upon it.

C. McCormick, *Handbook on the Law of Damages* § 164, at 641 (1935). The same formula used to determine a contractor's damages from an owner is used to determine a subcontractor's damages from a general contractor. 2 S. Stein, *Construction Law* para. 11.02[4][b], at 11-58 n.222 (1990).

Instead of following one of the damage calculations outlined by Professor McCormick, the court simply awarded McClain its anticipated profits on the entire contract less the full amount of the progress payments received. This calculation fails to address three relevant matters: (1) McClain's actual costs to complete the job, (2) the apportionment of the progress payments between cost and profit, and (3) the allocation of the risk that the job will take longer than originally anticipated.

Under the facts of this case, McClain's damages should not be derived from the total amount of the profits it originally planned to make on this job. The amount of these anticipated profits was based on McClain's assumption that the work would require twenty days to complete. This assumption was no longer valid when McClain stopped work because, by that time, McClain's crew had already worked fifteen days but had completed only 25% of the work. Clearly, McClain would not have been able to complete the remaining work within five days.

The record contains no proof concerning which of the parties would have absorbed the additional labor costs had McClain returned to finish the work. Since McClain did not seek a change order or later request delay or disruption damages, we can only presume that McClain planned to absorb the increased labor costs. Had it done so, its anticipated profits would have been reduced in direct proportion to the additional labor costs.

---

[8] Mr. McClain testified that his men laid 20,000 of the 78,000 bricks required for the job.

Similarly, McClain's damages should not be reduced by the progress payments it actually received unless the payments represented profit. Mr. McClain's uncontradicted testimony was that his company's payroll expenses for the three weeks its crew was on the job exceeded its draw requests. Accordingly, the record supports only one conclusion—that the progress payments were for costs not for profit. The trial court should not have reduced McClain's damages by the amount of the progress payments.

The trial court decided this case without a jury. Tenn. R. App. P. 13(b) and 36(a) authorize us to review its decision de novo and to grant the relief warranted by law and the facts. Even though McClain has not questioned the trial court's damage calculation on appeal, we have the responsibility to apply the controlling law whether or not cited or relied upon by either party. Tenn. R. App. P. 13(b), 36(a); *Nance v. Westside Hosp.*, 750 S.W.2d 740, 744 (Tenn. 1988); *City of Memphis v. IBEW, Local 1288*, 545 S.W.2d 98, 100 (Tenn. 1976).

While we favor the conservation of the judicial resources, we do not have sufficient evidence to calculate McClain's damages on our own. Accordingly, pursuant to Tenn. Code Ann. § 27-3-128 (1980),[9] we vacate the damage award and remand the case to the trial court for the calculation of the damages McClain incurred as a result of Kimbrough's unilateral termination of the contract.[10]

[806 S.W.2d 202]

C

Finally, we find no error with the trial court's refusal to reduce McClain's damage award by the cost Kimbrough incurred in completing the contract. Kimbrough incurred these costs because of its unilateral termination of the contract which prevented McClain from correcting any defects in its work and completing the job. Since Kimbrough's material breach occurred prior to McClain's failure to complete the job, Kimbrough is not entitled to recover the cost it incurred in completing the work. *Denver Ventures, Inc. v. Arlington Lane Corp.*, 754 P.2d 785, 788 (Colo. Ct. App. 1988); *John P. Saad & Sons, Inc. v. Nashville Thermal Transfer Corp.*, 715 S.W.2d 41, 47 (Tenn. 1986).

VI

We affirm the trial court's decision that McClain was damaged by Kimbrough's unilateral termination of the contract. We vacated the damage award and remand the case for the purpose of assessing McClain's damages in accordance with this opinion and for any other proceedings that may be required. We also tax the costs of this appeal in equal proportions to Kimbrough Construction Company and its surety and to Harrison McClain for which execution, if necessary, may issue.

VACATED AND REMANDED.

---

[9] Tenn. Code Ann. § 27-3-128 provides, in part:

The court shall also, in all cases, where, in its opinion, complete justice cannot be had by reason of . . . oversight without culpable negligence, remand the case to the court below for further proceedings, with proper direction to effectuate the objects of the order, and upon such terms as may be deemed right.

[10] McClain's damages should be limited to the damages stemming from Kimbrough's unilateral termination of the contract. Throughout these proceedings, McClain has not sought damages for the delay or disruption of its performance. Since it has failed to do so up to this point, it should not be permitted to do so when the case is remanded.

Chapter 14

Equity and Quasi-Contract

Chapter Objectives

The student will be able to:

- Use vocabulary regarding equitable remedies properly.
- Differentiate among the different types of equitable remedies and explain the basis for their award.
- Evaluate the plaintiff's chances for success in obtaining the different kinds of injunctive relief.
- Identify situations where the court will or will not order specific performance.
- Discuss the doctrine of promissory estoppel.
- Determine if/when a defendant has been "unjustly enriched."
- Explain the difference between a valuation of equitable damages based on quantum meruit and quantum valebant.
- Discuss the doctrine of "unclean hands."

This chapter will examine WHAT HAPPENS when contractual remedies are not available to a plaintiff DUE TO a defect in the formation or substance of the agreement and WHY these kinds of damages are made available. According to the rules of contractual remedies, unless there is objective certainty in the amount of monetary damages to be awarded pursuant to a valid contract, there is nothing the court can do to assist the plaintiff. Where there are no valid and

equity
The doctrine of fairness and justice; the process of making things balance or be equal between parties.

bright-line rules
A legal standard resolves issues in a simple, formulaic manner that is easy in application although it may not always be equitable.

black letter law
The strict meaning of the law as it is written without concern or interpretation of the reasoning behind its creation.

equitable remedies
A non-monetary remedy fashioned by the court using standards of fairness and justice.

irreparable harm
The requesting party must show that the actions of the defendant will cause a type of damage that cannot be remedied by any later award of the court.

injunction
A court order that requires a party to refrain from acting in a certain way to prevent harm to the requesting party.

temporary injunction
A court order that prohibits a party from acting in a certain way for a limited period of time.

permanent injunction
A court order that prohibits a party from acting in a certain way for an indefinite and perpetual period of time.

enforceable contractual obligations, but harm has occurred, the law of contracts must step aside to permit equitable remedies. There are instances where the parties have made contract-like promises and so should be given some sort of relief in order to avoid injustice on the "innocent" party. These equitable remedies often do not take the form of monetary damages, but rather are a unique species of performance obligations.

Having performed a strict contractual analysis of the plaintiff's case and a determination of the legal remedies available, the paralegal student may cry out: "But it doesn't seem *fair*." Contract law mutters "stuff and nonsense" and turns its back on this plea. However, the law of **equity** turns to listen to the complaint. Equity is the "softer" side of the law. It does not rely solely on **bright-line rules** and **black letter** contractual doctrines. Equity picks up where contract law leaves off. Considerations of fairness and justice prevail rather than the calculated principles of pure contract law. Equity seems to supplement and soften the hard edges of contract law.

"ACTION" DAMAGES

Money cannot buy happiness and sometimes it cannot give an aggrieved party an adequate remedy for the defendant's breach of contract. When a party's monetary damages, also referred to as "legal remedies," are inadequate to compensate for the harm incurred, the court has the ability to order alternative **equitable remedies** in the form of either (1) an *injunction* or (2) *specific performance*. These are "action" damages because they effectively force the defendant to act in some way to try to remedy the breach. An injunction requires the defendant to refrain from acting and specific performance requires the defendant to affirmatively perform some act.

It bears repeating that the court must find that the monetary remedies are insufficient to compensate the plaintiff. Fixing a set amount of money is definitive and contract law's desire for certainty prefers this type of remedy. Only after showing that the money will not fix or prevent harm can the plaintiff obtain an injunction or specific performance. The courts have been willing to consider the ability to collect upon the monetary judgment when determining whether to grant an injunction or order specific performance. "This remedy, however, is a discretionary one resting in equitable principles. Relief of this character rests, not upon what the court must do, but rather upon what, in view of all the circumstances, it ought to do." *Kilarjian v. Vastola*, 877 A.2d 372, 376 (N.J. Super. Ch. 2004).

Injunctions

If the performance of an act by the defendant would result in **irreparable harm** to the plaintiff, a court may enjoin the defendant from acting. The **injunction** may be granted either before or after the commencement of litigation, and it may be **temporary** or **permanent**.

A temporary injunction granted prior to the commencement of litigation is often referred to as a **TRO** (temporary restraining order). The party seeking the TRO must show that there is a high likelihood of the defendant committing some act that will not be able to be corrected or reversed after a preliminary hearing or a determination on the merits of the case. TROs may be issued without notice to the adverse party and, as they are such a drastic (and one-sided) measure, they are generally only in place for a maximum of 10 days and require that a bond be posted by the party seeking the relief. In that 10-day time period, a **preliminary hearing** will be scheduled so that the adverse party has an opportunity to be heard.

Once litigation has commenced, an application for a preliminary injunction is appropriate for the maintenance of the status quo until a final determination on the merits. In this way, the interests of both parties can be preserved. It is like a freeze has been put on the issue. Again, the party seeking the injunction must show that there is a likelihood that she will succeed and that the harm will be immediate and irreparable should the adverse party have the opportunity to act. The court then balances the potential harm to the plaintiff to the harm the restraint may cause to the defendant. This is often referred to as "balancing the equities"; a judge must make a fairness determination. "If enforcement of the contract will be attended with great hardship or manifest injustice, the court will refuse its aid. The decree, if rendered, must operate without injustice or oppression either to plaintiff or to defendant." *Kilarjian*, 877 A.2d at 376 (internal citations omitted).

TRO
A temporary restraining order that is issued prior to any hearing in the court.

preliminary hearing
An appearance by both parties before the court to assess the circumstances and validity of the restraining application.

Example

The town of Middleville publishes a solicitation for construction bids to erect a new bridge over the river. Several local contractors, including Guy's Construction Company and Lucky's Construction Company, have responded with bids to try to win the project. Guy's total bid was $100,500 based on a bid at $15 per foot for the steel beams; the project will require 6,700 linear feet of steel. Lucky's total bid was stated at $103,850 based on a bid of $14.50 per foot. The town, looking only at the total bid price, awarded Guy the project. Upon closer inspection, the mathematical error in Lucky's bid is revealed. The total price was calculated at $15.50 per foot instead of $14.50 per foot. Lucky contends that he is the low bidder based on the per foot price. Lucky learned of the award and filed for a TRO. Lucky asserts that he is entitled to the TRO because if the construction is permitted to go forward, Lucky will be irreparably harmed. He will have no chance to step in to prove that he was the lower bidder. After construction begins, it is too late to reverse the construction award. *See Landry/French Constr. Co. v. Lisbon Sch. Dep't*, No. AP-14-052 (Me. Super. 2014).

After a final determination on the merits has been made, a party may be granted a temporary or permanent injunction. This court order prohibits the defendant from taking certain specified actions for a period of time, as in the case of a temporary injunction, or for an unlimited period, as in the case of a permanent injunction.

Common examples of injunctions involve *covenants not to compete*. Covenants that bind companies and products are more commonly enforced than covenants that restrict a person's right to work. There are important public policy considerations that courts take into account when deciding whether to enforce a contractual provision that restricts trade or employment. The first hurdle is to determine that there is a valid underlying agreement to which the covenant attaches. If the employment agreement itself is invalid, then so is the covenant not to compete that is a part of it.

An employment contract may contain a provision that if the employee leaves the company, she will not go to work for a competitor. These clauses protect the company's interest in maintaining its trade secrets, client lists, and other proprietary information. Losing the employee does not mean that the company has to lose all of this kind of information. A covenant not to compete restricts the former employee from using this information for professional advantage by giving it to the new employer. If a former employee chooses to leave the original employer and work for a direct competitor of the original employer in breach of this covenant not to compete, the original employer can seek a TRO to prevent the immediate dissemination of this information; irreparable harm is presumed where trade secrets have been misappropriated. After filing a lawsuit to enforce the covenant not to compete, the court may issue a preliminary injunction to prevent the former employee from starting work for the competitor. This maintains the status quo until trial. At trial, the court may determine that the former employee is prohibited from working for a competitor in the state for two years. This is a temporary injunction. Permanent injunctions are not common in these situations as it is hard to prove that harm will continue indefinitely, and courts are unwilling to strip a person of the ability to earn a living in her chosen field.

> A covenant not to compete is reasonable only if the covenant: (1) is not greater than is necessary to protect the employer in some legitimate business interest; (2) is not unduly harsh and oppressive to the employee; and (3) is not injurious to the public.
>
> *Pinnacle Performance, Inc. v. Hessing*, 17 P.3d 308, 312 (Idaho 2001), *citing* Restatement (Second) of Contracts § 188 (1981).

> A covenant not to compete will be held unenforceable if the covenant is unreasonable in duration, geographical area, or scope of activity.
>
> *Id.*, *citing Magic Lantern Prods., Inc. v. Dolsot*, 892 P.2d 480, 482 (Idaho 1995).

A non-compete clause may look something like the one from *Pinnacle*:

> Non-Competition. Contractor [Hessing] agrees to not offer, sell, or trade his services directly to Company [Pinnacle] clients, both current and past, for a period of two (2) years from completion of Contractor's work for the Company, without first providing an opportunity to contract the work through the Company. . . .

Ultimately, the court in *Pinnacle* found that the covenant was not enforceable because it unreasonably restricted Hessing's employability. The restriction was not narrowly tailored to fit the employer's valid interest in protecting its relationships with clients.

SURF'S UP

EF Cultural Travel BV v. Explorica, Inc., 274 F.3d 577 (1st Cir. 2001). EF Travel sought equitable relief in the form of an injunction against Explorica for electronically "scraping" information from EF's website. In order to obtain the injunction, EF had to prove that there would indeed be some sort of damages that an injunction would prevent. Essentially, Explorica was taking private pricing and tour information from EF's server. While damages were hard to assess in terms of goodwill or stress on the system, the court permitted recovery of the costs for retaining a consultant to calculate the measure of damages for this unauthorized access. The court further explained that in cases of software access, there may be no damages as system administrators can fix the security breaches; the victims of these security breaches do suffer loss. *Id.* at 584. Because there were actual losses in the expense to retain consultants, the court found there was enough of a basis to grant injunctive relief.

It appears that there are two vast extremes with regard to damages in the "Web world": one where sellers can strip away all damages with the exception of a refund for expenses as in the *EF* case, and the other where the aggrieved and defrauded party is entitled to an extensive and permissive array of damages (recall *Creative Computing* in the last chapter). *See also Facebook, Inc. v. Power Ventures, Inc.*, 252 F. Supp. 3d 765 (N.D. Cal. 2017) (Facebook sued Power Ventures because the Defendants "scraped" Facebook's proprietary data without its permission by inducing Facebook users to provide their login. Defendants then displayed Facebook's material on power.com to its benefit. Facebook sought both monetary damages and equitable remedies.).

Specific Performance

On the opposite side from injunctions are orders for **specific performance**. Where injunctions say, "Stop that!" orders for specific performance say, "Do this!" Courts are even more reluctant to order specific performance because it requires compelling a party to act rather than just stopping them from acting. Forced labor is not a business in which courts want to get involved. To obtain an order for specific performance, the contract must be very clear as to the act to be compelled. The standard of proof for specific performance is greater than that of obtaining damages at law. Courts grant these orders where the subject matter of the contract is unique or irreplaceable. These usually involve the sale of

specific performance
A court order that requires a party to perform a certain act in order to prevent harm to the requesting party.

one-of-a-kind goods such as astronomical clocks,[1] puppies,[2] trademarks in Mexican hot sauces,[3] and oyster boats.[4] Additionally, courts consider all parcels of real estate unique, so specific performance is an appropriate remedy in the transfer of land. "An order of specific performance may be appropriate to enforce a contract for the sale of land because of the uniqueness of each parcel of real property." *Sullivan v. Porter*, 861 A.2d 625 (Me. 2004), *citing O'Halloran v. Oechslie*, 402 A.2d 67, 70 (Me. 1979) ("a justice may assume the inadequacy of money damages in a contract for the purchase of real estate and order the specific performance of the contract without an actual showing of the singular character of the realty").

However, just as the court of equity looks to render a judgment that is fair to the plaintiff, it will not do so at the expense of the defendant. The fairness must be present on both sides of the "v." If, in enforcing an order for specific performance, the defendant is faced with undue hardship, oppression, or injustice, the court, in its discretion, can refuse to order specific enforcement, even where it may seem appropriate. *See Kilarjian, supra*, 877 A.2d at 376-377 (The court refused to render an order for specific enforcement of a contract for sale of real estate.).

> Nevertheless, the court would render a heartless judgment to evict a woman whose health has deteriorated badly while the contract was pending, and wishes nothing more than to remain in her home during the most difficult days of her illness. While plaintiffs argue that assisted living or alternate living quarters may appear a logical alternative, that is not a decision for this court to make. In weighing the equities, although a difficult decision, they weigh in defendants' favor. If Chancery cannot exercise discretion in this circumstance, it is a sad day.

RESEARCH THIS

In your jurisdiction, find two cases regarding specific performance: one that ordered the defendant to perform the contractual obligations (or some variation thereof) and another that held that specific performance was not appropriate. What were the factual differences that resulted in these contradictory outcomes?

EYE ON ETHICS

Injunctive relief is particularly appropriate in unauthorized practice of law cases. Lawyers are bound by their jurisdiction's ethical codes to refrain from either assisting a non-lawyer to commit UPL or

---

[1] *Ruddock v. First Nat'l Bank of Lake Forest*, 559 N.E.2d 483 (Ill. App. 1990).
[2] *Bono v. McCutcheon*, 824 N.E.2d 1013 (Ohio App. 2005).
[3] *Madariaga v. Morris*, 639 S.W.2d 709 (Tex. App. 1982).
[4] *Lulich v. Robin*, 466 So. 2d 780 (La. App. 1985).

practicing in a jurisdiction in which they are not admitted. If a lawyer is found to be committing either of these acts, the court has injunctive power to order her to stop. *See Matter of Discipline of Droz*, 160 P.3d 881, 885 (Nev. 2007) ("Examples of penalties considered or imposed by other courts in situations similar to this case include public reprimands, a temporary or permanent prohibition on future admission, including pro hac vice admission, injunctive relief, contempt sanctions, fines, and payment of costs.").

Additionally, the ultimate sanction of disbarment is, in essence, a permanent injunction. The lawyer is prohibited from acting in a certain way within that jurisdiction. A court also, on the other side of the coin, may mandate actions by specific performance in requiring registration for pro bono service or a denying a lawyer's motion to withdraw from a case. In these situations, a lawyer must affirmatively act to complete a court-assigned task.

"COURT-ORDERED" SOLUTIONS

Where neither an injunction nor an order for specific performance is appropriate to solve the issue between the parties, a court can fashion a number of other remedies.

Declaratory Judgment

Where the issue between the parties is the status of or title to the subject matter, **declaratory judgment** is appropriate. Declaratory judgment is the court's determination of the rights and responsibilities of a party with respect to the subject matter of the controversy. The court's decree settles the matter in its entirety. No money needs to change hands; no title needs to pass. The parties came before the court because they are uncertain of where things stand, and the court has to clarify the situation so that the matter can be concluded. There is a requirement under this interpretive power that there be an actual case or controversy in front of the court. The court will not render an opinion that essentially will have no effect because it has only answered a hypothetical. In essence, parties cannot come to the court for advice; the court must have a real dispute with real results.

declaratory judgment
The court's determination of the rights and responsibilities of a party with respect to the subject matter of the controversy.

It is important to note that declaratory judgment is only appropriate where another legal remedy is not available or more appropriate. The action for declaratory judgment is limited to those situations where there is a genuine controversy as to the rights and status of the parties involved and a declaration of those rights as determined by the court will resolve the issue between the parties. A party may not clothe the issue as one for declaratory judgment and then try to collect monetary damages due to the determination of the court. In that instance, the party seeking relief should apply for the monetary damages as a legal remedy. Why would a party bring a declaratory action rather than one in law? The Declaratory Relief Acts permit the recovery of attorney's fees; therefore, if a party frames the issue as one for declaratory relief, she may be able to recover additional damages to which she would not normally be entitled. *See Park Cities Limited Partnership v. Transpo Funding Corp.*, 131 S.W.3d 654 (Tex. Ct. App. 2004) (The finance company properly brought an action for declaratory relief to determine who had legal title to four vehicles in question; the issue of ownership was the central problem to be resolved.).

SPOT THE ISSUE!

The law firm of Faith, Hope, and Joy (FHJ) telephoned Hire 'Em Company, a paralegal recruitment firm, in order to staff their expanding office. FHJ also put ads in the local classifieds to speed up the process. FHJ hired Emma Employee, a recent graduate of a local college who had previously registered with Hire 'Em for a different position, but who independently applied for this current position with FHJ. Hire 'Em filed a declaratory action seeking a determination as to whether a placement commission was due. Is this an appropriate equitable remedy? Why or why not?

Example

Farmer Fred wishes to sell part of his land to a real estate developer. There is some controversy with regard to the boundaries of the land as some squatters have decided that they have title to the land under adverse possession. The statutory requirement in this jurisdiction to claim rights in land under adverse possession is 20 years. These squatters have lived on this parcel for *approximately* 20 years and challenge the sale of what they believe to be their property. A suit for declaratory relief is appropriate. The court can determine the rights of the parties with respect to the ownership of the land. Once this declaration of right and title has been made, the parties can proceed accordingly.

Rescission and Restitution

rescission and restitution
A decision by the court that renders the contract null and void and requires the parties to return to the wronged party any benefits received under the agreement.

Where a party seeks to have the contract declared null and void, the court's remedial response is **rescission and restitution**. This equitable remedy is very similar to the consensual mutual rescission as discussed in Chapter 12. The difference here is the lack of mutuality. The plaintiff seeks a judgment of the court that she is relieved of her obligations due to the breach or other grievous conduct on the part of the defendant. The second component is also familiar to the paralegal student as it is the same as the calculation for restitutionary damages. If the plaintiff, relying on the defendant's promises, has changed her position, she is entitled to recover damages to make her whole again and to avoid unjust enrichment of the defendant.

Example

The Newlyweds have gone house hunting and have found a beautiful old Victorian home on the lake owned by the Waterstons. Months prior to putting their house on the market, the Waterstons "spruced up" their basement by installing all new sheetrock and tiling the floor. While this finished look would enhance their house, it also hid all the water damage to the cinderblock walls and concrete floor! The Newlyweds signed the sales contract and agreed that they would close on August 1st. They also hired a home inspector to look at the property. Due to the newly finished work, he could not see any water damage to the home. The Waterstons moved out of the house in July and told the Newlyweds they could start moving even though the parties had not actually closed. This generous gesture was offset by the discovery of the extensive water damage when Ned Newlywed was removing some of the sheetrock to change the layout of the rooms in the basement. The Newlyweds filed suit for *rescission* of the contract due to this material nondisclosure of water damage. They also sought *restitution* for the cost of the home inspection and moving costs.

Reformation

A **reformation** is akin to a court-ordered "accord and satisfaction" in that the writing does not reflect the reality of the transaction between the parties. The parties supposedly act in accordance with their individual understandings of the agreement. However, the writing does not accurately reflect this. In reformation, the court, instead of the parties, "revises" the contract to make the writing agree with the actual understanding of the parties. This is tricky territory for the court because it cannot construct a contract where there is no underlying mutual agreement. To reform a contract, evidence supporting the reformation must be clear and convincing so that the court is merely a scrivener, not a creator of the newly created document.

reformation
An order of the court that "rewrites" the agreement to reflect the actual performances of the parties where there has been some deviation from the contractual obligations.

Example

The Newlyweds found a new home built by Dave Developer, far away from the lake and not plagued by any water damage or other flaw. The closing went without a hitch and the Newlyweds moved in. Several months later, Dave approached them regarding a mistake in the deed. The deed's description of the property was inaccurate, actually conveying not only the Newlyweds' lot but also part of the adjoining lot. The surveyor had used an incorrect landmark to describe the property's boundaries. The Newlyweds refused to recover this parcel of land, even though they knew they had not contracted for it, so Dave was forced to bring a suit for reformation. The court reformed the deed to reflect the original and true understanding of the parties. *See, e.g., Hoffman v. Chapman*, 34 A.2d 438 (Md. 1943).

QUASI-CONTRACTS

Equity not only fashions a remedy not available under strict contract principles, it can actually fashion a contract substitute! No court can rewrite a contract. By its own terms, a contract must be a voluntary meeting of the minds of the parties involved. Equity deals with this "handicap" by creating a new creature called a **quasi-contract**, a contract created by law, not by the facts of the situation. It is a **pseudo-contract**, close to the real thing but still an imposter. Why do courts do this? It all boils down to issues of justice and fairness. These are contracts that the law implies exists between the parties where, under strict contract principles, it does not. They are also referred to as **implied-in-law** contracts. This is where the court substitutes its judgment for the intention of the parties with respect to consideration and available remedies.

> **quasi-contract/ pseudo-contract/ implied-in-law contract**
> Where no technical contract exists, the court can create an obligation in the name of justice to promote fairness and afford a remedy to an innocent party and prevent unearned benefits to be conferred on the other party.

SPOT THE ISSUE!

Jimmy Roughit entered into an agreement with Crump Development Corporation for the sale of some of Jimmy's land. Jimmy would like to retain the southernmost parcel so he could have a place to relax and sip margaritas all day (if only he could find his salt shaker!). This means that Jimmy would need an easement (permission to cross) over some of the property he is selling to Crump to access his remaining southern parcel.

Three days after the transfer of title to the property (which included the necessary easement), Crump decided to begin constructing elaborate landscaping that, when finished, will completely block Jimmy's access to his land.

Determine what actions Jimmy could take to preserve his interest and what remedies would be appropriate.

Promissory Estoppel

Unlike the two equitable remedies of injunctions and specific performance seen above, **promissory estoppel** does not require certainty in all the elements of contract. Indeed, this theory of relief only arises where there is no valid contract! Where a defect in formation would normally render the contract unenforceable under traditional contract principles, the court can look to the precepts of fairness and rely on the doctrine of promissory estoppel. "[P]romissory estoppel is an offensive, equitable cause of action frequently asserted by a party as an alternative to a breach of contract claim." *Dugas-Filippi v. JP Morgan Chase & Co.*, 971 F. Supp. 2d 802 (N.D. Ill. 2013).

Equity balances the harsh consequences of contract law. However, even equity has its limits as far as granting relief to every party coming before it. There must be (1) a **promise relied upon** by the other party (2) that the promisor knows the promisee will *reasonably* rely upon and (3) the

> **promissory estoppel**
> A legal doctrine that makes some promises enforceable even though they are not compliant with the technical requirements of a contract.

> **promissory reliance**
> A party's dependence and actions taken upon another's representations that he will carry out his promise.

promisee incurs a **substantial detriment** as a result of the reliance. Notice how the element of valid consideration is missing. This is often the case in promissory estoppel. That is why the court cannot apply contract principles to grant relief to the promisee. Additionally, the court requires substantial reliance upon the promise. Merely beginning performance is not enough. There must be a significant change in the promisee's position to merit a remedy absent a valid contract. Why do courts afford this type of remedy? To avoid injustice. Why is it called *promissory estoppel*? The promisor is stopped from denying his promise.

substantial detriment
The change in a party's position in reliance upon another's representations that, if unanswered, will work a hardship on that party.

Example

Doris lives in Mr. Roper's apartment complex and really would love to get a dog, but her lease agreement forbids pets. She talks to Mr. Roper about her desire for a canine companion and he tells her she is permitted to have a dog. Doris falls in love with an Afghan hound and spends $2,000 on him and an additional $500 on all the supplies. The other tenants love the dog and see him on a regular basis as Doris takes him for walks. Four years later, Mr. Roper decides he would like to rent Doris's apartment to another person who is willing to pay him more in monthly rent. Instead of waiting until Doris's lease runs out, Mr. Roper tells Doris that she is in violation of the lease by having the dog and she must leave immediately or else get rid of the dog. Of course, Doris is not willing to give up her beloved pet. Doris challenges his eviction notice. Mr. Roper's defense is the language in the lease prohibiting pets. The oral agreement between Doris and Mr. Roper was neither written nor supported by consideration; therefore, contract law principles do not apply. There is no contract regarding the dog. However, it would be unfair to make Doris give up her dog. The court can permit Doris to keep her pet without being in violation of the lease under promissory estoppel. Mr. Roper (1) *promised* her that she could have the pet and (2) knew that Doris was *reasonable* in relying on that promise and (3) in fact did rely on that promise to her *substantial detriment*. Doris paid $2,000 for the dog and much more for the pet supplies over the years and she has grown very attached to her pet. *See Royal Associates v. Concannon*, 490 A.2d 357 (N.J. Super. App. Div. 1985).

Prevention of Unjust Enrichment

The court in equity will prevent a party from taking advantage of another simply because there is no valid contract to enforce. Promissory estoppel focuses on the reliance of the promise, whereas the doctrine of **unjust enrichment** focuses on the unearned benefit received by the promisor. The court must find that (1) there was a *promise* made (2) that the promisor intended to *induce* the promisee to act in *reliance* thereon and (3) the promisee's actions conferred a *benefit* on the promisor. The promisee has fulfilled her part of the bargain, but, without a valid contract, the promisee cannot seek to enforce the promise

unjust enrichment
The retention by a party of unearned and undeserved benefits derived from his own wrongful actions regarding an agreement.

under contract principles. Equity steps in to save the day by disallowing the promisor to derive a benefit from the bargain while incurring no detriment. It simply offends one's sense of fairness to allow a party to take advantage of another and "get something for nothing." The promisor has been unjustly enriched at the expense of the promisee.

Example

George, the general contractor for a large building project, hires Tony to install some very expensive tile in the kitchen and baths of the house. Tony and George never discussed costs for labor and supplies; Tony figured that it would all work itself out as the project progressed. This assumption is a drastic failure in the formation stage; the agreement will fail as a contract for lack of consideration. Tony finishes the job and invoices George. However, although George has been paid by the owners, he has not paid Tony for his work. Tony sues for the cost of his labor and supplies under the agreement. The court cannot grant a contractual remedy as no contract exists. Equity can prevent unjust enrichment of George. George will not be permitted to keep the benefit of all the tile work without paying for it. It simply isn't fair.

quantum meruit
A Latin term referring to the determination of the earned value of services provided by a party.

quantum valebant
A Latin term referring to the determination of the market worth assignable to the benefit conferred.

How does the court determine the value of the promise where the agreement has failed due to lack of consideration? There are two perspectives: **quantum meruit** ("as much as he has deserved") and **quantum valebant** ("as much as they were worth"). Quantum meruit is the value of services rendered. In the example above, the value would be the amount of the invoice, say $8,500; that is the price that the promisee places on the benefit he conferred to the promisor. Alternatively, the court may determine that a more just valuation lies in quantum valebant, which is the value of the benefit received. This is the value to the benefited promisor. It is the amount of money the promisor has gained in taking advantage of the situation. In the example above, it is the amount of money received from the owner. If George is $10,000 richer because he failed to pay Tony, then under quantum valebant that amount is due and owing to Tony.

> The basic aim of [the various kinds of restitution] is to place the plaintiff in the same economic position as he enjoyed prior to contracting. Thus, unless specific restitution is obtained in Equity, the plaintiff's recovery is for the reasonable value of services rendered, goods delivered, or property conveyed less the reasonable value of any counter-performance received by him. The plaintiff recovers the reasonable value of his performance whether or not the defendant in any economic sense benefitted from the performance.

Farash v. Sykes Datatronics, Inc., 465 N.Y.S.2d 917, 920 (N.Y., 1983).

These methods of calculating damages should look familiar. Under contract principles, they are akin to expectation (quantum meruit) and restitution damages (quantum valebant).

IN-CLASS DISCUSSION

Loosely based on *Bander v. Grossman,* 161 Misc. 2d 119, 611 N.Y.S.2d 985 (N.Y. Cnty. Ct. 1994).

Frank's brother, Ernesto, has his own version of "flipping." Ernesto buys rare, antique automobiles, waits for the market to hit a peak, and then resells them at a profit. He has had much success doing this in the past. Ernesto learned of a 1965 Aston Martin in fair condition selling for a mere $80,000 from an antique car dealer. Ernesto thought this was a good deal since only 40 were ever made and only 20 were thought to be in existence at this time.

A valid contract was entered into with the seller and Ernesto was really looking forward to this acquisition; however, one glitch after another came up in the attempt to gain title to the vehicle. The contract was canceled by the seller, who later sold the car to Carl Buyer for $145,000. The market fluctuated greatly in price from the time the contract was canceled until trial. When Ernesto filed the complaint, the price was $250,000; during the two years between the filing of the complaint and trial, the price skyrocketed to $335,000; however, at the time of trial, the market fell off sharply and the car was valued at $125,000.

Tomorrow is the first day of trial, and your supervising attorney is pacing the floor of her office. She asks you, her most trusted paralegal, what your professional opinion is.

What is the FAIR remedy for Ernesto to recover? Specific performance? Is this still available as a remedy? If not, what equitable remedies are available and appropriate? What is your best estimation of the judge's opinion in this matter?

DOCTRINE OF "UNCLEAN HANDS"

None of these equitable remedies will be available to a party seeking relief if she comes to the court with **unclean hands**. Where the plaintiff is also guilty of some misconduct, the notions of justice under equitable principles will not allow a guilty party to complain of unfairness. Only a party who has not done any wrong to merit the mistreatment of the other party can appeal to the court to right the injustice that she may suffer.

The courts have not generally favored this doctrine without a clear showing of intent to do some wrong in relation to the agreement. Mistakes, omissions, and other intended consequences that may, in reality, turn out to be unfair are not considered "unclean" for equitable purposes. In *Schivarelli v. Chicago Transit Authority*, 823 N.E.2d 158 (Ill. App. 2005), a commercial lease was modified and there were inconsistencies between the prior agreements and the current lease regarding the responsibility to pay for utilities. The intention was for the tenant to pay for the utilities; however, for 14 years the transit authority, as the landlord, had been paying for them. In an action to recoup these expenses, the court

doctrine of unclean hands
A party seeking equitable remedies must have acted justly and in good faith in the transaction in question; otherwise, equitable remedies will not be available to a wrongdoer.

determined that the error was neither intentional nor fraudulent and, therefore, the transit authority had come to the court with clean hands and was entitled to have the contract reformed and be reimbursed for the utility expenses. While this bulk payment seems "unfair" in application to the tenants, "in determining whether a party acted with unclean hands, the court will look to the intent of the party, not the effect of its actions, and will only find unclean hands present if there has been fraud or bad faith." *Id.* at 168.

Example

Johnny Goodfella transferred the title to his property in the Hamptons to his cousin Vinny to avoid its being seized by the state as part of its judgment against him for racketeering. Vinny promised to return the title to the property once Johnny got out of prison. Five years later, after Johnny was released on parole, he asked Vinny to transfer the deed back to him. Vinny refused, so Johnny sought relief in the courts. Johnny was denied equitable remedies to force his cousin Vinny to reconvey the Hamptons property because he did not come to the court with "clean hands." The court would not grant him the fruit of his wrongdoing.

Equity permits a judge hearing a contractual dispute to fashion a fair remedy where the rules of contract law may not. After you, the paralegal, have reviewed a contract and accompanying dispute, a twofold analysis must ensue. First, a determination must be made by applying the principles of strict contract law. This includes examining all the factors from the formation of the contract, defenses, and calculation of damages. After this, a paralegal may conclude that either the "contract law" result renders the dispute's outcome unfair or no formal contractual relationship exists due to some flaw. At this time, the principles of fairness under equity can be applied to the situation.

Summary

Equitable principles allow a court to grant a remedy where justice requires but where contract law does not recognize a legal, monetary remedy. Where money does not adequately compensate an aggrieved party for the damages caused by a breach, a court may order the breaching party to act or refrain from acting in some way that will make up for the loss. An aggrieved party can apply for a *temporary restraining order*, a preliminary *injunction*, and/or a final injunction (either *temporary* or *permanent*) if without preserving the status quo she will suffer irreparable harm. If the only way to make the plaintiff whole is to force the defendant to carry out her contractual promises, the court may order *specific performance* as long as the contractual duties are specifically set forth in the agreement.

The court also may fashion a remedy in the form of

1. *Declaratory judgments*, where the court makes a determination of the rights and responsibilities of the parties with respect to the subject matter.
2. *Rescission and restitution*, where the court declares the contract null and void and gives the plaintiff damages to make him/her whole again.
3. *Reformation*, where the court changes the document to reflect the actual understanding of the parties.

Where no valid contract exists due to a defect in formation, usually a failure of consideration, the court can fashion its own agreement under *quasi-contract* theory. These are contracts *implied-in-law*. A party may be prohibited from denying the existence of an agreement under the doctrine of *promissory estoppel* where

1. A promise is relied upon by the aggrieved party, and
2. The promisor knows the promisee will reasonably rely upon it, and
3. The promisee incurs a *substantial detriment* as a result of the *reliance*.

A party also may be prevented from taking advantage of the aggrieved party by keeping a benefit conferred on him/her where the court finds that the promisor has been unjustly enriched if

1. There was a promise made
2. That the promisor intended to induce the promisee to act in reliance thereon and
3. The promisee's actions conferred a benefit upon the promisor.

How do courts determine the *value* of the promise under either promissory estoppel or *unjust enrichment* doctrines? A calculation can be made using either *quantum meruit* or *quantum valebant*.

Of course, none of these equitable principles applies unless the aggrieved party comes to the court with *clean hands*.

Key Terms

black letter law	quantum meruit
bright-line rules	quantum valebant
declaratory judgment	quasi-contract/pseudo-contract/
doctrine of unclean hands	implied-in-law contract
equitable remedies	reformation
equity	rescission and restitution
injunction	specific performance
irreparable harm	substantial detriment
permanent injunctions	temporary injunctions
preliminary hearings	TROs
promissory estoppel	unjust enrichment
promissory reliance	

Review Questions

VIVE LA DIFFÉRENCE!

In your own words, explain the difference between

1. Legal remedies and equitable remedies.

2. Injunctions and specific performance.

3. Promissory estoppel and prevention of unjust enrichment.

4. The two means of valuation, quantum meruit and quantum valebant.

5. Rescission and reformation.

EXPLAIN YOURSELF

All answers should be written in complete sentences.

1. Describe the process of obtaining injunctive remedies.

2. Explain the theory of recovery under quasi-contract.

3. Describe a situation where a court would probably find that specific performance is an appropriate remedy.

4. Give an example of a situation illustrating the doctrine of promissory estoppel.

5. Give an example of a situation illustrating the doctrine of unjust enrichment.

6. Describe a situation where a party would apply to the court for declaratory judgment.

"FAULTY PHRASES"

All of the following statements are FALSE; state why they are false and then rewrite them as true statements. Write a brief fact pattern that illustrates your answer.

1. Specific performance can always be ordered where the plaintiff's monetary remedies are too difficult to calculate.

2. Courts can never grant both legal remedies and equitable remedies in the same case.

3. Equity can rewrite a contract to conform to the standards of fairness.

4. Even though a party has committed some intentional wrongdoing, she can apply to the court for a remedy.

"WRITE" AWAY! PORTFOLIO ASSIGNMENT

Not only has Druid materially breached the contract and caused a monetary loss, but the workers also have started to harass Carrie and loiter on her lawn. They have begun to "salt the earth" and destroy her landscaping, hoping to ruin it for any future plantings as well. Are there any equitable remedies available to Carrie? If so, draft an application to the court for the appropriate measures to be taken.

Case in Point   EQUITABLE DAMAGES

193 Cal. Rptr. 409
143 Cal. App. 3d 571
TAMARIND LITHOGRAPHY WORKSHOP, INC., a California non-profit corporation, and June WAYNE, Plaintiffs, Cross-Defendants and Respondents,
v.
Terry SANDERS and the TERRY SANDERS COMPANY, a California corporation, Defendants, Cross-Complainants and Appellants.
Civ. 66492.
Court of Appeal, Second District, Division 5, California.
April 28, 1983.
As Modified on Denial of Rehearing
May 26, 1983.

Page 410

[143 Cal. App. 3d 572] Don Erik Franzen, Los Angeles, for defendants, cross-complainants and appellants.

Ball, Hunt, Hart, Brown & Baerwitz and Stephen A. Cirillo, Long Beach, for plaintiffs, cross-defendants and respondents.

STEPHENS, Associate Justice.

The essence of this appeal concerns the question of whether an award of damages is an adequate remedy at law in lieu of specific performance for the breach of an agreement to give screen credits. Our saga traces its origin to March of 1969, at which time appellant, and cross-complainant below, Terry Sanders (hereinafter "Sanders" or "appellant"), agreed in writing to write, direct and produce a motion picture on the subject of lithography for [143 Cal. App. 3d 573] respondent, Tamarind Lithography Workshop, Inc.[1] (hereinafter referred to as "Tamarind" or "respondent").[2]

---

[1]Terry Sanders as well as The Terry Sanders Company were both originally named as co-defendants and later became co-complainants in this action. For the purposes of our discussion, references to Terry Sanders are intended as references to both Terry Sanders and The Terry Sanders Company.

[2]Respondent June Wayne, who as the president of respondent Tamarind, was responsible for entering into the agreement on behalf of that company and is also to be included in all references to respondent Tamarind.

Pursuant to the terms of the agreement, the film was shot during the summer of 1969, wherein Sanders directed the film according to an outline/ treatment of his authorship, and acted as production manager by personally hiring and supervising personnel comprising the film crew. Additionally, Sanders exercised both artistic control over the mixing of the sound track and overall editing of the picture.

After completion, the film, now titled the "Four Stones for Kanemitsu," was screened by Tamarind at its tenth anniversary celebration on April 28, 1970. Thereafter, a dispute arose between the parties concerning their respective rights and obligations under the original 1969 agreement. Litigation ensued and in January 1973 the matter went to trial. Prior to the entry of judgment, the parties entered into a written settlement agreement, which became the premise for the instant action. Specifically, this April 30, 1973, agreement provided that Sanders would be entitled to a screen credit entitled "A Film by Terry Sanders."

Tamarind did not comply with its expressed obligation pursuant to that agreement, in that it failed to include Sanders' screen credits in the prints it distributed. As a result a situation developed wherein Tamarind and co-defendant Wayne filed suit for declaratory relief, damages due to breach of contract, emotional distress, defamation and fraud.

Sanders cross-complained, seeking damages for Tamarind's breach of contract, declaratory relief, specific performance of the contract to give Sanders screen credits, and defamation. Both causes were consolidated and brought to trial on May 31, 1977. A jury was impaneled for purposes of determining damage issues and decided that Tamarind had breached the agreement and awarded Sanders $25,000 in damages.[3]

The remaining claims for declaratory and injunctive relief were tried by the court. The court made findings that Tamarind had sole ownership rights in the [143 Cal. App. 3d 574] film, that "both June Wayne and Terry Sanders were each creative producers of the

film, that Sanders shall have the right to modify the prints in his personal possession to include his credits." All other prayers for relief were denied.

It is from the denial of appellant's request for specific performance upon which appellant predicates this appeal.

Since neither party is contesting the sufficiency of Sanders' $25,000 jury award for

Page 411

damages,[4] the central issue thereupon becomes whether that award is necessarily preclusive of additional relief in the form of specific performance, i.e., that Sanders receive credit on all copies of the film. Alternately expressed, the issue is whether the jury's damage award adequately compensates Sanders, not only for injuries sustained as a result of the prior exhibitions of the film without Sanders' credits, but also for future injuries which may be incurred as a result of any future exhibitions of the film without his credit. Commensurate with our discussion below, we find that the damages awarded raise an issue that justifies a judgment for specific performance. Accordingly, we reverse the judgment of the lower court and direct it to award appellant the injunctive relief he now seeks.

Our first inquiry deals with the scope of the jury's $25,000 damage award. More specifically, we are concerned with whether or not this award compensates Sanders not only for past or preexisting injuries, but also for future injury (or injuries) as well.

Indeed, it is possible to categorize respondent's breach of promise to provide screen credits as a single failure to act from which all of Sanders' injuries were caused. However, it is also plausible that damages awarded Sanders were for harms already sustained at the date of trial, and did not contemplate injury as a result of future exhibitions of the film by respondent, without appropriate credit to Sanders.

Although this was a jury trial, there are findings of facts and conclusions of law necessitated by certain legal issues that were decided by the court. Finding of Fact No. 12 states:

---

[3]The jury was asked to decide both Sanders' claim for breach of contract, as well as Tamarind's and Wayne's claim for contract breach, emotional distress, defamation and fraud. Tamarind was non-suited on its emotional distress and defamation claim, and also received unfavorable verdicts respecting its breach of contract claim and fraud claim.

[4]Respondent Tamarind concedes this fact in its brief by asserting that appellant's remedy at law (the $25,000 damage award) is adequate.

"By its verdict the jury concluded that Terry Sanders and the Terry Sanders Company are entitled to the sum of $25,000.00 in damages for all damages suffered by them arising from Tamarind's breach of the April 30th agreement." The exact wording of this finding was also used in Conclusion of Law No. 1. Sanders argues that use of the word "suffered" in the past tense is positive [143 Cal. App. 3d 575] evidence that the jury assessed damages only for breach of the contract up to time of trial and did not award possible future damages that might be suffered if the film was subsequently exhibited without the appropriate credit. Tamarind on the other hand, contends that the jury was instructed that if a breach occurred the award would be for all damages past and future arising from the breach. The jury was instructed: "For the breach of a contract, the measure of damages is the amount which will compensate the party aggrieved, for the economic loss, directly and proximately caused by the breach, or which, in the ordinary course of things, would be likely to result therefrom" and ". . . economic benefits including enhancement of one's professional reputation resulting in increased earnings as a result of screen credit, if their loss is a direct and natural consequence of the breach, may be recovered for breach of an agreement that provides for screen credit. Economic benefits lost through breach of contract may be estimated, and where the plaintiff [Tamarind], by its breach of the contract, has given rise to the difficulty of proving the amount of loss of such economic benefit, it is proper to require of the defendant [Sanders] only that he show the amount of damages with reasonable certainty and to resolve uncertainty as to the amount of economic benefit against the plaintiff [Tamarind]."

The trial court agreed with Tamarind's position and refused to grant the injunction because it was satisfied that the jury had awarded Sanders all the damages he was entitled to including past and possible future damages. The record does not satisfactorily resolve the issue. However, this fact is not fatal to this appeal because, as we shall explain, specific performance as requested by Sanders will solve the problem.

The availability of the remedy of specific performance is premised upon well

Page 412

established requisites. These requisites include: A showing by plaintiff of (1) the inadequacy of his legal remedy; (2) an underlying contract that is both reasonable and supported by adequate consideration; (3) the existence of a mutuality of remedies; (4) contractual terms which are sufficiently definite to enable the court to know what it is to enforce; and (5) a substantial similarity of the requested performance to that promised in the contract. (See *Henderson v. Fisher* (1965) 236 Cal. App. 2d 468, 473, 46 Cal. Rptr. 173, and Civ. Code, §§ 3384, 3386, 3390, 3391.)

It is manifest that the legal remedies available to Sanders for harm resulting from the future exhibition of the film are inadequate as a matter of law. The primary reasons are twofold: (1) that an accurate assessment of damages would be far too difficult and require much speculation, and (2) that any future exhibitions might be deemed to be a continuous breach of contract and thereby create the danger of an untold number of lawsuits.

[143 Cal. App. 3d 576] There is no doubt that the exhibition of a film, which is favorably received by its critics and the public at large, can result in valuable advertising or publicity for the artists responsible for that film's making. Likewise, it is unquestionable that the non-appearance of an artist's name or likeness in the form of screen credit on a successful film can result in a loss of that valuable publicity. However, whether that loss of publicity is measurable dollar wise is quite another matter.

By its very nature, public acclaim is unique and very difficult, if not sometimes impossible, to quantify in monetary terms. Indeed, courts confronted with the dilemma of estimating damages in this area have been less than uniform in their disposition of same. Nevertheless, it is clear that any award of damages for the loss of publicity is contingent upon those damages being reasonably certain, specific, and unspeculative.[5] (See *Ericson v. Playgirl, Inc.* (1977) 73 Cal. App. 3d 850, 140 Cal. Rptr. 921.)

---

[5]California codifies this doctrine in section 3301 of the Civil Code which provides in pertinent part:

"No damages can be recovered for a breach of contract which are not clearly ascertainable in both their nature and origin."

The varied disposition of claims for breach of promise to provide screen credits encompasses two schools of thought. On the one hand, there is the view that damages can be ascertained (to within a reasonable degree of certainty) if the trier of fact is given sufficient factual data. (See *Paramount Productions, Inc. v. Smith* (1937) 91 F.2d 863, cert. den. 302 U.S. 749, 58 S. Ct. 266, 82 L. Ed. 579.) On the other hand, there is the equally strong stance that although damages resulting from a loss of screen credits might be identifiable, they are far too imponderable and ethereal to define in terms of a monetary award. (See *Poe v. Michael Todd Co.* (S.D.N.Y.1957) 151 F. Supp. 801.) If these two views can be reconciled, it would only be by an independent examination of each case on its particular set of facts.

In *Paramount Productions, Inc. v. Smith*, supra, 91 F.2d 863, 866-867, the court was provided with evidence from which the ". . . jury might easily compute the advertising value of the screen credit." (Id., at p. 867.) The particular evidence presented included the earnings the plaintiff/writer received for his work on a previous film in which he did not contract for screen credits. This evidence was in turn easily compared with earnings that the writer had received for work in which screen credits were provided as contracted. Moreover, evidence of that artist's salary, prior to his receipt of credit for a play when compared with earnings received subsequent to his actually receiving credit, was ". . . if believed, likewise sufficient as a gauge for the measure of damages." (Id., at p. 867.)

[143 Cal. App. 3d 577] In another case dealing with a request for damages for failure to provide contracted for screen credits, the court in *Zorich v. Petroff* (1957) 152 Cal. App. 2d 806, 313 P.2d 118 demonstrated an equal awareness of the principle. The court emphasized ". . . that there was no evidence from which the [trial] court could have placed a value upon

Page 413

the screen credit to be given plaintiff as an associate producer. (Civ. Code, § 3301.)" (Id., at p. 811, 313 P.2d 118.) Incident to this fact, the court went on to surmise that because the motion picture which was at the root of the litigation was an admitted

financial failure, that screen credit, if given, ". . . could reasonably have been regarded as a detriment to him." (Id., at p. 811, 313 P.2d 118.)

At the other extreme, it has been held that failure to give an artist screen credit would constitute irreparable injury. In *Poe v. Michael Todd Co.*, supra, 151 F. Supp. 801, the New York District Court was similarly faced with an author's claim that his contractual right to screen credit was violated. The court held: "Not only would money damages be difficult to establish, but at best they would hardly compensate for the real injury done. A writer's reputation, which would be greatly enhanced by public credit for authorship of an outstanding picture, is his stock in trade; it is clear that irreparable injury would follow the failure to give screen credit if in fact he is entitled to it." (Id., at p. 803.)

Notwithstanding the seemingly inflexible observation of that court as to the compensability of a breach of promise to provide screen credits, all three cases equally demonstrate that the awarding of damages must be premised upon calculations, inferences or observations that are logical. Just how logical or reasonable those inferences are regarded serves as the determining factor. Accordingly, where the jury in the matter sub judice was fully apprised of the favorable recognition Sanders' film received from the Academy of Motion Picture Arts and Sciences, the Los Angeles International Film Festival, and public television, and further, where they were made privy to an assessment of the value of said exposure by three experts,[6] it was reasonable for the jury to award monetary damages for that ascertainable loss of publicity. However, pecuniary compensation for Sanders' future harm is not a fully adequate remedy. (See Rest., Contracts, § 361, p. 648)

We return to the remaining requisites for Sanders' entitlement to specific performance. The need for our finding the contract to be reasonable and supported by adequate consideration is obviated by the jury's determination of respondent's breach of that contract. The requisite of mutuality of remedy has been satisfied in that Sanders had fully performed his

---

[6]Those experts all rendered opinions that publicity received by someone with the credit "A film by" for a documentary similar to appellant's, which received similar honors, could be quantified in monetary terms between $50,000 and $150,000.

obligations pursuant to the agreement (i.e., release of all claims of copyright to the film and dismissal of [143 Cal. App. 3d 578] his then pending action against respondents). (See Civ. Code, § 3386.) Similarly, we find the terms of the agreement sufficiently definite to permit enforcement of the respondent's performance as promised.

In the present case it should be obvious that specific performance through injunctive relief can remedy the dilemma posed by the somewhat ambiguous jury verdict. The injunction disposes of the problem of future damages, in that full compliance by Tamarind moots the issue. Of course, violation of the injunction by Tamarind would raise new problems, but the court has numerous options for dealing with the situation and should choose the one best suited to the particular violation.

In conclusion, the record shows that the appellant is entitled to relief consisting of the damages recovered, and an injunction against future injury.[7]

Subsequent to the initial filing of this opinion, it was brought to this court's attention that Terry Sanders entered into a settlement agreement which it is alleged may have a mooting effect on the instant action.

The subject agreement, which was executed approximately one day after the initial

Page 414

posting of this opinion, is assertedly a general release from liability of both respondents and various insurance companies for both the instant action and a related action not a part of this appeal. Respondents submit that the import of the agreement, which is captioned "FULL RELEASE OF ALL CLAIMS," is to make the instant action moot, thus disposing of the issues before this court. Accordingly, respondents petitioned this court to dismiss the instant appeal or alternatively allow them to produce evidence in addition to their supporting declarations.

In opposition to respondents' request, appellants (Terry Sanders and The Terry Sanders Company) submit, by way of opposition declarations, that the subject settlement agreement did not in any way act as a release of their asserted rights to screen credits which comprise the core of this appeal. Specifically, appellants argue that the agreement only states that its effect is to release and discharge respondents from the monetary judgment in the instant action and makes no mention whatsoever concerning this appeal or the rights to screen credits. Appellants suggest by way of argument supported by documentation that said agreement was the product of negotiations in which appellants specifically made known that the agreement was not to affect or otherwise encompass the right to specific performance of the agreement to provide the screen credits involved in this appeal.

[143 Cal. App. 3d 579] Considering the extent of this controversy, in conjunction with our decision to reverse the judgment below, we think it in the best interests of all parties concerned for the trial court to determine what effect, if any, the agreement should have on the action. In effect, respondents' petition is tantamount to a motion to dismiss the entire action, as opposed to the mere dismissal of this appeal. It would appear that the trial court is the more appropriate forum to receive evidence and adjudicate the merits of this issue. If it were to reach a determination unfavorable to petitioners, it would be in position to grant the relief we have determined appellants are entitled to. On the other hand, a contrary determination by the trial court would still leave that court with the authority to take the action requested by petitioners.

The judgment denying appellants' prayer for injunctive relief is hereby reversed and the action, with the addition of this new issue, is remanded to the trial court to take appropriate action in conformity with the views expressed in this opinion, including the taking of additional evidence, oral or written, if deemed appropriate, on the motion to dismiss.

FEINERMAN, P.J., and HASTINGS, J., concur.

---

[7]Contrary to respondent's position, this disposition is not inconsistent with prevailing California authority. (See Lemat Corp. v. Barry (1969) 275 Cal. App. 2d 671, 679, 80 Cal. Rptr. 240, and Harvey v. White (1963) 213 Cal. App. 2d 275, 282, 28 Cal. Rptr. 601.)

VOCABULARY BUILDERS

Across

1 Damages that put the non-breaching party in as good a position as if the contract was not breached.
3 Restraining orders that maintain the status quo until a hearing.
6 Where no valid contract exists, but the court interprets one.
11 The defendant is prohibited from denying the contract under promissory _____.
14 The non-breaching party has a duty to lessen the amount of damages.
19 A "ceiling" on damages.
20 Natural and foreseeable damages.
25 Where the court determines the rights and responsibilities of the parties.
27 The breaching party must give back any benefit received from the non-breaching party.
29 The court declares the contract null.
31 The promisee must incur a substantial _____ in order to recover under promissory estoppel.
33 A type of potentially speculative damages.
35 Maintaining the current state of affairs.
36 Damages that punish the wrongdoer have a(n) _____ effect.
37 A quasi-contract is ____ __ ___.
38 The promisor intended to _____ the promisee to act.
39 The plaintiff must come to the court with _____ _____.

Down

2 Damages are calculated according to what a willing buyer and willing seller would agree to.
4 An injunction issued after trial.
5 A defendant will be denied the benefit of the quasi-contract where s/he has been _____.

7 Punitive damages may be awarded for a(n) _____ act accompanying the breach of contract.
8 The breaching party must pay for actions taken in _____ upon the contract promises.
9 Requiring a party to act is _____ performance.
10 Quantum _____ is the value of the plaintiff's services.
12 The injunction will last indefinitely.
13 The kind of harm that must ensue for a TRO to be issued.
15 A set amount of damages previously agreed upon by the parties in the contract.
16 Court-ordered cessation of defendant's actions.
17 The court's rewriting of the contract to reflect the parties' original intentions.
18 Treble damages allowed by statute is an example of _____damages.
21 Damages are awarded based on the non-breaching party's _____ of the benefit of the contract.
22 The price for substituted goods.
23 An injunction order before trial.
24 Damages that result from the breach but are not necessarily foreseeable.
26 _____ _____ are not awarded under the American rule.
27 To make the plaintiff whole again.
28 Damages that cannot be reasonably and objectively determined.
30 The value that the non-breaching party actually received for selling the goods to another buyer.
32 Principles of fairness and justice.
34 Quantum _____ is the value of the benefit received.

Fig. 14.1 (Number for internal reference only. Do not print). Crossword grid as shown on next page

Part Five

Article 2 of the Uniform Commercial Code

Chapter 15: The Uniform Commercial Code—Article 2: Sale of Goods and Dealings with Merchants

Chapter 15

The Uniform Commercial Code— Article 2: Sale of Goods and Dealings with Merchants

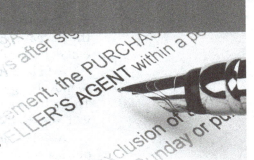

Chapter Objectives

The student will be able to:

- Use vocabulary regarding the UCC's transactions in goods properly.
- Identify the types of transactions covered by the UCC.
- Explain the different standards applicable to merchants and non-merchants under the UCC.
- Discuss the exceptions to formation defects that would otherwise invalidate the contract.
- Explain the battle of the forms.
- Differentiate between a firm offer and an option contract.
- Evaluate the potential warranties involved in a transaction.
- Discuss the options available to the buyer and seller upon breach.
- Identify the remedies available to each non-breaching party.

This chapter examines only one article of the 11 contained in the Uniform Commercial Code (UCC). It is important to note that the UCC is a model code written by experts and published by the American Law Institute (ALI). Each jurisdiction has the option to adopt the language of the UCC into its own legal codes. For the most part, the sections of the UCC have been adopted with local modifications in all of the states, the District of Columbia, and Puerto Rico. Therefore, it is easiest to discuss the UCC in this text with the caveat that the reader should refer to their own jurisdictional commercial code for authority.

Article 2 deals solely with transactions between merchants relating only to movable goods—those dealings that we normally associate with commerce. These transactions are usually sales; therefore, the remainder of the chapter will refer to them simply as such, unless otherwise noted.

Article 2 of the UCC is divided into seven sections. Each section deals with one aspect of commercial contracts for the sale of goods.

- Section 1 addresses the general construction of the code and gives definitions and intentions of this article.
- Section 2 deals with the formation of the contract.
- Section 3 addresses the obligations of the parties with respect to the transaction. This includes warranties and price, delivery, and allocation of risk.
- Section 4 is very brief and solely concerns the passage of title to the goods and will not be discussed in this chapter.
- Section 5 addresses performance obligations.
- Section 6 deals with the consequences of a breach.
- Section 7 describes the remedies available as a consequence of the breach.

Only a selection of the provisions of Article 2 will be discussed in this chapter. Many of the sections are compatible with the common law principles already familiar to the contract student; exceptions and technical requirements will be discussed in greater detail.

COVERED TRANSACTIONS

transactions in goods
A sale or other transfer of title to identifiable, tangible, movable things from a merchant to a buyer.

The best place to start is at the beginning. The UCC goes to great length to define all its terms clearly. Section 2-102 defines the scope of the UCC's application: "This Article applies to **transactions in goods**; it does not apply to any transaction which [operates as a security contract]." In other words, the agreement must relate to the sale/purchase of identifiable, tangible, movable things (a "good") that will change hands from merchant to buyer.

This article does not relate to a contract for the provision of services. A contract to purchase copper and PVC plumbing supplies is covered, whereas the contract for repair of your household plumbing is not, even though it includes the plumbing supplies. The primary purpose in the first contract is to procure goods, whereas the primary purpose in the second contract is to have the plumber supply his services and fix your pipes. Mixed contracts, those procuring both goods and services, need to be examined individually to determine the primary purpose of the agreement in order to determine whether the UCC applies. The courts have fashioned the **predominant factor test** to assist in making the assessment regarding mixed contracts for goods and services.

predominant factor test
An examination of a transaction to determine whether the primary purpose of the contract is the procurement of goods or services.

The predominant factor test is relied upon in the majority of jurisdictions as "it fulfills two of the purposes of the UCC by clarifying and simplifying the law." *Tacoma Athletic Club, Inc. v. Indoor Comfort Systems, Inc.*, 902 P.2d 175, 179 (Wash. App. 1995). Further, the element of actual "tangibility" is not necessary when the sale involves software or other electronic products. The court in *RRX Industries, Inc. v. Lab-Con, Inc.*, 772 F.2d 543, 546 (9th Cir. 1985), acknowledged that these electronic transactions must be considered on a case-by-case basis. "Here, the sales aspect of the transaction predominates. The employee training, repair services, and system upgrading were incidental to sale of the software package and did not defeat characterization of the system as a good." The alternate approach is to separate the contract into its two parts—services and goods—and then treat the provision of goods under the rules of the UCC and treat the provision of services under common law principles. However, this approach has been criticized because it tends to alter the intentions of the parties and inconsistencies result. By separating the two and treating them as separate transactions, it is possible to have a valid contract for the sale of goods under the UCC but have an invalid service agreement. Such an outcome in some cases might drastically alter the legal effect of the agreement as intended by the parties; indeed, it might even become impossible to perform. *See Insul-Mark Midwest, Inc. v. Modern Materials, Inc.*, 612 N.E.2d 550, 554 (Ind. 1993) ("The bifurcation approach seems less sensitive to parties' expectations. Rather, the effect of such approach is to break an agreement into two contracts, with one governed by the UCC and one by the common law. Such an outcome in some cases might drastically alter the legal effect of the agreement as intended by the parties.").

Even contracts that appear to be sales of goods have an element of service within them because labor is needed to create the good and transport it to its final destination. However, it is not these kinds of contracts that pose the most problems. Courts have the most problems where the purpose of the contract is mixed. The consumer desires both the good and the service. It must be determined which is incidental or subservient to the other. The court can look to the negotiations between the parties, the ratio of cost allocated to the service aspect versus the goods' value, and the other aspects of the agreement to determine whether the contract falls under the control of the UCC. *See Tacoma Athletic*, where the court found that the negotiations focused on the goods and named a specific manufacturer of the kinds of goods to be supplied, the goods made up approximately 80 percent of the total cost, and the written contract predominately listed the goods being sold.

SPOT THE ISSUE!

Bash Throwers, Inc., a company that provides "all inclusive" event packages consisting of accommodations, food, tables, flowers, entertainment, and all the other party goodies, entered into a agreement with Sara Smith (who was always trying to outdo her neighbors, the Joneses) to throw a huge block party. Sara is throwing the party in order to attract more clients to her real estate business. The food was to be the centerpiece of the entire experience. Sara prided herself on being a gourmand and spent the majority of her $25,000 budget on exotic delicacies and platters overflowing with food. On the day of the party, although the rest of the terms of the contract were complied with to a T, Bash showed up with hot dogs and hamburgers as the only food items. Sara wishes to file a complaint against Bash for a breach of contract under the UCC. What is your advice?

See *Fallsview Glatt Kosher Caterers, Inc. v. Rosenfeld*, 7 Misc. 3d 557, 794 N.Y.S.2d 790 (N.Y. City Civ. Ct. 2005).

Further, a contract may not involve either a provision of a service or a tangible, movable good. It may involve things that are not considered "goods" under the UCC, but rather are "personal property" governed by a separate set of rules. This is particularly applicable in the high-tech world we now live in. Intellectual property is a kind of personal property not contemplated under the UCC. *See Carcorp, Inc. v. Chesrown Oldsmobile-GMC Truck, Inc.*, 823 N.E.2d 34, 41 (Ohio App. 2004). The purpose of the contract was to transfer all the rights to the automobile dealership so that the buyer could sell GMC trucks—inarguably a movable, tangible good. However, the bulk of the agreement dealt with the transfer of the "incorporeal" intellectual personal property of the seller, including customer information gathered and analyzed by the seller, contract rights, and a favorable reputation in the community. The court determined that this contract was not governed under the UCC as a sale of goods. Remember to make the distinction between intellectual property rights and the actual software that may carry within it the intellectual property of the developer. Under the UCC, software programs are a good—the customer is buying a copy of the code that makes it work; on the other hand, if the developer were selling his rights to control that code in the software and then do whatever the buyer wished after purchase—that would be intellectual property and not a good under the UCC.

EYE ON ETHICS

It is undisputed that most of what an attorney does is provide services; therefore, those activities are not covered under the UCC. However, when an attorney is engaged in the sale of goods ancillary to her legal practice, those sales are not only governed by the relevant statute in the jurisdiction, but also by the ethical rules. Attorneys are consistently held to a higher standard of conduct, even when that conduct is not directly related to the provision of legal services. Further, if the attorney refers her clients to nonlegal businesses in which the attorney owns or has a financial interest, the attorney must inform her client that the attorney-client privilege will not apply in transactions with that distinct business. *See Ancillary Business Organizations; Transactions Between Lawyer and Client*, NY Eth. Op. 755 (N.Y. St. Bar. Ass'n Comm. Prof. Ethics).

MERCHANTS

Now that the subject matter, the goods, has been identified, it is important to define the parties who are governed by the UCC. Article 2 only applies where the seller is also a **merchant,** a person that "deals in goods of the kind or otherwise holds itself out by occupation as having knowledge or skill peculiar to the practices or goods involved in the transaction. . . ." A used car salesman is a merchant with respect to used cars but is not a merchant with respect to organic foods. "The concept of professionalism is heavy in determining who is a merchant under the statute. . . . The defined term 'between merchants,' used in the exception proviso to the statute of frauds, contemplates the knowledge and skill of professionals on each side of the transaction." *Harvest States Cooperatives v. Anderson*, 577 N.W.2d 381, 384 (Wis. App. 1998), *citing Sand Seed Serv. v. Poeckes*, 249 N.W.2d 663, 666 (Iowa 1977) (*quoting, Decatur Coop. Ass'n v. Urban*, 219 Kan. 171, 547 P.2d 323, 328 (1976) (The court made a determination that a casual farmer, one who only occasionally sold his wheat and in small amounts, was not a "merchant" under the UCC.). The frequency and experience of the party assist the court in making the determination, on a case-by-case basis, whether the UCC rules regarding "merchants" apply.

> **merchants**
> Persons who regularly deal in goods of the kind specified in the agreement. They hold themselves out as having special knowledge in their area.

Transactions are governed by slightly different standards if only the seller is a merchant or if both the seller and the buyer are merchants. An example of the special treatment of transactions "between merchants" is the UCC's Statute of Frauds § 2-201(2). The writing evidencing the transaction doesn't even need to be signed by the party against whom satisfaction is sought! How does this work? After their meeting, if Greg Grocer sends a fax over to Fred Farmer confirming the verbal agreement for the purchase of 12 bushels of Granny Smith apples, that writing is sufficient as against Fred if he fails to respond within 10 days of receipt of the confirmation. The UCC imposes the burden of timely responding and/or objecting to business correspondence on merchants.

FORMATION OF THE CONTRACT

Missing Terms Do Not Invalidate the Offer

Under common law principles, an offer must identify the parties, price, quantity, and time for performance. As indicated, the UCC has created a distinction between the two types of parties that could be involved in a covered transaction, merchants and non-merchants. The leniency of the UCC is evident as the writing may not sufficiently state, or may omit, some of the necessary terms.

Similar to common law, the UCC requires the quantity to be specified or at least to be objectively determinable from the terms of the agreement. This is where the resemblance ends, however. In order to preserve and encourage commercial transactions, the UCC does not require a price or time for performance term. Instead, a reasonable price and a reasonable time are made part and parcel of every covered contract unless otherwise specified in the agreement itself. Section 2-204 states that "even though one or more terms are left open a contract for sale does not fail for indefiniteness if the parties have intended to make a contract and there is a reasonably certain basis for giving an appropriate remedy."

Example
The Chic Boutique contacts Fabricland to place an order for seven bolts of cream satin to be used in the design of custom wedding gowns. This is the extent of their agreement. What happens when something goes wrong and one of the parties needs to sue for enforcement? Under common law principles, there is nothing to enforce. However, the UCC recognizes the agreement as commercially viable. Fabricland is under an obligation to ship the material in a timely manner according to the standards set forth in the garment industry and the Chic Boutique is under an obligation to pay a reasonable market price for the goods.

Indeed, even if the contract fails under these relatively permissible requirements, it still may be enforceable under section 2-201(3)(a). If the contract calls for the manufacture of **specialized goods**, those that can only be used by this one particular buyer, then the contract can be enforced despite failing under the UCC's Statute of Frauds. The manufacturer can recover for the time, labor, and materials expended as it started the process of creating these special goods. The courts have fashioned a four-part test to determine when this UCC exception applies:

> **specialized goods**
> A product made for a particular buyer with specifications unique to that buyer so that it could not be sold on the general market.

(1) the goods must be specially made for the buyer;
(2) the goods must be unsuitable for sale to others in the ordinary course of the seller's business;
(3) the seller must have substantially begun to have manufactured the goods or to have a commitment for their procurement; and
(4) the manufacture or commitment must have been commenced under circumstances reasonably indicating that the goods are for the buyer and prior to the seller's receipt of notification of contractual repudiation.

See Kalas v. Cook, 800 A.2d 553, 558 (Conn. App. 2002).

For example, Beaufort Biker calls Hadley Ravenson Motorcycles and orders a custom-made luxury bike that features Beaufort's business logos. Hadley, knowing Beaufort's reputation, begins to construct the bike immediately.

After thinking about it, Beaufort decides that his hair will get too messed up if he rides, so he calls to rescind. Hadley insists on payment for the bike, and the courts will most likely find in its favor since the goods are not suitable for sale to Hadley's other customers.

Modifications or Counteroffers Do Not Terminate the Offer

Another problem in the formative stage is the issue of counteroffers and terminations of offers. The common law recognizes only a perfect mirror image as acceptance of an original offer. Any deviation from the original offer's terms is considered a counteroffer. Not so in commercial transactions *between merchants*. Where additional or different terms are incorporated into the acceptance, they may become part of the contract. If the offeree intends to make a binding counteroffer, she must indicate that the original offeror must accept the new or different terms or else the deal is off.

Battle of the Forms

Now the situation exists where the writings of each merchant-party do not exactly match; a **battle of the forms** ensues under section 2-207. It is common for many businesses to use preprinted forms as the basis for the agreement because most of their transactions are similar. These forms contain "boilerplate" (standard) terms that are favorable to the party proposing to use the form. The terms can be changed to suit each agreement if the situation warrants it; however, many times this extra step is not taken.

The offeree's different or additional terms will become part of the contract unless

1. The offer expressly **limits acceptance** to the terms of the offer.
2. The new or different terms **materially alter** the essence of the agreement.
3. The offeror has already, or within a reasonable time, **objected** to those proposed new or different terms.

Why does the UCC allow such practice? Because merchants do it all the time. Merchants are held to a higher standard and knowledge of the way their industry works and handles routine commercial transactions. Merchants simply don't have the time to address every addition or minor deviation. Only to those that they object do they need to respond. It's the UCC's practicality that wins over common law's stringent nature. Therefore, the response acts as a counteroffer only if the offer specifically states that no deviations will be considered an acceptance of the offer. Further, courts have generally agreed that a "material alteration" is one that would surprise or impose a hardship upon the other party. Notification of the objection also must be made; otherwise, in this case, silence is acceptance of the new or modified terms. These factors clearly favor the formation of a contract.

battle of the forms
An evaluation of commercial writings whose terms conflict with each other in order to determine what terms actually control the performances due from the parties.

limitation of acceptance
A commercial offeror may specifically state that the offeree must accept all terms as set forth in the offer with no deviations.

material alteration
A change in the terms that would surprise or impose hardship on the other party if allowed to become a part of the agreement.

objection to terms
A merchant must state her disapproval of the offeree's new or different terms within a reasonable time, or else they are considered accepted by her.

The same principles apply to modifications to an agreement *after* the consummation of the contract. The modification does not require its own separate consideration. Section 2-206. The UCC is permitting leniency with regard to stringent enforcement of certain requirements in order to facilitate commercial transactions.

RESEARCH THIS

In your jurisdiction, find a case clearly defining and explaining what a "material" change to a contract is under the UCC. In your own words, what makes an additional or contradictory element "material enough" to avoid the formation of a sale of goods contract?

The thrust of all of this is the basic determination that the parties intended to enter into a contractual relationship. While the exact terms are not necessarily set forth in precise detail, the intent to be bound exists and can be shown through some sort of memorialization, including conduct. *See Superior Boiler Works, Inc. v. R.J. Sanders, Inc.*, 711 A.2d 628 (R.I. 1998).

> Prior to adoption of the Uniform Commercial Code, the common law "mirror image rule" held that an acceptance that did not precisely parrot the terms set out in the offer was never an acceptance but a mere counteroffer. This rigid requirement led to an unfortunate practice whereby commercial dealings too often degenerated into a "battle of the forms" in which the merchant sending the last written communication before performance would reap the spoils of the battle by having the "last shot" at inserting favorable boilerplate terms. Section 2-207 of the UCC effects a "radical departure" from the common-law rule. Under the UCC an acceptance that evinces that party's intent to be bound operates to create a contract with respect to the terms agreed upon even though the acceptance states additional or different terms.

> *Id.* at 633 (citations omitted).

The *Superior Boiler Works* court was faced with a situation where there were two different writings that evidenced the intent to enter into a contract. They disagreed on one material term, time for delivery. In fact, the terms were in direct conflict with one another. The court was faced with making a determination as to what term should be upheld.

> The problem is that § 6A-2-207(2) utterly fails to explicate the legal consequences of conflicting terms that are both material to the contract and objected to by at least one of the parties. The official comments and drafting history are at best ambiguous on this point. . . .
> Courts have taken three divergent approaches to this question. In brief the first approach treats "different" terms as a subgroup of "additional" terms. The result is that such different terms, when material, simply do not

become part of the contract and thus the original delivery term offered by Sanders would control. *See id.* (and cases cited therein). The second approach reaches the same result by concluding that "the offeror's terms control because the offeree's different terms merely fall out [of the contract]; § 2-207(2) cannot rescue the different terms since that subsection applies only to additional terms." Id. Finally, the third approach, aptly named the "knock-out rule," holds that the conflicting terms cancel one another, leaving a blank in the contract with respect to the unagreed-upon term that would be filled with one of the UCC's "gap-filler" provisions. Id. Here, the void relating to delivery time would be filled by § 6A-2-309(1), which reads, "The time for shipment or delivery . . . if . . . not agreed upon shall be a reasonable time."

We conclude that this approach best promotes the UCC's aim to abrogate the criticized common-law mirror image rule and its attendant last-shot doctrine and avoids "re-enshrin[ing] the undue advantages derived solely from the fortuitous positions of when a party sent a form." Because of the UCC's gap-filling provisions, we recognize that this approach might result in the enforcement of a contract term that neither party agreed to and, in fact, in regard to which each party expressed an entirely different preference. We note in response to this concern that the offeror and the offeree both have the power to protect any term they deem critical by expressly making acceptance conditional on assent to that term.

Id. at 634-635 (citations omitted).

SPOT THE ISSUE!

Fatima, the owner of an upscale fashion boutique, wishes to purchase Stella Shoes from the manufacturer for resale in her shop. Fatima faxes the following "order" to Stella:

> Fatima Boutique wishes to purchase 200 pair of top-quality leather high-heeled shoes per the catalogue. We would like the fall fashion assortment listed on page 12. Kindly confirm receipt of this facsimile.

Stella faxes the following document back to Fatima:

Order received. Seller to provide 200 shoes. Fall assortment. Shipment to be made August first via common carrier.

Seller disclaims any and all warranties. All disputes are to be submitted to binding arbitration.

What impact, if any, does the above "fine print" have on the terms of the agreement?

Firm Offers

What about consideration? There needs to be consideration for the original, underlying offer. However, the UCC has its own version of an option

firm offer
An option contract to keep the offer open between merchants that does not have to be supported by separate consideration in order to be valid.

contract—it is called a **firm offer**. *See* section 2-205. This offer cannot be retracted for a certain period of time, just like an option contract, but unlike an option contract, there is no need for it to be supported by its own consideration. Merchants essentially have given their word of honor to keep the offer open exclusively for the offeree for a set period of time. If no period of time is specified, then the UCC steps in again with its standard of reasonability. In any event, a firm offer will not stay open for longer than three months.

Silence as Acceptance

Acceptance of an offer usually requires an affirmative response from the offeree made in the manner prescribed by the offer. Section 2-206(1)(a) loosens this requirement in that any method of acceptance is invited unless otherwise stated in the offer. Additionally, silence can be acceptance under section 2-206(1)(b). To reflect the reality of commercial transactions, the UCC permits the shipment of goods to act as acceptance. The offeree has not transmitted an acceptance to the buyer's invitation to purchase the goods; in silence she has acted upon the offer. Most of us do not expect a commercial seller to call us after receiving our order to accept it. Shipment is the normal course of acceptance in this instance. On the receiver's side, silence is acceptance of the goods as conforming under the contact unless the buyer notifies the seller within a reasonable time. *Import Traders, Inc. v. Frederick Mfg. Corp.*, 117 Misc. 2d 305, 457 N.Y.S.2d 742 (N.Y. City Civ. Ct. 1983) (silence for five months after delivery is acceptance of the goods as conforming under the contract).

Warranties

warranty
A promise or representation by the seller that the goods in question meet certain standards.

When entering into the contract, the seller makes certain representations, or **warranties**, for the benefit of the buyer. The UCC imposes those warranties that are commercially fair and reasonable to expect and delineates the method to create or avoid other kinds of warranties. As in any circumstance, the parties, under freedom of contract principles, are able to specifically avoid any warranty. The UCC imposes a **warranty of title** under section 2-312. The seller is under an obligation to provide the buyer with goods that are freely transferable and not encumbered by any third-party interests.

warranty of title
The seller promises the buyer that the seller has the right to transfer the title free and clear of encumbrances to the buyer.

express warranty
A written representation by the seller as to the nature of the goods to be sold.

As part of the bargain, a seller may **expressly warrant** the goods she is selling. Any statements of facts or promises made by the seller to the buyer to induce the buyer to purchase the goods become part of the contract for sale. Items must conform to the description of the goods or any samples provided by the seller. An important distinction to be made is the difference between a statement of fact that is intended to induce the buyer to buy and goes to the "basis of the bargain" (section 2-313) and a statement of the seller's opinion of value or statements that are mere puffery and salesmanship. "[U]nder the UCC, a seller's statements to a buyer regarding goods sold, made during the bargaining process, are presumptively part of the basis of the bargain between the seller and buyer. Therefore, the burden is on the seller to prove that the resulting bargain did not rest at all on the seller's statements." *Torres v. Northwest Engineering Co.*, 949 P.2d 1004, 1015 (Haw. App. 1997). The distinction does not lie in the seller's intention to create a warranty. No intent is necessary; as long as the statements relate to the reason why the buyer is entering into the contract, they create an express warranty. Again, the objective, not the subjective, wins out in contract formation.

In addition to express warranties, **implied warranties** are included in the contract for sale unless they are specifically excluded. When a seller places an item on the market, she represents that the good is **merchantable**. Under section 2-314(2), goods are merchantable if they

> [p]ass without objection in the trade under the contract description; and

> (a) In the case of fungible goods, are of fair average quality within the description; and
> (b) Are fit for the ordinary purposes for which such goods are used; and
> (c) Run, within the variations permitted by the agreement, of even kind, quality and quantity within each unit and among all units involved; and
> (d) Are adequately contained, packaged, and labeled as the agreement may require; and
> (e) Conform to the promises or affirmations of fact made on the container or label if any.

implied warranty
An unwritten representation that is normally and naturally included by operation of law that applies to the goods to be sold.

merchantable
Goods must meet certain standards that are required in the relevant industry.

That's a very long way of saying that the goods should be of the same quality as the market requires and expects. For example, Belinda runs a dance school and purchases all her students' ballet slippers from Cinderella Slipper Company. Absent an express contract term disclaiming any and all warranties, the ballet slippers have an *implied warranty of merchantability*. They would not cause complaint in the industry and are of average quality for ballet slippers. The slippers should not vary from the contract specifications, and they should be packaged in a box or bag to prevent them from getting ripped or stained in delivery. Further, if the box or bag also states that they are leather, they should indeed be leather, not a synthetic material. This all boils down to getting what you expect and what you paid for.

Even more demanding is the **implied warranty for a particular purpose** under section 2-315. The goods may impliedly be warranted to a higher standard if the buyer made the seller aware of the particular use for which the good was being purchased. The buyer relies on the seller's skill and knowledge of her own product in order to obtain suitable goods. For example, Paul has been hired to paint a historic building in town. Unfamiliar with the materials used in the restoration, he contacts Bill Voilà, who sells specialty paints. Paul explains the project and Bill suggests an oil-based paint that mimics an antique milk paint finish common to the era of the house and true to the restoration. Bill has impliedly warranted the paint for use in Paul's application.

implied warranty for a particular purpose
If a seller has reason to know of the needs of the buyer in relation to the goods to be sold, the seller impliedly warrants the goods to that higher standard.

Had Paul simply walked in and asked for interior paint without mentioning the project, no warranty for fitness would exist.

A merchant may limit or exclude any and all warranties; however, the UCC prefers their existence in order to protect buyers. Section 2-316(1). Therefore,

conspicuous limitation or exclusion of warranties
A seller may specifically deny any warranties as long as the limitation or exclusion of the warranties is set forth in language that is understandable and noticeable by the buyer.

the UCC requires that the **limitation or exclusion of warranties** be **conspicuous**. Section 2-316(2). The term "as is" sufficiently signals the buyer that there may be some defects that the seller will not warrant. This "as is" language relates to the limitation, but it also must be conspicuous. This means that, in some way, the seller has brought the limitation language to the buyer's attention. "A term or clause is conspicuous when it is so written that a reasonable person against whom it is to operate ought to have noticed it. . . . Language in the body of a form is 'conspicuous' if it is in larger or other contrasting type or color." *Bailey v. Tucker Equipment Sales, Inc.*, 510 S.E.2d 904, 905-906 (Ga. App. 1999). Additionally, if the buyer has been given the opportunity to inspect the goods but chooses not to, the implied warranties do not apply to those defects that could have been detected by such an inspection. Section 2-316(3).

good faith obligation
Both buyers and sellers must deal with each other in a reasonable and fair manner without trying to avoid legitimate performance obligations.

Can a buyer return items that are merchantable and conform to the contract specifications? The usual answer is no. The buyer is under a **good faith obligation** to purchase the conforming goods. However, the parties may agree that the transaction is a **sale on approval** or a **sale or return**. Section 2-326. This first term allows a buyer to receive the goods and see if they meet her requirements. This may involve testing the good in its intended use. The title to the goods remains with the seller until the buyer accepts them. The second term deals with goods that are intended for resale. If the buyer fails to resell the goods, they are returned to the seller. This scenario is typical in college bookstores. The bookstore buys a specified number of textbooks for resale to students. Leftover, unsold texts are returned to the original seller. It is important to note that neither of these provisions relates to nonconforming goods for which an action for breach may lie.

sale on approval
The agreement may provide that the contract for sale is not consummated until the buyer receives and approves of the goods.

sale or return
The agreement provides that if the buyer is unable to resell the goods, she is permitted to return the unsold goods to the original seller.

SURF'S UP

The electronic equivalent of Article 2 of the UCC is the UCITA (Uniform Computer Information Transactions Act). Just like Article 2, UCITA is an attempt to codify the existing practices and give certainty and predictability to transactions covered by the act. UCITA covers transactions involving the sale of software licenses, access to databases (like Westlaw and Lexis-Nexis), software development, and the like. It does not cover the hardware used in computing; that is still the domain of the UCC because those things are movable, tangible goods, whereas digital information is not. This is where the first tricky part comes in. UCITA applies to the sale of CDs, drives, or other tangible media that are merely a way of transporting the electronic data contained on them. Blank CDs are goods under the UCC. It is important to understand what the main goal of the transaction is: the transfer of electronic information or a good upon which information can be stored.

Unlike the predominant factor test, the UCITA breaks the contract out into its component parts. Therefore, the UCITA and the UCC both may apply to the contract. Comment 4 to section 103 of the UCITA states:

a. *Computer Information and UCC Subject Matter.* If a transaction includes computer information and subject matter governed by an article of the Uniform Commercial Code, in the absence of contrary agreement, the general rule is that the rules of the Uniform Commercial Code apply to their subject matter and this Act applies to its subject matter. That rule is stated in subsection (b)(1), subsection (c), and subsection (d)(8). For example, under subsection (d)(8), Uniform Commercial Code Article 8, and not this Act, deals with investment securities, while Articles 4 and 4A, and not this Act, deal with payments, checks, and funds transfers. Under subsection (c), if there is a conflict between a provision of this Act and Article 9 of the Uniform Commercial Code, Article 9 prevails. This preserves uniformity in Article 9's application across a wide variety of personal property financing transactions.

b. *Computer Information and Goods.* Some transactions include goods and computer information. "Goods" is defined for purposes of this Act in Section 102. Generally, there is no overlap between goods and computer information since computer information and informational rights are not goods. *See, e.g., United States v. Stafford*, 136 F.3d 1109 (7th Cir. 1998); *Specht v. Netscape Communications Corp.*, 306 F.3d 17 (Fed. 2d Cir. 2002); *Fink v. DeClassis*, 745 F. Supp. 509, 515 (N.D. Ill. 1990) (trademarks, tradenames, advertising, artwork, customer lists, goodwill and licenses are not "goods"). A diskette is a tangible object but the information on the diskette does not become goods simply because it is copied on tangible medium, any more than the information in a book is governed by the law of goods because the book binding and paper may be Article 2 goods. *See, e.g., Grappo v. Alitalia Linee Aeree Italiane, S.p.A.*, 56 F.3d 427 (2d Cir. 1995); *Architectonics, Inc. v. Control Systems, Inc.*, 935 F. Supp. 425 (S.D.N.Y. 1996).

   (1) **General Rule.** If a transaction involves goods and computer information (e.g., a computer and software), the general rule is that Article 2 or Article 2A applies to the aspect of the transaction pertaining to the sale or lease of goods, but this Act applies to the computer information and aspects of the agreement relating to the creation, modification, access to, or transfer of it. Section 103(b)(1). Each body of law governs as to its own subject matter. Some describe this as a "gravamen of the action" standard. The law applicable to an issue depends on whether the issue pertains to goods or to computer information. A similar distinction exists in copyright law between ownership of a copy and ownership of the copyright. *See, e.g.,* 17 U.S.C. § 202; *DSC Communications Corp. v. Pulse Communications, Inc.*, 170 F.3d 1354 (Fed. Cir. 1999), cert. den. 528 U.S. 923 (1999).

   (2) **Exceptions to General Rule: Copy and Documentation.** There are exceptions to the general rule's gravamen test. Thus, this Act treats the medium that carries the computer information as part of the computer information and within this Act, whether the medium is a tangible object or electronic. This Act applies to the copy, documentation, and packaging of computer information; these are within the definition of computer

> information itself. Section 102. They are mere incidents of the transfer of the information.
>
> (3) ***Exceptions to General Rule: Embedded Programs***. If a computer program is embedded and contained in goods, the general rule ordinarily applies. This Act applies to the program, while goods law applies to the goods. In some cases, however, an embedded program is a mere part of the goods and this Act should not apply.

PERFORMANCE

identification of the goods to the contract
Once a seller has designated specific goods as the ones that will be delivered to the buyer, the buyer has a protectable interest in them.

The primary issues set forth in these sections deal with the identification of the goods to the contract and their subsequent delivery. Once the specific **goods have been identified** as the ones that will be sent to the buyer under the terms of the contract, the buyer has a protectable and insurable interest in them. This is particularly significant where the buyer has paid a portion of the price prior to delivery. Sections 2-501 and 2-502.

Once the goods have been designated for a particular buyer, they then must be delivered. (The extensive shipping methods and attendant requirements will not be explored in this chapter.) A seller may tender delivery by notifying the buyer of the time, place, and manner of delivery, permitting the buyer to make any necessary preparation for the arrival of the goods. A **tender of delivery** means that the goods are essentially at the disposal of the buyer. Section 2-503. It does not mean that the buyer has actual delivery to its front door. Upon tender of delivery, the buyer's obligation to pay for the goods arises. Section 2-507. This is also the point when the statute of limitations begins to run for any breach under the contract. A cause of action begins to accrue when tender of delivery is made. If it were otherwise, it "would lead to the absurd result that the period of limitations never begins to run in cases such as this where a plaintiff takes delivery and retains possession of goods for a considerable period of time before notifying the seller of possible defects." *Washington Freightliner, Inc. v. Shantytown Pier, Inc.*, 719 A.2d 541, 546 (Md. 1998).

tender of delivery
The seller is ready to transfer the goods to the buyer and the goods are at the disposal of the buyer.

inspect
The buyer must take steps to examine the goods to ensure they are of the type indicated in the contract. The seller must make the goods available for this purpose.

As sales of goods may involve buyers and sellers at a distance (rather than face-to-face immediate transactions), the buyer must have an opportunity to receive and **inspect** the goods to ensure conformance with the contract specifications. Section 2-513. Payment for goods prior to inspection (upon tender of delivery) does not mean that the buyer has accepted the goods, and the buyer has a right to all remedies for nonconformance. If the goods are found to be **nonconforming**, the seller may tell the buyer that she will **cure** the defect by delivering conforming goods within the allotted contract time. Section 2-508(1). This right to cure, or fix the problems with the performance, is *absolute* if the seller can do so within the original time for performance. Further, if the seller has reason to believe that the goods were in conformance with the contract, she may have a reasonable amount of additional time to cure the defect. Section 2-508(2). The court will judge

nonconforming
Goods that are not in reasonable compliance with the specifications in the contract.

cure
The seller is given a reasonable opportunity to fix the defects in the goods found by the buyer.

whether the right to cure exists "in the light of the absence of loss, risk or inconvenience" to the buyer. *Yttro Corp. v. X-Ray Marketing Ass'n, Inc.*, 559 A.2d 3, 7 (N.J. Super. App. Div. 1989).

BREACH

Upon improper delivery of nonconforming goods, the seller is in breach of the contract. It is the buyer's responsibility to establish proof of the breach and seasonably inform the seller. Section 2-607(4). Under section 2-601, the buyer may

(a) accept the whole;
(b) reject the whole;
(c) accept any commercial unit and reject the rest.

No matter what action the buyer chooses to take, all of the remedies for breach are still available.

Acceptance

Once the buyer has accepted the whole shipment or only part, and the seller has notice of the acceptance, the deal is final. Well, usually it is final. The UCC has carved out exceptions in accordance with commercial realities.

A buyer may **revoke the previous acceptance** if the seller had promised to cure the nonconformity but has failed to do so or if the seller had assured the buyer of conformity that in reality did not exist. Section 2-608(1). If the nonconformity was difficult to discover, the buyer must revoke within a reasonable time after she discovered or should have discovered the nonconformity. Section 2-608(2). These are the only reasons allowed for revoking acceptance. Merely changing your mind about accepting nonconforming goods is not permissible. Further, the buyer must pay the contract price for the goods that are accepted.

revocation of a previous acceptance
A buyer has the right to refuse to accept the seller's attempts at a cure if those attempts are still not in conformance with the contract requirements.

SPOT THE ISSUE!

Connie loves the outdoors and so she purchased a "pop-up" camper from Outdoor Abodes, Ltd., in June. She took delivery a few days later and noticed that it leaned slightly and the door wouldn't lock. She returned the camper to Outdoor, which replaced the lock and told her that "the leaning condition was normal for a pop-up camper." Due to her hectic work schedule, she was not able to go camping until late July. Not only would the door not lock, but it still leaned, and the sides and roof of the camper were unstable and swayed and, worst of all, the refrigerator did not work properly. Connie notified Outdoor of these problems. On her next trip in August, she noticed the same problems. On August 31st, Connie delivered the camper to Outdoor for repairs. This was the beginning of the repair saga. In late September, Connie went back to Outdoor for more repairs. Connie was upset; she wanted her money back, but, after talking to Outdoor, she agreed to let them do further repairs. When she went to pick up the camper after these repairs, it still leaned. Connie said she wanted her money back—effectively trying to revoke her acceptance. Outdoor asked for one more attempt to repair the camper. Connie picked it up in January—supposedly fixed. Connie noticed some differences in this camper and doesn't believe it is the one she purchased. Connie wants her money back. *See Head v. Phillips Camper Sales & Rental, Inc.*, 593 N.W.2d 595 (Mich. App. 1999).

commercial unit
A batch of goods packaged or sold together in the normal course of the relevant industry.

A note on accepting only part of the shipment: A **commercial unit** is a portion of the shipment that, if removed, does not affect the value of the remaining lot. For example, if pencils are only sold by the gross (a dozen dozen), a buyer must accept an entire gross or none; she cannot break it up. If the buyer wishes to accept the 100 pencils that are acceptable within the gross (144), the buyer must accept the entire lot of 144. Section 2-606(2). Recall that remedies for breach are still available. Permitting these types of actions allows commerce to continue and puts off resolution of the issues until the parties can deal with them. The speed of business is much faster than the speed of justice.

Rejection

Rejection must be made within a reasonable time after delivery. Section 2-602. If the rejection is not made within a reasonable time, it operates as an acceptance. The seller has a right to know of the rejection in order to take action to minimize the loss. The buyer also is under an obligation to minimize the potential losses of the seller in that she must take reasonable care of the rightfully rejected goods in her possession. The UCC goes so far as to impose a **duty to resell** them for the original seller if they are perishable goods or those that are likely to decline in value quickly. Section 2-602(1). The buyer must act in good faith in taking the necessary steps after rightful rejection. Fairness dictates that the good deeds also will be rewarded as the buyer is entitled to reimbursement for any out-of-pocket expenses incurred on behalf of preserving the seller's interest in the nonconforming goods. Section 2-602(2) and (3).

duty to resell
The UCC requires commercial sellers to try to resell the goods that have not been accepted by the original buyer.

actions inconsistent with rejection
A buyer must not do anything that is contrary to her previous refusal of the goods.

If a buyer rejects the goods but then takes an **action inconsistent** with this position, the rejection is not valid and will act as an acceptance. Generally speaking, this means that if a buyer seasonably states his rejection of the goods but then sells them on his accord for his own account and benefit, the rejection is no longer valid. The buyer has accepted the goods. This is distinguishable from the duty to resell on behalf of the seller's account as described above.

The court in *Ford v. Starr Fireworks, Inc.*, 874 P.2d 230 (Wyo. 1994), makes this point clearly. A wholesaler of fireworks (Ford) bought cases of fireworks to be distributed to his retail stores. When Ford received the fireworks from Starr, some of them appeared to be nonconforming and Ford notified Starr of his rejection. However, Ford sent some of the fireworks to his retail outlets and sold those to end consumers and other retailers. The court found that Ford exercised ownership of the rejected goods by selling some of the fireworks and by holding them in his retail outlets for an unreasonable amount of time. Ford's attempted rejection of these goods was ineffective. The *Ford* court made another finding that Ford could not recover for the "returned" fireworks as he did not follow the instructions given by the seller. Ford left the cases unattended outside Starr's downtown Denver business office. Therefore, the rejection of these goods was also ineffective.

The buyer is also under an obligation to **specify the reason(s) for the rejection**. The seller must not only know within a reasonable time that a defect exists, but what kind of defect. This information is critical in ascertaining whether the seller is able to cure. The UCC presumes that without stating the justification for rejection, the buyer is acting in bad faith, most likely looking to get out of a bad deal. The UCC tries to preserve the contract. The buyer must provide a good faith reason for rejection of the goods in order to be relieved of the obligation to pay for them and consummate the deal. Section 2-605. Goods do not have to be perfect; they must be merchantable.

> **specific reasons for rejection**
> The buyer is under an obligation to notify the seller within a reasonable time not only that the goods have been rejected but also the reasons for the refusal to accept the goods.

Adequate Assurances

In a "last ditch" effort to avoid a breach post-shipment, the UCC provides a mechanism for both buyers and sellers to ensure performance, or at least find out if a breach is likely *before* time for performance. Section 2-609 gives the parties a right to seek **adequate assurance** of performance where the party has reason to believe that the other will not be able to perform. This feeling of insecurity must be commercially reasonable. The "insecure" party may request in writing an assurance from the other party that performance will be forthcoming. Once this demand has been made, the insecure party may suspend her performance until the assurance is received. By permitting the suspension of obligations, the UCC has allowed the insecure party to lessen potential damages if the assurances are not forthcoming. *See Hornell Brewing Co., Inc. v. Spry*, 174 Misc. 2d 451, 664 N.Y.S.2d 698 (1997) (The Arizona Ice Tea supplier filed a suit against a former beer distributor, Spry, who wished to distribute Arizona products. Spry failed to provide adequate assurances when requested by Arizona. The court held that Arizona was within its rights to request the assurances because Spry was behind in paying invoices, had bounced checks, and failed to sell the original shipment of Arizona Ice Tea. Further, this failure to provide adequate assurances was anticipatory repudiation and Arizona was entitled to seek damages.).

> **adequate assurances**
> Either party may request the other to provide further guarantees that performance will be forthcoming if the requesting party has reasonable suspicion that the other may default.

If the adequate assurance is not provided within 30 days, the insecure party may treat it as a repudiation of the contract and seek damages, even if the time for performance is not yet due. That should sound familiar . . . something like anticipatory repudiation. Yes, but in an effort to encourage commercial transactions, the UCC gives merchants a tool to protect their interests under circumstances where the insecure party has reasonable doubts. This is a less-stringent standard than common law anticipatory repudiation, which requires an unequivocal statement of the intent not to go through with the agreement. Again, the UCC is simply addressing commercial reality. It is not likely that merchants are going to clearly and unequivocally state that they will not perform. Indeed, even while knowing that performance is nearly impossible, businesses will make promises in the vain attempt to salvage what they can from the deal. It is just the nature of the beast. Section 2-609 addresses this peculiarity.

Example

The Chic Boutique and Fabricland enter into a contract for seven bolts of cream satin to be used in the design of custom wedding gowns. Fabricland learns of Chic Boutique's declining sales and that another supplier has complained of slow payments from Chic. Fabricland is probably justified in requesting adequate assurances from Chic that payment will be made upon delivery. It is not commercially reasonable to gamble on this particular buyer's ability to pay where there are other potential customers who would like to purchase from Fabricland. It makes good business sense to protect the expectations of payment and sell to the better customers.

It is not only sellers who can become insecure. If Chic learns of Fabricland's habit of late or nonconforming deliveries, Chic can request adequate assurance of delivery. This way, Chic can procure the satin from another source in time to meet the deadline for fabrication of the gowns.

REMEDIES

The UCC disfavors finding a breach and gives both the buyer and seller options in order to preserve the contract. However, if that is not possible and a breach has occurred, the UCC also offers both the buyer and seller options as to the remedies available.

Seller's Remedies

insolvency
The inability to pay one's debts, which may result in a declaration of bankruptcy and put all contractual obligations on hold or terminate them.

The primary concern of sellers is the buyers' ability to pay. Upon the **insolvency** of a buyer, the seller may rightfully refuse to deliver unless the buyer pays in cash. Section 2-702(1). Further, if the goods were delivered on credit while the buyer was insolvent, the seller may demand that the buyer return the goods within 10 days of receipt. The seller does not assume the risk of buyers being able to pay. It is commercially reasonable to expect that a business placing an order should have the ability and intention to pay.

The UCC gives sellers the following options where the buyer has breached:

1. Withhold delivery. Section 2-703.
2. Stop delivery. Section 2-705.
3. Identify and complete manufacture of the goods in order to prepare them for resale or cease production and resell for salvage value. Section 2-704.

4. Resell and recover the difference. Section 2-706.
5. Recover damages caused by the breach or recover the contract price. Sections 2-708 and 2-709.
6. Cancel the contract. Section 2-703.

The first and last remedies need very little discussion as they are straightforward. Once a party is in breach, the other is relieved of her performance obligations (in these matters, shipment) and may choose to cancel the contract. Cancellation draws the relationship to a close and remedies can and will be pursued immediately.

If the seller has already shipped the goods via a carrier and they have not yet been "delivered," the seller has a right to stop the delivery in transit. Section 2-705. **Delivery** between merchants can mean several things: (1) receipt at the buyer's place of business, (2) acknowledgment of receipt at a warehouse at the disposal of the buyer, or (3) receipt of a negotiable instrument by the buyer giving title to the goods to the buyer. In order to stop delivery, the seller also must notify the carrier in a reasonable amount of time to be able to stop delivery. Any additional costs associated with the cessation of delivery must be paid for by the seller.

A seller also may be at a "manufacturing crossroad" if the buyer breaches during the middle of production. The seller must decide whether it makes more commercial sense to **finish the goods** and try to resell them to another customer or to halt production and try to resell what there is **for scrap or salvage** value. This determination must be made in a commercially reasonable manner and will depend on the facts surrounding not only the breach, but the current state of the market.

In any circumstance, the seller is under an obligation to mitigate damages; therefore, *resale* is often an option. The resale must be made in conformance with the UCC's requirement of good faith and commercial reasonableness. If the goods then sell for less than the contract price, the seller may recover the difference between what she actually received for the goods in resale on the market and the contract price. The seller also is entitled to any damages that accrue during the attempts at resale as *incidental damages* under section 2-710. If the seller manages to obtain a higher price for the resold goods, the seller keeps the profits with a smile and the buyer has no claim to that money. Section 2-706 sets forth particular requirements relating to the time, place, and manner of the resale; however, these requirements will not be set forth at length. Needless to say, the UCC frowns upon resale from the back of the truck on a lonely street at midnight.

Until now, the seller has retained control over the goods in question. What happens when the buyer is in control or possession of the goods and then refuses to pay? The seller has the right to recover the **price under the contract**. Section 2-709.

If the buyer improperly rejects the goods or repudiates, the seller can collect as damages the difference between the market price and the contract price along with incidental damages. Section 2-708. What is **market price**?

delivery
In commercial contracts, delivery may be accomplished by transferring actual possession of the goods, or putting the goods at the disposal of the buyer, or by a negotiable instrument giving the buyer the right to the goods.

finish or scrap
The seller has the option to either finish producing the partially manufactured goods or stop production and scrap the materials for their recycled value.

price under the contract
The seller has the right to collect the agreed-upon price for the goods where the buyer has possession, despite the market conditions at the time.

market price
The amount of money that another neutral party would pay for the goods on the open market.

Section 2-723 defines it as the price for the same goods at the same place prevailing at the time the seller learns of the breach. Market price can be shown by market quotes for the same goods in the same (or similar) geographical location.

Example

Julie contracts to purchase gold necklaces and bracelets from Guido. Guido manufactures and ships the goods to Julie's Jewelry Store in Santa Barbara, California. Julie improperly refuses to pay for the pieces and Guido sues for breach. The price of gold and custom-made jewelry varies daily within the affluent city of Santa Barbara. The market value must be determined by the cost of similar products in Santa Barbara, not just a global price or one from any random city in America.

A seller also may be entitled to *lost profits* if the market price for the goods does not put him/her in as good a position as performance would have. In other words, the market price is not enough to make the seller whole again (as if the breach did not occur).

Buyer's Remedies

The UCC gives buyers the following options where the seller has breached:

1. Recover any payments made.
2. "Cover" the loss by purchasing substitute goods.
3. Compel delivery of identified goods.
4. Recover damages caused by the breach.
5. Cancel the contract.

Similar to the seller's remedies, the buyer is entitled to be relieved of his/her performance obligation (to pay). If any payments have been made, the buyer is entitled to have that money back if no shipment has or will be tendered. If you get nothing, you should pay nothing. Additionally, the buyer also may choose to cancel the contract. It is the middle three options that will be explored further.

cover
The buyer can mitigate her losses from the seller's breach by purchasing substitute goods on the open market.

First, the buyer can **cover** the loss by purchasing substitute goods. Section 2-712. Should Guido fail to deliver the gold necklaces to Julie in Santa Barbara, Julie can take commercially reasonable measures to procure alternate necklaces and bracelets so her store has something to sell. Retailers cannot open a store without inventory!

The buyer is then entitled to the cost of the substituted goods over the contract price and any incidental damages incurred in obtaining them. The overarching standard of good faith applies here as well. The buyer must make a reasonable good faith effort to obtain goods of similar value and at a commercially reasonable price. Julie must make every effort to obtain the substitute goods as soon as she can to avoid further damages. The duty to mitigate damages places a burden on buyers to try to effect cover. The UCC does not mandate that all buyers must cover, but consequential damages will be reduced by the amount that could have been saved by covering. It is important to note that this provision applies to all covered transactions under the UCC, not just those between merchants.

A buyer may not be able to effectuate cover and, therefore, the measure of damages would be calculated using the market price at the time when the buyer learns of the non-delivery or repudiation. This assumes that there is a market price or, at the very least, a **spot sale** price that is determinable. A spot sale price is the price that a buyer would pay for goods of that kind in the buyer's location at the time of the breach (on the spot).

If there is no market for that kind of good, neither cover nor market price will assist in making the buyer whole again. Under those circumstances, where the goods are unique, the court may compel the seller to deliver the goods. An action for *specific performance* under the UCC is more liberally construed than under traditional contract law. It is commercially reasonable to expect a seller to perform on its promise as personal service is not at issue. Permitting specific performance to a buyer is equivalent to the seller's right to recover the price.

If the buyer has already accepted the goods, the buyer still has one last way to make him/herself whole again. Once the nonconformity has been established, the buyer may obtain damages in the amount equal to the difference between the **value of the goods as accepted** and the value they would have had if they were conforming to the contract specifications. Section 2-714. Essentially, the goods are not as warranted by the seller and the seller should be responsible for the diminution in value due to that defect.

spot sale
A purchase on the open market in that particular place at that particular time.

value of the goods as accepted
The buyer is entitled to a "set-off" for the difference between the price of the goods as specified in the contract and the actual price those goods would garner on the open market.

Example

Guido also sells diamonds to Julie. He tells her that they have all been GIA (Gemological Institute of America) certified as colorless and near flawless diamonds. Julie accepts the delivery of the diamonds but later learns that they are not GIA certified. This certification adds to the value of diamonds on the market. Julie can recover the difference between the price she paid for the diamonds (assuming they were GIA certified) and the value they have as uncertified diamonds.

In all cases, the buyer is entitled to *consequential* and/or *incidental damages* caused by the breach. These may be any commercially reasonable expenses incurred in the receipt, inspections, transporting, and care of rightfully rejected goods. Section 2-715. These expenses, along with any other damages resulting from the seller's breach, may be deducted from the price still due and owing under the contract. Section 2-717.

The UCC gives these various options for recovery to address the possible commercial situations that arise. The UCC shows its contractual heart by adhering to the goals of certainty. Both parties know the potential consequences of their actions.

IN-CLASS DISCUSSION

Loosely based on *LeSueur Creamery, Inc. v. Haskon, Inc.*, 660 F.2d 342 (8th Cir. 1981).

Finally, your love for cheese and paralegal education have merged! Your supervising attorney comes to you with the following facts and a plate of Wisconsin Cheddar and crackers:

Chester, an artisanal cheese maker, entered into a contract for the purchase of a commercial pasteurizer and related equipment from Louis, who was also to install the machinery. The installation and ongoing maintenance by a professional of the pasteurizing equipment is essential to the manufacture of cheese and achieving the related health standards.

Make an argument both for and against the application of the UCC to this transaction.

Are there any additional facts that would make a difference in the determination? What are they?

Assume that the UCC does cover this transaction. As Chester continued to use the machinery, he discovered that there were defects that reduced the amount of salable cheese Chester was able to produce.

Summary

Article 2 of the Uniform Commercial Code governs the sale of goods between both merchants and non-merchants. Some particular rules apply to dealings between merchants, persons holding themselves out as having particular knowledge or skills in goods involved in the transaction.

Formation. The UCC carves out several exceptions to formation defects that would otherwise render a contract invalid under common law principles:

1. Missing terms do not invalidate an offer.
2. Modifications or counteroffers do not terminate the offer.
3. Firm offers (option contracts) do not require consideration.
4. Silence can operate as acceptance.
5. Warranties are included in the transaction.

A seller can make either express or implied warranties. The implied warranties, unless conspicuously excluded, are merchantability and, if applicable, for a particular purpose.

Further, a buyer may be entitled to a sale on approval or sale or return to protect her interest in the transaction should the goods prove to be unsatisfactory, even if they conform to the contract specifications.

Performance. Once goods have been identified to the contract, the seller is under an obligation to perform and tender delivery. The buyer has the right to inspect the goods to ensure conformance and, if they are found to be unsatisfactory, the seller may have the right to cure the defect.

Breach. Upon improper delivery of nonconforming goods, the buyer may

1. Accept the whole.
2. Reject the whole.
3. Accept any commercial unit and reject the rest.

An acceptance can be revoked if the promise to cure is not performed by the seller. If the buyer chooses to reject the whole, she must state the particular reasons why the goods are being refused and may have the duty to resell the goods if they are perishable. Any action inconsistent with the rejection will operate as an acceptance.

If either the buyer or seller feels insecure about the other party's intentions or ability to perform under the contract, they may request adequate assurances to prevent a breach after shipment has occurred.

Remedies. A seller may refuse to ship goods to an insolvent buyer or request return of goods already shipped under such insolvency. Further, the seller has the following ways to deal with a buyer's breach:

1. Withhold delivery.
2. Stop delivery.
3. Identify and complete manufacture of the goods in order to prepare them for resale or cease production and resell for salvage value.
4. Resell and recover the difference.
5. Recover damages caused by the breach or recover the contract price.
6. Cancel the contract.

Likewise, a buyer has the following remedies:

1. Recover any payments made.
2. "Cover" the loss by purchasing substitute goods.
3. Compel delivery of identified goods.
4. Recover damages caused by the breach.
5. Cancel the contract.

All of the UCC's provisions governing the transactions in goods give certainty and clarity of action to the participants so they may act in good faith in a predictable, commercially reasonable manner.

Key Terms

actions inconsistent with acceptance	cover
adequate assurances	cure
battle of the forms	delivery
commercial unit	duty to resell
conspicuous	express warranty

finish or scrap	nonconformity
firm offer	objection to alteration in terms
good faith obligation	predominant factor test
identification of goods	price under the contract
implied warranty	revocation of previous acceptance
implied warranty for a particular purpose	sale on approval
	sale or return
insolvency	specialized goods
inspection	specify reasons for rejection
limitation of acceptance	spot sale
limitation or exclusion of warranties	tender of delivery
market price	transactions in goods
material alteration	value of goods as accepted
merchantable	warranty
merchants	warranty of title

Review Questions

EXPLAIN YOURSELF

All answers should be written in complete sentences. A simple "yes" or "no" is insufficient.

1. Carl, the used car salesman, assures Polly Packard that the car she is interested in is a "creampuff, "top-of-the-line," "mint condition" automobile. Has he created any warranties? Why or why not?

2. What is the difference between a warranty of merchantability and a warranty for a particular purpose?

3. When can a party seek "adequate assurances"?

4. Marty ordered 100 reams of colored construction paper for his after-school art workshops. Bulk construction paper is shipped in 12-ream bundles (the industry standard). The shipment comes and Marty opens the nine bundles (108 reams). Can he return the extra eight reams? Why or why not?

5. Tommy ordered 12 sushi-grade ahi tuna steaks for service in his restaurant the evening when celebrity Iron Chef Masaharu Morimoto will be dining. Freddy the Fishmonger fails to deliver by 3:00 p.m., the contractually specified time. Explore what damages could possibly be involved.

GO FIGURE

Calculate and explain the proper measure of damages in the following cases.

1. Guido sells Julie an antique watch for $10,000. However, contrary to Guido's assertions, the watch does not keep proper time. The nonfunctioning watch is still beautiful and Julie wishes to keep it.

2. Guido gives Julie quite a deal on a new Relax watch for $10,000. After receiving the watch, Julie discovers the face is defective. She purchases another one just like it from Wally at the cost of $13,575.

3. Julie receives the watch and it's perfect; however, she decides not to pay for it. On the date she receives the watch, its market value is $12,775.

4. Julie unjustly cancels the contract. Guido resells the watch for $8,999.

"FAULTY PHRASES"

All of the following statements are FALSE; state why they are false and then rewrite them as a true statement. Write a brief fact pattern that illustrates your answer.

1. In the battle of the forms, all additional terms become part of the offer unless they are promptly objected to in writing.

2. The purchase of dinner show tickets is always covered under the UCC. The good involved is the ticket.

3. The sale of trees standing on a certain piece of property is not a subject of the UCC because it deals with real estate.

4. As long as the price is mentioned in the contract, the other missing terms do not invalidate the offer under the UCC.

5. Without any other consideration, a merchant can make a firm offer to keep the contract open for six months.

6. All warranties can be disclaimed by the "fine print."

7. A contract can never limit the remedies available to the aggrieved party; everyone is entitled to be made whole.

8. A seller always has the right to try to cure the defect in the goods.

9. A buyer can always reject nonconforming goods.

10. Once a buyer pays for the goods, she has accepted them.

"WRITE" AWAY! PORTFOLIO ASSIGNMENT

Druid will need to enter into many agreements with subcontractors and suppliers in order to complete the work on Carrie's house. Draft a generic "purchase order" for Druid's use. Pay attention to the "between merchants" issues discussed in this chapter.

Case in Point

SCOPE OF UCC'S APPLICATION AND THE PREDOMINANCE TEST "GOODS AND SERVICES"

2013 Ohio 5542
ACTION GROUP, INC., Plaintiff-Appellant,
v.
NANOSTATICS CORPORATION, Defendant-Appellee.
No. 13AP-72
C.P.C. No. 11CVH-02-1991
Court of Appeals of Ohio Tenth Appellate District
Rendered: December 17, 2013

(REGULAR CALENDAR)

DECISION

Owens Law Office, and *Robert M. Owens,* for appellant.
Porter Wright Morris & Arthur, LLP, and *Colleen Marshall,* for appellee.
APPEAL from the Franklin County Court of Common Pleas
KLATT, P.J.

{¶ 1} Appellant, Action Group, Inc., appeals a judgment of the Franklin County Court of Common Pleas in favor of appellee, NanoStatics Corporation. For the following reasons, we affirm in part and reverse in part that judgment.

{¶ 2} NanoStatics is a production volume nanofiber company that creates nanofibers for commercial use. Action Group is a company that specializes in product development, manufacturing, and fulfillment.

{¶ 3} In early 2010, NanoStatics approached Action Group seeking its services in developing and manufacturing certain items, including a "head" and components to support the head. After the initial contact, Action Group's president, Frank Denutte, sent NanoStatics' president and CEO a letter dated February 8, 2010 that stated:

Page 2

I look forward to working with NanoStatics and servicing your needs in the initial research and development stage along with the production stage of your products. Below are research and development hourly rates for the initial development of your project. Labor will be billed at an hourly rate of $60 per hour and $90 per hour for over time hours. We will invoice these hours on a weekly basis until the initial development stage is complete. This hourly rate is significantly lower than our standard rate as we hope to develop a lasting relationship with you on this project. We are a service driven organization and this is a great opportunity to work in the field of nanotechnology. Once the initial development stage is complete, we will price our services at cost plus 30% on the production of your items. Our team is flexible on servicing many different industries and customers and with our teams in the local vicinity, we will be able to work with your organization effectively. Please sign and return this document as it will serve as our agreement on our services provided. . . .

(R. 131.) NanoStatics' president and CEO signed the letter.

{¶ 4} Using NanoStatics' specifications, Action Group worked on multiple iterations of the head. Ultimately, NanoStatics gave Action Group a computer model of a monolithic plastic head that it wanted produced. On September 30, 2010, representatives from NanoStatics visited Action Group's facility to inspect the monolithic plastic head and the supporting components. According to NanoStatics, its representatives determined that the monolithic plastic head had severe defects and was unusable. The NanoStatics representatives also determined that the supporting components did not conform to the tolerances and dimensions that NanoStatics had given Action Group. Due to the defects in the monolithic plastic head, NanoStatics rejected delivery of it. Although NanoStatics accepted delivery of some of the substandard components, it had to modify the design of its system to use those components.

{¶ **5**} On February 11, 2011, Action Group filed a breach-of-contract action against NanoStatics. In the complaint, Action Group alleged that "[NanoStatics] ordered [Action Group] to manufacture certain goods that were timely delivered to [NanoStatics] and accepted by [NanoStatics] without defect." (R. 1 at ¶ 6.) Action Group contended that

Page 3

NanoStatics breached its contract with Action Group by not paying for the goods provided, and that Nano-Statics owed Action Group $96,163.90.[1]

{¶ **6**} NanoStatics answered the complaint and asserted a counterclaim. According to NanoStatics' counterclaim, Action Group promised to develop and manufacture the items that NanoStatics ordered using procedures certified as compliant with ISO 9001:2008. ISO 9001:2008 is an internationally recognized industry standard for quality management systems. It specifies procedures that ensure the consistent production of items that meet customer or government specifications. A certification body may assess the quality management system of a particular company and, if that company has successfully implemented the requirements of ISO 9001:2008, the certification body will certify the company as ISO 9001:2008 compliant. Action Group has an ISO 9001:2008 certification.

{¶ **7**} In its counterclaim, NanoStatics averred that Action Group breached its express warranties that (1) Action Group would comply with its ISO 9001:2008 certified procedures, and (2) the monolithic plastic

head and supporting components would conform to the specifications NanoStatics provided. Additionally, NanoStatics alleged that Action Group's failure to conform to the specifications breached the parties' contract. Finally, NanoStatics claimed that, when Action Group supplied it with defective and nonconforming goods, Action Group breached various implied warranties, including the warranties of merchantability and fitness for a particular purpose.

{¶ **8**} On March 5, 2012, NanoStatics moved to compel full responses to its first set of interrogatories and requests for production. In part, NanoStatics sought discovery related to Action Group's ISO 9001:2008 certification. In response to the interrogatories and production requests related to the ISO 9001:2008 certification, Action Group had simply stated "[n]ot applicable" or "N/A." (R. 55.) Nano-Statics asked the trial court to order Action Group to answer the relevant interrogatories and production requests. Action Group did not respond to NanoStatics' motion to compel.

{¶ **9**} The trial court granted NanoStatics' motion to compel in an order dated April 13, 2012. The trial court required Action Group to provide complete responses to

Page 4

NanoStatics' first set of interrogatories and requests for production by April 26, 2012. The trial court also awarded NanoStatics reasonable attorney fees incurred in pursuing the discovery responses and in preparing and prosecuting the motion to compel. The trial court directed NanoStatics to file and serve an affidavit detailing its attorney fees. The trial court allowed Action Group 14 days to file and serve any objections to the attorney fees set forth in the affidavit.

{¶ **10**} In compliance with the trial court's order, NanoStatics' attorney submitted an affidavit stating that the attorney fees awarded in the April 13, 2012 order amounted to $6,067.50. Action Group did not object, or respond in any way, to the affidavit.

{¶ **11**} Following the trial court's April 13, 2012 order, Action Group provided NanoStatics with a link to an on-line storage site containing more than 300 pages of documents. According to NanoStatics, the vast majority of the 300 pages were neither responsive to the discovery requests nor relevant to

---

[1]Action Group also asserted claims arising from NanoStatics' hiring of a former Action Group employee. The trial court granted NanoStatics summary judgment on those claims, and Action Group does not appeal that ruling.

the case. For example, Action Group supplied Nano-Statics with instructions on how to assemble a door, documents related to work for other customers, and photographs of boxes prepared for shipment to other customers. Significantly, the on-line storage site did not contain requested documents such as Action Group's quality manual; a copy of Action Group's ISO 9001:2008 certificate; design and review notes related to the items manufactured for NanoStatics; internal communications regarding design issues, inspection, and testing records; or records for any of the raw materials purchased for use in the manufacture of the relevant items.

{¶ 12} In a letter dated May 8, 2012, NanoStatics' attorney informed Action Group's attorney of the deficiencies in Action Group's discovery responses. The letter contained a list of the documents that Nano-Statics sought, but Action Group had not provided. Action Group's attorney replied that "[m]y client says to the extent that documents exist on your request list, you have them already." (R. 91.)

{¶ 13} When NanoStatics' attorney deposed Frank Denutte, Action Group's president, she discovered that not only did many of the requested documents exist, but also that Denutte had no explanation for Action Group's failure to produce them. Denutte admitted that Action Group had an ISO 9001:2008 certificate, which hung in Action Group's lobby. The following colloquy about Action Group's certificate ensued:

Page 5

> Q: If you have a certificate, do you know why you have failed to produce it?
> A: No.
> Q: Can you produce it?
> A: I would assume so.
> Q: Why haven't you produced it?
> A: I don't have an answer.

(R. 95 at 63.)

{¶ 14} Denutte also acknowledged that Action Group had a quality manual. When asked why Action Group had not provided its quality manual to Nano-Statics, Denutte answered, "Same answer as before. I don't know." (R. 95 at 73.)

{¶ 15} On July 9, 2012, NanoStatics moved for dismissal of Action Group's claims because Action Group had failed to comply with the April 13, 2012 order compelling it to fully respond to NanoStatics' discovery requests. Citing to Denutte's deposition testimony, NanoStatics argued that Action Group's defiance of the April 13, 2012 order was willful and in bad faith.

{¶ 16} In its memorandum contra NanoStatics' motion to dismiss, Action Group first argued that it had turned over its quality manual. According to Action Group, NanoStatics introduced the quality manual as an exhibit during Denutte's deposition and used the manual to question Denutte. Next, Action Group blamed its discovery failures on Denutte's bout with multiple myeloma, which severely incapacitated him from May 2011 to June 2012.

{¶ 17} At the same time it responded to NanoStatics' motion to dismiss, Action Group moved for reconsideration of the portion of the April 13, 2012 order that awarded NanoStatics its attorney fees. Action Group advanced Denutte's illness as the basis for reconsidering that order and relieving Action Group of the obligation to pay the fees.

{¶ 18} In its reply to Action Group's memorandum contra and motion to reconsider, NanoStatics accused Action Group of misrepresenting the record. NanoStatics asserted that, despite Action Group's contention otherwise, Action Group had not produced its quality manual. The deposition exhibit that Action Group claimed was

Page 6

its quality manual was actually a copy of the ISO 9001:2008 requirements that was licensed to NanoStatics. Because NanoStatics did not know the specific procedures adopted in Action Group's quality manual, NanoStatics' attorney instead questioned Denutte using the universal standard set forth in the ISO 9001:2008 requirements.

{¶ 19} NanoStatics also attacked Action Group's claim that Denutte's illness was the cause of Action Group's failure to respond to NanoStatics' discovery requests. NanoStatics pointed out that Denutte testified during his deposition that Tracy Garner, Action Group's vice president and general manager, had access to the disputed documents and should have provided them to Action Group's attorney. Garner was the point person for ensuring that Action Group complied with the ISO 9001:2008 requirements. NanoStatics thus argued that Action Group could not rely on Denutte's illness as an excuse for failing to produce documents that Garner regularly worked with and relied on.

{¶ 20} In a decision and entry dated October 10, 2012, the trial court granted NanoStatics' motion to dismiss and denied Action Group's motion for reconsideration. The trial court found that documents that NanoStatics had requested existed, and that Action Group had failed to produce those documents. The trial court also found that Action Group had not offered any legitimate or reasonable explanation for its failure to provide the documents. In addition to dismissing Action Group's claims, the trial court ordered Action Group to pay the costs and attorney fees NanoStatics incurred for the preparation of the motion to dismiss, as well as the costs and attorney fees related to Action Group's failure to properly respond to discovery and its failure to obey the April 13, 2012 order.

{¶ 21} After the issuance of the October 10, 2012 decision and entry, NanoStatics' attorney submitted an affidavit stating that the attorney fees generated from dealing with discovery deficiencies and briefing NanoStatics' motion to dismiss totaled $15,379.25. Although Action Group had not responded to NanoStatics' attorney's first affidavit in support of attorney fees, it responded to the second. Action Group argued that NanoStatics sought fees for work that was not related to dealing with Action Group's discovery violations, and that the fees sought might be excessive. Action Group asked the trial court to deny NanoStatics its attorney fees or, alternatively, to hold a hearing to determine the appropriate amount of fees.

Page 7

{¶ 22} On November 16, 2012, NanoStatics moved for summary judgment on its counterclaim. NanoStatics cited two reasons justifying summary judgment. First, NanoStatics argued that the trial court should grant it summary judgment as a sanction for Action Group's discovery violations. Second, NanoStatics argued that it deserved summary judgment under the Civ.R. 56 standard. With regard to its claims for breach of the implied warranties, NanoStatics asserted that undisputed evidence established

that the monolithic plastic head was defective and that the head's defects rendered it unusable. Thus, NanoStatics contended, in manufacturing a head unfit for any use, Action Group breached the implied warranties of merchantability, as set forth in R.C. 1302.27, and fitness for a particular purpose, as set forth in R.C. 1302.28. NanoStatics also argued that the evidence established that Action Group had impliedly and expressly warranted that it would adhere to its ISO 9001:2008 certified procedures when developing and manufacturing the monolithic plastic head and the supporting components. Because Action Group admittedly did not follow those procedures, it breached those implied and express warranties.

{¶ 23} Action Group responded that the trial court had already sanctioned it for its failure to produce discovery and no additional sanction was warranted. As for NanoStatics' argument that it was entitled to summary judgment under Civ.R. 56, Action Group asserted that NanoStatics could not recover on its claims because they were based on Ohio's version of the Uniform Commercial Code ("UCC"), which did not govern the parties' contract. Action Group contended that the provision of services, not the sale of goods, was the predominant purpose of the parties' contract. As the UCC only applies to contracts for the sale of goods, Action Group maintained that NanoStatics could not establish any claim based on UCC provisions.

{¶ 24} In a decision granting NanoStatics' motion, the trial court concluded that NanoStatics was entitled to summary judgment pursuant to Civ.R. 56. The trial court issued a judgment, dated December 28, 2012, entering summary judgment for NanoStatics and ordering Action Group to pay $102,200 in damages and $21,446 in attorney fees.

{¶ 25} Action Group now appeals the December 28, 2012 judgment, and it assigns the following errors:

Page 8

[1.] The trial court did not issue a final appealable order.

[2.] The trial court erred by dismissing Action Group's claims.

[3.] The trial court erred by granting summary judgment in favor of NanoStatics.

[4.] The trial court erred by awarding attorneys' fees to NanoStatics.

{¶ 26} By Action Group's first assignment of error, it argues that the December 28, 2012 judgment is not a final, appealable order. Action Group first raised this argument in a motion, which we considered and denied. Accordingly, we overrule Action Group's first assignment of error.

{¶ 27} By Action Group's second assignment of error, it argues that the trial court erred in dismissing its claims as a discovery sanction. We disagree.

{¶ 28} Two Ohio Rules of Civil Procedure authorize the dismissal of claims for the failure to comply with a court order. Civ. R. 37(B)(2)(c) allows dismissal after a violation of an order to compel discovery:

> If any party . . . fails to obey an order to provide or permit discovery, including an order made under subdivision (A) of this rule . . . , the court in which the action is pending may make such orders in regard to the failure as are just, and among others the following: . . . (c) . . . [D]ismissing the action or proceeding or any part thereof[.]

Civ.R. 41(B)(1) permits a trial court to dismiss an action or claim where a plaintiff fails to comply with any court order, whether related to discovery or not.

{¶ 29} The decision to dismiss under Civ.R. 37(B)(2)(c) and 41(B)(1) is within the sound discretion of the trial court. *Quonset Hut, Inc. v. Ford Motor Co.*, 80 Ohio St. 3d 46, 47 (1997); *Toney v. Berkemer*, 6 Ohio St. 3d 455, 458 (1983). However, that discretion must be cautiously exercised. *Quonset Hut, Inc.* at 48. Before dismissing claims for violation of a discovery order, a trial court must find that the failure to comply is due to willfulness, bad faith, or any fault of the plaintiff. *Toney* at 458. Appellate courts will

Page 9

affirm the dismissal "when 'the conduct of a party is so negligent, irresponsible, contumacious or dilatory as to provide substantial grounds for a dismissal with prejudice for a failure to . . . obey a court order.'" *Quonset Hut, Inc.* at 48, quoting *Tokles & Son, Inc. v. Midwestern Indemn. Co.*, 65 Ohio St. 3d 621, 632 (1992).

{¶ 30} Here, Action Group argues that its violation of the order compelling discovery is not its fault, but instead, a consequence of Denutte's battle with cancer. We, like the trial court, reject this argument. Although Denutte may not have been well enough to collect the documents requested by NanoStatics, nothing precluded Action Group's vice president and general manager, Tracy Garner, from doing so. In his deposition, Denutte identified Garner as the person responsible for gathering documents responsive to NanoStatics' discovery requests. Now, on appeal, Action Group defends Garner's failure to carry out that responsibility by claiming that Garner did not have the comprehensive knowledge of Action Group's records that Denutte had.

{¶ 31} First, we doubt that Garner's lack of knowledge caused the discovery failures. In his deposition, Garner denied knowing that NanoStatics had requested a copy of Action Group's quality manual. Thus, it appears that poor communication, not lack of knowledge, led to the incomplete document production.

{¶ 32} Even if we accept Action Group's excuse as true, it does not entirely explain why Action Group failed to comply with the discovery order. Garner did not need Denutte's knowledge to locate the ISO 9001:2008 certificate hanging in Action Group's lobby or the quality manual in Garner's office. Nothing impeded Garner from providing a copy of those documents to Action Group's attorney so he could produce them in response to NanoStatics' discovery requests.

{¶ 33} Moreover, Denutte had resumed working at the time of his June 26, 2012 deposition. During that deposition, NanoStatics' attorney directly informed Denutte that it had requested Action Group's ISO 9001:2008 certificate and quality manual. Denutte promised to produce the quality manual within "two weeks, max." (R. 95 at 74.) Action Group's subsequent failure to deliver that document or, for that matter, other responsive documents, cannot be blamed on Denutte's illness.

{¶ 34} Based on the evidence in the record, we find that, at best, Action Group did not take its obligation to comply with the trial court's discovery order seriously. At worst,

Page 10

Action Group showed outright contempt for the order by supplying NanoStatics with hundreds of pages of irrelevant records and informing NanoStatics that it had produced all responsive documents, when it had not. Given Action Group's pattern of noncompliance and obfuscation, we conclude that the trial court did not abuse its discretion in dismissing Action Group's claims as a discovery sanction. Accordingly, we overrule Action Group's second assignment of error.

{¶ 35} By Action Group's third assignment of error, it argues that the trial court erred in granting NanoStatics summary judgment on its claims. We agree.

{¶ 36} Initially, we must address NanoStatics' contention that the trial court appropriately granted summary judgment as a discovery sanction. NanoStatics may have requested summary judgment as a Civ. R. 37(B)(2) sanction, but the trial court did not grant summary judgment on that basis. The trial court, instead, relied solely on Civ. R. 56 when deciding NanoStatics' motion for summary judgment. Consequently, in advocating before this court that summary judgment is appropriate under Civ. R. 37(B)(2), NanoStatics wants this court to expand the discovery sanction imposed by the trial court to include a judgment in NanoStatics' favor on its claims. We decline to do so. In this matter, we are tasked with reviewing the trial court's ruling, not deciding in the first instance matters left to the trial court's sound discretion. Thus, we turn to reviewing whether NanoStatics deserved summary judgment under Civ. R. 56.

{¶ 37} A trial court will grant summary judgment under Civ. R. 56 when the moving party demonstrates that: (1) there is no genuine issue of material fact; (2) the moving party is entitled to judgment as a matter of law; and (3) reasonable minds can come to but one conclusion when viewing the evidence most strongly in favor of the nonmoving party, and that conclusion is adverse to the nonmoving party. *Hudson v. Petrosurance, Inc.*, 127 Ohio St. 3d 54, 2010-Ohio-4505, ¶ 29; *Sinnott v. Aqua-Chem, Inc.*, 116 Ohio St. 3d 158, 2007-Ohio-5584, ¶ 29. Appellate review of a trial court's ruling on a motion for summary judgment is de novo. *Hudson* at ¶ 29. This means that an appellate court conducts an independent review, without deference to the trial court's determination.

Zurz v. 770 W. Broad AGA, L.L.C., 192 Ohio App. 3d 521, 2011-Ohio-832, ¶ 5 (10th Dist.); *White v. Westfall*, 183 Ohio App. 3d 807, 2009-Ohio-4490, ¶ 6 (10th Dist.).

Page 11

{¶ 38} Here, Action Group argues that the parties' contract is not governed by the UCC, and thus, it urges us to reverse the grant of summary judgment for NanoStatics on its UCC claims. Article Two of the UCC, adopted in Ohio as R.C. 1302.01 to 1302.98, applies to transactions for the sale of goods, not to service contracts. R.C. 1302.02; *Tubelite Co. v. Original Sign Studio, Inc.*, 176 Ohio App. 3d 241, 2008-Ohio-1905, ¶ 12 (10th Dist.); *Fox & Lamberth Ents., Inc. v. Craftsman Home Improvement*, 2d Dist. No. 21060, 2006-Ohio-1427, ¶ 25. Action Group contends that its contract with NanoStatics is a contract for services, not a contract for goods, so the UCC does not apply.

{¶ 39} In reply, NanoStatics asserts that whether the UCC is applicable is irrelevant. Regardless of the law applied, NanoStatics argues, it is entitled to summary judgment because Action Group supplied it with defective products. This argument would have been persuasive had NanoStatics supported it with law showing that the receipt of defective products entitles a party to recovery under both the UCC and common law. NanoStatics, however, points only to UCC provisions—R.C. 1302.27 (implied warranty of merchantability) and R.C. 1302.28 (implied warranty of fitness for a particular purpose)—to support its contention that the supply of defective products justifies summary judgment in its favor. Neither NanoStatics' motion for summary judgment nor its appellate brief identifies any other legal basis for recovery due to the receipt of defective goods. In order to prevail on any defective-goods claim, therefore, NanoStatics must establish that the UCC applies.

{¶ 40} A review of the parties' contract reveals that it is neither a contract solely for goods nor a contract solely for services, but a contract for both goods and services. The contract contemplates a "research and development stage," during which Action Group would provide NanoStatics with services, and a "production stage," during which Action Group would provide NanoStatics with goods. The parties, therefore, entered into hybrid transaction.

{¶ **41**} Despite the plain language of the contract, Action Group denies that the parties' transaction involved any sale of goods. Action Group argues that the contract does not include the sale of goods because it does not identify the specific goods purchased. Action Group also argues that the contract's failure to comply with the UCC's statute of frauds demonstrates that the parties did not intend for the contract to fall under

Page 12

the UCC. Action Group failed to make either of these arguments in the trial court. Generally, a party waives the right to raise an argument on appeal it could have raised, but did not, in earlier proceedings. *Niskanen v. Giant Eagle, Inc.*, 122 Ohio St. 3d 486, 2009-Ohio-3626, ¶ 34. Because Action Group did not assert its arguments before the trial court, it cannot now raise them on appeal.

{¶ **42**} When presented with a hybrid contract, Ohio courts, like the majority of courts, follow the predominant-purpose test to determine whether or not the UCC applies. *Carcorp, Inc. v. Chesrown Oldsmobile-GMC Truck, Inc.*, 159 Ohio App. 3d 87, 2004-Ohio-5946, ¶ 21 (10th Dist.); *DeHoff v. Veterinary Hosp. Operations of Cent. Ohio, Inc.*, 10th Dist. No. 02AP-454, 2003-Ohio-3334, ¶ 73. The predominant-purpose test examines "'whether the predominant factor and purpose of the contract is the rendition of service, with goods incidentally involved, or whether the contract is for the sale of goods, with labor incidentally involved.'" *Carcorp, Inc.* at ¶ 21, quoting *Allied Indus. Serv. Corp. v. Kasle Iron & Metals, Inc.*, 62 Ohio App. 2d 144, 147 (6th Dist. 1977). This test requires consideration of both the contractual language and extrinsic evidence, such as the circumstances surrounding the contract formation and the parties' performance of the contract. *Cranpark, Inc. v. Rogers Group, Inc.*, 498 Fed. Appx. 563, 568 (6th Cir. 2012); *Arlington Elec. Constr. v. Schindler Elevator Corp.*, 6th Dist. No. L-91-102 (Mar. 6, 1992); *accord* 1A Anderson, *Uniform Commercial Code*, Section 2-105:113 (3d Ed. 1996) ("As the making of the determination that a hybrid contract is predominantly a contract for the goods or predominantly for services requires what is basically a quantitative analysis, it is necessary

for the court to consider all circumstances of the case, the commercial or non-commercial setting in which the case arises, as well as the terms of the contract itself.").

{¶ **43**} Generally, whether a hybrid contract is predominately a contract for goods or services presents a factual question. *Mecanique C.N.C., Inc. v. Durr Environmental, Inc.*, 304 F. Supp. 2d 971, 976 (S.D. Ohio 2004); *Corporex Dev. & Constr. Mgt., Inc. v. Shook, Inc.*, 10th Dist. No. 03AP-269, 2004-Ohio-1408, ¶ 50, *rev'd on other grounds*, 106 Ohio St. 3d 412, 2005-Ohio-5409; *Valleaire Golf Club, Inc. v. Conrad*, 9th Dist. No. 03CA0006-M, 2003-Ohio-6575, ¶ 6. Where, however, there are no disputed facts for a fact finder to decide, it is proper for a trial court to rule as a matter of law on whether the

Page 13

contract is covered by Article Two of the UCC. *Mecanique C.N.C., Inc.* at 976-77; *Corporex Dev. & Constr. Mgt., Inc.* at ¶ 50-51; *Conrad* at ¶ 6.

{¶ **44**} Here, the parties do not identify any disputed facts relative to the question of whether the provision of goods or services predominates. Therefore, we must determine, as a matter law, the parties' primary purpose. After considering the contract and the testimony of Action Group's president and NanoStatics' president and CEO, we conclude that the parties' overall objective was the production of goods, i.e., the head and its supporting components. Those goods were what NanoStatics ultimately wanted and what Action Group promised to deliver.

{¶ **45**} True, Action Group performed a substantial amount of services for NanoStatics in the development of the head and components. However,

> virtually all commercial goods involve some type of service, 'whether design, assembly, installation, or manufacture.' . . . The mere fact that a manufacturer utilizes its effort and expertise in producing a good does not mean that the buyer is purchasing those services instead of the good itself. The question is whether the purchaser's ultimate goal is to acquire a product or procure a service.

Mecanique C.N.C., Inc. at 977, quoting *Neibarger v. Universal Coops., Inc.*, 439 Mich. 512, 536 (1992).

Therefore, spending significant time and resources to design or engineer the product sold does not transform a contract for goods into a contract for services. *BMC Industries, Inc. v. Barth Industries, Inc.*, 160 F.3d 1322, 1332 (11th Cir. 1998); *Republic Steel Corp. v. Pennsylvania Eng. Corp.*, 785 F.2d 174, 181 (7th Cir. 1986).

{¶ 46} Moreover, our conclusion is influenced by the way Action Group described its contract with NanoStatics in its complaint. How the parties characterize their contract is a factor that a court can consider in determining whether goods or services predominate. *Bamcor LLC v. Jupiter Aluminum Corp.*, 767 F. Supp. 2d 959, 972 (N.D. Ind. 2011); *Mitchell v. Speedy Car-X, Inc.*, 127 Ohio App.3d 229, 232 (9th Dist. 1998). In considering that factor, we find it significant that, in its complaint, Action Group portrayed the parties' contract as one for the manufacture of goods, not the rendition of services. (R. 1 at ¶ 4.) The complaint also alleged that NanoStatics ordered Action Group to manufacture goods, and that Action Group sought payment "for manufactured goods as requested by and delivered to [NanoStatics]." (R. 1 at ¶ 6, 40.)

Page 14

Thus, despite the hybrid nature of the parties' contract, Action Group initially characterized its dealings with NanoStatics as solely a transaction for the sale of goods.

{¶ 47} We recognize that Action Group later denied NanoStatics' averment in its counterclaim that the head and components were goods within the meaning of R.C. 1302.01(A)(8). Nevertheless, before NanoStatics introduced the question of the UCC's applicability, Action Group construed the contract as one for the provision of goods, not services.

{¶ 48} As the parties' contract is predominantly a contract for goods, the UCC applies. We thus turn to the question of whether NanoStatics met its burden under Civ.R. 56 to prove its entitlement to summary judgment on its UCC claims.

{¶ 49} As we stated above, NanoStatics sought and received summary judgment on its claims for breach of the implied warranties of merchantability and fitness for a particular purpose. NanoStatics argues that it is entitled to summary judgment on

both claims because Action Group supplied it with defective, unusable goods. However, NanoStatics has failed to present proof that it is entitled to summary judgment on its breach of implied warranty claims.

{¶ 50} We will first address NanoStatics' claim for breach of the implied warranty of merchantability. Pursuant to R.C. 1302.27(A), "[u]nless excluded or modified as provided in section 1302.29 of the Revised Code, a warranty that the goods shall be merchantable is implied in a contract for their sale if the seller is a merchant with respect to goods of that kind." R.C. 1302.27(B) sets forth the minimum criteria that goods must meet in order to be merchantable. Any failure of the goods to comply with the criteria set forth in R.C. 1302.27(B) is a breach of the implied warranty of merchantability.

{¶ 51} NanoStatics has not identified which of the six criteria the monolithic plastic head and supporting components failed to satisfy. However, of the six criteria, only the third arguably applies. Under that criterion, to be merchantable, goods must be "fit for the ordinary purposes for which such goods are used." R.C. 3102.27(B)(3). This criterion expresses a fundamental concept in the meaning of merchantability. UCC Official Comment, Section 2-314, Comment 8 (1961); 1 Hawkland & Rusch, *Uniform Commercial Code Series*, Section 2-314:3.

Page 15

{¶ 52} To show a breach of the third criterion, a plaintiff must first identify the ordinary purpose of the goods purchased. *Koken v. Black & Veatch Constr., Inc.*, 426 F.3d 39, 51 (1st Cir. 2005); *Bethlehem Steel Corp. v. Chicago E. Corp.*, 863 F.2d 508, 514-15 (7th Cir. 1988); *Elvig v. Nintendo of Am., Inc.*, D. Colo. No. 08-cv-02616-MSK-MEH (Sept. 23, 2010). "[T]he ordinary purposes for which goods are used . . . go to uses which are customarily made of the goods in question." UCC Official Comment, Section 2-315, Comment 2 (1961); *accord Koken* at 51; *Doll v. Ford Motor Co.*, 814 F. Supp. 2d 526, 544 (D. Md. 2011); *Conveyor Co. v. SunSource Technology Servs., Inc.*, 398 F. Supp. 2d 992, 1002 (N.D. Iowa 2005). Here, NanoStatics did not present any evidence explaining how the monolithic plastic head and supporting components worked, what they did, or their purpose. The record, therefore, contains no evidence of the ordinary, customary use of the head and components.

{¶ **53**} Moreover, given the evidence in the record, we question whether the head and components even have an ordinary purpose. The president of Action Group indicated in his deposition that the items Action Group manufactured for NanoStatics had never been manufactured before. Under such circumstances, the goods could not have any ordinary purpose, and thus, the implied warranty of merchantability based on fitness for ordinary purposes could not arise. *Norcold, Inc. v. Gateway Supply Co.*, 154 Ohio App. 3d 594, 2003-Ohio-4252, ¶ 23 (3d Dist.) (when no one had previously manufactured the parts at issue, "'no average or usual standards for determining ordinary performance or quality for the components can be determined'"); *accord Binks Mfg. Co. v. Natl. Presto Industries, Inc.*, 709 F.2d 1109, 1121-22 (7th Cir. 1983) (because the goods at issue were unlike any other goods previously manufactured, there was no ordinary purpose for the goods and no implied warranty of merchantability could exist); *Price Bros. Co. v. Philadelphia Gear Corp.*, 649 F.2d 416, 424 (6th Cir. 1981) (same).

{¶ **54**} In any event, NanoStatics has not come forward with any evidence regarding the ordinary purpose of the head and components. Such evidence is necessary to establish a breach of the standard of merchantability set forth in R.C. 1302.27(B)(3). Consequently, the trial court erred in granting Nano-Statics summary judgment on its claim for breach of the implied warranty of merchantability.

Page 16

{¶ **55**} We next consider NanoStatics' claim for breach of the implied warranty of fitness for a particular purpose. Under R.C. 1302.28,

[w]here the seller at the time of contracting has reason to know any particular purpose for which the goods are required and that the buyer is relying on the seller's skill or judgment to select or furnish suitable goods, there is unless excluded or modified under section 1302.29 of the Revised Code an implied warranty that the goods shall be fit for such purpose.

For an implied warranty of fitness for a particular purpose to arise, (1) the seller must have reason to know the buyer's particular purpose, (2) the seller must have reason to know that the buyer is relying on the seller's skill or judgment to select or furnish appropriate goods, and (3) the buyer must, in fact, rely on the seller's skill or judgment. *EBCO Mfg. Co. v. Eaton Corp.*, 10th Dist. No. 94APE08-1147 (Apr. 20, 1995); *Hollingsworth v. Software House, Inc.*, 32 Ohio App. 3d 61, 65 (2d Dist. 1986). "The heart of the concept is the justifiable reliance by the buyer on the seller's skill or judgment in providing goods for the buyer's special needs." Hawkland & Rusch, *Uniform Commercial Code Series*, Section 2-315:1.

{¶ **56**} In the case at bar, NanoStatics produced no evidence that it relied on Action Group's skill or judgment to provide it with appropriate products for its particular purpose. With regard to the monolithic plastic head, the evidence actually suggests the opposite. According to Action Group's president, Action Group constructed the monolithic plastic head by following a computer model provided by NanoStatics. When a buyer gives precise and complete specifications to the seller, the warranty of fitness for a particular purpose does not normally arise. *New Jersey Transit Corp. v. Harsco Corp.*, 497 F.3d 323, 329 (3d Cir. 2007); *Bethlehem Steel Corp.*, 863 F.2d at 516; *Lesnefsky v. Fischer & Porter Co.*, 527 F. Supp. 951, 956-57 (E.D. Penn. 1981); UCC Official Comment, Section 2-316, Comment 9; 3A Anderson, *Uniform Commercial Code*, Section 2-315:134 (3d Ed. 2002). In that situation, the buyer eschews reliance on the seller's skill or judgment to furnish the appropriate goods and, instead, requires the seller to follow the buyer's own judgment regarding what goods would best serve its purposes. *Bethlehem Steel Corp.* at 516; Anderson, Section 2-315:134.

{¶ **57**} Here, the evidence does not disclose the specificity of the computer model. Consequently, we cannot determine to what degree, if any, NanoStatics depended on

Page 17

Action Group to exercise its own judgment in manufacturing the monolithic plastic head. If the computer model left any construction details to Action

Group's discretion, NanoStatics could conceivably produce evidence that it relied on Action Group's skill and judgment to appropriately exercise that discretion. Nevertheless, at this stage in the proceedings, the record does not contain evidence establishing NanoStatics' reliance. The trial court, therefore, erred in granting NanoStatics summary judgment on its claim for breach of the implied warranty of fitness for a particular purpose.

{¶ 58} Now that we have addressed the claims based on the receipt of defective goods, we turn to NanoStatics' claims that Action Group breached implied and express warranties by failing to follow its ISO 9001:2008 certified processes. Like the defective-goods claims, the ISO claims lack sufficient evidentiary support.

{¶ 59} First, NanoStatics argues that Action Group breached an implied warranty that it would comply with its ISO 9001:2008 certified processes when manufacturing NanoStatics' goods. NanoStatics, however, does not identify any law or facts that establish such an implied warranty. Based on the facts of this case, we cannot see how such a warranty fits with either the implied warranties of merchantability or fitness for a particular purpose. Other implied warranties may exist. R.C. 1302.27(C) states that, "[u]nless excluded or modified as provided in section 1302.29 of the Revised Code, other implied warranties may arise from course of dealing or usage of trade." Conceivably, NanoStatics could prove that members of Action Group's trade regularly adhere to their ISO 9001:2008 certified processes, thus proving an implied warranty of ISO compliance. However, based on the evidence currently in the record, NanoStatics has not demonstrated any such implied warranty. The trial court, therefore, erred in granting NanoStatics summary judgment on its claim for breach of implied warranty.

{¶ 60} NanoStatics also argues that Action Group breached an express warranty that it would follow its ISO 9001:2008 certified processes when manufacturing NanoStatics' goods. R.C. 1302.26 sets forth three ways in which an express warranty may arise. Although NanoStatics does not specify which of the three ways applies here, only the first fits the facts that NanoStatics relies on. Under that way, "[a]ny affirmation of fact or promise made by the seller to the buyer which relates to the goods and becomes part of the basis of the bargain creates an express warranty that the goods shall conform to the

Page 18

affirmation or promise." R.C. 1302.26(A)(1). A seller does not need to use formal words such as "warrant" or "guarantee" to create a warranty. R.C. 1302.26(B). Any affirmation by the seller that forms the basis of the bargain may establish an express warranty. *Slyman v. Pickwick Farms*, 15 Ohio App. 3d 25, 27-28 (10th Dist. 1984). An affirmation forms the basis of the bargain if it "goes to the heart of the basic assumption between the parties." *Bobb Forest Prods., Inc. v. Morbark Industries, Inc.*, 151 Ohio App. 3d 63, 2002-Ohio-5370, ¶ 49 (7th Dist.).

{¶ 61} Here, if Action Group affirmed or promised that it would manufacture NanoStatics' goods using its ISO 9001:2008 certified processes, then an express warranty to that effect would arise. NanoStatics presented evidence that Action Group's website, business cards, and letterhead all state that Action Group is an ISO 9001:2008 certified company. Yet, the record contains no evidence that any Action Group representative told a NanoStatics representative that Action Group would be following its ISO 9001:2008 processes in manufacturing NanoStatics' goods. NanoStatics' president and CEO instead merely testified that he "fully expected that in its work on behalf of NanoStatics Action Group would follow the ISO certified processes." (R. 131 at ¶ 6.)[2]

{¶ 62} A buyer's understanding or expectation does not give rise to an express warranty. *Dow Corning Corp. v. Weather Shield Mfg., Inc.*, 790 F. Supp. 2d 604, 611 (E.D. Mich. 2011); 3A Anderson, *Uniform Commercial Code*, Section 2-313:45 (3d Ed. 2002). "As there must be a statement by the seller before it is necessary to determine whether that statement is a part of the basis of the bargain, it follows that the subjective beliefs of the buyer that are never

---

[2]In his deposition, Action Group's president seems to state that the ISO 9001:2008 certified processes apply only to mass production, not the manufacture of first-article goods like the goods produced for NanoStatics. Whether this is true or merely the president's belief, it explains the absence of any affirmation or promise from Action Group that it would follow the ISO 9001:2008 certified processes when fabricating the monolithic plastic head and supporting components.

communicated to the seller cannot be a part of the basis of the bargain." *Id.* Applying that rule here, we conclude that NanoStatics' president and CEO's expectation cannot create an express warranty. In the absence of an affirmation or promise that Action Group would manufacture NanoStatics' products in accordance with the ISO 9001:2008 certified processes, no express warranty to that effect could arise. The record contains no evidence of such an affirmation or promise. Accordingly, the trial

Page 19

court erred in granting NanoStatics summary judgment on its claim for breach of express warranty.

{¶ 63} In sum, we conclude that NanoStatics is not entitled to summary judgment on any of the grounds argued. Accordingly, we sustain Action Group's third assignment of error.

{¶ 64} By Action Group's fourth assignment of error, it argues that the trial court erred in granting NanoStatics attorney fees. For the most part, we find that the trial court did not err as alleged. To the extent that the trial court did err, that error did not prejudice Action Group.

{¶ 65} The trial court awarded NanoStatics attorney fees in two instances: (1) when it granted Nano-Statics' motion for an order to compel, and (2) when it granted NanoStatics' motion for dismissal as a discovery sanction. In each instance, after the trial court made the award, NanoStatics' attorney submitted affidavits setting forth her calculation of the amount of fees owed. The first affidavit lists that the amount owed as $6,067.50, and the second lists $15,379.25, for a total of $21,446.75. In its December 28, 2012 judgment entry, the trial court ordered Action Group to pay "$21,446.00 in attorneys' fees previously awarded by the Court." (R. 139.)

{¶ 66} Initially, we must address Action Group's argument that the December 28, 2012 judgment does not unambiguously award NanoStatics $21,446 in attorney fees. Action Group takes issue with the trial court's statement that attorney fees were "previously awarded," when the trial court had not previously determined any amount of attorney fees owed. We find this argument disingenuous. In its April 13, 2012 and October 10, 2012 entries, the trial court indisputably awarded attorneys fees, even if it did not state the

amount of those fees. In the December 28, 2012 judgment, the trial court set the amount of attorney fees "previously awarded" at $21,446. No ambiguity exists.

{¶ 67} Action Group next argues that the trial court erred in granting NanoStatics any attorney fees at all. We disagree.

{¶ 68} Pursuant to Civ.R. 37(A)(4), a trial court is generally required to award reasonable expenses incurred, including attorney fees, to the party who prevails on a motion for an order compelling discovery. *Cryer v. Cryer*, 10th Dist. No. 07AP-546, 2008-Ohio-26, ¶ 31; *Stratman v. Sutantio*, 10th Dist. No. 05AP-1260, 2006-Ohio-4712,

Page 20

¶ 29. Likewise, under Civ. R. 37(B)(2), a court is generally required to order the party who fails to obey a discovery order to pay the opposing party's reasonable expenses, including attorney fees. *Bellamy v. Montgomery,* 10th Dist. No. 11AP-1059, 2012-Ohio-4304, ¶ 11. Under both Civ. R. 37(A)(4) and 37(B)(2), a trial court may forego an award of attorney fees only if the court finds that the uncooperative party's actions are substantially justified or other circumstances make the award unjust. An appellate court reviews an award of attorney fees under either Civ. R. 37(A)(4) or 37(B)(2) for an abuse of discretion. *Bellamy* at ¶ 7; *Pegram v. Painter,* 5th Dist. No. 09 CA 59, 2010-Ohio-2934, ¶ 40.

{¶ 69} Here, Action Group argues that its president's ill health makes the award of attorney fees in the order to compel unjust. Parties generally assert such an argument as a reason to deny a motion for a discovery sanction. However, it could also serve as a reason why a trial court might decline to award attorney fees in an order to compel. If an extended illness of a key employee impacted the employer's ability to collect and transmit discovery, that illness could make an award of attorney fees unjust. We, however, find that argument unavailing here. As we stated above, the trial court rejected Action Group's illness excuse, and we concur with that rejection. We thus find no error in the trial court's decision to award NanoStatics attorney fees in the order to compel.

{¶ 70} We next turn to the award of attorney fees in the dismissal entry. Action Group did not address in its memorandum contra the request for attorney fees incorporated into NanoStatics' motion for dismissal. After NanoStatics' attorney filed an affidavit setting forth her calculation of the amount of attorney fees owed under the dismissal entry, Action Group only challenged the amount, not the appropriateness, of the attorney-fee award. A party who fails to raise an argument before the trial court waives the right to make that argument on appeal. *Niskanen,* 122 Ohio St. 3d 486, 2009-Ohio-3626, at ¶ 34. Because Action Group did not attack the appropriateness of the attorney-fee award before the trial court, it cannot undertake such an attack on appeal.

{¶ **71**} As a final matter, Action Group argues that the trial court erred in not articulating how it arrived at the amount of attorney fees to award NanoStatics. Action Group correctly states that the trial court did not state the evidentiary basis for its award. Nevertheless, the record contains evidence—namely, the affidavits of NanoStatics' attorney—that justify the amount awarded. The first affidavit states:

Page 21

13. . . . I reviewed all invoices related to this matter, calculating time reasonably connected to dealing with the discovery deficiencies and preparing NanoStatics' Motion to Compel and for Sanctions at $6,067.50. . . .
14. Given the amount of work performed[,] the level of experience of those who performed the work, [and] the nature and the complexity of pursuing resolution to this matter, $6,067.50 is a reasonable amount of attorneys' fees.

(R. 79.) The second affidavit states:

10. . . . I reviewed all invoices related to this matter, calculating time reasonably connected to dealing with the discovery deficiencies and briefing NanoStatics' Motion to Dismiss at $15,379.25. . . .
11. Given the amount of work performed[,] the level of experience of those who performed the work, [and] the nature and the complexity of pursuing resolution to this matter, $15,379.25 is a reasonable amount of attorneys' fees.

(R. 125.) The amounts listed in the two affidavits—$6,067.50 and $15,379.25—total $21,446.75. NanoStatics' attorney attached to each affidavit a table with entries that specify the date on which the work was performed, the name of the attorney that performed the work, the number of hours worked, the amount charged for those hours, and a description of the work performed.

{¶ **72**} We do not find persuasive Action Group's argument that the trial court did not rely on the affidavits and their attachments to determine the amount of attorney fees. Action Group points out that the trial court awarded NanoStatics $21,446 in attorney fees, not $21,466.75. Relying on the $0.75 difference between the amount set by the trial court and the amount testified to in the attorney's affidavits, Action Group contends the affidavits are not evidence supporting the trial court's award. We disagree. The $0.75 difference is not so great that it throws into question what evidence the trial court used to reach the amount of attorney fees awarded.

{¶ **73**} Even though we know what evidence the trial court used to calculate the attorney fees, we normally would require an explanation for why the trial court found $21,466 to be a reasonable amount. *Adams, Babner & Gitlitz, LLC v. Tartan Dev. Co. (West), LLC,* 10th Dist. No. 12AP-729, 2013-Ohio-1573, ¶ 18; *Jubilee Ltd. Partnership v.*

Page 22

Hosp. Properties, Inc., 10th Dist. No. 09AP-1145, 2010-Ohio-5550, ¶ 51-52. We impose this requirement to ensure our ability to meaningfully review the trial court's attorney-fee calculation. *Id.* We nevertheless conclude that the absence of an explanation does not warrant reversal in this case. A reviewing court will not disturb a judgment unless the error contained within is materially prejudicial to the complaining party. *Alternatives Unlimited-Special, Inc. v. Ohio Dept. of Edn.,* 10th Dist. No. 12AP-647, 2013-Ohio-3890, ¶ 39. As we will explain, Action Group has not shown that the alleged error—the absence of explanation—prejudices it.

{¶ **74**} When deciding the amount of an attorney-fee award, a trial court first multiplies the number of hours reasonably expended by the hourly fee, and then determines whether to modify that "lodestar" amount through consideration of the factors listed in Prof. Cond. R. 1.5. *Bittner v. Tri-Cty. Toyota, Inc.,* 58 Ohio St. 3d 143 (1991), syllabus (applying the predecessor to Prof. Cond. R. 1.5). Here, the trial court simply adopted the lodestar amount, without modification, as the reasonable amount of attorney fees to award. On appeal, Action Group advances no argument that this was error or that the amount awarded is unreasonable. Action Group does not challenge the reasonableness of the number of hours worked or the amount of the hourly rates, whether the hours worked were reasonably expended, or the trial court's failure to modify the lodestar amount based on the factors in Prof. Cond. R. 1.5. We require the trial court to articulate an analysis of those matters so that we can review that analysis in determining whether the result—the amount of attorney fees awarded—is reasonable. However, as Action Group has not alleged any supposed error in either the analysis or the result, we have no need to review the analysis. In other words, the trial court's failure to set forth a reasonableness analysis is irrelevant where the appellant does not argue on appeal that the amount awarded is unreasonable. Without such an argument, the lack of an explanation does not prejudice the appellant.

{¶ 75} In sum, we find no error argued in the fourth assignment of error justifies reversal. Therefore, we overrule the fourth assignment of error.

{¶ 76} For the foregoing reasons, we overrule the first, second, and fourth assignments of error, and we sustain the third assignment of error. We affirm in part and reverse in part the judgment of the Franklin County Court of Common Pleas, and we

Page 23

remand this case to that court for further proceedings in accordance with law and this decision.

Judgment affirmed in part and reversed in part; cause remanded.

TYACK and O'GRADY, JJ., concur.

VOCABULARY BUILDERS

Across

2 Buyers have a right to _____ the goods upon delivery.
3 The buyer is permitted to test the good without first accepting it.
7 Portion of the shipment.
10 The seller may have reason to know of the buyer's ___ _____ in purchasing the good.
11 Parties to the transaction must act in _____.
12 The goods are not as specified in the contract.
14 A seller may limit or _____ warranties.
18 The value of the goods at the time and place of the breach.
19 The seller makes certain representations to the buyer in order to complete the transaction.
21 Permits a seller to refuse to deliver the goods to the buyer.
22 Article 2 deals with the _____.
23 The seller agrees to take back what the buyer cannot resell.
24 Putting the goods at the disposal of the buyer.
25 Those type of goods that can only be used by one particular buyer.

26 Where the merchants' writings do not match.

Down

1 To purchase substitute goods.
2 Unspoken representation with regard to the good.
4 A party may feel insecure and request _____.
5 A statement of fact with regard to the good warranted.
6 A person with knowledge of the goods involved in the transaction.
8 The good is of acceptable average quality.
9 Goods are _____ as the ones that will be sent to the buyer under the contract.
13 A limit or exclusion of the warranty must be _____ _.
15 A buyer may have the _____ the goods for the seller if they are perishable.
16 Does not need consideration to be valid.
17 A seller must have _____ to a good in order to sell it.
20 Can act as acceptance under the UCC.

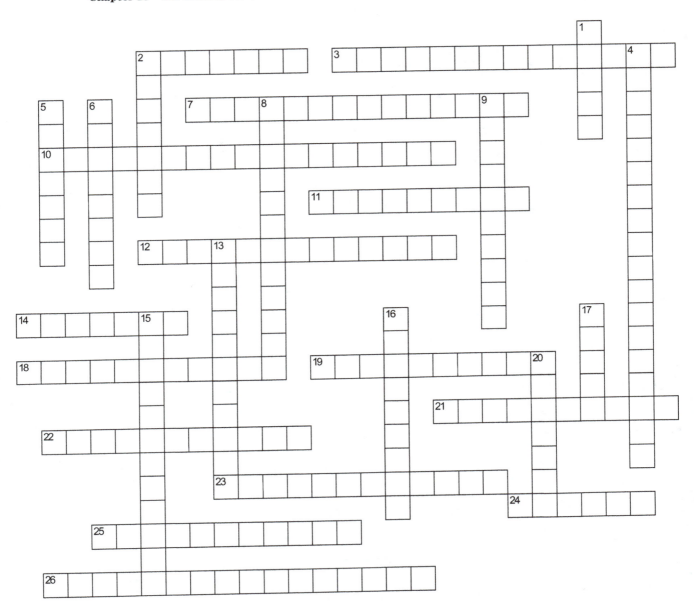

Appendix A

HOW TO PREPARE THE CASE BRIEF

First, the paralegal student needs to understand the importance of briefing cases and why this needs to be done properly. After the paralegal has completed collecting the relevant cases through research, the information needs to be summarized and analyzed. Briefed cases are a tool and the first step in the writing process toward the final trial brief. Case briefs are a tool in that they serve as a "cheat sheet"; if a case is briefed properly, no one should have to reread the original case opinion. Some judges have a propensity for verbosity and use of esoteric language. A paralegal's task is to see through that and simplify and clarify the opinion for future use in the office.

Second, how is the paralegal to accomplish this feat? The following is a relatively standard format for case briefing. Remember to write clearly, use your own words, and be concise.

1. The Facts

- You must identify what the material facts are—what's important. This should read like a story.
- There are two types of facts:
  - *Occurrence facts*—*what* happened between the parties that gave rise to the lawsuit.
  - *Procedural facts*—*what* happened to the case once it started its journey through the legal system. Most of the time this is how/why the case ended up at the appellate level.
- You must learn what is important in a case—for example, weather conditions in a contract dispute are irrelevant, but they can be vital to a car accident.
- Pay attention to what the court itself focuses on; these are the facts that make a difference as to how the law is applied in the case.
- Identify the role that each party plays. Is there a buyer and a seller? A realtor and a construction manager? Avoid using the actual names of the parties; it will only confuse and/or annoy the reader.

2. The Issue(s)

- This is *not* the guilt or innocence of a party. It doesn't matter what actually happened to the parties; what matters is how their situation was analyzed by the court.

- What is the correct legal standard to apply and was it applied properly at the trial level?
- You are looking for the reason *why* a certain legal standard was applied in that case and *how* the result was achieved.
- In this way, the researcher can determine how that same precedent can or should be applied in the instant case.
- It is most helpful to pose the issue as a question. Very frequently starting the question with "Whether . . ." is appropriate and helps to focus the reader.
- Break the issue down into its component parts. This may mean that you will have a set of numbered issues.

3. The Holding

This should be a short statement; essentially, it answers the question posed in the ISSUE section. Do not try to explain the answer here; that is for the next section.

- Identify the legal standard relied upon by the court.
- How did the court resolve the legal issue before it?
- Judges will look for statutory authority first; if there is none, then the judge will apply fundamental ideals of right and wrong (equity).
- If you have more than one question posed in the ISSUE section, you should answer each one separately here.

4. Reasoning (The most important part of the brief!)

- The court gives the reasons *why* the outcome (holding) is what it has determined. It will explain how the legal standard applies in that case. It is important to always apply the law to the facts. This is essential for you to determine how your case will turn out.
- Be sure to mention the relevant law relied upon by the court: "Pursuant to . . .", "In accordance with . . . ."
- The court may rely on several different theories in making its determination; be sure to discuss all of them.
- Treat this section as an educational discussion. Remember, you do not want to have to reread the original case.
- Also note how the court ultimately treated the case—its "Judgment." Did it affirm, reverse, or remand the case?

AN EFFECTIVE CASE BRIEF SHOULD GIVE THE READER ALL THE NECESSARY INFORMATION WITHOUT HAVING TO REFER TO THE TEXT OF THE CASE.

Case

Superior Court of Maine
Martin E. MOORE and COASTAL DESIGNERS
AND CONSULTANTS, INC., Plaintiffs
v.
OCTOBER CORPORATION and BOULOS
PROPERTY MANAGEMENT, Defendants
No. CV-02-045
Oct. 1, 2004
DECISION AND ORDER

ATWOOD, J.

I. INTRODUCTION

Pending before the court is the defendants' motion for partial summary judgment which seeks disposition in their favor on count I of the plaintiffs' second amended complaint. For their part, the plaintiffs oppose this motion but assert that because the contract at issue is unambiguous and because the defendants breached its terms, summary judgment ought to be entered for the plaintiffs on this count. Thus, each set of parties ask the court to resolve count I in its respective favor via the pending motion.[1] By this decision and order, the court will endeavor to address these competing requests.

II. FACTS

Based on the parties' submissions in support of, or in opposition to, the pending motion, the following facts or disputes of fact, may be found in the record.

October Corporation (October) purchased the former Pineland Center from the State in 2000 and decided to develop a dairy farm there which would include a dairy barn. It engaged Coastal Designers and Consultants ("CDC"), of whom plaintiff Martin E. Moore (Moore) is the principal, to design the dairy barn. On July 21, 2001, the defendants signed a

contract, which is the subject of the dispute in this case, by which CDC was to provide the design services for the dairy barn.

The contract, entitled "Standard Proposal Agreement for Construction Drawings" ("Agreement") was drafted by CDC and contained the following list of services it would provide:

- Site visit—Master planning session
- On site review of revised preliminary master plan, floor plans & elevations
- On site review meeting of revised preliminary plans
- On site review first draft of construction drawings & specifications
- On site review proof set of construction dwgs & specifications
- On site deliver & review construction drawings & specifications for contractor bid
- Assistance in selection of all finishing materials
- Assistance in selection of suppliers
- Assistance in selection of contractors
- Consultation during construction via telephone, fax & Federal Express
- Contractor bid review meeting
- Pre construction meeting w/G.C.

The contract also included the following relevant text under its section entitled "Standard Policy":

---

[1] Counts II and III which allege, respectively, Unjust Enrichment and Quantum Meruit, are not the subject of this motion and, therefore will survive this motion and, apparently, be in order for trial.

—A design fee of 10% will be charged based on the project construction cost excluding landscaping/bldg. permits fees

* * *

—In the event that the Owners stop this project for any reason, the Owners will only be responsible for the percentage of the drawings & specifications completed to date when we received notice to stop the project.
—The design fee will be charged for all portions of the project excluding landscaping & building permit.

Finally, the contract contained the following language as the payment schedule for the services that CDC would provide October:

PAYMENT SCHEDULE

#1.	Retainer at start of work	$ 7,500.00
#2.	Progress payment due & appreciated at preliminary drawing review meeting [Preliminary site plan layout floor plan & elevations]	$15,500.00
#3.	Progress payment due & appreciated at first draft construction drawing review meeting	$45,000.00
#4.	Progress payment due & appreciated at the proof set of construction dwg & specification review meeting	$40,000.00
#5.	Payment due & appreciated when bid documents are delivered [Dwgs. & specifications]	$42,000.00
#6.	Balance due [if any] balance of 10% design fee when contractor bid is obtained	$ Pending
#7.	Final payment due [if any] 10% design fee of change orders	$ Pending

The numbers cited above total $150,000 through step #5 in the schedule, namely when bid documents are delivered to the owner. The parties dispute the significance of this figure. The defendants say it represents 10%, CDC's fee, of a pre-contract budget estimate of $1,500,000 which would allow CDC to be paid $150,000 if October did not complete the project. DSMF, ¶ 24. Moore disagrees with this interpretation,

and asserts that his fee was to be 10% of the cost of construction, but agrees that the figure of $1.5 million came from a discussion with individuals from October or Boulos Property Management (Boulos) as to the possible scope of the project. PRSMF, ¶ 20. He also agrees that the Agreement "suggests that a $1.5 million dollar project would be the minimum project cost." *Id.* Moore also testified that when he filled out the payment schedule, he used the 10% figure to calculate the payment schedule and that that 10% was applied against a $1.5 million building figure which he had discussed with the defendants. DRSMF, ¶ 20.

Thereafter, CDC received payments #1 through #4 under the Agreement's payment schedule which totaled $108,000. It also received $23,692.50 for work outside the contract for the dairy processing plant.

On November 5, 2001, CDC provided the defendants with a set of design development drawings which the defendants characterize as "preliminary drawings," DSMF, ¶ 30, but which Moore refers to as "the first draft of construction drawings." PRSMF, ¶ 30. On this date, CDC submitted an invoice for progress payment #3 in the amount of $45,000. Apparently it was paid.

The defendants say they then wished to get a budget estimate of the cost of constructing the dairy barn as it was depicted on the November 5, 2001, plans so gave these "preliminary" plans to Pochebit, a construction company, to get this estimate for constructing the dairy barn. Pochebit responded in December of 2001 with an estimated budget price of over $2.8 million which was more than the defendants contemplated spending.

In reaching this figure, Michael White of Pochebit testified that he understood his firm's task was to "get a preliminary budget estimate for the project"; that it was "real preliminary . . . a high and a low type of estimate . . . it was a range." DSMF, ¶ 43.

The defendants further say that, based upon the costs given to them by Pochebit, they decided to look at various options, including "value engineering" for the dairy barn, to see if cost reductions could be made so that a variation of the November 5, 2001 plans could be constructed. DSMF, ¶ 44. The plaintiffs dispute this and assert that CDC provided Boulos with "90% complete" drawings on or about December 14, 2001, which, it believes, were given to Pochebit and used to discuss "value engineering."[2]

---

[2]The plaintiffs do not dispute the defendants' assertion at paragraph 41 of their statement of material facts that the latter gave

In February 2002, CDC was instructed to complete the drawings and specifications. CDC complied, and in February or March, 2002, CDC prepared the final drawings. The defendants claim that they gave this instruction so that they could use portions of the drawings in the event they decided to use value engineered plans. DSMF, ¶ 46. Moore denies this and states that he "was told that the project design was going to change dramatically due to the purchase of another dairy farm," . . . and that "what you have designed will not be built as Owner no longer has the need. I want, however, for you to finish your design work so that I can close out your contract." PRSMF, ¶ 46 (quoting Paul Ureneck of Boulos). Moore claims, without contradiction, that he replied to this, confirming that CDC would:

> . . . prepare 3 sets of final drawings and 3 specifications booklets & will plan on delivering these documents to your [sic] personally . . . . Immediately after that, I will prepare the above mentioned so that we can finalize my contract as per your request. The only item that will remain for you to do prior to construction is a professional engineers review that you chose not to do at this time.

> Id.

Moore was also told in February, 2002, that the defendants wanted to reduce the cost of the dairy barn from the budget estimate of $2.8 million.

On March 8, 2002, Moore faxed to Ureneck an invoice for $233,811 which he claimed then, and now, to be the balance due CDC based on the project construction cost provided by Pochebit. Moore calculated this figure by applying 10% to the figure developed by Pochebit.[3]

On March 20, 2002, Moore went to Boulos' office and may have then resubmitted the faxed invoice for $233,811. Boulos refused payment and Moore refused to release the final plans without that payment.

The defendants assert that the plaintiffs never submitted an invoice for $42,000 for payment #5 under the payment schedule. CDC takes the position that the invoice which it submitted included what would have been payment #5.

The defendants also say that if Moore had submitted an invoice for $42,000 with his plans on March 20, 2002, they would have paid that sum. The plaintiffs reply that while the parties negotiated over a fee for the defendants to obtain the final plans, it is their position that the contract called for final payment before the plans would be left and the defendants have rejected that interpretation of their agreement.

After March, 2002, the defendants decided to build "an entirely different dairy barn facility than that designed by Coastal." DSMF, ¶ 59. Once built, it had a construction costs of $1.2 million. The plaintiffs assert that the bam built has significant similarities to the dairy complex it designed.[4] PRSMF, ¶ 59.

III. DISCUSSION

All parties agree that the contract, the "Agreement," is unambiguous and therefore its interpretation is a question of law which must be decided by a court. *American Protection Ins. Co. v. Acadia Ins. Co.*, 2003 ME 6, ¶ 11, 814 A.2d 989, 993. In doing so, the interpretation "must be determined from the plain meaning of the language used and from the four corners of the instrument without resort to extrinsic evidence." *Id.* (quoting *Portland Valve, Inc. v. Rockwood Sys. Corp.*, 460 A.2d 1383, 1387 (Me. 1983)). The court must look at the whole instrument and the contract should "be constructed to give force and effect to all of its provisions." *Id.* at 12 (quoting *Acadia Ins. Co. v. Buck Constr. Co.*, 2000 ME 154, ¶ 9, 756 A.2d 515, 517).

The defendants argue that CDC did not have the option or the right to skip over payment step #5 and go

---

the November 5, 2001 plans to Pochebit early that month and that Pochebit continued to work on numbers in December. PRSMF, § 41.

It is unknown if there are two sets of plans, one that was submitted to Pochebit in November, 2001, the "preliminary" or "draft" plan, and a second "90% complete" plan that was developed later and given to Pochebit on or about December 14, 2001. *See* DSMF, ¶ 41, PRSMF, ¶¶ 40, 42(b), 44; DRSMF, ¶ 44. The defendants deny that there was a second set of plans and assert that the only set given to Pochebit was dated November 5, 2001. They support this contention with record references showing that there was no transmittal letter for any December plans, that an invoice of December 28, 2001, was for "proofing" the November 5 plans, and that no new plans were produced for the December 28 invoice. DRSMF, III, ¶ 40.

[3] *See* DSMF, Exh. B, which shows CDC's final statement and the calculations used which also involved a separate fee for a related project.

---

[4] The defendants correctly point out that this assertion is based on hearsay and ought not to be considered in the disposition of this motion. *Searles v. Trustees of St. Joseph's College*, 695 A.2d 1206, 1210, n.2.

to step #6 and be paid its 10% design fee which was to occur only upon the defendants' receipt of the contractor's bid. Instead, the defendants argue, CDC was required to turn over the final plans in return for the $42,000 payment specified at step #5. After this, the contract envisions that a contractor's bid would be submitted, based on the final plans which would have been turned over on this occasion. Thereafter, when the contractor's bid is accepted by the owner, the construction cost could be determined and the 10% payment could be calculated as payment #6. Thus, the defendants argue, payment #6 could only occur when the actual construction cost could be figured, and not before then, and that that step was contingent upon the receipt of the final plans. So, they reason, because the final plans were withheld, no construction bid could be obtained, and it is not possible to calculate the applicable percentage of the contractor's bid because none could be obtained without the final plans.

The defendants also argue that even if the court ventured outside the four corners of the Agreement and examined the undisputed facts extrinsic to this document, it would reach the same result. More particularly, the defendants say that in order for the plaintiffs to have any argument that it could skip step #5 and proceed to step #6 they would have to establish that the Pochebit figures constituted the "contractor bid" cited in step #6. The plaintiffs cannot accomplish this, it is claimed, because there is no evidence that what Pochebit submitted was "a contractor bid."

The record cited by the defendants supports this contention. As noted, infra, Michael White of Pochebit has testified without contradiction that his firm provided "a preliminary budget estimate for the project"; that it was "real preliminary . . . a high and a low type of estimate . . . it was a range." DSMF, ¶ 43. The defendants also point to evidence in the record that Moore appreciated that Pochebit's figures were an estimate. *See, e.g.,* DSMF, ¶ 39, PRSMF, ¶ 41. Thus, the evidence outside the contract would show that the figure against which CDC calculated the 10% design fee was not a contractor's bid, but, rather, an estimate used in the planning process for this project.[5] That being so, the plaintiffs may not use the

figure they have relied on from Pochebit to assess their design fee and bill the defendants. Instead, the defendants say, CDC had to wait until after they had turned in the final plans and then calculate its bill based on a bid which would, in turn, be based on those plans.

Finally, the defendants argue, because the plaintiffs refused to turn over the plans so that the defendants could solicit and obtain a contractor's bid, they have breached the agreement and cannot be awarded the damages they seek. This is because Maine law provides that a party who breaches a contract by providing less than full performance of all its material provisions cannot rely on that contract to secure payment thereunder, but must turn to equitable remedies such as *quantum meruit* to recover for his services. *Loyal Erectors, Inc. v. Hamilton & Son, Inc.,* 312 A.2d 748, 756 (Me. 1973).

The plaintiffs have assembled a variety of arguments to overcome the defendants' interpretation of the Agreement.

First among these is the contention that the parties executed a single, nonseverable contract in that, they say, the payment steps do not correlate to the value of the work performed at each step. Accordingly, the plaintiffs are entitled to be paid for the complete design drawings they were asked to, and did, tender on March 20, 2002. At this time they would say they had completed their part of the contract and, apparently, could skip step #5. This would be justified because the plaintiffs were told to complete the plans but that the owner would not be building the barn CDC designed. Thus, it may be said, there was to be no contractor's bid on those plans so that steps #5 and #6 could be skipped. Said differently, once CDC was told to complete the drawings but that the building would not be built as they designed so that no contractor would be bidding on it, CDC was entitled to be paid its final design fee. Further, because there would be no contractor's bid, the best means of determining that fee would be to use the estimate submitted by Pochebit to construct the barn. Otherwise, there would be no way under the contract to calculate this fee. This purports to be a fair interpretation of the contract because the defendants had the option of terminating it and paying for only the work done but, once they asked for the final plans, they were bound to pay for them as the contract specified.

---

[5] Even if it turned out to be correct that Pochebit provided two estimates, one in November, the other in December of 2001, there is no evidence that either represented its bid on the project. Accordingly, it may be said, neither would trigger payment steps #5 or #6.

However, as the plaintiffs have acknowledged, the contract for CDC's performance was not completed on the delivery of the plans. CDC was also responsible for having them reviewed by a structural engineer and CDC was also responsible for participating in the construction process. Plaintiffs' memorandum, p. 10. The plaintiffs say the defendants waived this performance because the former were told to complete the final plans at which time the defendants would "close out" the contract. Upon the contract being "closed out" then, the plaintiffs were entitled to be paid for their plans on delivery as the contract specified, i.e., "Blueprints will not be left without final payment." Agreement, p. 2. It is argued that the failure of the defendants to pay for these plans as the contract required is a breach of that contract because the plaintiffs were prepared to tender performance, outside the elements which had been waived, and the defendants refused to pay.[6] Upon that refusal, the plaintiffs say that under the quoted text of the contract they were entitled to retain the plans and not leave them without that final payment which action, therefore, would not constitute a breach on their part.

In the end, though, the parties' respective arguments, extrinsic evidence aside, amount to competing interpretations of the contract language and the ultimate question, what obligation under the contract did the defendants have when the plaintiffs tendered the final plans? Were the defendants required to pay the plaintiffs 10% of Pochebit's figures or was payment of $42,000 under step #5 called for?

In the court's view, the defendants' interpretation of the Agreement's provisions is the most persuasive. In this regard, a careful and fair reading of the payment schedule sheds light on the mutual obligations of the parties under the Agreement as here defined.

That schedule contemplated a series of payments culminating in a potential total of $150,000 which was 10% of a hypothetical $1.5 million building. Payment step #5, which calls for a $42,000 payment of the $150,000 total, can reasonably and logically be understood to mean that that payment would be made when the bid documents were delivered "[Dwgs & Specifications]" Agreement, p. 3; that is, when CDC delivered drawings and specifications sufficient to solicit construction bids, it was to be paid $42,000.

When the owner took the next step and obtained a contractor's bid, then CDC would be entitled to "Balance due [if any] balance of 10% design fee . . ." *Id.* But, as the defendants have argued, it was necessary to have the plans in order to obtain a contractor's bid and that the use of the phrase "if any" in this step meant that the $42,000 might well be the final payment if the contractor's bid was at or less than $1.5 million. By similar reasoning, if the owner decided not to go forward with the building, it would be required to pay CDC the amount due under step #5, i.e., the "final payment" which would complete the payments for the original, albeit hypothetical, building with a projected cost of $1.5 million.[7]

In this regard, the court concurs with the defendants' reading of the case of *Fay, Spofford & Thorndike, Inc. v. Massachusetts Port Authority*, 387 N.E.2d 206 (Mass. App. Ct. 1979) to the effect that a design contract which contains an early termination design fee calculated against a specified cost of construction, as here, means that that fee is to be paid even when the owner changes the scope of the project. So, here, the defendants would be required to pay CDC the full $150,000, the percentage of the projected cost of the barn that was agreed to when it decided to alter course. When the plaintiffs chose not to deliver the final plans, however, the defendants were relieved of this obligation.

Finally, it is worth addressing the plaintiffs' argument that the Agreement text which states, "Blueprints will not be left without final payment" means that the defendants were required to pay the final design fee, i.e., 10% of construction cost, when the blueprints were delivered, so that if that sum were not paid, the blueprints could be withheld.

Assuming, as the parties do, that "blueprints" and "bid documents" . . . [Dwgs & Specifications]

---

[6] The defendants have not argued that the plans CDC tendered were not fully satisfactory.

[7] The fairness of this interpretation is manifest. The designer receives 10% of the anticipated project cost and is relieved of any further obligations to the owners while taking no risk that the actual construction cost might end up being lower than was projected. In return, the owners get a full set of plans to do with as they may wish except, arguably, build the barn actually designed.

are synonymous, it would be illogical, as discussed, infra, to have the owners either commit to a bid or complete construction without having the blueprints first. Instead, as the defendants contend, it makes considerably more sense to interpret this text as requiring the payment of the sum in step #5, which was the projected "final payment," as the event at which the blueprints would be left and that payment tendered. The effect of this part of the contract would be carried out if the defendants refused to make that "final payment" at which time the blueprints would not be left.

In the end, the court endorses the defendants' interpretation of the Agreement, namely that it unambiguously required the plaintiffs to satisfy their end of the bargain by delivering final plans for payment #5, namely $42,000, and upon this event construction bids could be obtained, or the project abandoned. If the former, the plaintiffs would continue to be bound to the project and, perhaps, be compensated further if the final construction costs exceeded $1.5 million; if the latter, they would have been paid the full 10% of the original projected cost of the dairy barn.

In the court's view, based on the undisputed facts extrinsic to the contract, and the contract language by itself as here interpreted, the plaintiffs breached the Agreement by not delivering the final plans and, therefore, cannot succeed with a breach of contract claim which contradicts the court's interpretation of that document, although their equitable claims may meet with a different fate. *Loyal Erectors, Inc. v. Hamilton & Son, Inc.*, 312 A.2d 748, 756 (Me. 1973).

Accordingly, for the reasons stated herein, the clerk is DIRECTED to make the following entry:

Defendants' Motion for Partial Summary Judgment is GRANTED. Judgment is ENTERED for the defendants on count I of the Second Amended Complaint.

Sample Case Brief

MOORE v. OCTOBER CORPORATION, CV-02-045, SUPERIOR COURT OF MAINE, 2004

FACTS

Occurrence

October Corporation ("Owner") planned to develop a dairy farm and contracted with Moore, the principal of Coastal Designers and Consultants ("Designer"), to design the dairy barn, which was projected to cost $1.5 million. The contract set forth the tasks to be completed by the Designer and included a 10% design fee based upon the project's construction cost and a seven-step schedule indicating when the payments were due. The obligations of the Designer also included supervision of the progress of construction. The agreement also included a clause providing for payments due to the Designer in the event that the Owner stopped work on the project; in that case, the Owners were responsible only for the percentage of the drawings and specifications completed as of the date of notice of stoppage and the 10% final design fee for all parts of the contract based upon the estimated cost of $1.5 million ($150,000 total).

The Designer completed the first four tasks assigned to it and the Owner paid on them. Despite not having obtained the "final plans" from the Designer (step 5) and pursuant to step 6, the Owner contacted a construction company to obtain a preliminary building cost estimate. The cost estimate of $2.8 million was too high for the Owner and the barn would not be built. The Owner requested that the Designer finish the plans taking more economical options into consideration and "close out the contract." At this point, Owner claimed that Designer had not been paid on step 5 because the "final bid" drawings had not been turned over, on step 6 because the contractor's final bid had not been obtained, and on step 7 because the contract was breached by Designer's failures in steps 5 and 6. Designer claimed that because the Owner had decided not to build the barn, that steps 5 and 6 were not necessary and that the Designer was entitled to payment under the "stop work" clause—that is, 10% of the final project cost.

Procedural

This case before the court involved a motion for summary judgment from both parties regarding the resolution of the first count of the complaint relating to entitlement to final payment.

ISSUE

Whether the Designer was entitled to the final design fee of 10% of the construction costs pursuant to the "stop work" clause based upon either the original $1.5 million estimate or the construction estimate of $2.8 million?

Alternately, whether the Designer was owed only for the work and plans supplied at the point of stoppage because the Designer was in breach for not supplying the final plans?

HOLDING

The Designer was obligated to turn over the final plans pursuant to step 5 before any further payment obligations were due from the Owner. The Designer's breach of contract relieved the Owner from enforcement of the "stop work" clause in the contract.

REASONING

Courts look to the actual language of the agreement in interpreting a contractual dispute. The plain meaning of the contract indicates that the Designer was under an obligation to supply the final plans before he was entitled to payment #5. The Designer failed to supply final plans sufficient to base a bid upon and therefore a final construction bid could not be obtained. Even though the project was abandoned, the Owner requested the final plans to "close out the contract"; therefore, the originally contemplated progress payments would be followed and made.

Relying on *Fay, Spofford & Thorndike, Inc. v. Massachusetts Port Authority*, 387 N.E.2d 206 (Mass. App. Ct. 1979), the court determined that where a construction contract contains an early termination fee based upon a percentage of the estimated costs, that clause is enforceable. However, that clause is no longer in force when the Designer has breached the contract.

Partial Summary Judgment was entered in favor of the Owner based upon the first count of its complaint for the Designer's breach.

Appendix B

"WRITE" AWAY! FINAL PORTFOLIO PROJECT

How to Polish the Construction Contract

"*God is in the details.*" How appropriate that Ludwig Mies van der Rohe applied that philosophy to architecture, as it applies equally well to a construction contract—architecture put into practice.

Once the basics of the contract have been set forth, keep the following details in mind and polish the segments of the "Write" Away! exercise into a cohesive document. The additional forms may be referenced as exhibits to the contract.

- The title of the document should accurately reflect the nature of the transaction.
- Proper identification of the parties and the role that they play in the agreement. Be sure to include current phone, fax, e-mail contacts, and procedures for sending notices (in writing or electronically).
- Proper identification of the property, including block and lot numbers.
- Identify the parties' rights and liabilities and relationships to each other. Is the Owner entitled to access to the site during construction? Are there any indemnification or "hold harmless" clauses necessary or desirable?
- Cost, including all contingent costs associated with performance (fees, late charges, etc.). Be sure to delineate whose responsibility it is to pay these costs.
- Term of the contract—are there time limits associated with performance? How long will the contract be effective? Be sure to date the contract.
- Are there any conditions that must be satisfied? Are there financing conditions? Are there provisions for continued performance obligations despite the failure of the condition?
- Warranties and representations of the parties. The parties must be authorized to enter into the agreement and the subject matter can be properly transferred without encumbrances.
- Are there any specific exclusions to the subject matter of the contract?
- Is there any "boilerplate" language that must be changed?
- Risks of loss/failure of performance due to external factors are clearly delineated. Insurance requirements? Delay procedures?
- What are the standards to be applied to performance? What is "satisfactory performance"? Set forth the quantities, quality, method of determining price, inspection criteria, etc. Consider a "substitution policy" for both parties, services, and goods to be supplied.

- Time, place, and method of delivery of the goods or services and payment. This may include detailed schedules for work and payments.
- Definition of default and breach. Do the parties have an opportunity to "cure"? Is there a method in place to resolve disputes? Must the parties submit to arbitration?
- Remedies available to the non-breaching party. (Limitations in amount or liability of a party? Liquidated damages available?)

Once all of these factors have been incorporated, if appropriate, the next step is to ORGANIZE the terms of the contract. First, consider terms chronologically. Remedies should be the last section because it comes at the end of a dispute; the basics should come first to establish the grounds of a valid contract. Second, consider grouping related clauses together for ease of comprehension.

Glossary

ability to cure A breaching party may be able to fix the defective performance.

abuse of process Using the threat of resorting to the legal system to extract agreement to terms against the other party's will.

acceptance of services or goods Where an offeree has taken possession of the goods or received the benefit of the conferred services, he has been deemed to have accepted the offer.

accord and satisfaction An agreement to accept the imperfectly proffered performance as a fulfillment of the contractual obligations.

actions inconsistent with rejection A buyer must not do anything that is contrary to her previous refusal of the goods.

active concealment Knowingly hiding a situation that another party has the right to know and, being hidden from them, assumes that it does not exist.

adequate assurances Either party may request the other to provide further guarantees that performance will be forthcoming if the requesting party has reasonable suspicion that the other may default.

adequate compensation A party denied the benefit of his bargain may be paid or otherwise put in a position equivalent to where he would have been had performance been in compliance with the contractual terms.

adequate consideration Exchanges that are fair and reasonable as a result of equal bargaining for things of relatively equal value.

affirmative acts Knowing and conscious efforts by a party to the contract that are inconsistent with the terms of the agreement and that make contractual obligations impossible to perform.

affirmative defense An "excuse" by the opposing party that does not just simply negate the allegation, but puts forth a legal reason to avoid enforcement.

affirmative duty The law requires that certain parties positively act in a circumstance and not have to wait until they are asked to do that which they are required to do.

against the drafter Imprecise terms and/or ambiguous wording is held against the party who wrote the document as he was the party most able to avoid the problem.

American rule of attorney's fees and costs Expenses incurred by the parties to maintain or defend an action for the breach of contract are generally not recoverable as damages.

anticipation An expectation of things to come that has reasonable basis for the conclusion.

anticipatory repudiation Words or acts from a party to the contract that clearly and unquestionably state the intent not to honor his contractual obligations before the time for performance has arrived.

assertion of defenses Either the original parties or a third-party beneficiary has the right to claim any legal defenses or excuses that they may have as against each other. They are not extinguished by a third party.

assignee The party to whom the right to receive contractual performance is transferred.

assignment The transfer of the rights to receive the benefit of contractual performance under the contract.

assignor The party who assigns his rights away and relinquishes his rights to collect the benefit of contractual performance.

B

battle of the forms An evaluation of commercial writings whose terms conflict with each other in order to determine what terms actually control the performances due from the parties.

benefit conferred The exchange that bestows value upon the other party to the contract.

bilateral contract A contract in which the parties exchange a promise for a promise.

black letter law The strict meaning of the law as it is written without concern or interpretation of the reasoning behind its creation.

blackmail The extortion of payment based on a threat of exposing the victim's secrets.

breach A party's performance that deviates from the required performance obligations under the contract and for which the conforming party may seek recourse to the court.

bright-line rules A legal standard resolves issues in a simple, formulaic manner that is easy in application although it may not always be equitable.

C

cancel the contract The aggrieved party has the right to terminate the contractual relationship with no repercussions.

certainty The ability for a term to be objectively determined and evaluated by a party outside of the contract.

commercial unit A batch of goods packaged or sold together in the normal course of the relevant industry.

compensatory damages A payment to make up for a wrong committed and return the non-breaching party to a position where the effect of the breach has been neutralized.

complete integration A document that contains all the terms of the agreement and the parties have agreed that there are no other terms outside the contract.

concurrent condition An event that happens at the same time as the parties' performance obligations.

condition An event that may or may not happen upon which the rest of the performance of the contract rests.

condition precedent An event that happens beforehand and gives rise to the parties' performance obligations. If the condition is not satisfied, the parties do not have a duty to perform.

condition subsequent An event that, if it happens after the parties' performance obligations, negates the duty to perform. If the condition is satisfied, the parties can "undo" their actions.

conditional acceptance A refusal to accept the stated terms of an offer by adding restrictions or requirements to the terms of the offer by the offeree.

consent All parties to a novation must knowingly assent to the substitution of either the obligations or parties to the agreement.

consequential damages Damages resulting from the breach that are natural and foreseeable results of the breaching party's actions.

consideration The basis of the bargained for exchange between the parties to a contract that is of legal value.

conspicuous limitation or exclusion of warranties A seller may specifically deny any warranties as long as the limitation or exclusion of the warranties is set forth in language that is understandable and noticeable by the buyer.

contract of adhesion An agreement wherein one party has total control over the bargaining process and therefore the other party has no power to negotiate and no choice but to enter into the contract.

contradictory Evidence which is in conflict with the terms of the contract and inadmissible under the parol evidence rule.

counteroffer A refusal to accept the stated terms of an offer by proposing alternate terms.

course of dealing The parties' actions taken in similar previous transactions.

course of performance The parties' actions taken in reliance on the particular transaction in question.

covenant The promise upon which the contract rests.

covenant not to compete An employment clause that prohibits an employee from leaving his job and going to work for a competitor for a specified period of time in a certain geographical area.

covenant not to sue An agreement by the parties to relinquish their right to commence a lawsuit based on the original and currently existing cause of action under the contract.

cover The non-breaching party's attempt to mitigate damages may require that he purchase alternate goods on the open market to replace those never delivered by the breaching party. The non-breaching party can recover the difference in price between the market price and the contract price.

creditor A party to whom a debt is owed.

cure The seller is given a reasonable opportunity to fix the defects in the goods found by the buyer.

D

death or incapacity of a party An excuse for performance on a contract due to the inability of the party to fulfill his obligation.

declaratory judgment The court's determination of the rights and responsibilities of a party with respect to the subject matter of the controversy.

defects in formation Errors or omissions made during the negotiations that function as a bar to creating a valid contract.

delegant/delegator The party who transfers his obligation to perform his contractual obligations.

delegate/delegatee The party to whom the obligation to perform the contractual obligations is transferred.

delegation The transfer of the duties/obligations to perform under the contract.

delivery In commercial contracts, delivery may be accomplished by transferring actual possession of the goods, or putting the goods at the disposal of the buyer, or by a negotiable instrument giving the buyer the right to the goods.

deprived of expected benefit A party can reasonably expect to receive that for which he bargained; if he does not receive it, the breach is considered material.

destruction of subject matter Excuse of performance is based on the unforeseeable and unavoidable loss of the subject matter.

deterrent effect The authority to assess excessive fines on a breaching party often can dissuade a party from committing an act that would subject him to these punitive damages.

detriment incurred The exchange that burdens the party in giving the consideration to the other party to the contract.

detrimental effect A party's worsening of his position due to his dependence on the terms of the contract.

detrimental reliance An offeree has depended upon the assertions of the offeror and made a change for the worse in his position depending on those assertions.

disavowal A step taken by a formerly incapacitated person that denies and cancels the voidable contract and thereby makes it unenforceable.

divisibility/severability A contract may be able to be compartmentalized into separate parts and be seen as a series of independent transactions between the parties.

doctrine of unclean hands A party seeking equitable remedies must have acted justly and in good faith in the transaction in question; otherwise, equitable remedies will not be available to a wrongdoer.

donee A party to whom a gift is given.

dram-shop liability A bar keeper or owner who negligently over-serves alcohol to a patron who is visibly intoxicated may be liable for harm that the intoxicated person causes due to his inability to control his actions.

duress Unreasonable and unscrupulous manipulation of a person to force him to agree to terms of an agreement that he would otherwise not agree to.

duty A legal obligation that is required to be performed.

duty to resell The UCC requires commercial sellers to try to resell the goods that have not been accepted by the original buyer.

E

economic duress   The threat of harm to a party's financial resources unless demands are met.

equitable remedies   A non-monetary remedy fashioned by the court using standards of fairness and justice.

equity   The doctrine of fairness and justice; the process of making things balance or be equal between parties.

excessive and unreasonable cost   A court will only consider excusing performance based on impracticality if the additional expense is extreme and disproportionate to the bargain.

excused from performance   The non-breaching party is released from her obligations to perform due to the other party's breach.

executed   The parties' performance obligations under the contract are complete.

executory   The parties' performances under the contract have yet to occur.

existence of the subject matter   The goods to be transferred must exist at the time of the making of the contract.

expectation damages   A monetary amount that makes up for the losses incurred as a result of the breach that puts the non-breaching party in as good a position as he would have been had the contract been fully performed.

explanatory   Oral testimony is permitted to clarify the terms of the contract.

express conditions   Requirements stated in words, either orally or written, in the contract.

express contract   An agreement whose terms have been communicated in words, either in writing or orally.

express warranty   A written representation by the seller as to the nature of the goods to be sold.

extinguishment of liability   Once a novation has occurred, the party exiting the agreement is no longer obligated under the contract.

F

fiduciary relationship   A relationship based on close personal trust that the other party is looking out for one's best interests.

finish or scrap   The seller has the option to either finish producing the partially manufactured goods or stop production and scrap the materials for their recycled value.

firm offer   An option contract to keep the offer open between merchants that does not have to be supported by separate consideration in order to be valid.

firm offers under the UCC   An agreement made by a merchant-offeror, and governed by the Uniform Commercial Code, that he will not revoke the offer for a certain time period. A firm offer is not supported by separate consideration.

forbearance of a legal right   Consideration that requires a party to refrain from doing something that he has the legal right to do.

force majeure   An event that is neither foreseeable nor preventable by either party that has a devastating effect on the performance obligations of the parties.

foreseeability   The capacity for a party to reasonably anticipate a future event.

forfeiture   A loss caused by a party's inability to perform.

forgoing a legal right to sue   Valid consideration as it has recognized legal value to support a contractual obligation.

formal contract   An agreement made that follows a certain prescribed form like negotiable instruments.

four corners doctrine   A principle of contract law that directs the court to interpret a contract by the terms contained within the pages of the document.

fraud   A knowing and intentional misstatement of the truth in order to induce a desired action from another person.

frustration of purpose   Changes in the circumstances surrounding the contract may render the performance of the terms useless in relation to the reasons for entering into the contract.

freedom of contract The doctrine that permits parties to make agreements on whatever terms they wish with few exceptions.

G

gift Bestowing a benefit without any expectation on the part of the giver to receive something in return and the absence of any obligation on the part of the receiver to do anything in return.

good consideration An exchange made based on love and affection, which have no legal value.

good faith obligation Both buyers and sellers must deal with each other in a reasonable and fair manner without trying to avoid legitimate performance obligations.

guarantee An agreement in which a third party assures the repayment of a debt owed by another party.

guarantor A party who assumes secondary liability for the payment of another's debt. The guarantor is liable to the creditor only if the original debtor does not make payment.

I

identification of the goods to the contract Once a seller has designated specific goods as the ones that will be delivered to the buyer, the buyer has a protectable interest in them.

identity or quality of the subject matter The goods to be transferred must be described with sufficient clarity to allow an outside third party to recognize them.

ignore the repudiation If the repudiating party has not permanently made his performance impossible, the aggrieved party can wait to see if the repudiator changes his mind and does perform.

illegal scheme A plan that uses legal steps to achieve an illegal result.

illusory promise A statement that appears to be a promise but actually enforces no obligation upon the promisor because he retains the subjective option whether or not to perform on it.

immediate right to commence a lawsuit The aggrieved party does not have to wait until the time when performance would be due under the contract term where there has been an anticipatory repudiation.

implied contract An agreement whose terms have not been communicated in words, but rather by conduct or actions of the parties.

implied in fact Conditions that are not expressed in words but that must exist in order for the terms of the contract to make sense and are assumed by the parties to the contract.

implied in law Conditions that are not expressed in words but are imposed by the court to ensure fairness and justice as a result of its determination.

implied warranty An unwritten representation that is normally and naturally included by operation of law that applies to the goods to be sold.

implied warranty for a particular purpose If a seller has reason to know of the needs of the buyer in relation to the goods to be sold, the seller impliedly warrants the goods to that higher standard.

impossibility An excuse for performance based upon an absolute inability to perform the act required under the contract.

impracticality An excuse for performance based upon uselessness or excessive cost of the act required under the contract.

incapacity The inability to act or understand the actions that would create a binding legal agreement.

incidental beneficiaries Persons who may derive some benefit from the performance of a contract but who were not intended to directly benefit from the performance.

incidental damages Damages resulting from the breach that are related to the breach but not necessarily directly foreseeable by the breaching party.

infancy doctrine The generally accepted doctrine of contract law that permits minors to avoid contractual obligations under a public policy that minors need to be protected from potentially unfair or unscrupulous terms due to their lack of sophistication.

injunction A court order that requires a party to refrain from acting in a certain way to prevent harm to the requesting party.

insolvency   The inability to pay one's debts, which may result in a declaration of bankruptcy and put all contractual obligations on hold or terminate them.

inspect   The buyer must take steps to examine the goods to ensure they are of the type indicated in the contract. The seller must make the goods available for this purpose.

intent   Having the knowledge and desire that a specific consequence will result from an action.

intent to deceive   The party making the questionable statement must plan on the innocent party's reliance on the first party's untruthfulness.

intent of the parties   Almost always the controlling factor in determining the terms and performance of an agreement.

intoxication   Under the influence of alcohol or drugs which may, depending on the degree of inebriation, render a party incapable of entering into a contractual relationship.

irreparable harm   The requesting party must show that the actions of the defendant will cause a type of damage that cannot be remedied by any later award of the court.

irrevocable offers   Those offers that cannot be terminated by the offeror during a certain time period.

K

knowing and intentional   A party must be aware of and plan on the outcome of his words or actions in order to be held accountable for the result.

knowledge of the offer   An offeree must be aware of the terms of the offer in order to accept it.

L

lapse of time   An interval of time that has been long enough to affect a termination of the offer.

"last in time = first in right"   A principle in law that favors the most current activity or change with respect to the transaction as it is most likely the most reflective of the intent of the parties.

legal remedy   Relief provided by the court to a party to redress a wrong perpetrated by another party.

legal value   Having an objectively determinable benefit that is recognized by the court.

legislation   Regulations codified into laws by Congress.

letter of intent/nonbinding offer   A statement that details the preliminary negotiations and understanding of the terms of the agreement but does not create a binding obligation between parties.

limitation of acceptance   A commercial offeror may specifically state that the offeree must accept all terms as set forth in the offer with no deviations.

limitation of damages   An amount of money agreed upon in the original contract as the maximum recovery the non-breaching party will be entitled to in the event of a breach.

liquidated damages   An amount of money agreed upon in the original contract as a reasonable estimation of the damages to be recovered by the non-breaching party.

loss of subject matter   The nonexistence of the subject matter of the contract, which renders it legally valueless and unable to be exchanged according to the terms of the contract.

lost profits   A calculable amount of money that the non-breaching party would have made after the execution of performance under the agreement but that has not been realized due to the breach.

M

mailbox rule   A principle of contract law that sets the time of acceptance of an offer at the time it is posted and the time of rejection of an offer at the time it is received.

malum prohibitum   An act that is "prohibited" by a rule of law.

market price   The objective worth placed on the subject matter in the open marketplace for similar products.

material   An element or term that is significant or important and relates to the basis for the agreement and affects a party's decision whether or not to enter into the contact.

material alteration   A change in the terms that would surprise or impose hardship on the other party if allowed to become a part of the agreement.

medicinal side effects Under the influence of over-the-counter or prescription drugs having an impact on a person's mental capacity which may render a party incapable of entering into a contractual relationship.

meeting of the minds A legal concept requiring that both parties understand and ascribe the same objective and subjective meaning to the terms of the contract.

mental duress The threat of harm to a party's overall well-being or a threat of harm to loved ones that induces stress and action on the party of the threatened party.

mentally infirm Persons not having the capacity to understand a transaction due to a defect in their ability to reason and, therefore, who do not have the requisite mental intent to enter into a contract.

merchantable Goods must meet certain standards that are required in the relevant industry.

merchants Businesspersons who have a certain level of expertise dealing in commercial transactions regarding the goods they regularly sell.

mere request for a change A party's interest in renegotiating the terms of the contract does not amount to anticipatory repudiation.

merger Combining previous obligations into a new agreement.

merger clause Language of a contract that indicates that the parties intend to exclude all outside evidence relating to the terms of the contract because it has been agreed that all relevant terms have been incorporated in the document.

minors Persons under the age of 18; once a person has reached 18, they have reached the age of majority.

mirror image rule A requirement that the acceptance of an offer must exactly match the terms of the original offer.

misrepresentation A reckless disregard for the truth in making a statement to another in order to induce a desired action.

mitigate To lessen in intensity or amount.

modification A change or addition in contractual terms that does not extinguish the underlying agreement.

moral obligation A social goal or personal aspiration that induces a party to act without any expectation of a return performance from the recipient.

mutual mistake An error made by both parties to the transaction; therefore, neither party had the same idea of the terms of the agreement. The contract is avoidable by either party.

mutual rescission An agreement by mutual assent of both parties to terminate the contractual relationship and return to the pre-contract status quo.

mutuality of assent Both parties must objectively manifest their intention to enter into a binding contract by accepting all of the terms.

mutuality of contract Also known as "mutuality of obligation"—is a doctrine that requires both parties to be bound to the terms of the agreement.

mutuality of obligation Also known as "mutuality of contract"; it is a doctrine that requires both parties to be bound to performance obligations under the agreement.

N

necessities Goods and services that are required; basic elements of living and employment.

nominal consideration The value of the things exchanged are grossly disproportionate to each other so that very little is given in exchange for something of great value.

nominal damages A small amount of money given to the non-breaching party as a token award to acknowledge the fact of the breach.

nonconforming Goods that are not in reasonable compliance with the specifications in the contract.

nondisclosure The intentional omission of the truth.

novation An agreement that replaces previous contractual obligations with new obligations and/or different parties.

O

objection to terms A merchant must state her disapproval of the offeree's new or different terms within a reasonable time, or else they are considered accepted by her.

objective Impartial and disinterested in the outcome of the dispute.

objective impracticality A party's performance is excused only when the circumstances surrounding the contract become so burdensome that any reasonable person in the same situation would excuse performance.

objectively determinable The ability of the price to be ascertained by a party outside of the contract.

objectively reasonable A standard of behavior that the majority of persons would agree with or how most persons in a community generally act.

obligor The original party to the contract who remains obligated to perform under the contract.

offer A promise made by the offeror to do (or not to do) something provided that the offeree, by accepting, promises or does something in exchange.

offeree The person to whom an offer is made.

offeror The person making the offer to another party.

option contracts A separate and legally enforceable agreement included in the contract stating that the offer cannot be revoked for a certain time period. An option contract is supported by separate consideration unless it is between merchants and controlled by the UCC.

output contract An agreement wherein the quantity that the offeror desires to purchase is all that the offeree can produce.

P

parol evidence Oral testimony offered as proof regarding the terms of a written contact.

parol evidence rule A court evidentiary doctrine that excludes certain types of outside oral testimony offered as proof of the terms of the contract.

partial breach A failure of performance that has little, if any, effect on the expectations of the parties.

partial integration A document that contains the essential terms of the contract but not all the terms that the parties may have or need to agree upon.

partial performance/substantial beginning An offeree has made conscientious efforts to start performing according to the terms of the contract. The performance need not be complete nor exactly as specified, but only an attempt at significant compliance.

partial performance doctrine The court's determination that a party's actions taken in reliance on the oral agreement "substitutes" for the writing and takes the transaction out of the scope of the Statute of Frauds and, thus, can be enforced.

parties The persons involved in the making of the contract. There must be at least two; one to make the offer and the other to accept it.

past consideration A benefit conferred in a previous transaction between the parties before the present promise was made.

performance prevented If a party takes steps to preclude the other party's performance, then the performance is excused due to that interference.

permanent injunction A court order that prohibits a party from acting in a certain way for an indefinite and perpetual period of time.

physical duress The threat of bodily harm unless the aggressor's demands are met.

plain meaning rule Courts will use the traditional definition of terms used in a contract if those terms are not otherwise defined in the agreement.

pledge to charity A legally enforceable gift to a qualifying institution.

poor judgment Contract law does not allow avoidance of performance obligations due to a mistake that was simply a bad decision on the part of one party.

positively and unequivocally In order to treat a party's statement as an anticipatory repudiation, the statements or actions from the potential repudiator must clearly and unquestionably communicate that intent not to perform.

predominant factor test An examination of a transaction to determine whether the primary purpose of the contract is the procurement of goods or services.

preexisting duty An obligation to perform an act that existed before the current promise was made that requires the same performance presently sought.

preliminary hearing An appearance by both parties before the court to assess the circumstances and validity of the restraining application.

present obligation The performances under the contract must not have been carried out but must still be executory in order to be available for a novation.

price The monetary value ascribed by the parties to the exchange involved in the contract.

price under the contract The seller has the right to collect the agreed-upon price for the goods where the buyer has possession, despite the market conditions at the time.

prior or contemporaneous agreements These negotiations and resulting potential terms are governed by the principles of the parol evidence rule.

privity A relationship between the parties to the contract who have rights and obligations to each other through the terms of the agreement.

promisee The party to whom the promise of performance is made.

promisor The party who makes a promise to perform under the contract.

promissory estoppel A legal doctrine that makes some promises enforceable even though they are not compliant with the technical requirements of a contract.

promissory reliance A party's dependence and actions taken upon another's representations that he will carry out his promise.

proper dispatch An approved method of transmitting the acceptance to the offeror.

punitive damages An amount of money awarded to a non-breaching party that is not based on the actual losses incurred by that party, but as a punishment to the breaching party for the commission of an intentional wrong.

Q

quantum meruit A Latin term referring to the determination of the earned value of services provided by a party.

quantum valebant A Latin term referring to the determination of the market worth assignable to the benefit conferred.

quasi-contract/pseudo-contract/implied-in-law contract Where no technical contract exists, the court can create an obligation in the name of justice to promote fairness and afford a remedy to an innocent party and prevent unearned benefits to be conferred on the other party.

R

ratification A step taken by a formerly incapacitated person that confirms and endorses the voidable contract and thereby makes it enforceable.

reasonable Comporting with normally accepted modes of behavior in a particular instance.

reasonable assignment A transfer of performance obligations may only be made where an objective third party would find that the transfer was acceptable under normal circumstances and did not alter the rights and obligations of the original parties.

reformation An order of the court that "rewrites" the agreement to reflect the actual performances of the parties where there has been some deviation from the contractual obligations.

rejection A refusal to accept the terms of an offer.

reliance A party's dependence and actions based on the assertions of another party.

reliance damages A monetary amount that "reimburses" the non-breaching party for expenses incurred while preparing to perform her obligations under the agreement but lost due to the breach.

resale value The non-breaching party's attempt to mitigate damages may require that he sell the unaccepted goods on the open market. The non-breaching party can recover the difference in price between the market price and the contract price.

requirements contract An agreement wherein the quantity that the offeror desires to purchase is all that the offeror needs.

rescission and restitution A decision by the court that renders the contract null and void and requires the parties to return to the wronged party any benefits received under the agreement.

restitution damages A monetary amount that requires the breaching party to return any benefits received under the contract to the non-breaching party to ensure that the breaching party does not profit from the breach.

retract the repudiation Until the aggrieved party notifies the repudiator or takes some action in reliance on the repudiation, the repudiator has the right to "take it back" and perform on the contract.

revocation The offeror's cancellation of the right of the offeree to accept an offer.

revocation of a previous acceptance A buyer has the right to refuse to accept the seller's attempts at a cure if those attempts are still not in conformance with the contract requirements.

right to transfer The party supplying the goods must have the legal title (ownership) or legal ability to give it to the receiving party.

S

sale on approval The agreement may provide that the contract for sale is not consummated until the buyer receives and approves of the goods.

sale or return The agreement provides that if the buyer is unable to resell the goods, she is permitted to return the unsold goods to the original seller.

severability of contract The ability of a court to choose to separate and discard those clauses in a contract that are unenforceable and retain those that are.

sham consideration An unspecified and indeterminable recitation of consideration that cannot support an exchange.

signed by the party to be charged The writing that purports to satisfy the Statute of Frauds must be signed by the party against whom enforcement is sought.

silence In certain circumstances, no response may be necessary to properly accept an offer.

solicited offer An invitation for members of a group to whom it is sent (potential offerors) to make an offer to the party sending the information (the potential offeree).

specialized goods A product made for a particular buyer with specifications unique to that buyer so that it could not be sold on the general market.

specific performance A court order that requires a party to perform a certain act in order to prevent harm to the requesting party.

specific reasons for rejection The buyer is under an obligation to notify the seller within a reasonable time not only that the goods have been rejected but also the reasons for the refusal to accept the goods.

speculative damages Harm incurred by the non-breaching party that is not susceptible to valuation or determination with any reasonable certainty.

spot sale A purchase on the open market in that particular place at that particular time.

standards of good faith and fair dealing A party's performance will be judged in light of the normal or acceptable behavior displayed generally by others in a similar position.

statutory authority The legislature of a jurisdiction may codify certain actions as subject to punitive damages if they occur in conjunction with a contractual breach.

subsequent agreements Negotiations and potential terms that are discussed after the agreement has been memorialized are not covered by the parol evidence rule.

subject matter The bargained-for exchange of goods and/or services that forms the basis for the contract.

substantial beginning An offeree has made conscientious efforts to start performing according to the terms of the contract. The performance need not be complete nor exactly as specified, but only an attempt at significant compliance.

substantial compliance A legal doctrine that permits close approximations of perfect performance to satisfy the contractual terms.

substantial detriment The change in a party's position in reliance upon another's representations that, if unanswered, will work a hardship on that party.

substituted agreement A replacement of a previous agreement with a new contract with additional but not inconsistent obligations.

substituted goods The products purchased on the open market that replace those not delivered by the breaching party.

sufficient consideration The exchanges have recognizable legal value and are capable of supporting an enforceable contract. The actual values are irrelevant.

supervening illegality A change in the law, during the time in which the contract was executory, governing the subject matter of the contract that renders a previously legal and enforceable contract void and therefore excusable.

supplemental Evidence which adds to, but does not contradict, the original agreement is admissible under the parol evidence rule.

supplemental agreements Those writings of the parties are those that naturally add to, but do not conflict with, the original terms of the partially integrated contract.

surety A party who assumes primary liability for the payment of another's debt.

T

transactions in goods A sale or other transfer of title to identifiable, tangible, movable things from a merchant to a buyer.

technical terms, specifications, or trade/business custom Parol evidence is permitted to explain the meaning of special language in the contract as the parties understood it if the plain ordinary meaning of the language was not intended or was ambiguous.

temporary injunction A court order that prohibits a party from acting in a certain way for a limited period of time.

tender of delivery The seller is ready to transfer the goods to the buyer and the goods are at the disposal of the buyer.

tender of performance The offeree's act of proffering the start of his contractual obligations. The offeree stands ready, willing, and able to perform.

third-party beneficiary A person, not a party to the contract, who stands to receive the benefit of performance of the contract.

time for performance A condition that requires each party be given a reasonable time to complete performance.

time of the essence A term in a contract that indicates that no extensions for the required performance will be permitted. The performance must occur on or before the specified date.

tortious A private civil wrong committed by one person as against another that the law considers to be punishable.

total breach A failure of performance that has a substantial effect on the expectations of the parties.

transfer of interest In a purchase agreement, a preliminary requirement is that the seller has legal title to the subject matter and authority to transfer it to the seller. If the seller transfers his interest to a third party, this preliminary requirement can no longer be met.

TRO A temporary restraining order that is issued prior to any hearing in the court.

U

unconscionable So completely unreasonable and irrational that it shocks the conscience.

under the influence Persons who do not have the capacity to understand a transaction due to overconsumption of alcohol or the use of drugs, either legal or illegal, and, therefore, who do not have the requisite mental intent to enter into a contract.

undue influence Using a close personal or fiduciary relationship to one's advantage to gain assent to terms that the party otherwise would not have agreed to.

unforeseen circumstances Occurrences that could not be reasonably forecast to happen.

unilateral contract A contract in which the parties exchange a promise for an act.

unilateral mistake An error made by only one party to the transaction. The contract may be avoided only if the error is detectable or obvious to the other party.

unjust enrichment The retention by a party of unearned and undeserved benefits derived from his own wrongful actions regarding an agreement.

usage of the trade Actions generally taken by similarly situated parties in similar transactions in the same business field.

V

value The worth of the goods or services in the transaction as determined by an objective outside standard.

value of the goods as accepted The buyer is entitled to a "set-off" for the difference between the price of the goods as specified in the contract and the actual price those goods would garner on the open market.

V + E + L − M − R = D Value + Expenses + Losses − Mitigation − Received value = Damages

vested   Having a present right to receive the benefit of the performance when it becomes due.

void   A transaction that is impossible to be enforced because it is invalid.

voidable   Having the possibility of avoidance of performance at the option of the incapacitated party.

voidable obligation   A duty imposed under a contract that may be either ratified (approved) or avoided (rejected) at the option of one or both of the parties.

voluntary destruction   If a party destroys the subject matter of the contract, thereby rendering performance impossible, the other party is excused from his performance obligations due to that termination.

voluntary disablement   If a party takes steps to preclude his own performance, then the performance due from the other party is excused due to that refusal/inability to perform.

voluntary repayment of debt   An agreement to pay back a debt that cannot be collected upon using legal means because the obligation to make payments has been discharged.

W

waiver   A party may knowingly and intentionally forgive the other party's breach and continue her performance obligations under the contract.

warranty   A promise or representation by the seller that the goods in question meet certain standards.

warranty of title   The seller promises the buyer that the seller has the right to transfer the title free and clear of encumbrances to the buyer.

writing to satisfy the Statute of Frauds   A document or compilation of documents containing the essential terms of the agreement.

Index

A

Abuse of process, 202
Acceptance, 67–92
  affirmative, 69–70
  of bilateral contracts, 71–77
  cardinal change doctrine, 68–69
  case in point, 90–92
  communication of, 80
  conditional, 15
  of counteroffers, case in point, 84–89
  limitations on, 421
  mailbox rule, 71–77. *See also*
    Mailbox rule
  mirror image rule, 68–71
  mutual assent, 70
  partial performance as, 77–80
  reliance on, 77–78
  of services or goods, 71
  silence as, 70–71, 424
  solicited offers, 71
  substantial beginnings, 15, 77–80
  tender of performance, 79
  under UCC, 429–430
  under UETA, 75–76
  of unilateral contracts, 77–80
Accord and satisfaction, 330–332,
  341–349
"Action" damages, 390–395
  injunctions, 390–393. *See also*
    Injunctions
  specific performance, 393–395
Active concealment, 207
Adequate assurances, 258, 431–432
Adequate compensation for breach, 263
Adequate consideration, 48
Advertisements, 22–35
Affirmative acts of anticipatory
  repudiation, 259
Affirmative defenses, 165–194
  capacity, 165–173, 286–287. *See also*
    Capacity
  illegality, 17–19, 173–178, 289–291. *See*
    also Illegality
Affirmative duties, 205–207
Alimony payments, 97
Ambiguous terms, 224–225
American Law Institute (ALI), 416
American rule of attorneys' fees and
  costs, 377

Antenuptial agreements, 151
Anticipation, 258
Anticipatory repudiation, 258–262
  adequate assurances, 258
  affirmative acts, 259
  cancellation of contract, 260–261
  ignoring repudiation, 260–261
  lawsuit, immediate right to
    commence, 260
  positive and unequivocal statements,
    258–259
  retractions of, 261
  transfers of interest, 258–259
As-is provisions, 206
Assent, mutual, 4–5
Assignees/assignors, 121
Assignment, 120–125. *See also* Delegation
  assignment, defined, 120
  case in point, 128–131
  compared to delegation, 122
  crytpo contracts, 124
  e-commerce, 124
  obligor, 121
  prohibition of, 122
  reasonable assignment, 123
Attorney-client relationship. *See*
  Ethics issues
Attorneys' fees and costs, 377–379
Automated transactions, 8

B

Bargained for exchanges, 41–42
Battle of the forms, 421–423
Beneficiaries
  incidental, 114–115
  intended, 114–115
  third-party, 113–137. *See also*
    Assignment; Delegation;
    Third-party interests
Benefit conferred, 42
Bilateral contracts
  acceptance of, 71–77. *See also*
    Acceptance
  mirror image rule, 68
Black letter law, 44, 145, 300, 390, 403
Blackmail, 202
Blockchain. *See* Crypto contracts
Breaches of contract, 257–282
  ability to cure, 263

adequate compensation, 263
anticipatory repudiation, 258–262. *See*
  also Anticipatory repudiation
crypto contracts issues, 264
defined, 6, 258
deprivation of expected benefit, 263
divisibility, 269–270
ethics issues, 266–267
excused from performance, 264
fair dealing standard, 263
forfeitures, 263
good faith standard, 263
intention of parties, 264, 269
material elements or terms, 262
materiality, 262–269, 276–282
nonconformity, 429
objectivity and, 263
partial breaches, 264
separate assent, 269–270
severability, 269–270
software licensing and, 262–263
substantial compliance, 263–264
total breaches, 264
under UCC, 429–431
waivers, 270–272
Bright line rules, 390
Business custom, 226–228
Buyer's remedies, UCC, 434–436

C

Calculation of damages, 365–368,
  372–375, 383–388
Cancellation of contract, 260–261
Cannabis industry, 289–290
Capacity, 166–173
  case in point, 181–184
  crypto contracts and, 175
  death or incapacity of parties, 16,
    286–287
  disavowal of incapacity, 167
  dram-shop liability, 172
  e-commerce and, 167
  infancy doctrine, 166
  intoxication, 171–173
  invalid contractual purpose, 171–173
  legislative exceptions, 169
  malum in se, 173–174
  malum prohibitum, 174
  medicinal side effects, 171–173

481

Capacity (*cont.*)
  mental infirmity, 166, 169–171
  minors, 47, 166–169
  necessities exceptions, 168–169
  offers and, 16–17
  ratifications and, 166
  under the influence, 166, 171–173
  voidable transactions, 166
  void transactions, 166
Cardinal change doctrine, 68–69
Cases in point
  acceptance, 90–92
  accord and satisfaction, 341–349
  advertisements and offers, 22–35
  assignment, 128–131
  attempts to rescind, 36–40
  capacity, 181–184
  conditions, 106–112
  counteroffers and acceptance, 84–89
  damages, calculation and award of,
    383–388
  equitable damages, 405–409
  fraud in the inducement, 213–220
  frustration of purpose, 304–312
  illegality, 185–194
  impossibility of performance, 298–303
  legally sufficient consideration, 56–66
  novations or modifications, 350–356
  parol evidence and rules of
    construction, 243–250
  predominance test, UCC, 440–452
  Statute of Frauds and partial
    performance, 159–164
  supervening illegality, 313–324
  third-party beneficiaries, 131–135
  trade usage, 238–242
Certainty of terms, 6–12, 16, 142–143, 222
Changes by agreement of parties, 325–358
  accord and satisfaction, 330–332,
    341–349
  cardinal change doctrine, 68–69
  consent, 333
  covenant not to sue, 327–328, 328*f*
  e-commerce, 337
  ethics issues, 327
  extinguishment of liability, 333
  forgoing legal right to sue, 331–332
  mergers, 332
  modifications, 335–337, 350–356
  mutual rescission, 326–328
  novations, 332–335, 350–356
  present obligations, 333
  releases, 328–330, 329*f*
  substituted agreements, 332–335
Charities, pledges to, 51
Commercial units, defined, 430
Communication of offers, 12–13
Compensatory damages, 361–388. *See
  also* Damages

Complete integration, 229
Concealment, 207
Conditional acceptance, 15
Conditional fee arrangements, 95–96
Conditions, 93–112
  case in point, 106–112
  compared to covenants, 94
  concurrent, 97–98
  consideration, attached to, 49
  creation, methods of, 98–103
  crypto contracts, 99
  defined, 93–94
  ethical considerations, 95–96
  express, 98–99
  implied in fact, 100
  implied in law, 100–102
  precedent, 94–96
  subsequent, 96–97
  time for performance, 102–103
  types of, 94–98
Consent of parties, 333
Consequential damages, 370–371, 435
Consideration, 41–66
  adequate, 48
  benefit conferred as, 42
  case in point, 56–66
  compared to gifts, 44
  compared to guarantees, 52
  compared to illusory promises, 44
  compared to moral obligations, 44, 52
  compared to preexisting duties, 46–47
  conditions attached to, 49
  crypto contracts, 43
  defined, 41–42
  detriment incurred as, 42
  duty owed to third person as, 46
  e-commerce, 50–51
  ethics issues, 50
  excluded exchanges, 44–48
  forbearance of legal right as, 42–43
  forgoing legal right to sue as, 331–332
  formal contracts, 52
  good consideration, 48–49
  legal value, 42–48
  minors and, 167
  mutuality of obligation/contract, 44
  new or different, 47
  nominal, 48
  past consideration, 46
  pledges to charities, 51
  rules of construction for, 231
  sham, 49
  special agreements, 51–52
  sufficient, 48–51
  unforeseen circumstances and, 47
  voidable obligations, 47
  voluntary repayment of debt, 51–52
Conspicuous limitations of
  warranties, 426

Construction, rules of. *See* Rules of
  construction
Contemporaneous or prior
  agreements, 233
Contract formation
  acceptance, 67–92. *See also* Acceptance
  conditions, 93–112. *See also*
    Conditions
  consideration, 41–66. *See also*
    Consideration
  defects in, 139–220, 230. *See also*
    Defects in formation
  missing terms and, 419–421
  offers, 3–40. *See also* Offers
  third-party interests, 113–137. *See also*
    Third-party interests
Contract price, 433
Contracts
  adhesion contracts, 201–203
  bilateral, 5–6
  elements of, 7–12. *See also* Contract
    formation
  employment, 6, 123. *See also*
    Employment contracts
  executory/executed, 12
  express, 13
  failure of performance, 255–258. *See
    also* Failure of performance
  formal, 52
  implied, 13
  lease agreements. *See* Lease
    agreements
  option contracts, 18
  output contracts, 11
  parties to, 7–8, 16–17
  personal services contracts, 7
  purpose of, 291–292
  quasi-contracts, 398. *See also* Equity
    and quasi-contracts
  real estate. *See* Real estate contracts
  remedies, contract law, 6, 359–412. *See
    also* Damages; Equity and quasi-
    contracts
  remedies, UCC, 413–456. *See also*
    Remedies, UCC
  requirements contracts, 11
  severability, 177–178
  third-party interests. *See* Third-party
    interests
  UCC, Article 2, 415–456. *See also*
    Uniform Commercial Code
    (UCC), Article 2
  unilateral, 5–6, 77–80. *See also*
    Unilateral contracts
  void, 166
  voidable, 166
Contradictory evidence, 228, 230
Controlled Substances Act, 289–290
Costs, excessive and unreasonable, 284

Counteroffers
case in point, 84–89
mirror image rule, 68–69
termination of contract and, 15
under UCC, 421
Course of dealing, 226
Course of performance, 226
Court-ordered solutions, 395–397
Covenants
compared to conditions, 94
not to compete, 149–150, 176, 392–393
not to sue, 327–328, 328*f*
Covering losses, 374, 434
Creditors, 117–120
Crypto contracts
ambiguity, 228
conditions, 99
consideration, 43
contracts of adhesion, 202–203
excuses of law, 290
inflexibility, 264
introduction, 8
liquidated damages, 376
mailbox rule, 76–77
mistakes, 198–199
rules of construction, 232
substituted agreements/novations, 333
third-party interests, 125
Cure under UCC, 429
Custom, 226–228

D

Damages, 361–388. *See also* Equity and
quasi-contracts; Remedies, UCC
action, 390–395
American rule of attorneys' fees and
costs, 377
attorneys' fees and costs, 377–379
calculation of, 365–368, 372–375
case in point, 383–388
compensatory damages, 365–368
consequential damages, 370–371, 435
crypto contracts, 376
e-commerce, 374–375
equity and quasi-contracts, 389–412. *See
also* Equity and quasi-contracts
ethical considerations, 378–379
expectation damages, 365–366
incidental damages, 370–371, 433, 435
limitation of, 377
liquidated damages, 375–376
lost profits, 362–363
mitigation of, 368–370
nominal damages, 372
not recoverable, 362–365
punitive damages, 364–365
reliance damages, 367–368
restitution damages, 366–367
for sale of goods under UCC, 373–374

speculative damages, 362–364
Dating sites, consideration issues, 50–51
Dealings with merchants, 415–456. *See
also* Uniform Commercial Code
(UCC), Article 2
Death or incapacity of parties, 16, 286–287
Debt, voluntary repayment of, 51–52
Debt of another, agreement to pay, 52,
152–153
Declaratory judgment, 395–396
Declaratory Relief Act, 395–396
Defects in formation, 139–220
capacity, 165–173. *See also* Capacity
defined, 230
illegality, 173–178. *See also* Illegality
meeting of the minds, 195–220. *See
also* Meeting of the minds
rules of construction, 221–253. *See also*
Rules of construction
Statute of Frauds, 141–164. *See also*
Statute of Frauds
Defenses
affirmative, 165–194. *See also* Capacity;
Illegality
formative, 195–220. *See also* Meeting of
the minds
third-party interests, 120
Delegants/delegators, 121
Delegates/delegatees, 121
Delegation, 120–125. *See also* Assignment
compared to assignment, 122
compared to novations, 334
defined, 120
prohibition of, 122
Delivery, 433
Deprivation of expected benefit, 263
Deterrent effect of punitive damages, 364
Detrimental effect, 197
Detrimental reliance, 15
Detriment incurred, 42
Disavowal, 167
Divisibility, 269–270
Divorce settlements, 269–270
Doctrine of unclean hands, 401–402
Domestic relations mediation, 152
Donees, 117–118
Dram-shop liability, 172
Duress, 200–203
Duties
affirmative, 205–207
defined, 368
to mitigate damages, 368–370
owed to third person, 46
preexisting, 46
to resell, 430

E

E-commerce
acceptance of contract, 75–76

business custom and usage in, 227
calculating damages, 374–375
changes by agreement of parties, 337
dating sites, consideration issues,
50–51
end-user license agreements, 292
injunctions, 393
insurance policies, 124
meeting of the minds, 198
minors and, 167
online auction site agreements, 99
software licensing, 262–263
Statute of Frauds and, 143–144
UCITA and UCC, 426–428
UETA, 7–8, 75–76
Economic duress, 201
Electronic agents, 8
Elements of contract. *See* Contract
formation
Employment contracts
accord and satisfaction, case in point,
341–349
assignment of, 123
at-will, 6
conditions, case in point, 106–112
consideration, case in point, 56–60
covenants not to compete, 149, 176,
392–393
drafting exercise, 11
mitigation of damages, 370
Statute of Frauds and, 148–149
third party beneficiaries, case in point,
131–135
unilateral/bilateral, 6
Equity and quasi-contracts, 389–412
action damages, 390–395
black letter law, 390
bright line rules, 390
case in point, 405–409
court-ordered solutions, 395–397
covenants not to compete, 149, 176,
392–393
declaratory judgments, 395–396
equitable remedies, 390
equity, defined, 390
implied-in-law contracts, 398
injunctions, 390–393
irreparable harm, 390
permanent injunctions, 391
preliminary hearings, 390
promissory estoppel, 398–399
promissory reliance, 398–399
pseudo-contracts, 398
quantum meruit, 400
quantum valebant, 400
quasi-contracts, 398
reformation, 397
rescission and restitution, 396–397
specific performance, 393–395

Equity and quasi-contracts (*cont.*)
    substantial detriment, 399
    temporary injunctions, 390
    TROs, 391
    unauthorized practice of law, 394–395
    unclean hands doctrine, 401–402
    unjust enrichment, prevention of,
        399–401
Ethics issues
    attorney-attorney relationships,
        266–267
    attorney-client contracts, 10
    business transactions with clients, 70,
        229–230
    conditional fee arrangements, 95–96
    continuing legal education, 291
    domestic relations mediations, 152
    fee arrangements, 50
    illegal schemes by clients, 175–176
    incapacity of attorney, 287
    insurance policies, 116–117
    malpractice claims, 378–379
    rescission, 327
    sale of goods by attorneys, 418–419
    unauthorized practice of law, 394–395
    undue influence, 204
Evidence
    contradictory, 228, 230
    explanatory, 228
    parol, 228–233. *See also* Parol evidence
Excessive and unreasonable costs, 284
Exclusion of warranties, 426
Excuse of performance, 283–324
    continuing legal education
        requirements and, 290
    crypto contracts, 290
    death or incapacity of parties, 286–287
    destruction of subject matter, 287–289
    end-user license agreements, 292
    excessive and unreasonable costs, 284
    force majeure, 289
    forfeiture, 295–296
    frustration of purpose, 291–292,
        304–312
    impossibility, 285–291, 298–303
    impracticality, 284–285
    insolvency, 294–295
    performance prevented, 293–294
    supervening illegality, 289–291, 313–324
    voluntary destruction, 293–294
    voluntary disablement, 293–294
Executed contracts, 12
Executory contracts, 12
Existence of subject matter, 197
Expectation damages, 365–366
Expected deprivation of benefits, 263
Explanatory evidence, 228
Express contracts, 13
Extinguishment of liability, 333

F
Failure of performance
    breaches of contract, 257–282. *See also*
        Breaches of contract
    changes by agreement of parties,
        325–358. *See also* Changes by
        agreement of parties
    excuse of performance, 283–324. *See
        also* Excuse of performance
Fair dealing standard, 263
Fee-splitting agreements, 267–269
Fiduciary relationships, 203–204
Finish or scrap, 433
Firm offers, 18, 423–424
Forbearance of legal rights, 42–43
Force majeure, 289
Foreseeability, 197
Forfeiture, 263, 295–296
Forgoing legal right to sue, 331–332
Formal contracts, 52
Formation of contracts. *See* Contract
        formation
Forms, battle of, 421–423
Four corners doctrine, 222–226
Fraud, 204–208
    active concealment, 207
    affirmative duties, 205–207
    as-is provisions, 206
    case in point, 213–220
    intent to deceive, 204–205
    nondisclosure, 205–207
Freedom of contract, 222, 379
Fruits of the land, sales of, 146
Frustration of purpose doctrine, 291–292,
        304–312

G
Gambling, 174
Gifts, 44, 51
Good consideration, 48–49
Good faith standard, 263
Goods. *See* Sale of goods
Guarantees, 52, 152–153
Guarantor, 153

I
Identification of goods to the
        contract, 428
Illegality
    case in point, 185–194
    covenants not to compete, 176
    ethics and, 175–176
    formation of contracts, 173–178
    illegal schemes, 174
    severability of contracts, 177–178
    supervening, 17–19, 289–291, 313–324
Illinois Rules of Professional
        Responsibility, 267–269
Illusory promises, 9, 44

Immediate right to commence
        lawsuit, 260
Implied contracts, 13
Implied-in-fact conditions, 100, 155
Implied-in-law
    conditions, 100–102
    contracts, 398
Implied warranties, 425
Impossibility of performance, 16,
        285–291
    case in point, 298–303
    death or incapacity, 286–287
    destruction of subject matter,
        287–289
    force majeure, 289
    supervening illegality, 289–290
Impracticality of performance, 284–285
Incapacity. *See* Capacity
Incidental beneficiaries, 114–115
Incidental damages, 370–371, 433, 435
Infancy doctrine, 166
Injunctions, 390–393
    covenants not to compete, 392–393
    permanent, 391
    temporary/TROs, 390
Insanity, 16–17. *See also* Capacity
Insolvency, 294–295, 432
Insurance policies
    assertion of defenses, 120
    assignment, case in point, 128–130
    attorney conflicts of interest and,
        116–117
    beneficiary's right to sue, 117
    crypto contracts for, 125
    death or incapacity of party, 286
    e-commerce and, 124
    forbearance of right to sue, 42–43
    illegality, case in point, 313–324
    incapacity of policy holder, 286
    rules of construction for, 225
    third-party interests, 114
Integration of agreements, 228–229
Intended beneficiaries, 114–115
Intent
    battle of the forms, 421–423
    breaches of contract, 264
    to deceive, 204–205
    meeting of the minds, 195–220. *See
        also* Meeting of the minds
    third-party beneficiaries, 114–115
Intoxication, 171–173
Irreparable harm, 390
Irrevocable offers, 18, 77–78, 185–194

J
Joint venture agreements, 146–147

K
Knowledge of offer, 69

L

Last in time = first in right principle, 224
Lawsuit, immediate right to
    commence, 260
Lease agreements
    consideration, case in point, 61–66
    delegation, subleases and, 121–122, 124
    divisibility of, 269
    duty to mitigate, 369
    frustration of purpose, 291–292
    mailbox rule and, 72
    with minors, 166, 168–169
    partial performance, case in point,
        159–164
    promissory estoppel, 399
    Statute of Frauds and, 145
    substitute agreements/novations, 334
    unclean hands doctrine, 401–402
Legal remedies, 6, 359–412
    compensatory and related damages,
        361–388. *See also* Damages
    equity and quasi-contracts, 389–412. *See
        also* Equity and quasi-contracts
    under UCC, 432–436. *See also*
        Remedies, UCC
Legal value, 18, 42–44
Legislation on contracts with minors, 169
Letters of intent, 15
Limitation of damages, 377
Liquidated damages, 375–376
Loan sharking, 174
Lost profits, 362–363

M

Mailbox rule, 71–77
    change of mind by offeree, 74
    email delivery, 72
    option contracts exception, 75
    proper dispatch, 71–72
    rejection of offer, 73–74
    reliance, 74–75
    revocation of offer, 73
Malum in se, 173–174
Malum prohibitum, 174
Market price, 373, 433–435
Marriage, 150–152
    domestic relations mediation and, 152
    prenuptial agreements, 150–151
    unmarried couples, agreements
        between, 151
Material alteration, 421
Material breaches, 262–269, 276–282
Material terms/materiality, 197, 262
Medicinal side effects, 171–173
Meeting of the minds, 195–220
    crypto contracts, 198–199, 202–203
    defined, 7, 196
    duress, 200–203
    e-commerce, 198

fraud and misrepresentation, 204–208.
    See also Fraud
mutual mistakes, 9–10, 197–200
unconscionability, 208–209
undue influence, 203–204
unilateral mistakes, 196–197
Memorandum of Understanding (MOU),
    144–145
Mental duress, 201
Mental infirmity, 166
Merchantability, 425
Merchants, 226, 419–420
Mere request for change, 261
Mergers, 232, 332
Minors
    capacity of, 166–169
    legislative exceptions, 169
    necessities exceptions, 168–169
    voidable obligations, 47
Mirror image rule, 68–71
    acceptance of services or goods, 71
    affirmative acceptance, 69–70
    cardinal change doctrine, 68–69
    knowledge of offer, 69
    silence as acceptance, 70–71
Misrepresentation, 204–208. *See also* Fraud
Mistakes, 196–200
    in crypto contracts, 198–199
    mutual, 197–200
    unilateral, 196–197
Mitigation of damages, 368–370
Modifications, 350–356, 421
Moral obligations, 44, 52
Mortgages. *See* Real estate contracts
MOU (Memorandum of Understanding),
    144–145
Mutual assent, 4–5, 70
Mutuality of contract/obligation, 4–5, 44
Mutual mistakes, 197–200
    detrimental effect, 197
    existence of subject matter, 197
    foreseeability, 197
    identity or quality issues, 197, 199–200
    material terms, 197
    ownership issues, 199–200
    poor judgment, 197
    right to transfer, 197
    subject matter, existence of, 197,
        199–200
Mutual rescission, 326–328

N

Natural catastrophes, 289
Necessities, incapacity and, 168–169
Nominal consideration, 48
Nominal damages, 372
Nonbinding offers, 15
Nonconformity, 429
Nondisclosure, 205–207

Nonmaterial breaches, 262–269, 276–282
Non-Negotiable Confidential Disclosure
    Agreement (NDA), 144–145
Novations, 332–335
    compared to delegation, 334
    crypto contracts, 333
    renegotiations and, 333–334

O

Objections to terms, 421
Objective impracticality, 285
Objectively determinable price, 9
Objectively reasonable standard, 4–5
Objectivity and breach of contract, 263
Obligors, 121
Offerees, 3, 12–13
Offerors, 3
Offers, 3–40
    attempt to rescind, case in
        point, 36–40
    case in point, 22–35
    certainty of terms, 6–12
    communication of, 12–13
    conditional acceptance, 15
    counteroffers, 15, 68–69, 84–89, 421
    death of party, 16
    defined, 4
    destruction or loss of subject
        matter, 17
    detrimental reliance, 15
    e-commerce, 7–8
    firm offers, 18, 423–424
    incapacity, 16–17
    irrevocable, 18, 77–78, 185–194
    knowledge of, 69
    letters of intent, 15
    method of creation, 13
    mutual assent, 4–5
    nonbinding, 15
    parties to, 7–8
    price, 8–9
    reasonability standard, 4–5
    rejection of, 15, 73–74
    revocation of, 14, 73
    solicited, 71
    subject matter, 9–11
    substantial beginnings, 15
    supervening illegality, 17–19
    termination of, 13–19. *See also*
        Termination of offers
    time for performance, 11–12
    time of the essence clauses, 12
Online auction site agreements, 99
Option contracts
    defined, 18
    firm offers, 423–424
    mailbox rule and, 75
    tender of performance, 79
Output contracts, 11

P

Parol evidence, 228–233
  admissibility of, 228–229
  case in point, 243–250
  consideration, 231
  contradictory evidence, 228
  defects in formation, 230
  ethics issues, 229–230
  explanatory evidence, 228
  integration, 228–229
  merger clauses and, 232
  parol evidence rule, 228
  prior or contemporaneous
    agreements, 233
  specifications, 231
  Statute of Frauds and, 231–232
  subsequent agreements, 233
  supplemental agreements, 229
  supplemental evidence, 229
  technical terms, 231
  trade/business custom, 231
Partial breaches, 264
Partial integration, 229
Partial performance doctrine, 154–156,
    159–164
Parties to contract, 7–8, 16–17
Past consideration, 46
Performance, 428–429
  cure, 429
  failure of, 255–358. *See also* Failure of
    performance
  identification of goods, 428
  inspection, 428
  nonconforming goods, 428–429
  prevented, 293–294
  tender of delivery, 428
Permanent injunctions, 391
Personal property, UCC, 418
Personal services contracts, 7
Persons under the influence, 166, 171–173
Physical duress, 201
Plain meaning rule, 223
Pledges to charities, 51
Poor judgment, 197
Positive and unequivocal statements,
    258–259
Predominant factor test, 417, 440–452
Preexisting duties, 46–47, 69
Preliminary hearings, 390
Prenuptial agreements, 150–151
Present obligations, 333
Prevention of unjust enrichment, 399–401
Price, 8–9
  under the contract, 433
  objectively determinable, 9
  UCC definition, 153–154
Prior or contemporaneous
    agreements, 233
Privity, 114

Professional responsibility. *See*
    Ethics issues
Promisees, 114
Promises, illusory, 9
Promisors, 114
Promissory estoppel, 398–399
Promissory reliance, 398–399
Property rentals. *See* Lease
    agreements
Pseudo-contracts, 398
Punitive damages, 364–365

Q

Quantum meruit, 400
Quantum valebant, 400
Quasi-contracts, 398

R

Ratification, 166
Real estate contracts
  acceptance, case in point, 90–92
  ambiguous terms in, 224–225
  conditions, 49, 100
  death or incapacity of party, 286
  declaratory relief, 396
  nondisclosure, 205–207
  novations or modifications, case in
    point, 350–356
  partial performance, 15, 154–155
  reliance damages, 367
  specific performance, 394
  time of the essence clauses, 12
Reasonability standard, 4–5
Reformation, 397
Rejection of offers
  defined, 15
  mailbox rule and, 73–74
  under UCC, 430–431
Releases, 328–330
Reliance, 74–75, 77–80
Reliance damages, 367–368
Remedies, contract law, 359–412
  compensatory damages, 361–388. *See*
    also Damages
  equity and quasi-contracts,
    389–412. *See also* Equity and
    quasi-contracts
Remedies, UCC, 432–436
  buyer's, 434–436
  consequential damages, 435
  contract price, 433
  covering the loss, 434
  delivery, 433
  finish or scrap, 433
  incidental damages, 433, 435
  insolvency, 432
  market price, 433–435
  resale, 433
  seller's, 432–434

  spot sales, 435
  value of goods as accepted, 435
Renegotiations, 333–334
Requirements contracts, 11
Resale, 433
Resale value, 374
Rescission
  case in point, 36–40
  mutual, 326–328
  restitution and, 396–397
Resell, duty to, 430
Restatement (Second) of Contracts, 4, 14,
    94, 117, 148, 263
Restatement (Second) of Torts, 206
Restitution
  damages, 366–367
  rescission and, 396–397
Retraction of repudiation, 261
Revocation
  defined, 14
  mailbox rule, 73
  of previous acceptance, 429
Right of transfer, 197
Right to sue, 117–120, 331–332
Rules of construction, 221–253
  ambiguous terms, 224–225
  big picture, 224
  business custom, 226–228
  certainty of terms, 222
  complete integration, 229
  for consideration, 231
  course of dealing, 226
  course of performance, 226
  crypto contracts, 228, 232
  e-commerce, 227
  four corners doctrine, 222–226
  freedom of contract, 222
  last in time = first in right
    principle, 224
  parol evidence, 228–233, 243–250. *See*
    also Parol evidence
  plain meaning rule, 223
  trade usage, 226–228, 238–242
Rules of Professional Responsibility. *See*
    Ethics issues

S

Sale of goods, 415–456. *See also* Uniform
    Commercial Code (UCC),
    Article 2
  on approval, 426
  covering losses, 374, 434
  damages related to, 373–374
  goods valued over $500, 153–154
  identification of goods, 428
  market price, 373
  remedies, UCC, 432–434
  resale value, 374
  sale or return, 426

specialized goods, 420–421
spot sales, 435
substituted goods, 374
value as accepted, 435
value of goods, 373
Severability, 177–178, 269–270
Sham consideration, 49
Signature requirements, 144–145
Silence as acceptance, 70–71, 123, 424
Smart contracts. *See* Crypto contracts
Software licensing, 262–263
Solicited offers, 71
Special agreements, 51–52
Specialized goods, 420–421
Specific performance, 393–395
Specific reasons for rejection, 431
Speculative damages, 362–364
Spot sales, 435
Statute of Frauds, 141–164
    applicability of, 145–156
    case in point, 159–164
    covenants not to compete, 149–150
    debt of another, agreements to pay,
        152–153
    domestic relations mediation, 152
    e-commerce and, 143–144
    guarantees, 152–153
    implied in fact conditions, 155
    joint venture agreements, 146–147
    marriage contracts, 150–152. *See also*
        Marriage
    parol evidence and, 231–232
    partial performance doctrine, 154–156
    performance within one-year
        requirement, 148–150
    real property interests, transfer of,
        145–147
    sale of goods valued over $500,
        153–154
    signature requirement, 144–145
    state law and, 142
    stock transfers, 147
    sureties, 152–153
    writing requirement, 142–145
Statutory authority, punitive
    damages, 364
Stock transfers, 147
Subject matter, 9–11
    destruction or loss of, 17
    existence of, 197
    identity or quality of, 197
Subleases, 121–122, 124
Subsequent agreements, 233
Substantial beginnings, 15, 77–80
Substantial compliance, 263–264
Substantial detriment, 399
Substituted agreements, 332–335
Substituted goods, 374
Sufficient consideration, 48–51

Supervening illegality, 17–19, 289–291,
    313–324
Supplemental agreements, 229
Sureties, 152–153

T
Temporary injunctions, 390
Temporary restraining orders (TROs), 391
Tender of delivery, 428
Tender of performance, 79
Termination of offers, 13–19
    death of party, 16
    detrimental reliance, 15
    lapse of time, 14
    rejection, 15, 73–74
    revocation, 73
    substantial beginnings, effect of, 15
Third-party beneficiaries, 114
Third-party creditor beneficiary contract,
    117–118
Third-party interests, 113–137
    assertion of defenses, 120
    assignees/assignors, 121
    assignment, 120–125, 128–131
    case in point, 131–135
    creditors, 117–120
    crypto contracts, 125
    delegants/delegators, 121
    delegates/delegatees, 121
    delegation of contractual rights and
        obligations, 120–125
    donees, 117–118
    e-commerce, 124
    employment contracts, 123
    ethics issues, 116–117
    incidental beneficiaries, 114–115
    intended beneficiaries, 114–115
    obligors, 121
    privity, 114
    promisees, 114
    promisors, 114
    reasonable assignment, 123
    right to sue, 117–120
    third-party beneficiary, defined, 114
    types of, 114–117
    vested contracts, 118–119
Time of the essence clauses, 12
Time-related conditions
    concurrent conditions, 97
    conditions precedent, 94–95
    conditions subsequent, 96–97
    lapse of time, termination due to, 14
    performance, time for, 11–12, 102–103
    third-party beneficiaries right to sue,
        119–120
    time of the essence clauses, 12
Tortious acts, 365
Total breaches, 264
Trade usage, 226–228

Transactions in goods, 415–456. *See
    also* Uniform Commercial Code
    (UCC), Article 2
Transfer of interest, 197, 258–259. *See
    also* Assignment
TROs (temporary restraining orders), 391

U
UCC. *See* Uniform Commercial Code,
    Article 2
UCITA (Uniform Computer Information
    Transactions Act), 124, 426–428
UETA. *See* Uniform Electronics
    Transactions Act
Unclean hands doctrine, 401–402
Unconscionability, 208–209
Undue influence
    ethics issues, 204
    fiduciary relationships, 203–204
Unequivocal statements, 258–259
Unforeseen circumstances, 47
Uniform Commercial Code (UCC),
    Article 2, 415–456
    acceptance, 429–430
    adequate assurances, 431–432
    battle of the forms, 421–423
    breaches, 429–431
    commercial units, 430
    compensatory and related damages,
        373–374
    contract formation, 419–429
    counteroffers, 421
    covered transactions, 416–419
    cures, 429
    duty to resell, 430
    e-commerce regulation, 426–428
    ethics issues for attorneys, 418–419
    firm offers, 423–424
    merchants, 419–420
    missing terms, 419–421
    modifications, 421
    objections to terms, 421
    overview, 416
    performance, 428–429. *See also*
        Performance
    personal property, rules for, 418
    predominant factor test, 417, 440–452
    price, defined, 153–154
    rejections, 430–431
    remedies, 432–436. *See also*
        Remedies, UCC
    revocation of previous acceptance, 429
    sale of goods valued over $500, 153–
        154
    silence as acceptance, 70–71, 424
    specialized goods, 420–421
    transactions in goods, 416
    value, defined, 153–154
    warranties, 424–428. *See also* Warranties

Uniform Computer Information Transactions Act (UCITA), 124, 426–428
Uniform Electronic Transactions Act (UETA)
    acceptance, 5–6, 75–76
    application of traditional contract doctrines, 175
    capacity and, 175
    definitions, 7–8
    e-commerce regulation and, 426–428
    meeting of the minds, 198
    writing requirements, 143–144
Unilateral contracts
    acceptance of, 77–80
    mirror image rule, 68
    partial performance, 77–80
    substantial beginnings, 77–80
    tender of performance, 79
Unilateral mistakes, 196–197
Unjust enrichment, prevention of, 399–401
Unmarried couples, agreements between, 151

Unreasonable and excessive costs, 284
Usage of trade, 226–228
Usury, 174

V
Value
    of goods, 373
    of goods as accepted, 435
    goods valued over $500, 153–154
    legal value, 42–48
    resale value, 374
    UCC definition, 153–154
V + E + L – M – R = D formula, 372
Vested contracts, 118–119
Voidable contracts, 166
Voidable obligations, 47
Voidable transactions, 166
Void contracts, 166
Void transactions, 166
Voluntary destruction, 293–294
Voluntary disablement, 293–294
Voluntary repayment of debt, 51–52

W
Waivers, 270–272
Warranties, 424–428
    conspicuous limitations of, 426
    exclusions of, 426
    express warranties, 424–425
    good faith obligations, 426
    implied warranties, 425
    implied warranties for particular purpose, 425
    limitation or exclusion of, 425–426
    merchantability, 425
    sales on approval, 426
    sales or returns, 426
    of title, 424
Wills, 114–118, 170, 203–204
Writing requirements
    Statute of Frauds, 142–145
    UETA, 143–144
Wrongful acts, 201